ENCYCLOPEDIA
OF THE
U.S. SUPREME COURT

ENCYCLOPEDIA
OF THE
U.S. SUPREME COURT

Volume I

Abington School District v. Schempp — Fugitive slaves

Editors
Thomas T. Lewis
Mount Senario College

Richard L. Wilson
University of Tennessee at Chattanooga

Managing Editor
R. Kent Rasmussen

Project Editor
Rowena Wildin

SALEM PRESS, INC.
PASADENA, CALIFORNIA   HACKENSACK, NEW JERSEY

Editor in Chief: Dawn P. Dawson

Managing Editor: R. Kent Rasmussen	*Project Editor:* Rowena Wildin
Production Editor: Joyce I. Buchea	*Assistant Editor:* Andrea E. Miller
Research Supervisor: Jeffry Jensen	*Research Assistant:* Jeff Stephens
Acquisitions Editor: Mark Rehn	*Assistant Photograph Editor:* Philip Bader
Layout: William Zimmerman	*Photograph Production:* Yasmine Cordoba

Design and Graphics: James Hutson

Encyclopedia of the U.S. Supreme Court / editors, Thomas T. Lewis, Richard L. Wilson.
    p. cm.
    Includes bibliographical references and index.
    ISBN 0-89356-097-9 (set : alk. paper) — ISBN 0-89356-098-7 (vol. 1 : alk. paper) — ISBN 0-89356-099-5 (vol. 2 : alk. paper) — ISBN 0-89356-148-7 (vol. 3 : alk. paper)
    1. United States. Supreme Court—Encyclopedias. 2. United States. Supreme Court—Biography. I. Title: Encyclopedia of the United States Supreme Court. II. Lewis, Thomas T. (Thomas Tandy) III. Wilson, Richard L., 1944-

KF8742.A35 E53 2000
347.73´26–dc21

00-032217

First printing

Contents

Publisher's Note ix
Introduction xi
Contributors xv

Abington School District v. Schempp 1
Ableman v. Booth 1
Abortion 2
Abrams v. United States 6
Academic freedom 7
Adair v. United States 8
Adams, John Quincy 9
Adamson v. California 10
Adarand Constructors v. Peña 10
Adderley v. Florida 11
Adkins v. Children's Hospital 11
Administrative assistant to chief justice 11
Administrative law 12
Admiralty and maritime law 13
Advertising of lawyers 16
Advisory opinions 17
Affirmative action 17
Age discrimination 21
Agostini v. Felton 23
Agricultural issues 23
*Akron v. Akron Center for Reproductive
    Health* 26
Albemarle Paper Co. v. Moody 26
*Albertson v. Subversive Activities Control
    Board* 27
Alien land laws 27
Alien rights and naturalization 28
*Allegheny County v. American Civil Liberties
    Union Greater Pittsburgh Chapter* 32
Allgeyer v. Louisiana 33
American Bar Association Committee
    on Federal Judiciary 33
American Civil Liberties Union 34
*American Communications Association v.
    Douds* 37
Americans United for Separation of
    Church and State 37
Antelope, The 38
Antitrust law 38
Appellate jurisdiction 42
Appointment and removal power 45
Aptheker v. Secretary of State 47
Argersinger v. Hamlin 47
Arizona v. Fulminante 47

*Arlington Heights v. Metropolitan Housing
    Development Corp.* 48
Articles of Confederation 48
Ashwander v. Tennessee Valley Authority 49
Assembly and association, freedom of 50
Automobile searches 52
Automobile Workers v. Johnson Controls 53

Bad tendency test 55
Badger, George E. 55
Bail 56
Bailey v. Drexel Furniture Co. 57
Baker v. Carr 58
Baldwin, Henry 58
Ballard v. United States 59
Ballew v. Georgia 60
Bank of Augusta v. Earle 60
Bank of the United States v. Deveaux 60
Bankruptcy law 60
Barbour, Philip P. 62
Barenblatt v. United States 63
Barker v. Wingo 63
Barnes v. Glen Theatre 64
Barron v. Baltimore 64
Bates v. State Bar of Arizona 65
Batson v. Kentucky 65
Beard, Charles Austin 66
Belle Terre v. Boraas 67
Benton v. Maryland 67
Berman v. Parker 67
Betts v. Brady 68
Bickel, Alexander 68
Bigelow v. Virginia 69
Bill of attainder 70
Bill of Rights 71
Birth control and contraception 76
Black, Hugo L. 78
Black, Jeremiah S. 80
Black Monday 81
Blackmun, Harry A. 82
Blair, John, Jr. 84
Blatchford, Samuel 85
BMW of North America v. Gore 86
*Board of Education of Oklahoma City v.
    Dowell* 86
Boerne v. Flores 87
Bolling v. Sharpe 87
Bork, Robert H. 87

Boudinot, Elias 88
Bowers v. Hardwick 88
Bowsher v. Synar 89
Boyd v. United States 89
Bradford, Edward A. 90
Bradley, Joseph P. 91
Bradwell v. Illinois 92
Brandeis, Louis D. 93
Brandeis Brief 95
Brandenburg v. Ohio 95
Branzburg v. Hayes 96
Brecht v. Abrahamson 96
Breedlove v. Suttles 96
Brennan, William J., Jr. 97
Brewer, David J. 100
Breyer, Stephen G. 101
Briefs 102
*Briscoe v. Bank of the Commonwealth of
    Kentucky* 103
British background to U.S. judiciary 103
British Law Lords 107
Bronson v. Kinzie 109
Brown, Henry B. 109
Brown v. Board of Education 110
Brown v. Maryland 112
Brown v. Mississippi 112
Buchanan v. Warley 113
Buck v. Bell 113
Buckley v. Valeo 114
Budd v. New York 114
Bunting v. Oregon 115
Bureaucratization of the judiciary 115
Burger, Warren E. 116
Burr, Aaron. 120
Burstyn v. Wilson 120
Burton, Harold H. 121
Burton v. Wilmington Parking Authority . . . 122
Butler, Charles Henry 122
Butler, Pierce. 123
Butler, United States v. 124
Butz v. Economou 125
Byrnes, James F. 125

Calder v. Bull 127
California, United States v. 127
California v. Acevedo 127
Campbell, John A. 128
Cantwell v. Connecticut 129
Capital punishment 129
Capitalism 135

Cardozo, Benjamin N. 138
Carolene Products Co., United States v. . . . 139
Carroll v. United States. 140
Carswell, G. Harrold 140
Carter v. Carter Coal Co. 141
Catron, John 141
Censorship 142
Cert pool 145
Certiorari, writ of 145
Chafee, Zechariah, Jr. 148
Champion v. Ames. 149
Chaplinsky v. New Hampshire 149
Charles River Bridge v. Warren Bridge . . . 150
Chase, Salmon P. 150
Chase, Samuel 152
Cherokee Nation v. Georgia. 154
*Chicago, Burlington, and Quincy
    Railroad Co. v. Chicago.* 154
*Chicago, Milwaukee, and St. Paul
    Railway Co. v. Minnesota.* 155
Chicago v. Morales. 155
Chief justice 156
Chimel v. California. 159
Chinese Exclusion Cases 159
Chisholm v. Georgia 160
Choate, Joseph H. 160
Church of Lukumi Babalu Aye v. Hialeah . . . 161
Circuit courts of appeals. 161
Circuit riding. 163
Citizenship 164
Civil law. 167
Civil Rights Acts 168
Civil rights and liberties 171
Civil Rights Cases 173
Civil Rights movement. 173
Civil War 175
Clark, Tom C. 180
*Clark Distilling Co. v. Western Maryland
    Railway Co.* 181
Clarke, John H. 182
Classic, United States v. 183
Clear and present danger test. 183
Clerk of the Court 184
Clerks of the justices 186
Clifford, Nathan 187
Clinton, Bill 188
Clinton v. City of New York. 191
Clinton v. Jones 192
Cohen v. California 192
Cohen v. Cowles Media Co. 193

Cohens v. Virginia 193
Coker v. Georgia 194
Cold War 194
Colegrove v. Green 196
Coleman v. Miller 196
Collector v. Day 197
Collegiality 197
Columbus Board of Education v. Penick 198
Comity clause 198
Commerce, regulation of 199
Commercial speech 202
Common carriers 204
Common law 205
Common law, federal 206
*Communist Party v. Subversive Activities
   Control Board.* 206
Concurring opinions 207
Conference of the justices. 208
Congress, arrest and immunity of
   members of 210
Congress, qualifications for 210
Congressional power of investigation. 210
Congressional power to enforce
   amendments 212
Conkling, Roscoe 214
Conscientious objection. 214
Conscription 216
Constitution, U.S. 217
Constitutional amendment process. 221
Constitutional Convention 225
Constitutional interpretation 227
Constitutional law 231
Constitutionalism 234
Contempt power of Congress 235
Contempt power of courts. 236
Contract, freedom of 236
Contracts clause 238
Cooley, Thomas M. 239
*Cooley v. Board of Wardens of the Port of
   Philadelphia* 240
Cooper v. Aaron 240
Copyright. . . . . , . . 241
Corporations. 242
Corrigan v. Buckley 243
Corwin, Edward S. 244
Counsel, right to 244
Counselman v. Hitchcock. 246
Court of Justice of the European
   Communities 246
Court-packing plan 248

Courts of appeals 250
Cox v. Louisiana. 251
Cox v. New Hampshire 252
Coyle v. Smith 252
Craig v. Boren 252
Craig v. Missouri 253
Cranch, William 253
Criminal syndicalism. 254
Crittenden, John J.. 254
Crow Dog, Ex parte 255
Cruel and unusual punishment. 256
Cruikshank, United States v. 257
*Cruzan v. Director, Missouri Department
   of Health* 257
*Cumming v. Richmond County Board of
   Education.* 258
Cummings v. Missouri 258
Curator 259
Curtis, Benjamin R. 259
*Curtiss-Wright Export Corp., United
   States v.*. 260
Cushing, Caleb. 261
Cushing, William. 261

Dallas, Alexander J. 263
Dames and Moore v. Regan 263
Daniel, Peter V. 264
Darby Lumber Co., United States v.. 264
Dartmouth College v. Woodward 265
Davis, Bancroft 265
Davis, David 266
Davis, John W. 267
Davis v. Bandemer. 267
Davis v. Beason 268
Day, William R.. 268
Debs, In re. 269
Decision making 270
Declaration of Independence. 271
DeJonge v. Oregon 272
Delegation of powers 273
Democracy 274
Dennis v. United States. 276
Desegregation 277
*DeShaney v. Winnebago County Department
   of Social Services* 279
Dillon v. Gloss 279
Disability of justices 280
Dissents. 281
Diversity jurisdiction 284
Dobbins v. Erie County 285

Dodge v. Woolsey 285
Doe v. Bolton 286
Dolan v. City of Tigard 286
Dombrowski v. Pfister 286
Double jeopardy 287
Douglas, William O. 288
Due process, procedural 290
Due process, substantive 292
Duncan v. Kahanamoku 294
Duncan v. Louisiana 295
Duplex Printing Co. v. Deering 295
Duvall, Gabriel 295
Dworkin, Ronald 296

E. C. Knight Co., United States v. 297
Edelman v. Jordan 297
Edmonson v. Leesville Concrete Co. 298
Education 298
Edwards v. Aguillard 301
Edwards v. California 302
Edwards v. South Carolina 302
Eichman, United States v. 302
Eighteenth Amendment 303
Eighth Amendment 304
Eisenstadt v. Baird 304
Elastic clause 305
Elections 305
Eleventh Amendment 309
Elfbrandt v. Russell 310
Ellsworth, Oliver 311
Elrod v. Burns 312
Employment discrimination 312
*Employment Division, Department of
    Human Resources v. Smith* 314
Engel v. Vitale 314
Environmental law 315
Epperson v. Arkansas 318
Equal protection clause 319
Erie Railroad Co. v. Tompkins 323
Ernst, Morris L. 323
Escobedo v. Illinois 324
Espionage acts 324
Euclid v. Ambler Realty Co. 326
Evans v. Abney 327
*Everson v. Board of Education of Ewing
    Township* 327
Evolution and creationism 327

Ex post facto laws 329
Exclusionary rule 330
Executive agreements 332
Executive immunity 334
Executive privilege 336
Extrajudicial activities 338

Fairfax's Devisee v. Hunter's Lessee 342
Family and children 342
Fay v. Noia 345
Federal Tort Claims Act 345
Federalism 346
Federalist, The 350
Feiner v. New York 352
*Feist Publications v. Rural Telephone
    Service Co.* 352
Ferguson v. Skrupa 352
Fetal rights 353
Field, Stephen J. 354
Fifteenth Amendment 356
Fifth Amendment 358
Finality of decision 362
Financing political speech 363
First Amendment 365
First Amendment absolutism 368
First Amendment balancing 369
First Amendment speech tests 371
*First English Evangelical Lutheran Church
    of Glendale v. County of Los Angeles* 372
First Monday in October 373
First National Bank of Boston v. Bellotti 373
Fiscal and monetary powers 374
Flag desecration 375
Flast v. Cohen 378
Fletcher v. Peck 379
Florida v. Bostick 379
Foreign affairs and foreign policy 380
Fortas, Abe 381
Fourteenth Amendment 383
Fourth Amendment 386
Frank v. Mangum 389
Frankfurter, Felix 389
French Constitutional Council 391
Freund, Ernst 393
Frontiero v. Richardson 393
Frothingham v. Mellon 394
Fugitive slaves 394

Publisher's Note

Within the vast framework of the American federal system of government, the U.S. Supreme Court stands out as a uniquely powerful institution. Though comprising only nine unelected members, it alone can overturn the actions of every other branch of government, at all levels. Any decision by any elected executive officer—from a small-town mayor to the president of the United States— any legislation enacted by any elected body—from a city council to the Congress of the United States—can be invalidated by the Supreme Court. By contrast, only two methods exist to overturn unpopular Court decisions: The Court can reverse its own rulings, or the Congress or state conventions can initiate the long and difficult process of constitutional amendment. Since the Court began in 1789, it has reversed itself many times; however, opponents to its decisions have managed to get the Constitution amended only a handful of times. There is no other institution quite like the Supreme Court—in the United States or anywhere else in the world.

What limits are there to the power of this very special institution? What impact has it actually had on the nation's constitutional history? What manner of people have sat on its benches and how did they get there? How does the Court actually function? These and many other questions are the subject matter of *Encyclopedia of the Supreme Court*. This three-volume set is designed to meet the growing need among students and members of the general public for clear, authoritative, and up-to-date information about the Court.

The 1,075 topics treated in individual essays in these volumes have been selected, formatted, and written with the needs of nonspecialist readers in mind. Emphasis throughout the set is on clear explanations of subjects, supported by illuminating graphics and illustrations. Essays range in length from 250 to 3,000 words and contain several distinct component parts. All essays open with specially formatted top-matter sections, whose content varies according to essay type. The core of every essay is a clear discussion of its subject, whose relevance to the Supreme Court is constantly stressed. This is followed by from three to ten alphabetically arranged cross-references to related articles. Essays of 1,000 or more words append

brief lists of recommended readings, and essays of 2,000 or more words provide annotated discussions of the recommended readings. All essays are signed by their authors, whose names and affiliations are listed in the list of contributors at the front of volume 1.

Essay topics are thoroughly linked by cross-references. A Categorized List of Entries following the appendix section at the back of volume 3 groups related essays under broad subject headings. Despite these aids, each essay is written to stand on its own as much as possible. Essay top matter is presented in a concise, ready-reference format that provides the most essential information at a glance. Top matter in each of the 189 biographical essays, for example, opens with its subject's full name, brief identification, full birth and death information, and a summary statement of the person's significance in Court history. The top matter in essays on justices adds exact dates of the justices' Court service and identifies the presidents who appointed them. In addition to essays covering the Court's 109 justices, there are biographical essays on all failed nominees, all Supreme Court reporters, important attorneys who have argued before the Court, scholars on constitutional law, and U.S. presidents with close ties to the Court.

In the more than two centuries since the Court first convened, it has passed down thousands of decisions in individual cases. Many of its decisions contain broad rulings that have become part of the law of the land. Indeed, some decisions—such as *Brown v. Board of Education* (1954) on school desegregation, *Miranda v. Arizona* (1966) on protection against self-incrimination, and *Roe v. Wade* (1973) on abortion rights—have materially affected the lives of millions of Americans. Court cases are thus part of U.S. constitutional history, and it is impossible to understand the workings of the Supreme Court without a study of them.

Encyclopedia of the Supreme Court devotes 548 essays to the most important, or most representative, decisions the Court has made. The cases are arranged alphabetically, under the names by which they are most commonly known, such as *Brown v. Board of Education*. To ensure precise identification in top matter, case names are followed by the standard citations given in *United States Reports*. Essay top matter also provides the dates the Court passed down the decisions, concise summaries of issues involved, and brief statements of the cases' significance. The bodies of the essays themselves are mostly brief; they emphasize how the cases fit into constitutional history and touch on details that illuminate the workings of the Court and the opinions of its justices. Additional references to cases—including hundreds of cases not covered in individual essays—can be found in the index.

Encyclopedia of the Supreme Court contains 74 essays on types of law (such as administrative law, bankruptcy law, and state constitutions), individual pieces of legislation, and clauses and amendments to the U.S. Constitution. Top matter on essays on these subjects provides, as appropriate, the dates the laws were passed, brief descriptions, and summaries of their significance. Closely related to essays of this type are 131 essays on broad issues, such as abortion, academic freedom, corporations, education, and race and discrimination. These essays examine how the Court has treated important issues throughout its history. Emphasis here, as in the set as a whole, is on the Court itself. For example, the essay on "Civil rights and liberties" is not so much an overview of civil rights and liberties in the country in general, as it is an examination of how the Supreme Court has treated these issues throughout its own history. In this regard, *Encyclopedia of the Supreme Court* also contains 38 essays on specific historical events and eras, such as the Civil War, Reconstruction, and Japanese American relocation during World War II.

A unique feature of this set is its international perspective. A core essay titled "International perspectives on the Court" compares the U.S. Supreme Court with national courts in other countries and shows how the Court has influenced foreign court systems. Other essays offer more detailed comparisons between the U.S. Supreme Court and the highest courts in Canada, France, Germany, and Great Britain, as well as the Court of Justice of the European Communities.

The mechanics of how the Supreme Court works and procedural matters of it and of the court system generally are covered in another 80 essays. Included in this broad category are such subjects as staff positions, basic terminology (such as "Briefs," "Cert pool," and "Certiorari"), and broad concepts related to the Court's powers and practices (such as "Judicial powers," "Rules of the Court," and "Workload"). Readers are also encouraged to consult the 266-term Glossary at the end of the third volume.

In addition to the Glossary, volume 3's appendix section includes an annotated Bibliography and a discussion of Internet resources on the Court that offers a selection of Web site addresses. A table of federal statutes consolidates basic information on selected laws. Information on the justices can be found in two tables: one lists them in order of their appointments; the other lists them alphabetically and provides capsule information on their vital dates, appointments, and Court careers. The history of the Court is condensed in the Time Line, which provides dates of justices' nominations, confirmations, and oaths of office, as well as many details on legislation, court cases, and other relevant facts. The set concludes with two indexes: an index of cases (including those not covered in individual essays) and a general subject index.

Having the encyclopedia written by a large number of contributors helps ensure balance in the viewpoints behind its contents. More than 220 scholars generously contributed their time and talents to *Encyclopedia of the Supreme Court*. We thank them all for their contributions. A complete list of their names and affiliations appears in volume 1. We particularly wish to thank Thomas T. Lewis of Mount Senario College and Richard L. Wilson of the University of Tennessee at Chattanooga for offering their expertise, advice, and enthusiasm as the project's editors. Professor Wilson would also like to add his thanks to the staff of the Lupton Library at the University of Tennessee at Chattanooga for their assistance in many aspects of his research, expressing special gratitude to Neil Coulter, Sarla Murgai, William Prince, and Maria Rankin.

Introduction

Foreign observers have long been impressed with the power of judges in the United States. In 1834, following his visit to the young republic, French aristocrat Alexis de Tocqueville concluded that the real "American aristocracy" resided in the judiciary, and he noted: "Scarcely any political question arises in the United States that is not resolved, sooner or later, into a judicial question." In the twentieth century, the role of judges in American political life has continued to grow. Among other functions, judges resolve disputes that involve millions of dollars, they supervise the criminal justice system, and they make authoritative interpretations about the meanings of constitutional texts and legislative statutes.

The Supreme Court stands at the apex of the U.S. judiciary. Whenever a legal question relates to the U.S. Constitution, decisions of the lower courts can be appealed to the Supreme Court. However, Supreme Court decisions can be reversed only under one of three conditions: an addition of a new constitutional amendment, which is difficult to achieve; a change in the membership of the Court, which depends on the health and age of the justices; or the possibility that one or more of the justices might decide differently in a future case, which is relatively rare.

Every human society faces the very difficult problem of establishing and maintaining order. One approach for achieving order is to provide unlimited powers to individual people, based either on their physical strength, virtue, charisma, or inheritance. Although sometimes tolerable for short periods, political systems relying on individual characteristics tend to become arbitrary and despotic. Another approach at seeking order is to institutionalize a system of limited government based on impersonal rules, which is commonly called a rule of law. Historically, such systems have used laws that were either written or unwritten, but a system of written laws clearly promotes greater objectivity and continuity. Although the origins of written codes can be traced as far back as the codes attributed to Hammurabi and Moses, a major step forward came with the creation of the Roman legal system, culminating in the Byzantine emperor Justinian's codification during the sixth century.

As a legal and political institution, the U.S. Supreme Court is a product of many historical developments and influences. Probably the most profound long-term influence was the British form of limited government, or constitutionalism, that gradually emerged from the medieval period, with the Magna Carta of 1215 requiring that even the king follow the established "law of the land." Although the British Parliament acquired supremacy in matters of legislation during the seventeenth century, judges under the common law had considerable discretion in interpreting both parliamentary statutes and unwritten traditions. The common-law practice of recognizing judicial precedents, or *stare decisis*, meant that British judges had more authority and discretion than did judges of the civil-law tradition on the continent. In the famous *Dr. Bonham's Case* of 1610, jurist Sir Edward Coke even went so far as to suggest that parliamentary acts were void if they contradicted the established principles of the common law. More than a century later, French jurist Montesquieu, whose *Spirit of the Laws* overly simplified the British system, advocated a system of separation of powers that envisioned an independent judiciary with a great deal of authority.

During the eighteenth century, American colonists opposed to British policies were able to exploit the ideas of jurists such as Coke and Montesquieu, and the result was a new American conception of constitutionalism. In 1761, when James Otis denounced a parliamentary act authorizing general writs of assistance, he quoted the *Bonham* case and insisted that the act was void because it was contrary to natural equity and the established constitution. Following the Seven Years' War of the mid-eighteenth century, Americans increasing relied upon Otis's constitutional theory in order to protest the new taxes that they detested. The American theory of a normative and fixed constitution that was separate from, and superior to, parliamentary legislation was an innovation. For Americans, however, the theory was not altogether novel, as colonial charters and compacts had long resembled fixed constitutional arrangements.

With the American Revolution, therefore, it is not especially surprising that eleven of the thirteen new states took the innovative step of adopting written constitutions contained in single documents. Because Americans were suspicious of both legislative and executive power, moreover, it was almost inevitable that judges soon began to consider themselves to be constitutional guardians. Even before the U.S. Constitution was formulated, the high courts of New Jersey, North Carolina, and Rhode Island had ruled that legislative acts were unconstitutional and therefore void. The concept of judicial review, sometimes called the "judicial veto," had become fairly widespread by this time. In *The Federalist*, No. 78, for example, Alexander Hamilton wrote that the courts under the proposed national constitution would have the duty "to declare all acts contrary to the manifest tenor of the Constitution void." Hamilton appeared to mean that the courts would have the power to strike down only laws that were contrary to the clear language of the constitutional text. The idea that judges should have wide discretion to strike down legislative statutes based on controversial interpretations of the Constitution was not a part of the legal discourse of the eighteenth century.

Some form of judicial review appears to have been implied in the Constitution drafted in 1787. Its third article authorized the Supreme Court to make final judgments about cases and controversies arising under the Constitution, federal laws, and federal treaties. Its sixth article, moreover, proclaimed the Constitution to be the "supreme law of the land," with federal statutes and treaties also part of the supreme law as long as they are made in conformity with the principles of the Constitution. In the famous case of *Marbury v. Madison* (1803), the Supreme Court clearly and firmly established its authority to overturn congressional statutes it considers to have violated these principles.

The application of judicial review has been controversial throughout American history. Even Thomas Jefferson, the primary drafter of the Declaration of Independence, had reservations about it. He argued that because the three branches of the federal government had *equal* powers to interpret the Constitution, allowing the Supreme Court to be the ultimate arbiter of the Constitution would lead to "the despotism of an oligarchy."

By the end of the twentieth century, almost no one seriously suggested an end to judicial review; however, Americans continued to debate about whether the justices should exercise "self-restraint"

or actively promote their own visions about a just and free society. This ongoing debate is related to several fascinating questions about interpretation. Some jurists argue that the Court should base its interpretations on an analysis of the text itself. Other jurists emphasize the intention of the Framers. Still others think that interpretations should utilize extratextual concepts such as natural law or contemporary philosophy. In this encyclopedia, needless to say, there are many entries about the art of interpretation and related topics.

Americans sometimes argue about whether it is the role of the Supreme Court to make laws. On one hand, the first article of the Constitution states that "all legislative powers herein granted shall be vested in a Congress." However, the Framers appeared to recognize that the term "law" was broader than the term "legislation." Within the common-law tradition, after all, judges often relied on case law, in which people were punished for disobeying judge-made laws. In the American legal system, legislatures make statutes, but constitutional law is primarily the work of the Supreme Court.

It is helpful to recognize a distinction between the constitutional text and constitutional law. The words in the Fourteenth Amendment, for example, have not changed since the amendment's adoption in 1868. The amendment's legal meanings, however, have changed in fundamental ways on numerous occasions. In *Plessy v. Ferguson* (1896), for example, the Court held that racially segregated trains were entirely compatible with the amendment's equal protection requirements. However, in the well-known case of *Brown v. Board of Education* (1954), the Court ruled that the equal protection clause required that de jure segregation of public schools be eliminated.

The Supreme Court's interpretations of the term "due process of law" have changed in even more dramatic ways. As Charles Evans Hughes said in a 1907 speech: "We are under a Constitution, but the Constitution is what the judges say it is." Whatever one thinks about the influences of the Supreme Court, it is impossible to deny that the doctrine of judicial review has allowed the Court to play a major role in American political life.

During the twentieth century, it has become commonplace to describe the American political system as a "constitutional democracy." Clearly some inherent tensions arise when there is an attempt to unite the concepts of judicial review and democracy within a single system, at least if the latter term is taken to mean the will of the majority. In order to unite the two concepts, it is usually assumed that the majority has the right to determine public policy within a constitutional framework, but that the majority does not have the right to violate constitutional rules, especially those that protect individual rights and preserve democratic procedures. The American polity aspires to be a system of representative democracy, with an emphasis on the selection of representatives and leaders in free and competitive elections. If the Supreme Court arrives at an "incorrect" decision that is not accepted by the majority of citizens, it is very possible that the decision will eventually be reversed by the democratic process. However, sometimes the public gradually accepts the Court's point of view.

The Framers of the U.S. Constitution were not concerned about whether there were contradictions between democracy and judicial review, in part because they were fearful of unrestrained majoritarian government. Indeed, the Framers rarely used the term "democracy," which they tended to associate with the disorder and the tyranny of the majority. Rather, they preferred the word "republic," by which they had in mind a system that included representation based on free elections and widespread participation by adult male citizens—at least those male citizens who owned some property. The Supreme Court, armed with the power of judicial review, has played an important role in the expansion of the democratic idea during the last two centuries.

For the first century and a half of its existence, the notion of judicial review was not well received outside the United States. European powers rejected the notion for at least two reasons. First, they usually assumed that ultimate sovereignty resides in the government, not in a constitution. Second, proponents of democracy usually assumed that the courts would hinder the will of the majority and defend the economic interests of wealthy elites. The Marxist-Leninist ideology was especially incompatible with concepts such as constitutionalism and judicial review. People committed to a Marxist-Leninist system concentrated on trying to change the economic foundations of society, and they usually assumed that the legal system was simply a superstructure that must change to adapt to the needs of society. The very term "dictatorship of the proletariat" denoted a rejection of limited government.

In a speech delivered in 1999, Chief Justice William H. Rehnquist observed that in recent years the institution of judicial review "has been one of the most widely imitated of American institutions." Japan and the Federal Republic of Germany, under the influence of American occupations, were among the first countries to adopt the practice. In spite of traditional French suspicions of judicial power, the government of France's Fifth Republic eventually established a French Constitutional Council with a limited power of judicial review. Although Canada has a parliamentary system based largely on the British model, the addition of the Canadian Charter of Rights and Freedoms in 1982 allowed that nation's Supreme Court to overturn parliamentary acts based on broad constitutional interpretations. After the collapse of the Soviet Union, nearly all the Eastern European countries that were a part of the Soviet bloc established independent judiciaries empowered to protect individual rights and prevent governmental abuses. As the European Union has taken shape, moreover, it has recognized the advantages of having a high court with the authority to interpret the requirements of the European Charter.

This *Encyclopedia of the U.S. Supreme Court* contains articles about all aspects of the Court and its influences on American society, both now and in the past. Readers will find discussions of procedural matters and concepts in separate entries. Especially important are the issues addressed by the Court. Readers wishing to research a particular issue will not need to know the names of the relevant cases, but they may look up the general topics, which will include cross-references with the major cases listed. Readers will also be able to find biographies of all justices of the Court, as well as short biographies of those nominated but not confirmed by the Senate. Likewise, there are entries about the presidents and their impacts on the Court, as well as entries about influential jurists and legal scholars.

The articles of this encyclopedia have been written for general readers, especially the patrons of public, middle and high school, and university libraries across North America and beyond. For readers studying legal topics for the first time, the concepts and terminology can be quite challenging, if not overwhelming. The contributors to the encyclopedia have attempted to use standard and clear English and to define words that might be unfamiliar. Readers who do not understand the meanings of key words are encouraged to consult the glossary and the index.

Although the focus of this reference set is on the Supreme Court rather than the Constitution, many of the most significant decisions of the Court are devoted to interpretations of the constitutional text. Readers will find entries on all the statements of the Constitution that have elicited judgments by the Court. In the twentieth century, certainly, the Court has given special attention to the Bill of Rights, as well as several of the other twenty-seven amendments that have been added during the last two hundred years. The Court also interprets legislative statutes, overturning them if they are deemed to violate some constitutional provision. This work, therefore, provides considerable information about the major statutes that have been examined and interpreted by the Court.

Thomas T. Lewis
Richard L. Wilson

Contributors

Nobuko Adachi
Illinois State University

Bethany Andreasen
Minot State University

Earl R. Andresen
University of Texas at Arlington

John Andrulis
Western New England College

Paula C. Arledge
Northeast Louisiana University

Gayle R. Avant
Baylor University

Charles F. Bahmueller
Center for Civic Education

Carl L. Bankston III
Tulane University

Paul Bateman
Southwestern University School of Law

Patricia A. Behlar
Pittsburg State University

Bernard W. Bell
Rutgers Law School

Sara C. Benesh
University of New Orleans

Alvin K. Benson
Brigham Young University

Mark L. Berlin
University of Ottawa

Milton Berman
University of Rochester

Steve D. Boilard
Sacramento, California

Michael W. Bowers
University of Nevada at Las Vegas

Timothy S. Boylan
Winthrop University

P. J. Brendese III
State University of New York at Albany

Saul Brenner
University of North Carolina at Charlotte

Beau Breslin
Skidmore College

Richard A. Brisbin, Jr.
West Virginia University

Joseph V. Brogan
La Salle University

Kenneth H. Brown
Northwestern Oklahoma State University

Thomas W. Buchanan
Plymouth, Indiana

Fred Buchstein
John Carroll University

Mary Louise Buley-Meissner
University of Wisconsin at Milwaukee

Michael H. Burchett
Limestone College

Edmund J. Campion
University of Tennessee

Bradley C. Canon
University of Kentucky

Martin D. Carcieri
University of North Florida

Beau David Case
Ohio State University

Christine R. Catron
St. Mary's University

Gilbert T. Cave
Lakeland Community College

H. Lee Cheek, Jr.
Brewton-Parker College

Carl P. Chelf
Western Kentucky University

Bradley Stewart Chilton
University of North Texas

Jim D. Clark
Richland College

Thomas Clarkin
Lake Hills, Texas

Douglas Clouatre
Kennesaw State University

Alisa White Coleman
University of Texas at Arlington

Susan Coleman
West Texas A&M University

William H. Coogan
University of Southern Maine

Michael L. Coulter
Grove City College

David A. Crain
South Dakota State University

Edward R. Crowther
Adams State College

Gilbert Morris Cuthbertson
Rice University

Rebecca Davis
Georgia Southern University

Robert C. Davis
Pikeville College

Frank Day
Clemson University

Ione Y. DeOllos
Ball State University

Thomas E. DeWolfe
Hampden-Sydney College

Gordon Neal Diem
Advance Education and Development Institute

L. Mara Dodge
Westfield State College

Steven J. Dunker
Northeastern State University

William V. Dunlap
Quinnipiac University School of Law

Philip A. Dynia
Loyola University

Robert P. Ellis
Worcester State College

Kevin Eyster
Madonna University

Daryl R. Fair
College of New Jersey

Michael P. Federici
Mercyhurst College

John E. Finn
Wesleyan University

Alan M. Fisher
California State University at Dominguez Hills

Dale L. Flesher
University of Mississippi

Tonya K. Flesher
University of Mississippi

John Fliter
Kansas State University

Michael Flynn
Nova Southeastern University Law School

Carol G. Fox
East Tennessee State University

Michael J. Garcia
Arapahoe Community College

Janet E. Gardner
University of Massachusetts at Dartmouth

Robert P. George
Princeton University

Phyllis B. Gerstenfeld
California State University at Stanislaus

Evan Gerstmann
Loyola Marymount University

Louis Gesualdi
St. John's University

Richard A. Glenn
Millersville University

Robert Justin Goldstein
Oakland University

Nancy M. Gordon
Amherst, Massachusetts

Robert F. Gorman
Southwest Texas State University

Lewis L. Gould
University of Texas at Austin

Diana R. Grant
California State University at Stanislaus

Donald E. Greco
Baylor University

William C. Green
Morehead State University

Cherie Gregoire
Siena College

Steven P. Grossman
University of Baltimore School of Law

John Gruhl
University of Nebraska at Lincoln

Michael Haas
California State University at Fullerton

Pamela D. Haldeman
Mount St. Mary's College

Irwin Halfond
McKendree College

Timothy L. Hall
University of Mississippi

Nelson L. Henning
Cedarville College

Diane Andrews Henningfeld
Adrian College

John R. Hermann
Trinity University

Mark L. Higgins
Wayne State College

L. Lynn Hogue
Georgia State University College of Law

Barbara Holden-Smith
Cornell University School of Law

Kenneth M. Holland
University of Memphis

Louis M. Holscher
San Jose State University

Eric Howard
Los Angeles, California

Harvey Gresham Hudspeth
Mississippi Valley State University

John C. Hughes
Saint Michael's College

Patricia Jackson
Davenport College

Robert Jacobs
Central Washington University

Dwight Jensen
Marshall University

Bruce E. Johansen
University of Nebraska at Omaha

Alan E. Johnson
Brecksville, Ohio

Dale W. Johnson
Southern Wesleyan University

Gae R. Johnson
Northern Arizona University

Herbert A. Johnson
University of South Carolina School of Law

Ronald Kahn
Oberlin College

Sugwon Kang
Hartwick College

Thomas M. Keck
University of Oklahoma

Robert Keele
The University of the South

Kimberley H. Kidd
King College

East Tennessee State University

Marshall R. King
Maryville University at St. Louis

F. E. Knowles, Jr.
Central Methodist College

Samuel Krislov
University of Minnesota

David J. Langum
Cumberland School of Law of Samford University

James E. Lennertz
Lafayette College

Paul Lermack
Bradley University

David W. Levy
University of Oklahoma

Thomas T. Lewis
Mt. Senario College

Lester G. Lindley
Nova Southeastern University

Matthew Lindstrom
Siena College

Janet Alice Long
Pasadena, California

James J. Lopach
University of Montana

David C. Lukowitz
Hamline University

Nicholas C. Lund-Molfese
Salve Regina University

William Shepard McAninch
University of South Carolina School of Law

Siobhan McCabe
Siena College

Joseph M. McCarthy
Suffolk University

Dana P. McDermott
Martinsburg, West Virginia

Priscilla H. Machado
United States Naval Academy

Thomas C. Mackey
University of Louisville

Edgar J. McManus
Queens College

Kelly J. Madison
California State University at Los Angeles

Eduardo Magalhaes III
Simpson College

Patrick Malcolmson
St. Thomas University

Robin Sakina Mama
Monmouth University

Martin J. Manning
United States State Department

David E. Marion
Hampden-Sydney College

John Austin Matzko
Bob Jones University

Berenice Mejia
Siena College

Albert P. Melone
Southern Illinois University at Carbondale

Joseph A. Melusky
St. Francis College

Kurt X. Metzmeier
University of Kentucky College of Law

Ken Millen-Penn
Fairmont State College

Andrea E. Miller
Glendale, California

Mark C. Miller
Clark University

Robert D. Mitchell
Northeastern University

Wayne D. Moore
Virginia Polytechnic Institute and State University

William V. Moore
College of Charleston

C. Morin
California State University at Chico

Robert P. Morin
California State University at Chico

Kenneth F. Mott
Gettysburg College

Sharon K. O'Roke
Oklahoma City University School of Law

William Osborne
Florida International University

William A. Paquette
Tidewater Community College

Cheryl Pawlowski
University of Northern Colorado

Bruce G. Peabody
University of Texas at Austin

William D. Pederson
Louisiana State University

Nis Petersen
New Jersey City University

J. P. Piskulich
Oakland University

Oliver B. Pollak
University of Nebraska at Omaha

Maureen J. Puffer-Rothenberg
Valdosta State University

Steven Puro
St. Louis University

Steven J. Ramold
University of Nebraska at Lincoln

R. Kent Rasmussen
Thousand Oaks, California

John David Rausch, Jr.
West Texas A&M University

Edward A. Riedinger
Ohio State University

John R. Rink
University of Wisconsin at Platteville

Stephen F. Rohde
Los Angeles, California

Francine Sanders Romero
University of Texas at San Antonio

William G. Ross
Cumberland School of Law of Samford University

Paul F. Rothstein
Georgetown University School of Law

Irene Struthers Rush
Los Osos, California

Kurt M. Saunders
California State University at Northridge

Sean J. Savage
Saint Mary's College

J. Christopher Schnell
Southeast Missouri State University

Kathleen Schongar
The May School

Rose Secrest
Signal Mountain, Tennessee

Gregory N. Seltzer
Villa Julie College

Stephen J. Shapiro
University of Baltimore School of Law

Elizabeth Algren Shaw
Cleveland, Ohio

Christopher Shortell
Los Angeles, California

R. Baird Shuman
University of Illinois at Urbana-Champaign

Michael J. Siler
California State University at Los Angeles

Donald C. Simmons, Jr.
Mississippi Humanities Council

Brian P. Smentkowski
Southeast Missouri State University

Christopher E. Smith
Michigan State University

Chuck Smith
West Virginia State College

Jane Marie Smith
Slippery Rock University

Bes Stark Spangler
Peace College

Arthur K. Steinberg
Livingstone College

Barry M. Stentiford
Grambling State University

Robert J. Stewart
California Maritime Academy

Glenn L. Swygart
Tennessee Temple University

Donald G. Tannenbaum
Gettysburg College

Steven C. Tauber
University of South Florida

G. Thomas Taylor
University of Maine

Carol Tebben
University of Wisconsin at Parkside

Jeffrey E. Thomas
Kansas City School of Law at University of Missouri,

Susan L. Thomas
Hollins University

Paul B. Trescott
Southern Illinois University

David Trevino
Ohio Northern University

Dean Van Bibber
Fairmont State College

Joanne LeBlanc Verity
Edmond, Oklahoma

Theodore M. Vestal
Oklahoma State University

Dean Wagstaffe
Florida International University

William T. Walker
Chestnut Hill College

Peter Wallenstein
Virginia Polytechnic Institute and State University

Spencer Weber Waller
Brooklyn Law School

Annita Marie Ward
Salem-Teikyo University

Bradley C. S. Watson
Saint Vincent College

Donald A. Watt
Southern Arkansas University

Marcia J. Weiss
Point Park College

Jamison Wilcox
Quinnipiac University School of Law

Rowena Wildin
South Pasadena, California

Lou Falkner Williams
Kansas State University

Richard L. Wilson
University of Tennessee at Chattanooga

Michael Witkoski
Columbia, South Carolina

Philip R. Zampini
Westfield State College

ENCYCLOPEDIA
OF THE
U.S. SUPREME COURT

A

Abington School District v. Schempp

CITATION: 374 U.S. 203
DATE: June 17, 1963
ISSUE: School prayer
SIGNIFICANCE: This decision reaffirmed the Supreme Court's 1962 ruling that made it unconstitutional for public schools to sponsor prayers or Bible readings.

Writing for an 8-1 majority, Justice Tom C. Clark reiterated the Supreme Court's position in *Engel v. Vitale* (1962) that the government could not promote religion by sponsoring public school prayers or Bible readings. In *Abington*, the American Civil Liberties Union helped the Schempps challenge a Pennsylvania law requiring public schools to begin each day by reading Bible verses. In the companion case, *Murray v. Curlett* (1963), nationally known atheist Madalyn Murray (later O'Hair) attacked a Baltimore city statute providing for a daily reading in the city schools of the Lord's Prayer or a passage from the Bible. Unlike the situation in *Engel*, the government did not write the prayer and used the readings without comment, but the Court still found both laws an impermissible promotion of religion.

Although two new justices participated in *Abington*, the outcome remained the same as *Engel*. Justice Potter Stewart wrote the Court's lone dissent, arguing that the free exercise clause should be given preferred status to avoid inherent conflicts with the establishment clause. The Court sought to minimize criticism by having Clark, a politically moderate southern Presbyterian, write the Court's opinion and Justices Arthur J. Goldberg (Jewish) and William J. Brennan, Jr. (Roman Catholic) write strong concurrences, but widespread public criticism continued from religious groups against the Court for interfering with religion.

Richard L. Wilson

SEE ALSO *Engel v. Vitale*; *Epperson v. Arkansas*; *Illinois ex rel. McCollum v. Board of Education*; Religion, establishment of; School prayer; *Wallace v. Jaffree*.

Madalyn Murray (later O'Hair) and her sons, William (left) and Garth, stand outside the Supreme Court a few months before the Court banned prayer in public schools in Murray v. Curtlett *(1963), a companion case to* Abington School District v. Schempp. *(AP/Wide World Photos)*

Ableman v. Booth

CITATION: 21 How. (62 U.S.) 506
DATE: March 7, 1859
ISSUE: Supremacy of federal courts over state courts
SIGNIFICANCE: The Supreme Court held that the Fugitive Slave Law of 1850 was constitutional and ruled that a state court may not issue a writ of *habeas corpus* to release a person from federal custody.

Joshua Glover, a fugitive slave from Missouri, found work in a Wisconsin mill. Under the Fugitive Slave Law of 1850, the U.S. commissioner in Milwaukee issued an order for Glover's arrest. An angry group of about one hundred men broke into the Milwaukee jail and rescued Glover, who escaped to Canada. Sherman Booth, a dynamic speaker who edited an antislavery newspaper, was convicted in federal court for taking part in the rescue. Not long after, the Wisconsin supreme court declared the 1850 law invalid, and one judge of the court issued a writ of *habeas corpus* to have Booth released. The court's action was appealed to the U.S. Supreme Court.

Writing for a unanimous Court, Chief Justice Roger Brooke Taney reaffirmed the authority of the federal government to capture runaway slaves and ruled that a state court lacked jurisdiction over a person in federal custody. In response, Wisconsin's supreme court split evenly concerning whether or not to recognize federal supremacy in the matter. Taney's opinion on federal supremacy was upheld in *Tarble's Case* (1872), and that aspect of the decision remains good law.

Thomas T. Lewis

SEE ALSO Federalism; Fugitive slaves; *Jones v. Van Zandt; Prigg v. Pennsylvania.*

Abortion

DESCRIPTION: Intentional expulsion or removal of the fetus from the womb except for the purpose of accomplishing a live birth or removing a dead fetus from the womb.

SIGNIFICANCE: With its controversial decision in *Roe v. Wade* (1973), the Supreme Court declared that women had the right to have an abortion, which it later interpreted to prohibit laws that unduly burdened a woman's ability to choose an abortion until the third trimester of pregnancy.

Scarcely any constitutional issue provoked more controversy in the last half of the twentieth century than the issue of whether the U.S. Constitution protected a woman's right to obtain an abortion. On some issues during this period, such as racial segregation, the Supreme Court was able to guide the country toward an ultimate consensus. However, on the issue of abortion, the Court was unable to accomplish such closure. The two major political parties partially defined themselves by reference to their respective attitudes toward this question, often using the abortion issue as a litmus test for their evaluation of potential Supreme Court justices. Protesters marked the anniversary of the Court's original abortion decision with vigils in front of the Court. Legislators, both federal and state, proposed an endless series of laws that would restrict or at least discourage abortions. In the last decade of the twentieth century, the Court stood by its original declaration that the right to abortion was protected by the Constitution. Nevertheless, the Court redefined the standard to be used in evaluating laws relating to abortion with the effect of increasing the ability of state and federal lawmakers to regulate in this controversial area.

Before the Right to Abortion. Prior to the nineteenth century, laws regulating abortions were virtually unknown because the procedure was extraordinarily dangerous and this danger operated as a deterrent, making abortion-banning laws largely superfluous. However, improved medical techniques in the nineteenth century made abortions more common and prompted state lawmakers to prohibit them. By the middle of the twentieth century, abortion, except when necessary to protect the pregnant woman's life, was illegal everywhere in the United States.

Beginning in the middle of the twentieth century, however, the Supreme Court determined that not all state laws bearing on issues of procreation were immune from constitutional scrutiny. In *Skinner v. Oklahoma* (1942), the Court determined that a state law providing for compulsory sterilization of certain habitual criminals amounted to an unconstitutional discrimination in violation of the Fourteenth Amendment's equal protection clause. The Court concluded that certain rights were sufficiently fundamental to require the government to demonstrate an overwhelmingly persuasive justification before depriving selected people of these rights. Though the Constitution nowhere specifically enumerates a right to procreation, the Court nevertheless concluded that this right was sufficiently fundamental to require strict scrutiny of the sterilization law. Finding no compelling purpose served by the law, the Court declared it unconstitutional.

Two decades later, the Court again turned to a consideration of whether the Constitution protected individuals from state laws that intruded into matters relating to procreation. *Griswold v. Connecticut* (1965) called upon the Court to determine the constitutionality of a state law prohibiting use of contraceptives. By the early 1960's this kind of law was extraordinarily rare, prompting Justice

Potter Stewart to characterize it as "exceedingly silly," but its constitutional infirmity was not immediately apparent. Justice William O. Douglas, though, writing for the Court, concluded that the right to use contraceptives lay within a zone of privacy protected by penumbras of various constitutional provisions. Other justices argued in concurring opinions that the right to use contraceptives was a species of the liberty protected from undue deprivations by the Fourteenth Amendment's due process clause. Justices Hugo L. Black and Stewart dissented. Black, in particular, challenged the majority's willingness to use the due process clause to scrutinize the reasonableness of laws affecting rights not specifically enumerated in the Constitution. He accused the majority of resurrecting the same form of substantive due process employed by the Court earlier in the century in cases such as *Lochner v. New York* (1905), which invalidated what the Court viewed as unreasonable restrictions on the freedom of contract.

The Abortion Ruling. The Court's holding in *Griswold* suggested that the Constitution protected a zone of privacy relating to matters of procreation, though the justices remained divided in their views of precisely where to root this right of privacy in the Constitution's text. Such controversy as the case engendered, however, was mostly abstract because an overwhelming majority of states had long since abandoned laws against the use of contraceptives. When the Court turned to the subject of abortion in *Roe v. Wade* (1973), however, it confronted prohibitions against abortion that were still in force in a majority of the states. The decade before *Roe* had seen some change in state laws relating to abortion. The 1962 Model Penal Code, drafted by the American Law Institute and followed by some states, allowed for abortions in cases involving rape or serious birth defects. A few states—New York, Alaska, and Hawaii—had repealed their antiabortion laws. However, a majority of states retained significant restrictions on the ability of women to obtain abortions, and in *Roe*, the Court swept aside virtually all these laws.

Justice Harry A. Blackmun, writing for the majority, concluded that the right of privacy previously recognized in cases such as *Griswold* was

Activists on both sides of the abortion question demonstrate in 1993 outside the Supreme Court, which was hearing arguments in a case involving protesters who block access to abortion clinics. (AP/Wide World Photos)

broad enough to encompass a woman's right to an abortion. He located the constitutional right of privacy in the Fourteenth Amendment's due process clause, which protected against deprivations of life, liberty, or property without due process of law. Finding the right to abortion fundamental, he determined that the government could not abridge the right without satisfying a strict review, which entailed demonstrating that the abridgment was necessary to serve some compelling governmental interest and that it was the least restrictive means of achieving that interest.

Using this formulation, Blackmun turned to the interests purportedly served by state abortion regulations: protecting the health of the pregnant woman and protecting the potential life of the unborn fetus. Blackmun suggested that no consensus existed as to when human life began and that, in any event, the fetus was not a "person" entitled to constitutional protection. Dividing pregnancy into three trimesters, Blackmun concluded that in the first trimester of pregnancy, neither a state's interest in the health of the pregnant woman nor its interest in the potential life of a fetus justified restrictions on abortion. In the second trimester, though, he found abortions sufficiently dangerous to the health of the pregnant woman to justify such regulations as necessary to protect the woman's health. Finally, after viability, in the third trimester, Blackmun reasoned that the state's interest in the potential life of the fetus was sufficiently weighty to justify a prohibition against all abortions except those necessary to preserve the life or the health of the pregnant woman. The abortion right thus established by *Roe* was virtually absolute during the first three months of pregnancy, subject only to regulations designed to protect the woman's health during the second three months, and subject to prohibition to protect the fetus during the last three months.

Responses to the Ruling. Though the Court's decision in *Roe* was widely hailed in some quarters of American life, criticism of the Court's decision was immediate and vociferous. Some legal scholars argued that the Court substituted its judgment on a controversial issue for the judgment of political majorities without constitutional justification. They agreed with Justice Black's claim in *Griswold* that the Court's use of the due process clause to evaluate the reasonableness of laws affecting rights not specifically protected by the Constitution resurrected in liberal political garb the same spirit that had inspired conservative justices to invalidate laws restricting the unenumerated right to contract in the first part of the twentieth century. Scholars supportive of the result in *Roe* argued that the Court's reasoning was correct. The problem with cases such as *Lochner*, they argued, was not that they protected unnamed fundamental rights, but that they designated the right to contract as fundamental. In contrast, they agreed with the Court that the right of privacy, including the right of a woman to choose to have an abortion, was indeed fundamental and should be protected from unreasonable legislative interference.

The Court's decision in *Roe* prompted the emergence of a right-to-life movement dedicated to overturning it, whether by constitutional amendment, legislative action, or reconstitution of the Court itself. Politicians opposed to the Court's ruling responded by proposing legislation and a constitutional amendment that would declare the fetus a "person" and therefore subject to constitutional protection. Neither the legislation nor the amendment succeeded in gaining passage, however. Opponents of the decision eventually turned their attention to the composition of the Court that had rendered the decision in *Roe* and, especially during the 1980's, attempted to screen nominees to the Court as to whether they approved or disapproved of *Roe*'s reasoning. This effort also produced only limited success. In the meantime, legislatures—especially at the state level—passed a variety of legislation that did not entirely prohibit abortions but placed a variety of obstacles in the paths of women seeking to exercise their right to seek an abortion. It remained to be seen after *Roe* whether such regulations would pass constitutional muster.

Post-*Roe* Abortion Regulations. In the fifteen years immediately after the *Roe* decision, abortion regulations generally found a cool welcome in the Court. Relying on the trimester scheme announced in *Roe*, the Court generally invalidated all laws that restricted the ability of women to obtain an abortion before the last trimester of pregnancy. For example, the Court declared laws requiring a spouse's consent to an abortion unconstitutional in *Planned Parenthood of Central Missouri v. Danforth* (1976). Restrictions on various abortion techniques were also invalidated, as were requirements that abortions be performed in hospitals as opposed to clinics. Moreover, the Court was initially hostile to laws designed to discourage abortions, such as those requiring a waiting period before a woman obtained an abortion or those requiring physicians to provide specific counsel to patients about the dangers of the abortion procedure.

The Court upheld a few forms of abortion regulation. It sustained the constitutionality of laws requiring parental consent when the woman seeking an abortion was a minor as long as the law also provided a means for the minor to obtain the consent of a judge rather than her parents. More significantly, the Court held that the right to an abortion did not include the right to have an abortion financed at public expense. In *Harris v. McRae* (1980), the Court upheld the constitutionality of the Hyde Amendment (1976), a federal law that prevents the use of Medicaid funds to pay for abortions except where necessary to save the pregnant woman's life. A majority of the Court, in an opinion by Justice Stewart, distinguished between laws that impeded a woman's right to seek an abortion and laws that simply declined to facilitate that right. According to the Court, although the federal or state governments could not take away a woman's right to an abortion, they nevertheless need not subsidize it.

A Conservative Turn. During President Reagan's two terms of office in the 1980's, he made it a priority to nominate justices to the Court who would favor overruling *Roe v. Wade*. He partially achieved this purpose by appointing Justice William H. Rehnquist—one of the original dissenters in *Roe*—as chief justice upon the retirement of Chief Justice Warren E. Burger. Late in his second term, President Reagan attempted to appoint Robert H. Bork, an outspoken critic of *Roe*, to fill the seat on the Court vacated by Justice Lewis F. Powell, Jr., only to have the Senate reject the nomination. Nevertheless, Reagan's other nominees—Sandra Day O'Connor, Antonin Scalia, and Anthony M. Kennedy—were all viewed as representing some measure of dissatisfaction with the decision in *Roe*.

By the close of the 1980's, some reconsideration of *Roe* seemed imminent. In *Webster v. Reproductive Health Services* (1989), a majority of the Court appeared to reject a rigid view of the trimester analysis of *Roe* by upholding a requirement that fetuses be tested for viability after twenty weeks of pregnancy. Under *Roe*, twenty weeks, being within the second trimester, fell within a period when the state's interest in the potential life of the fetus was insufficient to justify any impediment to a woman's abortion right. Four justices were prepared to overrule *Roe* explicitly on this point. Justice O'Connor concurred in the result but was unwilling to repudiate *Roe*'s trimester approach completely.

In the wake of the decision in *Webster*, observers of the Court speculated that a majority of the justices were poised to revisit *Roe*. Four justices remained solidly behind the precedent—William J. Brennan, Jr., Thurgood Marshall, John Paul Stevens, and Blackmun–and dissented vigorously from the holding in *Webster*. Standing on the opposite side were Chief Justice Rehnquist and Justices Scalia, Kennedy, and Byron R. White. Justice O'Connor stood in the middle—apparently willing to reconsider at least some aspects of *Roe v. Wade*. In the years immediately following *Webster*, President George Bush added two more justices to the Court to replace staunch defenders of *Roe*. Justice David H. Souter took the seat formerly held by Brennan, and Justice Clarence Thomas filled the seat vacated by Marshall. These appointments seemed likely to tip the balance against continued adherence to the principles of *Roe v. Wade*.

The Revolution That Was and Was Not. In 1992 a Court largely reconstituted from its composition at the time of *Roe* considered a cluster of abortion regulations in *Planned Parenthood of Southeastern Pennsylvania v. Casey*, including a requirement that women seeking an abortion wait at least twenty-four hours after being given information by a physician about the nature of the abortion procedure, the fetus's developmental stage, and alternatives to abortion. The Court also considered a requirement that married women notify their husbands of their intent to have an abortion. The widely anticipated decision of the Court proved to frustrate many prognostications about its likely result and to satisfy neither those who wished to abolish the *Roe*-given right to abortion nor those who wished to defend it against all government restrictions on the abortion procedure.

Three justices joined to write the opinion for the Court: O'Connor, Kennedy, and Souter. The first major element of their opinion was to reaffirm the basic holding of *Roe v. Wade* that the Constitution guaranteed the right to abortion. With an eye to the profound political controversy still surrounding abortion nearly two decades after *Roe*, the justices argued that adherence to the core of the Court's previous holding was necessary to sustain the Court's legitimacy and to prevent it from appearing to bow to political pressure. They were joined in this reaffirmation of *Roe* by Justices Blackmun and Stevens. However, the Court's opinion, while not overruling *Roe*, nevertheless substantially revised the formulation originally adopted by the Court in *Roe*. Instead of the trimester scheme, which prevented laws from interfering with a woman's choice to have an abortion except to protect her health after the first trimester and to protect the fetus after the second trimester, the Court focused on whether a particular law amounted to an undue burden on the right to abortion. Under this formulation, some regulations of abortion might be undertaken throughout a pregnancy. Applying this new test, a majority of the Court found that the twenty-four-hour waiting period was not an undue burden, but that the spousal notification was an unconstitutional burden on a woman's right to an abortion.

FURTHER READING

Abortion: The Supreme Court Decisions, edited by Ian Shapiro (Indianapolis, Ind.: Hackett, 1995), collects the major legal decisions defining the current constitutional law concerning abortion. For further background, readers may consult *The Abortion Controversy: A Documentary History*, edited by Eva R. Rubin (Westport, Conn.: Greenwood, 1994), which includes both Supreme Court materials and other important political documents relating to abortion, and *Abortion: A Reference Handbook*, by Marie Costa (2d ed., Santa Barbara, Calif.: ABC-CLIO, 1996), which offers a variety of background information concerning the abortion controversy, including a chronology of abortion laws from ancient times to the present, biographies of those involved in the abortion debate, and a variety of statistics concerning abortion. A variety of sources treat the historical context of the Court's abortion decisions. *Liberty and Sexuality: The Right to Privacy and the Making of "Roe v. Wade,"* by David J. Garrow (New York: Macmillan, 1994), is a sweeping history of the cases and controversies leading up to the Court's decision. *"Roe v. Wade": The Untold Story of the Landmark Supreme Court Decision That Made Abortion Legal*, by Marian Faux (New York: Macmillan, 1988), focuses more specifically on the trial and appeal of *Roe* itself.

The interplay between the Court and other social actors may be explored in Lee Epstein and Joseph F. Kobylka's *The Supreme Court and Legal Change: Abortion and the Death Penalty* (Chapel Hill: University of North Carolina Press, 1992), which emphasizes the role that legal arguments played in constitutional cases involving abortion and the death penalty, and in Neal Devins's *Shaping Constitutional Values: Elected Government, the Supreme Court, and the Abortion Debate* (Baltimore, Md.: Johns Hopkins University Press, 1996), which explores the relationship between the Court and politics with respect to the abortion controversy. *Abortion: The Clash of Absolutes*, by Harvard Law School professor Laurence H. Tribe (New York: Norton, 1992), presents a summary of the constitutional issue from the standpoint of a position protective of abortion rights. Mary Ann Glendon's *Abortion and Divorce in Western Law* (Cambridge, Mass.: Harvard University Press, 1987) provides an international perspective on the issue of divorce by comparing the Court's treatment of the issue with the results of decisions in the courts of other nations. Finally, *Wrath of Angels: The American Abortion War,* by James Risen and Judy L. Thomas (New York: Basic Books, 1998), is an illuminating account of the abortion protest movement inaugurated by the Court's decision in *Roe v. Wade.*

Timothy L. Hall

SEE ALSO *Akron v. Akron Center for Reproductive Health;* Birth control and contraception; Blackmun, Harry A.; Due process, substantive; Fetal rights; Fourteenth Amendment; *Griswold v. Connecticut;* Judicial scrutiny; Nominations to the Court; *Planned Parenthood of Southeastern Pennsylvania v. Casey; Reese, United States v.; Roe v. Wade;* Webster, Daniel.

Abrams v. United States

CITATION: 250 U.S. 616
DATE: November 10, 1919
ISSUE: Freedom of speech
SIGNIFICANCE: Oliver Wendell Holmes, in his dissent to this 1919 case in which the Supreme Court upheld convictions of Russian anarchists on sedition charges, clarified and limited the clear and present danger test he had created.

In a 7-2 decision, the Supreme Court upheld the conviction and lengthy prison terms of five Russian anarchists who had written and distributed English- and Yiddish-language leaflets criticizing the United States for sending troops to Russia during the 1917 Bolshevik Revolution. The anarchists were indicted under the Sedition Act of 1918, which made it a crime to criticize the government or advocate disruption of the war effort.

Justice Oliver Wendell Holmes had previously written the unanimous opinions in *Schenck v. United States* (1919) upholding the 1917 Espionage Act and *Debs v. United States* (1919) upholding the 1918 Sedition Act. After being criticized by influential friends, he dissented in *Abrams,* setting the limits of what he meant by the clear and present danger test. Holmes insisted that the test required a readily apparent, imminent danger before the government could restrict speech. His *Abrams* dissent is regarded as one of his best and is widely quoted, but it did not persuade a majority of the other justices. The Court struggled for decades with varying definitions of the clear and present danger test before it adopted the direct incitement test in *Brandenburg v. Ohio* (1969).

Richard L. Wilson

SEE ALSO Bad tendency test; *Brandenburg v. Ohio*; Clear and present danger test; *Gitlow v. New York*; Holmes, Oliver Wendell; *Schenck v. United States*; Speech and press, freedom of; *Stromberg v. California*; *Whitney v. California*.

Academic freedom

DESCRIPTION: Ability to freely exchange ideas and concepts in an academic setting.

SIGNIFICANCE: The Supreme Court has never granted academic freedom full constitutional status. It has ruled both for and against the protection of academic freedom on the basis of the First and Fourteenth Amendments.

In many rulings, the Supreme Court recognized that citizens possess constitutional rights of free speech and due process. However, when these citizens were faculty members at academic institutions, the Court also obligated them to respect their responsibilities to their students, their academic community, and society in general. In early cases such as *Gitlow v. New York* (1925) and *Whitney v. California* (1928), the Court struggled with the standard for judging constitutionality of state laws or actions that were being challenged as violations of the free speech clause of the First Amendment. The Court upheld convictions for subversive advocacy in both *Gitlow* and *Whitney* and ruled that the defendants' First Amendment rights had not been violated. The dissent issued in *Gitlow* by Justice Oliver Wendell Holmes joined by Justice Louis D. Brandeis became the test by which the Court determined what speech was allowable. The justices stressed that speech should be protected unless it creates a clear and present danger. In *Stromberg v. California* (1931), Stromberg's lawyers used the clear and present danger test in their arguments before the Court, which overturned Stromberg's conviction by a state court on a charge of displaying a red (communist) flag at a youth camp.

Two Supreme Court decisions in 1952 focused on the First Amendment rights of teachers. Both cases, *Adler v. Board of Education* and *Wieman v. Epdegraff*, involved teachers being discharged because of membership in subversive organizations. In *Adler*, the Court upheld New York's Feinberg Law, which banned teachers who belonged to subversive organizations from public schools. Justice Sherman Minton reasoned that because teachers shape the attitudes of young minds toward the society in which they live, the state has a vital concern in protecting schools from subversive organizations. In the dissent, Justices William O. Douglas and Hugo L. Black wrote of their concern for censorship and threat to First Amendment rights. This concern for constitutional freedoms would be echoed by Justice William J. Brennan, Jr., in *Keyishian v. Board of Regents* (1967). In *Wieman v. Epdegraff*, the Court overruled an Oklahoma statute that disqualified people from teaching or other public employment solely on the basis of membership in a subversive organization and not whether they had knowledge of its purposes and activities. The Oklahoma statute was ruled unconstitutional under the due process clause. Justice Felix Frankfurter endorsed the issue of academic freedom for teachers at all levels.

The Warren Court. As chief justice, Earl Warren led the Court in landmark decisions guaranteeing First Amendment protections. In *Shelton v. Tucker* (1960), the Court declared unconstitutional a New York statute that required teachers to disclose all organizational affiliations. In *Keyishian v. Board of Regents*, it struck down sections of the Feinberg Law that had been upheld in *Adler* and established broad First Amendment protections for academic freedom for college faculty. In the majority opinion, Justice Brennan stressed the importance of academic freedom for all people, not just for teachers.

The Court's ruling in *Epperson v. Arkansas* (1968) extended academic freedom to precollegiate levels as it negated an Arkansas law prohibiting the teaching of evolution. The Court ruled on the basis of the First Amendment prohibition against religious establishment and therefore did not set a precedent for free speech rights for elementary and secondary schools. Free speech protection would not be extended to the precollegiate level until *Tinker v. Des Moines Independent Community School District* (1969).

Burger-Rehnquist Eras. Justices appointed by Presidents Richard M. Nixon and Ronald Reagan (Warren E. Burger, William H. Rehnquist, Lewis F. Powell, Jr., and Sandra Day O'Connor) formed the core of a new majority on the Burger and Rehnquist Courts. Under these chief justices, the Court would issue opinions contradicting rulings that had previously limited the authority of school-governing officials. In *Ambach v. Norwick* (1979), two teachers from Scotland and Finland challenged the New York statute that denied certification to foreign nationals who were not in the process of attaining U.S. citizenship. In writing the majority opinion, Justice Powell stressed the role of the school as an agency for socialization and the importance of the influence of the teacher in this process. The teachers argued on the grounds of academic freedom, but the Court ruled on the basis of an equal protection case under the Fourteenth Amendment rather than a free speech case under the First Amendment. The *Ambach* case, which describes the political socialization of schools, was cited by both sides in *Island Trees School District v. Pico* (1982). Justices Brennan and Harry A. Blackmun asserted in the majority opinion that judicial review of book removals from libraries is warranted in order to prevent First Amendment violations. In their dissent, Justices Burger, Powell, and Rehnquist argued that it is not unconstitutional for school officials to remove from the library books that contain expressions of values that are not shared by the community.

Hazelwood School District v. Kuhlmeier (1988) was a milestone in supporting the authority of school officials. The case involved a Missouri high school principal who removed articles from a school newspaper. The Court ruled that the newspaper was part of the school curriculum and was rightfully under the control of the school. The Court did not view the principal's action as a First Amendment violation.

University of Pennsylvania v. Equal Employment Opportunity Commission (1990) placed a different twist on the typical academic freedom argument. The University of Pennsylvania denied tenure to an associate professor who then filed a charge with the Equal Employment Opportunity Commission alleging discrimination in violation of Title VII of the Civil Rights Act of 1964. When a subpoena was issued requesting tenure-review files of the professor and of five other male faculty members, the university filed suit. The university argued that the files would jeopardize a common-law privilege against disclosure of confidential peer review materials and would violate the faculty members' First Amendment rights, including academic freedom. The Court rejected this position and ruled that a university does not enjoy a special privilege regarding peer review files.

FURTHER READING

Menard, Louis. *The Future of Academic Freedom.* Chicago: University of Chicago Press, 1996.

Poch, Robert. *Academic Freedom in American Higher Education: Rights, Responsibilities, and Limitations.* Washington, D.C.: George Washington University Press, 1993.

Whitson, James Anthony. *Constitution and Curriculum.* London: The Falmer Press, 1991.

Gae R. Johnson

SEE ALSO *Epperson v. Arkansas*; First Amendment; Fourteenth Amendment; *Gitlow v. New York*; *Keyishian v. Board of Regents*; *Stanley v. Georgia*; *Tinker v. Des Moines Independent Community School District*; Warren, Earl; *Whitney v. California*.

Adair v. United States

CITATION: 208 U.S. 161
DATE: January 27, 1908
ISSUE: Freedom of contract
SIGNIFICANCE: The Supreme Court severely limited the extent to which the federal government could protect the rights of workers.

The Erdman Act of 1898 made it illegal to discharge or punish employees for union activity. Its main purpose was to prohibit yellow dog contracts, which required workers to agree not to join a labor union. By a 7-2 vote, the Supreme Court ruled that the Erdman Act deprived persons of their substantive liberty guaranteed in the due process clause of the Fifth Amendment. Justice John Marshall Harlan, speaking for the majority, used the theory of freedom of contract, or the right of individuals to enter into labor agreements without governmental interference. In dissent, Justices Joseph McKenna and Oliver Wendell Holmes argued that the Constitution did not prohibit reasonable legislation promoting fairness in collective bargaining.

In *Coppage v. Kansas* (1915), the Court used the *Adair* precedent to strike down state laws protecting workers' rights to join unions. Progressives of the day were outraged by such decisions, while conservatives praised the Court for preventing class warfare. In 1937 the Court reversed the precedents of *Coppage* and *Adair* when it upheld the constitutionality of the Wagner Act (1935), a New Deal law protecting the right of collective bargaining.

Thomas T. Lewis

SEE ALSO Contract, freedom of; Due process, substantive; Labor; *Lochner v. New York*; *National Labor Relations Board v. Jones and Laughlin Steel Corp.*; New Deal.

Adams, John Quincy

IDENTIFICATION: Sixth president of the United States (1825-1829)
NOMINATIONS TO THE COURT: Two, one confirmed
BORN: July 11, 1767, Braintree (later Quincy), Massachusetts
DIED: February 21, 1848, Washington, D.C.
SIGNIFICANCE: A strong advocate of a powerful federal judiciary, Adams was unable as president to make appointments that strengthened the Supreme Court.

John Quincy Adams. (Library of Congress)

ADAMS'S APPOINTMENTS TO THE COURT		
Year	*Nominee*	*Result*
1826	Robert Trimble	confirmed
1828	John J. Crittenden	no action

Admitted to the Massachusetts bar as a young man, Adams found the practice of law tedious and boring. Discontinuing his practice after four years to become a diplomat, he resumed practice between 1801 and 1809 while continuing to pursue a political career, including a term in the U.S. Senate. During this time, Adams argued several commercial cases before the Supreme Court. In *Fletcher v. Peck* (1810), he argued against the validity of Georgia's recission of a land grant when the case first came before the Court, but he did not participate in the final arguments that led to the Court's ruling in favor of the position that Adams had earlier espoused. While serving as ambassador to Russia in 1811, Adams was appointed by President James Madison to serve as an associate justice of the Supreme Court and was confirmed by the Senate in a voice vote. He rejected the appointment because he preferred to remain in politics. After continuing his diplomatic career, he served as secretary of state from 1817 to 1825.

As president, Adams failed to convince Congress to adopt his proposal for a comprehensive program of "internal improvements" that would have strengthened the federal government. He was no more successful in helping to enhance federal power through his Supreme Court nominations. His nomination of Robert Trimble of Kentucky in 1826 was influenced by Trimble's staunch defenses of federal power during his service as a lower federal judge at a time when states' rights advocates in Kentucky were fiercely attacking federal power. Although Trimble continued to defend federal power as a justice, his impact was slight because he died after only two years. Adams nominated John Crittenden of Kentucky to replace Trimble in December, 1828, but the Senate refused to act on the nomination, which was made after Adams had been defeated for reelection.

Adams later served in the House of Representatives, where he championed the cause of the abolition of slavery. In 1841 he appeared once more before the Court to successfully argue the case of Africans who sought freedom from Spanish slave traders in *United States v. The Amistad* (1841).

FURTHER READING

Ross, William G. "The Legal Career of John Quincy Adams." *Akron Law Review* 23 (Spring, 1990): 415-453.

William G. Ross

SEE ALSO Crittenden, John J.; *Fletcher v. Peck*; Slavery; Trimble, Robert.

Adamson v. California

CITATION: 332 U.S. 46
DATE: June 23, 1947
ISSUE: Incorporation doctrine
SIGNIFICANCE: Reaffirming that the Fifth Amendment privilege against self-incrimination was not applicable to the states, the Supreme Court reiterated that the due process clause of the Fourteenth Amendment incorporated only those procedural rights considered essential to a fair trial.

When tried for murder, Admiral D. Adamson did not testify, because of his prior criminal record. The district attorney, as permitted by applicable state law at the time, told the jury that Adamson's refusal to testify was a good reason to infer his guilt. The Supreme Court had earlier permitted this practice in *Twining v. New Jersey* (1908). After Adamson was convicted, his attorney argued that permitting the prosecutorial comment was a violation of the Fifth Amendment. A 5-4 majority of the Court upheld the conviction, based on the long-standing doctrine that the Fourteenth Amendment did not require the states to honor all the privileges and protections of the Bill of Rights.

Adamson is notable primarily because of Hugo L. Black's long dissent, which used historical data to argue for the "total incorporation" of the entire Bill of Rights into the Fourteenth Amendment. Justice Felix Frankfurter's concurring opinion defended the alternative theory of "selective incorporation." Although subsequent Courts have never accepted Black's perspective, the privilege against self-incrimination was made binding on the states in *Malloy v. Hogan* (1964). This privilege was interpreted to prohibit prosecutorial comment on a defendant's failure to testify in *Griffin v. California* (1965).

Thomas T. Lewis

SEE ALSO *Barron v. Baltimore*; Constitutional interpretation; Fifth Amendment; *Griffin v. California*; Incorporation doctrine; *Malloy v. Hogan*; *Palko v. Connecticut*; *Twining v. New Jersey*.

Adarand Constructors v. Peña

CITATION: 515 U.S. 200
DATE: June 12, 1995
ISSUE: Affirmative action
SIGNIFICANCE: The Supreme Court required lower courts to use the standards of "strict scrutiny" when examining any preferences based on race.

The Federal Highway Division provided premiums to general contractors for awarding contracts to firms owned by members of racial minorities recognized as having experienced social and economic disadvantages. Although the Adarand Constructors company was the lowest bidder for one construction project, the award was made to a Hispanic-owned company. Adarand sued, claiming that this race-based preference violated the Fifth Amendment guarantee of equal protection. In *Richmond v. J. A. Croson Co.* (1989), the Supreme Court had required "strict scrutiny" on racial classifications at the state and local levels, but it had applied "intermediate scrutiny" for federal programs in *Metro Broadcasting v. Federal Communications Commission* (1990). The court of appeals used the more lenient standard and upheld the government's policy.

However, the Supreme Court overturned the lower court's decision. Speaking for a 5-4 majority, Justice Sandra Day O'Connor held that all racial classifications must be analyzed under the strict scrutiny standard, which required such classifications to be "narrowly tailored measures that further compelling governmental objectives." Contradicting what many authorities had written, O'Connor denied that strict scrutiny would always be "fatal in fact." Although the *Adarand* decision did not end all affirmative action, it did increase the probability that federal programs involving preferences would be challenged and invalidated.

Thomas T. Lewis

SEE ALSO Affirmative action; *Fullilove v. Klutznick*; Judicial scrutiny; *Metro Broadcasting v. Federal Communications Commission*; *Richmond v. J. A. Croson Co.*; *Texas v. Hopwood*.

Adderley v. Florida

CITATION: 385 U.S. 39
DATE: November 14, 1966
ISSUE: Freedom of assembly
SIGNIFICANCE: Supreme Court Justice Hugo L. Black underscored a distinction between speech and action in upholding the conviction of civil rights demonstrators.

Justice Hugo L. Black, writing for a five-member majority, upheld the conviction of civil rights protesters who demonstrated directly on the grounds of a county jail in Tallahassee, Florida, where demonstrations had never been permitted. Reading the First Amendment literally, Black found that it allowed a government to protect jails and courthouses from demonstrations if it did so consistently. Assembly, he argued, is not an absolute right but conditioned by the inclusion of the word "peaceably" in the First Amendment.

Although often regarded as a civil libertarian, Black disappointed many liberals with his opinion in this case. His critics failed to perceive that his so-called "absolute standard" was logically compatible with a distinction between speech, which was absolutely protected, and assembly, which was limited by the Constitution's use of the word "peaceably" and could never be so absolutely protected. Justice William O. Douglas, Black's frequent partner in dissent, disagreed with him in this case and was joined by Chief Justice Earl Warren and Justices William J. Brennan, Jr., and Abe Fortas.

Richard L. Wilson

SEE ALSO Assembly and association, freedom of; Black, Hugo L.; *Brandenburg v. Ohio*; *Hague v. Congress of Industrial Organizations*; Time, place, and manner regulations.

Adkins v. Children's Hospital

CITATION: 261 U.S. 525
DATE: April 9, 1923
ISSUE: Minimum-wage laws

SIGNIFICANCE: This decision, in which the Supreme Court struck down a minimum-wage law, was a prime example of the Court's commitment to the freedom of contract doctrine and laissez-faire principles.

In 1918 Congress established a board with authority to set minimum wages for women and minors in the District of Columbia. The stated purpose of the law was to protect women and minors from conditions of poverty that would be "detrimental to their health and morals." Children's Hospital, a private institution paying less than the minimum wage, argued that the law was a violation of the due process clause of the Fifth Amendment. In a 6-3 vote, the Supreme Court agreed with the hospital's position. Justice George Sutherland, speaking for the majority, based the ruling on two doctrines: substantive due process and freedom of contract. Although the government could exercise its police power to prevent specific evils, freedom of contract was "the general rule and restraint the exception." Sutherland found that the law was demeaning to women, especially in view of the political equality that had resulted from the Nineteenth Amendment. In addition, any law that considered only the needs of workers was unjust to the needs of the employer.

Chief Justice William H. Taft, usually a defender of substantive due process, dissented in the *Adkins* case. He emphasized that the Court had earlier approved of laws mandating a maximum-hour workday and a time-and-a-half provision for overtime, and he argued that there were no fundamental differences between regulations of hours and of wages. He insisted that the Court should not overturn laws that were simply considered to be based on "unwise or unsound" economic theories. In 1937 a majority of the justices agreed with Taft's dissent in *West Coast Hotel Co. v. Parrish*.

Thomas T. Lewis

SEE ALSO *Bunting v. Oregon*; Contract, freedom of; Due process, substantive; Labor; *Morehead v. New York ex rel. Tipaldo*; Taft, William H.; *West Coast Hotel Co. v. Parrish*.

Administrative assistant to chief justice

DESCRIPTION: A person who assists the chief justice in a multitude of administrative duties.

Significance: Position was created in 1972 to assist Chief Justice Warren E. Burger with his increasing nonjudicial obligations.

The chief justice assigns various duties to the administrative assistant, who is assisted by a small support staff. These duties include conducting research for the chief justice's public addresses and statements, acting as a intermediary between the chief justice and others, such as Congress, the executive branch, and the state courts, and "monitoring of literature and developments in the fields of judicial administration and court improvement." The administrative assistant also aids the chief justice in responsibilities to the Federal Judicial Center, the Judicial Conference, and the Smithsonian Institution.

Other duties include helping the chief justice prepare the Supreme Court's budget, drafting personnel policies, and resolving problems concerning the Court's staff. The administrative assistant also recruits new staff and officers of the Court. Further responsibilities include managing the judicial internship program at the Court and directing the judicial fellows program, started by Warren E. Burger in 1973. After the position was created, four people have filled the capacity of administrative assistant to the chief justice.

Andrea E. Miller

See also Burger, Warren E.; Chief justice; Clerk of the Court; Staff of the Court.

Administrative law

Description: Branch of law governing those who implement public policy when they are acting in their official capacity.

Significance: Through administrative law, courts prevent administrative agencies and officials from exceeding their legitimate authority. The Supreme Court, in various cases, determined whether specific administrative procedures violated the due process clause.

Administrators, those who carry out public policy, have discretion in how they fulfill their responsibilities. Their discretion, however, is limited by the U.S. Constitution. If they are state administrators, their discretion is limited by both the U.S. Constitution and their state constitutions. The Supreme Court does not enforce the commands of a state constitution—that is the job of state courts—but it does enforce the language of the Fifth and Fourteenth Amendments prohibiting federal and state officials from denying life, liberty, or property, without due process of law. Administrative law, therefore, has a constitutional component.

Administrative law also has a statutory component. When administrators attempt to carry out public policy, they are doing what they believe they have been authorized to do by a legislative enactment. For example, Congress may have enacted a statute to regulate a particular industry and given the Environmental Protection Agency (EPA) responsibility for implementing the law. A corporation subject to the law might recognize Congress's constitutional authority to enact such legislation but challenge EPA regulations on grounds that the agency misinterpreted what Congress authorized it to do. If such a challenge reached the Court, it would be up to the Court to interpret the meaning of the statutory language. In other words, the Court would be second-guessing the administrative agency, and its interpretation of the law would be binding on the agency.

Administrative Due Process. A major constitutional concern of the Court is ensuring that administrative procedures treat people fairly. In *Goldberg v. Kelly* (1970), within the context of welfare rights, the Court noted that Congress had established the policy of providing welfare payments to people who had demonstrated their poverty. Though funded by the federal government, the policy was carried out by the states, and the Court held that a state could not terminate payments to welfare recipients without first according them a hearing in which they had an opportunity to establish their continued eligibility. The state procedure permitted a hearing after the termination of payments, but the Court found that a posttermination hearing did not satisfy the requirements of due process. Moreover, the Court specified several procedural rights that due process required in a pretermination hearing, procedures similar to those used in a court trial. Such hearings, whether they come before or after an administrative action, are called administrative adjudications.

The Court did not, however, interpret due process as requiring that all administrative adjudications contain every procedure that the *Goldberg* case mandated in the welfare rights context. Instead, it interpreted administrative due process flexibly. The Court required that administrators use fair procedures, but in *Mathews v. Eldridge* (1976), it also recognized that what is required for fairness is not the same in all administrative situations.

Judicial Deference. Although the constitutional claim of due process plays an important role in the Court's administrative law decisions, the Court did not overlook the need for effective government and tried to avoid tying the hands of administrators so that they are unable to carry out public policy efficiently. In the welfare case, for example, the Court was cognizant of the administrators' responsibility to protect the taxpayers' money. In the *Goldberg* case, the balance tipped in favor of due process. However, in cases involving statutory interpretation, the Court often shows deference to administrators and recognizes that they are specialists in their fields while most justices are not educated in chemistry, physics, biology, or medicine. Such technical knowledge would be necessary if the Court were wisely or intelligently to supersede administrators' interpretations of how they should carry out the laws entrusted to them by Congress, laws such as the various clean-air acts or the Occupational Safety and Health Act (1970).

In the 1970's the federal courts went through a period in which they rejected a deferential role, and their activism received scholarly criticism. In *Vermont Yankee Nuclear Power Corp. v. Natural Resources Defense Council* (1978), the Court endorsed a deferential approach when it reversed an activist lower court decision regarding administrative rule making under the Administrative Procedure Act of 1947. In *Chevron, U.S.A. v. Natural Resources Defense Council* (1984), the Court accepted the EPA's interpretation of regulatory legislation rather than imposing a contrary interpretation. When the Court takes a deferential approach, the agency interpretation must merely be reasonable for the Court to accept it.

Interest groups actively try to influence the way that agencies interpret regulatory laws. Therefore, when the Court decides administrative law cases, it is functioning in the political process as well as the legal process.

In the course of carrying out their duties, administrators may inadvertently cause harm to citizens. For much of U.S. history, citizens could not sue the government. However, as a result of the Federal Tort Claims Act of 1946, it became possible, under certain circumstances, to bring a lawsuit against a government agency. This created a new dimension of administrative law. The Court's interpretation of this statute over the years had considerable impact on the relationship between administrators and citizens.

FURTHER READING

Cann, Steven J. *Administrative Law.* Thousand Oaks, Calif.: Sage, 1995.

Mashaw, Jerry L. *Due Process in the Administrative State.* New Haven, Conn.: Yale University Press, 1985.

Melnick, R. Shop. *Regulation and the Courts: The Case of the Clean Air Act.* Washington, D.C.: Brookings Institution, 1983.

O'Brien, David M. *What Process Is Due? Courts and Science-Policy Disputes.* New York: Russell Sage Foundation, 1987.

Patricia A. Behlar

SEE ALSO *Butz v. Economou*; Due process, procedural; Federal Tort Claims Act; *Goldberg v. Kelly*; *Marshall v. Barlow's*; Stevens, John Paul.

Admiralty and maritime law

DESCRIPTION: Laws and international treatises governing marine navigation and commerce, the transportation over water of property and people, and other issues involving navigable waters, including oceans, gulfs, coastal regions, and inland waterways.

SIGNIFICANCE: The Supreme Court's constitutional mandate is to promote the United States' interest by applying uniform rules to safeguard and conserve the surrounding oceans and inland waterways for trade, navigation, fishing, recreation, marine ecosystems, offshore oil and gas development, scientific research, national security, and scenic beauty.

Article III, Section 2, of the U.S. Constitution provides that federal judicial power shall extend to "all cases of admiralty and maritime jurisdiction." Virtually every admiralty and maritime case in the United States is fundamentally a matter of constitutional law. Nowhere, however, does the Constitution or any act of Congress define the nature and limits of this national jurisdiction.

The preponderance of Supreme Court decisions and legal scholarship interpret the language of the clause and its placement within the Constitution as stipulating only the courts that can decide maritime cases. The clause does not delegate to the Court the authority to develop its own rules of decision. In the Court's view, the Constitution gives Congress the power to enact and amend maritime laws.

Jurisdiction. The Framers of the Constitution gave the Court exclusive prerogative to determine the appropriate jurisdiction for maritime cases so that there would be only one body of maritime laws. Uniform maritime laws foster the nation's economic health and security. Most major trading countries, including the United States, have laws (called cabotage laws) to assure reliable domestic shipping service and a maritime capability subject to national control in times of war or other emergency. The conflicting state laws found in colonial America were detrimental to the development and prosperity of the new country.

The words "admiralty" and "maritime" are virtually synonymous. Historically, though, the term "maritime" referred to oceans and other vast bodies of water, whereas "admiralty" referred to the judges who presided over the English courts and American colonies.

The relationship of an event or occurrence to a vessel or to navigable waters often determines the boundaries of U.S. admiralty jurisdiction. In many cases, however, admiralty jurisdiction rests in whole or in part on finding that the event or occurrence has a "maritime flavor." The key to determining a maritime flavor lies in determining whether the lack of a uniform national law or regulation governing this matter will have a substantial effect on the shipping industry. The measurement of the effect includes determining the availability of manpower, customers, and capital from within the United States, and the willingness of foreign carriers to traffic within ports of the United States. This standard determines whether a matter falls in federal or state jurisdiction. In contract matters, for example, admiralty jurisdiction depends on the nature of the transaction. In matters involving alleged wrongful acts, injury, or damage (or the law of torts), jurisdiction depends on the locality. In tort actions, plaintiffs must show the activity giving

rise to the incident had a substantial relationship to a traditional maritime activity such as the injury of a person on an unseaworthy vessel.

Settling Admiralty Disputes. In 1789 Congress enacted the Judiciary Act to exercise its constitutional mandate to establish a system of federal courts with exclusive jurisdiction in admiralty matters. These courts became, in effect, the ultimate arbiters of admiralty disputes. No separate courts of admiralty were created.

Federal district court judges decide whether a case will be decided under federal or state law. When national interests are at stake, the Court has ruled that state maritime interests must bow to federal law. State laws that threaten the uniformity of national maritime law and the national interest are unconstitutional. Under the maritime but local doctrine, where a matter is maritime, but there is neither federal law nor a perceived need for uniformity, a court may use state law to decide the case. Congress added a saving to suitors clause that allowed state courts to have jurisdiction where a common-law remedy existed.

During World War I, the Court clarified which courts may hear maritime cases and what law governs the disposition of such cases. In *Southern Pacific Co. v. Jensen* (1917) and *Chelentis v. Luckenbach Steamship Co.* (1918), the Court established a two-step test for determining maritime jurisdiction and legal principles and rights. The first step is to determine whether the focus of a case is an admiralty and maritime cause of action. Such a claim may exist under the federal maritime case law governing the jurisdiction of tort and contract actions in admiralty or by virtue of a federal law. In addition, the Court has indicated states may modify or supplement federal maritime law, but they may not flatly contradict it or deprive any person of a substantive federal right. Assuming such a cause of action exists, the second step is for a judge to determine whether the case belongs in state court or federal district court.

Although admiralty jurisdiction includes the sea and other navigable waters, the sea is the primary domain of the admiralty jurisdiction. The bulk of maritime law is federal. Much of it is international in scope. The majority of maritime controversies relate to vessels, and most transactions concerning or involving ships and navigation are within admiralty jurisdiction. Admiralty cases are filed either against the property (*in rem*) or against individuals and their organizations (*in personam*). Plaintiffs have the option of filing an *in personam* action in either federal or state court. The right to proceed *in rem* is the distinctive and exclusive remedy of the federal courts exercising admiralty jurisdiction. No state can confer jurisdiction on its courts to proceed *in rem* for any cause of action within admiralty jurisdiction. According to the Court, the Constitution prohibits Congress from delegating such a power to a state. State legislatures cannot constitutionally restrict federal jurisdiction but can only ensure that other remedies, if applicable, remain available.

The basis of the *in rem* proceeding is the maritime lien, or a claim on a property as security for payment of a just debt. The difference between the maritime lien and other liens is that the maritime lien is generally independent of possession and remains in effect even if the property is sold. Although a personal maritime liability may exist without a lien, the lien itself may be on the property even though the owner of the vessel is not liable. The vessel in question is taken into custody of the court. The owner of the vessel in contention will normally post a bond, thus securing release of the vessel. If the lien is upheld, the vessel is sold at a court auction, with the proceeds going to the plaintiff up to an amount sufficient to satisfy the lien.

Maritime law regulates the rights and obligations of the states and relations with foreign states. The reach of admiralty law extends to all navigable waters, including rivers, streams, and lakes, as long as the body of water has an interstate nexus. Without such federal power, domestic and foreign participants in maritime shipping and commerce would be subject to varying state laws, which could have an adverse effect on the nation's maritime commerce, natural resources, and shipping.

Admiralty jurisdiction is determined by either the waters/vessel test or the activity or type of lawsuit test. Admiralty jurisdiction extends to all waters, with or without tides, salt or fresh, natural or artificial, which are navigable in interstate or foreign water commerce. Federal statutes define a watercraft as a contrivance capable of being used as a means of transportation over water. Lawsuits that fall within admiralty jurisdiction include contracts for the transportation of goods and passengers, contracts for repairs and supplies furnished to vessels such as towage, and contracts for the services of sea personnel.

Origins. Maritime law is among the oldest branches of law in the world. U.S. admiralty law developed from British admiralty courts present in most of the American colonies. At the time of the Revolutionary War, each state maintained its own admiralty courts. The Articles of Confederation gave the Continental Congress jurisdiction to hear appeals over cases involving the seizure of foreign vessels and their prize cargoes. These courts functioned separately from courts of law and equity, which were resorted to when statute and common laws proved unjust.

During the early history of the federal judiciary, each federal district court had three dockets—law, equity, and admiralty. If a matter was based on federal admiralty jurisdiction, the case would be placed on the admiralty docket and decided by special admiralty rules interpreted by a judge "sitting in admiralty" and lawyers called "proctors in admiralty." With the passage of the Judiciary Act, though, Congress placed admiralty under the jurisdiction of the federal district courts. By the mid-1940's, the federal district courts with separate admiralty dockets had discontinued them. Although admiralty law shares much in common with civil law, it is separate from it.

Admiralty and maritime law developed in response to the practical problems and controversies of trade and commerce, including commerce, fishing, and navigation. Trade requires dependable and uniform laws and courts. State law yields to the uniform federal maritime law to preserve harmony in the multifarious transactions on the ocean, seas, lakes, and rivers. Traditionally, admiralty courts had jurisdiction over maritime contracts that included such contracts as charter-parties, contracts for maritime services (building, supplying, and navigating ships), and contracts between shipowners.

Not all maritime matters are controlled by federal law. The Court, in *Romeo v. International Terminal Operating Co.* (1959), said the states and federal government have joint roles that correspond to the realities of power, interest, and national power. The states have wide regulatory power, especially in the areas of maritime torts and contracts.

Because the coasts and oceans of the United States are a highly valued geographical asset and biological resource, laws protect them in the interests of the public. In *Shively v. Bowlby* (1894), the Court ruled that lands under navigable waters are owned in the public trust for the benefit of all the people. The protection has grown to include recreational sites, fish and wildlife habitats, aquatic life, lands preserved for scientific purposes, and lands devoted to the enjoyment of natural scenic beauty.

Procedural differences existed between maritime cases and other civil proceedings until 1966, when the Court approved amendments to the Federal Rules of Civil Procedure that brought admiralty and maritime procedural rules into accord with those used in other civil suits. On the admiralty side of the court, litigants, however, are still not entitled to trial by jury either by constitutional or statutory right.

The Court's exclusive prerogative to determine what matters fall within admiralty and maritime jurisdiction exists to ensure uniformity in maritime law. Uniformity is the key to the nation's prosperity and security. As the ultimate arbiter of maritime matters, the Court balances the uses of maritime resources with the conservation of those resources. The Court's constitutional mandate is to safeguard, protect, and restore the nation's stake in its navigable waterways.

FURTHER READING

The body of law on the sea and waterways is voluminous. For an overview, read Frank L. Maraist's *Admiralty in a Nutshell* (3d ed., St. Paul, Minn.: West Publishing, 1996). Readers will find the discussion of the origin and development of the Court's jurisdiction in maritime matters insightful. Significant Court decisions are analyzed and explained in layman's terms. To understand the origin of the Court's admiralty jurisdiction, refer to *Modern Constitutional Law* (2d ed., St. Paul, Minn.: West Group, 1997). For a comprehensive analysis of all facets of admiralty and maritime law, turn to the multivolume *Benedict on Admiralty* (New York: Matthew Bender, 1999), edited by Steven F. Friedell. Erastus C. Benedict published the first edition more than 150 years ago. Updates are published as significant developments occur in maritime law. Another useful multivolume work is Thomas J. Schoenbaum's *Admiralty and Maritime Law* (2d ed., St. Paul, Minn.: West Publishing, 1994). Donna R. Christie discusses the Court's impact on coastal and ocean resource development, preservation, and regulation in *Coastal and Ocean Management Law in a Nutshell* (St. Paul, Minn.: West Publishing, 1994). For a concise summary of the Court's authority in admiralty and maritime cases, read David P. Currie's *Federal Jurisdiction in a Nutshell* (St. Paul, Minn.: West Publishing, 1990).

Fred Buchstein

SEE ALSO *Bates v. State Bar of Arizona*; Constitutional interpretation; Delegation of powers; *Genesee Chief v. Fitzhugh*; Judiciary Act of 1789; Lower federal courts; State courts; States' rights; Understanding tests.

Advertising of lawyers

DESCRIPTION: Promotion of a lawyer's or law firm's services in any media including television and radio commercials, outdoor billboards, newspapers or magazines, and direct mailings where a fee was paid for placement.

SIGNIFICANCE: Until 1977 all advertising by individual lawyers or established law firms was tightly regulated by state bar associations and state supreme courts. Supreme Court decisions after 1977 reduced various restrictions on advertising in the legal profession.

In 1977 the Supreme Court addressed the limitations on advertising for lawyers in *Bates v. State Bar of Arizona*. The decision centered on the right of a legal firm to advertise in newspapers and other media, which was prohibited under the Arizona state supreme court's disciplinary rule. The Court found in favor of the defendant, viewing the restrictions placed on the law office as infringements of the First Amendment and contrary to the Sherman Antitrust Act of 1890. In delivering the opinion of the Court, Justice Harry A. Blackmun stated that "advertising does not provide a complete foundation on which to select an attorney. . . . The alternative—the prohibition of advertising—serves only to restrict the information that flows to consumers."

In subsequent decisions, the Court focused on the use of illustrations in advertisements (*Zauderer v. Office of Disciplinary Counsel*, 1985) and the use of direct mailings toward potential new clients (*Shapero v. Kentucky Bar Assn.*, 1988). In both cases, the limitations on advertising by lawyers and law firms were reduced.

Robert D. Mitchell

SEE ALSO Blackmun, Harry A.; First Amendment; *Goldfarb v. Virginia State Bar*; Sherman Antitrust Act; State courts.

Advisory opinions

DESCRIPTION: Judicial decisions issued about a hypothetical case, usually at the request of the legislative or executive branch to determine the constitutionality of proposed legislation.

SIGNIFICANCE: The Supreme Court stated that the federal courts will not issue advisory opinions but will rule only on actual cases and controversies.

Advisory opinions allow legislatures and executive officials to determine issues of constitutionality before proposed legislation is enacted. Although these opinions are commonly issued by some state and many foreign courts, the U.S. Supreme Court stated that the federal courts will rule only on actual controversies and not on hypothetical issues.

The prohibition on advisory opinions from U.S. federal courts dates from very early in U.S. history. On July 18, 1793, President George Washington sought an advisory opinion from the Supreme Court regarding the interpretation of the 1778 Franco-American Treaty. On August 8, 1793, the justices of the Court wrote a letter to formally decline to provide the requested advice, citing separation of powers concerns. Chief Justice John Jay stated that the justices were "judges of a court in the last resort" and should refuse to issue opinions except as a result of normal litigation undertaken by real parties in an actual conflict.

This ruling reinforced the independence of the federal courts and reaffirmed the attorney general's role as legal adviser to the president. However, this prohibition does not apply to the states, and some state constitutions do allow the state courts to issue advisory opinions.

Mark C. Miller

SEE ALSO Constitutional interpretation; Extrajudicial activities; Jay, John; Judicial review; Separation of powers; Standing; Washington, George.

Affirmative action

DESCRIPTION: Programs of governmental agencies or private institutions designed to provide members of racial and ethnic minorities and women with access to opportunities in education and employment.

SIGNIFICANCE: Because of discrimination against women and minority members, governmental agencies, businesses, and educational institutions gave them special opportunities, which some people criticized as discriminating against nonminority members. A divided Supreme Court struggled with the question of when such programs are acceptable.

Affirmative action is a highly controversial means of pursuing equal access to resources in education and employment. Although the term affirmative action first appeared in an official document in an executive order issued by President Lyndon B. Johnson in 1965, affirmative action did not emerge as a government policy until the 1970's. In *Griggs v. Duke Power Co.* (1971), the Supreme Court ruled that discrimination could be judged to exist when business practices resulted in limiting opportunities for minorities, even if there had been no evidence of intent to discriminate on the part of the employer. This altered the definition of discrimination, making it a matter of built-in racial bias.

Duke Power Company required either a high-school diploma or a passing grade on a general intelligence test for a job in its power plant. Fewer black applicants than white applicants passed this test. The plaintiffs argued that in this case, educational credentials and test results had no direct relevance to job performance, so no justification existed for a job requirement that disproportionately affected members of the minority race. The Court, under Chief Justice Warren E. Burger, found that employment practices that exclude African American job seekers and are not related to job performance are indeed discriminatory.

The concept of built-in discrimination established by *Griggs* helped lay the groundwork for political efforts to dismantle unintended barriers to full participation in American society. Affirmative action, according to the official government definition, involved action to overcome past or present barriers to equal opportunity. Two of the most obvious ways of overcoming such barriers were establishing quotas of minority members or women to be hired or admitted to educational programs and creating set-asides, positions reserved for minority members or women. These remedies, however,

In 1995 students in San Francisco marched to protest the University of California's plans to dismantle affirmative action programs in its nine-campus system. Earlier that year, the Supreme Court ruled that such programs must be necessary to meet a compelling state interest. (Reuters/Blake Sell/Archive Photos)

met with challenges by those in groups not benefiting from affirmative action, who charged that they were suffering from officially sanctioned discrimination.

In 1971 a Jewish man named DeFunis applied for admission to the University of Washington Law School but was rejected. The law school followed a practice of dividing its applicants into two categories, minority group members and majority group members, using lower standards for admitting minority group members. If DeFunis had been black, American Indian, or Latino, his test scores and grades would have gained him entry. He sued, claiming that his rights to equal legal protection, guaranteed by the Fourteenth Amendment, had been violated.

DeFunis v. Odegaard came before the Court in 1974. However, DeFunis had been admitted to the law school after a lower court found in his favor, and the school had said that he would be allowed to graduate, regardless of the Court's ruling. The Court ruled the case moot because a ruling would not affect the outcome for the plaintiff, and it dismissed the appeal. Justice William O. Douglas wrote

a dissent expressing his view that DeFunis had indeed been denied equal protection under the law.

Increasing Challenges. Although the Court did not have to rule on preferential treatment of protected categories of people in the DeFunis case, challenges to affirmative action increased through the 1970's. One of the objections was the claim that affirmative action violated Title VII of the Civil Rights Act of 1964, which forbids discrimination on the basis of race. Many critics maintained that preferential treatment of minority group members could be viewed as discrimination against those who were not minority group members. In *United Steelworkers of America v. Weber* (1979), the court ruled that Title VII's prohibition against racial discrimination does not condemn all private, voluntary race-conscious affirmative action plans. Kaiser Aluminum and Chemical Corporation and the United Steelworkers Union maintained a training program. As long as the percentage of African Americans among Kaiser's plant employees was less than the percentage of African Americans in the local workforce, half of the openings on this program were reserved for African Americans. Brian Weber, a white man who had not been allowed to enter the training program, sued, claiming that he had been a victim of racial discrimination.

Justice William J. Brennan, Jr., writing for the majority of justices, maintained that Congress had not intended Title VII to prohibit private, voluntary efforts to overcome long-established patterns of racial discrimination in employment. In addition, the Fourteenth Amendment did not apply in this case because it did not involve any governmental actions. Whites, in Brennan's view, were not handicapped by the policy regarding the training program because no whites were fired and whites still had opportunities for advancement.

The best-known challenge to affirmative action to come before the Court was *Regents of the University of California v. Bakke* (1978). Alan Bakke was a white man who had been denied admission to the

University of California medical school at Davis. In 1972 the thirty-two-year-old Bakke was a Marine Corps veteran who had served in Vietnam and an engineer at a research center of the National Aeronautics and Space Administration (NASA) near Palo Alto, California. While working at NASA, he decided to become a medical doctor. He took classes to prepare himself for medical school and served as a volunteer in a local hospital emergency room.

Despite high scores on the Medical College Admissions Test and strong letters of recommendation, Bakke was rejected by the University of California and ten other schools to which he applied. Bakke wrote to the chairman of admissions at the University of California, Davis, requesting reconsideration, charging that racial minority members who were less qualified than he had been admitted through a special admissions program. Bakke reapplied for early admissions in 1973 and prepared to sue if he was again rejected. In the summer of 1974 Bakke's suit was officially filed in Yolo County Superior Court.

Bakke became one of the most celebrated court cases of the decade. It provoked national debate over affirmative action and brought wide attention to the practice of setting aside places in businesses or educational institutions for minority members. The California supreme court found that Bakke had suffered racial discrimination. In November, 1976, the Board of Regents of the University of California voted to appeal the decision to the Supreme Court.

Four justices, led by Justice Brennan, voted not to hear the case. Five chose to hear it, however, and it went on the Court docket. Ultimately, the Court reached a split decision. Four justices concluded that the University of California had clearly violated both the equal protection clause of the Fourteenth Amendment and the Civil Rights Act of 1964. Four other justices disagreed and wanted to uphold the constitutionality of taking race into consideration for education or employment. The swing vote, Justice Lewis F. Powell, Jr., essentially divided his decision. He sided with the four who maintained that the minority set-aside program at Davis was unconstitutional; however, he also stated that although racial quotas were unacceptable, race could be taken into consideration. The majority opinion, written by Brennan, incorporated Powell's ambivalence. It

stated that it was constitutional to take race into account to remedy disadvantages resulting from past prejudice and discrimination, but that race alone could not be the basis for making decisions about opportunities in employment or education.

After *Bakke*. Many legal scholars believe that *Bakke* established an unclear precedent. Although it did uphold the basic principle of affirmative action, it also left the door open for challenges to specific affirmative action policies. As a part of the 1977 Public Works Employment Act, Congress set aside 10 percent of all federal appropriations for public works contracts for minority contractors and subcontractors. This legislation came before the Court in *Fullilove v. Klutznick* (1980). Once again, a controversial issue split the members of the Court.

One of the differences between *Fullilove* and earlier affirmative action cases was that it involved the actions of Congress, which may act with greater power and authority than a private employer or a local school board and is also charged with seeking the present and future welfare of the nation. Chief Justice Burger's opinion, joined by Justices Powell and Byron R. White, recognized this, stating that Congress has the power to act to remedy social evils and that there was a compelling governmental interest in seeking to counteract the deep-rooted disadvantages of minority contractors. Thurgood Marshall, joined by Justices Brennan and Harry A. Blackmun, wrote a concurring opinion arguing that the actions of Congress were constitutional because the set-aside provision was related to the congressionally approved goal of overcoming racial inequality. Justices Potter Stewart, William H. Rehnquist, and John Paul Stevens disagreed. Stewart and Rehnquist maintained that an unconstitutional practice could not be constitutional simply because it came from Congress rather than from a lesser source and that the set-aside involved distributing governmental privileges based on birth. Stevens objected to the governmental favoring of some groups over others and pointed out that those who were likely to benefit most were the least disadvantaged members of minority groups, such as successful black or Hispanic businesspeople. Thus, although *Fullilove* established once more the principle of affirmative action, it also made it clear that there were fundamental disagreements on the principle, even among the justices.

Two major issues emerged from the *Fullilove* decision. One was the concept that affirmative action policies undertaken by the government merit a special deference because of the constitutional authority of Congress to make laws. The second was that because affirmative action is a means of pursuing governmental policies, agencies and organizations must be able to demonstrate that their affirmative action programs serve a compelling governmental interest. This second point placed the burden of justifying affirmative action programs on those seeking to establish the policies. Those seeking to pursue affirmative action policies must be able to demonstrate that these policies are narrowly designed to compensate for past discrimination or to bring about a clearly defined goal. For this reason, the Court decided in *Mississippi University for Women v. Hogan* (1982) that a college could not deny men entry into a nursing program on the grounds that this was intended to compensate women for past discrimination. On the other hand, when past discrimination could be clearly demonstrated, affirmative action policies were deemed acceptable. A requirement in Alabama that one black state trooper be promoted for every promotion of a white state trooper was upheld by the Court in *United States v. Paradise* (1987) because it could be demonstrated that underrepresentation of African Americans at high ranks was caused by past discrimination by the Alabama Department of Public Safety. In *Richmond v. J. A. Croson Co.* (1989), however, the Court ruled that the Richmond city government's minority business utilization plan failed to provide appropriate statistical data showing systematic underrepresentation of minority-owned businesses. Therefore, the Court found that the plan was not narrowly tailored to remedy the effects of prior discrimination and failed to demonstrate a compelling government interest for awarding a certain percentage of contracts to minority-owned businesses. Both the concept of the special status of Congress and of the legitimacy of affirmative action for compelling governmental interests were upheld in *Metro Broadcasting v. Federal Communications Commission* (1990), in which a majority of justices ruled that minority preference policies of the Federal Communications Commission were acceptable because they met both criteria.

Limits on Affirmative Action. During the 1990's there were a number of public challenges to affirmative action, notably in the Texas and California systems of higher education, where controversial laws passed in 1997 made it illegal to give preferential treatment to members of protected groups. Affirmative action proponent Marshall left the Court in 1991, and new justices appointed by Presidents Ronald Reagan and George Bush—including Sandra Day O'Connor, Anthony M. Kennedy, Antonin Scalia, and Clarence Thomas—appeared to be largely unsympathetic to affirmative-action-style policies. In his book on affirmative action and the Court, Lincoln Caplan observed that in the middle to late 1990's Chief Justice Rehnquist and Justices O'Connor, Kennedy, Scalia, and Thomas never voted to uphold an affirmative action program based on race. Thomas, the only African American among these justices, was the strongest and most open opponent of the preferential treatment of minorities, which he derided as "racial paternalism." The limiting of affirmative action appeared in *Adarand Constructors v. Peña* (1995), in which the Court expanded the idea that programs had to serve a compelling interest. Affirmative action programs, the court ruled, must be observed with the strictest scrutiny and must be necessary to meet a compelling state interest.

By the end of the twentieth century, many observers were predicting that the Court would make a ruling that would end affirmative action. This perception made some defenders of affirmative action policies reluctant to bring cases before the Court. This happened, for example, in the case of Sharon Taxman. Taxman, a white teacher, had been laid off from her job by the school district of Piscataway, New Jersey, in 1991. The school district needed to reduce its teaching force and had to choose between Taxman and an equally qualified black teacher. Because black teachers were underrepresented in the district, the school system used its voluntary affirmative action program to decide between the two teachers. Taxman sued, claiming racial discrimination. The case was poised to go to the Court in late 1997. Fear that a Court ruling in favor of Taxman would further weaken affirmative action led civil rights groups to support the Piscataway School Board's decision to pay Taxman a $433,000 settlement in November, 1997, rather than risk an unfavorable Court decision.

The Court also showed a reluctance to hear affirmative action cases at the end of the twentieth century. In March, 1999, the Court refused to hear a case regarding a program in Dallas, Texas, that had been intended to benefit minority firefighters. A lower court, the Fifth Circuit Court of Appeals, earlier found that there was insufficient evidence of a historical pattern of discrimination against minorities in Dallas to justify preferential promotions for minority candidates. The two justices who had been appointed by President Bill Clinton, Stephen G. Breyer and Ruth Bader Ginsburg, issued a written dissent urging the majority of justices to take the case. Nevertheless, the Court let the decision of the lower court stand. Many observers maintained that this case and others like it sent the message that the majority on the Court saw racial preferences as a dying and disfavored strategy.

FURTHER READING

Up Against the Law: Affirmative Action and the Supreme Court (New York: Twentieth Century Fund Press, 1997) is a short introduction to the role of the Supreme Court in the American debate over affirmative action that also offers explanations of the practices and consequences of affirmative action programs. A great deal has been written on the *Bakke* case. Timothy J. O'Neill's *"Bakke" and the Politics of Equality: Friends and Foes in the Classroom of Litigation* (Middletown, Conn.: Wesleyan University Press, 1981) is a detailed study of the case and of the political forces on both sides. Readers who want to know about the *Bakke* case should consult *Behind "Bakke": Affirmative Action and the Supreme Court* (New York: New York University Press, 1988) by Bernard Schwartz. *The Color-Blind Constitution* (Cambridge, Mass.: Harvard University Press, 1992) attempts to discover the history of the argument that the Constitution prohibits racial classifications by agencies of the government. The last chapter, "Benign Racial Sorting," is particularly useful to those interested in the arguments surrounding affirmative action issues. For the ideas behind questions of racial preferences, readers may want to consult *Equality and Preferential Treatment* (Princeton, N.J.: Princeton University Press, 1972). This is a collection of essays by professors of law and philosophy that attempt to present arguments for and against racial, ethnic, or gender preferences in schooling or employment. Although the book is a little old, its arguments continue to be relevant. Dinesh D'Souza's *Illiberal Education: The Politics of Race and Sex on Campus* (New York: Free Press, 1991), a work strongly opposed to affirmative action, presents a view of affirmative action policies in universities before these began to be scaled back. *The Shape of the River: Long-Term Consequences of Considering Race in College and University Admissions* (Princeton, N.J.: Princeton University Press, 1998) by William G. Bowen and Derek C. Bok provides a positive view of affirmative action in higher education.

Carl L. Bankston III

SEE ALSO *Adarand Constructors v. Peña*; Employment discrimination; *Fullilove v. Klutznick*; *Griggs v. Duke Power Co.*; *Mississippi University for Women v. Hogan*; Private discrimination; Race and discrimination; *Regents of the University of California v. Bakke*; *Richmond v. J. A. Croson Co.*; School integration and busing; *Texas v. Hopwood*; Thomas, Clarence; *United Steelworkers of America v. Weber.*

Age discrimination

DESCRIPTION: Unequal treatment of adults or denial of services, access, or benefits based on age.

SIGNIFICANCE: The Supreme Court, composed of middle-aged and older jurists, usually ruled to protect people over forty from age discrimination although it approved some mandatory early retirement policies.

The Age Discrimination in Employment Act (ADEA) of 1967 banned workplace discrimination against those between ages forty and sixty-five. The ADEA, which built on a provision in Title VII of the Civil Rights Act of 1964, allowed employers to take action based on age when it is a "bona fide occupational qualification reasonably necessary to the normal operation of the particular business." In 1974 Congress extended the ADEA to state and local governments. In 1975 Congress passed the Age Discrimination Act (ADA), prohibiting discrimination on the basis of age in programs or activities that receive financial assistance from the federal government. After 1975, age discrimination complaints no longer went to the Department of Labor but instead could be filed with the Equal Employment Opportunity Commission (EEOC), which in turn sent cases to state civil rights agencies that monitored age discrimination.

In *Oscar Mayer v. Evans* (1979), the Supreme Court ruled five to four that a complaint need not be filed first with a state agency; a state agency complaint and a federal court lawsuit could be filed concurrently. In *Astoria Federal Savings and Loan Association v. Solomino* (1991), the Court unanimously held that those dissatisfied with state agency findings could sue in federal court. States' rights advocates, who wanted to prevent private parties from suing state governments on the basis of federal laws, were in the minority when the Court ruled five to four in *Equal Employment Opportunity Commission v. Wyoming* (1983) and *Johnson v. Mayor and City Council of Baltimore* (1985). The 1999 case *Alden v. Maine*, based on the Federal Labor Standards Act of 1938, suggested that the Court might eventually reverse itself.

Mandatory Retirement. Pursuant to the Fourteenth Amendment, which guarantees equal justice under the law, the Court ruled on various challenges to the ADA. However, it interpreted the act quite narrowly. In *Massachusetts Board of Retirement v. Murgia* (1976), the Court ruled seven to one that the state's mandatory retirement of police officers

In 1999 eighty-four-year-old former Woolworth employee Katherine Zajac talks to the press in New York about an age discrimination lawsuit filed by the Equal Employment Opportunity Commission. The Supreme Court's rulings have generally protected the rights of older workers. (AP/ Wide World Photos)

at age fifty was reasonable, accepting the argument that physical abilities decline over time. In *United Air Lines v. McMann* (1977), the Court voted seven to two that compulsory retirement for those reaching age sixty who received especially generous retirement plans was not contrary to the act.

In 1978 Congress amended the ADA to prohibit most employers from requiring mandatory retirement before the age of seventy, with no cap for federal workers. Nevertheless, in *Vance v. Bradley* (1979), the Court ruled eight to one that retirement of foreign service officers at age sixty was reasonably necessary because of the stress of overseas work. Because the law exempted policy-making officials, the Court ruled seven to two that Missouri could retire judges at age seventy in *Gregory v. Ashcroft* (1991). Although the amendment did not overturn the Federal Aviation Administration rule that pilots and copilots must retire at age sixty, in *Western Air Lines v. Criswell* (1985), the Court unanimously disallowed involuntary retirement of flight engineers (those who monitor the cockpit's side-facing instrument panel) at age sixty because the company refused to provide specific medical evidence of unfitness. Trans World Airlines (TWA), however, gave younger pilots and copilots medical fitness exams, and those who flunked were immediately reassigned as flight engineers. In *Trans World Airlines v. Thurston* (1985), the Court unanimously ruled that TWA could not force those who passed, upon approaching sixty, to follow a different procedure—to await reassignment as flight engineers on the basis of seniority.

Other Rulings. The Court has been generous about monetary damages paid to victims of age discrimination. In *Thurston*, reaffirmed unanimously in *Hazen v. Biggins* (1993), the Court ruled that victims of age discrimination may collect damage settlements, such as back pay, when an employer recklessly disregards the ADA. In *McKennon v. Nashville Banner* (1995), an employer admitted to firing a worker because of age, and the Court ruled unanimously that damages were warranted even though the employee was later discovered to have engaged in misconduct that would have been grounds for termination anyway.

Sometimes a factor other than age can affect older people more than younger people. In *Markam v. Geller* (1981), the Court refused to review a lower court's decision that age discrimination occurred when a school district hired a twenty-six-year-old teacher instead of a fifty-five-year-old teacher despite a policy of hiring less experienced teachers to save money. In *Hazen,* however, the Court noted that the text of the ADA specifically allows employers to operate a bona fide seniority system. In *O'Connor v. Consolidated Coin Caterers* (1996), the Court unanimously held that age discrimination may apply whenever a person fired is substantially older than the person hired, even if the latter is over forty.

In 1990 because some employers were placing undue pressure on workers to retire early, Congress passed the Older Workers Benefit Protection Act. In *Oubre v. Entergy* (1998), the Court ruled six to three that an employee did not have to forfeit an early termination incentive bonus before pursuing a lawsuit based on the act when the employer did not first give the worker enough information or time to deliberate on whether to accept the bonus.

FURTHER READING

Aiken, Lewis R. *Aging: An Introduction to Gerontology.* Thousand Oaks, Calif.: Sage Publications, 1995.

Butler, Robert N. *Why Survive? Being Old in America.* New York: Harper & Row, 1975.

Coni, Nicholas. *Aging: The Facts.* New York: Oxford University Press, 1992.

Department of Labor. *The Older American Worker— Age Discrimination in Employment: Report to Congress under Section 715 of the Civil Rights Act of 1964.* Washington, D.C.: Government Printing Office, 1965.

Eglit, Howard. "Health Care Allocation for the Elderly: Age Discrimination by Another Name?" *Houston Law Review* 26 (October, 1989): 8113-8900.

Equal Employment Opportunity Commission. *Age Discrimination.* Washington, D.C.: Government Printing Office, 1998.

Hushbeck, Judith C. *Old And Obsolete: Age Discrimination and the American Worker, 1860-1920.* New York: Garland Press, 1989.

Nichols, Barbara, and Peter Leonard, eds. *Gender, Aging and the State.* New York: Black Rose Books, 1994.

Michael Haas

SEE ALSO Employment discrimination; Fourteenth Amendment; Reversals of Court decisions by Congress; Suspect classifications.

Agostini v. Felton

CITATION: 521 U.S. ___, 117 S.Ct. 1997
DATE: June 23, 1997
ISSUE: Establishment of religion
SIGNIFICANCE: The Supreme Court held that the establishment clause did not prevent the use of public funds for sending public school teachers into parochial schools to provide remedial services.

In *Aguilar v. Felton* (1985), the Supreme Court voted five to four to strike down a program in which public school teachers went to private schools to provide a variety of secular services for disadvantaged students. Emphasizing the separationist viewpoint, the majority explained that the program might convey a message of governmental endorsement of religion. After *Aguilar,* New York continued the program by providing remedial services in parked vans near the private schools. In 1995 the parents of affected students went to federal court asking for the reversal of *Aguilar,* which appeared inconsistent with several recent decisions.

In *Agostini v. Felton,* a 5-4 majority of the justices agreed with the petitioners and overturned *Aguilar.* Using an interpretation of the *Lemon* test (developed in *Lemon v. Kurtzman,* 1971) that favored accommodationists, Justice Sandra Day O'Connor argued that the placing of public employees in parochial schools did not result in any state-sponsored indoctrination nor did it constitute any symbolic union between government and religion. In dissent, Justice Ruth Bader Ginsburg argued that it was impossible to draw a clear line between religious and secular instruction in religious schools.

Thomas T. Lewis

SEE ALSO *Everson v. Board of Education of Ewing Township; Lemon v. Kurtzman;* Religion, establishment of.

Agricultural issues

DESCRIPTION: Matters relating to the production of food crops from the land and the raising of livestock.

SIGNIFICANCE: The Supreme Court did not devote much attention to agriculture before the New Deal because farming was regarded as a local activity. However, after the Court was reconstituted with more liberal justices, it viewed many agricultural issues as part of the national economy and therefore federal questions.

As long as agriculture was largely a subsistence activity, it was generally held to be a matter of purely local concern in which the states had exclusive jurisdiction. However, as agriculture became increasingly commercialized, especially after the Civil War (1861-1864) when the national railroad network was completed, matters affecting agriculture through commerce in farm products came increasingly to the Supreme Court's attention.

The first of the agriculture-related cases to come before the Court were the *Slaughterhouse Cases* (1873). Louisiana butchers protested a law that granted monopoly status to a meat-slaughtering facility, claiming it was unconstitutional because it violated individual rights guaranteed by the Thirteenth and Fourteenth Amendments. The Court upheld the Louisiana law; however, a justice in a dissenting opinion stated his view that the Fourteenth Amendment offers protections from state interference.

The second case before the Court involved the regulation of trade in agricultural commodities, specifically through regulation of grain elevators. Many state legislatures, especially in the Midwest, were dominated by politicians representing farming interests. Those interests, often organized through societies of farmers known as the Grange, pressed for regulation of the large commercial interests that affected the sale of their agricultural crops. The most important of these were the proprietors of grain elevators, generally railroads, who held a local monopoly. Under pressure from the farmers, states passed legislation regulating the actions, including price setting, of the grain elevators and the railroads that owned them. The railroad owners believed that such laws restricted the freedom of contract and should be beyond the reach of state laws because the railroads that owned the elevators were engaged in interstate commerce. They appealed to the courts, and the issue reached the Court in the Granger cases, notably *Munn v. Illinois* (1877). Although the Court had long tenaciously defended freedom of contract, in this case it allowed the state regulation of businesses that were "affected with the public interest," a category that

included grain elevators. In another important decision, *Wabash, St. Louis, and Pacific Railway Co. v. Illinois* (1886), the Court ruled that the power to regulate businesses such as railroads engaged in interstate commerce belonged properly with the federal government, and some experts believe that this decision triggered the passage, by Congress, of the Interstate Commerce Act of 1887.

The Court, although generally conservative in its outlook, responded to the demands of society for the regulation of commercial products that involved the health and safety of the public. The Pure Food and Drug Act of 1906 was upheld by the Court in *Hipolite Egg Co. v. United States* in 1911. In *Hipolite*, the Court gave expression to a federal police power when the commerce in question was undeniably interstate. In 1915 in *Hadacheck v. Sebastian*, the Court ruled that the states had the power to condemn diseased animals, even without compensation.

In *Frost v. Oklahoma Corporation Commission* (1929), the Court indirectly recognized the special status of farm cooperatives. Although the Court ruled in favor of Frost, an individual, instead of the cooperative cotton ginning company licensed to compete with Frost by the Oklahoma Corporation Commission, it recognized that true agricultural cooperatives enjoyed certain freedoms that did not extend to private companies operating for profit.

New Deal Legislation. Agricultural issues played a prominent part in the Court's reaction to the attempts of Franklin D. Roosevelt to deal with the effects of the Depression. In 1933 Congress passed the Agricultural Adjustment Act, which paid farmers to take land out of production, in an effort to reduce the supply of farm products so that prices would rise. In *United States v. Butler* (1936), the Court ruled the act to be unconstitutional on the grounds that it was being used to transfer income from one segment of society to another, in the process depriving the states of the authority retained by them under the Constitution. The Court, by a 6-3 majority, held that this kind of regulation was inappropriate because agriculture was essentially a local activity.

Roosevelt brought about an effective reconstitution of the Court by replacing seven of its justices between 1937 and 1941, exchanging the Court's extreme conservatism for a more liberal outlook. Even before the shift, in *St. Joseph Stock Yards Co. v.*

United States (1936), the Court had indicated that it would accept some agricultural regulations if the Agriculture Department would develop procedural rules that applied uniformly, thus assuring the fairness of administrative actions. In 1938 Congress passed a second Agricultural Adjustment Act, funded by the U.S. Treasury, not by taxes levied specifically on some special interests. The Court in effect approved the second Agricultural Adjustment Act in *Mulford v. Smith* (1939). In addition, in *Wickard v. Filburn* (1942), the Court effectively granted the federal government the right to regulate any agricultural operations, even those that clearly did not involve interstate commerce, on the grounds that even agricultural commodities withheld from the market had an implicit effect on the national market in agricultural products. In the same year, in *United States v. Wrightwood Dairy Co.*, the Court allowed federal regulation of intrastate commerce when such commerce directly related to interstate commerce.

After 1937 the Department of Agriculture developed an elaborate system of market regulation of the commerce in agricultural products, to which the Court made few objections. The Court, however, did police some agricultural operations that appeared to be taking advantage of exemptions from antitrust rules provided as long ago as the Capper-Volstead Act (1922) for farm cooperatives. For example, in *United States v. Borden Co.* (1939), the Court ruled that a cooperative lost its antitrust exemption if it included members who were not primary agricultural producers, and again, in *Case-Swayne v. Sunkist Growers* (1967), that "agriculture" meant primary agricultural producers. Because Sunkist included commercial packing houses among its members, it did not qualify as an exempt agricultural cooperative. In *Maryland v. Virginia Milk Producers Association* (1960), agricultural cooperatives using predatory pricing lost their antitrust protection, and in *Farmers Reservoir and Irrigation Co. v. McComb* (1949), the Court ruled that an irrigation business did not qualify as "agriculture."

Marketing orders (under which producers of various agricultural products have been effectively compelled to join cooperatives that set prices for the product and exclude nonmembers from participation) have generally passed Court muster, but some orders have produced controversy and in a few cases litigation. The system provides for the participants to underwrite, from their sales receipts, some of the costs of administering the marketing orders. One of the most controversial of the marketing orders has been that governing milk, which attempted to set prices based in part on the distance of the ultimate market from the primary dairy region of the United States in Wisconsin and Minnesota. This system has led to complaints from some dairy groups that they cannot recover higher production costs because the pricing is tied to the primary dairy area where production costs are low. In Massachusetts, to stem the loss of dairy farmers, the Massachusetts Dairy Equalization Fund was created to help Massachusetts dairy farmers meet the higher costs of dairying in New England. However, in *West Lynn Dairy v. Healy* (1994), the Court ruled that it was impermissible to have a system that helped farmers in one state at the expense of those from other states.

Another challenge to the system of marketing orders was brought in *Dan Glickman v. Wileman Bros. and Elliott, et al.* (1997), in which it was alleged that the assessments imposed under the orders, used in part for generic advertising of the crop, infringed on the First Amendment rights of those required to pay the assessments. In a 5-4 decision, the Court upheld the marketing orders, including the assessment to pay for generic advertising, because it did not push any particular producer's product and did not push any particular political viewpoint. Moreover, the Court found that the marketing orders did not prevent any participant from advertising his or her own particular products or viewpoints. Hence the marketing orders did not violate the First Amendment guarantee of free speech.

FURTHER READING

The best general account of agricultural law is Donald B. Pedersen and Keith G. Meyer's *Agricultural Law in a Nutshell* (St. Paul, Minn.: West Publishing, 1995). The book contains a long list of cases, the overwhelming majority of which were heard either in state courts or in the lower federal courts, but a few did reach the Supreme Court. Elder Witt's *Congressional Quarterly's Guide to the U.S. Supreme Court* (Washington, D.C.: Congressional Quarterly, 1990) is a vast compendium, with a brief historical introduction and a discussion of the various powers of the government. The major decisions of the Court appear with other relevant documents. The book contains a subject index and a list of cases at the rear. John R. Schmidhauser deals with the issue of the Court's effect on federal-state relations in *The Supreme Court as Final Arbiter in Federal-State Relations, 1789-1957* (Chapel Hill: University of North Carolina Press, 1958). Lawyers J. W. Looney and Donald B. Uchtmann's *Agricultural Law: Principles and Cases* (New York: McGraw-Hill, 1990) looks at the law and agriculture, but the cases cited are mostly either in the lower federal courts or in state courts. Paul R. Benson's *The Supreme Court and the Commerce Clause, 1937-1970* (New York: Dunellen, 1970), covers the willingness of the Court to expand the application of the commerce clause. *Liberty Under Law: The Supreme Court in American Life* (Baltimore, Md.: Johns Hopkins University Press, 1988) by William M. Wiecek treats the evolution of the Court's authority under its various leaders.

Nancy M. Gordon

SEE ALSO Alien land laws; *Butler, United States v.*; Commerce, regulation of; Contract, freedom of; First Amendment speech tests; *Mulford v. Smith*; *Munn v. Illinois*; Roberts, Owen J.; *Slaughterhouse Cases*; *Wabash, St. Louis, and Pacific Railway Co. v. Illinois*; *Wickard v. Filburn*.

Akron v. Akron Center for Reproductive Health

CITATION: 462 U.S. 416
DATE: June 15, 1983
ISSUE: Abortion
SIGNIFICANCE: Reaffirming the strict scrutiny approach established in 1973, the Supreme Court ruled that a city ordinance imposed unjustifiable restrictions on a woman's exercise of a fundamental constitutional right.

An ordinance of Akron, Ohio, required that all abortions after the first trimester be performed in hospitals, that abortions not be performed before a twenty-four-hour waiting period, that physicians should advise patients that "the unborn child is a human life from the moment of conception," that parents of unmarried minors must consent for abortions to be performed, and that all fetal remains must be disposed of in a "humane and sanitary" way. By a 6-3 vote, the Supreme Court struck

down all the provisions. It found that the hospital and waiting-period requirements unnecessarily increased the cost of abortions and that the information requirement was designed to persuade women not to have abortions. In addition, the disposal requirement was "impermissibly vague," implying that a fetus had a right to a burial.

The most notable aspect of *Akron Center* was Justice Sandra Day O'Connor's dissenting opinion, which criticized the trimester approach and argued that restrictions on abortions should be allowed unless they placed an "undue burden" on the woman's decision.

Thomas T. Lewis

SEE ALSO Abortion; Due process, substantive; Fundamental rights; Judicial scrutiny; *Ohio v. Akron Center for Reproductive Health*; Privacy, right to; *Roe v. Wade*.

Albemarle Paper Co. v. Moody

CITATION: 422 U.S. 405
DATE: June 25, 1975
ISSUE: Employment discrimination
SIGNIFICANCE: Based on Title VII of the Civil Rights Law of 1964, the Supreme Court found that an employer's screening tests were discriminatory and that the employer must provide back pay for employees who suffered monetary loss due to racial discrimination.

African American employees in a North Carolina paper mill, the Albemarle Paper Company, charged that the company's preemployment tests and seniority system perpetuated the discrimination that had existed before the passage of Title VII, and they sought back pay relief. By a 7-1 vote, the Supreme Court ruled in favor of the employees. Because the tests were judged to be not sufficiently job related to be valid, they had to be discontinued. The awarding of back pay, moreover, provided an appropriate incentive for compliance with the law. The *Albemarle Paper Co.* decision provided a useful framework for resolving numerous claims under Title VII.

Thomas T. Lewis

SEE ALSO Civil Rights acts; Employment discrimination; *Griggs v. Duke Power Co.*; Race and discrimination.

Albertson v. Subversive Activities Control Board

CITATION: 382 U.S. 70
DATE: November 15, 1965
ISSUE: Freedom of assembly and association
SIGNIFICANCE: In this case, one of a series of decisions undermining 1950's anticommunist legislation, the Supreme Court struck down registration provisions of the 1950 McCarran Act.

The Supreme Court unanimously ruled that the Subversive Activities Control Board could not prosecute Communist Party members for failing to register with the board as mandated by the McCarran Act of 1950. The Court held that forced registration meant self-incrimination in other prosecutions. Even provisions granting registrants immunity from prosecution were inadequate to protect Communist Party members from violations of their Fifth Amendment right against self-incrimination.

In an earlier decision, *Communist Party v. Subversive Activities Control Board* (1961), the Court had upheld the registration provisions of the act but declined to reach a conclusion on whether anyone could be prosecuted for refusing to register. Many legal authorities correctly surmised that the Court might not actually allow prosecutions. When enforcement of the act was attempted, the Court blocked it. Recognizing that the act was unenforceable, President Richard M. Nixon and Congress allowed the board to expire in the early 1970's.

Richard L. Wilson

SEE ALSO *Aptheker v. Secretary of State*; Assembly and association, freedom of; Cold War; *Communist Party v. Subversive Activities Control Board*; *Dennis v. United States*; *Scales v. United States*; Self-incrimination, immunity against; *Yates v. United States*.

Alien land laws

DESCRIPTION: State laws prohibiting Asian immigrants from owning real property, particularly agricultural land, mainly on the basis that they were "aliens ineligible to citizenship."
SIGNIFICANCE: In various cases, the Supreme Court upheld alien land laws and the constitutionality of denying naturalized citizenship to Asians.

In the late 1800's numerous Japanese migrated to California, where many of them became farmers. They cultivated land, irrigating it when necessary, and helped develop California's fruit and vegetable industry. However, their success was perceived as a threat by parts of the farming population, and in 1913 California made it illegal for "aliens ineligible to citizenship" (at that time, primarily Japanese and other Asian immigrants) to own land or lease it for more than three years. Because it takes three years for strawberry plants to produce berries suitable for market, this law negatively affected Japanese immigrants, whose strawberry farms were producing 70 percent of the state's total strawberry output. In 1920 the state passed a law prohibiting aliens from leasing land, buying land through corporations, or purchasing it in the name of U.S.-born (and therefore citizen) children. A 1923 amendment strictly limited cropping contracts (under which aliens farmed for wages). Consequently, land ownership among Japanese immigrants decreased from 74,768 acres to 41,898, and leased land dropped from 192,150 acres to 76,397. California's alien land laws became a model for similar laws passed by fourteen other states.

In 1923 the Supreme Court upheld alien land laws in four separate cases. In *Terrace v. Thompson*, the Court upheld a Washington state statute prohibiting citizens from leasing land to Japanese immigrants. *Porterfield v. Webb* involved a similar statute in California. In *Webb v. O'Brien*, the Court found sharecropping agreements between citizens and aliens to be illegal, and in *Frick v. Webb*, it upheld a statue prohibiting aliens from owning stock in certain types of agricultural corporations. Furthermore, two Court cases in 1922—*Yamashita v. Hinkle* and *Ozawa v. United States*—upheld the constitutionality of denying naturalized citizenship to Japanese immigrants.

However, in *Oyama v. California* (1948), the Court declared California's 1920 alien land law to be "outright racial discrimination" and in violation of the equal protection clause of the Fourteenth Amendment. In 1952 the McCarran-Walter Act granted Japanese immigrants the right to naturalized citizenship. State referendums officially repealed the remaining alien land laws, with the last law reversed in Washington state in 1966.

Mary Louise Buley-Meissner

SEE ALSO Agricultural issues; Alien rights and naturalization; Citizenship; Fourteenth Amendment; Immigration law; Japanese American relocation; Property rights; Race and discrimination.

Alien rights and naturalization

DESCRIPTION: The rights held by people who are not citizens of the United States and the process by which people who are not citizens become citizens.

SIGNIFICANCE: The Supreme Court played a critical role in determining the rights of both resident aliens, noncitizens legally living in the United States, and undocumented aliens, noncitizens in the country illegally. The Court also influenced the rights of aliens to become citizens and to maintain citizenship.

The U.S. Constitution touches on the definition of citizenship only indirectly and makes no provisions for how aliens, or noncitizens, may become citizens. Moreover, although the amendments to the Constitution enumerate rights, it is not clear to what extent these rights apply to people who live in the United States but are not U.S. citizens. Because the Supreme Court is entrusted with interpreting the Constitution and establishing whether laws are consistent with this document, it has played a critical role in determining the rights of aliens.

Exclusion and Deportation. Congress has the constitutional power to decide which noncitizens may enter the United States and who may be excluded. During the first century of the nation's existence, Congress made little use of its power to restrict immigration. One of the earliest pieces of immigration legislation was the Chinese Exclusion Act of 1882, which barred the entry of Chinese laborers for a period of ten years. The Supreme Court upheld the right of Congress to exclude an entire national group from entering the country in *Chae Chan Ping v. United States* (1889) and in *Fong Yue Ting v. United States* (1893).

In theory, Congress could exclude all aliens from entering the United States because there is no constitutional right to immigration. Prior to entry, aliens have no constitutional rights. In *Chew v. Colding* (1953), the Court ruled that those who have successfully entered the country are protected by First Amendment rights to free speech, Fourth Amendment protections against unreasonable searches and seizures, and Fourteenth Amendment guarantees of equal protection of the law. Outside of the United States, however, these protections do not apply. The lack of constitutional rights by aliens seeking entry became clear in *Shaughnessy v. United States ex rel. Mezei* (1953). Ignatz Mezei was a Romanian citizen who was a resident of the United States for twenty-five years. He returned to Romania to visit his mother in 1948. When he attempted to re-enter the United States, first an immigration inspector and then the U.S. attorney general ordered him excluded. He was held on Ellis Island, which the Court ruled was "on the threshold" of U.S. territory. His confinement there could not be considered a violation of the Fourth Amendment because he was not in U.S. territory. The Court affirmed this principle in *United States ex rel. Knauff v. Shaughnessy* (1950), in which the German wife of an U.S. citizen was denied entry into the United States and held for months on Ellis Island. The Knauff-Mezei doctrine, that aliens outside the United States do not have constitutional protection, continued to be in effect, but the Court moderated it somewhat in the following years. In *Landon v. Plasencia* (1982), the Court ruled that an alien who has established legal resident status in the United States does not lose that status merely by traveling overseas and may be deported but not excluded.

Congress has consistently excluded individuals on political grounds, such as association with a government opposed to the United States or membership in a political organization thought to be opposed to U.S. interests. Writers, artists, and intellectuals have often been among those excluded on these grounds. In 1969 the Justice Department refused to grant a visa to the Belgian journalist Ernest Mandel, who had been invited to speak at universities in the United States. Citing the Chinese Exclusion Act, the Court upheld the right of Congress to determine on political grounds who can be admitted to the country.

In deportation, a noncitizen who has already entered the United States, either legally or illegally, is denied the right to remain and sent back to the country of origin. The Court officially recognized the right of Congress to enact deportation laws in the 1892 case *Nishimura Ekiu v. United States*. Aliens facing deportation enjoy more rights than those who are excluded because the former are actually in U.S. territory. Undocumented aliens, those in the United States illegally, make up the bulk of the deportations from U.S. soil. Deportation proceedings are not considered trials but civil procedures, so those being deported do not have all the safeguards given to defendants in criminal trials.

Being an undocumented alien is in itself a reason for deportation. However, resident aliens are also subject to deportation. In *Marcello v. Bonds* (1952), the Court upheld the government's right to deport a resident alien for violation of a marijuana law years earlier. In *Galvan v. Press* (1954), the Court approved the deportation of Juan Galvan, a resident alien, for having been a member of the Communist Party, even though it was a legal party at the time that Galvan was a member.

Rights to Employment. A number of Court rulings have affirmed the right of aliens residing legally in the United States to employment without discrimination by state or federal regulation. The Fourteenth Amendment to the Constitution, ratified in 1868, requires that all states give equal protection of the laws to all persons residing within their jurisdictions. In *Yick Wo v. Hopkins* (1886), the Court struck down a San Francisco city ordinance aimed at preventing Chinese nationals from operating laundries on the grounds that this was a violation of the Fourteenth Amendment. Four decades later, in *Truax v. Raich* (1915), the Court ruled unconstitutional an Arkansas statute that limited the number of aliens that any employer could hire. Citing *Yick Wo*, the Court ruled that the language of the Fourteenth Amendment included noncitizens under its protection. The Court's decision observed that the right to work at common occupations was essential to the personal freedom that the amendment was intended to secure. Further, it observed that the power to control immigration is given by the Constitution to the federal government. If a state limits the opportunity for immigrants to earn a living, the state effectively limits immigration, which it does not have the authority to do.

The Court has permitted both state and federal governments to refuse employment to noncitizens in some circumstances. The job of police officer, for example, may be restricted to citizens only. In *Foley v. Connelie* (1978), the Court upheld a New York state law that allowed only citizens to become state troopers. Chief Justice Warren E. Burger, who wrote the decision in this case, explained that police officers are found throughout American soci-

Outside a federal courthouse in Seattle in 1999, a young girl whose brother was detained by the Immigration and Naturalization Service for more than two years protests the agency's indefinite detention of people. The Supreme Court plays a significant role in determining the rights of aliens. (AP/Wide World Photos)

ety and exercise wide powers over those U.S. citizens who have contact with them. Similarly, in *Cabell v. Chavez-Salido* (1982), the Cousrt upheld a California statute requiring probation officers and those in similar occupations to be U.S. citizens. The idea that governmental positions of authority and responsibility can be restricted on the basis of citizenship was also extended to teachers in *Ambach v. Norwick* (1979). In this case, the Court gave its support to a New York statute that prohibited giving permanent teacher certification to an alien unless the alien demonstrated an intention to become a U.S. citizen.

In general, the Court has ruled against barring noncitizens from civil service jobs, but it has left state and federal governments the right to exclude foreigners from civil service positions when there are compelling political reasons to do so. In *Sugarman v. Dowell* (1973), the Court struck down a New York law that allowed only citizens to get competitive civil service jobs because people holding high-level and elective positions, who were in the most sensitive and authoritative positions, were exempted. In *Hampton v. Mow Sun Wong* (1976), the Court ruled that a regulation of the federal Civil Service Commission that prohibited noncitizens from taking civil service jobs violated the Fourteenth Amendment guarantee of equal legal protection. However, the Court also indicated that the regulation would be permissible if it came from the president or Congress, rather than from a mere governmental agency.

The Court has distinguished between employment discrimination on the basis of ethnic or racial background and discrimination in employment on the basis of citizenship by private employers. Although discrimination against noncitizens by state or federal government is usually prohibited by the Fourteenth Amendment guarantee of equal protection, the employment policies of private employers are not laws and therefore are not covered by this guarantee. In private employment, employers are prohibited from discriminating on the basis of race, color, sex, religion, or national origin by Title VII of the Civil Rights Act of 1964. None of these prohibitions, however, keeps private employers from discriminating on the basis of citizenship. In *Espinoza v. Farah Manufacturing Co.* (1972), the Court ruled that Farah Manufacturing Company's decision to hire only U.S. citizens was not equivalent to discrimination on the basis of national origin because the company did employ large numbers of Americans of Mexican descent, the primary national origin of the noncitizens who were refused employment.

Rights to Public Education and Public Assistance. By definition, noncitizens who are in the United States illegally do not have the right to employment. However, the Court has issued rulings that have recognized the rights of both resident aliens and undocumented aliens to some of the other advantages of American society. One of the advantages of residence in the United States is access to the U.S. system of free public education. By the early twentieth century, free and compulsory public schools had been established in all areas of the United States. The right of children of noncitizen immigrants to attend these schools was widely accepted. Indeed, the "Americanization" of children from various ethnic backgrounds was seen by Americans in many areas with large immigrant populations as an important function of public education.

The right of children of illegal immigrants to education at the public expense was a much more controversial issue, particularly as popular concern over illegal immigration increased from the late 1960's onward. This issue came before the Court in the controversial case of *Plyler v. Doe* (1982). A section of the Texas Education Code allowed school districts in Texas to either prohibit undocumented alien children from attending public schools or to charge the families of these children tuition.

Those who opposed the Texas statute maintained that employers in the state deliberately attracted illegal immigrant labor and that keeping undocumented aliens out of the school system would help to maintain a permanently disadvantaged and undereducated class of workers. Those who supported it pointed out that undocumented aliens could not expect to enjoy the benefits of a society when they were in that society illegally. They also claimed that if the Court upheld the statute, states would be obligated to extend every public benefit to all illegal immigrants who managed to escape capture. In its 1982 decision, the Court for the first time explicitly stated that undocumented aliens did enjoy the equal protection of the law guaranteed by the Fourteenth Amendment and that the Texas statute was therefore unconstitutional. However, Justice William J. Brennan, Jr., who delivered the decision, also stated that some public benefits can be denied to adult illegal immigrants because adult aliens in the United States without proper documents are intentionally breaking the law.

Although the right of resident aliens to public education has been widely accepted, their right to public assistance has been controversial. The case *Graham v. Richardson* (1971) dealt with the right of aliens to receive welfare benefits. The petitioners in this case challenged two state statutes: an Arizona statute requiring individuals receiving disability benefits to be U.S. citizens or residents for a minimum of fifteen years and a Pennsylvania statute that denied general assistance benefits to noncitizens. The Court ruled that the states could not restrict to citizens the benefits of tax revenues to which aliens had also contributed because this would violate the equal protection clause of the Fourteenth Amendment. However, the Court also observed that the federal government had the power to set policies toward immigrants. This made it possible for Congress to restrict access of resident aliens to some welfare benefits in 1996.

Rights of Suspected Illegal Aliens. The Immigration and Naturalization Service (INS) is charged by Congress with regulating the movement of aliens into the United States. This means that INS officers have the power to detain, interrogate, and arrest those suspected of having entered the United States illegally. However, the Fourth Amendment guarantees to all those on U.S. soil—citizens or noncitizens—freedom from unreasonable searches and seizures. Because many Americans living near the Mexican border are of Mexican or Hispanic ancestry, moreover, the duty of the INS to find suspected illegal aliens raises the continual danger that Mexican or Hispanic Americans will be placed under suspicion without justification. In making rulings on issues in this area, the Court had to balance the duties of immigration officers with the Fourth Amendment rights of suspected illegal aliens.

One of the chief limitations on the detention of suspected illegal aliens resulted from the case of *Almeida-Sanchez v. United States* (1973). In this case, the Court ruled that immigration officials could not use roving patrols far from the border to stop vehicles without a warrant or probable cause. This meant that immigration officers had to be able to demonstrate that a search by a roving patrol took place either at the border or at the equivalent of a border, such as an airport.

The practice of detaining suspected illegal aliens because of appearance or language is a difficult matter because it can easily be seen as discrimination against members of minority groups in the United States. The District of Columbia circuit court, in *Cheung Wong v. Immigration and Naturalization Service* (1972), ruled that immigration officers were justified in stopping and interrogating two individuals who did not speak English and who were Chinese in appearance outside of a restaurant that was suspected of employing illegal immigrants. This issue came before the Court in *United States v. Brignoni-Ponce* (1975). The Court ruled that roving patrols could stop vehicles to question suspected illegal aliens, but they could not use appearance alone as a justification for stopping people. Race or apparent ancestry alone was not enough cause for an officer to detain an individual. In *Brignoni-Ponce*, though, the Court did allow officers to take ancestry into consideration along with other factors when deciding to investigate the legal status of a suspected alien.

Naturalization and Denaturalization. Resident aliens who are not U.S. citizens may become citizens through naturalization. The conditions under which an alien may become a citizen are determined by Congress, and the power of Congress to set these conditions has been continually affirmed by the Supreme Court. The first Naturalization Act, passed in 1790, restricted citizenship through naturalization to "free white persons" of good character. Before the Civil War (1861-1865), nonwhites born on U.S. soil were considered ineligible for citizenship. With the passage of the Fourteenth Amendment, nonwhites born in the United States were granted U.S. citizenship, but people who were not of European ancestry continued to be ineligible for naturalization. The Court upheld this racial restriction on naturalization in the case of *Ozawa v. United States* (1922). Takao Ozawa had immigrated to the United States as a child in 1894, graduated from Berkeley High School, and attended the University of California. When Ozawa applied for citizenship at the U.S. District Court for the Territory of Hawaii, the court ruled that he was qualified for citizenship in every way except one: He was not white. On appeal, the Supreme Court ruled that Ozawa was not entitled to naturalization as a U.S. citizen because he was not of European descent. Although the United States no longer has naturalization policies that intentionally discriminate on the basis of race, this is a result of legislation rather than of judicial rulings on discrimination in naturalization.

Naturalization laws continue to require that new citizens support the basic form of government found in the United States. Those who, during a ten-year period before application for naturalization, were members of anarchist, Communist, or other organizations considered subversive may be barred from citizenship. The Court placed some limitations on these political restrictions in *Schneiderman v. United States* (1943).

Just as Congress determines the conditions under which individuals may be naturalized, it also historically determined the conditions under which they may be denaturalized, or stripped of their naturalized citizenship. Before the late

1950's, the Court usually did not question the right of Congress to take citizenship from the foreign born. However, in *Trop v. Dulles* (1958), Chief Justice Earl Warren recognized the seriousness of denaturalization when he observed that deprivation of citizenship could be seen as a violation of "the principles of civilized treatment." In *Schneider v. Rusk* (1964), the Court ruled that naturalized citizens could not lose their citizenship merely for living outside of the United States for extended periods of time. The greatest judicial limitation on denaturalization came in *Afroyim v. Rusk* (1967), in which a Polish-born citizen's citizenship was removed for voting in an Israeli election. The Court ruled that Congress has no constitutional power to remove citizenship without the voluntary renunciation of the individual concerned. After this case, denaturalization has been limited to cases in which the government can prove that a foreign-born person obtained citizenship illegally or fraudulently.

FURTHER READING

One of the most informative works on the rights of aliens is *Without Justice for All: The Constitutional Rights of Aliens* (Westport, Conn.: Greenwood Press, 1985) by Elizabeth Hull. *The Rights of Aliens and Refugees: The Basic ACLU Guide to Alien and Refugee Rights* (Carbondale: Southern Illinois University Press, 1990) by David Carliner, Lucas Guttentag, Arthur C. Helton, and Wade Henderson is a practical handbook on the rights of noncitizens put together by the American Civil Liberties Union. Gerald L. Neuman's *Strangers to the Constitution: Immigrants, Borders, and Fundamental Law* (Princeton, N.J.: Princeton University Press, 1996) is an academic consideration of problems in applying U.S. constitutional law to noncitizens and discusses case law interpretations of immigrant rights. In *Rights Across Borders: Immigration and the Decline of Citizenship* (Baltimore, Md.: Johns Hopkins University Press, 1998), sociologist David Jacobson argues that the growth of immigrant populations in the United States and other countries has led to the granting of rights formerly reserved to citizens. He maintains that this has weakened the status of citizenship. *U.S. Immigration Law* (Dallas: Pearson Publications, 1998) by Jeffrey A. Helewitz is a thorough introduction to the immigration law of the United States that includes historical background and cases.

Carl L. Bankston III

SEE ALSO Alien land laws; *Chinese Exclusion Cases*; Citizenship; Immigration law; Japanese American relocation; *Plyler v. Doe*; *Trop v. Dulles*; *Yick Wo v. Hopkins*.

Allegheny County v. American Civil Liberties Union Greater Pittsburgh Chapter

CITATION: 492 U.S. 573
DATE: July 3, 1989
ISSUE: Separation of church and state
SIGNIFICANCE: The Supreme Court held that a Christmas display focusing predominantly on religious symbols violated the establishment clause of the First Amendment.

In *Lynch v. Donnelly* (1984), the Supreme Court voted five to four to approve a government-sponsored nativity scene that also included a reindeer, a clown, and a Santa Claus house. The majority found that the display was in conformity with the demands of the three-part *Lemon* test established in *Lemon v. Kurtzman* (1971). Justice Sandra Day O'Connor joined the majority because she concluded that the effect of the display was not to convey a message of either endorsing or disapproving a religion.

The *Allegheny County* case involved two holiday displays located on public property in Pittsburgh. The first was a pious nativity scene without any secular symbols. The judges voted five to four that this display was unconstitutional. Justice Harry A. Blackmun's opinion, which O'Connor joined, was based on the "no endorsement of religion" standard. The same 5-4 majority approved of the second display, a menorah placed next to a Christmas tree. Blackmun asserted that the second display did not promote any religious message. The requirement for including some secular symbols in a seasonal display is sometimes called the "Christmas tree rule." Justice Anthony M. Kennedy, a dissenter, wanted to rule on the basis of whether there was any "coercion." The case illustrated the deep divisions of the justices when interpreting the establishment clause.

Thomas T. Lewis

SEE ALSO Agostini v. Felton; *Lemon v. Kurtzman*; *Lynch v. Donnelly*; Religion, establishment of.

Allgeyer v. Louisiana

CITATION: 165 U.S. 578 (1897)
DATE: March 1, 1897
ISSUE: Freedom of contract
SIGNIFICANCE: The Supreme Court first used the freedom of contract doctrine to overturn a state law as unconstitutional.

In order to regulate insurance businesses, Louisiana prohibited its residents from entering into most types of insurance contracts with companies located outside the state. Allgeyer and Company was fined $1,000 for making such a contract with a New York firm. By a 9-0 vote, the Supreme Court ruled that the law unconstitutionally violated the liberty of citizens to enter into business contracts without unwarranted interference by the state. Writing for the Court, Justice Rufus W. Peckham explained that his opinion was based on the concept that substantive economic liberties were protected by the due process clause of the Fourteenth Amendment. Further, having earlier ruled that insurance was not a form of commerce, the Court could not base the decision on the issue of state jurisdiction.

Although *Allgeyer* recognized the authority of states to regulate private companies, it insisted that states must justify the reasonableness of all such regulations. Freedom of contract was to be the rule, with exceptions allowed only when clearly necessary to protect the safety, health, or welfare of the public. Through the next four decades, the *Allgeyer* precedent provided a theoretical basis for overturning numerous laws that regulated terms of employment—such as laws requiring maximum working hours or minimum wages. The Court finally stopped giving special protection for the freedom of contract doctrine in *West Coast Hotel Co. v. Parrish* (1937).

Thomas T. Lewis

SEE ALSO Contract, freedom of; Due process, substantive; Labor; *Lochner v. New York*; *West Coast Hotel Co. v. Parrish*.

American Bar Association Committee on Federal Judiciary

FOUNDED: 1946
DESCRIPTION: Standing committee of the American Bar Association (ABA) that evaluates the qualifications of prospective candidates and presidential nominees for the federal bench, including the Supreme Court.
SIGNIFICANCE: Presidents typically consult the ABA Committee on Federal Judiciary before they formally nominate individuals as Supreme Court justices, and the Senate Judiciary Committee routinely asks the committee for nominee evaluations. The committee's evaluations of the professional qualifications of prospective judicial officers carry considerable weight.

The ABA committee directs its attention to the professional qualifications of nominees, defined as their integrity, professional competence, and judicial temperament. Because the Supreme Court is at the head of the judicial hierarchy, the committee employs its criteria with a view toward obtaining justices with exceptional ability.

Evaluations. Procedures for evaluating nominees for the Supreme Court differ somewhat from those employed for other federal judgeships although the general operating principles are consistent. In the investigation of Supreme Court nominees, unlike the procedure for examining other federal judge candidates, all fifteen members of the committee take part. The committee interviews those who are most likely to have information on candidates, including judges, practicing attorneys in all sectors of the law, law professors and deans, and representatives of legal associations and organizations. The legal writings of prospective nominees are examined by law professors working together to evaluate the intellectual qualities of the prospective nominees. As a cross-check on the findings of the professors, teams of practicing attorneys also examine the writings, which include scholarly articles, judicial opinions if the candidates are or have been judges, and briefs of counsel authored by the prospective justices.

The committee employs three ratings in reporting evaluations of Court nominees: "well qualified," "qualified," and "not qualified." First, the committee's ratings are submitted in confidence to the attorney general. If the president forwards the nomination to the Senate, then the committee reports its findings to the Senate Judiciary Committee. At the confirmation hearings, an ABA committee member, without revealing the source of its findings, makes a formal presentation reporting on the reasons for the committee's evaluation.

Committee Makeup and Politics. The ABA president appoints each member of the committee for staggered three-year terms. No member may serve more than two terms. The committee typically has fifteen members, one of whom is an at-large member, and the rest are chosen from all twelve judicial circuits to ensure geographical balance. Although the committee draws members from all over the nation, the ABA leadership generally comes from the upper reaches of the highly stratified legal profession. Critics of the ABA argue that the elite of the legal profession seek to populate the bench with judges and justices that share their view of the world.

Throughout most of the organization's history, ABA leaders were responsible for resolutions and congressional lobbying activities that aligned them with the more conservative elements within the U.S. political culture. For example, sixteen former ABA presidents opposed the 1916 nomination of Louis D. Brandeis to the Supreme Court because of his liberal views. Although this incident took place thirty years before the establishment of the ABA standing committee, the committee produced some controversial judgments that reinforced the image of the ABA as a conservative organization. For example, in 1969 after it became known that Circuit Court of Appeals Judge Clement Haynsworth, Jr., a Richard M. Nixon nominee to the Supreme Court, sat in cases involving corporations in which he owned stock and that he misled the Senate Judiciary Committee about his business activities, the ABA committee met for a second time and reaffirmed its original favorable assessment of the South Carolinian. Then, the ABA board of governors, in an unprecedented move, met to consider overriding the committee. However, the board decided it did not possess the authority under the ABA constitution and bylaws.

During the 1980's, conservative forces in Congress charged that the ABA committee reflected liberal political biases when evaluating the qualifications of prospective judges and justices. Conservatives were particularly upset with the committee because four members found President Ronald Reagan's nominee, Robert H. Bork, to be "unqualified." However, although one member voted "not opposed," the others found the advocate of consti-

tutional originalism to be "well qualified." Conservative convictions that the ABA had become a bastion of liberal thought were reinforced when in 1990 the ABA's house of delegates voted to endorse the right to privacy and a woman's right to choose an abortion. Then, in 1991, the ABA Committee on the Federal Judiciary gave President George Bush's nominee, Clarence Thomas, the lowest rating given a Court nominee since 1955: Twelve members voted him "qualified" and two "not qualified."

The ABA has endeavored to portray itself as an objective, public-service-oriented organization that is not interested in promoting partisan policy goals. The ABA Committee on Federal Judiciary clearly plays an important role in the process of selecting judges and justices.

FURTHER READING

Abraham, Henry J. *Justices, Presidents, and Congress: A Political History of Appointments to the Supreme Court.* 4th ed. Lanham, Md.: Rowman & Littlefield, 1999.

American Bar Association. *The Standing Committee on Federal Judiciary: What It Is and How It Works.* Chicago: Author, 1991.

Goldman, Sheldon. *Picking Federal Judges: Lower Court Selection From Roosevelt Through Reagan.* New Haven, Conn.: Yale University Press, 1997.

Grossman, Joel B. *Lawyers and Judges: The ABA and the Politics of Judicial Selection.* New York: John Wiley and Sons, 1965.

Melone, Albert P. *Lawyers, Public Policy, and Interest Group Politics.* Washington, D.C.: University Press of America, 1977.

Slotnick, Elliot, "The ABA Standing Committee on Federal Judiciary: A Contemporary Assessment." *Judicature* 66 (1983): 348-362, 385-393.

Albert P. Melone

SEE ALSO Judicial codes and rules; Nominations to the Court; Presidential powers; Senate Judiciary Committee.

American Civil Liberties Union

FOUNDED: 1920
DESCRIPTION: A nonprofit, nonpartisan organization dedicated to upholding the Bill of Rights and defending the civil liberties and civil rights of all Americans.

SIGNIFICANCE: Appearing before the Supreme Court more often than any other organization except the federal government itself, the ACLU has been involved in an estimated 80 percent of the landmark cases brought before the Court after 1920.

The ACLU was founded in 1920 by Roger Baldwin and other Progressive-era activists. It grew out of earlier organizations that had opposed the entry of the United States into World War I (1917-1918) and had upheld the rights of conscientious objectors when little popular support existed for defending these dissenters' rights. At the time of the ACLU's founding, the Supreme Court had never upheld a free speech claim under the First Amendment but instead had repeatedly ruled that the Bill of Rights limited only the federal government and did not apply to the states. Therefore, states were free to ignore the First Amendment. Only gradually was the Court persuaded to adopt the philosophy of selective incorporation, in which various provisions of the Bill of Rights were applied to the states. The ACLU developed the legal arguments for many of these landmark decisions.

Early Victories and Defeats. The ACLU's first victory before the Court came in *Gitlow v. New York* (1925). Benjamin Gitlow, a socialist, had been sentenced to prison for distributing a radical pamphlet calling for world proletarian revolution. Although the Court upheld Gitlow's conviction, it accepted the argument set forth by ACLU lawyer Walter H. Pollak that liberty of expression was a right that should be protected against state infringement. The significance of this case was not immediately recognized, and the ACLU's annual report characterized it as a defeat.

Because of the conservative nature of the Court, the ACLU leadership remained divided over the extent to which it should be relied on for the protection of civil liberties. Felix Frankfurter, a member of the ACLU National Committee, argued that legislative protec-tion of civil liberties provided a more secure and democratic foundation. What the Court could give, it could just as easily take away. Baldwin was also suspicious of legal strategies and focused his attention on direct action, particularly in support of labor. However, in 1931 ACLU lawyers successfully argued in *Stromberg v. California* that the conviction of a communist for displaying a red flag should be overturned because it violated the First Amendment. The decision represented the first time in the Court's history that it ruled a state law unconstitutional on free speech grounds. In the 1930's the ACLU launched a broad anticensorship campaign that focused on movie censorship, artistic expression, and the right to disseminate information regarding birth control. By the late 1930's a growing number of legal victories fueled the ACLU's increasing turn toward legalism. In 1941 the organization hired its first full-time staff attorney.

The ACLU first came to national attention with the 1926 Scopes "Monkey" trial. It had offered legal assistance to anyone willing to challenge a Tennessee law prohibiting the teaching of evolution. Although biology teacher John T. Scopes was convicted, the trial brought widespread publicity and support to the fledgling organization. The issues of academic freedom and the separation of church

The American Civil Liberties Union celebrates a favorable Supreme Court ruling in Jersey City, New Jersey, in 1939. The ACLU helps bring numerous cases involving civil liberties before the Court. (Library of Congress)

and state would remain central to the ACLU. During the 1930's and 1940's it sponsored key cases involving the rights of Jehovah's Witnesses. Later, in the landmark ACLU-sponsored cases of *Engel v. Vitale* (1962) and *Abington School District v. Schempp* (1963), the Court struck down "nondenominational" school prayer and in-school Bible reading.

The ACLU's commitment to civil liberties faltered in the 1940's and 1950's. During World War II (1941-1945), it unsuccessfully argued two cases involving Japanese internment, *Korematsu v. United States* (1944) and *Hirabayashi v. United States* (1943), yet refused to permit its lawyers to directly challenge the constitutionality of the internment orders. During the 1950's the ACLU succumbed to anticommunist hysteria, prohibiting communists from serving on its board. Although it filed *amicus* briefs in cases involving the Smith Act, an antisubversive law adopted in 1940, it refused to directly represent communists.

Expanding Rights for All Americans. By the 1960's the ACLU had resumed its unwavering defense of freedom of speech, winning such landmark cases as *Tinker v. Des Moines Independent Community School District* (1969) and *Brandenburg v. Ohio* (1969). The ACLU's "absolutist" position on free speech, which supported Nazis, Ku Klux Klan members, and communists, developed amidst many internal debates. In one of the most controversial cases in its history, the ACLU supported the right of American Nazis to march through a Chicago suburb where many Holocaust survivors lived. The ACLU's challenge was ultimately upheld in *Smith v. Collin* (1978). The ACLU's support for the rights of criminal suspects also generated public hostility. In the 1960's the ACLU argued or directly influenced many of the most important decisions involving police conduct and the rights of the accused, including *Mapp v. Ohio* (1961), *Gideon v. Wainwright* (1963), *Escobedo v. Illinois* (1964), and *Miranda v. Arizona* (1966).

ACLU leadership played an important part in developing the legal strategy that resulted in the landmark *Brown v. Board of Education* (1954) decision and subsequently argued numerous cases supporting school desegregation, civil rights protesters, and affirmative action. During the 1970's and 1980's the ACLU's Voting Rights Project played a critical role in the judicial enforcement of the 1965 Voting Rights Act, filing lawsuits against nearly two

hundred jurisdictions. The ACLU also stood at the forefront of women's rights and participated in two-thirds of cases involving gender discrimination heard by the Court. Ruth Bader Ginsburg, general counsel to the ACLU's Women's Rights Project, pioneered in gender equity litigation in the 1970's. In 1971 the ACLU argued *United States v. Vuitch*, the first abortion rights case before the Court.

The ACLU was at the forefront of expanding legal and constitutional protections to groups that have traditionally been denied their rights, including women, minorities, students, juveniles, prisoners, the disabled, mental patients, welfare recipients, immigrants, criminal suspects, and homosexuals. By the late 1990's the ACLU had a national office in New York City, a legislative office in Washington, D.C., and autonomous affiliates in all fifty states staffed by more than sixty full-time lawyers. It sponsored national projects devoted to specific civil liberties issues such as AIDS, capital punishment, education reform, privacy and technology, reproductive freedom, and workplace rights. Combining litigation with lobbying and public education, the ACLU helped create whole new areas of constitutional law and doctrine and played a pivotal role in the twentieth-century "rights revolution."

FURTHER READING

Garey, Diane. *Defending Everybody: A History of the American Civil Liberties Union.* New York: TV Books, 1998.

Lamson, Peggy. *Roger Baldwin: Founder of the American Civil Liberties Union.* Boston: Houghton Mifflin, 1976.

Murphy, Paul L. *World War I and the Origin of Civil Liberties in the United States.* New York: W. W. Norton, 1979.

Reitman, Alan. *The Pulse of Freedom: American Liberties, 1920-1970's.* New York: W. W. Norton, 1975.

Walker, Samuel. *In Defense of American Liberties: A History of the ACLU.* New York: Oxford University Press, 1990.

L. Mara Dodge

SEE ALSO Abortion; Desegregation; Evolution and creationism; First Amendment absolutism; *Gideon v. Wainwright*; *Gitlow v. New York*; Japanese American relocation; *Miranda v. Arizona*; Pollak, Walter H.; Religion, establishment of; Smith Act; Speech and press, freedom of; *Stromberg v. California*; War and civil liberties.

American Communications Association v. Douds

CITATION: 339 U.S. 382
DATE: May 8, 1950
ISSUES: Freedom of speech; freedom of assembly; interstate commerce
SIGNIFICANCE: At the height of the Cold War, the Supreme Court upheld the portions of the Taft-Hartley Act (1947) that required labor union leaders to sign an affidavit affirming that they were not presently members of the Communist Party.

The Communications union, which had a record of some Communist Party infiltration, charged that the registration provisions of the Taft-Hartley Act of 1947 violated the freedoms provided by the First Amendment. Speaking for a 5-1 majority, Chief Justice Fred M. Vinson interpreted the law as an attempt to prevent disruptive strikes in interstate commerce, a legitimate interest of Congress. Using an ad hoc balancing approach, Vinson made a distinction between freedom of speech, protected by the First Amendment, and political association, a form of action that deserved less protection than the communication of ideas.

Douds may be contrasted with *United States v. Brown* (1965), in which the Supreme Court struck down a more restrictive law that prohibited people from serving as labor leaders if they had been affiliated with the Communist Party during the previous five years.

Thomas T. Lewis

SEE ALSO Clear and present danger test; Cold War; *Cumming v. Richmond County Board of Education*; First Amendment; Labor; Speech and press, freedom of.

Americans United for Separation of Church and State

FOUNDED: 1947
DESCRIPTION: Private organization that, using legal channels, attempts to prevent any governmental aid to religious schools or social service providers.
SIGNIFICANCE: Beginning in the 1950's, Americans United became involved in litigation in the

Parents voice their opposition to a state law involving school vouchers in front of the Florida supreme court in Tallahassee in 1999. Although not involved in this case, the organization Americans United for Separation of Church and State supports similar litigation designed to prevent religious schools from benefiting from government funds. (AP/Wide World Photos)

Supreme Court and other federal and state courts to prevent religiously sponsored schools and social service providers from obtaining direct or even indirect financial benefits from the government.

After the Supreme Court handed down its decision in *Everson v. Board of Education of Ewing Township* (1947), permitting states to provide bus transportation for parochial school children, a group led by Bromley Oxnam, a prominent Methodist bishop, and Paul Blanshard, the controversial author of polemical books warning that "Catholic power" was a threat to U.S. freedom, founded Protestants and Other Americans United for Separation of Church and State. In recent years, the group renamed itself Americans United for Separation of Church and State and is often referred to simply as Americans United.

Americans United sponsors litigation, provides legal counsel, and submits friend-of-the-court briefs in an effort to persuade the Supreme Court to interpret the First Amendment's prohibition of "laws respecting an establishment of religion" to prevent *any* governmental aid to religiously sponsored schools or social service providers. Its influence can be seen in *Lemon v. Kurtzman* (1971), in which the Court set guidelines for interpreting cases on establishment clause grounds. The organization was more successful in opposing direct aid to parochial schools than in preventing indirect benefits, such as tax credits, to the families of parochial school children. Key tests of the organization's strength are likely to come in future cases involving school vouchers and governmental support to religion-sponsored agencies to combat poverty, drug addiction, and other social evils.

From its beginning, Americans United has been controversial. Supporters contend that it is a nonpartisan champion of religious freedom. Critics insist that it pursues a secularist liberal political agenda motivated by animus against conservative religious believers, particularly Roman Catholics and evangelical Protestants.

Robert P. George

SEE ALSO *Everson v. Board of Education of Ewing Township*; First Amendment; Religion, establishment of; Religion, freedom of; School prayer.

Antelope, The

CITATION: 10 Wheat. (23 U.S.) 66
DATE: March 16, 1825
ISSUES: Natural law; international law
SIGNIFICANCE: While acknowledging that the slave trade was contrary to principles of natural justice, the Supreme Court nevertheless recognized the authority of sovereign nations to enact laws allowing the practice.

Pirates seized a Spanish vessel, *The Antelope*, carrying a large cargo of African slaves. A U.S. naval ship subsequently captured the ship with its cargo and took it to Savannah, Georgia. Spanish and Portuguese slave traders sued to have their property restored. Because Congress had outlawed U.S. participation in the slave trade in 1808, many jurists argued that the captured slaves should be repatriated to Africa.

Chief Justice John Marshall's opinion for the Supreme Court had three parts. First, the "abhorrent" trade in slaves was indeed "contrary to the law of nature"; however, the trade, long accepted throughout the world, was not condemned by the positive law of nations. Second, the United States had no power to impose its laws on other countries; therefore, a ship captured in a time of peace must be restored with its cargo. Third, based on the evidence for the claims of ownership, some of the slaves were returned to the Spanish claimants, and the remainder were repatriated to the American Colonization Society's colony in Liberia.

Thomas T. Lewis

SEE ALSO *Cooley v. Board of Wardens of the Port of Philadelphia*; *Johnson and Graham's Lessee v. McIntosh*; Natural law; Slavery.

Antitrust law

DESCRIPTION: Set of statutes regulating economic competition by prohibiting anticompetitive agreements, monopolization, attempted monopolization, conspiracies to monopolize, and mergers and acquisitions that may tend to substantially injure competition.

Microsoft chairman Bill Gates responds to a question during a 1998 Senate Judiciary Committee hearing to determine if his company was restricting the efforts of other Internet software providers. The following year, Microsoft was judged to be a monopoly. Although agencies enforce antitrust laws, the Supreme Court maintains an active role in interpreting them. (AP/Wide World Photos)

SIGNIFICANCE: After the Sherman Antitrust Act was passed in 1890, the Supreme Court defined the scope of antitrust law and interpreted its wording and intent, delineating the permissible bounds of business behavior.

The Sherman Antitrust Act of 1890 was a broad statute prohibiting various forms of attempted and actual monopolies and agreements that restrained trade. The act allowed people who suffered injuries to their business and property to recover three times their actual damages, plus attorney fees and costs. One of the principal purposes of antitrust laws was to give the federal courts jurisdiction to create a federal common law of competition.

Interpreting the Antitrust Acts. In the early 1900's, the Supreme Court engaged in a long-running battle to define the scope of the interstate and foreign commerce subject to the Sherman Antitrust Act and to define the act's key words. The Court's early interpretations focused on whether the act prohibited all restraints of free trade or only those that were unreasonable under the common law. It also considered what, if anything, constituted a reasonable restraint of trade.

In *Standard Oil Co. v. United States* (1911), the Court adopted the rule of reason, under which only agreements that unreasonably restrained competition were unlawful under the Sherman Act. The uncertainty of the rule of reason led to great criticism of the Court by both defenders and critics of the antitrust laws. The *Standard Oil* decision also prompted Congress, in 1914, to enact the Clayton Act, which listed more specific types of antitrust offenses, and to create the Federal Trade Commission, a federal agency with the power to prohibit "unfair methods of competition."

The Court began to define categories of offenses that were per se unreasonable and hence illegal under the ruling reached in *Standard Oil.* Virtually all price-fixing agreements were unlawful if it could be proved that an agreement between competitors had been reached as to the price of goods or services being bought or sold by those firms. It would be no defense that the firm operated in an industry where competition produced unusual or even harmful results, that the competitors had agreed on a "reasonable" price, or even that the firms lacked the power to raise prices pursuant to their agreement.

This trend condemning price-fixing agreements culminated in *United States v. Socony-Vacuum Oil Co.* (1940), which held that all price agreements between competitors were per se unlawful under the Sherman Act. The Court subsequently extended per se treatment to a wide variety of both horizontal and vertical agreements (agreements between manufacturers of similar products and between manufacturers and suppliers or distributors, respectively). Per se rules were created or modified to condemn agreements between competitors as to the territories or customers they served in *Timken Roller Bearing Co. v. United States* (1951), maximum- and minimum-price agreements between competitors in *Arizona v. Maricopa County Medical Society* (1982), maximum- and minimum-price agreements between sellers and their customers in *Albrecht v. Herald Co.* (1968), certain types of group boycotts in *Klor's v. Broadway-Hale Stores* (1959), so-called tying agreements that required a customer to take one product or service in order to obtain another in *United States v. Northern Pacific Railway Co.* (1958), and most nonprice vertical agreements between sellers and their customers limiting the territory or manner in which goods or services could be sold in *United States v. Arnold, Schwinn and Co.* (1967). In each of these cases, the Court cited the effect on consumers and competitors and the leading economic thinking of the times to justify the use of per se rules that did not permit the defendant to argue that its particular agreement might, on balance, promote, rather than injure, competition.

During this same period, the Court also struggled with the concept of how the Sherman and Clayton Acts applied to mergers and acquisitions. Neither act had proved effective in stemming the tide of mergers that periodically swept the nation. In 1950 Congress passed the Celler-Kefauver Act, which eliminated most of the technical loopholes in the Clayton Act and made it clear that the antitrust laws prohibited any merger or acquisition that had the tendency to injure competition. Beginning with the *Brown Shoe Co. v. United States* decision in 1962, the Court held in an unbroken string of victories for the government that virtually any quantitatively substantial merger would violate the antitrust laws if the government could show that the market shares of the merging firms and overall industry concentration would increase as a result of the merger or acquisition.

An Economic Analysis. The increasing severity of these court-made antitrust rules in the 1950's, 1960's, and early 1970's led to a backlash of scholarly criticism focused on the negative economic effects of the Court's antitrust jurisprudence. Prominent law and economics scholars such as Richard Posner and Robert H. Bork, each of whom later became influential judges, argued that the Court's antitrust decisions were inconsistent with what they argued was the principal purpose of the antitrust laws—to increase wealth, consumer welfare, and economic efficiency.

The Court quickly proved receptive to this economically oriented style of antitrust analysis. In the area of agreements between competitors, the Court retained the basic per se rule against hardcore price-fixing agreements but showed an increasing willingness to look under the surface of agreements to determine whether the agreement contained any plausible procompetitive justification that merited further inquiry. In a number of cases, including *National Society of Professional Engineers v. United States* (1978), *Broadcast Music v. Columbia Broadcasting System* (1979), and *National Collegiate Athletic Association v. Board of Regents of the University of Oklahoma* (1984), the Court ultimately condemned anticompetitive agreements between competitors relating to price but only after the type of searching inquiry that would not be possible under a true rule of per se illegality. At the same time, the Court quickly condemned agreements between competitors relating to price in *Federal Trade Commission v. Superior Court Trial Lawyers Association* (1990) or territory in *Jay Palmer et al. v. BRG of Georgia et al.* (1990), if they lacked a plausible procompetitive justification, regardless

---

MAJOR ANTITRUST CASES AND LEGISLATION

Date	Action	Significance
1890	Sherman Antitrust Act	Banned every "contract, combination . . . or conspiracy" in restraint of trade or commerce.
1898	*United States v. Addyston Pipe and Steel Co.*	Ruled that an agreement to set prices was illegal because it gave the parties power to set unreasonable prices.
1904	*Northern Securities v. United States*	Supreme Court ruled against holding companies that control the stock of competing companies.
1911	*Standard Oil Co. v. United States*	Supreme Court ordered the breakup of Standard Oil.
1911	*United States v. American Tobacco Co.*	Supreme Court ordered the breakup of American Tobacco Company. Along with the Standard Oil case, established the "rule of reason" approach to antitrust prosecution.
1914	Clayton Antitrust Act	Specified actions that are subject to antitrust prosecution.
1914	Federal Trade Commission Act	Established the Federal Trade Commission as an administrative agency to police "unfair methods of competition."
1920	*United States v. U.S. Steel Corp.*	Supreme Court ruled that size alone, in the absence of abuse of power, did not make a monopoly illegal.
1921	*American Column and Lumber Co. v. United States*	Ruled that competitors could be convicted if they had discussed prices and later set identical prices, even if no agreement to do so had been reached.
1936	Robinson-Patman Act	Specified the types of price discrimination that are illegal.

Date	Action	Significance
1936	*International Business Machines Corp. v. United States*	Established conditions under which it is illegal to tie the sale of one product to the sale of another.
1937	Miller-Tydings Act	Exempted manufacturers and retailers from prosecution for agreeing to set minimum prices if the states in which they operate allow such agreements.
1938	Wheeler-Lea Act	Strengthened enforcement powers of the Federal Trade Commission.
1945	*United States v. Aluminum Co. of America* (Alcoa)	Supreme Court ordered breakup of Alcoa, ruling that a monopoly is illegal even if not accompanied by abuse of power.
1948	*Federal Trade Commission v. Cement Institute*	Supreme Court ruled illegal agreements by producers to base prices on manufacturing costs plus transportation from a given location (base-point pricing).
1950	Celler-Kefauver Act	Clarified the Clayton Antitrust Act, making it enforceable against mergers accomplished by sale of assets in addition to those accomplished by sale of stock.
1967	*Federal Trade Commission v. Procter & Gamble Co.*	Supreme Court forced Procter & Gamble to divest itself of Clorox because P&G's market power could have allowed Clorox to dominate the bleach market.
1976	Antitrust Improvements Act	Allows state attorneys general to sue on behalf of residents.
1976	*United States v. American Telephone and Telegraph Co.*	Ruled that even though the company was subject to regulation it still was subject to antitrust prosecution. The decision led to the breakup of AT&T.

of the precise test or label being utilized by the Court.

Other per se rules were modified to require a showing of substantial market power before the practice would be condemned as per se unreasonable. For example, the Court modified the per se rule in both tying cases (*Jefferson Parish Hospital Dist. No. 2 v. Hyde*, 1984) and group boycotts (*Northwest Wholesale Stationers v. Pacific Stationery and Printing Co.*, 1985) to require the plaintiff to prove that the defendant enjoyed substantial market power before any liability be imposed. It is difficult to characterize such rules as per se liability because they recognize that these arrangements are not inevitably anticompetitive under all circumstances and typically require the proof of the relevant product and geographic market and the defendant's power within that market, all complicated

factual issues that the original per se rule was designed to avoid.

Vertical Agreements. The most significant changes were in vertical restraints dealing with the distribution of products and services. In *Continental T.V. v. GTE Sylvania* (1977), the Court held that all vertical restraints, other than those dealing with price, would be judged under the full rule of reason, weighing the pro- and anticompetitive effects of the arrangements before rendering judgment under the antitrust laws. As a practical matter, the vast majority of such restricted distribution systems became lawful as a result of this decision.

Although vertical agreements dealing with price were nominally per se unreasonable, they became very difficult to prove. The Court in *Business Electronics Corp. v. Sharp Electronics Corp.* (1988) narrowed the definition of vertical price-fixing agreements subject to the per se rule, leaving everything else subject to the more generous *Sylvania* rule of reason approach. In *Monsanto Co. v. Spray-Rite Service Corp.* (1984), the Court narrowed the type of evidence that plaintiffs could show to demonstrate unlawful vertical price fixing. In *Atlantic Richfield Co. v. USA Petroleum Co.* (1990), the Court limited who could sue for unlawful vertical price fixing. Finally, in *State Oil Co. v. Khan* (1997), the Court reversed one of its earlier precedents and held that maximum vertical price fixing would be treated under the full rule of reason because it was not inevitably anticompetitive and had the potential to help consumers in certain cases.

After *Sylvania*, the Court generally restricted antitrust liability by increasing the substantive and procedural hurdles necessary for either the government or private plaintiffs to prevail. Notable decisions include *Brooke Group Ltd. v. Brown and Williamson Tobacco Corp.* (1993), which limited liability for predatory pricing to those situations in which the defendant has both priced below some appropriate measure of cost and has the ability in the real world to recoup any losses and actually exercise monopoly power following the demise of its competitors. Few plaintiffs were able to prevail under this demanding standard.

Although the center of antitrust activity shifted from the courts to the enforcement agencies, the Court remained actively involved in shaping antitrust law and policy. It continued the trend of shrinking the categories of offenses that are per se unlawful in *NYNEX Corp. v. Discon* (1998) and of narrowly interpreting exemptions and immunities to the antitrust laws, while ensuring that state and local governments could regulate or avoid competition without undue interference from the federal antitrust laws. Despite a general trend toward limiting federal legislative and regulatory power over the economy, the Court preserved the antitrust laws as the preeminent use of the commerce clause, holding that the antitrust statutes extend to the full limit of the power of Congress over both interstate and foreign commerce.

The Court is the final arbiter of the legality of business behavior that affects competition as was intended by Congress in 1890. The precise rules and the tests used by the courts changed over the years in line with the current political and economic thinking. Antitrust law always looked toward economics as a source of wisdom although not as the only factor in deciding the evolution of the legal rules that set the ground rules for the market. The Court uses antitrust law as a flexible instrument determining the bounds between lawful competition and unlawful collusion or exploitation of market power to the detriment of competition and competitors.

FURTHER READING

For an overview of the history of the antitrust laws see Rudolph J. R. Peritz's *Competition Policy in America 1888-1992* (New York: Oxford University Press, 1996) and Hans B. Thorelli's *The Federal Antitrust Policy* (Baltimore, Md.: Johns Hopkins University Press, 1955). For the leading treatises on antitrust doctrine and the Court decisions discussed in this article, see Philip Areeda and Donald Turner's *Antitrust Law* (3 vols., Boston: Little, Brown, 1978) and *Antitrust Law Developments* (4th ed., 2 vols., Chicago: American Bar Association, 1997). The classic economic analyses of the antitrust laws can be found in Robert H. Bork's *The Antitrust Paradox: A Policy at War with Itself* (2d ed., New York: Free Press, 1993) and Richard A. Posner's *Antitrust Law: An Economic Perspective* (Chicago: University of Chicago Press, 1976). The leading analysis of the application of U.S. antitrust law to international business is Spencer Weber Waller's *James R. Atwood and Kingman Brewster's Antitrust and American Business Abroad* (3d ed., New York: Clark Boardman Callaghan, 1997).

Spencer Weber Waller

SEE ALSO Bork, Robert H.; Corporations; *Debs, In re*; *Loewe v. Lawlor*; *Northern Securities Co. v. United States*; Sherman Antitrust Act; *Standard Oil Co. v. United States*; *Swift and Co. v. United States*.

Appellate jurisdiction

DESCRIPTION: Power given to the Supreme Court by Article III, section 2, of the U.S. Constitution, as further defined by federal statute, to review and revise the final decisions of the highest state courts and to review cases from the U.S. court of appeals.

SIGNIFICANCE: The Court's appellate jurisdiction was an important factor in the uniformity and development of law in the United States and is the primary mechanism by which the supremacy clause of the U.S. Constitution is given effect.

The Supreme Court's power, including its appellate jurisdiction, originates in the U.S. Constitution. As one of the three coordinate branches of the federal government, it is the judicial arbiter of the Constitution, exercising appellate authority for this purpose over both state and federal courts. Without the Court's appellate jurisdiction, the Framer's concern for the rule of law and the supremacy of the Constitution and the statutes passed pursuant to it would have no practical effect.

All federal courts, including the Supreme Court, are courts of limited jurisdiction. As such, the federal courts are limited to hearing only certain types of cases under constitutional and statutory limits. Article III, section 2, of the U.S. Constitution limits federal court jurisdiction to cases arising under the Constitution, the laws of the United States, and treaties. It also extends jurisdiction to cases affecting ambassadors and consuls and to cases of admiralty and maritime jurisdiction. The Constitution also extends jurisdiction to controversies to which the United States is a party, controversies between two or more states, controversies between citizens of different states (known as diversity jurisdiction), and controversies between a state or its citizens against a foreign state or its citizens.

The Constitution also differentiates between the original and appellate jurisdiction of the Court. Original jurisdiction is the power of a court to hear and determine a matter before any other court does. The Supreme Court has this power with regard to cases affecting ambassadors, consuls, and those in which a state is a party. The remaining jurisdiction of the Court is appellate. Although Congress may not expand or curtail the Court's original jurisdiction, the Constitution left the nature and scope of the Court's appellate jurisdiction largely undefined. This flexibility resulted in many significant changes in the way in which the Court exercised its power to review and revise lower court decisions.

Traditionally, appellate jurisdiction has two purposes. The first is error correction. On appeal, rulings can be examined to ensure that they are correct and that the procedures that safeguard the substantial rights of the litigants were followed. The second purpose is to announce, clarify, and

harmonize the rules of decision employed in a legal system. This is known as development of the law. Thus, appellate jurisdiction is concerned not only with the impact of a decision on a particular set of litigants but also with the impact on the affairs of persons other than the parties to the case it is deciding. In a system in which there are two levels of appeal, the error correction function is usually left to the first appellate level, and the law development function is left to the appellate court of last resort. In the United States, the Supreme Court's role has gradually changed from that of error correction to that of law development.

Congressional Regulation. Congress did not waste much time enacting its first major legislation dealing with the federal judiciary. In the same year in which the Constitution was ratified, Congress passed the Judiciary Act of 1789. This act provided for basic appellate jurisdiction and created a three-tier judiciary staffed by Supreme Court justices and district court judges. The act established a circuit court consisting of one district court judge and two Supreme Court justices who would literally "ride the circuit" to hear cases and appeals from district court decisions. It also provided for appellate jurisdiction in the Supreme Court over civil cases from the circuit court in which the amount in controversy was in excess of two thousand dollars. (The Supreme Court did not have jurisdiction to hear appeals in criminal cases until 1889.) The act also gave the Court appellate jurisdiction to reexamine and "reverse or affirm" a final decision from the highest state court in which a decision in the suit could be had, where the validity of a federal law or a right was drawn into question and the decision was against validity.

During the United States' first century, the Court was virtually the only federal appellate court. The Court was required to rule on all appeals brought from lower federal courts as well as those brought from state courts under the Judiciary Act of 1789. The only way to gain appellate review in the Court under the Judiciary Act of 1789 was by "writ of error" (later known as appeal). Under this method, sometimes called a "writ of right," the Court was obligated to hear an appeal once it determined it had jurisdiction over the subject matter. As the United States grew, the caseload of the Court began to swell. Data available starting in 1880 shows the number of cases filed in the Court increased tenfold. If the obligatory writ of right or appeal system had prevailed, the Court would certainly have had trouble managing such a caseload.

Appeals of Right Curtailed. The Court acknowledged the significant power Congress has to expand or contract its appellate jurisdiction in *Daniels v. Chicago and Rock Island Railroad Co.* (1866). This does not mean, however, that the members of the Court have no influence over Congress when it comes to legislation affecting the Court's appellate jurisdiction. Indeed, members of the Court actually had a hand in drafting one of the major pieces of legislation affecting the Court's appellate jurisdiction in the twentieth century. Under the Judiciary Act of 1925, the appeal of right was significantly curtailed and was replaced by what was eventually to become virtually the only avenue of appeal to the Court, the writ of certiorari. The groundwork for this shift from direct appeals to discretionary appeals was laid in 1891, when Congress created a new level of courts between the circuit and district courts and the Supreme Court. The Judiciary Act of 1891 provided for Supreme Court review over decisions of the new appeals court if the appeals court judges certified a case to the Court or the Court granted review by writ of certiorari. Automatic appeal was still allowed, however, in cases involving constitutional questions, treaties, jurisdictional questions, capital crimes, and conflicting laws.

Continuing this trend, the Judiciary Act of 1925 limited the appeal of right for cases from the appeals courts to those in which the appeals court held a state law invalid under the Constitution or federal laws. Appeals of right remained, however, for appeals from district courts in a small number of categories: antitrust, appeals by the United States under the Criminal Appeals Act, suits to enjoin enforcement of state laws, and suits to enjoin enforcement of Interstate Commerce Commission orders. This act and subsequent statutes that further limited the availability of appeals of right to the Court, reflected an important shift in the philosophical view of the Court's function. Instead of error correction, the Court was to focus its efforts on cases raising issues of broad public interest.

By 1988, the trend of limiting appeals of right was nearly complete. In the 1988 Act to Improve the Administration of Justice, Congress virtually eliminated the Court's nondiscretionary appellate jurisdiction. Today, the right of appeal exists only in cases that are required to be determined by a district court of three judges. The vast remainder of the Court's appellate jurisdiction is through the writ of certiorari, which is granted or denied at the discretion of the Court.

Standards for Granting Certiorari. A review on writ of certiorari is granted "only when there are special and important reasons," according to the Supreme Court's rule 17. The rule goes on to list the types of reasons that may be considered by the Court in deciding whether to grant certiorari in a particular case. Some of the types of reasons justifying certiorari to a court of appeals are where a court of appeals decides a matter in conflict with another court of appeals, where a court of appeals has decided a matter in conflict with the decision of a state's highest court, and where an appeals court has drastically departed from the usual course of judicial proceedings. Certiorari is also justified when the court of appeals or a state's highest court has decided an important question of federal law that has never been decided by the Supreme Court or has decided a federal question in a way that conflicts with previous Court decisions. However, the rule makes it clear that the Court retains the discretion to deny certiorari even in cases that fall within these categories. A less formal rule employed by the Court in making certiorari decisions is the rule of four. Under this rule, a case is accepted for full review only if four members of the Court feel that it merits such consideration. However, it is employed, this power to select the cases over which the Court will exercise its appellate jurisdiction gives the Court considerable influence over the speed and direction of the law's development.

In fact, the percentage of cases that the Court selects for appellate review fell steadily in the second half of the twentieth century. From the 1980's to the 1990's, the percentage of cases in which certiorari was granted dropped from around 10 percent to around 3 percent. For example, 2,441 petitions for certiorari were filed in 1992, and only 83 were granted.

The cases accepted for review also can reflect certain social trends. In 1933 cases involving due process made up only 5.2 percent of total cases accepted for review, whereas in 1987 those cases amounted to 29.6 percent of the Court's docket. A similar trend can be seen in the increase in cases involving federal rights. Those cases represented about 1 percent of total cases in 1933, but nearly 11 percent in 1987. Other policy areas in which growth can be seen are equality, government benefits, and separation of governmental powers. The percentage of cases involving foreign affairs, federal regulation, economic regulation, state regulation, and internal revenue has steadily decreased.

FURTHER READING
One of the best sources for a summary of the appellate jurisdiction of the Court, as well as reprints of source documents such as the U.S. Constitution, the Judiciary Acts, and Supreme Court rules is Elder Witt's *Congressional Quarterly's Guide to the Supreme Court* (2d ed., Washington, D.C.: Congressional Quarterly, 1990). An excellent primer on appellate jurisdiction in general is Robert J. Martineau's *Appellate Practice and Procedure* (St. Paul, Minn: West Publishing, 1987). Statistical information on the Court and its decisions can be found in *The Supreme Court Compendium*, written by Lee Epstein, Jeffrey A. Segal, Harold J. Spaeth, and Thomas G. Walker (Washington, D.C.: Congressional Quarterly, 1994). The Federal Judicial Center has several helpful publications, in particular, *Creating the Federal Judicial System* by Russell R. Wheeler and Cynthia Harrison (2d ed., Federal Judicial Center, 1994). In-depth information about the historical background of the Court's appellate jurisdiction, including reproduction of some source materials in the Framers' own hands, can be found in Julius Goebel, Jr.'s *History of the Supreme Court of the United States: Antecedents and Beginnings to 1801* (New York: Macmillan, 1971).

Sharon K. O'Roke

SEE ALSO Certiorari, writ of; Circuit courts of appeals; Circuit riding; Courts of appeals; Diversity jurisdiction; Judiciary Act of 1789; Judiciary Acts of 1801-1925; Oral argument; Review, process of.

Appointment and removal power

DESCRIPTION: Authority to appoint and discharge persons from nonelective positions in the federal government

SIGNIFICANCE: The U.S. Constitution's provisions regarding the appointment and removal of Supreme Court justices influences the composition of the Court and affects its independence

from Congress and the president, the other two branches of government.

The U.S. Constitution describes the power to appoint government officials in some detail. Article II, section 2, clause 2, provides that the president shall appoint ambassadors (and other diplomats), Supreme Court justices, and "all other Officers of the United States," with the "Advice and Consent of the Senate." The president nominates people to fill these positions, and the Senate then approves or rejects these nominations by majority vote. The Senate usually confirms nominations of executive branch officials but sometimes rejects them. The level of deference given the president by the Senate has varied over time. However, when the Senate is not in session, the Constitution authorizes the president to fill vacancies in federal offices without the Senate's approval. These "recess appointments" last until the end of the Senate's next annual session.

The Constitution also authorizes Congress to vest the power to appoint "inferior Officers" in "the President alone, the Courts of Law, or in the Heads of Departments." Thus, many federal officials can be appointed without Senate confirmation. The Court held that low-level positions, held by the vast majority of federal employees, are not covered by Article II, and thus Congress may vest power to hire such employees largely without restriction. In addition, congressional appointments of legislative branch officers are not subject to Article II appointment procedures.

Though difficult constitutional issues rarely arise with respect to the appointment power, in *Buckley v. Valeo* (1976) the Court had to decide whether members of the congressional leadership could appoint some of the members of the Federal Elections Commission, whose responsibilities included enforcement of federal campaign finance laws. The Court held that because the members exercised more authority than legislative branch appointees could wield and qualified as "officers of the United States," the traditional Article II requirement of appointment by the president had to be observed.

Removal Power. The power to remove appointed officials outside of the legislative or judicial branches has produced significant controversy. The Constitution does not expressly discuss the power to remove officials, except to provide for re-

The 1986 nomination of William H. Rehnquist, an antiabortion conservative, caused members of the National Organization for Women to organize a protest outside the federal courthouse in New York. (AP/Wide World Photos)

moval of any "Civil Officer of the United States" upon impeachment by the House of Representatives and conviction by the Senate. Federal officials are almost never removed by impeachment. Shortly after the Constitution's adoption, the question of the president's power to remove government officials arose. The Senate concluded that the president could remove federal officials without its "advice and consent." The right to remove officials serving in the executive branch is generally thought to inhere in the "executive power" of the United States, which the Constitution vests in the president.

The increased complexity of the government and the expansion of the role of administrative agencies beginning in the New Deal in the 1930's unsettled the understanding of the locus of the removal power. In *Humphrey's Executor v. United States* (1935), the Court recognized that some agencies, such as the Federal Trade Commission, exercised a type of judicial and legislative power in addition to the executive powers delegated to them by the president. The Court ruled that because commissioners exercised quasi-legislative and quasi-judicial powers that the president lacked the exclusive right to exercise, Congress could establish fixed terms for appointees to commissions such as the Federal Trade Commission and prevent the president from discharging them during those terms except for "good cause." Thus, some appointees had some independence from the president be-

cause the president could not discharge them over policy differences. In *Morrison v. Olson* (1988), involving the constitutionality of a statute that authorized appointment of independent counsel to investigate and, if warranted, prosecute high governmental officials, the Court held that special circumstances could justify limiting the president's power to remove even some officials who were exercising purely executive functions, such as investigating and prosecuting crimes.

Mistretta v. United States (1989) illustrates the removal power puzzles that can be created by the complexities of modern government. *Mistretta* involved a challenge to the U.S. Sentencing Commission, which had been created as an "independent commission in the Judicial Branch" to establish guidelines limiting the discretion judges exercised in sentencing criminal defendants. The president could remove commission members only for good cause. The Court upheld that limitation on the president's removal power, arguing that the president has never exercised the kind of authority Congress granted the Sentencing Commission.

Unlike officials at least nominally in the executive branch of government, Court justices and other judges appointed to judgeships created under Article III of the Constitution, namely federal district court and federal court of appeals judges, hold their offices during "good behavior" and may be removed only by impeachment.

FURTHER READING

Aman, Alfred C., Jr., and William T. Mayton. *Administrative Law*. St. Paul, Minn.: West Publishing, 1993.

Carter, Stephen L. *The Confirmation Mess: Cleaning Up the Federal Appointments Process*. New York: Basic Books, 1994.

Tribe, Laurence H. *God Save This Honorable Court: How the Choices of Supreme Court Justices Shape Our History*. New York: Random House, 1985.

Bernard W. Bell

SEE ALSO *Bowsher v. Synar; Buckley v. Valeo; Humphrey's Executor v. United States;* Impeachment of judges; Judicial codes and rules; *Mistretta v. United States; Morrison v. Olson;* New Deal; Nominations to the Court; Separation of powers.

Aptheker v. Secretary of State

CITATION: 378 U.S. 500
DATE: June 22, 1964
ISSUE: Freedom of association; right to travel
SIGNIFICANCE: In this case, one of a series that undermined 1950's anticommunist legislation, the Supreme Court overturned the communist registration provision in the 1950 McCarran Act.

A six-vote liberal majority on the Supreme Court voided the part of the 1950 McCarran Act requiring Communist Party members to register with the Subversive Activities Control Board. This registration provision was upheld in *Communist Party v. Subversive Activities Control Board* (1961), but the Court said it would rule on the constitutionality of the registrations only if enforcement were attempted. The government had previously tried to block the issuance of passports to communists and other subversives under the 1926 Passport Act, but this was stricken as unconstitutional in *Kent v. Dulles* (1958).

Writing for the Court, Justice Arthur J. Goldberg called the statute overly broad, pointing out that the right to travel outside the United States, while not absolute, was valuable and that this act banned travel for subversive organization members without regard to the purpose of their travel and whether or not they were active or knowing members of the organization.

Richard L. Wilson

SEE ALSO *Albertson v. Subversive Activities Control Board;* Assembly and association, freedom of; *Communist Party v. Subversive Activities Control Board; Dennis v. United States; Scales v. United States;* Travel, right to; *Yates v. United States.*

Argersinger v. Hamlin

CITATION: 407 U.S. 25
DATE: June 12, 1972
ISSUE: Right to counsel for indigent defendants
SIGNIFICANCE: The Supreme Court ruled that the Sixth and Fourteenth Amendments mandate that states must provide a poor defendant with a lawyer at the time of trial if the defendant could be imprisoned for any period of time.

In *Gideon v. Wainwright* (1963), the Supreme Court held that states must provide counsel for indigent defendants in felony cases. However, it was not clear whether this expanded right to an attorney applied to misdemeanor cases. Then the Court decided in 1968 that defendants had a right to a jury trial when they faced incarceration for six months or more. In this context, Argersinger was not provided counsel when he was convicted and sentenced to three months in jail for the misdemeanor of carrying a concealed weapon.

By a 9-0 vote, the Court reversed Argersinger's conviction. Writing for the majority, Justice William O. Douglas developed the one-day rule, which triggers the right to counsel whenever a person is deprived of liberty for even one day. The *Argersinger* decision was ambiguous about whether the right to counsel applied whenever a defendant was charged with a crime that could result in a jail term. The Court clarified the issue in *Scott v. Illinois* (1979), holding that counsel must be provided only if conviction would actually result in imprisonment.

Thomas T. Lewis

SEE ALSO Counsel, right to; Due process, procedural; *Johnson v. Louisiana;* Sixth Amendment.

Arizona v. Fulminante

CITATION: 499 U.S. 279
DATE: March 26, 1991
ISSUE: Coerced confessions
SIGNIFICANCE: The Supreme Court ruled that when an involuntary confession is erroneously admitted in a criminal trial, an appellate court may confirm the conviction if it decides that the defendant would have been found guilty on the strength of the other evidence.

Before the *Fulminante* decision, if a person was convicted in a trial in which a coerced confession was admitted, the conviction was automatically reversed, regardless of the other evidence used in the trial. When Orestes Fulminante was in prison, a fellow inmate, an informant for the Federal Bureau of Investigation, promised to protect Fulminante from violent prisoners if he would describe the murder of the young girl. At Fulminante's trial for the murder, the prosecution used the account he gave to the informant in combination with other evidence, and Fulminante was found guilty of first-degree murder.

The justices agreed that the confession had been coerced and that it should have been excluded from the trial. Disagreeing on almost everything else, the justices issued two rulings. In regard to the central issue, Chief Justice William H. Rehnquist, speaking for a 5-4 majority, held that use of a coerced confession may be excused as a "harmless error" if other evidence is adequate to support a guilty verdict. Rehnquist argued that the Supreme Court had accepted harmless error analysis is regard to other "trial errors" just as detrimental to a defendant. Justice Byron R. White, speaking for a different 5-3 majority, ruled that the impact of Fulminante's confession had not been shown to be harmless beyond a reasonable doubt. This ruling meant that Fulminante was entitled to a new trial in which his confession would not be admitted.

Thomas T. Lewis

See also *Brown v. Mississippi*; Due process, procedural; Exclusionary rule; Fifth Amendment; *Harris v. New York*; Self-incrimination, immunity against.

Arlington Heights v. Metropolitan Housing Development Corp.

Citation: 429 U.S. 252
Date: January 11, 1977
Issue: Racial discrimination by a governmental agency
Significance: The Supreme Court reaffirmed the principle that a governmental policy will not be judged unconstitutional solely because it has a disproportionate impact on a particular race.

A nonprofit developer wanted to construct low- and moderate-income housing units in a largely white suburb of Chicago. A major goal of the project was to promote racial integration in the community. The suburb's board of trustees refused to rezone the region for multiple-family dwellings, thus killing the project. The federal court of appeals ruled that the denial of rezoning violated the Fourteenth Amendment because its "ultimate ef-

fect" was discrimination against racial minorities. By a 7-1 vote, the Supreme Court reversed the lower court's ruling. Based on the recent precedent, *Washington v. Davis* (1976), Justice Lewis F. Powell, Jr., explained that proof of a "racially discriminatory intent" was necessary in order to establish a constitutional violation. From the official minutes and other evidence of the case, Powell concluded that the challengers had "simply failed to carry their burden of showing that discriminatory purpose was a motivating factor in the Village's decision."

Thomas T. Lewis

See also Equal protection clause; Jones v. Alfred H. Mayer Co.; Race and discrimination; *San Antonio Independent School District v. Rodriguez*; *Washington v. Davis*; Zoning.

Articles of Confederation

Date: 1781
Description: First written blueprint for organizing a compact of the American colonies.
Significance: The Articles of Confederation provided the first American system of government, although they did not create a judicial system. They also were a precursor to the Tenth Amendment.

Drafted in stages from 1776 to 1777 but not ratified until 1781, the Articles of Confederation extended and revised the existing understanding of diffused authority and state autonomy. Richard Henry Lee, Samuel Adams, John Dickinson, and Roger Sherman, among others, assisted in the drafting of the document. Although regarded in 1781 as a reliable constitution, the accepted modern view of the articles is that they were a dismal failure in all respects. The articles could not provide for a system of popular rule or supply the young regime with the security measures that were needed to ensure its survival. The critics of the articles usually cite the plan's inability to endow a national government with the power to levy taxes or regulate commerce, thereby discouraging all efforts at national cohesion. The articles, in other words, embodied the political tensions within American politics during the period between the signing of the Declaration of Independence and the Constitutional Convention.

The articles possessed the means for affirming popular rule, diffusing political authority, and allowing for a system of government. As in the case of the Declaration of Independence, the articles perpetuated the original design for the territorial division of the country, into independent and sovereign states, a "perpetual union." Article II described the nature of the alliance: "Each state retains its sovereignty, freedom and independence, and every power, jurisdiction, and right, which is not by the Confederation expressly delegated to the United States in Congress assembled." Articles III and IV, antecedents of the Tenth Amendment, affirmed the nature of their "league of friendship" and provided for the extradition of fugitives. Article V presented a system of representation for the states in Congress that allowed for each state to have no less than two and no more than seven delegates. Articles VI and VII concerned limitations on the states regarding the conducting of foreign affairs and national security. Article VIII detailed how the costs of war would be defrayed and Article IX outlined the powers of Congress, the only branch of government established by the document. The last four articles discussed various aspects of the "perpetual" union.

The articles confirmed the centrality of the states, thus placing the relationship between the governed and the government at the state level instead of the national level. The articles also provided that the respective states, not the federal government, would protect citizens' privileges and immunities. As a genuine precursor to the Tenth Amendment (which reserved for the states or the people those powers not delegated to the United States by the Constitution), the articles limited the power of the federal government and strengthened state prerogatives.

FURTHER READING

Hoffert, Robert W. *A Politics of Tension: The Articles of Confederation and American Political Ideas.* Boulder: University Press of Colorado, 1991.

Jensen, Merrill. *The Articles of Confederation.* 1940. Reprint. Madison: University of Wisconsin Press, 1970.

Moore, Wayne D. *Constitutional Rights and Powers of the People.* Princeton, N.J.: Princeton University Press, 1996.

H. Lee Cheek, Jr.

SEE ALSO Constitution, U.S.; Constitutional Convention; Declaration of Independence; Federalism; State action; State constitutions; States' rights; Tenth Amendment.

Ashwander v. Tennessee Valley Authority

CITATION: 297 U.S. 288
DATE: February 17, 1936
ISSUE: Constitutionality of the Tennessee Valley Authority (TVA)
SIGNIFICANCE: The Supreme Court upheld the constitutionality of the TVA, including its right to sell electricity. In a concurring opinion, Justice Louis D. Brandeis formulated influential guidelines concerning when the Court will decide constitutional questions.

When the TVA sold "surplus power" to a private utility company, minority shareholders went to court to annul the agreement. Speaking for an 8-1 majority, Chief Justice Charles Evans Hughes argued that the TVA had been built for national defense and for the improvement of navigation, which were legitimate interests of the national government. He added that Article IV, section 3, of the U.S. Constitution authorized Congress to dispose of property legally acquired. Dissenting, Justice James C. McReynolds accused the majority of using a fictitious rationale, since the main purpose of the TVA was to produce and sell electricity.

Although concurring with the decision, Justice Brandeis argued that the Supreme Court should not have even addressed the constitutional question because the case involved only an internal dispute among shareholders. He codified rules for the Court to follow. First, the Court will not determine constitutional questions in a friendly, nonadversarial proceeding; second, the Court will not anticipate an issue of constitutional law; third, the Court will not decide a constitutional question unless necessary to resolving the case at hand; fourth, the Court will not formulate a principle of constitutional law broader than necessary for resolving the case; fifth, the Court will not decide on the validity of a statute unless a plaintiff has been injured by its operation; and sixth, before deciding that a statute is unconstitutional, the Court will first ascertain whether a reasonable interpretation of the statute permits avoidance of the constitutional issue.

Although not always followed, justices commonly refer to the *Ashwander* rules, or Brandeis rules, as established standards. At times the rules have encouraged the justices to exercise a degree of self-restraint, and sometimes they have served as an excuse to avoid awkward or difficult questions.

Thomas T. Lewis

SEE ALSO Brandeis, Louis D.; Constitutional interpretation; Judicial powers; Judicial self-restraint.

Assembly and association, freedom of

DESCRIPTION: The right of the people to gather peaceably and to associate with anyone they desire.

SIGNIFICANCE: The Supreme Court has generally upheld the freedom of assembly and association, although it has upheld time, place, and manner restrictions on demonstrations, picketing, and similar gatherings.

The First Amendment to the Constitution prohibits Congress from making any law that limits "the right of the people peaceably to assemble," but the Constitution does not mention freedom of association. Freedom of association has been inferred, however, from freedom of assembly, and the guarantees of the Bill of Rights, of which the First Amendment is part, have been inferred to apply to the states. Therefore, subject to the interpretation of the Supreme Court, all laws, whether state or federal, that unduly restrict freedom of assembly and association are unconstitutional.

The only explicit restriction on these freedoms is the word "peaceably"; mobs and other groups intent on violence or destruction of property lie outside constitutional protection, as do picketers who physically oppose those who wish to cross picket lines. The freedoms also impinge on trespassing laws that protect the rights of private owners of property, resulting in issues of legal interpretation. Additionally, the Court has upheld laws requiring the licensing of parades and other large assemblies that, although taking place in public areas, may disrupt traffic or otherwise place an undue burden on local authorities. The Court has made further distinctions between public and private places. Quasi-public or quasi-private places, such as college campuses and privately owned areas open to the general public, have been defined regarding the limitations of the right of assembly. How such limitations are to be interpreted and applied have been and continue to be the subject of litigation that is often controversial.

Interpretations. The general standard that the Court applies to the question of the right of assembly is the same that it applies to speech: time, place, and manner. For example, the noisy demonstration that is legal in a park outside a public library may be considered illegal if it takes place inside the library. As the Court stated in *United States Postal Service v. Greenburgh Civic Associations* (1981): "The

---

COURT RULINGS RESTRICTING AREAS WHERE ASSEMBLIES ARE PERMITTED

Date	Case	Areas designated as restricted
1966	*Adderley v. Florida*	Special access roads to jails and courthouses
1972	*Flower v. United States*	Army bases
1976	*Greer v. Spock*	Military bases
1990	*United States v. Kokinda*	U.S. Post Office property sidewalks (plurality ruling)
1992	*International Society for Krishna Consciousness v. Lee*	Airports

COURT RULINGS EXPANDING PROTECTED AREAS FOR ASSEMBLIES

Date	Court case	Protected areas
1937	*Hague v. Congress of Industrial Organizations*	Public streets and meeting halls
1963	*Edwards v. South Carolina*	State capitol steps
1965	*Cox v. Louisiana*	Streets, sidewalk near courthouse or State Capitol
1972	*Chicago Police Department v. Mosley*	Streets, sidewalk near school
1972	*Chief, Capitol Police v. Jeanette Rankin Brigade*	Lafayette Park, Washington, D.C.
1975	*Southeastern Promotions v. Conrad*	Municipal Auditorium
1982	*United States v. Grace*	Steps of U.S. Supreme Court Building
1987	*Board of Airport Commissioners of Los Angeles v. Jews for Jesus*	Central Airport Terminal could not be declared "First Amendment Free Zone" to prohibit solicitations and canvassing
1988	*Boos v. Barry*	Streets, sidewalks within 500 feet of embassy

First Amendment does not guarantee access to property simply because it is owned or controlled by the government." This statement should be compared, however, with one from *Hague v. Congress of Industrial Organizations* (1939), that whether streets or parks are publicly or privately owned, "they have immemorially been held in trust for the use of the public for purposes of assembly and discussing public questions." The conflict between these two statements is to be resolved by examination of the intent that the government has in limiting the assembly in question. In *Perry Education Association v. Perry Local Educators' Association* (1983), the Court stated that the government may "reserve a forum for its intended purposes as long as the regulation is reasonable and not an effort to suppress expression merely because public officials oppose the speaker's view." Perry concerned a dispute between two teachers' unions. Under the employment contract, Perry Educational Association (PEA) had access to the interschool mail system and teacher mail boxes. The bargaining agreement also provided that access rights to the mail facilities were not available to any rival union. A rival union, Perry Local Educators' Association filed suit, contending that PEA's preferential access to the internal mail system violated the First Amendment. The Supreme Court ruled that the PEA's contract provision did not violate the First Amendment.

Freedom of association—in particular, political association, including membership in communist organizations—has been examined in similar ways. In such cases as *Yates v. United States* (1957), the Court explicitly rejected the idea that membership in a group indicates guilt by association. Communist groups are not the only ones whose memberships were subject to government scrutiny. In *National Association for the Advancement of Colored People v. Alabama* (1958), for example, the National Association for the Advancement of Colored People was able to enforce its right to free and private association, in particular to keep its membership rolls out of the hands of Alabama officials. Such protection, however, does not extend to groups that a government can demonstrate are engaged in illegal activities. The Court has upheld the careful application of federal antigang laws that make it a crime to belong to a group engaged in criminal enterprise.

Private organizations that discriminate according to sex, race, or other criteria have defended themselves on First Amendment grounds, with varying degrees of success. In general, the Court has placed greater emphasis on laws against discrimination than on the right to association, especially regarding large associations that have few restrictions on membership. In *Roberts v. United States Jaycees* (1984), the Court reasoned that the Jaycees lacked the distinctive characteristics, such as small size, identifiable purpose, selectivity in membership, and perhaps seclusion from the public eye that might afford constitutional protection to the organization's exclusion of women. In *Rotary International v. Rotary Club of Duarte* (1987), the Court upheld a California law that prevented Rotary International from excluding women from membership, and in *New York State Club Association v. City of New York* (1988), the Court upheld a New York City law prohibiting discrimination based on race, creed, sex, and other categories in places "of public accommodation, resort, or amusement." The court held that the law applied to clubs of more than 400 members providing regular meal service and supported by nonmembers for trade or business purposes.

A landmark case touching on freedom of association is *Griswold v. Connecticut* (1965). Griswold gave medical advice to married people regarding birth control and was convicted of breaking a Connecticut law prohibiting the use of birth control and the giving of medical advice about birth control. The Supreme Court declared the Connecticut law an unconstitutional violation of the right of privacy. The Constitution makes no mention of such a right, but in Griswold the Court reasoned that such a right flowed from the right to association. Put broadly, the government did not have the authority to tell people what they could talk about with whom. Thus the "right to be left alone is the beginning of all freedoms" could be inferred to freedom of association.

Abortion clinic protests, specifically the tactics employed by those opposed to abortion to prevent entrance to clinics, have generated various cases touching on freedom of assembly. In *Bray v. Alexandria Clinic* (1993), for example, the Court held that picketers in front of an abortion clinic did not violate the rights of those accessing the clinic to equal protection of the law because the picketers' methods did not rise to the level of "hinderance" considered illegal. On the other hand, the convictions of abortion clinic protesters who are too aggressive in their methods, particularly those that rise to physical confrontation, have been upheld in various courts.

FURTHER READING

Abernathy, M. Glenn. *The Right of Assembly and Association*. Columbia: University of South Carolina Press, 1981.

Gutmann, Amy, ed. *Freedom of Association*. Princeton, N.J.: Princeton University Press, 1998.

Murphy, Paul L. *Rights of Assembly, Petition, Arms, and Just Compensation*. New York: Garland, 1990.

Shiffrin, Steven H., and Jesse H. Choper. *The First Amendment: Cases, Comments, Questions*. St. Paul, Minn.: West Publishing, 1996.

Eric Howard

SEE ALSO *Adderley v. Florida*; *Cox v. New Hampshire*; *Griswold v. Connecticut*; *Hague v. Congress of Industrial Organizations*; *National Association for the Advancement of Colored People v. Alabama*; States' rights; Time, place, and manner regulations; *Yates v. United States*.

Automobile searches

DESCRIPTION: The inspection by police and other government agents of the interiors of motor vehicles to look for evidence of unlawful activity.

SIGNIFICANCE: Starting with its 1925 ruling, the Supreme Court made it progressively easier for police and other government agencies to engage lawfully in searches of motor vehicles by interpreting the search and seizure requirements of the Fourth Amendment in a manner that clearly distinguishes the search of a vehicle from that of a residence or a container.

The framers of the Fourth Amendment were concerned about protecting people from unlawful government searches and seizures of their "houses" and "effects" when they drafted the amendment in the late eighteenth century. When the automobile became prominent in U.S. society more than a century later, the Supreme Court had to decide how the words and principles of the Fourth Amendment should be applied to searches of cars and other motor vehicles.

Beginning with its decision in *Carroll v. United States* (1925), the Court has consistently held that where there is probable cause that an automobile contains evidence of a crime, the police may search that vehicle without a search warrant. Unlike houses, automobiles are mobile and therefore the police may not have time to obtain a warrant before the vehicle and any evidence contained within it disappear, the Court reasoned. As the Court applied the warrant requirement of the Fourth Amendment differently to automobiles than to houses, inevitably the question arose as to whether the search of a motorhome would be treated as that of a house or an automobile. In *California v. Carney* (1985), the Court held that in most cases, the potential mobility of a motorhome obviates the need for the police to obtain a search warrant.

Searches of effects, such as containers, generally are subject to the same warrant requirement that applies to house searches. The Court was thus confronted with the question of whether to require the police to obtain a warrant before searching a container located in an automobile. In a series of cases culminating in *California v. Acevedo* (1991), the Court held that when the police have probable cause that a container in an automobile contains criminal evidence or that the evidence is located somewhere in the automobile and can fit into the container, they may search the container without obtaining a warrant.

The Court has also authorized police searches of automobiles in situations in which there was no probable cause that there was criminal evidence within the automobile. After lawfully arresting the occupant of a vehicle, the police may search the passenger area of that vehicle, including the glove compartment or items within the passenger area. According to the Court's decision in *New York v. Belton*, (1981), such a search is permissible to prevent the arrested person from grabbing a weapon or disposing of evidence. Additionally, when police properly impound a vehicle, they are allowed to search all parts of the vehicle in order to inventory its contents, as the Court held in *South Dakota v. Opperman* (1976). In *United States v. Di Re* (1999), the Court held that officers who stopped a driver for a traffic violation and saw evidence of drugs were allowed to search everything in the automobile and the private effects of a passenger.

FURTHER READING

Quick, Bruce D. *Law of Arrest, Search, and Seizure: An Examination of the Fourth, Fifth, and Sixth Amendments to the United States Constitution.* Rev. ed. Bismarck, N.D.: Attorney General's Office, Criminal Justice Training and Statistics Division, 1987.

Regini, Lisa A. "The Motor Vehicle Exception: When and Where to Search." *FBI Law Enforcement Bulletin* 68, no. 7 (July, 1999): 26-32.

Savage, David G. "Privacy Rights Pulled Over: Cops Get More Power to Search Personal Effects in Vehicles." *American Bar Association Journal* 85 (June, 1999): 42-44.

Steven P. Grossman

SEE ALSO *California v. Acevedo*; *Carroll v. United States*; Exclusionary rule; Fourth Amendment; *Michigan v. Long*; *New York v. Belton*; Privacy, right to; *Ross, United States v.*; Search warrant requirement.

Automobile Workers v. Johnson Controls

CITATION: 499 U.S. 187
DATE: March 20, 1991
ISSUE: Gender issues
SIGNIFICANCE: Based on an interpretation of the Pregnancy Discrimination Act of 1983, the Supreme Court struck down a private company's fetal-protection policy that barred all women with childbearing capacity from jobs involving significant lead exposure.

The Pregnancy Discrimination Act of 1983, an amendment to Title VII of the Civil Rights Act of 1964, required that pregnant employees must be "treated the same" as other employees unless there was a bona fide occupational qualification for different treatment. By a 6-3 vote, the Supreme Court held that there was no bona fide occupational qualification justification for Johnson Controls' policy of exclusion. Justice Harry A. Blackmun's majority opinion emphasized that the policy did not seek to protect the future children of all employees equally because it did not apply to male employees despite evidence of the debilitating effect of lead exposure on the male reproductive system. In addition, he wrote that the 1983 act permitted a safety exception only in instances in which the employee's sex or pregnancy actually interfered with the worker's ability to perform the job and that decisions about the welfare of future children must be left to parents rather than the employer. Rejecting the argument about the need of the company to protect itself from tort liability, Blackmun noted that the Occupational Safety and Health Administration required safety standards designed to minimize the risk to an unborn child and that it would be difficult for a court to find liability without negligence.

Thomas T. Lewis

SEE ALSO Civil Rights acts; Employment discrimination; Gender issues; Private discrimination.

B

Bad tendency test

DESCRIPTION: A test first applied by the Supreme Court in 1919 according to which speech that had a "tendency" to incite unlawful acts was not constitutionally protected.

SIGNIFICANCE: Throughout much of the twentieth century, the Court used the bad tendency test broadly to restrict speech critical of the U.S. government or its policies.

Although usually associated with *Debs v. United States* (1919), the bad tendency test actually has its genesis in *Schenck v. United States* (1919). In that case, the Supreme Court decided that Charles Schenck, a leader of the Socialist party, was guilty of a conspiracy to violate the 1917 Espionage Act by distributing flyers denouncing the draft. As part of the opinion in *Schenck*, Justice Oliver Wendell Holmes made it clear that not all speech can or should be protected by invoking the now-famous example of a person yelling "fire" in a crowded theater. Drawing the line between protected and unprotected speech, however, has proven difficult. In *Schenck*, the Court established the following test for determining whether speech should be protected:

> The question in every case is whether the words used are used in such circumstances and are of such a nature as to create a clear and present danger that they will bring about substantive evils that Congress has a right to prevent.

As applied, this test was far less protective of free speech than the term "clear and present danger" might suggest. No showing of present danger was required in *Schenck* or subsequent cases. The Court held that if the "tendency and intent" of the speech was to encourage illegal action, then the speech was not protected by the First Amendment. Furthermore, the Court was often willing to *assume* a bad tendency and intent if the speech was critical of the government or its policies. The bad tendency test was notoriously applied just weeks after *Schenck* in *Debs v. United States*, when the perennial presidential candidate Eugene Debs was convicted of conspiracy for telling a crowd that he was sympathetic toward those who were trying to obstruct the draft. He was sentenced to ten years in prison for the crime.

Almost immediately, the test came under fire, with Justice Holmes dissenting against the test's application in *Abrams v. United States* (1919). His was a lone voice, however, and the bad tendency test continued to be applied. For example, in *Gitlow v. New York* (1925), *Whitney v. California* (1927), and *Dennis v. United States* (1951), members of either the Socialist or Communist Parties were convicted of breaking the law because they were found to have advocated illegal action by distributing flyers or assembling in groups.

Although the Court employed various First Amendment tests after *Debs*, it did not begin to seriously move away from the substance of the bad tendency test until *Yates v. United States* in 1957. In *Yates*, the Court reversed the conspiracy convictions of fourteen "second-string" Communist Party officials, drawing a line between advocacy of an abstract principle and advocacy of action. Even so, it was not until 1969, in *Brandenburg v. Ohio*, that the Court finally abandoned the bad tendency test completely and developed the modern, highly protective standard for freedom of speech.

FURTHER READING

Chafee, Zechariah, Jr. *Free Speech in the United States.* Cambridge, Mass.: Harvard University Press, 1941.

Downs, Donald. *Nazis in Skokie.* Notre Dame, Ind.: University of Notre Dame Press, 1985.

Greenawalt, Kent. *Speech, Crime and the Uses of Language.* New York: Oxford University Press, 1989.

Evan Gerstmann and Christopher Shortell

SEE ALSO *Abrams v. United States*; *Brandenburg v. Ohio*; Clear and present danger test; *Dennis v. United States*; Espionage acts; First Amendment speech tests; *Gitlow v. New York*; Holmes, Oliver Wendell; *Schenck v. United States*; Unprotected speech; *Whitney v. California*; *Yates v. United States*.

Badger, George E.

IDENTIFICATION: Supreme Court nominee (1853)
NOMINATED BY: Millard Fillmore

BORN: April 17, 1795, New Bern, North Carolina

DIED: May 11, 1866, Raleigh, North Carolina

SIGNIFICANCE: A prominent lawyer and jurist, Badger was nominated by U.S. president Millard Fillmore to replace Supreme Court Justice John McKinley, who had died. In spite of his impeccable qualifications, political considerations prevented his confirmation.

Badger achieved prominence as one of the foremost legal minds of the mid-nineteenth century, rivaled only by Supreme Court Justice Joseph Story. After serving as a judge on the North Carolina superior court, he argued more than seven hundred cases before the U.S. Supreme Court. As a member of the U.S. Senate, he was regarded as an unsurpassed authority on constitutional law.

In 1853, after the death of U.S. Supreme Court Justice John McKinley, President Millard Fillmore sought to install Badger, a Whig, on the Court. Fillmore's lame duck status, however, offered little political weight to the nominee, who faced opposition from a Democratic-controlled Senate. Southern Democrats were especially wary of Badger's nationalism. Custom required at that time that Court justices also preside over designated federal circuit courts; the less politically charged excuse was made that Badger was not a resident of the circuit for which he would be responsible. Badger's nomination was not confirmed by his fellow senators. Like Learned Hand a century later, the candidate widely considered most qualified to serve on the Court was blocked by partisan concerns.

Janet Alice Long

SEE ALSO Hand, Learned; McKinley, John; Nominations to the Court; Story, Joseph.

Bail

DESCRIPTION: Money posted by persons accused of crimes as security for their appearance at trial. The U.S. Constitution offers guarantees against excessive bail, which were interpreted and generally upheld by the Supreme Court.

SIGNIFICANCE: Because of the inherent unfairness of subjecting an unconvicted person to a long, indefinite period of imprisonment, the Court has attempted to ensure that the accused is not unreasonably detained. Denial of bail or excessive bail is also thought to be an unreasonable impediment of the accused person's right to prepare a defense.

The use of bail has been a part of the Anglo-American criminal justice system since the English Bill of Rights of 1689 gave protections against excessive bail. The founders of the American republic counted the right to a just bail among the essential liberties. The Eighth Amendment to the U.S. Constitution guarantees that "excessive bail shall not be required." A stronger expression of the contemporary feeling about bail is found in the Northwest Ordinance of 1787, which declared that "all persons shall be bailable, unless for capital offenses, where the proof shall be evident, or the presumption great."

In 1895 the Supreme Court first affirmed the importance of a right to reasonable bail in *Hudson v. Parker*. Writing for the majority, Justice Horace Gray noted that a key principle of the U.S. justice system was "the theory that a person accused of a crime shall not, until he has been finally adjudged guilty . . . be absolutely compelled to undergo imprisonment or punishment." However, an earlier decision, *McKane v. Durston* (1894), limited the scope of this decision by ruling that the Eighth Amendment's bail provision did not apply to state courts.

The Court in *Stack v. Boyle* (1951), a case involving twelve Communist Party leaders accused of conspiracy, was concerned that excessive bail hampered the accused's right to a vigorous defense. The Court held that "the traditional right to freedom before conviction permits the unhampered preparation of a defense. Unless the right to bail is preserved, the presumption of innocence, secured after centuries of struggle, would lose its meaning." The Court determined that the purpose of bail is to "serve . . . as assurance of the presence of an accused. Bail set at a figure higher than an amount reasonably calculated to fulfill this purpose is excessive under the Eight Amendment." However, the next year, in *Carlson v. Landon* (1952), the Court in a 5-4 vote found that not all detentions were subject to bail, and Congress had the power to define cases in which bail was not allowed. The *Carlson* case was a civil case involving the detention of aliens before a deportation hearing.

Preventive Detention. Traditionally, the sole justification for jailing an accused but otherwise presumed innocent person before trial was to assure that the individual did not flee. It was generally not believed to be proper to deprive people of their liberty on the grounds that they may commit future crimes when they have not been convicted of a crime. The constitutional protection of the rights of the accused person has clashed in recent years with the desire by federal authorities to "preventively detain" persons accused of federal crimes to prevent them from engaging in criminal activities. One concern is the fear that members of criminal organizations freed on bail might harass and intimidate witnesses, thereby corrupting the judicial process.

The rise of international terrorism and drug trafficking led Congress to pass the Bail Reform Act of 1984, which allows a federal judge to consider preventive detention of a person accused of a federal crime if he or she finds that "no conditions or combination of conditions will reasonably assure the appearance of the [defendant] as required and the safety of any person before trial." The act allows a federal prosecutor to ask a judge to hold a defendant without bail indefinitely if the prosecutor can make a showing that the person poses a threat to others.

The Act Examined. The constitutionality of the Bail Reform Act was determined by the Court in *United States v. Salerno* (1987). *Salerno* involved two defendants indicted for racketeering and denied bail under the provisions of the act. One of the accused was alleged by prosecutors to be the "boss" of the Genovese crime family and the other a high-ranked "captain." The crimes included several counts of extortion and conspiracy to murder. The Court examined whether the bail reforms violated the defendant's constitutional right to be free from excessive bail, but it rejected the claim that *Stack* applied to the case. Limiting the scope of *Stack,* the Court found that the right to bail had never been considered absolute and that persons accused of capital crimes and at risk of flight had long been subject to bail restrictions and upheld the act. The Court noted that although "in our society liberty is the norm, and detention prior to trial or without trial is the carefully limited exception," the Bail Reform Act fell "within that carefully limited exception." The Count determined that the "numerous procedural safeguards" adequately protected against abuse of the act.

FURTHER READING
Duker, William F. "The Right to Bail: A Historical Inquiry." *Albany Law Review* 42 (1977): 33-120.
Goldkamp, John S. "Danger and Detention: A Second Generation of Bail Reform." *Journal of Criminal Law and Criminology* 76 (Spring, 1985): 1-74.
Metzmeier, Kurt X. "Preventive Detention: A Comparison of Bail Refusal Practices in the United States, England, Canada, and Other Common Law Nations." *Pace International Law Review* 7 (Spring, 1996): 399-438.

Kurt X. Metzmeier

SEE ALSO British background to U.S. judiciary; Counsel, right to; Eighth Amendment; Northwest Ordinance.

Bailey v. Drexel Furniture Co.

CITATION: 259 U.S. 20
DATE: May 15, 1922
ISSUES: Regulation of manufacturing; dual federalism
SIGNIFICANCE: The Supreme Court ruled that Congress could not use its taxing power to impose regulations on production, which were powers reserved to the states by the Tenth Amendment.

In *Hammer v. Dagenhart* (1918), the Supreme Court struck down the first federal child labor statute as an unconstitutional use of the commerce power. In response, Congress enacted the Keating-Owen Child Labor Act of 1919, which imposed a 10 percent tax on the net profits of companies employing children under the age of fourteen. Supporters of the law noted that the Court had approved of a prohibitive excise tax on oleomargarine in *McCray v. United States* (1904).

In *Bailey,* the justices voted eight to one to strike down the law. Chief Justice William H. Taft's opinion for the majority declared that the "so-called" tax was really a disguised regulation designed to stop child labor. To allow taxes to be used for such purposes, he declared, would give Congress almost unlimited powers and "completely wipe out the sovereignty of the states." In *McCray,* the Court had approved of a tax that provided only "incidental restraint and regulation," but the child labor tax, in contrast, had a "prohibitory and regulatory effect." Modern commentators usually find that Taft's distinction lacks merit. Although the *Bailey* decision remained good law for two decades, the Court rejected its theoretical foundations in *Mulford v. Smith* (1939).

Thomas T. Lewis

SEE ALSO *Butler, United States v.*; Federalism; Labor; *McCray v. United States*; *Mulford v. Smith*; Police powers; Taxing and spending clause; Tenth Amendment.

Baker v. Carr

CITATION: 369 U.S. 186
DATE: March 26, 1962
ISSUE: Reapportionment
SIGNIFICANCE: The Supreme Court ruled for the first time that legislative malapportionment was not a political question but an issue that could be considered by the courts.

Justice William J. Brennan, Jr., wrote the 6-2 majority opinion in this landmark case, ignoring warnings from Justices Felix Frankfurter and John Marshal Harlan II that the Supreme Court was entering a political thicket with this decision. The Court overturned *Colegrove v. Green* (1946) and ruled that the federal courts had jurisdiction to hear legislative reapportionment cases regarding states such as Tennessee, which had not reapportioned its legislative seats in more than sixty years.

Baker did not actually reapportion any districts, nor did it set forth standards for states to follow. The one person, one vote principle, not enunciated until *Gray v. Sanders* (1963), was not applied to congressional redistricting until *Wesberry v. Sanders* (1964) nor applied to all legislative houses including the state senates until *Reynolds v. Sims* (1964). These cases opened the door to a flood of litigation over the next two decades as citizens in urban areas filed suit to force rural-dominated legislatures to reapportion themselves.

The long-term impact of this decision was to correct a situation that apparently could not be corrected by the ordinary political process. As more Americans moved to urban areas, rural areas became underpopulated and overrepresented in state legislatures. In most states, rural domination was so great that the legislature had a majority of rural representatives who blocked any realistic chances of reapportioning their states. Because state legislatures also draw congressional district lines, this malapportionment extended to the national level. Reapportionment had historically been regarded as a political question beyond the reach of the federal courts, but this decision reversed that legal standard.

Richard L. Wilson

SEE ALSO *Colegrove v. Green*; Gerrymandering; *Gray v. Sanders*; *Kirkpatrick v. Preisler*; *Mahan v. Howell*; Political questions; Representation, fairness of; *Reynolds v. Sims*; *Wesberry v. Sanders*.

Baldwin, Henry

IDENTIFICATION: Associate justice (January 11, 1830-April 21, 1844)
NOMINATED BY: Andrew Jackson
BORN: January 14, 1780, New Haven, Connecticut
DIED: April 21, 1844, Philadelphia, Pennsylvania
SIGNIFICANCE: As a justice, Baldwin supported states' rights and viewed slaves as property, without civil rights.

After receiving a Doctor of Laws degree from Yale University in 1797, Baldwin studied under Alexander J. Dallas in Philadelphia and was admitted to the bar. He then headed west to Ohio, getting only as far as Pittsburgh, where he settled, becoming a distinguished citizen. People there considered him intelligent, energetic, and witty.

In 1805 he moved to Crawford County in northwestern Pennsylvania, where he ran for Congress and, in 1817, became a member of the U.S. House of Representatives. He supported high tariffs and disagreed vehemently with rural Jeffersonians. Suffering from ill health, Baldwin resigned from the House in 1822.

By 1828 his health had improved, and he served as adviser to Andrew Jackson, subsequently elected president and, in 1829, inaugurated for the first of his two terms. Jackson rewarded Baldwin's support when the death of Bushrod Washington created a vacancy on the Supreme Court. Jackson passed over several promising jurists to nominate Baldwin, who was easily confirmed.

Baldwin recounted his philosophical outlook as a justice in *A General View of the Origin and Nature of the Constitution and Government of the United States* (1837). In this booklet, he portrayed himself as moderate. He was a notable dissident in Chief

Henry Baldwin. (Max Rosenthal/Collection of the Supreme Court of the United States)

Justice John Marshall's Court. Baldwin supported states' rights, favoring interstate commerce unfettered by federal regulation. Although he voted with pronorthern justices on matters involving slavery, he nevertheless viewed slaves as property lacking the civil rights of America's white citizens. In cases that tested the right of the federal government to overrule the sovereignty of individual states, he consistently supported the rights of states to make and enforce their own laws. This attitude explains in part his stand regarding the ownership of slaves.

Baldwin's spirited dissent in *Ex parte Crane* (1831) objected to strengthening the power of federal courts to issue writs of mandamus, orders issued by superior courts to lower courts. He was convinced that the Court, through judicial and political sensitivity, could determine which powers belonged to the individual states and which to the federal government.

As he aged, Baldwin became increasingly irascible, often disturbing the much-heralded equanimity of the Marshall Court. In 1831 Baldwin dissented in seven cases, a record unparalleled in the Marshall Court. Baldwin's eccentricity eventually became an embarrassment. He sometimes re-

sorted to violent behavior, presumably stemming from an obsessive-compulsive disorder. Plagued for years by financial difficulties, Baldwin died in 1844, penniless and paralyzed, in Philadelphia.

FURTHER READING

Abraham, Henry Julian. *Justices and Presidents: A Political History of Appointments to the Supreme Court.* 3d ed. New York: Oxford University Press, 1992.

Wagman, Robert J. *The Supreme Court: A Citizen's Guide.* New York: Pharos Books, 1993.

R. Baird Shuman

SEE ALSO Dallas, Alexander J.; Jackson, Andrew; Marshall, John; Separation of powers; States' rights; Washington, Bushrod.

Ballard v. United States

CITATION: 329 U.S. 187
DATE: December 9, 1946
ISSUE: Sex discrimination
SIGNIFICANCE: The Supreme Court held that women may not be excluded from jury service in federal trials taking place in states where women were eligible for service under state law.

After Edna Ballard, a leader of the "I Am" movement, was convicted for fraudulent use of the mails, she appealed her conviction on the grounds that the federal courts in California systematically excluded women from juries. At the time federal law required federal courts to maintain the same jury requirements as those of state courts. Although California made women eligible for juries, the state courts did not summon women to serve, and the federal courts in California followed the same practice.

By a 5-4 vote, the Supreme Court reversed Ballard's conviction. Speaking for the majority, Justice William O. Douglas reasoned that the various federal statutes on the topic demonstrated that Congress desired juries to represent a cross section of the community. Because women were eligible for jury service under California law, they must be included in the federal trial juries. Although the Ballard decision was an interpretation of congressional statutes, its reasoning was used to arrive at basically the same requirement under the Sixth Amendment in *Taylor v. Louisiana* (1975).

Thomas T. Lewis

SEE ALSO Gender issues; *Hoyt v. Florida*; Jury composition and size; Sixth Amendment; *Taylor v. Louisiana*.

Ballew v. Georgia

CITATION: 435 U.S. 223
DATE: March 21, 1978
ISSUE: Jury size
SIGNIFICANCE: The Supreme Court held that juries must be composed of a minimum of six persons.

Historically, the Anglo-American trial jury has been composed of twelve members. In *Williams v. Florida* (1970), nevertheless, the Supreme Court approved of the use of six-person juries in all noncapital cases. The state of Georgia, attempting to save time and money, instituted a five-person jury for misdemeanor cases. By a 9-0 vote, the Court ruled that five-person juries were inconsistent with the demands of due process. Justice Harry A. Blackmun's opinion for the majority cited studies showing that the purpose and functioning of the jury "is seriously impaired" if the size is reduced to less than six members. Blackmun concluded that at least six jurors was necessary to promote group deliberation and to "to provide a representative cross section of the community."

Thomas T. Lewis

SEE ALSO Due process, procedural; Jury composition and size; Sixth Amendment; *Williams v. Florida*.

Bank of Augusta v. Earle

CITATION: 38 U.S. 519
DATE: March 9, 1839
ISSUE: Comity clause
SIGNIFICANCE: The Supreme Court recognized that the comity clause gave corporations a conditional right to do business in other states, but it also allowed states to regulate or even prohibit such business by explicit legislation.

An Alabama citizen refused to pay the bills of exchange of an out-of-state bank on the grounds that a foreign corporation had no legal right to make and enforce contracts in Alabama. The bank responded that a corporation, like a citizen, was guaranteed basic privileges and immunities in all the states, including the right to conduct business.

Writing for an 8-1 majority, Chief Justice Roger Brooke Taney ruled in favor of the bank. The comity principle was operative in the absence of clear laws to the contrary, which was the situation in Alabama. Taney refused to recognize corporations as possessing all the rights of natural persons. Based on the *Bank of Augusta* principle, state legislatures enacted a great deal of legislation restricting business practices of out-of-state corporations. Although it never overturned the decision, the Supreme Court has subsequently held that regulations must not impose an undue burden on interstate commerce.

Thomas T. Lewis

SEE ALSO Comity clause; Commerce, regulation of; Federalism; Privileges and immunities.

Bank of the United States v. Deveaux

CITATION: 5 Cranch (9 U.S.) 61
DATE: March 15, 1809
ISSUE: Citizenship of corporations
SIGNIFICANCE: The Supreme Court held that although a corporation was a citizen for the purpose of diversity jurisdiction, the location of its citizenship was determined by the citizenship of its shareholders.

The Bank of the United States attempted to sue a Georgia tax collector for recovery of property. The issue was whether the bank (as a corporation) could sue in federal court under diversity of citizenship jurisdiction. The Supreme Court's unanimous ruling made the suit impossible, because some of the bank's shareholders lived in Georgia. The *Deveaux* restriction on diversity jurisdiction was overruled in *Louisville, Cincinnati, and Charleston Railroad Co. v. Letson* (1844), which recognized corporate citizenship in the state granting the charter.

Thomas T. Lewis

SEE ALSO Citizenship; Corporations; Diversity jurisdiction; *Louisville, Cincinnati, and Charleston Railroad Co. v. Letson*.

Bankruptcy law

DESCRIPTION: Federal statutes that allow consumers and businesses unable to meet their financial obligations to discharge their debts and start over economically. Article I, section 8, clause 4, of the U.S. Constitution stipulates that Congress shall establish "uniform Laws on the subject of Bankruptcies throughout the United States."

SIGNIFICANCE: The Supreme Court hears appeals on issues that began in bankruptcy courts and applies bankruptcy court rules.

Business and personal finance is beset with a degree of unpredictability. Under capitalism, private individuals, public institutions, small businesses, partnerships, and major corporations sometimes face changes in the marketplace, technology, and consumer preferences that decrease income and profits, creating financial crises. Congress, in response to economic downturns, increasingly complex commercial transactions, expanding credit, and a larger number of entrepreneurships, produced major bankruptcy legislation in 1800, 1841, 1867, and 1898.

A 1970 joint resolution of Congress created the Bankruptcy Commission, with members appointed by the president, chief justice, and Congress. In 1978 Congress passed the Bankruptcy Reform Act, which, with subsequent amendments, created laws that balanced creditor and debtor interests. The nine chapters in the code occupy nearly five hundred pages in *Bankruptcy Code, Rules, and Forms* (St. Paul, Minn.: West Publishing, 1999), and the ten chapters on rules fill nearly three hundred pages. After its passage, more than sixty bankruptcy cases have been decided by the Supreme Court.

Bankruptcy court, district court, bankruptcy appellate panel, and court of appeals judges may differ in their interpretations of legislative history, legislation, rules, and the plain meaning of the text. Some court watchers believe sufficient scope exists for judges to engage in policy making while ostensibly interpreting the text of bankruptcy laws. Most bankruptcy cases reach the Supreme Court because of conflicting results on substantially identical facts reached by the various courts of appeals. The Court, seeking uniformity within the federal system, usually makes narrow decisions.

The constitutionality of the 1978 bankruptcy laws was raised in *Northern Pipeline Construction Co. v. Marathon Pipe Line Co.* (1982). Before 1978, the bankruptcy court employed semijudicial referees. The 1978 code created Article I nontenured judges, whose salaries could be reduced and who served for renewable fourteen-year terms but gave them Article III powers, which the Court held unconstitutional.

Definitions and Procedures. Bankruptcy legislation, particularly chapter 11, has historically been concerned with businesses and corporations. In the twentieth century, personal consumer bankruptcies, chapter 7 and 13, became far more numerous than business cases. The Court in *Local Loan Co. v. Hunt* (1933) stated that honest debtors should have "a new opportunity in life and a clear field for future effort." *Toibb v. Radloff* (1991) and *Johnson v. Home State Bank* (1991) expanded bankruptcy relief. In the 1990's the Court chipped away at the debtor-favorable 1978 bankruptcy laws and began to favor creditors, a trend paralleled by various legislative changes.

Grogan v. Garner (1991) established a preponderance of the evidence test for determining fraud rather than a clear and convincing evidence test, an issue visited again in *Field v. Mans* (1995). *Union Bank v. Wolas* (1991) reiterated the plain language approach to interpreting statutes. Although "willful and malicious injury" is not dischargeable, the court in *Kawaauhau v. Geiger* (1998) distinguished between intentional and reckless torts. Deadlines, like statutes of limitation, are very important. *Barnhill v. Johnson* (1992) set the standard for computing a ninety-day period on the writing of a check, *Taylor v. Freeland and Kronz* (1992) dealt with trustee objections to exemptions, and *Pioneer Investment Services Co. v. Brunswick Associates Ltd. Partnership* (1993) dealt with deadlines for filing proofs of claim.

Property. The bankrupt debtor generally does not pay more for property than it is worth. Creditors dislike this and assert that mortgages in real estate should be treated differently than liens on cars, equipment, jewelry, and other consumer items. Lien stripping was the subject of *Dewsnup v. Timm* (1992) and *Nobelman v. American Savings Bank* (1993). *BFP v. Resolution Trust Corp.* (1994) established that when a property is sold at a noncollusive sale, such as an auction, it is presumed to satisfy the requirement of "reasonably equivalent value." Even if it sells for much less than its appraisal, the sale is not a fraudulent conveyance (transfer of ownership of property). In *Associates Commercial Corp. v. Rash* (1997), the Court in distinguishing between retail and wholesale value of property, settled on replacement value. Secured claims, debts with collateral, are to be paid interest (adequate protection) according to *United Savings Association of Texas v. Timbers of Inwood Forest Associates* (1988), *United States v. Ron Pair Enterprises* (1989), and *Rake v. Wade* (1993).

In *United States v. Whiting Pools* (1983), the Court held that property seized by the Internal Revenue Service before the bankruptcy filing was property of the estate, and in *Patterson v. Shumate* (1992) it determined that Employee Retirement Income Security Act-qualified pension funds were not property of the estate.

Other Issues. The federal system, the balance between state and federal government, increasingly protects governments from being sued without their permission. *Hoffman v. Connecticut Department of Income Maintenance* (1989), *United States v. Nordic Village* (1992), and *Seminole Tribe v. Florida* (1996) expanded the immunity and authority of governments and limited the ability of debtors and the trustees to bring government agencies into the bankruptcy. The trend in sovereign immunity cases appears to detract from the bankruptcy court status as a national forum for debt resolution.

The wide range of Court decisions indicates the pervasiveness of economic issues and the bankruptcy court's role in American economic life. The Court has made decisions regarding taxes, transportation and common carriers, the absolute priority rule (an important creditor protection in devising chapter 11 reorganization plans), and family law regarding property settlements in divorces.

Public and legislative dissatisfaction with Court decisions may result in corrective legislation. In *Pennsylvania Department of Public Welfare v. Davenport* (1990), the Court held that criminal restitution could be discharged (and therefore, not paid), and Congress passed the Violent Crime Control and Law Enforcement Act of 1994, making restitution nondischargeable. When *Christians v. Crystal Evangelical Church* (1997) threatened religious liberty and tithing, Congress passed the Religious Liberty and Charitable Donation Protection Act of 1998.

FURTHER READING

Gross, Karen. *Failure and Forgiveness, Rebalancing the Bankruptcy System.* New Haven, Conn.: Yale University Press, 1997.

Sullivan, Teresa A., Elizabeth Warren, and Jay Lawrence Westbrook. *As We Forgive Our Debtors: Bankruptcy and Consumer Credit in America.* New York: Oxford University Press, 1989.

Oliver B. Pollak

SEE ALSO Common carriers; Courts of appeals; Eleventh Amendment; *Ogden v. Saunders*; Property rights; Reversals of Court decisions by Congress; *Seminole Tribe v. Florida.*

Barbour, Philip P.

IDENTIFICATION: Associate justice (May 12, 1836-February 25, 1841)
NOMINATED BY: Andrew Jackson
BORN: May 25, 1783, Barboursville, Virginia
DIED: February 25, 1841, Washington, D.C.
SIGNIFICANCE: During his five years on the Supreme Court, Barbour supported states' rights over the authority of the federal government.

Barbour began practicing law in 1802. He was elected to Congress in 1814, where he served as Speaker of the House from 1821 to 1823. In *Cohens v. Virginia* (1821), he unsuccessfully argued before

Philip P. Barbour. (George Healy/Collection of the Supreme Court of the United States)

the Supreme Court that a defendant had no right of appeal from a state court to a federal court. He left Congress in 1825, served as a state judge, then returned to Congress in 1827. In 1829 he unsuccessfully introduced a bill requiring five out of seven Supreme Court justices to agree in constitutional cases. In 1830 he was appointed a federal judge by President Andrew Jackson.

Jackson nominated Barbour to the Court on December 28, 1835. He was confirmed by the Senate on March 15, 1836, and took the oath of office on May 12. During his relatively brief career on the Court, he usually agreed with the majority as it turned away from supporting the power of the federal government over the states. In *New York v. Miln* (1837), a case involving the power of a state over ships entering harbors from other states or nations, he wrote that "the authority of a state is complete, unqualified and exclusive." His few dissents from the majority came in cases that involved restrictions of states' rights.

Rose Secrest

SEE ALSO Jackson, Andrew; *New York v. Miln*; States' rights.

Barenblatt v. United States

CITATION: 360 U.S. 109
DATE: June 8, 1959
ISSUES: Congressional power of investigation; freedom of association
SIGNIFICANCE: The Supreme Court upheld a conviction for contempt of Congress, ruling that the public's interest in opposing communist infiltration outweighed a person's limited First Amendment right to refuse to answer questions.

When Lloyd Barenblatt, a college professor, appeared before the House Un-American Activities Committee, he refused to answer questions that dealt with his political beliefs and associations. Rather than relying on the Fifth Amendment, he alleged that the questions infringed on his right to free expression under the First Amendment. The Supreme Court had appeared to give some support to such a claim in *Watkins v. United States* (1957). Barenblatt was convicted of contempt of Congress.

Speaking for a 5-4 majority, Justice John M. Harlan II used a balancing of interests approach.

Although Harlan acknowledged that the First Amendment in some circumstances protects a person "from being compelled to disclose his associational relationships," he concluded that Barenblatt's particular claim was outweighed by the public's interest in exposing communist subversion. In contrast to the situation in *Watkins*, Harlan found that the subcommittee had explained the relevance of the questions and had not attempted to pillory witnesses. The Barenblatt decision was never overruled. In *Eastland v. United States Servicemen's Club* (1975), the Court strengthened the prerogatives of congressional committees by expansively reading the speech or debate clause. When dealing with state investigations, on the other hand, the Court has tended to demonstrate greater concern for protecting First Amendment values.

Thomas T. Lewis

SEE ALSO Assembly and association, freedom of; Cold War; Congressional power of investigation; Contempt power of Congress; First Amendment balancing; *Watkins v. United States.*

Barker v. Wingo

CITATION: 407 U.S. 514
DATE: June 22, 1972
ISSUE: Right to speedy trial
SIGNIFICANCE: To decide whether a trial was delayed for an unreasonable period of time, the Supreme Court established a balancing test with four factors: length of the delay, reasons for the delay, the defendant's assertion of the right to a speedy trial, and prejudice to the defendant from the delay.

Two defendants, Barker and Manning, were charged with a brutal murder. Because the case against Manning was very strong, he was tried first, then he was to be a witness in Barker's trial. As a result of difficulties in prosecuting Manning, the trial of Barker was delayed for five years from the time of his arrest. After being found guilty, Barker appealed on the grounds that the long delay violated his right to a speedy trial. His lawyers referred to *Dickey v. Florida* (1970), in which an eight-year delay had been found to be unconstitutional.

The Supreme Court unanimously rejected Barker's claim. Justice Lewis F. Powell, Jr.'s opinion for the majority was based on a balancing test. The delay of the trial, while long, was not unreasonable in view of the unavailability of an important witness; the defendant had been slow to register objections to the delay; and there was no evidence that the delay caused any prejudice in the trial.

Much of the public disagreed with the *Barker* opinion. In 1974 Congress passed the Speedy Trial Act, requiring federal trials to take place one hundred days after an arrest. Most states have enacted similar laws.

Thomas T. Lewis

SEE ALSO *Klopfer v. North Carolina*; Reversals of Court decisions by Congress; Scalia, Antonin; Sixth Amendment; Speedy trial.

Barnes v. Glen Theatre

CITATION: 501 U.S. 560
DATE: June 21, 1991
ISSUE: Expressive conduct

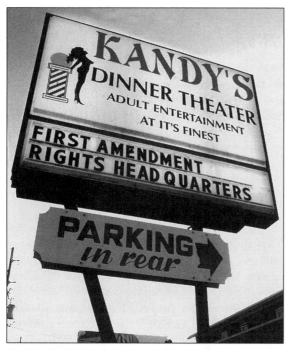

In March 2000, the Supreme Court ruled against this Erie, Pennsylvania, club featuring all-nude dancers. The Court ruled that although nude dancing was expressive conduct, as it had found in Baines v. Glen Theatre, *the local authorities could make ordinances against nudity under their police powers to protect the public health and safety.* (AP/Wide World Photos)

SIGNIFICANCE: While reaffirming that nude dancing is expressive conduct protected by the First Amendment, the Supreme Court nevertheless upheld a state's general ban on complete nudity in public places.

In *Schad v. Borough of Mount Ephraim* (1981), the Supreme Court held that nonobscene nude dancing was a protected form of expression that could not be entirely prohibited throughout an entire community. Indiana's public decency statute prohibited complete nudity in all public places. Two adult-entertainment establishments in South Bend, Indiana, wanted to feature "totally nude dancing," but the decency statute required that the dancers wear pasties and G-strings.

Although the Court upheld the law by a 5-4 majority, Chief Justice William H. Rehnquist spoke for a plurality when he argued that the law was not expressly designed to prevent erotic expression and that the law only placed an incidental limitation on expression. The statute, he wrote, was essentially a time, place, and manner regulation, in keeping with the test set forth in *United States v. O'Brien* (1968). Observing that nudity had historically been proscribed by common law, he concluded that a ban on nudity furthered the state's substantial interest in protecting public morality and public order. In a concurrence, Justice David H. Souter argued that the law legitimately prevented secondary effects of nude dancing, such as prostitution.

Justice Byron R. White's dissent argued that the very purpose of the law was to prohibit the expression of a nonobscene erotic message; therefore, the law should be scrutinized with the compelling state interest test.

Thomas T. Lewis

SEE ALSO *Argersinger v. Hamlin*; *O'Brien, United States v.*; Obscenity and pornography; Speech and press, freedom of; Unprotected speech.

Barron v. Baltimore

CITATION: 32 U.S. 243
DATE: February 16, 1833
ISSUES: Incorporation doctrine; property rights
SIGNIFICANCE: The Supreme Court held that the Bill of Rights did not protect citizens from actions by their state governments, a ruling that stood largely unaltered until the 1920's.

The First Amendment begins with the word "Congress," apparently making the federal government its only target, but none of the other amendments in the Bill of Rights include this language. John Barron, a Baltimore businessperson, sought to test the possibility that the Fifth Amendment in the Bill of Rights might protect him from actions of the Maryland state government.

The city of Baltimore repaired the streets and dumped the leftover construction materials into the water near the wharf Barron owned, raising the bottom of the bay so much that ships could no longer dock there, depriving Barron of his property interest in his livelihood without due process or just compensation. Barron sued Baltimore to recover damages, but Baltimore was a subunit of Maryland, whose constitution, unlike the U.S. Constitution, did not provide a guarantee against eminent domain.

Because Barron could not succeed in Maryland courts, he turned to the federal courts. However, the Supreme Court ruled that the Fifth Amendment applied only to the federal government and not to the states and that therefore Barron was not entitled to protection against state action under this amendment. After *Barron*, the courts applied this ruling consistently. Although the passage of the Fourteenth Amendment would seem to have reversed this decision, the Court did not initially agree, essentially continuing *Barron* in force until justices holding different views began to serve on the Court in the 1920's. Gradually, the incorporation doctrine effectively overturned the principles set out in *Barron*.

Richard L. Wilson

SEE ALSO Bill of Rights; Due process, procedural; Due process, substantive; Fourteenth Amendment; *Hurtado v. California*; Incorporation doctrine; Marshall, John; Property rights; Takings clause.

Bates v. State Bar of Arizona

CITATION: 433 U.S. 350
DATE: June 27, 1977
ISSUE: Commercial speech
SIGNIFICANCE: The Supreme Court held that states could not prohibit lawyers from advertising the prices of routine legal services.

In 1974 lawyers John Bates and Van O'Steen placed an advertisement in a newspaper that announced "legal services at very reasonable fees" and listed several examples. Because the Arizona bar association's ethics code prohibited such advertisements, the two lawyers were censored and suspended from legal practice for one week. They appealed on First Amendment grounds. Meanwhile, the Supreme Court, in *Virginia Pharmacy Board v. Virginia Citizens Consumer Council* (1976), struck down a state law that made it illegal for pharmacists to advertise the prices of prescription medications. For the Court, Justice Harry A. Blackmun explained that the First Amendment protected the right of pharmacists to communicate truthful information about lawful products and services.

In *Bates*, the justices voted five to four to extend the *Virginia Pharmacy Board* principles to commercial advertising by lawyers. Justice Blackmun's majority opinion held that the protection of commercial speech under the First Amendment outweighed any possible "adverse effect on professionalism." He noted that the decision did not endorse in-person solicitation of clients or advertisements about the quality of legal services. Also, he recognized the need to restrain false, deceptive, or misleading advertising as well as the legitimacy of reasonable time, place, and manner regulations.

After *Bates*, the Court endorsed several restrictions on the commercial speech of lawyers. In *Florida Bar v. Went for It* (1995), for example, the Court upheld the Florida bar's prohibition of written solicitations to personal injury victims for thirty days following an accident or natural disaster.

Thomas T. Lewis

SEE ALSO Advertising of lawyers; Commercial speech; *Edmonson v. Leesville Concrete Co.*; *Goldfarb v. Virginia State Bar*; Story, Joseph; *Williams v. Mississippi*.

Batson v. Kentucky

CITATION: 476 U.S. 79
DATE: April 30, 1986
ISSUE: Jury composition
SIGNIFICANCE: The Supreme Court ruled that the equal protection clause of the Fourteenth Amendment forbids a prosecutor from using peremptory challenges to remove potential jurors because of their race.

James Batson, an African American, was indicted for second-degree burglary. When the judge conducted a voir dire examination (preliminary check of suitability and qualifications) of the potential jurors, the prosecutor used his peremptory challenges to remove all four African Americans from the panel, resulting in an all-white jury. The Supreme Court had refused to disturb the same development in *Swain v. Alabama* (1965). After Batson's conviction, nevertheless, his lawyers asserted that the process of jury selection violated his rights to equal protection and to a jury drawn from a cross section of the community.

By a 7-2 majority, the Court accepted Batson's claim. Speaking for the majority, Justice Lewis F. Powell, Jr., remanded the case and instructed the trial court to require the prosecutor to justify the exclusion of members of the defendant's race from the jury. If the prosecutor were unable to give a racially neutral explanation, Batson's conviction would have to be reversed. Powell's opinion formulated a framework for future voir dire proceedings. The basic idea is that a pattern of exclusion based on race creates an inference of discrimination. Once such an inference is established, the prosecutor has the burden of showing that the peremptories are not discriminatory. Emphasizing that the Constitution does not guarantee a right to peremptory challenges, Powell wrote that potential jurors may not be eliminated simply because of the assumption that people of a particular race might be more sympathetic to a particular defendant. Thus, Powell's opinion requires color-conscious rather than color-blind procedures in jury selection, and it tends to encourage the use of racial quotas.

The *Batson* principles have been significantly expanded. In *Powers v. Ohio* (1991), the Court held that criminal defendants may object to race-based peremptory challenges even if the defendant and the excluded jurors do not belong to the same race. Later that year, in *Edmondson v. Leesville Concrete Co.*, the Court applied the *Batson* framework to the selection of juries in civil trials. In *Georgia v. McCollum* (1992), the Court decided that the *Batson* ruling applies to defense attorneys. In *J. E. B. v. Alabama* (1994), moreover, the Court held that the equal protection clause prohibits discrimination in jury selection on the basis of gender.

Thomas T. Lewis

SEE ALSO Due process, substantive; Jury, trial by; Jury composition and size; *Powers v. Ohio.*

Beard, Charles Austin

IDENTIFICATION: Historian and political scientist
BORN: November 27, 1874, near Knightstown, Indiana
DIED: September 1, 1948, New Haven, Connecticut
SIGNIFICANCE: One of the most widely read scholars of the twentieth century, Beard claimed that the Constitution was a political document and that the justices, individuals with faults and personal feelings, could err in their interpretations.

Born the son of a North Carolina Unionist Quaker who had fled to Indiana during the Civil War (1861-1865), Beard graduated from DePauw University in 1898. In 1900 he married Mary Ritter of Indianapolis, before moving to Oxford, England, to work with a socialist to found a worker's college. In 1902 Beard returned to the United States to complete a Ph.D. degree at Columbia University and join the faculty.

Beard published historical works and texts primarily concerned with economic interpretations of U.S. history. In *The Rise of American Civilization* (1927), he criticized the Founders as merchant-creditors who were more concerned about protecting their own interests than the rights of others. His other works, including *The Supreme Court and the Constitution* (1912) and *An Economic Interpretation of the Constitution of the United States* (1913), were criticized for implying that the Founders were motivated by class interests. Beard praised, for example, the Jackson-appointed judges on the Supreme Court because they "broke down the historic safeguards thrown around property rights by the letter of the Constitution and the jurisprudence of John Marshall." Modern historians classify Beard, along with Oliver Wendell Holmes and John Dewey, as among the more prominent intellectual and cultural elite reformers of the late nineteenth and early twentieth century who called for legislative and judicial reforms designed to protect the poor and limit the abuses of big business.

Donald C. Simmons, Jr.

SEE ALSO Holmes, Oliver Wendell; Jackson, Andrew; Marshall, John.

Belle Terre v. Boraas

Citation: 616 U.S. 1
Date: April 1, 1974
Issues: Right of privacy; substantive due process
Significance: The Supreme Court upheld the constitutionality of a local zoning ordinance that prohibited most unrelated groups from living together in a single-unit dwelling.

The owner of a house in the small village of Belle Terre, New York, leased it to six unrelated college students. When cited for violating a zoning ordinance, the owners and tenants went to court, claiming that the ordinance violated their constitutional right of privacy. Speaking for a 7-2 majority, Justice William O. Douglas used the rational basis test of economic and social legislation, and found the ordinance to be a valid exercise of the community's police power. The ordinance bore a rational relationship with a permissible governmental objective of maintaining a quiet place to raise a family. In dissent, Justice Thurgood Marshall argued that the ordinance infringed on fundamental rights of privacy and association and that the village had the burden of showing a "compelling and substantial" justification for the infringement.

Although upholding the ordinance, the *Belle Terre* decision demonstrated the Supreme Court's developing commitment to the doctrine of substantive due process, requiring that any restraints on liberty must be justified by an adequate state interest. The decision should be compared with *Moore v. City of East Cleveland* (1977), in which the Court struck down an ordinance that had the effect of prohibiting an extended family from living together.

Thomas T. Lewis
See also Assembly and association, freedom of; Due process, substantive; *Griswold v. Connecticut*; Judicial scrutiny; *Moore v. City of East Cleveland*; Privacy, right to; Zoning.

Benton v. Maryland

Citation: 395 U.S. 785
Date: June 23, 1969
Issue: Double jeopardy
Significance: The Supreme Court ruled the Fifth Amendment protection against double jeopardy applied to the states through the due process clause of the Fourteenth Amendment.

In a 7-2 vote, the Supreme Court overturned *Palko v. Connecticut* (1937) and struck down Benton's second conviction in Maryland courts as a violation of his Fifth Amendment rights. Justice Thurgood Marshall, in the opinion for the Court, stated that the double jeopardy provisions of the Fifth Amendment applied to the states through the incorporation doctrine of the Fourteenth Amendment, and therefore, a person who had been acquitted of a crime in a state court could not be tried again for the same crime.

In *Palko*, the Court had allowed double jeopardy in Connecticut, saying that the only rights that applied to the states under the due process clause of the Fourteenth Amendment were those closely related to the concept of "ordered liberty." In reversing *Palko*, the Court recognized that although it had earlier not believed that a double jeopardy conviction was a universally "shocking" violation of justice, a prohibition against double jeopardy was, in fact, a long-standing practice that was fundamental to the American system of justice.

Richard L. Wilson
See also Bill of Rights; Double jeopardy; Due process, procedural; Fourteenth Amendment; Incorporation doctrine; *Lanza, United States v.*; *Palko v. Connecticut*; *Ursery, United States v.*

Berman v. Parker

Citation: 348 U.S. 26
Date: November 22, 1954
Issue: Public use doctrine
Significance: The Supreme Court interpreted the term "public use" to refer to any policy that reasonably promotes the public interest, providing legislatures with great discretion in deciding how to use the eminent domain power.

The District of Columbia Redevelopment Act of 1945 used the eminent domain power to condemn land for slum eradication and for beautification projects. Some of the land was sold to private developers, who developed it according to the urban renewal plan. A landowner challenged the constitutionality of the statute. He argued that the property was not taken for public use because it was sold to private interests and for the purpose of beautification.

By a 9-0 vote, the Supreme Court upheld the statute. Speaking for the Court, Justice William O. Douglas suggested that eminent domain might be used to advance any of the legitimate purposes of government. The term "public use" did not imply that the property must be publicly owned or used directly by the general public. Reaffirming several Court precedents, Douglas wrote that the role of the judiciary in the matter is "extremely narrow." The Court would not substitute its judgment for a legislature's judgment about what constitutes a public use, but it would insist only that the use must not be "palpably without reasonable foundation."

Subsequent decisions have endorsed Douglas's broad understanding of the public use doctrine, the most notable case being *Hawaii Housing Authority v. Midkiff* (1984).

Thomas T. Lewis

See also *Hawaii Housing Authority v. Midkiff*; Property rights; Public use doctrine; Takings clause; Zoning.

Betts v. Brady

Citation: 316 U.S. 455
Date: June 1, 1942
Issue: Right to counsel
Significance: Until the *Betts* ruling was reversed in 1963, indigent criminal defendants in state trials did not have the constitutional right to a lawyer's assistance.

Betts, a poor defendant prosecuted for robbery in Maryland, asked his trial court to appoint a lawyer for his defense. The local policy, however, was to appoint counsel only in cases of murder or rape. After his conviction, Betts filed *habeas corpus* petitions, alleging that his rights under the Sixth Amendment had been violated. The lower courts rejected his petitions, based on the principle that the first eight amendments generally applied only to the federal government. The Supreme Court then granted certiorari.

The issue before the Court was whether the right to counsel should be incorporated into the due process clause of the Fourteenth Amendment. The justices voted six to three to uphold the lower courts. Speaking for the majority, Owen J. Roberts noted that most states did not require appointment of counsel in all criminal trials, and he argued that counsel was not necessary for a fair trial in Betts's circumstances. Counsel was required only in special situations such as *Powell v. Alabama* (1932), when illiterate defendants had been charged with a capital offense.

Three dissenters—Hugo L. Black, William O. Douglas, and Frank Murphy—argued that the constitutional right to counsel should be recognized in *all* criminal trials. In *Gideon v. Wainwright* (1963), the Court finally accepted the position of the dissenters.

Thomas T. Lewis

See also Certiorari, writ of; Counsel, right to; Due process, procedural; Fourteenth Amendment; *Gideon v. Wainwright*; *Hague v. Congress of Industrial Organizations*; Incorporation doctrine; Indigent criminal defendants; *Powell v. Alabama*; Sixth Amendment.

Bickel, Alexander

Identification: Legal scholar
Born: December 17, 1924, Bucharest, Romania
Died: November 7, 1974, New Haven, Connecticut
Significance: Legal scholar Bickel prepared a memo on his research of the equal protection clause in preparation for the ruling in *Brown v. Board of Education* (1954), a pivotal civil rights case before the Supreme Court.

Bickel was a constitutional scholar, Yale law professor, and jurist of the Frankfurter school arguing judicial restraint. He arrived in the United States in 1938. After brilliant academic years at City University of New York and Harvard Law School, he served as law clerk to Justice Felix Frankfurter during the 1952 term when *Brown v. Board of Education* was first under consideration. Partly to secure more time for the Supreme Court to achieve what he believed was a necessary unanimity, Frankfurter asked Bickel to undertake research on the original understanding of the equal protection clause and convinced the Court to withhold decision pending reargument on this issue. Bickel's 1954 memo concluded that the framers of the Fourteenth Amendment conceived equal protection in different terms from those accepted in the mid-twentieth century but had deliberately chosen broad and malleable terms. His memo (revised) was published in the *Harvard Law Review* and remains a standard reference. Whether it influenced the Court or not, it helped the Court pause and find agreement in its ultimate decision.

In 1956 he joined the Yale law school faculty where he taught until his death. In that year he published a research volume regarding Justice Louis D. Brandeis's scrupulous attention to procedural correctness. His most influential book, *The Least Dangerous Branch* (1962), examined judicial restraint. In this work, he argued that *Marbury v. Madison* (1803) was a flawed and unconvincing opinion and that judicial review cannot be adequately defended on logical, historical, or legal grounds. The Court's function is actually to constrain unprincipled legislation, but it earns that right by validating most provisions and by adroitly choosing the occasion for exercising its majoritarian power. Avoidance of confrontation as well as adherence to principle are the "passive virtues" superior to quixotic efforts to overuse the paper powers the Court has only on a limited basis.

These themes were elaborated upon in a number of works, especially *The Supreme Court and the Idea of Progress* (1970) in which he pessimistically predicts reversal of the major Warren Court achievements. Gerald Gunther, in an impressive attack, suggested that the Bickel approach tells the Court to save its power for some mythical big issue that will never come. The Court pretends to protect but retreats when crises develop. Others—like Robert H. Bork—see Bickel as a seminal figure in understanding the nuanced balance of powers in the U.S. system, although mistaken in his failing to embrace an "original understanding" as the primary and decisive rule for constitutional law.

A high point in Bickel's career was as lawyer for *The New York Times* in the Pentagon Papers case (*New York Times Co. v. United States*, 1971). He agreed to argue only if he were allowed to acknowledge there were situations in which government could regulate expression, and the case is decided on that nonabsolutist basis. Bickel was a fervent advocate of community governance of schools and the police and saw such local-ethnic devolution as the cure for inner-city and racial antagonism. His conservative legal posture was based primarily on his view of the separation of powers, and his politics

were quite different from those assumed by Court watchers.

FURTHER READING

Bork, Robert. *The Tempting of America*. London: Free Press, 1990.

Gunther, Gerald. "The Subtle Vices of the Passive Virtues." *Columbia Law Review* 64 (1964).

Samuel Krislov

SEE ALSO *Brown v. Board of Education*; Judicial review; Judicial self-restraint; *New York Times Co. v. United States*.

Bigelow v. Virginia

CITATION: 421 U.S. 809
DATE: June 16, 1975
ISSUE: Commercial speech
SIGNIFICANCE: The Supreme Court declared that the First Amendment protects commercial advertising to "some degree" and overturned a state statute prohibiting advertisements of abortion services.

In 1971 the Virginia Weekly of Charlottesville published an advertisement for an organization that helped women obtain legal abortions in the state of New York. The newspaper's editor, Jeffrey Bigelow, was convicted for violating a state statute that made it a misdemeanor to encourage or help a woman to have an abortion. Bigelow argued that the statute infringed on his free press rights under the First Amendment. In response, the state referred to *Valentine v. Chrestensen* (1942), in which the Supreme Court ruled that the First Amendment placed no restrictions on governmental regulations of "purely commercial advertising."

By a 7-2 vote, the Court overturned the statute and greatly limited the *Valentine* ruling. Justice Harry A. Blackmun's opinion for the Court emphasized that the spirit of the First Amendment favors the widespread dissemination of information and opinions. Blackmum noted that the advertisement contained truthful information about a legal service. The Court refused to decide the extent to which states might regulate commercial advertisements, especially those dealing with harmful activities. It was clear, nevertheless, that commercial speech merited a lesser degree of constitutional protection than political and religious speech.

Subsequent to *Bigelow*, the Court issued a series of decisions, such as *Bates v. State Bar of Arizona* (1977), that continued to expand First Amendment protection for commercial advertising. In *Forty-four Liquormart v. Rhode Island* (1996), the Court struck down a state ban on the advertising of alcoholic beverage prices, even though the Twenty-first Amendment gives states broad authority to regulate the sale of the product.

Thomas T. Lewis

SEE ALSO Abortion; *Bates v. State Bar of Arizona*; Commercial speech; Speech and press, freedom of; Time, place, and manner regulations.

Bill of attainder

DESCRIPTION: Legislative act that, without a trial, conveyed punishment on a person guilty of a seditious act, later was generalized to mean any law that punishes a person or group without a trial.

SIGNIFICANCE: The U.S. Constitution prohibits Congress from passing bills of attainder. The Supreme Court determined that Congress was also barred from passing bills of pains and penalties, which convey punishments short of death for seditious acts.

The bill of attainder, along with the bill of pains and penalties, was employed by the British Parliament in the sixteenth and seventeenth centuries. The bill of attainder condemned people to death without due process and often denied their heirs the right to inherit any properties they owned. The bill of pain and penalties sentenced people to punishments short of the death penalty such as banishment or seizure of their possessions, again without a trial. During the American Revolution, some states passed bills of attainder or bills of pains and penalties against people disloyal to the American cause.

Nonetheless, many of the Framers of the Constitution found bills of attainder objectionable because they viewed it to be the role of the courts, judging individual cases, rather than the legislature, to determine punishment. James Madison, in *The Federalist* (1788), No. 44, found bills of attainder to be "contrary to the first principles of the social compact." Article I, section 9, clause 3, of the U.S. Constitution prohibits the federal government from passing bills of attainder; Article 1, section 10, clause 1, prohibits the states from doing the same. The Supreme Court interpreted these clauses as covering bills of pains and penalties as well and grouped the two under the term "bill of attainder." In modern usage, bills of attainder refer to legislative acts that punish a person or group without a trial.

In *Calder v. Bull* (1798), the Court stated that the prohibition against ex post facto laws (such as bills of attainder) dealt only with civil and not criminal cases. Given the due process clause and the Bill of Rights, the distinction between civil and criminal law is not applicable to modern jurisprudence. However, the Court's early interpretation was not an uncommon sentiment among the Founders.

In the twentieth century, attainder became an issue in cases in which legislation was passed to impose punishment of any kind on individuals or members of specific groups rather than to regulate for a legitimate purpose. Legislators must scrutinize bills carefully to avoid legislation being found a bill of attainder. For example, the Court held, in *United States v. Lovett* (1946), that appropriation bills cannot speak of denying funds to "subversives" because such a designation reflects punishment through an ex post facto conviction and is a denial of due process. Attainder violates due process because it predetermines guilt. In *Beazell v. Ohio* (1925), the court stated that statutory ex post facto changes in trial procedures or the application of the legal rules are a violation of due process and constitutional violation.

In *United States v. Brown* (1965), the Court invalidated a federal statute banning Communist Party members from becoming officers in a union in order to minimize the danger of politically motivated strikes that would possibly harm the national economy. The Court found the law a bill of attainder and therefore in violation of the Constitution. It argued that the determination of whether a specific person's activities were dangerous conduct was to be made by the judiciary, not by Congress. In making the law, the Court said, Congress erred by attributing the undesirable trait (likelihood to cause a political strike) to members of a specific group, the Communist Party. The Court ruled that the bill of attainder clause was intended as a "safeguard against legislative exercise of the judicial function or more simply—trial by legislature."

FURTHER READING

Chaffee, Zechariah. *Three Human Rights in the Constitution of 1787.* Lawrence: University of Kansas Press, 1956.

Galligan, Denis J. *Due Process and Fair Procedures: A Study of Administrative Procedures.* New York: Oxford University Press, 1996.

Perry, Richard L., ed. *Sources of Our Liberties: Documentary Origins of Individual Liberties in the United States Constitution and Bill of Rights.* New York: Associated College Presses, 1959.

Arthur K. Steinberg

SEE ALSO Due process, procedural; Ex post facto laws; Jury, trial by; *Lovett, United States v.*; *Nixon v. Administrator of General Services*; Separation of powers.

Bill of Rights

DATE: 1791

DESCRIPTION: First ten amendments to the U.S. Constitution, guaranteeing individual rights, such as freedom of speech, freedom of the press, separation of church and state, the right to counsel, the right against self-incrimination, and due process.

SIGNIFICANCE: The Bill of Rights has posed an endless series of challenges for the Supreme Court to interpret the scope of personal liberties and the limits of government power.

When the Constitutional Convention adjourned in September, 1787, and submitted its new Constitution to a curious public, three of the remaining delegates refused to sign the new charter. One, George Mason of Virginia, declared that he would "sooner chop off this right hand than put it to a constitution without a Bill of Rights." Fearing that Mason and other Antifederalists might scuttle the ratification of the new Constitution, James Madison promised his fellow Virginians that if they supported the new charter (and elected him to the First Congress), he would sponsor a Bill of Rights. Each side kept its end of the bargain.

In December, 1791, the Bill of Rights was ratified, launching more than two hundred years of Supreme Court decisions interpreting, defining, and refining the nature of the relationship between the government and its citizens.

The Constitution was essentially a plan of government, establishing the legislative, executive, and federal branches and delineating their powers and responsibilities. Although the Constitution purported to grant only limited powers to Congress to pass laws in specified areas, it also provided that Congress had the authority to "make all Laws which shall be necessary and proper for carrying into Execution the foregoing Powers, and all other Powers vested by this Constitution in the Government of the United States, or in any Department or Officer thereof." This elastic catch-all clause worried those who feared that the Constitution would install an all-powerful national government, free to dominate the people and the states. It was the Bill of Rights that gave these critics some measure of solace that the new federal government would not become the same tyrannical seat of power that they had so recently fought to escape.

From the outset, the Supreme Court played a special role in giving meaning to the Bill of Rights. In March of 1789, Thomas Jefferson wrote to Madison that "the Bill of Rights is necessary because of the legal check which it puts into the hands of the judiciary." Jefferson was referring to a "legal check" on unwarranted government interference with the rights of the citizens.

The Bill of Rights touches on every realm of human affairs. It has fallen to the Supreme Court to interpret its elusive and elastic language. In every generation, the Court has been called on to grapple with the challenge of applying its 413 words, written in the late eighteenth century, to circumstances unknown to the authors, arising in the nineteenth, twentieth, and twenty-first centuries. The Bill of Rights protects both substantive and procedural rights. In contrast to the Constitution itself, which says what the government *can* do, the Bill of Rights says what the government *cannot* do.

First Amendment. The most powerful articulation of individual rights against government intrusion is found in the First Amendment, which is considered by many to be the most important of all the Amendments. The opening words speak volumes about the purpose and intent of the Bill of Rights: "Congress shall make no law . . . " These five words set the tone for all that follows. However, the simplicity is deceiving and the Supreme Court has the responsibility of deciding which laws pass constitutional muster and which do not.

Specifically, under the First Amendment, Congress is prohibited from making laws "respecting an establishment of religion or prohibiting the free exercise thereof." In one phrase, the First Amendment simultaneously guarantees the right of individuals to follow the beliefs and practices of their chosen religious faiths, while at the same time, it prohibits the government from singling out any particular religious denomination as a state-sponsored church. The First Amendment built what Jefferson called a "wall of separation" between church and state.

The free exercise and establishment clauses generated great consternation for the Court on controversial issues. From prayer in school to religious symbols on public property, from religious invocations at high school graduations to vouchers using public funds to subsidize parochial schools, the Court struggled to ensure that government remains neutral, but not hostile, in matters of religion.

The First Amendment next prohibits Congress from "abridging the freedom of speech, or of the press, or the right of the people peaceably to assemble, and to petition the Government for a redress of grievances." No portion of the Bill of Rights has engaged the Court's attention with more intensity, drama, and public interest than its protection of freedom of expression and freedom of assembly. Volumes have been written about how and why the Court decided whether particular speech or gatherings are constitutionally protected.

No majority of Supreme Court justices ever treated the protections guaranteed by the First Amendment as absolute. Instead, the Court recognized exceptions for obscenity, libel, criminal solicitation, perjury, false advertising, and fighting words. Within and beyond these categories, the Court has shifted, especially in times of war or during external threats, from the protection of wide-open, robust debate to the punishment of controversial ideas.

Second Amendment. The Second Amendment has been controversial; however, it was addressed by the Court only on rare occasions. It is popularly known for guaranteeing "the right of the people to keep and bear arms." However, in its most significant pronouncement, the Court unanimously held that this right is qualified by the opening phrase which reads: "A well regulated Militia, being necessary to the security of a free State . . . " In the light of that limitation, most recently the Court declined to hear an appeal from a lower court ruling upholding a municipal ban on hand guns.

Third Amendment. The Third Amendment, prohibiting the quartering of soldiers in private houses in times of peace without the consent of the owner, or in times of war, except as prescribed by law, while vitally important when it was written, is no longer the subject of serious Court review.

Fourth Amendment. The Fourth Amendment is a catalogue of important personal rights that the Court has sought to interpret by balancing the right of privacy against the legitimate needs of law enforcement. It begins by declaring that the "right of the people to be secure in their persons, houses, papers, and effects, against unreasonable searches and seizures, shall not be violated." The very presence of the undefined term "unreasonable" has required the Court to delve into every manner of search and seizure, developing specific rules that police must follow in order to avoid the exclusion of evidence at trial. The Court has repeatedly articulated that the consequence for an illegal search or seizure is suppression of the evidence, thereby creating an incentive for police to scrupulously follow constitutional requirements.

The Fourth Amendment also guarantees that "no Warrants shall issue, but upon probable cause." Here again the Court developed rules to determine whether probable cause exists. In essence, the Court uses a standard of reasonableness based on all of the facts and circumstances surrounding a challenged search or arrest. The Court places itself in the position of the reasonable police officer, relying on particularized suspicion and past experience, but rejecting mere hunches or guesswork.

Fifth Amendment. The Fifth Amendment also protects the rights of persons charged with crimes. It prohibits double jeopardy ("subject for the same offence to be twice put in jeopardy of life or limb"), self-incrimination (being "compelled in any criminal case to be a witness against himself"), denial of due process (being "deprived of life, liberty, or property, without due process of law"), and a taking without compensation (having "private property . . . taken for public use without just compensation"). The Court takes these rights very seriously because they set critical boundaries on what government may do in prosecuting crime.

Sixth Amendment. The Sixth Amendment protects the rights of persons charged with criminal vi-

THE BILL OF RIGHTS

Amendment I

Congress shall make no law respecting an establishment of religion, or prohibiting the free exercise thereof; or abridging the freedom of speech, or of the press, or the right of the people peaceably to assemble, and to petition the Government for a redress of grievances.

Amendment II

A well regulated Militia, being necessary to the security of a free State, the right of the people to keep and bear Arms, shall not be infringed.

Amendment III

No Soldier shall, in time of peace be quartered in any house, without the consent of the Owner, nor in time of war, but in a manner to be prescribed by law.

Amendment IV

The right of the people to be secure in their persons, houses, papers, and effects, against unreasonable searches and seizures, shall not be violated, and no Warrants shall issue, but upon probable cause, supported by Oath or affirmation, and particularly describing the place to be searched, and the persons or things to be seized.

Amendment V

No person shall be held to answer for a capital, or otherwise infamous crime, unless on a presentment or indictment of a Grand Jury, except in cases arising in the land or naval forces, or in the Militia, when in actual service in time of War or public danger; nor shall any person be subject for the same offence to be twice put in jeopardy of life or limb, nor shall be compelled in any criminal case to be a witness against himself, nor be deprived of life, liberty, or property, without due process of law; nor shall private property be taken for public use without just compensation.

Amendment VI

In all criminal prosecutions, the accused shall enjoy the right to a speedy and public trial, by an impartial jury of the State and district wherein the crime shall have been committed; which district shall have been previously ascertained by law, and to be informed of the nature and cause of the accusation; to be confronted with the witnesses against him; to have compulsory process for obtaining witnesses in his favor, and to have the assistance of counsel for his defence.

Amendment VII

In Suits at common law, where the value in controversy shall exceed twenty dollars, the right of trial by jury shall be preserved, and no fact tried by a jury shall be otherwise reexamined in any Court of the United States, than according to the rules of the common law.

Amendment VIII

Excessive bail shall not be required, nor excessive fines imposed, nor cruel and unusual punishments inflicted.

Amendment IX

The enumeration in the Constitution, of certain rights, shall not be construed to deny or disparage others retained by the people.

Amendment X

The powers not delegated to the United States by the Constitution, nor prohibited by it to the States, are reserved to the States respectively, or to the people.

olations. Often mischaracterized as mere "technicalities" protecting the "guilty," Sixth Amendment rights were included in the Bill of Rights because the Founders had lived under a government that frequently arrested, jailed, convicted, and punished individuals without any semblance of fairness or justice.

Under the Sixth Amendment, the accused has a "right to a speedy and public trial." Both elements of this right are very important. The right to a trial is of little value if the accused is kept in jail for several months or years waiting to be tried. Generally speaking, unless the accused waives the time limit, he or she is entitled to go to trial within sixty days after arrest. Likewise, a "public" trial is vital to ensure that an overzealous prosecutor or corrupt judge does not trample on the rights of the accused. Exposing criminal trials to the bright light of public scrutiny allows the general public and the press to observe the proceedings and see for themselves whether the accused is getting a fair trial. The days of the notorious "Star Chamber," where Englishmen were tried in secret, are a thing of the past.

Anyone accused of a crime is also entitled to "an impartial jury" chosen from the geographical area where the crime was committed. The Sixth Amendment guarantees that no one may sit on a jury if he or she has a demonstrable bias or prejudice against the accused, either individually, or because of his or her gender, race, religion, ethnicity, or any other immutable characteristic. Generally, trial judges go to great lengths to question prospective jurors in order to ferret out those who cannot discharge their duties in an impartial manner.

Anyone accused of a crime has a right under the Sixth Amendment "to be informed of the nature and cause of the accusation." Obviously, in order to defend himself, the accused must know what he is being accused of so that he can establish an alibi or find witnesses who may assist in proving his innocence. Only by knowing the charges can the accused's attorney challenge the sufficiency of the indictment of the validity of the statute or regulation involved.

Closely allied to this right is the important right under the Sixth Amendment "to be confronted with the witnesses against him." An accused is entitled to know who will testify against him or her so that the accused and his or her lawyer can prepare adequate cross-examination. From experience, the Founders knew that it is more difficult to lie to another's face than to do so when the other person is not present.

Also, under the Sixth Amendment, an accused has the right "to have compulsory process for obtaining witnesses in his favor." In other words, the accused has the right to subpoena other persons and require them to come to court to testify and to bring papers and documents. Because the government already has this power, this right ensures a level playing field, where an accused can force reluctant witnesses to present evidence that may exonerate him or her or prove that a witness for the prosecution is lying. Without this right, an accused would be confined to presenting only testimony or documents from persons who voluntarily chose to take the time to come to court.

Finally, and perhaps most importantly, the Sixth Amendment guarantees the accused the right "to have Assistance of Counsel for his defense." No person should face a criminal trial without competent legal counsel at his or her side. Only attorneys trained in the rules of evidence and trial procedures can adequately navigate through the complexities of a criminal trial. Indeed, so vital is the right to legal counsel that the law requires the state to provide a lawyer free of charge for the most serious crimes where the accused cannot afford one.

It is worth noting, before leaving the Sixth Amendment, that it contains no reference to the fundamental principle—considered the very foundation of Anglo-Saxon law—that one is innocent until proven guilty. Indeed, the presumption of innocence appears nowhere in the Bill of Rights or the Constitution. Yet, this essential right has repeatedly been recognized by the courts and remains a vital guarantee of American justice.

Seventh Amendment. The Seventh Amendment provides that in civil cases in federal courts at common law, where the value in controversy exceeds twenty dollars, "the right of trial by jury shall be preserved." Essentially, any civil case that entitled a litigant to a jury in 1791 still entitles the litigant to a jury today. Numerous rules (too extensive to be discussed here) have been developed by the courts to determine which civil claims must be tried before a jury and which may not.

The Seventh Amendment also guarantees that once a fact has been decided by a jury, it may not be otherwise reexamined in any federal court, except as provided by common law. Here again, because juries were viewed by the Founders as a protection against injustice and tyranny, it was important to ensure that once a jury had decided the facts in a case, a judge could not overturn that finding, except in limited circumstances provided in the common law.

Eighth Amendment. Further protections for criminal defendants are found in the Eighth Amendment, beginning with the guarantee that "excessive bail shall not be required." Persons awaiting trial are entitled to be released from jail, provided they post reasonable bail, in cash or property, which will be returned as long as they appear in court where required. The prohibition against excessive bail ensures that an accused is not arbitrarily detained because a judge has set an unreasonably high bail.

Closely related is the Eighth Amendment's prohibition against "excessive fines." This provision ensures that once convicted, an individual will be fined in proportion to his or her crime or in keeping with guidelines for similar offenses under similar circumstances.

The most important provision of the Eighth Amendment states that "cruel and unusual punishment" shall not be inflicted. This prohibition limits the kinds of punishment that can be imposed on those convicted of crimes. It proscribes punishment grossly disproportionate to the severity of a crime, and it imposes substantive limits on what can be made criminal and punished as such. At its most basic level, the prohibition against cruel and unusual punishment was intended to eliminate torture and other barbaric methods of punishment, although as recently as 1963, twenty lashes as part of the sentence for robbery was found not to be in violation of the Eighth Amendment.

By far, the most serious—and controversial—application of the prohibition on cruel and unusual punishment came in 1972 when the Court used it to strike down the death penalty (which was then reinstated four years later). The Court found that to the extent the death penalty was administered in an arbitrary and capricious manner, amounting to little more than a lottery, it constituted cruel and unusual punishment in violation of the Eighth Amendment.

Generally, in determining whether a punishment is cruel and unusual, the courts consider a variety of factors, including the age of the defendant, the attitude of the defendant, the availability of less severe punishments, contemporary standards of decency, the frequency of imposition, the disparity in punishments for the same or lesser crimes, the proportionality to the offense, the inhuman shocking or barbarous nature of the punishment, and the totality of the circumstances.

Ninth Amendment. One of the least known but most important provisions of the Bill of Rights is the Ninth Amendment, which in simple but meaningful terms states that the "enumeration in the Constitution, of certain rights, shall not be construed to deny or disparage others retained by the people." In many ways, these twenty-one words speak volumes about the very nature of the United States' constitutional democracy.

As set forth in the Declaration of Independence, people are born with certain inalienable rights. They are not granted their rights by a benevolent government; they are born with those rights and they establish governments in order to preserve and protect them. Thus, people speak of the Bill of Rights as "guaranteeing" constitutional rights, not "creating" them.

The Founders firmly believed in those principles. Indeed at first, the drafters of the Constitution did not include a Bill of Rights because they did not contemplate that the Constitution posed any threat to the inalienable rights of all citizens. However, as noted at the outset, many feared that a new and powerful national government would seize all the power it could, thereby jeopardizing personal rights and liberties.

However, when James Madison set about to draft the Bill of Rights during the First Congress in 1789, he faced a dilemma: How could he write a comprehensive list of *all* rights enjoyed by Americans without the risk of leaving some out? The solution was the Ninth Amendment. There, Madison, with utter simplicity, stated that the fact that "certain rights" were enumerated in the Constitution did not mean that "others retained by the people" were denied or disparaged. Consequently, any analysis of constitutional rights cannot stop by merely examining the specific rights; the "certain rights" spelled out in the first eight amendments. One must go further to determine whether there are "others retained by the people."

One of the most profound applications of the Ninth Amendment relates to the right of privacy. Few rights are more important to Americans than the right to be let alone, yet the right to privacy is nowhere mentioned in the Constitution or the Bill of Rights. To some extent, the entire Constitution and Bill of Rights express a right to privacy, that is, a set of limited and enumerated powers delegated to the government, with all other powers and rights held by the people. When the Supreme Court in the 1960's and 1970's began to address laws restricting contraception and abortion, it found that the right of privacy was rooted in several amendments, including the First, Fourth, Fifth, and Ninth, and what it called the "penumbras" emanating from all of the amendments.

Trivialized by certain judges and scholars as a mere "water blot" on the Constitution, the Ninth Amendment, on serious examination, may well reflect the true meaning of the Bill of Rights.

Tenth Amendment. Parallel to the Ninth Amendment, the Tenth Amendment rounds out the Bill of Rights. It provides that the "powers not delegated to the United States by the Constitution, nor prohibited by it to the States, are reserved to the States respectively, or to the people." Thus, as all *rights* not expressed in the Constitution are retained by the people, all *powers* not delegated to the federal government are reserved to the individual States or to the people. The Tenth Amendment reemphasizes the *limited* nature of the national government, underscoring the fact that the government possesses only the powers expressly delineated in the Constitution and no others.

The Tenth Amendment is rather obscure on the question of whether the reserved powers belong to the states or to the people. This was surely intentional. Having made his point that the national government was a creature of limited powers, Madison and his colleagues left it to others, including state legislatures, state courts, and the people themselves to sort out their respective relationships when it came to these reserved powers.

The Bill of Rights continues to serve the majestic purposes for which it was written more than two hundred years ago. Sometimes with intentional ambiguity, often with passionate eloquence and always with elusive simplicity, the Bill of Rights represents one of the most masterful declarations of individual rights and civil liberties in human history.

Yet, as a charter written by people to last the test of time, the Bill of Rights demands continuous study and interpretation to meet the challenges of the next century.

FURTHER READING

Don Nardo's *The Bill of Rights* (San Diego, Calif.: Greenhaven Press, 1998) provides an overview of the original debate over the need for a bill of rights and explores some of the later debates about rights. Books that examine the origins of the Bill of Rights include Akhil Reed Amar's *The Bill of Rights: Creation and Reconstruction* (New Haven, Conn.: Yale University Press, 1998), Leonard Levy's *Origins of the Bill of Rights* (New Haven, Conn.: Yale University Press, 1999), and *The Essential Bill of Rights: Original Arguments and Fundamental Documents* (Lanham, Md.: University Press of America, 1998), edited by Gordon Lloyd and Margie Lloyd. Works that examine the legacy of the Bill of Rights include Ellen Alderman and Caroline Kennedy's *In Our Defense: The Bill of Rights in Action* (New York: Bard, 1998), *The Bill of Rights, the Courts and the Law: The Landmark Cases that Have Shaped American Society* (3d ed., Charlottesville, Va.: Virginia Foundation for the Humanities and Public Policy, 1999) by Lynda Butler et al., and Nat Hentoff's *Living the Bill of Rights: How to Be an Authentic American* (New York: HarperCollins, 1998). *1791-1991: The Bill of Rights and Beyond* by the Commission on the Bicentennial of the United States Constitution, edited by Herbert M. Atherton et al. (Washington, D.C.: Commission on the Bicentennial of the U.S. Constitution, 1990) provides an interesting look back at the Bill of Rights.

Stephen F. Rohde

SEE ALSO British background to U.S. judiciary; Constitution, U.S.; Eighth Amendment; Fifth Amendment; First Amendment; Fourth Amendment; Incorporation doctrine; Jefferson, Thomas; *Lovett, United States v.*; Ninth Amendment; Second Amendment; Seventh Amendment; Sixth Amendment; Tenth Amendment; Third Amendment.

Birth control and contraception

DESCRIPTION: The temporary or permanent prevention of pregnancy by barrier devices, hormonal pills and implants, surgery, spermicides, intrauterine devices, or other means.

In 1914 the federal government indicted Margaret Sanger for violating the 1873 law against distributing birth-control information but later dropped the charges against her to avoid making her a public martyr. (AP/Wide World Photos)

SIGNIFICANCE: The Supreme Court's landmark 1965 ruling struck down a law preventing the distribution of contraceptives to married couples and established an implied constitutional "right of marital privacy." This right to privacy was cited in the 1973 ruling that found state antiabortion laws unconstitutional.

In the 1800's some Christians viewed contraception as immoral, believing that its widespread use would lead to promiscuity, marital infidelity, divorce, child abandonment, and abortion. In the mid-nineteenth century several states passed statutes banning the dissemination and use of contraceptives. In 1873 Congress enacted a law forbidding the sending of contraceptives or information about them through the mail.

Early in the twentieth century, Margaret Sanger and others began campaigning for public acceptance of birth control and the repeal of laws against contraception. Some campaigners viewed contraception as an instrument of women's liberation, some sought the freedom to have sex without fear of pregnancy, and others were principally motivated by eugenic goals.

By the 1940's most states permitted physicians to prescribe contraceptives. Nonprescription distribution of contraceptives was still legally restricted although these laws were rarely enforced. Procontraception groups challenged these restrictions on contraceptives in federal courts. Their initial efforts were unsuccessful. In *Gardner v. Massachusetts* (1938), *Tileston v. Ullman* (1943), and *Poe v. Ullman* (1961), the Supreme Court supported legislation placing restrictions on contraceptive use and distribution.

In *Griswold v. Connecticut* (1965), however, the Court struck down a state law that forbade the distribution of contraceptives to and their use by married couples. Writing for the Court, justice William O. Douglas claimed that the statute violated a "right of marital privacy," which was found in "penumbras formed by emanations" from various specific Bill of Rights guarantees. In concurring opinions, several justices proposed alternative justifications for the holding. Most notably, Arthur J. Goldberg suggested treating marital contraception as an "unenumerated right" under the Ninth Amendment.

In dissent, Hugo L. Black and Potter Stewart argued that nothing in the text, logic, structure, or original understanding of the Constitution prevents a state from restricting contraception pursuant to its police power to protect public health, safety, and morals. They faulted the majority for substituting an allegedly enlightened judicial view of the requirements of public morality for the contrary judgment of the elected representatives of the people of Connecticut.

Griswold purported to protect the institution of marriage against legal interference with spousal decisions about birth control. In *Eisenstadt v. Baird* (1972), the Court ruled that this right to privacy extended to individuals, married or single, who wished to use contraceptives. A year later, the right of privacy was invoked in a ruling against state laws forbidding abortion in *Roe v. Wade* (1973).

Opponents of judicial activism criticized the Court's invalidation of laws against contraceptives as a step toward judges injecting their personal views about morality and public policy into the Constitution. Supporters of the right of privacy doctrine were disappointed by the Court's unwillingness to expand the doctrine beyond decisions about child-bearing to embrace consensual sex generally. In *Bowers v. Hardwick* (1986), the Court upheld laws against homosexual sodomy despite the rulings in the contraception cases.

FURTHER READING

Appleby, Brenda Margaret. *Responsible Parenthood: Decriminalizing Contraception in Canada.* Toronto: University of Toronto Press, 1999.

Critchlow, Donald T. *Intended Consequences: Birth Control, Abortion, and the Federal Government in Modern America.* New York: Oxford University Press, 1999.

Mason, J. K. *Medico-legal Aspects of Reproduction and Parenthood.* Brookfield, Vt.: Dartmouth, 1990.

Robert P. George

SEE ALSO Abortion; Black, Hugo L.; *Bowers v. Hardwick*; Douglas, William O.; *Eisenstadt v. Baird*; Family and children; Gender issues; Goldberg, Arthur J.; *Griswold v. Connecticut*; Judicial activism; Marriage; Privacy, right to; *Roe v. Wade*.

Hugo L. Black. (AP/Wide World Photos)

Black, Hugo L.

IDENTIFICATION: Associate justice (August 19, 1937-September 17, 1971)

NOMINATED BY: Franklin D. Roosevelt

BORN: February 27, 1886, Harlan, Alabama

DIED: September 25, 1971, Bethesda, Maryland

SIGNIFICANCE: During his thirty-four years on the Court, Black led the drive to make the rights of the Constitution's first eight amendments binding on the states, while working vigorously to expand constitutional rights, especially in the areas of free speech and civil rights.

The son of a poor storekeeper in rural Alabama, Black took a keen interest in both books and politics at a young age. Although a disciplinary incident prevented him from graduating from high school, he studied for a year in medical school and then transferred to the University of Alabama's law school. Immediately after earning his law degree at the age of twenty, he began to practice law in the city of Birmingham. Orienting his practice toward working people and labor unions, he became one of Alabama's most successful personal injury lawyers. His courtroom style combined fiery presenta-

tions and detailed knowledge of relevant facts. He joined many civic organizations, and despite his religious skepticism, he taught a popular adult class at a Baptist church. He also served as a part-time police court judge in 1910-1911.

Political Career. In 1914 Black was elected prosecutor of Alabama's Jefferson County. He effectively emptied a large docket, and he once prosecuted police officers for forcing confessions from African American defendants. He joined the Army during World War I and rose to the rank of captain but never left the United States. After returning to Birmingham, he married and had three children. Meanwhile, his law practice flourished.

Black was a member of the Ku Klux Klan from 1923 to 1925 and was elected to the U.S. Senate with Klan support in 1926. Like other southern populists of the time, he campaigned on the theme of promoting economic justice for the poor and the weak. Because the Republican Party controlled Congress during Black's first Senate term, he spent much of his time pursuing his interests in history and philosophy. However, the Democratic Party's electoral triumph in 1932 gave him the opportunity to exercise a leadership role in the Senate.

As Democratic Party whip in the Senate, Black played a crucial role in helping to pass President Franklin D. Roosevelt's New Deal legislation. He was also a leading force in congressional investigations of lobbying practices and misappropriation of government subsidies. Black sponsored the earliest minimum-wage and maximum-hours law. A long-time critic of the Supreme Court's economic conservatism, he bitterly resented the Court's striking down of New Deal legislation and enthusiastically supported Roosevelt's Court-packing plan.

Appointment to the Court. On August 12, 1937, Roosevelt named Black to fill the first Supreme Court vacancy that opened during his presidency. A mere five days later, the Senate confirmed Black's nomination by a vote of sixty-three to sixteen. Black served on the Court until failing health forced his resignation on September 25, 1973. He died just eight days later.

As an associate justice, Black argued that framers of the Fourteenth Amendment (1868) had intended to incorporate all the rights guaranteed by the first eight amendments into their new amendment. For that reason, he argued, those rights should apply to the state governments, as they already did to the federal government. In his view, the Fourteenth Amendment's "liberty" and "privileges or immunities" meant the states should have the full protections of the Bill of Rights. Defending this position in his dissent in *Adamson v. California* (1947), he amassed an impressive amount of historical material, but critics observed that he ignored contradictory evidence. On this issue, he often came into conflict with Justice Felix Frankfurter, who argued that the Fourteenth Amendment applied selective guarantees based on their fundamental fairness. Black never persuaded a majority of his colleagues to accept his principle of total incorporation but succeed in launching the piecemeal incorporation of most of the specific rights of the first eight amendments. By the time he retired in 1971, the debate over incorporation had largely ended, and most provisions of the Bill of Rights had been applied to the states.

Particular Rights. Believing that the First Amendment's guarantees of freedom of speech and press were at the heart of a free government, Black accepted the "preferred position" of these freedoms in the 1940's. He vigorously argued that all speech and writing was absolutely protected from governmental sanction. Like his close friend on the Court, William O. Douglas, he believed that this protection extended to all forms of obscenity, and he therefore refused to review adult movies to determine if they were obscene. At the same time, Black made a sharp distinction between conduct and verbal expression, and did not generally support the notion of "symbolic speech." In *Tinker v. Des Moines Independent Community School District* (1969), his bitter dissent insisted that the First Amendment did not protect any right of children to wear controversial political symbols in the public schools.

Black endorsed Thomas Jefferson's view that the First Amendment erected a wall separating church and state and that governmental funds must never support religious institutions. He wrote the majority opinion in *Everson v. Board of Education of Ewing Township* (1947), which theoretically applied this understanding of the establishment clause to the states, while permitting states to pay transportation costs to parochial schools. Many southerners were outraged when Black wrote *Engel v. Vitale* (1962), forbidding state-sponsored prayers in public schools.

In criminal trials, Black generally took an expansionist view on the Fifth and Sixth Amendments. One of his first majority opinions, *Johnson v. Zerbst* (1940), held that counsel must be provided for indigent defendants in federal prosecutions. In *Betts v. Brady* (1942), he registered a strong dissent when the majority refused to apply the principle to the states. Twenty years later, Black saw *Betts* overturned, and he had the honor of writing for a unanimous court in the famous case of *Gideon v. Wainwright* (1963). Black's views on the Fourth Amendment were more restrained. In *Katz v. United States* (1967), for example, he argued that personal conversations were not protected under the amendment.

Equal Protection. Black consistently took a firm stand against Jim Crow racial discrimination. When the school segregation cases were first argued in the early 1950's, he was one of only four justices to vote to overturn *Plessy v. Ferguson* (1896). His opinion in *Griffin v. County School Board of Prince Edward County* (1964) firmly rejected attempts to avoid compliance with school desegregation and declared that the "time for mere 'deliberate speed' had run out." In cases such as *Shapiro v. Thompson*

(1969), however, he opposed the application of the strict scrutiny test in equal protection claims not involving racial discrimination. In his later years, Black angered liberals when he argued in dissent that the Constitution did not provide any guarantee that citizens could engage in civil rights protests on private property.

Black has been especially criticized for his majority opinion in *Korematsu v. United States* (1944), which upheld the forced removal and internment of Japanese Americans living on the West Coast after the United States entered World War II. Although there was no real evidence that Japanese Americans had posed a threat to national security, Black continued to insist that the decision was justified by the exigencies of war. Ironically, Black's *Korematsu* opinion later had a liberal influence as the Court's first reference to race as a suspect classification that should be subjected to the "most rigid scrutiny."

Constitutional Philosophy. In his book, *A Constitutional Faith* (1968), Black expressed a quasi-religious devotion to the text of the Constitution. A critic of judicial discretion, he argued that judges should base their decisions on a literal reading of the Constitution, while taking into account the intent of the Framers. Called a "judicial positivist," he opposed subjective interpretations in which justices found unenumerated rights in either natural law, substantive due process, or the Ninth Amendment. Believing that judges were fallible, he never placed a high value on judicial precedents. During his early career, he denounced the concept of a probusiness "liberty of contract," just as he later became a vociferous critic of an unenumerated "right to privacy." When the Court overturned a law prohibiting the sale of contraceptives in *Griswold v. Connecticut* (1965), Black wrote a strong dissent, accusing the majority of reviving the excesses of the early twentieth century *Lochner v. New York* (1905) era, when the Court intervened excessively in commerce laws.

FURTHER READING

Roger K. Newman's *Hugo Black: A Biography* (New York: Pantheon, 1994) is a scholarly and well-written study of Black's life and career. James Magee's *Mr. Justice Black: Absolutist on the Court* (Charlottesville: University Press of Virginia, 1980) presents a critical analysis of his judicial philosophy, with an emphasis on his absolutist views on free expression For an interesting comparative approach, see James Simon's *The Antagonists: Hugo Black, Felix Frankfurter and Civil Liberties in Modern America* (New York: Simon & Schuster, 1989). For a detailed study of his career until 1937, see Virginia Van der Veer Hamilton's *Hugo Black: The Alabama Years* (Baton Rouge: Louisiana State University Press, 1972). Hugo Black, Jr., presents a delightful look at the man in *My Father: A Remembrance* (New York: Random House, 1975). Irving Dilliard edited a collection of many of his Supreme Court opinions in *One Man's Stand for Freedom: Mr. Justice Black and the Bill of Rights* (New York: Alfred A. Knopf, 1963). Other recommended works include Tony Freyer's *Hugo L. Black and the Dilemma of American Liberalism* (Glenview, Ill.: Scott, Foresman, 1990); Howard Ball's *Hugo L. Black: Cold Steel Warrior* (New York: Oxford University Press, 1998); Michael Parrish's *New Deal Justice* (New York: Random House, 1998); and Tinsley Yarbrough's *Mr. Justice Black and His Critics* (Durham, N.C.: Duke University Press, 1988).

Thomas T. Lewis

SEE ALSO Constitutional interpretation; Court-packing plan; Due process, substantive; First Amendment absolutism; Fourteenth Amendment; Frankfurter, Felix; Incorporation doctrine; New Deal; Race and discrimination; Religion, establishment of; Roosevelt, Franklin D.

Black, Jeremiah S.

IDENTIFICATION: Supreme Court nominee (1861), Supreme Court reporter (1861-1864)
NOMINATED BY: James Buchanan
BORN: January 10, 1810, Stony Creek, Pennsylvania
DIED: August 19, 1883, York, Pennsylvania
SIGNIFICANCE: Although Black was a respected judge, his nomination to the Supreme Court was rejected, possibly because of political reasons. He also served as Court reporter and argued cases before the Court.

Black was admitted to the bar in 1830 and appointed president judge of the court of common pleas of Pennsylvania in 1842. He was elected to that state's supreme court in 1851 and chosen chief justice. In 1857 he was appointed attorney general

Jeremiah S. Black. (Library of Congress)

by President James Buchanan. As attorney general, Black prosecuted cases involving California land titles that led to the reversal of district court decisions by the Supreme Court, enforced slave trade and fugitive slave laws, and in an official opinion, advised Buchanan on the powers of the president in suppressing rebellion. He became secretary of state on December 17, 1860, three days before South Carolina seceded.

Buchanan nominated Black, a Democrat, to the Court on February 5, 1861, less than a month before the inauguration of Abraham Lincoln. Although Black was known as an able and competent jurist, having twice been elected to Pennsylvania's supreme court, the nomination failed by one vote, twenty-five to twenty-six, on February 21, 1861.

Black was appointed reporter to the Supreme Court in December, 1861, and prepared two volumes of reports during his three years of service. Later, as an able member of the Supreme Court bar, he participated in the landmark decisions of *Ex parte Milligan* (1866) and *Ex parte McCardle* (1869), opposing the government's violations of civil rights and the Reconstruction Acts.

Susan Coleman

SEE ALSO Civil War; Fugitive slaves; *McCardle, Ex parte*; *Milligan, Ex parte*; Nominations to the Court; Reporters, Supreme Court.

Black Monday

DATE: May 27, 1935

DESCRIPTION: The day the Supreme Court struck down three pieces of New Deal legislation, signaling to President Franklin D. Roosevelt that his programs to cope with the Great Depression faced legal jeopardy.

SIGNIFICANCE: The Court's decision that economic emergencies did not enlarge governmental powers meant that many of the New Deal programs would probably not pass Court scrutiny. The ruling led the Roosevelt administration to craft programs more closely tailored to the Constitution and helped set the stage for the president's Court-packing plan in 1937.

In an attempt to bring order to the chaotic economy, President Franklin D. Roosevelt developed an economic recovery plan called the New Deal, which relied heavily on federal regulation and legislation. He signed numerous statutes, including the National Industrial Recovery Act (NIRA) in 1933 and the Frazier-Lemke Farm Bankruptcy Act in 1934. The NIRA set minimum wages and maximum hours and established a host of fair practice standards for business, created by business and labor leaders with the assistance of government lawyers. These standards, which were to be enforced by the government, affected even intrastate business concerns. The Frazier-Lemke act provided debt relief to bankrupt farmers. In addition, Roosevelt enlarged the role of economic regulatory commissions and sought to control independent commissions by removing members opposed to his New Deal.

Although the Supreme Court initially accepted some New Deal programs, on Monday, May 27, 1935, known as Black Monday, it handed down three unanimous decisions striking down major aspects of Roosevelt's plan.

In *Schechter Poultry Corp. v. United States* (1935), the Court held that poultry codes of the NIRA were unenforceable because the Constitution gave the federal government power to regulate only interstate commerce, not commerce within a state.

The facts of the case involved local production of kosher chickens, and the government could not demonstrate a reasonable connection of this intrastate activity to interstate commerce. Many similar NIRA codes were thus invalidated. The Roosevelt administration claimed that the Court had too narrowly defined commerce, much as it had in its decision in *United States v. E. C. Knight Co.* (1895).

In *Louisville Joint Stock Land Bank v. Radford* (1935), the Court invalidated the Frazier-Lemke act. The Court ruled that the act, which limited the power of owners to foreclose on debtors, transferred the property rights of the owner to the buyer, violating the takings clause of the Fifth Amendment.

In *Humphrey's Executor v. United States* (1935), the Court placed limits on presidential power to remove and appoint members of independent regulatory commissions. The court held that Congress had created such commissions to be independent of the executive branch. For the president to interfere with their independence by removing those members who hold opposing views, without congressional warrant, violated the separation of powers.

Supporters of the New Deal roundly criticized the Court for failing to recognize the need for flexibility and experimentation in dealing with the Great Depression. A report by the Brookings Institution at the time, and subsequent scholarly opinion, has suggested that some New Deal programs such as the NIRA were, in fact, seriously flawed. Black Monday caused Roosevelt to try other approaches to bring about economic recovery, including income tax reform, and in 1937 to attempt to pack the Court with justices who favored New Deal programs.

FURTHER READING

Irons, Peter. *The New Deal Lawyers.* Princeton, N.J.: Princeton University Press, 1983.

Leuchtenburg, William E. *The Supreme Court Reborn: The Constitutional Revolution in the Age of Roosevelt.* New York: Oxford University Press, 1995.

Edward R. Crowther

SEE ALSO Commerce, regulation of; Court-packing plan; *Humphrey's Executor v. United States*; New Deal; *Schechter Poultry Corp. v. United States*.

Blackmun, Harry A.

IDENTIFICATION: Associate justice (June 9, 1970-June 30, 1994)

NOMINATED BY: Richard M. Nixon

BORN: November 12, 1908, Nashville, Illinois

DIED: March 4, 1999, Arlington, Virginia

SIGNIFICANCE: Blackmun wrote the 7-2 majority decision in the controversial abortion case, *Roe v. Wade* (1973). In twenty-four years on the Supreme Court, he left his mark on disparate constitutional disputes involving federalism, criminal law, commercial speech, and the rights of aliens.

Blackmun was raised in St. Paul, Minnesota, leaving to take his undergraduate and law degrees at Harvard University in 1929 and 1932, respectively. He had a lifelong interest in medicine and was general counsel to the Mayo Clinic in Minnesota from 1950 to 1959. In 1959 President Dwight D. Eisenhower appointed him to the U.S. Court of Appeals for the Eighth Circuit. He was President Richard M. Nixon's third choice for a position on the Supreme Court, winning confirmation as a justice after the unsuccessful nominations of Clement Haynsworth, Jr., and G. Harrold Carswell.

On the Court. Many thought that Blackmun would reinforce Nixon's drive to move the Court in a more conservative direction than had characterized it since the 1950's. Initially this proved to be the case, with Blackmun generally voting to support governmental authority in criminal justice and free speech matters. He voted to support the death penalty in *Furman v. Georgia* (1972) and again in *Gregg v. Georgia* (1976) despite personal discomfort with the practice. His personal views did not crystallize into firm opposition to capital punishment until late in his career. He dissented in *New York Times Co. v. United States* (1971), siding with the Nixon administration in its efforts to prevent publication of the Pentagon Papers. He also dissented in *Cohen v. California* (1971), siding with the state in its effort to curb vulgar and offensive speech. However, in *Bates v. State Bar of Arizona* (1977), Blackmun wrote the majority decision striking down legal ethics guidelines that prevented lawyers from advertising their services. In addition to its First Amendment implications, the case in essence ended the claim of the U.S. legal profession to the relatively unrestricted power of self-regulation.

Despite his early sympathy with the general police power of the state, Blackmun's most renowned shift away from this view also came early in his Court career. In *Roe v. Wade* (1973), Blackmun relied on the putative right to privacy implied by the Fourteenth Amendment's due process clause to support a woman's right to abortion absent state interference (except in matters relating to maternal health) in the first trimester of pregnancy. Blackmun constructed his decision at least partially around research he had conducted at the Mayo Clinic in the summer of 1972. He later characterized the decision as a landmark in the drive to emancipate women.

Later in his career, Blackmun passionately dissented in the case of *Webster v. Reproductive Health Services* (1989), in which, he claimed, the Court had allowed the government to intrude improperly on what he believed to be the freedom of women to control their bodies. In *Planned Parenthood of Southeastern Pennsylvania v. Casey* (1992), Blackmun, dissenting in part, openly lamented what he claimed to be the dangers to individual liberty that would follow his retirement if one more anti-*Roe* justice were appointed to a Court narrowly divided on the abortion issue. In *Bowers v. Hardwick* (1986), Blackmun wrote a stinging dissent from the Court's refusal to extend the right to privacy to homosexual sodomy. Blackmun claimed that the fundamental "right to be let alone" was under assault in the case and that the majority's understanding of privacy and other constitutional issues was cramped.

Blackmun's concern for individual rights also manifested itself early on in his majority opinion in *Graham v. Richardson* (1971), holding alienage to be a suspect classification under the Fourteenth Amendment. By so holding, the Court made any governmental classifications based on alienage subject to the highest level of judicial scrutiny. He generally supported the rights of aliens against state discrimination in subsequent alienage cases.

In *Regents of the University of California v. Bakke* (1978), Blackmun voted against the application of strict scrutiny to racial classifications that are not stigmatizing, thus in effect, casting a vote in favor of governmentally sponsored affirmative action.

In general, by the 1980's, Blackmun had firmly joined the Court's liberal camp, often voting with

Harry A. Blackmun. (AP/Wide World Photos)

Justices William J. Brennan, Jr., and Thurgood Marshall. He opposed prayer in public schools on establishment clause grounds. In *Garcia v. San Antonio Metropolitan Transit Authority* (1985), Blackmun reinforced the Court's dominant interpretation of the commerce clause, writing the majority opinion that eliminated virtually all judicial limitations on Congress's power under this clause. The decision allowed federal economic regulation of areas in which state jurisdiction had traditionally been supreme. Many observers argued that this opinion—later effectively overturned by *United States v. Lopez* (1995)—rendered federalism largely inoperable.

Constitutional Philosophy. Blackmun's steady shift from moderate conservatism to judicial liberalism, conjoined with his largely pragmatic, nontheoretical approach to issues, makes it difficult to characterize his constitutional philosophy. Blackmun has been viewed as a centrist blessed with the virtue of moderation and a judicial activist bent on reinterpreting the Constitution to suit his own views. How he is characterized often varies with the constitutional philosophy of the person making the characterization.

FURTHER READING

Brennan, William J., et al. "A Tribute to Justice Harry A. Blackmun." *Harvard Law Review* 108, no. 1 (November, 1994).

Hair, Penda D. "Justice Blackmun and Racial Justice." *Yale Law Journal* 104, no. 1 (October, 1994).

Reuben, Richard C. "Justice Defined." *ABA Journal* 80 (July, 1994).

Rosen, Jeffrey. "Sentimental Journey: The Emotional Jurisprudence of Harry Blackmun." *The New Republic* 210, no. 18 (May 2, 1994).

Bradley C. S. Watson

SEE ALSO Abortion; Alien rights and naturalization; Capital punishment; Commerce, regulation of; Commercial speech; *Garcia v. San Antonio Metropolitan Transit Authority*; *Lopez, United States v.*; *Roe v. Wade*; *Webster v. Reproductive Health Services*.

Blair, John, Jr.

IDENTIFICATION: Associate justice (February 2, 1790-October 25, 1795)
NOMINATED BY: George Washington
BORN: 1732, Williamsburg, Virginia
DIED: August 31, 1800, Williamsburg, Virginia

John Blair, Jr. (Library of Congress)

SIGNIFICANCE: One of the original members of the Supreme Court, Blair worked to strengthen the powers of the federal government over the individual states.

Blair graduated in 1754 from the College of William and Mary. In 1755 and 1756 he studied law at the Middle Temple in London. He established a law practice in Williamsburg, Virginia, and in 1765 was elected to represent the College of William and Mary in Virginia's House of Burgesses.

As a burgess, Blair opposed Patrick Henry's 1765 Stamp Act as too radical a move. However, after the British Crown dissolved the burgesses in 1769 and 1770, Blair sided with fellow Virginians advocating independence. He helped create Virginia's new government as a delegate to the Virginia Convention in 1776 and was chosen as a general court judge. A series of court appointments followed. His most memorable decision came while sitting on the First Court of Appeals, when he and his fellow judges ruled in *Virginia v. Caton* (1782) that the court had the power to determine the constitutionality of legislative acts. This decision helped set the stage for a strong Supreme Court a few years later.

In 1787 Blair was a delegate to the Constitutional Convention and voted for the adoption of the Constitution. After the new government formed, President George Washington nominated Blair as one of the original five associate justices of the Supreme Court; Blair was confirmed by the Senate two days later.

Perhaps the most far-reaching decision of Blair's career was in *Chisholm v. Georgia* (1793), when he sided with the majority view that a citizen might bring suit against states in federal court. Blair's opinion demonstrated his belief in the Constitution as the supreme legal authority in the nation and strengthened the federal government's power over the states. The unfavorable reaction to this decision helped usher in the Eleventh Amendment, which restricted federal court power to hear suits against states brought by aliens or citizens of other states.

Early justices, in addition to their duties on the Supreme Court, presided over circuit courts. In Middle Circuit Court in 1792, Blair and fellow judges ruled in *Collet v. Collet* (1792) that if the U.S. government naturalized a citizen, states must accept that decision, once again strengthening the power of the central government over that of individual states.

Because of failing health and exhaustion brought on by riding the judicial circuit, Blair retired from the bench in 1796 to return to Williamsburg, where he died in 1800.

FURTHER READING

Friedman, Leon, and Fred L. Israel, eds. *The Justices of the United States Supreme Court: Their Lives and Major Opinons.* 5 vols. New York: Chelsea House, 1997.

Marcus, Maeva, and James Perry, eds. *The Documentary History of the Supreme Court of the United States, 1789-1800.* New York: Columbia University Press, 1985.

Carol G. Fox

SEE ALSO *Chisholm v. Georgia;* Circuit riding; Constitutional Convention; Constitutional interpretation; Eleventh Amendment; Federalism.

Blatchford, Samuel

IDENTIFICATION: Associate justice (April 3, 1882-July 7, 1893)

NOMINATED BY: Chester A. Arthur

BORN: March 9, 1820, New York, New York

DIED: July 7, 1893, Newport, Rhode Island

SIGNIFICANCE: Known as a workhorse, Blatchford wrote 430 opinions in his eleven years on the Supreme Court. In an 1892 decision, he extended the interpretation of the Fifth Amendment by emphasizing that it prevented a person from giving evidence in any criminal case.

Blatchford graduated as class valedictorian from Columbia College in 1837. He began studying law in his father's New York office, but soon was asked to serve as the private secretary of New York governor William Seward. In 1842 Blatchford was admitted to the New York bar and practiced in New York City with his father for the next three years. Subsequently, he became a law partner with Seward, which contributed greatly to Blatchford's later success.

In 1852 Blatchford began compiling reports of federal court decisions and ultimately published twenty-four volumes of previously uncollected decisions of the U.S. Court of Appeals for the Second

Samuel Blatchford. (Library of Congress)

Circuit. He also published *Blatchford's and Howland's Reports* (1855) of admiralty cases decided between 1827 and 1837 in the district court for the southern district of New York, as well as *Blatchford's Prize Cases* (1865), which covered prize cases in circuit and district courts of New York from 1861 to 1865. Between 1867 and 1872, Blatchford served as a federal district judge for the southern district of New York. He was then elevated to the U.S. Court of Appeals for the Second Circuit.

After Roscoe Conkling and George F. Edmunds each declined invitations to fill a vacancy in the Supreme Court, President Chester A. Arthur nominated Blatchford on March 13, 1882. Blatchford was easily confirmed in the Senate two weeks later. Being a judicial moderate, Blatchford usually supported the majority opinions of the Court, writing only two dissents out of his 430 opinions. Known as one of the hardest-working and most productive justices ever to sit on the Court bench, he also became known for his encouragement of younger members of the legal profession and for his kind, patient, courteous manner.

In 1890 Blatchford was cast into the national spotlight when he wrote the pivotal opinion for

Chicago, Milwaukee, and St. Paul Railway Co. v. Minnesota. Blatchford claimed that it was unconstitutional for a government-established commission to have the last word in whether railway rates were fair or not. He argued that it violated the railway's right to due process. However, less than two years later in *Budd v. New York* (1892), Blatchford ruled that the legislature could indeed set rates for businesses that affect the public interest. His contradictory decisions were highly criticized. However, he demonstrated his wisdom in *Counselman v. Hitchcock* (1892), when he broadly interpreted the Fifth Amendment's right against self-incrimination, giving individuals increased protection against federal authority.

Alvin K. Benson

SEE ALSO Admiralty and maritime law; *Budd v. New York*; *Chicago, Milwaukee, and St. Paul Railway Co. v. Minnesota*; Conkling, Roscoe; *Counselman v. Hitchcock*; Fifth Amendment.

BMW of North America v. Gore

CITATION: 116 S.Ct. 1589
DATE: May 20, 1996
ISSUES: Excessive damage awards; substantive due process
SIGNIFICANCE: The Supreme Court held that a punitive damage award of five hundred times the amount of actual damages was "grossly excessive" and therefore contrary to the due process clause of the Fourteenth Amendment.

After Ira Gore purchased a new BMW, he found that it had been repainted by the manufacturer. Alleging fraud according to Alabama law, Gore brought suit against BMW for failure to disclose a defect. He was awarded $4,000 in compensatory damages and $2 million in punitive damages. By a 5-4 margin, the Supreme Court found that BMW's conduct was not egregious enough to justify such an extreme sanction. Writing for the Court, Justice John Paul Stevens emphasized that there must be a "reasonable relationship" between a punitive damages award and any conceivable harm that the plaintiff might suffer. In dissent, Justice Antonin Scalia criticized the expansion of the substantive due process doctrine to include jury decisions in civil suits.

Thomas T. Lewis

SEE ALSO Civil law; Due process, substantive; *Gertz v. Robert Welch.*

Board of Education of Oklahoma City v. Dowell

CITATION: 498 U.S. 237
DATE: January 15, 1991
ISSUE: School integration and busing
SIGNIFICANCE: The Supreme Court held that federal district courts may end court-supervised busing plans when the "effects of past intentional discrimination" have been removed "as far as practicable" and a local school board has complied with a desegregation order for a "reasonable period of time."

In 1985 the Oklahoma City school district requested dissolution of a desegregation decree that had been in effect for nineteen years. Approving the request, the district judge observed that the school board had done nothing to promote residential segregation for twenty-five years and that it had bused students in good faith for more than a decade. The court of appeals reversed the judgment because the majority of children in the district continued to attend one-race schools, reflecting demographic residential patterns mostly developed after the decree had gone into effect. By a 5-3 vote, the Court ruled in favor of the district judge's decision. Chief Justice William H. Rehnquist argued that desegregation decrees had never been intended to "operate in perpetuity" and that the tradition of local control over public schools justified the dissolution of court-supervised desegregation plans as long as present residential segregation was a result of private decisions and economic factors rather than official policies.

The Court amplified the *Dowell* decision in *Freeman v. Pitts* (1992), holding that district judges have discretion to withdraw supervision of school districts once officials have shown good faith compliance with a court-ordered desegregation plan, even if some vestiges of de jure segregation continued.

Thomas T. Lewis

SEE ALSO *Missouri v. Jenkins*; Race and discrimination; School integration and busing; Segregation, de facto; State action; *Swann v. Charlotte-Mecklenburg Board of Education.*

Boerne v. Flores

CITATION: No. 95-2074
DATE: June 25, 1997
ISSUES: Separation of powers; freedom of religion
SIGNIFICANCE: In striking down the Religious Freedom Restoration Act of 1993, the Supreme Court declared that congressional enforcement powers in the Fourteenth Amendment may not be used to override the Court's interpretations of the Constitution.

In *Sherbert v. Verner* (1963), the Supreme Court required a compelling state interest as justification for any indirect restraint on religion. In *Employment Division, Department of Human Resources v. Smith* the Court allowed the states more discretion when balancing claims of religious freedom against the states' interests in enacting and enforcing reasonable laws of general application. Congress responded to the controversial *Smith* decision with the Religious Freedom Restoration Act of 1993, which required states to apply the more demanding *Sherbert* standards. A Roman Catholic Church in Boerne, Texas, desired to replace its old and small church building, but the city had classified the structure as an historic landmark that must be preserved. The bishop sued in federal court, asserting that the 1993 act prevented the city from interfering with the church's decision to construct a new building.

By a 6-3 vote, the Court ruled that the 1993 act was unconstitutional. Justice Anthony M. Kennedy's opinion argued that section 5 of the Fourteenth Amendment gave Congress the power only to enforce the rights protected by the amendment, not to decree the substantive meaning of the amendment. The clear intent of the 1993 act was to veto a constitutional interpretation made by the Court. Kennedy insisted that such a challenge to the Court's proper authority is contrary to the U.S. tradition of separation of powers. Three justices dissented from the majority's continued support for the *Smith* decision.

Thomas T. Lewis

SEE ALSO *Employment Division, Department of Human Resources v. Smith*; Judicial scrutiny; Religion, freedom of; Reversals of Court decisions by Congress; Separation of powers; *Sherbert v. Verner.*

Bolling v. Sharpe

CITATION: 347 U.S. 479
DATE: May 17, 1954
ISSUES: Segregation; substantive due process
SIGNIFICANCE: The Supreme Court unanimously held that de jure segregation by the federal government violated the due process clause of the Fifth Amendment.

The *Bolling v. Sharpe* decision dealt with school segregation in Washington, D.C., and was announced the same day as *Brown v. Board of Education* (1954). The equal protection clause of the Fourteenth Amendment did not apply to acts of Congress, so the two cases had to be considered separately. Speaking for the Supreme Court, Chief Justice Earl Warren implicitly used a substantive due process interpretation of the Fifth Amendment. He stated that because segregation in education was not reasonably related to a proper governmental function, it imposed a burden on African American children that constituted "an arbitrary deprivation of their liberty." Ironically, Warren referred to the Japanese American relocation cases, in which the Court's opinions had recognized an "equal protection component" in the concept of due process. *Bolling* established that the federal government and the states are usually accountable to the same standards in equal protection cases.

Thomas T. Lewis

SEE ALSO *Brown v. Board of Education*; Due process, substantive; Education; *Hirabayashi v. United States*; Race and discrimination.

Bork, Robert H.

IDENTIFICATION: Supreme Court nominee (1987)
NOMINATED BY: Ronald Reagan
BORN: March 1, 1927, Pittsburgh, Pennsylvania
SIGNIFICANCE: One of the most bitterly contested appointments in U.S. judicial history, Bork's nomination to the Supreme Court created the precedent that a nominee's judicial philosophy could be a subject of intense scrutiny by the Senate.

On July 1, 1987, President Ronald Reagan, a Republican, announced that he would nominate

Former president Gerald R. Ford (left) introduces Supreme Court nominee Robert H. Bork, (center) to the Senate. Senator Robert Dole also commented on Bork's qualifications. (AP/Wide World Photos)

Bork, a former judge on the United States Court of Appeals for the District of Columbia, to fill the position on the Supreme Court vacated by retiring Justice Lewis F. Powell, Jr. The nomination elicited immediate and bitter response not only in the Democrat-controlled Senate but also from liberal and radical groups throughout the country. They were alarmed by Bork's well-known conservative views on legal matters, particularly because he embraced the principle of judicial restraint and original intent, and were also suspicious of his opinions concerning civil rights, free speech, and the right of privacy and of his alleged pro-business orientation. Normally, Senate hearings examine only a nominee's academic and judicial credentials, judicial temperament, and personal integrity. On these matters, Bork had a sterling record. However, the Senate, in a departure from customary behavior, closely scrutinized his judicial philosophy, including his political views. The Senate's Judiciary Committee eventually voted not to recommend Bork by a 9-5 vote, and the full Senate voted on October 23, 1987, against his confirmation by a 58-42 margin.

David C. Lukowitz

SEE ALSO Judicial self-restraint; Nominations to the Court; Original intent; Powell, Lewis F., Jr.; Privacy, right to; Reagan, Ronald.

Boudinot, Elias

IDENTIFICATION: Statesman and lawyer
BORN: May 2, 1740, Philadelphia, Pennsylvania
DIED: October 24, 1821, Burlington, New Jersey
SIGNIFICANCE: Boudinot, a New Jersey politician, was the first lawyer admitted to the Supreme Court bar.

Descended from a Huguenot family that fled France following the Revocation of the Edict of Nantes, Elias was the fourth Boudinot of that name. Trained in the law, he entered politics during the Revolution, serving in the New Jersey assembly and helping to ensure its support of the war effort.

In 1777 the Continental Congress appointed Boudinot commissary-general of prisoners. He became a close associate of George Washington. In November of 1777 Boudinot was elected to the Continental Congress, where he served until 1784. He signed the 1783 peace treaty with Great Britain. He was a member of a committee to draft plans for a federal court of appeals as well as rules governing state admiralty courts. The court of appeals apparently operated briefly during the period of the Confederation but was replaced by the Supreme Court in the 1789 Constitution. Boudinot was also a member of a committee appointed by the Constitutional Convention to consider the amendments proposed by James Madison that became the Bill of Rights. In February, 1790, he became the first attorney to practice before the Supreme Court. He was elected to the first, second, and third Congresses, and in 1795, he became director of the U.S. mint, resigning in 1805.

Nancy M. Gordon

SEE ALSO Bill of Rights; Constitutional Convention; Courts of appeals.

Bowers v. Hardwick

CITATION: 478 U.S. 186
DATE: June 30, 1986

ISSUES: Gay and lesbian rights; right of privacy

SIGNIFICANCE: The Supreme Court held that the U.S. Constitution does not protect a right to engage in consensual homosexual conduct.

By 1986 the Supreme Court had established that the due process clauses of the Fifth and Fourteenth Amendments protect a fundamental right to generic privacy, especially in personal choices relating to marriage, procreation, and child rearing.

Proponents of gay rights argued that the right of privacy should be extended to provide protection for homosexual practices, which would invalidate all legislation proscribing such practices. Michael Hardwick, in the privacy of his own bedroom, was arrested for violating Georgia's antisodomy law. Hardwick, with the assistance of the American Civil Liberties Union, used the arrest to challenge the constitutionality of the Georgia statute.

By a 5-4 vote, the Court upheld the statute. Speaking for the majority, Justice Byron R. White argued that the Court should be cautious about expanding the number of liberties based on the doctrine of substantive due process, and that the liberties protected under the doctrine should be limited to those that are "implicit in the concept of ordered liberty" and those that are "deeply rooted in this Nation's history and tradition." White noted that as late as 1961, all fifty states had criminalized homosexual conduct and that half of the states continued to do so. He warned against "judge-made constitutional law having little or no cognizable roots in the language or design of the Constitution."

In a concurring opinion, Justice Lewis F. Powell, Jr., wrote that the actual imposition of a criminal penalty for homosexual conduct would be contrary to the principles of the Eighth Amendment. After retiring, Powell told law students that he had "probably made a mistake" in voting with the majority.

Thomas T. Lewis

SEE ALSO Due process, substantive; Gay and lesbian rights; *Griswold v. Connecticut*; Privacy, right to; *Romer v. Evans.*

Bowsher v. Synar

CITATION: 478 U.S. 714
DATE: July 7, 1986

ISSUE: Separation of powers

SIGNIFICANCE: The Supreme Court ruled that it was unconstitutional for Congress to invest one of its own legislative officers with powers belonging to the executive branch.

Faced with continuing budget deficits, Congress set annual ceilings for deficits in the Balanced Budget and Emergency Deficit Control Act of 1985. If Congress failed to make the necessary budget cuts, the statute authorized the comptroller general to instruct the president concerning where to make the reductions. Representative Mike Synar and eleven other members of Congress challenged the constitutionality of the statute in the Supreme Court.

Speaking for a 7-2 majority, Chief Justice Warren E. Burger wrote that Congress could not delegate the comptroller general with powers to make decisions properly belonging to the president. Because the comptroller general was an agent of Congress and independent of the executive departments, the statute encroached on the president's duty to execute the laws. Thus, Burger's opinion relied on the relatively narrow principle of separation of powers and avoided the much broader nondelegation doctrine, which would have had great implications for the modern administrative state. Burger approved of the fallback provision of the 1985 statute, which allowed Congress to make the final budget decision by joint resolution, subject to presidential veto.

Thomas T. Lewis

SEE ALSO Appointment and removal power; Delegation of powers; Presidential powers; Separation of powers.

Boyd v. United States

CITATION: 116 U.S. 616
DATE: February 1, 1886
ISSUES: Fourth and Fifth Amendments; exclusionary rule
SIGNIFICANCE: The Supreme Court made expansive interpretations of the constitutional guarantees against compulsory self-incrimination and unreasonable searches and seizures.

The federal government charged New York merchants George Boyd and Edward Boyd with a civil offense for importing plate glass without paying the required duty. Using a federal statute, officials obtained a court order instructing the Boyds to produce the invoices for the goods. When the invoices were used as evidence, the Boyds claimed that the government had violated their rights under the Fourth and Fifth Amendments. The government argued that there had been no physical invasion of property and that the amendments applied only to criminal trials.

A unanimous Supreme Court ruled in favor of the Boyds and found part of the customs statute unconstitutional. Justice Joseph P. Bradley reasoned that the Fourth and Fifth Amendments combined with the common law to protect "the sanctity of a man's house and the privacies of life." The Fourth Amendment protected individuals from any procedures that had the same effect as a physical search. It applied to all proceedings with government penalties and permitted searches only for contraband articles not for mere evidence of an illegal action. A warrantless seizure, moreover, violated the Fifth Amendment prohibition against compulsory self-incrimination. Bradley declared that the courts should guard against any "stealthy encroachments" of constitutional rights.

The *Boyd* decision was a watershed in providing a liberal interpretation of privacy rights by joining the Fourth and Fifth Amendments to common law principles. Also, the decision initiated the development of the exclusionary rule. *Boyd*'s mere evidence rule, however, was eventually abandoned in *Warden v. Hayden* (1967).

Thomas T. Lewis

SEE ALSO Exclusionary rule; Fifth Amendment; Fourth Amendment; Search warrant requirement; Self-incrimination, immunity against; *Weeks v. United States.*

Bradford, Edward A.

IDENTIFICATION: Supreme Court nominee (1852)

NOMINATED BY: Millard Fillmore

BORN: September 27, 1814, Connecticut

DIED: November 22, 1872, Paris, France

SIGNIFICANCE: President Millard Fillmore, a member of the Whig Party who sought compromise on the divisive issue of slavery, nominated Bradford to the Supreme Court, but the largely

Edward A. Bradford. (Library of Congress)

proslavery Democratic Senate took no action on the nomination, thus leaving Bradford unconfirmed.

Bradford was in Connecticut and educated in the North, but he became prominent as a lawyer in New Orleans after moving there in 1836. President Millard Fillmore nominated Bradford for the Supreme Court after the death of John McKinley, a southerner. Bradford's politicized nomination was followed by those of two southerners, George E. Badger and William C. Micou, whose nominations also were not successful. Franklin Pierce, after succeeding Fillmore to the presidency, was able to succeed in replacing McKinley with John A. Campbell.

Bradford and Micou later joined a law firm with Judah P. Benjamin, a U.S. senator from Louisiana who became a member of the Confederate cabinet.

Eric Howard

SEE ALSO Badger, George E.; Campbell, John A.; McKinley, John; Micou, William C.; Nominations to the Court.

Bradley, Joseph P.

IDENTIFICATION: Associate justice (March 23, 1870-January 22, 1892)

NOMINATED BY: Ulysses S. Grant

BORN: March 14, 1813, Berne, New York

DIED: January 22, 1892, Washington, D.C.

SIGNIFICANCE: As a Supreme Court justice, Bradley often dissented when the Court favored states' rights over the power of the national government to regulate the economy. However, he voted with the majority to restrict the ability of Congress and the Constitution to protect women and African Americans from discrimination.

The eldest of twelve children born to a poor farming couple, Bradley inherited a lifelong love of learning from his parents. By the time he was sixteen, he had read most of the books in the town's library, taught himself algebra, and become a teacher in his local school. However, it was not until he was twenty years old that he began college. Always a hardworking student with a broad range of interests, he graduated from Rutgers College in three years. Originally intending to study theology, Bradley soon turned to the study of law. After graduation, he apprenticed for the bar in the office of a Newark, New Jersey, lawyer.

Soon after his admission to the bar in 1839, Bradley rose to prominence in the New Jersey legal community. He spent most of his legal career as counsel for a number of railroads, eventually becoming general counsel, secretary of the board, and a member of the Executive Committee of the Joint Companies of New Jersey (which included the Camden and Amboy Line). Although New Jersey was a predominately Democratic state, Bradley joined the new Republican Party before the Civil War (1861-1865).

Appointment to the Court. On February 7, 1870, President Ulysses S. Grant nominated Bradley and William Strong to the two vacancies on the Supreme Court created by the resignation of Justice Robert C. Grier and enactment of the Judiciary Act of 1869, which restored the Court to its pre-Civil War membership of nine. On March 21, the Senate confirmed Bradley's nomination by a vote of forty-six to nine. He was sworn in two days later and served on the Court until January 22, 1892.

The appointments of Bradley and Strong came at a time when the Court was grappling with the important constitutional question of Congress's power to enact the Legal Tender Act of 1862. The Act required creditors to receive paper money issued by the United States in payment of debt. Although there is no evidence that Grant appointed Bradley and Strong with this issue in mind, both of these new justices voted to uphold the constitutionality of the act.

Fourteenth Amendment and Reconstruction. During his twenty-one-year service on the Court, Bradley participated in many of the decisions that endured as bedrock principles of states' rights. Therefore, although Bradley initially voted against the Court's evisceration of the privileges and immunities clause of the Fourteenth Amendment, he later became a solid member of the majority, sometimes writing for the Court, in cases repudiating Reconstruction legislation designed to protect the rights of newly freed African Americans to equality under the law. He also was a chief architect of the modern doctrine that the states are immune from suit in federal courts.

During Bradley's service, the Court had the task of defining the scope of the Fourteenth Amend-

Joseph P. Bradley (Library of Congress)

ment. In the Court's first decision, the *Slaughter-house Cases* (1873), a majority of the Court severely limited the reach of the privileges and immunities clause. In dissent, Bradley contended that the clause protected businesses from unreasonable state regulations. However, in *Bradwell v. Illinois* (1873), he voted with the majority to reject Myra Bradwell's Fourteenth Amendment challenge to an Illinois statute that barred women from practicing law. The case is as well known for Bradley's concurring opinion as it is for the result. Bradwell had no right to practice law, in Bradley's view, because "[t]he paramount destiny and mission of women are to fulfill the noble and benign offices of wife and mother. This was the law of the Creator."

Through a series of decisions, from 1870 to 1886, the Court contributed to the dismantling of Congress's Reconstruction plan and to the interweaving of racial segregation into the nation's social fabric. Bradley played a key role in these developments, generally by voting with the majority in cases such as *United States v. Cruikshank* (1876), which limited Congress's power to enforce the Fourteenth Amendment against the states, and *Baldwin v. Franks* (1876), which, along with *United States v. Harris* (1882), restricted Congress's authority to enact legislation protecting voting rights from state interference.

More specifically, Bradley helped make racial segregation immune from constitutional and congressional attack with his opinion in the *Civil Rights Cases* (1883), holding the Civil Rights Act of 1875 unconstitutional. Here, Bradley argued that neither the Thirteenth nor the Fourteenth Amendment gave Congress the power to enact the statute. Private discrimination, Bradley reasoned, was not a badge or incident of slavery that Congress could outlaw without "running the slavery argument into the ground." As to the Fourteenth Amendment, he argued, Congress could reach only discrimination carried on by the state itself, not the private acts of inns, theaters, and railroads. Bradley even suggested that the Civil Rights Act amounted to Congress treating African Americans as "the special favorite of the laws."

State Sovereign Immunity. The civil rights of African Americans was not the only question to plague the Court in the aftermath of the Civil War. The Court also confronted the vexing question of whether the southern states could escape from their war debts in a number of cases between 1883 and 1890. Here, Bradley's influence was large; he wrote the majority opinion for the Court in the most important of these cases, *Hans v. Louisiana* (1890). *Hans*, which is the cornerstone of the Court's modern Eleventh Amendment jurisprudence, stands for the proposition that the Constitution protects a state's sovereign immunity from suit in federal court. The soundness of the history and logic Bradley employed to reach the decision in *Hans* was questioned by numerous constitutional scholars and even other justices of the Court.

FURTHER READING

Fairman, Charles. "Mr. Justice Bradley." In *Mr. Justice*, edited by Allison Dunham and Phillip B. Kurland. Chicago: University of Chicago Press, 1956.

———. *Reconstruction and Reunion, 1864-88, Part I*. New York: Macmillan, 1971.

Friedman, Leon. "Joseph Bradley." In *The Justices of the Supreme Court: Their Lives and Major Opinions*, edited by Leon Friedman and Fred L. Israel. 5 vols. New York: Chelsea House, 1997.

Jacobs, Roger. *Memorials of the Justices of the Supreme Court of the United States.* Vol. 1. Littleton, Colo.: Fred B. Rothman, 1981.

Barbara Holden-Smith

SEE ALSO *Civil Rights Cases*; Eleventh Amendment; Fourteenth Amendment; Gender issues; *Legal Tender Cases*; Race and discrimination; Reconstruction; Strong, William.

Bradwell v. Illinois

CITATION: 16 Wall. (83 U.S.) 130
DATE: April 15, 1873
ISSUE: Sex discrimination
SIGNIFICANCE: The Supreme Court upheld a state's denial of the right of women to enter a profession traditionally reserved for men.

Myra Bradwell studied law with her attorney husband, and she edited and published the *Chicago Legal News*, a leading publication of the Midwest. Although she had passed the bar exam, her application for a state license to practice law was rejected solely because of her sex. She argued that her rights under the privileges and immunities clause of the Fourteenth Amendment were violated. By an 8-1 vote, the Supreme Court rejected her claim. Speaking for the Court, Justice Samuel F. Miller applied the restrictive interpretation of the Fourteenth Amendment that he had announced the previous day in the *Slaughterhouse Cases*. The granting of licenses to practice law was entirely in the hands of the states and therefore not related to any question of national citizenship. In a concurring opinion, Joseph P. Bradley noted: "The natural and proper timidity and delicacy which belongs to the female sex evidently unfits it for many of the occupations of civil life."

Although the Illinois supreme court allowed Bradwell to practice law in 1890, it was not until *Reed v. Reed* (1971) that the Court applied the Fourteenth Amendment to overturn discriminatory laws based on sex.

Thomas T. Lewis

SEE ALSO Equal protection clause; Gender issues; Privileges and immunities; *Reed v. Reed*; *Rostker v. Goldberg*.

Brandeis, Louis D.

IDENTIFICATION: Associate justice (June 5, 1916-February 13, 1939)

NOMINATED BY: Woodrow Wilson

BORN: November 13, 1856, Louisville, Kentucky

DIED: October 5, 1941, Washington, D.C.

SIGNIFICANCE: Brandeis's focus on the facts of the case was part of a philosophy of sociological jurisprudence. His sympathy for the weak and poor and opposition to big corporate and government control helped shape the political response to both the excesses of corporate America and government incursions against personal liberties.

Except for three years spent in Central Europe, Brandeis's formative years were not much different from those of other successful middle-class youth. He came from a very tightly knit, hard-working Bohemian German Jewish family and followed the American dream. He was an outstanding student at Harvard Law School and developed a commercial law practice in Boston.

The practice flourished, a testimony to Brandeis's skills as a lawyer: mastery of detail, logic of argument, clarity of communication, and focus on goals. His reputation spread and his wealth grew.

Louis D. Brandeis. (Library of Congress)

Along the way, however, he became interested in protecting the rights of those who were disadvantaged and suffered from the damages caused by rapid industrialization and the immense power of the new corporate giants.

The Two Passions. Much of Brandeis's work revolved around one central idea—the evil of bigness. He was convinced that excessive size and power were evil and incorrect. Bigness led to abuse of power and to corruption; moreover, it was inefficient, not just for the individual company but also for the society because it stifled competition.

For Brandeis, the issue was not simply economic—it was a moral crusade. Early on, in Boston, he started to fight big corporations: the railroad company that sought to monopolize the local railway, big banks, and utility companies. As his practice grew, Brandeis became more involved in public law, offering his service for free—a very uncommon practice then. His success in the courtroom led to wider contacts and to cases across the county, of sufficient repute that he was called the "people's lawyer." In one such case, *Muller v. Oregon* (1908), Brandeis prepared a very detailed, long legal brief explaining in much detail the impact on women of working long hours. This practice became known as a Brandeis Brief.

Brandeis's success in attacking big corporations and big government brought him into contact with leading Progressives. Although raised a progressive, antislavery Republican, he later switched to the increasingly liberal Democrats and became close to Woodrow Wilson. Brandeis consulted closely with the president and became one of the architects for Wilson's "New Freedom" program, basically regulation of business excesses, including the Clayton Act, a 1914 antitrust statute.

The second major passion was Zionism. Raised without formal religion and with little identification as a Jew, Brandeis became committed to Zionism as an adult. Over the course of his lifetime, he became the most well-known leader of the American Zionist movement and a major activist on the world scene. His commitment to a Jewish state was built on his sympathy for the poor persecuted Jews of Eastern Europe and their need for a place of refuge.

On the Court. Brandeis's reputation preceded him to the Supreme Court. He examined closely the facts of the cases and continued to be unsympathetic to large institutions. Nevertheless, he learned to use judicial restraint. He believed that the Court should not usurp the role of the legislature and that the national government should not suppress attempts by the state legislatures to regulate their economies. However, he also thought that no level of government should infringe on personal liberty.

Brandeis challenged and eventually convinced the Court to stop using the due process clause of the Fourteenth Amendment to strike down economic legislation, including regulation of child labor, as an infringement on the freedom of contract. He dissented in a number of cases that struck down New Deal legislation; again, the Court came around to his position. Ironically, Brandeis personally opposed much of this legislation because it created too strong a national government.

Brandeis also helped reverse the rule whereby federal courts could not ignore state law in favor of federal common law, in *Erie Railroad Co. v. Tompkins* (1938). This rule had allowed commercial litigants to move their cases to the federal courts where they could evade state commercial regulation.

In the area of civil liberties, however, Brandeis did believe that the Constitution set out strictures on the government that also applied to the states, especially in the matter of speech. It was not the government's business to regulate what the people heard; Brandeis believed that the people were eventually capable of making the right decisions.

Dissenting in *Gilbert v. Minnesota* (1920), Brandeis suggested that the liberty guaranteed by the Fourteenth Amendment extended beyond property rights to include personal freedoms such as those found in the Bill of Rights. Five years later, in *Gitlow v. New York* (1925), the Court accepted this idea, at least for freedom of speech. Later, many of the other provisions of the Bill of Rights were incorporated and applied to the states. Brandeis later wrote one of the most eloquent defenses of free expression in *Whitney v. California* (1927). Beyond free speech, Brandeis argued for the inclusion of privacy as one of the fundamental rights. Brandeis's powerful dissent in the wiretapping case *Olmstead v. United States* (1928) was used forty years later to protect privacy against a series of limitations set by the states, including the right to an abortion.

Brandeis's reputation and words long outlived him on the Court. Few justices had as strong an impact on the guidelines for preparing legal briefs and the acceptance of the relevance of sociological facts. Years later, his vision of personal liberty became accepted as the dominant constitutional standard.

FURTHER READING

Dawson, Nelson L., ed. *Brandeis and America.* Lexington: University of Kentucky, 1989.

Mason, Alpheus T. *Brandeis: A Free Man's Life.* New York: Viking, 1946.

Paper, Lewis J. *Brandeis.* Englewood Cliffs, N.J.: Prentice-Hall, 1983.

Strum, Philippa. *Brandeis: Beyond Progressivism.* Lawrence: University of Kansas, 1993.

Urofsky, Melvin. *A Mind of One Piece: Brandeis and American Reform.* New York: Scribners, 1971.

Alan M. Fisher

SEE ALSO Brandeis Brief; *Erie Railroad Co. v. Tompkins*; Incorporation doctrine; *Muller v. Oregon*; *Olmstead v. United States*; Progressivism; *Whitney v. California*; Wilson, Woodrow.

Brandeis Brief

DATE: 1908

DESCRIPTION: Lengthy summarization of a case before the Supreme Court prepared by Louis D. Brandeis in defense of an Oregon law that limited the length of the workday for women in certain industries.

SIGNIFICANCE: The Brandeis Brief was a defining moment in the history of the Supreme Court. Instead of limiting his defense of reform legislation to current law, Brandeis used Progressive social and economic values as the basis for his defense. The success of his effort led to his methodology being employed by many others.

The Ku Klux Klan's right to express its views, however unpleasant to some others, was challenged in several cases, including Brandenburg v. Ohio *(1969). In this 1999 photo, the head of the New York Civil Liberties Union defends the Klan's right to hold a rally outside the state supreme court.* (AP/ Wide World Photos)

Eight years before he joined the Supreme Court himself, Brandeis gained national attention with the lengthy brief he prepared while counsel for the defense in *Muller v. Oregon* (1908). A Progressive, Brandeis was retained to defend Oregon's 1903 reform law limiting the length of the workday for women in certain industries. After a cursory two-page review of the legal issues, Brandeis advanced a comprehensive and persuasive argument that validated the Oregon law. Supported by a team of researchers, Brandeis used statistics, medical reports, and other studies to develop a brief that reflected the sociological approach favored by Progressivism. The court found in favor of his brief, thereby giving tacit approval to this method of argumentation. President Woodrow Wilson appointed Brandeis as associate justice on the Supreme Court in 1916.

William T. Walker

SEE ALSO Brandeis, Louis D.; Briefs; Gender issues; Labor; *Muller v. Oregon*; Progressivism.

Brandenburg v. Ohio

CITATION: 395 U.S. 444

DATE: February 27, 1969

ISSUES: Freedoms of speech and assembly

SIGNIFICANCE: The Supreme Court overturned the conviction of a man under a criminal syndicalism statute, ruling that the advocacy of illegal action could be punished only if it was likely to produce imminent lawless action.

Clarence Brandenburg, a Ku Klux Klan member, was convicted of violating a criminal syndicalism statute for appearing in a television report brandishing a shotgun and advocating racial strife. The Supreme Court, in a unanimous unsigned *per curiam* decision, found it unconstitutional for a state to impose a criminal syndicalist statute punishing the mere advocacy of the overthrow of the U.S. government.

This ruling overturned *Whitney v. California* (1927), in which the Court had upheld a similar statute, and brought an end to fifty years of largely futile efforts to make the vague clear and present danger test of *Schenck v. United States* (1919) work in varying circumstances. At times, this test allowed the government to prosecute for speech that demonstrated a bad tendency or, as in *Dennis v. United States* (1951), for plans to publish unpopular views. By insisting that the government must demonstrate that the action was likely to incite imminent lawless action before prosecuting, the Court provided a much more concrete test that substantially strengthened free speech and validated the imminence test suggested in Justice Oliver Wendell Holmes's dissent in *Abrams v. United States* (1919).

Richard L. Wilson

SEE ALSO *Abrams v. United States*; Bad tendency test; Clear and present danger test; Criminal syndicalism; *Dennis v. United States*; First Amendment; *Gitlow v. New York*; *Schenck v. United States*; Symbolic speech; *Whitney v. California*.

Branzburg v. Hayes

CITATION: 408 U.S. 665
DATE: June 29, 1972
ISSUE: Freedom of speech
SIGNIFICANCE: The Supreme Court ruled that the First Amendment did not provide journalists with a special testimonial privilege not enjoyed by other citizens.

Paul Branzburg, a reporter of a Louisville newspaper, wrote a series of articles about traffic in illegal drugs, using information from drug users who insisted on their anonymity. Subpoenaed by a grand jury, he refused to answer questions about his confidential sources. The Supreme Court consolidated the case with those of two other journalists who had refused to provide information to grand juries. By a 5-4 vote, the Court found that requiring their testimony was not an unconstitutional infringement on the freedom of the press. Justice Byron R. White's plurality opinion concluded that the public interest in law enforcement outweighed any incidental burden that journalists might have in obtaining confidential information. Throughout U.S. history, White wrote, the press had "operated without protection for press informants." In response to the media's vehement opposition to the *Branzburg* decision, some twenty-six states enacted shield laws allowing reporters to refuse to divulge their sources in limited circumstances.

Thomas T. Lewis

SEE ALSO *Cohen v. Cowles Media Co.*; Grand jury; Newsroom searches; Speech and press, freedom of.

Brecht v. Abrahamson

CITATION: 507 U.S. 619
DATE: April 21, 1993

ISSUES: *Habeas corpus*; Miranda rights
SIGNIFICANCE: When federal courts review challenges to trial errors involving Miranda violations, the Supreme Court held that the courts may overturn convictions only when the errors result in "a substantial and injurious effect or influence" on the outcome of the trial.

In a trial that resulted in Todd Brecht's conviction on charges of first-degree murder, the prosecutor made statements that were contrary to the Supreme Court's binding interpretations of *Miranda v. Arizona* (1966). The Court had previously held that the state had the burden of proving beyond a reasonable doubt that any constitutional error was harmless. In *Brecht*, a 5-4 majority of the Court voted to expand the "harmless error" standard in cases involving Miranda rights. Chief Justice William H. Rehnquist's opinion for the majority had the result of shifting the burden of proof from the state to the defendant filing a petition for a *habeas corpus* hearing in federal court.

Thomas T. Lewis

SEE ALSO Appellate jurisdiction; Habeas corpus; Miranda rights; *Miranda v. Arizona*.

Breedlove v. Suttles

CITATION: 302 U.S. 277
DATE: December 6, 1937
ISSUE: Poll tax
SIGNIFICANCE: The Supreme Court upheld the constitutionality of a state's poll tax that did not treat all people equally.

A Georgia law levied a poll tax of one dollar per year on all people between the ages of twenty-one and sixty, except for the blind and women who had not registered to vote. Payment of the tax was a prerequisite for voter registration. A white male citizen asserted that the law was an invidious discrimination, contrary to the principles of the Fourteenth and Nineteenth Amendments. The Supreme Court unanimously rejected the claim. In the opinion for the Court, Justice Pierce Butler declared that the exclusions from tax liability were reasonable in view of the special circumstances of the exempted groups. Butler also noted that the use of poll taxes as a condition for voting had long been accepted in U.S. traditions. The *Breedlove* decision was overturned in *Harper v. Virginia State Board of Elections* (1966).

Thomas T. Lewis

SEE ALSO Ex post facto laws; *Harper v. Virginia State Board of Elections*; Poll taxes; Twenty-fourth Amendment; Vote, right to.

Brennan, William J., Jr.

IDENTIFICATION: Associate justice (October 16, 1956-July 20, 1990)

NOMINATED BY: Dwight D. Eisenhower

BORN: April 25, 1906, Newark, New Jersey

DIED: July 24, 1997, Arlington, Virginia

SIGNIFICANCE: Supreme Court justice Brennan created a legal philosophy designed to advance the dignity of all people. The goal of his jurisprudence of "libertarian dignity" was a highly egalitarian and pluralistic order that extended broad protection for freedom of expression and individual self-determination.

The son of an Irish Catholic immigrant, Brennan graduated from the University of Pennsylvania (1928) and Harvard Law School (1931). He drew inspiration from his father who rose from laboring as a boiler attendant soon after arriving from Ireland in 1890 to become a city commissioner and director of public safety in Newark, New Jersey. After a tour of duty in World War II (1941-1945) and promotion to the rank of colonel in the U.S. Army, Brennan, a Democrat, soon found himself elevated to the New Jersey superior court in 1949 by Republican Governor Alfred Driscoll, then to the state supreme court in 1952.

Four years later, President Dwight D. Eisenhower, another Republican, announced that he had selected Brennan to fill Justice Sherman Minton's seat on the U.S. Supreme Court. The appointment of Brennan, a moderate Democrat, occurred during the height of the presidential campaign of 1956 and had definite political overtones. His selection was expected to be well received by Catholics in the Northeast and by Eisenhower Democrats. Brennan's emergence as a leader of the Court's liberal bloc by the early 1960's, however, led Eisenhower to regret his decision. By the time Brennan announced on July 20, 1990, that he was retiring from the Court for reasons of failing health, his authorship of trailblazing First and Fourteenth Amend-

ment decisions had made him the leading liberal jurist of the last half of the twentieth century. From affirmative action to gender discrimination to general freedom of expression, Brennan's opinions chartered new ground for post-New Deal America. For his efforts, he received the Medal of Freedom, the nation's highest civilian award, from President Bill Clinton on November 30, 1993. In a tribute to Brennan, Associate Justice Byron R. White bluntly declared that his former colleague would be remembered "as among the greatest Justices who have ever sat on the Supreme Court."

Role of the Judiciary. The foundational pillars of Brennan's jurisprudence can be found in his thoughts on the power of the judiciary and on the oath of office taken by judicial officials. Brennan's judicial activism was a product of the conviction that it is not possible to accept the deficiencies of U.S. politics, some in the form of unchecked majoritarianism, and simultaneously be faithful to the Constitution. His willingness to cast judges as active participants in the process of adjusting the

William J. Brennan, Jr. (AP/Wide World Photos)

meaning of the Constitution to suit new challenges and new times is a hallmark of his jurisprudence. He defended an expansive interpretation of the federal *habeas corpus* power and of rules of justiciability such as standing requirements that affect when and how the courts may use their authority. His aim was to open up the judicial department to the largest number of possible claimants. His opinion for the Court in *Baker v. Carr*, a 1962 Tennessee malapportionment case, opened the door to judicial review of challenges to state electoral arrangements. In 1971 Brennan invited aggrieved parties to use the courts for redress in cases involving federal officials who historically had been shielded from suits by the sovereign immunity doctrine (*Bivens v. Six Unknown Named Narcotics Agents*, 1971).

Of particular concern to Brennan were threats posed by the modern administrative state. Writing in dissent in a 1976 disabilities case in which the claimant asserted a constitutional right to an oral hearing before the suspension of benefits under the Social Security program, Brennan rejected the government's appeal to costs and the sufficiency of post-termination procedures (*Mathews v. Eldridge*, 1976). Lurking behind his defense of judicial superintendence of the constitutional system was a belief that the judicial oath represented a sacred obligation to work for the achievement of a society based on the principle of libertarian dignity. He once declared that members of the legal profession should not rest until they have done everything within their power to ensure that the judicial system does not contribute to the denial of rights or perpetuate suffering due to unredressed injuries.

First Amendment. The process of freeing expression from significant restraints was initiated before Brennan joined the Court. What came of age with his assistance was a vigorous judicial defense of self-expression that challenged the constitutional bona fides of restraints historically associated with promoting respect for political institutions (flag desecration laws) or protecting the American way of life (libel and obscenity regulations). A relatively early articulation of Brennan's views on freedom of expression appears in his opinion in *New York Times Co. v. Sullivan* (1964), a civil rights-related case that challenged a judgment rendered against the *Times* under an Alabama libel law. Declaring that "debate on public issues should be uninhibited, robust and wide-open," Brennan set out the now famous "malice rule" that requires public officials to show that allegedly offensive statements are made with "'actual malice'—that is, with knowledge that [they are] false or with reckless disregard of whether [they are] false or not" in order to recover damages. The effect was to make it extremely difficult for public officials to win libel cases. With the chilling effect of these types of suits reduced, the visual and print media enjoyed a measure of freedom unparalleled in U.S. history. Brennan extended the effects of *Sullivan* in 1971 in *Rosenbloom v. Metromedia* with a ruling that applied the malice test to a civil libel action based on a radio broadcast about a person's involvement in an event of public interest. The "public interest" principle significantly expanded the malice rule beyond its original application to public officials.

Brennan reaffirmed his commitment to preserving a wide-open public forum two years after *Rosenbloom* in a dissent in *CBS v. Democratic National Committee* (1973) in which he asserted that the preservation of "an uninhibited marketplace of ideas" requires that people have access to "forums of communication" that will permit the widest possible dissemination of their views. In the Pentagon Papers case, *New York Times Co. v. United States* (1971), he argued that the Court should make it extremely difficult for the government to enjoin the publication of information even about secret military affairs. The defense of uninhibited expression led him to overturn state and national efforts to restrict flag burning as a form of expression in his final years on the Court. When the Court in 1978 permitted the Federal Communications Commission to place a warning in the file of a radio station that had aired a "Filthy Words" monologue by comedienne George Carlin during daytime hours, Brennan characterized the ruling as "another in the dominant culture's inevitable efforts to force groups who do not share its mores to conform to its way of thinking, acting, and speaking." Five years earlier, he had dissented in two obscenity and pornography cases, *Miller v. California* and *Paris Adult Theatre I v. Slaton*, on the grounds that the states should exercise little control over the entertainment habits of consenting adults. For Brennan, the republic of the First Amendment must not only permit but also really invite people to "flout majoritarian conventions." He believed that it was up to the people to decide whether they wished to engage in provocative communication or hear such expression from others. His frankly stated ideal was a "marketplace unsullied by the censor's hand."

Fourteenth Amendment. Justice Brennan's role in articulating and defending expansive interpretations of due process and equal protection principles under the Fourteenth Amendment was similar to that he had played in interpreting First Amendment law. He skillfully used the due process and equal protection language of the Fourteenth Amendment to bring about an expansion in the sphere of individual rights and liberties. Brennan's major contribution in the Fourteenth Amendment due process area was not in first-time incorporation cases but in cases that went beyond questions having to do with whether specific Bill of Rights guarantees apply to state action. For example, Brennan defended pretermination hearings in welfare and disability benefits cases such as *Goldberg v. Kelly* (1970). In like fashion, he did not author separate opinions in groundbreaking substantive due process cases such as *Griswold v. Connecticut* (1965) and *Roe v. Wade* (1973), but he actively lobbied for extending the principles of these cases in *Cruzan v. Director, Missouri Department of Health* (1990) and *DeShaney v. Winnebago County Department of Social Services* (1989).

Notwithstanding the importance of Brennan's opinions in procedural and substantive due process cases, it is his authorship of major opinions dealing with the use of racial and gender classifications in equal protection clause cases that is principally responsible for the reputation he acquired in Fourteenth Amendment law. Brennan understood the potential of the equal protection principle for changing the United States. Especially noteworthy in this regard was his willingness to extend Congress almost unfettered power under section 5 of the Fourteenth Amendment to strike at discriminatory practices. He championed the so-called "benign" use of racial categories to remedy the lingering effects of historical discrimination in *Regents of the University of California v. Bakke* (1978) and *Metro Broadcasting v. Federal Communications Commission* (1990).

In *Katzenbach v. Morgan*, a 1966 voting rights act case, he combined the power of the necessary and proper clause with the deference applied in commerce clause cases to enhance the power of the federal government to address equal protection claims. It was Brennan who led the way in urging the Court to treat gender distinctions as inherently suspect in *Frontiero v. Richardson* (1973). He was as impatient with delays in purging outdated gender distinctions from the law as he was with delays in making good on the promise to end racial segregation in *Green v. County School Board of New Kent County* (1968).

Libertarian Dignity. By addressing the difficulties associated with New Deal-style coalitional politics (such as perpetuation of discriminatory practices and malapportionment) and the modern bureaucratic state, Justice Brennan's jurisprudence can be viewed as an effort to complete the work of the political and judicial liberals who preceded him. His conviction that the United States could satisfy its historical destiny only when it was fully reconciled to being a "facilitative, pluralistic" society and not an "assimilative, homogeneous" one was matched by the belief that the country had reached a point in its development when practice might be expected to fulfill the high demands of theory. His opinions make clear that he believed the time had come to insist on government action that liberated the human will by removing or weakening constraints on the pursuit of preferred lifestyles while also compensating the victims of such constraints, for example, indigents or illegitimate children. Believing that government has a moral obligation *to do* whatever it *can do* to ensure comprehensive protection for all rights and redress for all grievances, Brennan had no difficulty in concluding that government officials can be guilty of sins of omission as well as of commission.

Although leading Founders such as George Washington and James Madison were careful to guard the capacity of the government to govern the people and defended institutions and practices that pointed the people in the direction of law-abidingness, Brennan shrank what government might do in the name of self-defense while inviting people to affirm their individual dignity through robust and uninhibited expression. It is not unreasonable to ask whether Brennan was demanding a better world than political life can offer. It is, however, the purity of Brennan's defense of the ideal of authentic individualism that warrants his identification as one of the major figures of American liberalism in the twentieth century.

FURTHER READING

Peter Irons's *Brennan vs. Rehnquist* (New York: Alfred A. Knopf, 1994) uses the comparative method to accentuate the distinctive qualities of Brennan's jurisprudence and the role that he played as the dominant liberal justice during the last half of the twentieth century. *The Jurisprudence of Justice William J. Brennan, Jr.: The Law and Politics of "Libertarian Dignity"* by David E. Marion (Lanham, Md.: Rowman & Littlefield, 1997) presents a sober constitutionalist view of Brennan's opinions by offering frequent comparisons with the political and legal thinking of James Madison, John Marshall, Alexis de Tocqueville, and Abraham Lincoln. For a careful review of the events surrounding Brennan's appointment to the Court, see Stephen Wermiel's "The Nomination of Justice Brennan: Eisenhower's Mistake? A Look at the Historical Record," *Constitutional Commentary* 11 (Winter, 1994-1995): 515-537. A useful account of Brennan's first decade on the Court appears in Stephen J. Friedman's "William Brennan," in *The Justices of the United States Supreme Court, 1789-1969: Their Lives and Major Opinions*, edited by Leon Friedman and Fred L. Israel (New York: Chelsea House, 1969). Brennan summarized his own thoughts on constitutional evolution and interpretation in "Reason, Passion, and 'the Progress of the Law,'" *Cardozo Law Review* 10 (1988): 3-23 and "Address to the Text and Teaching Symposium," in *The Great Debate: Interpreting Our Written Constitution* (Washington, D.C.: The Federalist Society, 1986).

David E. Marion

SEE ALSO Constitutional interpretation; Due process, procedural; Due process, substantive; First Amendment; Flag desecration; Incorporation doctrine; Judicial activism; Judicial powers; Obscenity and pornography; Race and discrimination; Suspect classifications.

Brewer, David J.

IDENTIFICATION: Associate justice (January 6, 1890-March 28, 1910)

NOMINATED BY: Benjamin Harrison

BORN: June 20, 1837, Smyrna, Asia Minor (later Izmir, Turkey)

DIED: March 28, 1910, Washington, D.C.

SIGNIFICANCE: In more than two decades on the Supreme Court, Brewer was the intellectual

David J. Brewer. (Library of Congress)

leader of an activist majority that regularly declared unconstitutional government-imposed labor and industrial regulations and interpreted the Constitution to protect private property and economic laissez-faire.

Although born in Asia to New England missionary parents, Brewer returned to Connecticut in 1839, where he was reared in a climate of wealth and privilege. After graduating from Yale University at the age of eighteen, Brewer attended Albany Law School and was admitted to the bar in 1858. Shortly thereafter, he moved to Kansas to practice law in Leavenworth. Brewer served as commissioner of the federal circuit court, probate court judge, state district court judge, Kansas Supreme Court justice, and federal Eighth Circuit Court of Appeals judge.

In December, 1889, Brewer was nominated to the Supreme Court by President Benjamin Harrison. His nomination was approved in the Senate by a vote of fifty-two to eleven, and he took his seat on January 6, 1890. Brewer's record on the Court is a mixed one, although he is primarily remembered for his devotion to the protection of private property and his opposition to government regulation of the economy, labor unions, and laws protecting working people.

Writing the majority opinion for *In re Debs* (1895), Brewer upheld the power of the government to stop labor strikes. In *Lochner v. New York* (1905), he joined the majority in declaring unconstitutional a state law that established the maximum number of hours per day that bakers could work. In *United States v. E. C. Knight Co.* (1895), he joined the majority in reading the Sherman Antitrust Act of 1890 so that many monopolies would remain untouched by it. However, it was Brewer who wrote the unanimous opinion in *Muller v. Oregon* (1908) upholding a maximum-hour workday law for women employed in laundries.

On race issues, Brewer's record was similarly mixed. Although he opposed slavery and favored the rights of Asian immigrants (*United States v. Wong Kim Ark*, 1898) and American Indians (*Brown v. Steele*, 1880), he also held in favor of segregated railway cars (*Louisville, New Orleans & Texas Railway Co. v. Mississippi*, 1890) and voted to uphold a state law prohibiting integrated classrooms in private schools and colleges (*Berea College v. Kentucky*, 1908). Likewise, he also voted to uphold a Virginia law prohibiting women from joining the bar (*In re Lockwood*, 1894).

FURTHER READING

Brodhead, Michael J. *David J. Brewer: The Life of a Supreme Court Justice, 1837-1910.* Carbondale: Southern Illinois University Press, 1994.

Gillman, Howard. *The Constitution Besieged: The Rise and Demise of Lochner Era Police Power Jurisprudence.* Durham, N.C.: Duke University Press, 1993.

Michael W. Bowers

SEE ALSO *E. C. Knight Co., United States v.*; Labor; *Lochner v. New York*; *Louisville, New Orleans, and Texas Railway Co. v. Mississippi*; *Muller v. Oregon*; *Wong Kim Ark, United States v.*

Breyer, Stephen G.

IDENTIFICATION: Associate justice (August 3, 1994-   )

NOMINATED BY: Bill Clinton

BORN: August 15, 1938, San Francisco, California

SIGNIFICANCE: An expert in a wide range of regulatory fields, including antitrust, environmental, and administrative law, Breyer repeatedly re-

Stephen G. Breyer. (AP/Wide World Photos)

jected the reasoning of the more conservative majority in a series of important constitutional cases.

In 1964 Breyer graduated magna cum laude from Harvard Law School and worked as a clerk for Supreme Court justice Arthur J. Goldberg until 1967, when he took a job in the U.S. Department of Justice as a special assistant. Later in 1967 Breyer returned to Harvard Law School as a professor and in 1973 served as an assistant special prosecutor in the Watergate investigation. In 1980 he took a seat on the U.S. First Circuit Court of Appeals and later became its chief judge.

On March 13, 1994, President Bill Clinton nominated Breyer to fill Harry A. Blackmun's vacated seat on the Supreme Court. Confirmed by the Senate by a vote of eighty-seven to nine, Breyer began serving during the 1994 opening session of the Court. Although initially inexperienced in constitutional issues, he contributed to Court decisions with his understanding of the legal aspects of economic regulation, environmental issues, and administrative law. Considered a moderate and a pragmatist, Breyer has focused on the human impact of legal decisions, believing that constitutional interpretation must adapt to changing world conditions.

Alvin K. Benson

SEE ALSO Blackmun, Harry A.; Circuit courts of appeals; Clinton, Bill; Goldberg, Arthur J.

Briefs

DESCRIPTION: Written arguments submitted to the Supreme Court by the parties in the cases and other interested individuals or organizations. The documents are called briefs because the Court limits the scope and length of documents it permits to be filed.

SIGNIFICANCE: Briefs present the case to the Court in a clear and concise manner. As the first contact of the Court with the case, briefs have great influence on the justices.

Of the thousands of certiorari petitions filed each year, only about one hundred twenty cases are selected to be heard by the Supreme Court. Therefore, the importance of the briefs filed to the Court cannot be overstated. Although oral argument may provide a dramatic stage for presenting the case, the written briefs contain the advocate's best efforts in written persuasion, and the Court will have scrutinized the briefs before hearing oral argument.

Content of the Brief. Various briefs are filed with the Court. Each is required to be bound with a particular binding: blue for petitioner, red for respondent, yellow for reply briefs, green for *amicus curiae* briefs, gray for the solicitor general's briefs, and tan for appendices briefs. Under the Court rules, the briefs are generally limited to fifty pages and must adhere to certain requirements of order, format, and content. The brief for the petitioner, for example, must include the following sections in the order stated: Questions Presented, List of Parties and Corporations, tables of Contents and Authorities, Opinions Below, Jurisdiction, Statutes Involved, Statement of the Case, Summary of the Argument, Argument, and Conclusion. Although the Argument is the longest section in the brief, two sections in the preliminary parts of the brief are vitally important. In the Questions Presented section, counsel articulates the exact questions raised in the appeal, and in the Statement of the Case, counsel establishes the factual foundation on which the argument is based. Both these preliminary sections, although short, must provide the Court with a clear overview of the brief's position.

The Argument section of the brief thoroughly explains and promotes the party's position. An effective argument is written in clear, plain English and is well organized. Mere citation of cases never supplants the careful analysis and application of those cases to the issue before the Court. The analysis of a cited case involves demonstrating its relevance to the appeal, an analysis of the cited case's reasoning, and a demonstration of its application to the issue at hand, usually by analogizing the facts of the decided case to the facts of the issue now before the Court. The Argument will discuss not only favorable precedent but also that which opposes the proposition advanced. Because a decision by the Court usually has far-reaching policy implications, briefs must also contain persuasive policy arguments that illustrate the reasonableness of the argument promoted.

Some of the rhetorical devices used in the Argument section can be traced to classical antiquity where the term "rhetoric" was more closely attached to legal argument than it is today. Although these early arguments were indeed oral arguments, many of those rhetorical devices are seen in the Argument sections of effective briefs, including not only the discovery of available arguments but also their arrangement and rebuttal. Hence it is not unusual to identify various rhetorical devices being used by the skillful advocate.

Order and Procedure. The petitioner's brief is filed first, followed by the respondent's brief, which is followed in turn by the petitioner's reply brief. The petitioner's brief faces some special problems in that the petitioner's brief is written and filed without seeing the respondent's brief. Hence the petitioner must anticipate the arguments and the cases that the opposition may plan to use. The lawyer is also under an ethical obligation governed by the Code of Professional Responsibility, which requires that a lawyer disclose to the Court legal authority that is directly adverse to the client's position. Apart from the ethical obligation, it is effective advocacy to include hostile precedent because it provides the brief writer with an opportunity to present these cases in a light that still illuminates the strength of the position argued. Here the advocate must distinguish the unfavorable precedent from the present case on its facts, establish that the reasoning of the case is flawed, or show that to adopt the holding of the case would be bad policy. To overlook unfavorable precedent would play into the opposition's hands. The petitioner, by filing its brief first, has the advantage of defining the issues first so that the respondent must redirect the Court's attention rather than just argue the respondent's position. Well-written respondent's briefs are more than mere responses to the petitioner's brief; they are also able to weave their affirmative arguments into that response. Finally, the petitioner also has the right to a reply brief, a shorter brief, usually no more than twenty-five pages, that attempts to rebut arguments raised in the respondent's brief, somewhat similarly to the way the petitioner uses rebuttal on oral argument.

In a departure from tradition, in 1997 a brief in compact disk format was filed with the Court. This brief contained internal hypertext markup language (html) with electronic links to the record and cases cited in the brief.

Amicus curiae ("friend of the court") briefs are filed by individuals or organizations that, although not a party to the appeal, have an interest in the appeal. These briefs are filed only with the permission of both the party the brief favors and the Court. Controversial issues usually invite such briefs. Most *amicus* briefs are filed by the solicitor general on behalf of the federal government. In some years the Court may see as many as three thousand such briefs.

FURTHER READING

Aldisert, Ruggero J. *Winning on Appeal: Better Briefs and Oral Argument.* Notre Dame, Ind.: National Institute for Trial Advocacy, 1996.

Stern, Robert L., Eugene Gressman, and Stephen M. Shapiro. *Supreme Court Practice.* 6th ed. Washington, D.C.: Bureau of National Affairs, 1986.

United States Supreme Court. *Landmark Briefs and Arguments of the Supreme Court of the United States.* Washington, D.C.: University Publications of America, 1893-   .

Paul Bateman

SEE ALSO Brandeis Brief; Conference of the justices; Oral argument; Review, process of; Rules of the Court; Solicitor general.

Briscoe v. Bank of the Commonwealth of Kentucky

CITATION: 11 Pet (36 U.S.) 257
DATE: February 11, 1837
ISSUE: Fiscal and monetary powers

SIGNIFICANCE: Reflecting Chief Justice Roger Brooke Taney's bias toward states' rights, the Supreme Court allowed a state-owned bank to issue notes for public circulation as legal tender.

The U.S. Constitution prohibited states from issuing bills of credit, but the exact meaning of the term was unclear. In *Craig v. Missouri* (1830), the Supreme Court ruled that interest-bearing certificates issued by a state were unconstitutional bills of credit. In *Briscoe v. Bank of the Commonwealth of Kentucky*, however, the justices voted six to one to allow a state-owned bank to issue circulating notes. Justice John McLean wrote for the Court that the notes at issue were not unconstitutional because they were not issued directly by the state or backed by the faith and credit of the state. The justices at the time were very sensitive to the rights of the states and recognized the need for a circulating medium following the demise of the Bank of the United States. The decision allowed for greater state controls over banking and currency in the years before the Civil War.

Thomas T. Lewis

SEE ALSO Capitalism; *Craig v. Missouri*; Full faith and credit; States' rights; Taney, Roger Brooke.

British background to U.S. judiciary

DESCRIPTION: British ideas concerning common law and natural law and the English people's attempts to establish political and civil rights under a monarchy guided the Founders in forming the ideology and procedures of the new nation's judicial system.

SIGNIFICANCE: Although it has evolved over the years, the U.S. judicial system, including the Supreme Court, is deeply rooted in the philosophy and institutions of the British judiciary. Its emphasis on the rights of individuals reflects the ideas of British legal reformers who tried to restrain a monarchy wielding arbitrary power.

Selectively drawing from the British legal tradition as it existed in the late eighteenth century, the Founders created a system designed to limit political power and protect fundamental individual rights, while guaranteeing uniform interpretation of federal law in the diverse states.

The cornerstone document of British and U.S. judicial development is the Magna Carta (1215), an agreement forced on King John by irate barons. Among other things, the Magna Carta established the principle that no individual could be deprived of life, liberty, or property except by "the lawful judgment of his peers and by the law of the land." Also *habeas corpus* (production of charges and evidence) was made mandatory. The Magna Carta became the basis for civil liberties and the right to a fair jury trial in England. It eradicated previous feudal practices of trial by ordeal and trial by combat. It also set up the Court of Common Pleas (permanently residing at Westminster) as distinct and separate from the King's Bench. Still there was much joint jurisdiction. After 1215, new legal thought emanated from the King's Bench, while Common Pleas remained conservative. Writs were organized to try to standardize justice and bring common law into synchronization with equity. Also within a century of the signing of the Magna Carta, because of economic transformation during the

Edward Coke produced a four-volume set of scholarly treatises on common law that helped appellate courts determine how the law should be interpreted. (Courtesy of Art & Visual Materials, Special Collections Department, Harvard Law School Library)

Renaissance period, the Court of Exchequer emerged. This new court had jurisdiction over all revenue cases related to the British Crown. For the United States, the Exchequer Court would become the model for separate, financially oriented courts such as the Court of Claims, the Tax Court, and the Court of Customs and Patent Appeals.

Another important work in the development of British law was Edward Coke's four-volume set of scholarly treatises on common law, *The Institutes of the Laws of England* (1628-1644), although many did not relish his less than lucid writing style. The work was a major study of legal statutes, criminal law, and legal jurisdiction. Such treatise writers were extremely important in an age without standardized court reporting because their conclusions produced awareness in appellate courts about how the law of the land should be interpreted. Coke served under the Stuart kings as chief justice of the Court of Common Pleas (1606) and chief justice of the King's Bench (1613-1616). Coke believed law to be sovereign, even above kings, and that the common law would keep life and country secure for each English person. Coke used common law to struggle against ecclesiastical and royal prerogative courts, often using a loose interpretation of the Magna Carta to support his conclusions. He had the courage to invoke higher law, even against parliamentary statutes, thus setting the precedent for judicial review. Thomas Jefferson viewed Coke as essential to the understanding of law.

The Importance of Rights. Coke helped write the Petition of Right (1628), which banned abuses by the Stuart kings such as imprisonment without cause and implementing taxes without parliamentary consent. When Charles I refused to abide by these principles, Parliament passed the Grand Remonstrance (1640), which listed and condemned Charles's abuse of power. Both documents became the basis for the Declaration of Independence. They also spelled out types of abuses to be avoided in the creation of the new nation by writing a constitution restraining potential abuses of power at both the state and national level.

When the last Stuart king, James II, refused to learn the lessons of British legal evolution, he was overthrown in a nearly Bloodless Revolution (1688), justified by John Locke's social contractual theories. The new monarchs, William and Mary, were asked to sign a Bill of Rights (1689) that gave inviolable political and civil rights to the people and recognized Parliament's political supremacy. Excessive bail and cruel and unusual punishment were banned, and juries were to be impanelled to prevent tampering. A person arrested was to be assumed innocent until proven guilty. Protestant citizens had the right to bear arms, and parliamentary elections and speech in Parliament were to be free. Similar principles were enumerated a century later in the Bill of Rights to the U.S. Constitution, a document that became the basis for Supreme Court decisions about whether actions taken, even at the highest levels of government, violated basic individual rights. The English Bill of Rights was so influential that many American states adopted their own bill of rights before the federal government was organized.

Almost half the signers of the Declaration of Independence were lawyers, and the document borrowed heavily from the second of Locke's *Two Treatises of Government* (1690), which defined unalienable rights to life, liberty, and property accorded by natural law. According to Locke, people even had the right to form a new government if the former one produced a long series of abuses destructive of natural rights. He advocated the separation of powers but viewed the judiciary as part of the executive power. Partially for this reason, the last resort for clemency in criminal cases in the United States is the governor for each state and the president for the nation as a whole.

Lawyers also made up more than half of the delegates to the federal Constitutional Convention of 1787. With law libraries few and bare, most practiced law under primitive conditions. However, if they had one law book, it was William Blackstone's *Commentaries on the Laws of England* (1765-1769), a well-written survey of the principles of common law as derived from important decisions in British case law. Blackstone viewed law as supreme to any and all individuals, including the chief executive. For Blackstone, law operated under the principle of equality as set by the law of nature. Therefore, individuals endowed with reason could uncover those actions that were inconsistent with natural law or that threatened those natural rights given to each individual by nature and nature's god. In short, Blackstone was defining "unalienable rights" that would lead to individual happiness and the common good. He also viewed all human laws as

William Blackstone created a well-written survey of the principles of common law as derived from important decisions in British case law. He viewed law as operating under the principle of equality as set by the law of nature. (Courtesy of Art & Visual Materials, Special Collections Department, Harvard Law School Library)

falling under supreme law. It was a short step from Blackstone's conclusions to a Supreme Court.

The importance of British documents in setting rules of law that all reasonable people could follow oriented the American colonists toward writing similar documents, leading to the writing of the Constitution itself, the accompanying Bill of Rights, and the establishment of a Supreme Court in the Judiciary Act of 1789. The Founders wanted to make sure that the written provisions were understood and carried out in a uniform way.

Historical Evolution. Britain's legal philosophy and fundamental documents did not emerge in a vacuum. Rather they were the product of slow evolution over many centuries. From early medieval times, English law was common law, which was unwritten law based on tradition and customs. What mattered most in common law was getting to the facts of the case, usually through oaths in which others swore to evidence. Penalties for damages were determined by a person's worth to the community, an idea that became the basis of torts in

Anglo-American law. For major crimes, oaths were sworn before twelve leading nobles, a process that became the basis of the grand jury system. An important principle handed down by Anglo-Saxon England was that the law originated from the understood customs of the people. To make such customs more clearly known, King Alfred (849-899) issued dooms.

When William the Conqueror established Norman rule in England, he confirmed the customary Anglo-Saxon laws. Yet with the introduction of feudalism, nobles established their own manorial courts, the church established ecclesiastical courts, and the king established his own court, presided over by members of his household. After a period of civil war and lawlessness, Henry II (1154-1189) took responsibility for bringing about the king's peace in England. After organizing England into six circuits, he sent out itinerant judges to dispense standardized justice. He also used writs to transfer cases from manorial courts to the king's court, allowed direct appeals to his own court, and placed clerical crimes of a secular nature under the king's court. By the end of his reign, professional judges were emerging, principles of equity were assimilated into common law, and England was developing a concept of common courts and superior appellate courts. Because the control of law was a good means of centralizing power, Henry II made sure that the king's court sat at the apex. Jurisdictional disputes continued, however, and powerful nobles did not want to be subject to the king's law. Hence within a generation of Henry's death, conflict came to a head with the signing of the Magna Carta.

The dynamic conflict between royal law, common law, and equity principle produced a small number of influential legal theorists, the most influential of which was Henry de Bracton (1215-1265), the first judge to collect and record thousands of decisions in his court, thus inaugurating the use of the most recent precedents in making legal judgments. His *Concerning the Laws and Customs of England* (1250-1258), the first study of how the common law evolved, held that principles of law could be deduced from particular cases. Although he held that all legal jurisdiction was derived ultimately from the Crown, the individual serving as king derived his power from the law and was subject to it.

Practices. By the second half of the eighteenth century, English law had a great number of practices that the Founders chose to duplicate. English law contained countless kinds of appeals calling for different pleadings and forms. The high courts expounded the law, while the lower courts decided the cases following rules and principles articulated by the superior appellate courts. For the superior courts, decisions did not have to be based on precedents but also incorporated higher principles of equity and natural law. The U.S. Supreme Court with its powers of judicial review and the appellate court system followed similar imperatives.

In relation to the colonies, the British gave the Privy Council the right to review court work of the individual colonies to see if any fundamental aspects of British law were violated. The Privy Council had the right to declare such actions null and void. Although the colonists hated such actions, this power was given in 1789 to the Supreme Court over state courts of the former colonies.

To ensure their independence, U.S. Supreme Court justices were appointed for life. However, they were subject to impeachment for cause, a process pioneered by the British parliament. In the newly formed United States, Congress had the power to pass new statutes that superseded previous laws, just as Parliament had. However, Congress was expected to stay within the basic precepts set down by the Constitution and could have its actions nullified by the Court. This process of judicial review did not exist in Britain, where law lords in the House of Lords acted as the final court of appeals.

Strongly influenced by British judicial development in its foundation, the U.S. judiciary evolved, determining its own path during the nineteenth and twentieth centuries. However, at the first session of the Supreme Court on February 2, 1790, the justices dressed in clothing similar to that worn by English justices. They were cloaked not only in English costumes but also English principles, procedures, and practices.

FURTHER READING

A general starting point is Bernard Schwartz's *The Law in America: A History* (New York: McGraw-Hill, 1974), which provides a highly readable survey in chapters 1-3. Another excellent overview is Lawrence M. Friedman's *A History of American Law* (New York: Simon & Schuster, 1973). Gordon S. Wood's classic, *The Creation of the American Republic 1776-1787* (Chapel Hill: University of North Carolina Press, 1969), contains an in-depth view of the evolution of U.S. law as a selective choosing process from the British tradition. For the development of English law, J. H. Baker's *An Introduction to English Legal History* (3d ed., London: Butterworths, 1990) remains the most reliable source. An understanding of both common law and the British legal theorists who influenced U.S. law can be obtained from James R. Stoner, Jr.'s *Common Law and Liberal Theory: Coke, Hobbes, and the Origins of American Constitutionalism* (Lawrence: University Press of Kansas, 1992). Wayne Bartee and Alice Bartee's *Litigating Morality: American Legal Thought and Its English Roots* (New York: Praeger, 1992) provides interesting comparisons of U.S. and British legal viewpoints regarding sex, insanity, punishment, and legal ethics. Russell Kirk's *America's British Culture* (New Brunswick, N.J.: Transaction, 1993) makes meaningful cultural contrasts in a highly readable format. For a well-written though opinionated study of the philosophical foundations of the Supreme Court and the reasoning behind early decisions, read Matthew J. Franck's *Against the Imperial Judiciary: The Supreme Court vs. the Sovereignty of the People* (Lawrence: University Press of Kansas, 1996).

Irwin Halfond

SEE ALSO Appellate jurisdiction; Bill of Rights; Common law; Constitution, U.S.; Declaration of Independence; Impeachment of judges; International perspectives on the Court; Judiciary Act of 1789; King, Edward; Natural law; Supreme Court of Canada.

British Law Lords

DESCRIPTION: Great Britain's court of last resort, composed of eleven distinguished jurists named by the British prime minister to life peerage in the House of Lords.

SIGNIFICANCE: Unlike the U.S. Supreme Court, the British Law Lords lack the power to declare the actions of other British national institutions unconstitutional, but they do have a modest power of judicial review by interpreting statutes and treaties.

The Law Lords are the court of last resort in Great Britain and, in this way, they are the closest institution in Britain to the U.S. Supreme Court. Despite the similarities between the British and U.S. common law systems in both theory and practice, the differences between the Law Lords and the Supreme Court are significant.

At the top of the U.S. court system is the nine-member Supreme Court, while the British court of last resort contains eleven Law Lords. The Law Lords are distinguished judges appointed by the prime minister to be life peers in the House of Lords. With life tenure, the Law Lords have nearly the same immunity from removal that U.S. justices have, except that there is no regularly recognized power of impeachment in Britain. Instead of sitting as a unified bank of jurists, the Law Lords sit on cases in panels of three to five judges. The remainder of the Law Lords use a convention that regards the judgment of the three- or five-member panels as equivalent to rulings produced by all eleven lords. In theory, all the members of the House of Lords serve as the court of last resort, so this convention actually extends to the entire body. If an unusually large number of cases arise, the House of Lords may delegate its judicial power to the Lord Chancellor, retired law lords, or even other distinguished jurists among their members. The Law Lords are simply appointed by the Prime Minister in contrast to the American procedure of the president nominating and the Senate confirming the appointments of justices. Despite what might seem to be the more politicized process in Britain, the Law Lords appointed so far have not been narrow partisans; for customary practice requires them to be very distinguished in the law.

Both Britain and the United States accept basic principles of the common law, relying on judge-made decisions to a greater degree than they do on detailed codes as in Roman or code systems. Within that common-law tradition, Britain and the United States diverged after the American revolution and the ratification of the U.S. Constitution in that the United States came to rely more on statutory law than common law. The most obvious example is the decision to have a written constitution, or a "super" statute, replacing common law on the federal level and setting a "super" statutory standard against which all other statutes could be measured. Although the British refer to themselves as a constitu-

COMPARISON OF THE HIGHEST U.S. AND BRITISH COURTS

	United States	Great Britain
Name of court	Supreme Court	Law Lords of House of Lords
Power of judicial review?	yes	no
Number of judges	9	11, sitting in panels of 3 or 5
How selected	presidential appointment with Senate confirmation	prime minister appointments
Length of terms	life	life
Legal tradition	common law	common law
Written constitution	yes	no
Criminal system	adversarial	adversarial
Bill of rights	yes	no*
Degree of protection of the accused	moderate	low
Habeas corpus	yes, for 48 hours	no
Type of review	concrete; cases and controversies only may be brought by citizens; no abstract jurisdiction; no advisory opinions	concrete; cases and controversies only may be brought by citizens; no abstract jurisdiction; no advisory opinions

*As a signatory of the European Charter on Human Rights, Great Britain is subject to a form of judicial review from the European Court on Human Rights.

tional government, the British have no single document that can form the basis for judicial review.

Judicial Review. Clearly the U.S. and British judicial system differ in the United States' use of judicial review, which allows courts to strike down laws as being at variance with the Constitution. Unlike the U.S. system of separation of powers, the British maintain that Parliament is supreme; therefore, no constitution is higher and no institution exists to declare laws unconstitutional. Because there is no British constitution, there is naturally no Bill of Rights to protect the rights of the accused as there is in the United States. For example, the Constitution provides the guarantee of a writ of *habeas corpus* that does not exist in Britain. Britain's accused are not normally incarcerated for long periods without a trial, but occasionally people have been held for long periods without being charged with a crime. In such cases, no British court could declare the government's action unconstitutional.

To say that British courts cannot declare a law unconstitutional is not to say the courts are powerless, for they have the common-law power to interpret parliamentary statutes. Although they never declare parliamentary enactments unconstitutional, their interpretation is broad enough to include limits they derive from the "traditional" constitution included in the common law. Judicial review is also present in the British system in that the entire British government has signed treaties making it a part of the European Community and accepting the authority of the Court of Justice of the European Community and the European Court of Human Rights to enforce Britain's obligations under the treaties. Some antecedents to judicial review existed in Britain before the founding of the United States, but the United States carried judicial review much further with the U.S. Constitution. As judicial review becomes more popular globally, the concept is slowly being introduced into Britain in a form never previously seen.

FURTHER READING

Cappelletti, Mario. *The Judicial Process in Comparative Perspective.* Oxford: Clarendon Press, 1989.

Glendon, Mary Ann, Michael Wallace Gordon, and Christopher Osakwe. *Comparative Constitutional Legal Traditions in a Nutshell.* St. Paul. Minn.: West Publishing, 1982.

Kommers, Donald, and John Finn. *American Constitutional Law: Essays, Cases, and Comparative Notes.* Belmont, Calif.: Wadsworth, 1998.

Murphy, Walter F., and Joseph Tanenhaus. *Comparative Constitutional Law: Cases and Commentaries.* New York: St. Martin s Press, 1977.

Rasmussen, Joel, and Joel C. Moses. *Major European Governments.* 9th ed. Belmont, Calif.: Wadsworth, 1995.

Richard L. Wilson

SEE ALSO British background to U.S. judiciary; Common law; Constitutional law; Court of Justice of the European Communities; Delegation of powers; Democracy; Federalism; French Constitutional Council; German Federal Constitutional Court; International perspectives on the Court; Judicial review; Rule of law; Separation of powers; Supreme Court of Canada.

Bronson v. Kinzie

CITATION: 42 U.S. 311
DATE: February 23, 1843
ISSUES: Contracts clause; property rights
SIGNIFICANCE: Based on the contracts clause, the Supreme Court overturned debtor-relief laws restricting the rights of creditors to foreclose on mortgages.

Although the Supreme Court under Chief Justice Roger Brooke Taney sometimes limited the scope of the contract clause, *Bronson v. Kinzie* demonstrated its continuing commitment to enforce property rights under the clause. With the Panic of 1837, several states passed laws providing relief for debtors unable to make mortgage payments. Illinois passed two such laws.

By a 6-1 vote, the Court ruled that the contract clause prohibited state legislatures from modifying the terms of an existing mortgage. The purpose of the clause, wrote the chief justice, "was to maintain the integrity of contracts, and to secure their faithful execution throughout this Union." Although the *Bronson* precedent was upheld for many years, it was almost entirely abandoned in *Home Building and Loan Association v. Blaisdell* (1934).

Thomas T. Lewis

SEE ALSO *Charles River Bridge v. Warren Bridge*; Contracts clause; Ex post facto laws; *Home Building and Loan Association v. Blaisdell*; Nixon, Richard M.; *Powell v. Alabama*; *Sturges v. Crowninshield.*

Brown, Henry B.

IDENTIFICATION: Associate justice (January 5, 1891-May 28, 1906)
NOMINATED BY: Benjamin Harrison
BORN: March 2, 1836, South Lee, Massachusetts
DIED: September 4, 1913, Bronxville, New York
SIGNIFICANCE: Appointed to the Supreme Court largely for his expertise in admiralty law, Brown ultimately was remembered as the author of the 1896 opinion upholding the legality of "separate but equal" facilities for blacks and whites.

Born into a wealthy merchant family in South Lee, Massachusetts, Brown graduated from Yale University in 1856. He moved to Detroit, Michigan, three years later and studied law at a private law office, subsequently completing his legal education by attending lectures at both Harvard and Yale. Admitted to the bar in 1860, Brown was appointed deputy U. S. marshall for Michigan one year later and in 1868 resigned his position to begin a lucrative private practice in Detroit.

Republican Brown made an unsuccessful bid for Congress before securing an appointment by President Ulysses S. Grant as U.S. District Court judge for eastern Michigan. Appointed in 1875, he acquired a nationwide reputation as an authority on admiralty law. The large number of admiralty cases arising out of shipping on the Great Lakes made *Brown's Admiralty Reports* universally accepted as the final word on that area of the law. He also became a regular lecturer on that topic at Michigan University.

Henry B. Brown. (Library of Congress)

Appointed to the Supreme Court by Benjamin Harrison in 1890, Brown took his seat on January 5, 1891. He acquired a reputation for impartiality, patience, courtesy, and a willingness to admit past errors during his fifteen years of service. Justice Brown was viewed as a moderate who favored property rights over civil rights. Concurring with the majority in *Lochner v. New York* (1905), he rejected New York's maximum-hour workday law as a violation of contractual freedom. Brown also joined the Court in its unanimous ruling destroying the power of the Sherman Antitrust Act of 1890 in *United States v. E. C. Knight Co.* (1895). He was the only northern justice to vote to uphold the legality of the income tax in *Pollock v. Farmers' Loan and Trust Co.* (1895) and authored opinions sanctioning the acquisition of Puerto Rico by the United States. However, Brown's most famous (or infamous) opinion was in the 1896 case of *Plessy v. Ferguson*. By upholding a Louisiana statute allowing for "separate but equal" facilities in that state's public transportation system, he in effect incorporated the concept of Jim Crow into the U.S. Constitution and thus initiated a constitutional crisis that was not to begin to correct itself until the *Brown v. Board of Education* decision of 1954.

Brown's abilities were severely impaired when a malady cost him his sight in his right eye in 1900 and rendered him unable to work without the assis-

tance of others. The next year, Brown was further weakened by the death of his wife of thirty-seven years. Brown remarried in 1904 and retired from the bench two years later.

FURTHER READING

Glennon, Robert Jerome. *Justice Henry Billings Brown: Values in Tension.* Denver: University of Colorado Law Review, 1971.

Harvey Gresham Hudspeth

SEE ALSO Admiralty and maritime law; *Insular Cases*; *Plessy v. Ferguson*; *Pollock v. Farmers' Loan and Trust Co.*

Brown v. Board of Education

CITATION: 347 U.S. 483
DATE: May 17, 1954
ISSUE: Desegregation
SIGNIFICANCE: The Supreme Court unanimously held that de jure (legally mandated) segregation of the public schools was prohibited by the equal protection clause of the Fourteenth Amendment.

Following the Civil War (1861-1865), racial segregation in public accommodations and education—through so-called "Jim Crow" laws—was one of the major tools of the southern states for maintaining a social system of white supremacy. In *Plessy v. Ferguson* (1896), the Supreme Court allowed state-mandated racial segregation based on the separate but equal doctrine. In *Cumming v. Richmond County Board of Education* (1899), the Court simply ignored the equal part of the doctrine when it allowed a community to maintain a public high school for white students without any similar institution for African Americans. In *Gong Lum v. Rice* (1927), the Court explicitly recognized the "right and power" of the states to require segregation in the public schools.

The Challenge Begins. In the 1930's the Legal Defense Fund of the National Association for the Advancement of Colored People (NAACP) began to mount a serious challenge to the constitutionality of Jim Crow laws in education. Rather than confronting *Plessy* directly, the NAACP first concentrated on equality of opportunity at publicly funded law schools. Decisions such as *Missouri ex rel. Gaines v. Canada* (1938) and *Sweatt v. Painter* (1950) indicated that the Court would insist on substantial equality of educational opportunity. In *McLaurin v. Oklahoma State Regents for Higher Education* (1950), the Court recognized that the policy of required separation was sometimes relevant to educational equality. With these victories, Thurgood Marshall and other NAACP lawyers decided that the time was ripe to question the constitutionality of segregation in elementary and secondary education.

Linda Carol Brown, an eight-year-old black girl, was not allowed to attend the all-white school in her neighborhood of Topeka, Kansas. Her parents did not want her to be bused to the all-black school, which was far from home, and they filed a suit charging a violation of the Fourteenth Amendment. When the case was appealed to the Supreme Court, it was consolidated with similar cases from South Carolina, Virginia, Delaware, and Washington, D.C. The cases were listed in alphabetical order, so that the name *Brown v. Board of Education* appeared first. The cases were first argued in December, 1952. Marshall and other NAACP lawyers emphasized the psychological and sociological evidence of negative effects from mandated segregation. In defense of segregation, the school districts invoked *Plessy* and claimed that their all-black schools either had or would soon have equal funding for facilities and teachers' salaries.

The Court's Response. Because of the great opposition to school integration in the South, the justices recognized the desirability of presenting a united front in both the decision and the opinion. At least six of the justices agreed that *Plessy* should be reversed, but they strongly disagreed about how rapidly to proceed. One justice, Stanley F. Reed, argued on behalf of the continuation of *Plessy*, and another justice, Robert H. Jackson, wanted to move very cautiously and appeared determined to write a concurring opinion if the majority opinion were too critical of the Court's past approval of segregation. Deciding that it needed more information about the original intention of the Framers and ratifiers of the Fourteenth Amendment, the Court scheduled a second argumentation of the cases for December, 1953. That summer, Chief Justice Fred M. Vinson, a moderate who was hesitant to order massive desegregation, unexpectedly died, and he was quickly replaced by the popular governor of California, Earl Warren. After Brown was reargued, Warren convinced his colleagues to de-

fer the question of relief, and he skillfully consulted with the various justices in order to get a consensus. About a week before the decision was announced, Jackson decided not to issue a concurrence and Reed agreed not to dissent.

Warren's opinion for the Court, written in thirteen paragraphs of nontechnical language, declared that segregation in public education was "inherently unequal" and therefore unconstitutional. The public interpreted racial segregation of students "as denoting the inferiority of the Negro group," generating among African Americans "a feeling of inferiority as to their status in the community that may affect their hearts and minds in a way unlikely ever to be undone." Warren found that the historical evidence about the original intent of the Fourteenth Amendment was "inconclusive." Even if the Framers and ratifiers had not intended to prohibit segregation in education, they had wanted to provide equal rights for public services, and the

Thurgood Marshall (center) stands on the steps of the Supreme Court with the other lawyers of the Legal Defense Fund, NAACP, who argued Brown v. Board of Education. *(AP/Wide World Photos)*

experiences of the twentieth century demonstrated that segregated schools were incompatible with the goal of equality. Formal education in the twentieth century, moreover, was much more important for a person's life chances than it had been when the Fourteenth Amendment was written.

Implementing Desegregation. The following year, in a decision commonly called *Brown II*, the Court addressed the issue of implementing desegregation. The NAACP wanted to proceed rapidly with firm deadlines, and the states warned that rapid desegregation would lead to withdrawal from the public schools and acts of violence. The Court settled on a cautious and ambiguous formula, requiring that segregation end "with all deliberate speed." The implementation of *Brown II*, which left much discretion to federal district judges, proceeded somewhat slowly for the first ten years. In *Alexander v. Holmes County* (1969), the Court abandoned the deliberate speed formula and ordered an immediate end to all remaining de jure segregation.

Brown is probably the most momentous and influential civil rights case of the twentieth century. In effect, the decision meant the eventual elimination of all state-sanctioned segregation. When *Brown* was announced, its implications were unclear in regard to the constitutionality of freedom of choice plans and de facto segregated schools based on housing patterns. The Court began to move beyond the issue of de jure segregation in *Green v. County School Board of New Kent County* (1968), ruling that previously segregated school districts had an "affirmative duty" to take the steps necessary to promote racially integrated schools.

FURTHER READING

Kluger, Richard. *Simple Justice: The History of "Brown v. Board of Education" and Black America's Struggle for Equality.* New York: Alfred A. Knopf, 1976.

Martin, Waldo. *"Brown v. Board of Education": A Brief History with Documents.* Boston: Bedford/St. Martin's, 1998.

Sarat, Austin, ed. *Race, Law, and Culture: Reflections on "Brown v. Board of Education."* New York: Oxford University Press, 1997.

Whitman, Mark. *Removing a Badge of Slavery: The Record of "Brown v. Board of Education."* Princeton: Wiener, 1992.

Thomas T. Lewis

SEE ALSO *Bolling v. Sharpe*; Desegregation; Fourteenth Amendment; Legal Defense Fund, NAACP; *Martin v. Hunter's Lessee*; National Association for the Advancement of Colored People; *Plessy v. Ferguson*; Property rights; Race and discrimination; *Schechter Poultry Corp. v. United States*; Segregation, de jure; Separate but equal doctrine; Warren, Earl.

Brown v. Maryland

CITATION: 12 Wheat. (25 U.S.) 419
DATE: March 12, 1827
ISSUE: State taxes
SIGNIFICANCE: The Supreme Court held that a state tax on imported goods that were still in the original packaging and not mixed with other goods violated both the imports-exports and the commerce clause.

A Maryland statute required importers of foreign goods to purchase a license. The state claimed that a license tax on the importer was different from a tax on the import itself. By a 6-1 vote, the Supreme Court struck down the law. Chief Justice John Marshall enunciated the original packaging rule, which said that as long as imported goods were in the original packaging, a state tax was an unconstitutional violation of both the imports-exports and the commerce clause. Once imported goods became mixed up with other property, the state could tax them. This ruling enhanced federal powers without permanently insulating imported goods from state taxation.

In 1869 the Court decided that the original packaging rule did not apply to goods moving in interstate commerce. In *Michelin Tire Corp. v. Wages* (1976), the Court almost entirely abandoned the rule when it allowed states to assess nondiscriminatory property taxes on foreign imports in storage.

Thomas T. Lewis

SEE ALSO Commerce, regulation of; State taxation; *Woodruff v. Parham.*

Brown v. Mississippi

CITATION: 297 U.S. 278
DATE: February 17, 1936
ISSUES: Coerced confessions; defendants' rights
SIGNIFICANCE: The Supreme Court held that the due process clause of the Fourteenth Amend-

ment prohibited states from using criminal confessions obtained by means "revolting to the sense of justice."

In the early 1930's, three African American tenant farmers in Mississippi were convicted of murdering a white planter. The main evidence was their confessions. At trial, police officers admitted that they had employed brutal whippings and threats of death to obtain the confessions. The defendants, nevertheless, were convicted and sentenced to be hanged. The Mississippi supreme court upheld the constitutionality of their trials and convictions.

By a 9-0 vote, the Supreme Court reversed the state court's ruling. Chief Justice Charles Evans Hughes's opinion held that coerced confessions violated a principle "so rooted in the traditions and conscience of our people as to be ranked as fundamental." At the same time, however, the Court reaffirmed that the self-incrimination clause of the Fifth Amendment was not binding on the states. Despite its modest requirements, *Brown* was the first in a line of cases requiring fundamental fairness for the use of confessions in state trials.

Thomas T. Lewis

SEE ALSO *Arizona v. Fulminante*; Due process, substantive; *Escobedo v. Illinois*; Fifth Amendment; *Harris v. New York*; Incorporation doctrine; Miranda rights; Self-incrimination, immunity against.

Buchanan v. Warley

CITATION: 245 U.S. 60
DATE: November 5, 1917
ISSUE: Housing discrimination
SIGNIFICANCE: Emphasizing property rights, the Supreme Court struck down state laws that mandated racial segregation in housing.

Early in the twentieth century, many southern cities enacted ordinances that mandated residential segregation. Louisville, Kentucky, prohibited both African Americans and European Americans from living on blocks where the majority of residents were persons of the other race. The National Association for the Advancement of Colored People arranged a sale of property to test the law. Although the Supreme Court had consistently sanctioned segregation, it ruled unanimously that the Louisville ordinance was unconstitutional. In his opin-

ion for the Court, Justice William R. Day stated that the ordinance was an unreasonable restriction on the liberty of all people to buy and sell property, as protected by the due process clause of the Fourteenth Amendment. The decision showed that the protection of property rights and economic liberty could sometimes have the effect of promoting civil equality.

The *Buchanan* decision, however, was of limited impact for two reasons. First, it did not question the constitutionality of de jure racial segregation in areas such as education and transportation. Second, many private citizens began to enter into racially restrictive contracts, which were not rendered unenforceable until *Shelley v. Kraemer* (1948).

Thomas T. Lewis

SEE ALSO Contract, freedom of; Housing discrimination; Property rights; *Shelley v. Kraemer*.

Buck v. Bell

CITATION: 274 U.S. 200
DATE: May 2, 1927
ISSUE: Compulsory sterilization
SIGNIFICANCE: This case upheld the authority of states to require sterilization of any person deemed to be mentally defective.

In 1924 the Virginia legislature passed a statute that required the sexual sterilization of many "feebleminded" persons in state mental institutions. The law provided for procedural rights, including a hearing, appointment of a guardian, approval of an institution's board, and appeals to the courts. The superintendent of the Virginia State Colony for Epileptics and Feebleminded recommended sterilization for Carrie Buck, who was classified as feebleminded and a "moral delinquent." Because Buck's mother and daughter were also alleged to be mentally deficient, she was considered an ideal test case for the law. After state courts decided in favor of the state's position, the Supreme Court upheld the lower court decisions by an 8-1 vote.

Justice Oliver Wendell Holmes, writing for the opinion for the majority, found that the law did not violate any principles of equal protection and that its procedural guarantees were more than adequate. Accepting the eugenics notions of the day, Holmes argued that if society could call on its "best citizens" to sacrifice their lives in war, it could "call upon those who already sap the strength of the State for these lesser sacrifices." In this context, he made the notorious statement that "three generations of imbeciles are enough." Holmes had no way of knowing that Carrie Buck's child was the result of a rape and that she had actually done acceptable work in school until withdrawn by her guardians to do housework.

Subsequent to *Buck v. Bell*, many states passed similar sterilization laws, and more than fifty thousand persons were sterilized nationwide. The practice of sterilization, however, was generally discontinued by the 1970's. Although *Buck* was never directly overturned, it was based on eugenics theories later considered invalid and appears inconsistent with several of the Court's decisions upholding reproductive freedom.

Thomas T. Lewis

SEE ALSO Birth control and contraception; Equal protection clause; Fundamental rights; Gender issues; Privacy, right to; *Skinner v. Oklahoma.*

Buckley v. Valeo

CITATION: 424 U.S. 1
DATE: January 30, 1976
ISSUE: Campaign finance
SIGNIFICANCE: The Supreme Court held that Congress cannot limit the amount of money candidates for political office contribute to their own campaigns, although the Court permitted other limits on campaign spending.

This complex, confusing, unsigned Supreme Court opinion was a decision rendered by shifting groups of five justices on the several sections of the case that voided parts of the 1971 Federal Election Campaign Act. Five out of eight justices actually dissented in part (Justice John Paul Stevens did not participate), so only three justices fully supported the decision. The Court struck down limits on how much individuals could contribute to their own campaigns as an improper infringement on free speech but upheld limits on what others could contribute directly to federal legislative campaigns. The Court also ruled unconstitutional Congress's plan to appoint a majority of the Federal Election Commission, stating that it violated the clause that reserved appointment power for the president.

The Court approved public funding for campaigns but said that if a candidate accepted public funding, limits would be permissible. The Court allowed federal income tax checkoff funds for presidential primary candidates on a matching basis and for presidential general election candidates on a full-funding basis. In the 1985 case, *Federal Election Commission v. the National Conservative Political Action Committee*, the Court made it clear that limits could not be placed on those spending their own money independently to help a government-funded candidate.

Richard L. Wilson

SEE ALSO Bill of Rights; Delegation of powers; Elections; Financing political speech; First Amendment; *First National Bank of Boston v. Bellotti*; Political parties; *Rutan v. Republican Party of Illinois.*

Budd v. New York

CITATION: 143 U.S. 517
DATE: February 29, 1892
ISSUE: Regulation of private businesses
SIGNIFICANCE: The Supreme Court reaffirmed that state legislatures had great discretion in regulating businesses "affected with a public interest."

In 1888 the New York legislature passed a statute establishing maximum rates that grain elevators might charge. The Supreme Court had approved similar regulations of large and strategic businesses in *Munn v. Illinois* (1877), but it had ruled that rates of regulatory commissions were subject to judicial review in *Chicago, Milwaukee, and St. Paul Railway Co. v. Minnesota* (1890).

In *Budd*, the justices voted six to three to approve the New York law. State legislatures, in contrast to regulatory commissions, had the authority to decide on the fairness of rates without judicial review. The dissenters argued that the law violated the rights to property and liberty protected by the due process clause of the Fourteenth Amendment. The Court read *Munn* and *Budd* narrowly early in the twentieth century, but legislative discretion was restored during the New Deal period.

Thomas T. Lewis

SEE ALSO *Chicago, Milwaukee, and St. Paul Railway Co. v. Minnesota*; Due process, substantive; *Legal Tender Cases*; *Nebbia v. New York*; Property rights; *Wolff Packing Co. v. Court of Industrial Relations.*

Bunting v. Oregon

CITATION: 243 U.S. 426
DATE: June 12, 1917
ISSUE: Maximum-hour laws
SIGNIFICANCE: In upholding a state's maximum-hour law, the Supreme Court weakened but did not overturn the freedom of contract doctrine.

An Oregon law of 1913 established a maximum ten-hour working day for all men and women who worked in factories, mills, and other manufacturing plants. The law required time-and-a-half pay for any additional hours. Bunting, foreman of a mill, was convicted of violating the law. After Louis D. Brandeis was named to the Supreme Court, the National Consumers' League obtained the services of Felix Frankfurter to defend the constitutionality of the law. In *Muller v. Oregon* (1908), the Court had upheld a maximum-hour law for women, but it had stated that such a policy could not be justified if applied to men. By a 5-3 vote, nevertheless, the Court upheld the 1913 law as a reasonable way to preserve the health of workers. Although the majority of the justices were strongly opposed to minimum-wage laws, they approved of the time-and-a-half provision as a penalty designed to discourage overtime work, not as a regulation of wages. Justice Joseph McKenna's opinion for the majority was wholly inconsistent with the reasoning and conclusion of *Lochner v. New York* (1905), but the opinion omitted any reference to *Lochner.* Despite *Bunting*, the Court reaffirmed its commitment to the freedom of contract doctrine in *Adkins v. Children's Hospital* (1923).

Thomas T. Lewis

SEE ALSO *Adkins v. Children's Hospital*; *Allgeyer v. Louisiana*; Brandeis, Louis D.; Contract, freedom of; Due process, substantive; Labor; *Lochner v. New York*; *Muller v. Oregon*.

Bureaucratization of the judiciary

DESCRIPTION: Development of an administrative body within the federal judiciary.
SIGNIFICANCE: The bureaucratization of the federal judiciary and Supreme Court allowed the courts to distance themselves from the administrative power of the executive branch, giving them greater control over their own budgets and dockets.

Administrative capabilities developed more slowly in the courts than in either the legislative or executive branches. One of the first laws passed by Congress was the 1789 Judiciary Act. The act established lower federal district courts and the structure of the federal legal system for the next century. Throughout most of the nineteenth century, limited federal jurisdiction meant that the lower district courts were frequently underworked, while the Supreme Court was able to maintain its caseload without difficulty.

The bureaucracy that existed in the federal court system was confined to patronage positions controlled by each federal judge. There was no centralized authority over these judges, and the Supreme Court had limited oversight power. The budgets for the courts were drawn up by the Justice Department with little input from the judges. This decentralized system of justice functioned effectively until Congress created regulatory agencies whose decisions could be reviewed by federal courts. Suddenly district courts were overwhelmed with cases involving challenges to regulatory schemes. The backlog of cases prompted Congress to pass the 1891 Judiciary Act and add a layer of courts to the federal system. The circuit courts of appeals, which oversaw the work of district judges, reduced the Supreme Court's appellate caseload.

The 1925 Judiciary Act took an additional step in limiting the Supreme Court's workload by giving the justices control over their docket. After 1925 the justices could decide which cases they would hear. However, even after gaining control over the docket, the judiciary had little control over the administration of the court system. The Justice Department continued to act as the administrator of the courts. The U.S. attorney general was responsible for determining salaries of clerks and other support staff, hiring marshals, and auditing the use of federal money by district judges. The Justice Department also investigated judicial misconduct. In an effort to clear clogged dockets, the department also assigned judges to different circuits or districts.

Disagreements with the Justice Department prompted judges to try to remove administrative power from the department. With the appointment of William H. Taft to chief justice, control over administration became a major issue.

Three Administrative Institutions. One of Taft's first steps was the formation of the Judicial Conference of the United States in 1922. The conference, which consists of the chief justice, federal appeals court judges, and district court judges, meets twice a year to discuss issues and problems within the federal judiciary. The conference's main role is to propose changes in the dispensation of justice, suggest legislation, and prepare a budget for the entire judiciary. The conference uses committees to study some specific problems. For example, Chief Justice William H. Rehnquist formed a committee to explore reform of the *habeas corpus* process. Chaired by former Justice Lewis F. Powell, Jr., the committee proposed limiting *habeas* appeals to federal courts, a suggestion made into law in 1995. Also, the conference's budget committee proposes to Congress the appropriations for the courts for each fiscal year.

With the conference in place, the judiciary moved to assert more administrative control over its budget and working conditions. A 1939 law formed the Administrative Office of the U.S. Courts. The legislation asserted judicial control over the courts' own budgets and appropriations. The office also audited expenditures, distributed resources, planned the construction or purchase of court buildings, and kept records of the decisions and issues before the courts. The office also provided information that the conference could use in making legislative suggestions to Congress. The 1939 legislation eliminated direct Justice Department control over the judiciary and placed it within the powers of an appointed official who worked for the courts.

A third institution created to aid federal courts in administration was the Federal Judicial Center. Formed in 1967, the center studied legal issues and methods of adjudication. The center conducts studies of management techniques used in federal courts and oversees whether judges are implementing the policies handed down by the Judicial Conference. The center also conducts training sessions for new judges, providing them information on how to efficiently dispense their caseloads. Each of these institutions placed more administrative control in the hands of judges and made the judiciary more independent of executive or legislative control. It also made the courts more efficient and able to hear more cases each year.

Internal Changes. As the federal courts became more efficient, it placed greater pressure on the Supreme Court, which was eventually forced to bureaucratize its own work. Chief Justice Warren E. Burger initiated reforms of the Court to handle the increased workload. In 1972 the Court began pooling the writs of certiorari to help process the thousands of certiorari petitions received by the justices each year. The petitions in the cert pool are divided equally among the clerks of the participating justices. The clerks prepare summaries of the petitions and distribute them among the other chambers. By dividing the tasks among the different chambers, the Court reduced the workload for each chamber and streamlined the process for determining whether certiorari should be granted in a case.

The Burger Court also experienced an increase in the clerical support for each justice. The number of law clerks increased to three per justice, and each chamber was provided the resources to hire an administrative staff. As a miniature bureaucracy formed within each chamber, the Court began to operate on the lines of nine individual law firms.

As the demands on the federal judiciary became greater, the judges created a bureaucracy that allowed for more efficient administration of justice.

FURTHER READING

Carp, Robert, and Ronald Stidham. *The Federal Courts.* Washington, D.C.: Congressional Quarterly, 1985.

Fish, Peter. *The Politics of Federal Judicial Administration.* Princeton, N.J.: Princeton University Press, 1973.

Surrency, Erwin. *History of the Federal Courts.* New York: Oceana, 1987.

Douglas Clouatre

SEE ALSO Burger, Warren E.; Certiorari, writ of; Clerk of the Court; Conference of the justices; Judiciary Act of 1789; Judiciary Acts of 1801-1925; Taft, William H.

Burger, Warren E.

IDENTIFICATION: Chief justice (June 23, 1969-September 26, 1986)

NOMINATED BY: Lyndon B. Johnson

BORN: September 17, 1907, St. Paul, Minnesota

DIED: June 25, 1995, Washington, D.C.

SIGNIFICANCE: Burger, who spent seventeen years on the Supreme Court, served the longest term as chief justice in the twentieth century, earning high praise for his achievement in judicial administration. As a jurist, Burger was most noted for his opinions on the separation of powers, desegregation, religion, obscenity, and procedure.

Burger was the fourth of seven children born to Charles Joseph and Katharine (Schnittger) Burger. His father worked as a railroad cargo inspector and salesman. Burger described his mother as running an "old-fashioned German house," instilling "common sense" in her children. Burger always loved the U.S. Constitution and wanted to be a lawyer, even as a young boy. Suffering from polio at age eight, he was kept home from school for a year, and his teacher brought many biographies of great judges and lawyers for the boy to read.

In high school, Burger was president of the student council, editor of the school paper, and a letterman in hockey, football, track, and swimming. He earned a scholarship from Princeton University but turned it down to stay at home and help support his family. Attending night school at the University of Minnesota from 1925 to 1927, he was president of the student council. He attended night classes at the St. Paul College of Law (later the William Mitchell College of Law) and graduated with his LL.B. magna cum laude in 1931. He sold life insurance while attending evening classes in college and law school.

Political Career. Burger started working in a law firm in 1931, made partner in 1935, and taught law at his alma mater. During the course of his law work, he met Republican Harold E. Stassen. Burger organized Stassen's successful campaign for governor in 1938.

In 1948 Burger went to the Republican Party National Convention, where he met Richard M. Nixon, another Stassen supporter. At the 1952 Republican convention, when Dwight D. Eisenhower emerged as a leading presidential hopeful, Burger was the key figure in a floor decision shifting Stassen support to ensure Eisenhower's nomination on the first ballot. Eisenhower was favorably impressed and in 1953 Burger was appointed U.S. assistant attorney general.

On June 21, 1955, Eisenhower nominated Burger to a judgeship on the District of Columbia Circuit Court of Appeals. His confirmation was stalled when discrimination charges were made by em-

Warren E. Burger. (Robert Oakes/Collection of the Supreme Court of the United States)

ployees whom Burger had fired for incompetence. Burger was finally sworn in on April 13, 1956. Burger developed an early interest in court administration and worked with the American Bar Association to create an efficient and competent federal judiciary. His critique of "moral neglect" by the Supreme Court in decisions on insanity and self-incrimination gained him national attention.

Appointment to the Supreme Court. On May 21, 1969, Burger was nominated as chief justice by President Nixon. Burger was to be the "law and order" appointee for whom Nixon had campaigned. He was confirmed by a Senate vote of seventy-four to three on June 9, 1969, with numerous endorsements from leaders of the American Bar Association and other bar groups. Departing chief justice Earl Warren swore him in on June 23, 1969.

Burger served seventeen court terms as chief justice, a tenure as chief justice exceeded only by John Marshall, Roger Brooke Taney, and Melville W. Fuller. On June 17, 1986, President Ronald Reagan announced Burger's resignation and the nomination of William H. Rehnquist to succeed Burger.

On September 26, 1986, at age seventy-eight, Burger officially retired as chief justice.

Burger and Judicial Administration. Even Burger's critics admit that he accomplished more in the area of judicial administration than anyone in U.S. legal history. Burger's greatest accomplishment was his innovation of improvements in judicial operations.

Burger contributed to judicial administration in at least six major areas. He added new administrative support to the Court with an administrative assistant to the chief justice, judicial fellows, public relations professionals, librarians, clerks, and vast improvements to the law library and technology of the Court. He continued his efforts with the American Bar Association in judicial education programs with the National Judicial College. He developed the Federal Judicial Center and National Center for State Courts to gather data on courts, research judicial reforms, and train and inform the judiciary. He convened lectures and colloquia to bring together key decision makers to discuss judicial administration. He urged training in actual legal skills and litigation practice in law schools, continuing education for lawyers, and programs such as the American Inns of Court. Burger is considered the father of alternative dispute resolution and court mediation, arbitration, and other alternatives to litigation.

Burger believed the greatest threat to the Court was its case docket overload, which had climbed from 4,202 cases and 88 signed opinions in the 1969 term to 5,158 cases and 161 signed opinions in the 1985 term. Burger was successful in lobbying Congress to limit the Court's mandatory jurisdiction docket, narrow federal three-judge court jurisdiction, place sanctions against attorneys for abuse of process, and create a special Court of Appeals for the Federal Circuit for expertise in patent, copyright, and trademark. He was not successful in such reforms as an Intercircuit Tribunal to take a burden off the Court for resolving conflicts between the federal circuits. Burger wanted a central judicial administrator similar to the Lord Chancellor of England, which did not come to fruition.

Burger as a Jurist. Burger proved to be difficult to categorize as a jurist. He was supposed to have been "Nixon's man" and lead the Court in a conservative revolution. Instead he rejected Nixon's arguments for executive privilege, limited congres-

sional oversight of the bureaucracy, joined to establish abortion rights, upheld school busing, and defended freedom for religious minorities. Some analyses conclude that Burger was neither conservative nor liberal but pragmatic and concerned with street-level implementation and administrative aspects of decisions. He was more concerned with efficiency and democratic accountability than in preserving tradition or some other conservative impulse.

As chief justice, Burger wrote 265 opinions of the Court in addition to separate concurring and dissenting opinions. Although this was a high output, most of his opinions have not endured as landmark decisions. Greatly distracted by judicial administration matters, Burger tended to assign the landmark decisions to others, and he believed in a limited role of the judiciary in resolving public controversies. However, he was most noted for three opinions on the separation of powers in the federal government, as well as a few opinions on desegregation, religion, obscenity, and procedure.

Separation of Powers. Burger's lifelong love for the Constitution is demonstrated by three landmark decisions on separation of powers. In *United States v. Nixon* (1974), a unanimous Court ruled against President Nixon and ordered him to comply with subpoenas of the special prosecutor investigating the Watergate Hotel burglary and other crimes. Burger rejected Nixon's argument of executive privilege to keep confidential the tape recordings of White House discussions. Separation of powers was preserved by the Court not only by affirming the special prosecutor's power of subpoena over the president but also in this "declaration of independence" of the Court by Burger and three other justices appointed by Nixon.

In *Immigration and Naturalization Service v. Chadha* (1983), Burger preserved separation of powers between Congress and the federal bureaucracy by striking down the legislative veto. The legislative veto allowed Congress to delegate duties to the Immigration and Naturalization Service to decide to deport individual aliens yet also revoke the specific immigration service decision to deport Mr. Chadha in a one-house legislative action. Although used by Congress in more than two hundred statutes since the 1930's, Burger reasoned that separation of powers did not allow Congress to take back agency decisions in this piecemeal fashion.

Bowsher v. Synar (1986) was Burger's last opinion of the Court. The Gramm-Rudman-Hollings Act of 1985 had created the office of comptroller general to identify spending reductions as mandated by the statute to balance the federal budget, an executive function. However, the comptroller general was removable from office by Congress. Burger concluded this crossover of function and removal powers was unconstitutional.

Other Landmark Decisions. Burger upheld the use of busing and other remedies to desegregate public schools in *Swann v. Charlotte-Mecklenburg Board of Education* (1971). He also developed a three-part constitutional test for public benefits to religion in *Lemon v. Kurtzman* (1971). Burger defended the freedom of religious minorities in *Wisconsin v. Yoder* (1972), refusing to require Amish parents to send their children to public high schools. His definition of obscenity in *Miller v. California; Paris Adult Theatre v. Slaton* (1973) allowed for local "contemporary community standards" rather than national definitions of obscenity. Other landmark decisions by Burger are not as popularly known to the general public but concern more technical court procedures, such as jurisdiction, and are in keeping with his intense interests in judicial administration.

Critics. Burger gathered many critics in his long tenure as chief justice. Scholars such as Vincent Blasi, in *The Burger Court: The Counter-Revolution That Wasn't* (1983), described him as a man of limited capacity with no discernable coherent philosophy. Burger's working-class background, night-school legal education, and pragmatic philosophy have all been subject to intense personal attack. Bob Woodward and Scott Armstrong in *The Brethren: Inside the Supreme Court* (1979) present a dismal portrait of Burger's leadership on the Court, alleging that even the old friendship between Harry A. Blackmun and Burger went sour. Justices Thurgood Marshall, John Paul Stevens, Potter Stewart, and Blackmun publicly aired their complaints about the Court's conflicts along with bitter personal criticisms of Burger.

However, Justice William J. Brennan, Jr., credited Burger with "boundless considerateness and compassion for the personal and family problems of every member of the Court" that kept relations cordial between justices of sharply divided philosophies. Justice Powell also claimed that good rela-

tions and comradeship existed between justices, and Justice Blackmun claimed to remain Burger's best friend to the end.

A Man and the Constitution. Before resigning from the Court, Burger was appointed chairman of the Commission on the Bicentennial of the Constitution of the United States by President Reagan in 1985. After resigning as chief justice, he regularly worked double shifts on the commission through the bicentennial of the ratification of the Bill of Rights in 1991. Burger believed it was more than coincidence that the two-hundredth birthday of the Constitution on September 17, 1987, was also his eightieth birthday. He described the greatest decisions of the Court in a book, *It Is So Ordered: A Constitution Unfolds* (1995).

FURTHER READING

Burger's personal papers are at the William Mitchell School of Law in St. Paul, Minnesota, and library staff at the Loyola University School of Law prepared *Warren E. Burger: A Bibliography of Works Written by and About the Chief Justice* (New Orleans, La.: Loyola University School of Law, 1984). Burger's account of his time on the Supreme Court is *It Is So Ordered: A Constitution Unfolds* (New York: W. Morrow, 1995). The Philippine Bar Association released a tribute book of Burger's opinions: *Significant Supreme Court Opinions of the Honorable Warren E. Burger, Chief Justice of the United States* (Manila, Philippines: Philippine Bar Association, 1984). In spite of Burger's importance on the Court, few scholarly biographies exist. Stanley H. Friedelbaum has a scholarly and well-written chapter on Burger's life on the Court in *The Burger Court: Political and Judicial Profiles*, edited by Charles Lamb and Steven Halpern (Urbana: University of Illinois Press, 1991). Carl Tobias surveyed Burger's many contributions to judicial administration in "Warren Burger and the Administration of Justice," *Villanova Law Review* 41 (December 15, 1996): 505-519. Phillip Craig Zane focused on Burger's concurring and dissenting opinions in his study, "An Interpretation of the Jurisprudence of Chief Justice Warren Burger," *Utah Law Review* 1995 (Fall, 1995): 975-1008. A symposium in *Oklahoma Law Review* 45 (Spring, 1992): 1-168, was entitled "The Jurisprudence of Chief Justice Warren E. Burger" and included scholarly analyses of Burger's opinions in several areas of law. Other related books by scholars that examine the Burger Court include Arthur L. Galub's *The Burger Court, 1968-1984* (Millwood, N.Y.: Associated Faculty Press, 1986), Vincent Blasi, ed., *The Burger Court: The Counter-Revolution That Wasn't* (New Haven, Conn.: Yale University Press, 1983), and Francis Graham Lee, ed., *Neither Conservative nor Liberal: The Burger Court on Civil Rights and Liberties* (Malabar, Fla.: R. E. Krieger, 1983). Popular books tend to focus on criticism of the Burger Court but give some insights into Burger's life. They include Bob Woodward and Scott Armstrong's *The Brethren: Inside the Supreme Court* (New York: Avon Books, 1979), Herman Schwartz's *The Burger Years: Rights and Wrongs in the Supreme Court, 1969-1986* (New York: Viking Press, 1987), and Bernard Schwartz's *The Ascent of Pragmatism: The Burger Court in Action* (Reading, Mass.: Addison-Wesley, 1990). Of course, many fine tributes and symposia have been assembled both surrounding Burger's retirement from the Court in 1986 and upon his death in 1995. The more complete of these tributes, such as *Texas Law Review* 74 (December, 1995): 207-236 and *William Mitchell Law Review* 22 (Fall, 1996): 1-65, feature writings by fellow justices, law clerks, judicial fellows, and close professional colleagues.

Bradley Stewart Chilton

SEE ALSO Blackmun, Harry A.; *Bowsher v. Synar*; Bureaucratization of the judiciary; Chief justice; *Immigration and Naturalization Service v. Chadha*; *Lemon v. Kurtzman*; *Miller v. California*; Nixon, Richard M.; *Nixon, United States v.*; Separation of powers; *Swann v. Charlotte-Mecklenburg Board of Education*.

Burr, Aaron

IDENTIFICATION: Vice president of the United States (1801-1805)

BORN: February 6, 1756, Newark, New Jersey

DIED: September 14, 1836, Staten Island, New York

SIGNIFICANCE: A politician, adventurer, and vice president of the United States, Burr presided over the impeachment trial of Justice Samuel Chase in the Supreme Court in 1805. Two years later, he was tried and acquitted of treason by Chief Justice John Marshall on circuit.

Burr was born into a distinguished family and studied theology and law at Princeton University, grad-

uating with honors in 1772. Following the Revolutionary War, he was admitted to the New York bar in 1782.

The 1800 presidential electoral college deadlocked between Burr and Thomas Jefferson, and the election was thrown to the House of Representatives. On the thirty-sixth ballot, Jefferson was chosen president and Burr vice president.

In 1804 Vice President Burr challenged Alexander Hamilton to a duel because, by Burr's standards, Hamilton had defamed him. Hamilton was killed in the duel, and Burr became a fugitive. He fled to the southwest where he envisaged a grand empire made up of Mexico and the states west of the Allegheny Mountains, which he thought would secede.

Burr returned to Washington to preside over the impeachment trial of Justice Samuel Chase in 1805. He ran the trial as a model of decorum and fairness, and Chase was not impeached. In the meantime, Burr's plan for a southwestern empire collapsed, and he was indicted for treason. His trial was presided over by Chief Justice John Marshall on circuit. Marshall was under pressure to convict Burr, but he narrowly interpreted the Constitution regarding treason, ruling that acts of treason required two witnesses. Burr was acquitted in September, 1807, but his public life was over.

Kenneth H. Brown

SEE ALSO Chase, Samuel; *Federalist, The*; Hamilton, Alexander; Jefferson, Thomas; Marshall, John; Martin, Luther; Treason; Wirt, William.

Burstyn v. Wilson

CITATION: 343 U.S. 495

DATE: May 26, 1952

ISSUE: Freedom of speech

SIGNIFICANCE: The Supreme Court held, for the first time, that films were a medium for expressing ideas and therefore deserved a degree of protection under the First and Fourteenth Amendments.

The film in question, *The Miracle*, was an Italian import that told the story of a peasant girl who, after being seduced by a stranger, gave birth to a son she believed to be Jesus Christ. The New York censors ruled that the film was "sacrilegious," and it was banned from the state. The practice of film censorship had been approved by the Supreme Court in its first ruling on films, *Mutual Film Corp. v. Industrial Commission of Ohio* (1915), which held that films were not covered by any constitutional guarantee of free expression because they were "business pure and simple."

The Court unanimously reversed the 1915 ruling and ruled that the vague concept "sacrilegious" was unacceptable as a standard for prior restraint. Justice Tom C. Clark's opinion for the majority argued that pre-exhibition censorship was justified only in exceptional cases, and that standards must not permit unfettered discretion by censors. Clark acknowledged that films, because of their special potential for harm, might enjoy less First Amendment protection than printed materials, but he refused to discuss whether states had a legitimate interest in censoring pornographic films.

Associate justice Harold H. Burton (right) poses with his family. (Library of Congress)

The prerogative of states to engage in film censorship was further restricted in *Roth v. United States* (1957), when the Court narrowly defined obscenity and ruled that any nonobscene expression of ideas was protected by the First and Fourteenth Amendments. In *Freedman v. Maryland* (1965), the Court continued to allow censorship of films but only under stringent procedures that include prompt judicial review.

Thomas T. Lewis

SEE ALSO Censorship; Obscenity and pornography; Prior restraint; *Roth v. United States*; Speech and press, freedom of.

Burton, Harold H.

IDENTIFICATION: Associate justice (October 1, 1945-October 13, 1958)

NOMINATED BY: Harry S Truman

BORN: June 22, 1888, Jamaica Plain, Massachusetts

DIED: October 28, 1964, Washington, D.C.

SIGNIFICANCE: Burton was the first Republican appointed as an associate justice on the Supreme Court by a Democratic president. Known for his thoroughness and for keeping tension among the justices to a minimum, Burton was a strong supporter of the Court's efforts in civil rights cases.

Burton graduated from Bowdoin College in 1909 and from Harvard Law School in 1912. For the next two years, he engaged in a private legal practice in Cleveland, Ohio, and then worked as legal counsel for a series of public utilities in Utah and Idaho. During World War I he served in an infantry regiment of the U.S. Army, achieved the rank of captain, and was awarded the Purple Heart and the Belgian Croix de Guerre.

After the war Burton and his wife returned to Cleveland, where he again established a private practice. In 1928 Burton was elected to one term as a Republican in the Ohio House of Representatives. From 1929 to 1932 he also served as the director of law for Cleveland. After serving a term as acting mayor of Cleveland from 1931 to 1932, Burton was elected mayor in 1935 and was reelected twice. In 1940 he was elected to the U.S. Senate, serving for four years and becoming a close associate of fellow senator Harry S Truman.

On September 19, 1945, Burton was nominated to the Supreme Court by President Truman, a

Democrat. Chief Justice Harlan Fiske Stone gave his advance approval of Burton, believing that his legislative experience would be helpful in establishing legislative intent in many cases. In his thirteen years on the Supreme Court, Burton wrote ninety-six majority, fifty dissenting, and fifteen concurring opinions. Wanting his opinions to be quickly and clearly understood, his writing style was direct and simple. His thoroughness required a vast amount of research by himself and his clerks.

Burton strongly supported the government in cases against subversion. He also strongly supported the Court's efforts in civil rights cases. For example, in *Henderson v. United States* (1950), he concluded that all people should be treated without discrimination in the operation of public transportation regulated by federal statutes. In labor cases, Burton typically upheld the rights of states to limit the picketing activities of unions. Burton and Justice Felix Frankfurter believed that picketing was not protected as a freedom of expression. In *Toolson v. New York Yankees* (1953), a case in which the Court reaffirmed the antitrust exemption of major league baseball, Burton dissented on the grounds that baseball should be treated as a big business. In addition to his duties on the Court, Burton wrote many articles about Court history, Chief Justice John Marshall, and the Supreme Court building.

Alvin K. Benson

SEE ALSO Antitrust law; *Brown v. Board of Education*; Frankfurter, Felix; Housing of the Court; Marshall, John; Subversion; *Yates v. United States*.

Burton v. Wilmington Parking Authority

CITATION: 365 U.S. 715
DATE: April 17, 1961
ISSUE: State action
SIGNIFICANCE: The Supreme Court held that a state agency may not lease public property to a private restaurant on terms inconsistent with the equal protection clause of the Fourteenth Amendment.

In *Burton*, the Supreme Court was asked to decide on the constitutionality of a segregated private restaurant located within a parking garage owned and operated by the city. William Burton, an African American, sued the city agency after he was denied service in the restaurant. By a 6-3 vote, the Court found that the city's association with the restaurant was sufficient to make it a party to the discrimination in violation of the Fourteenth Amendment. *Burton* illustrates the willingness of the Court under Chief Justice Earl Warren to expand the definition of state action in support of the Civil Rights movement. The public/private distinction became much less important after the Civil Rights Law of 1964 prohibited racial discrimination in private businesses open to the public. The doctrine of state action, nevertheless, continues to have significance in cases involving private clubs, as in *Moose Lodge v. Irvis* (1972).

Thomas T. Lewis

SEE ALSO Equal protection clause; *Moose Lodge v. Irvis*; Private discrimination; Race and discrimination; *Shelley v. Kraemer*; State action.

Butler, Charles Henry

IDENTIFICATION: Supreme Court reporter (1902-1916)
BORN: June 18, 1859, New York, New York
DIED: February 9, 1940, Washington, D.C.
SIGNIFICANCE: A lawyer who handled international affairs, Butler initially was pleased with his position as Supreme Court reporter but later found it somewhat boring.

Butler attended Princeton University but left before graduating. He studied law in his father's office, was admitted to the New York bar in 1882, and practiced law in New York in 1902. In 1898 he was a legal expert for the Fairbanks-Herschell Commission, which fixed the permanent boundary between Alaska and Canada. In December, 1901, Butler represented claimants before the Spanish Treaty Claims Commission on the responsibility of Spain for the destruction of the U.S.S. *Maine* in Havana harbor and the assumption of the United States of Spain's pecuniary liability for the injuries to, and death of, her officers and crew.

In 1902 Butler was appointed reporter of decisions for the Supreme Court; he produced volumes 187 to 241 of the *United States Reports*. However, his attitude toward the position evolved from enthusiasm in the beginning to a later sense that the reporter's job was monotonous and obscure. While Supreme Court reporter, Butler was appointed a delegate to the Hague Peace Conference in 1907 that dealt with international arbitration. He resigned from the Court in 1916 and practiced law in Washington, D.C., until his death.

Butler's publications include *Our Treaty with Spain: Triumphant Diplomacy* (1898), *Freedom of Private Property on the Sea from Capture During the War* (1899), *Treaty Making Power of the United States* (1902), *Index Digest of Opinions Delivered and Cases Decided by the Supreme Court of the United States During October Terms 1902, 1904 and 1905 and Reported in Volumes 187-202 Inclusive, United States Reports with a Table of Cases* (1906), and *A Century at the Bar of the Supreme Court of the United States* (1942).

Martin J. Manning

SEE ALSO Reporters, Supreme Court; Reporting of opinions; *United States Reports*.

Butler, Pierce

IDENTIFICATION: Associate justice (January 2, 1923-November 16, 1939)

NOMINATED BY: Warren G. Harding

BORN: March 17, 1866, Pine Bend, Minnesota

DIED: November 16, 1939, Washington, D.C.

SIGNIFICANCE: During seventeen years on the Supreme Court, Butler supported Court decisions that limited the authority of the states and the federal government to regulate private businesses. In the 1930's he was one of the Court's Four Horsemen, who consistently held New Deal legislation regulating economic affairs to be unconstitutional.

The son of Irish immigrants, Butler was raised on a farm in Dakota County, Minnesota. In 1887 he received a bachelor's degree from Carleton College. Admitted to the Minnesota Bar in 1888, Butler served from 1890 to 1896 as a prosecuting attorney for Ramsey County, Minnesota. He then entered private practice representing corporate clients and excelled as a courtroom attorney. In 1908 he was elected president of the Minnesota State Bar Association. He specialized in defending railroads in valuation cases that determined railroad rates and gained a national reputation when he defended the railroads before the Supreme Court in the *Minnesota Rate Cases* (1913).

On November 22, 1922, President Warren G. Harding named Butler to fill the vacancy created

Pierce Butler. (Library of Congress)

by Justice William R. Day's resignation. On December 21, 1922, Butler was confirmed by a Senate vote of sixty-one to eight. He took the oath on January 2, 1923, and served on the Court until his death on November 16, 1939.

During his Court tenure, Butler consistently supported laissez-faire legal doctrines that upheld the right of private businesses to operate without regulation by state and federal law. He voted against government regulation in every case involving freedom of contract that was decided by a divided Court. In rate and valuation cases involving railroads and utilities, Butler voted for the corporate position in all eighteen cases decided by a divided Court between 1924 and 1939. In 1935 and 1936 Butler and Justices George Sutherland, Willis Van Devanter, and James C. McReynolds were known as the Four Horsemen of the Court because they consistently voted together in Court decisions that held President Franklin D. Roosevelt's New Deal legislation regulating economic affairs to be unconstitutional.

The most significant Court opinion written by Butler was *Morehead v. New York ex rel. Tipaldo* (1936). His majority opinion in a 5-4 decision held that New York's law providing a minimum wage for women workers and minors was unconstitutional because it violated the due process clause of the Fourteenth Amendment, imposing an unconstitutional state interference with the freedom of contract between an employee and an employer. This decision, coming soon after Court decisions that held federal economic legislation unconstitutional, meant that both federal and state governments had minimal constitutional authority to regulate economic affairs. These Court decisions led to President Roosevelt's attack on the Court after his landslide reelection in 1936. The outcome was the judicial revolution of 1937, when moderate justices joined economic liberals on the Court to overturn laissez-faire precedents in Court decisions. When Justice Butler died in 1939, Roosevelt chose an economic liberal, Frank Murphy, as his successor.

FURTHER READING

Brown, Francis Joseph. *The Social and Economic Philosophy of Pierce Butler.* Washington: Catholic University Press, 1945.

Danelski, David J. *A Supreme Court Justice Is Appointed.* New York: Random House, 1964.

Friedman, Leon, and Fred L. Israel, eds. *The Justices of the United States Supreme Court: Their Lives and Major Opinions.* 5 vols. New York: Chelsea House, 1997.

Jim D. Clark

SEE ALSO Commerce, regulation of; Contract, freedom of; Contracts clause; Court-packing plan; Due process, substantive; Fourteenth Amendment; *Morehead v. New York ex rel. Tipaldo;* New Deal; Property rights; Roosevelt, Franklin D.

Butler, United States v.

CITATION: 297 U.S. 1
DATE: January 6, 1936
ISSUE: Taxing and spending clause
SIGNIFICANCE: The Supreme Court struck down the regulatory features of the Agricultural Adjustment Act (AAA) of 1933 as inconsistent with the Tenth Amendment, while at the same time interpreting the general welfare clause as pro-

viding an independent source of congressional power to spend public money for public purposes.

The first Agricultural Adjustment Act, in order to counter the devastating effects of the Great Depression on agricultural prices, authorized the payment of subsidies to farmers in exchange for a reduction in the production of agricultural commodities. The funding for the payments came from a processing tax levied on the processors of the commodities. William Butler and other receivers of a cotton processing company refused to pay the tax.

By a 6-3 vote, the Supreme Court ruled that the tax was unconstitutional. Speaking for the majority, Justice Owen J. Roberts argued that the processing tax was not a true tax for raising revenue but part of a system for regulating agricultural production, which was a power reserved to the states under the Tenth Amendment. In this part of his opinion, Roberts simply reaffirmed *Bailey v. Drexel Furniture Co.* (1922). Roberts then considered whether the subsidies could be justified by the general welfare clause. Although he found that Congress had broad authority to appropriate funds for the general welfare, he denied that Congress could impose regulations as a condition for receiving the funds.

In a famous dissent, Justice Harlan Fiske Stone argued that the act was a valid application of the taxing and spending power of Congress and referred to Roberts's opinion as "a tortured construction of the Constitution." Declaring that the Court should exercise self-restraint, Stone wrote: "Courts are not the only agencies of government that must be assumed to have the power to govern."

Although *Butler* expressed a preference for limited government, its interpretation of the general welfare clause provided later justification for the Social Security Act and other federal programs. In *Mulford v. Smith* (1939), Justice Roberts wrote the majority opinion that upheld the Agricultural Adjustment Act of 1938, despite its great similarity to the act of 1933.

Thomas T. Lewis

SEE ALSO Agricultural issues; *Bailey v. Drexel Furniture Co.;* Court-packing plan; General welfare clause; Judicial self-restraint; *Mulford v. Smith;* New Deal; *South Dakota v. Dole;* Taxing and spending clause; Tenth Amendment.

Butz v. Economou

CITATION: 438 U.S. 478
DATE: June 29, 1978
ISSUE: Executive immunity
SIGNIFICANCE: The Supreme Court held that high officials of the executive branch, with rare exceptions, do not have absolute immunity from civil suits.

Economou, a commodities dealer, filed a civil suit for $32 million, claiming that Secretary of Agriculture Butz had entered a false claim against him because of his criticisms of the department's policies. Citing Supreme Court precedents, Butz responded that he had absolute immunity from such a suit. Speaking for a 5-4 majority, however, Chief Justice Byron R. White declared that executive officials are entitled only to qualified good-faith immunity. Thus, officials are liable for damages if their illegal actions actually deprived a person of clearly established rights or if they acted with malicious intention in an attempt to cause harm or to deprive a person of constitutional rights. The Court allowed for exceptions for prosecutors and judicial officials within administrative agencies.

In *Harlow v. Fitzgerald* (1982), the Court modified the *Economou* ruling by eliminating the malicious intention test as a basis for bringing suits against officials. In *Harlow*'s companion case, *Nixon v. Fitzgerald* (1982), the Court found that the president did have absolute immunity for any actions stemming from his official duties.

Thomas T. Lewis

SEE ALSO *Clinton v. Jones*; Executive immunity; *Nixon, United States v.*; Separation of powers.

Byrnes, James F.

IDENTIFICATION: Associate justice (July 8, 1941-October 3, 1942)
NOMINATED BY: Franklin D. Roosevelt
BORN: May 2, 1879, Charleston, South Carolina
DIED: April 9, 1972, Columbia, South Carolina
SIGNIFICANCE: A judicial conservative who believed that the Supreme Court's role was to interpret rather than make law, Byrnes served on the Court for slightly more than a year although

James F. Byrnes. (Library of Congress)

his career in politics and public service lasted more than forty years.

Byrnes's first job in a career in politics and public service that spanned more than forty years was as a messenger boy in a law office. In 1900 he became the official court reporter in Aiken County, South Carolina. In 1903 he was admitted to the bar; the same year, he became editor and publisher of the *Aiken Journal and Review.* He was first elected to the U.S. House of Representatives in 1910 by a fifty-seven-vote margin. He served in this position until 1924, when he ran for the U.S. Senate but was defeated. After practicing law for six years, he again ran for the Senate and was elected. He served there for nearly eleven years until President Franklin D. Roosevelt nominated him for an associate justice seat on the Supreme Court. On June 12, 1941, the Senate unanimously confirmed his nomination.

During his tenure on the Court, Byrnes followed a philosophy of judicial conservatism. As a strict constructionist, he believed that the role of the Court was to interpret rather than to make law. He regarded the Court as the defender of the Constitution against actions by the president or Congress that violated that document. However, he believed that the activism of the Court had resulted in a situation in which Congress and the president had to defend the Constitution against the usurpation of legislative power by the Court itself. His best-known decision while on the Court was *Edwards v. California* (1941), in which he nullified a California statute that prohibited indigents from entering the state.

Byrnes served on the Court for slightly more than a year. In October, 1942, he resigned to head the wartime Office of Economic Stabilization. In May, 1943, he became director of war mobilization. President Roosevelt referred to Byrnes as his "assistant president"; however, Roosevelt did not select Byrnes as his running mate in 1944 because he was advised that a southern segregationist on the ticket would hurt his chances for reelection. Byrnes did, however, accompany Roosevelt to Yalta and Harry S Truman to the Potsdam Conference. He also served as Truman's secretary of state from July, 1945, to January, 1947. In 1946 *Time* magazine named him its "Man of the Year"—an honor it gave to persons having the greatest impact on the year's news. From 1951 to 1955 Byrnes served as governor of South Carolina. In 1953 he was appointed by President Dwight D. Eisenhower as a delegate to a session of the United Nations.

As governor of South Carolina, Byrnes concentrated on equalizing school funding for black and white schools in order to meet the Court's doctrine of separate but equal. When the Court declared the policy unconstitutional in *Brown v. Board of Education* (1954), Byrnes criticized the court for reversing the long-standing doctrine.

FURTHER READING

Brown, Walter J. *James F. Byrnes of South Carolina: A Remembrance.* Macon, Ga.: Mercer University Press, 1990.

Byrnes, James F. *All in One Lifetime.* New York: Harper, 1958.

Robertson, David. *Sly and Able: A Political Bibliography of James F. Byrnes.* New York: W. W. Norton, 1994.

William V. Moore

SEE ALSO Constitutional interpretation; *Edwards v. California*; Executive privilege; Judicial activism; Roosevelt, Franklin D.

C

Calder v. Bull

CITATION: 3 Dall. (3 U.S.) 368
DATE: August 8, 1798
ISSUES: Ex post facto laws; judicial review; natural law
SIGNIFICANCE: While ruling that the ex post facto limitation did not apply to civil laws, the Supreme Court justices debated the concepts of judicial review and natural law.

The Connecticut legislature passed a resolution that granted a new hearing in a probate trial. The disappointed litigants, Calder and his wife, contended that the resolution was an ex post facto law, which was prohibited to the states by the U.S. Constitution. By a 4-0 vote, the Supreme Court concluded that the term "ex post facto" applied only to retroactive criminal laws and not to laws dealing with civil matters. After much controversy, the Court reaffirmed this definition in *Collins v. Youngblood* (1990).

In *Calder*, the justices wrote seriatim opinions, discussing possible ways to decide the case. Justice Samuel Chase denied the "omnipotence" of the legislatures and asserted that "the very nature of our free Republican governments" will override and invalidate laws contrary to fundamental principles of "reason and justice." Justice James Iredell answered that judges did not have any right to invalidate a statute simply because they might consider it "contrary to the principles of natural justice," but he explicitly recognized the duty of the Court to strike down legislative acts that violate the Constitution. Beginning in the 1820's, the Court has assumed the validity of Iredell's theoretical perspective, but the natural law approach has sometimes reappeared, most often in the form of substantive due process.

Thomas T. Lewis
SEE ALSO Ex post facto laws; Judicial review; Natural law; Nominations to the Court.

California, United States v.

CITATION: 332 U.S. 19
DATE: June 23, 1947

ISSUE: Tidelands oil controversy
SIGNIFICANCE: The Supreme Court held that the federal government, not the states, had full dominion and mineral rights over the three-mile strip of submerged coastal lands.

The United States sued California in order to establish federal sovereignty over the offshore area three miles seaward from the low-water mark. Until then, the states had exercised de facto control over the area. The question was important because of huge oil and gas reserves that were being discovered. Speaking for a 6-3 majority, Justice Hugo L. Black found that the federal government had always possessed dominion over the entire coastal waters, even if it had allowed the states to control a three-mile strip. Black noted that the U.S. Constitution authorized Congress to decide the issue. Following an angry debate, Congress enacted the Submerged Lands Act of 1953, which gave title of the offshore lands to the coastal states.

Thomas T. Lewis
SEE ALSO *Powell v. Alabama*; Public lands; Reversals of Court decisions by Congress; States' rights; Tidelands oil controversy.

California v. Acevedo

CITATION: 500 U.S. 565
DATE: May 30, 1991
ISSUE: Automobile searches
SIGNIFICANCE: The Supreme Court held that the police may search either an automobile or a closed container in an automobile without a search warrant provided that the search is supported by probable cause.

The *Acevedo* decision established "one clear-cut rule" for searches of both automobiles and containers within automobiles. After 1925 the Supreme Court had allowed the police to stop and search moving vehicles on probable cause without a search warrant. In *United States v. Chadwick* (1977), however, the Court held that the police needed a warrant to search a sealed container, even when the container was located in an automobile. Then in *United States v. Ross* (1982), the Court allowed the police to search any containers that happened to be located in an automobile that was being searched on the basis of probable cause. The combination of *Chadwick* and *Ross* often confused judges and the police.

When the police observed Charles Acevedo put a brown bag into the trunk of his car, they had probable cause to think that the bag contained marijuana. Although the police had no other justification to search the car, they nevertheless took the bag from the trunk and opened the bag without getting a warrant. California courts, in conformity with *Chadwick*, ruled that the marijuana in the bag could not be used as evidence in a criminal trial. By a 6-3 vote, however, the Supreme Court reversed the *Chadwick* ruling. Justice Harry A. Blackmun's majority opinion argued that the Fourth Amendment's protection of privacy should not depend on "coincidences" such as whether the probable cause referred to the automobile or to the container.

Thomas T. Lewis

SEE ALSO Automobile searches; *Carroll v. United States*; Exclusionary rule; Fourth Amendment; *Ross, United States v.*; Search warrant requirement.

John A. Campbell. (Handy Studios/Collection of the Supreme Court of the United States)

Campbell, John A.

IDENTIFICATION: Associate justice (April 11, 1853-April 30, 1861)

NOMINATED BY: Franklin Pierce

BORN: June 24, 1811, Washington, Georgia

DIED: March 12, 1889, Baltimore, Maryland

SIGNIFICANCE: Campbell's opinion in the 1857 case involving slave Dred Scott cast him as a proslavery Southerner. As a lawyer before the Supreme Court in 1873, he argued that the Fourteenth Amendment should be used to limit state police powers in cases involving slaughterhouses.

A native of Georgia and graduate of the University of Georgia, Campbell moved to Alabama in 1830. A Democrat, he served in the state's legislature and practiced law, earning a reputation for sound arguments and superior writing. He began to argue cases before the Supreme Court in 1850, gaining favorable national attention.

Although Campbell defended states' rights and opposed abolitionism, he opposed Southern nationalists and only mildly endorsed slavery. His moderation made him attractive to Northern Democrats, and his Southern birth garnered support from Southern Democrats. Therefore, President Franklin Pierce nominated him to fill a seat on the Court that had been open for nearly a year. The sectional politics that marked his appointment colored his career on the bench.

As a justice, Campbell voted with the majority in *Scott v. Sandford* in 1857, which declared that Dred Scott remained a slave although he had resided in a free state. Campbell's vote in this case made him staunchly proslavery in many people's minds, but what he actually wrote in his opinion reveals a somewhat more moderate stance. He consistently argued that Congress could enact only laws pursuant to the powers enumerated in the Constitution. Although its Article IV gave Congress power to "make all needful Rules and Regulations" for territories under its jurisdiction, this power did not extend to interfering with the "relations of the master and slave." However repugnant in result, Campbell's opinion was not different in reasoning from his dissent in *Dodge v. Woolsey* (1856), in which he chided the Court for extending regulatory authority over state-chartered corporations without strict constitutional warrant.

Campbell used his office to back the national government to its fullest. In 1858 he convened a grand jury in Mobile to stop the filibustering expedition by William Walker, because filibustering violated the neutrality laws of the United States. The following year, he joined the other members of the Court in overturning the interposition of the Wisconsin supreme court in a matter involving the Fugitive Slave Act of 1850 because that act rested upon a specific constitutional authority and, under the Constitution, was the supreme law of the land.

Campbell resigned in 1861, the first year of the Civil War, and served for a time as assistant secretary of war for the Confederate States of America. In private practice after the war, Campbell represented butchers in New Orleans who ran afoul of a state law to regulate their trade. In the *Slaughterhouse Cases* (1873), Campbell held that the Louisiana regulation overextended police powers and interfered with the right to earn a living, making it an unreasonable law that wrongfully harmed an insular segment of the population. Campbell's novel use of the Fourteenth Amendment was rejected in this case but within two decades was embraced by the Court.

FURTHER READING

Saunders, Robert, Jr. *John Archibald Campbell: Southern Moderate, 1811-1889.* Tuscaloosa: University of Alabama Press, 1997.

Siegel, Martin. *The Taney Court, 1836-1864.* New York: Associated Faculty Press, 1987.

Edward R. Crowther

SEE ALSO Civil War; *Scott v. Sandford*; *Slaughterhouse Cases*; Taney, Roger Brooke.

Cantwell v. Connecticut

CITATION: 310 U.S. 296
DATE: May 30, 1940
ISSUE: Freedom of religion
SIGNIFICANCE: The Supreme Court broadly interpreted the religious exercise clause of the First Amendment and held that the clause was applicable to the states through the Fourteenth Amendment.

Newton Cantwell, an active member of the Jehovah's Witnesses, went door to door trying to make converts. A few people complained about his diatribes against the Catholic Church. Cantwell was arrested and convicted for violating a state law that required a license for soliciting funds.

By a 9-0 vote, the Supreme Court reversed the conviction and invalidated the law. Justice Owen J. Roberts's opinion for the Court emphasized that the Constitution protected religious conduct such as proselytizing. He wrote that a state may reasonably regulate the time, place, and manner of activities to prevent fraud or disorder, but it cannot entirely forbid unpopular conduct. The Connecticut law constituted a form of religious censorship because it gave public officials excessive discretion for approving or rejecting applications for licenses.

Thomas T. Lewis

SEE ALSO Incorporation doctrine; Jehovah's Witnesses; Religion, freedom of; Time, place, and manner regulations.

Capital punishment

DESCRIPTION: The killing of a convict by the state for purposes of punishment or to reduce future crime.

SIGNIFICANCE: The death penalty, although infrequently applied, has symbolic importance and has sharply polarized public opinion. The Supreme Court entered this fray only briefly, first to restrict executions, then to permit capital punishment, increasingly free of federal court supervision.

During the colonial period and the founding of the United States, the execution of convicts was not only routine but also a public spectacle. The hangman's noose, a humane alternative to beheading, was employed with a liberality that would disturb modern sensibility. In eighteenth century England, for example, it is estimated that approximately 240 crimes were punishable by death, with the sentence commonly carried out in the town squares. In contrast to millennia of practice, the nineteenth and twentieth centuries have seen a gradual civilization of punishment. Incarceration replaced execution for most crimes. Hangings were removed from public view and placed instead behind prison walls. The abolition of physical tor-

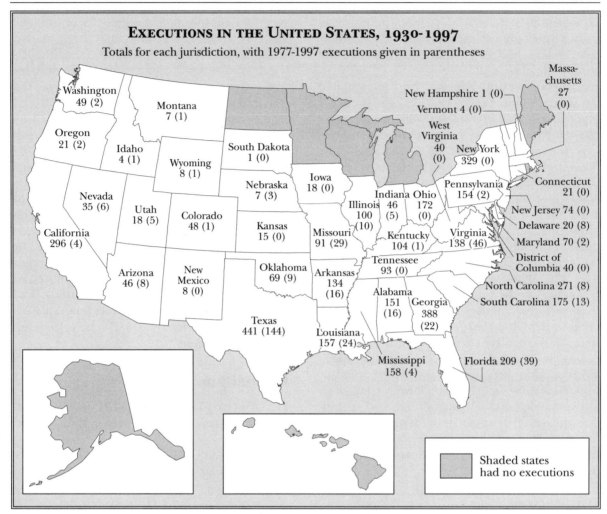

EXECUTIONS IN THE UNITED STATES, 1930-1997
Totals for each jurisdiction, with 1977-1997 executions given in parentheses

Washington 49 (2)
Oregon 21 (2)
Montana 7 (1)
Idaho 4 (1)
Wyoming 8 (1)
South Dakota 1 (0)
Nevada 35 (6)
Utah 18 (5)
Colorado 48 (1)
Nebraska 7 (3)
Iowa 18 (0)
California 296 (4)
Arizona 46 (8)
New Mexico 8 (0)
Kansas 15 (0)
Oklahoma 69 (9)
Missouri 91 (29)
Illinois 100 (10)
Indiana 46 (5)
Ohio 172 (0)
Kentucky 104 (1)
Tennessee 93 (0)
Arkansas 134 (16)
Texas 441 (144)
Louisiana 157 (24)
Mississippi 158 (4)
Alabama 151 (16)
Georgia 388 (22)
Florida 209 (39)
New Hampshire 1 (0)
Vermont 4 (0)
West Virginia 40 (0)
New York 329 (0)
Massachusetts 27 (0)
Connecticut 21 (0)
New Jersey 74 (0)
Delaware 20 (8)
Maryland 70 (2)
District of Columbia 40 (0)
Pennsylvania 154 (2)
Virginia 138 (46)
North Carolina 271 (8)
South Carolina 175 (13)

Shaded states had no executions

Note: There were 4,291 total executions, 1930-1997, including 33 prisoners executed in the federal system. The total for 1977-1997 of 432 prisoners executed includes no federal executions.
Source: U.S. Department of Justice, Bureau of Justice Statistics, *Capital Punishment 1997* (December, 1998).

ture as a legitimate part of punishment followed, eventually culminating in efforts to also circumscribe the infliction of psychological pain. Thus, the noose was replaced by electrocution, followed by the gas chamber, and more recently by lethal injection, all in a search of a humane method of depriving the convict of life, as the ultimate punishment. In the eyes of many ethicists, legal scholars, and moral leaders, the fulfillment of this historical trend would be the abolition of capital punishment altogether. In the United States, one of the last democratic nations retaining the death penalty, this debate has often acquired a constitutional dimension.

The Death Penalty and the Constitution. It is clear from the text of the Constitution that the Framers envisioned executions as a part of their legal regime. The Fifth Amendment provides that "no person shall be held to answer for a capital or otherwise infamous crime" absent an indictment by a grand jury. It further provides that no person shall "be subject for the same offense to be twice put in jeopardy of life and limb" nor be "deprived of life, liberty, or property without due process of law." The Fourteenth Amendment, adopted after the Civil War, similarly commands that no state shall deny any person "life, liberty, or property, without due process of law." Proponents of a contractual constitution, interpreted according to the historical intent of its Framers, are on apparently solid ground when they contend that the Constitution, in principle, sanctions capital punishment.

Opponents of the death penalty point to the same pair of due process clauses, promises of legal fairness, to condemn the application of the death penalty as arbitrary, capricious, even, in the words of Justice Potter Stewart, "freakishly imposed." They also point to the Fourteenth Amendment's requirement that states accord all persons the "equal protection of the laws" and raise questions concerning possible racial bias in the meting out of death sentences. Finally, and most tellingly, the Eighth Amendment's proscription of "cruel and unusual punishments" might provide a flat ban on capital punishment. The latter seems to have been adopted to end corporal punishments or the infliction of torture. However, in *Weems v. United States* (1910), the Supreme Court held that a constitutional principle "to be vital must be capable of wider application than the mischief which gave it birth." Abolitionists contend that these clauses create evolutionary constitutional rules, progressively driven by contemporary moral theory, that now proscribe the death penalty, regardless of accepted practice at the time of their adoption.

Judicial appeals to contemporary morality are always risky, especially regarding an emotionally contentious subject such as capital punishment. However, it is difficult to reconcile the death penalty, as practiced in the United States, with any of the common theoretical justifications for punishment. The death penalty is obviously not intended to accomplish the rehabilitation of the offender. There is little evidence in support of any general deterrence produced by the death penalty beyond that already achieved by incarceration and considerable evidence against the claim. Incapacitation of dangerous or repeat offenders can also be accomplished by means short of execution. Retribution, the theory that crime is a moral offense that must be redressed by the infliction of proportional pain to expiate the original offense, might justify capital punishment for heinous crimes, especially first-degree murder. The biblical injunction of "an eye for an eye and a tooth for a tooth" is a concise summary of retributive punishment. The problem is that retribution, if consistently followed, is a nondiscretionary punishment—a sentence pro-

portional to the crime *must* be carried out, with no room for mercy or selection. Proponents of capital punishment who appeal to retribution would have to countenance the execution of all defendants convicted of crimes for which capital punishment is authorized. The result would be a rate of executions unprecedented in U.S. history. Public opinion overwhelmingly supports capital punishment. However, polls and jury behavior also show that Americans want the death sentence to be employed sparingly.

The modern Court's initial foray into death penalty law was not encouraging to abolitionists. In *Louisiana ex rel. Francis v. Resweber* (1947), the Court rejected the contention that a second attempt at executing a prisoner, the electric chair having malfunctioned the first time, was either double jeopardy or cruel and unusual punishment. Despite the Court's permissive attitude, the number of execu-

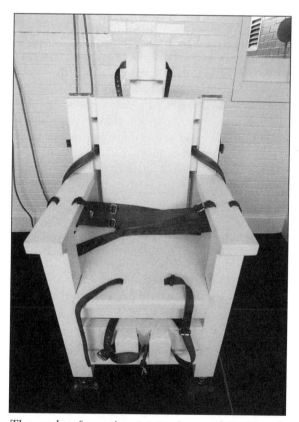

The number of executions per year increased significantly in the late 1990's, especially in southern states, such as Alabama. Pictured here is the electric chair at Holman Prison in Atmore, Alabama. (AP/Wide World Photos)

tions in the United States was already in decline. National statistics on executions date only from 1930, with 1935 the largest single year, with 199 executions. By the 1960's this number had declined to a trickle. Since the early 1980's, however, the number of annual executions in the United States has again been rising, especially in southern states. Sixty-eight executions were carried out in 1998.

The Death Penalty Moratorium. Encouraged by the Court's activism in civil rights and defendants' rights cases, death penalty opponents in the 1960's began a campaign to enlist the Court in the cause of abolition. The Legal Defense Fund (LDF) of the National Association for the Advancement of Colored People, later joined by the American Civil Liberties Union, orchestrated a threefold attack on capital punishment. First, the routine exclusion of "scrupled" jurors, those opposed to the death penalty on principle, was said to result in nonrepresentative juries skewed toward conviction and execution. Second, the determination of guilt and passing of sentence in a single trial procedure put defendants in an untenable position of having to offer evidence in mitigation of a crime they also contended they did not commit. Finally, the nearly complete discretion accorded juries in deciding when to impose death (the only sentencing question juries are called on to decide) resulted in an unpredictable, arbitrary, and discriminatory application of the death penalty.

In *Witherspoon v. Illinois* (1968), the Court banned the blanket exclusion of all scrupled jurors merely by virtue of their voicing objections to capital punishment. The state could still exclude those who would automatically or invariably vote against a death sentence, but not those expressing only "general objections" to capital punishment. The practical result of *Witherspoon* was to require commutation or resentencing of nearly all death sentences for prisoners then on death row. Until further litigation sorted out all potential *Witherspoon* claims, a de facto moratorium on capital punishment had been achieved. From 1967 until 1977, no executions were carried out in the United States.

Further LDF challenges to capital punishment were in the works. In *Furman v. Georgia* (1972), a fragmented Court adopted the third LDF critique of the death penalty as then practiced in all the states authorizing capital punishment, that unguided jury discretion produced arbitrary results.

Only Justices William J. Brennan, Jr., and Thurgood Marshall held capital punishment to be cruel and unusual punishment per se in contravention of the Eighth Amendment. Dissenters William H. Rehnquist, Warren E. Burger, Lewis F. Powell, Jr., and Harry A. Blackmun found no constitutional prohibition to unbridled jury discretion to mete out death and would have deferred on the issue to state legislative politics (although the latter eloquently expressed personal misgivings concerning capital punishment). This left Justices William O. Douglas, Potter Stewart, and Byron R. White to cast limited but decisive votes against Georgia's capital punishment statute. Douglas expressed concerns that the death penalty was applied disproportionately to poor and socially disadvantaged defendants, in effect reading into the Eighth Amendment an equality requirement. Stewart held that the rare imposition of death made capital punishment cruel and unusual in the minority of cases in which it was imposed. White agreed, arguing that its infrequency deprived the death penalty of any deterrent effect or ability to meet the test of retribution. For the first time, the Court had struck down a death sentence as cruel and unusual punishment. However, the long-term impact of *Furman* depended on the continued support of either Justice White or Justice Stewart, both centrists whose opposition to capital punishment seemed weak.

Public reception of *Furman* was immediate and hostile. Within a few years, thirty-five states had reenacted death penalty statutes purporting to meet the Court's objections. Three possibilities seemed available in the wake of *Furman*. States could enact mandatory death penalty statutes, imposing death in all cases where the death penalty was available, without discretion. This seemed to meet the objections of the Douglas, Stewart, and White bloc but would also have resulted in a large number of executions. A second option was to forgo death as a punishment altogether, but this seemed politically unlikely given the climate of public opinion. The third option was to enact guided discretion statutes, supplying juries with a host of aggravating and mitigating circumstances that would be considered in a separate sentencing phase of the trial, following a previous determination of guilt. This procedure met the LDF's second challenge to capital punishment, that the combined procedures for determining guilt and sentence imposed untenable choices on the defense. It also seemed to meet the issue of jury discretion head on, with neither the unpopular abolition of capital punishment nor the volume of executions that might follow adoption of mandatory capital punishment laws.

These laws came under the Court's scrutiny in *Gregg v. Georgia* (1976). Actually a compendium of five cases testing mandatory death penalty statutes in North Carolina and Louisiana and guided discretion statutes in Georgia, Texas, and Florida, *Gregg* also resulted in a badly fragmented Court. Justices Brennan and Marshall continued their per se opposition to the death penalty. Chief Justice Burger, along with Rehnquist, Blackmun, and White, voted to uphold all five death penalty regimes. As with *Furman*, the Court's decision rested on the centrists, now Justices Stewart, Powell, and John Paul Stevens. They approved of Georgia's death penalty regime, requiring a bifurcated procedure that separated the determination of guilt from the passing of sentence. In addition, before death could be imposed, a jury had to find beyond a reasonable doubt that at least one of ten aggravating circumstances had been met. Mitigating circumstances were also to be considered, and all death sentences were subject to mandatory appeal. Thus, a death penalty regime based on guided jury discretion now passed constitutional muster. The decision for a companion case, *Woodson v. North Carolina* (1976), specifically banned mandatory death sentences.

It is not at all clear that the death penalty regime approved in *Gregg* is able to meet the objections of jury discretion and arbitrary application of capital punishment that underlie *Furman*. Although subsequent litigation struck down jury guidelines that were deemed too vague, juries were still called on to consider unique circumstances pertaining to each case. Further inconsistency was introduced into the application of the death penalty through such practices as prosecutorial charging discretion, plea bargaining, and executive clemency. It thus appeared that *Gregg* marked a changed political sentiment on the part of the Court, perhaps even, as a practical matter, overruling *Furman*. With the decision in *Gregg*, the Court signaled a green light to executions. The death penalty moratorium came to an end in January of 1977, when the state of Utah executed Gary Gilmore by firing squad.

Race and the Death Penalty. The interest of the LDF in capital punishment should have surprised no one. It was long known that the death penalty was applied most frequently to society's outcast groups, especially the poor and members of minority groups. Over half of the convicts executed for all capital crimes between 1930 and 1995 were African Americans, far exceeding their proportion of the nation's population. Even more striking, of the 450 executions for rape between 1930 and 1965, more than 90 percent involved African American convicts. Criminologist Marvin Wolfgang, in a 1966 study, found that of 119 convicted rapists executed in twelve southern states between 1945 and 1965, 110 were black. The question remained as to whether these discrepancies could be explained by nonracial factors, such as a propensity to commit more heinous crimes.

A research team lead by David Baldus studied more than 2,400 criminal homicide cases in Georgia, from 1973 to 1980, tried under the death penalty regime approved in *Gregg*. Taking account of more than 230 separate characteristics of each case, they employed sophisticated statistical analysis to weigh the effect of each in producing death sentences. Their results found that, when adjusted for legitimate nonracial factors, the race of the *defendant* did not result in a strikingly disproportionate application of the death penalty. However, a strong correlation was uncovered between the race of the *victim* and the passing of a capital sentence.

In raw numbers, white or black killers of white victims were eleven times more likely to receive the death penalty than were killers of African American victims. Even when nonracial variables were factored in, killers of black victims were executed 4.3 times as often as were killers of whites. The discrepancy was inexplicable, except by the inference that race prejudice continued to affect the death penalty regime, even after *Gregg*. In fact, the race of the victim proved to be a stronger predictor of a capital sentence than such factors as the defendant's prior history of violence, that the victim was a police officer, or that the killing occurred during an armed robbery. The supposition drawn from these results was that prosecutors, when faced with the killer of an African American victim, were less likely to seek the death penalty or more likely to accept a plea bargain eliminating death. Alternatively, juries, even guided statutorily by nonracial aggravating and mitigating circumstances, were less likely to impose death for the killing of a black victim, perhaps valuing the life of a black person less highly than that of a white victim.

These data formed the basis for the LDF's next challenge to capital punishment, in *McCleskey v. Kemp* (1987), as violating both the Eighth Amendment and the equal protection clause of the Fourteenth Amendment. Such a disparate racial impact would seem to call into question the effectiveness of *Gregg* in eliminating the arbitrary or discriminatory factors in applying the death penalty that had informed *Furman*. However, writing for the Court, Justice Powell held that to make an equal protection claim, McCleskey had to demonstrate that either the Georgia legislature or the jury in his particular case was motivated by racial animus or a discriminatory purpose. The social background data revealed in the Baldus study were insufficient to make even a prima facie case that McCleskey had personally suffered from racial discrimination and, in any event, were more appropriately considered in a legislative forum. Similarly the discrepancy revealed in the Baldus study was insufficient to demonstrate a violation of the Eighth Amendment because it did not offend society's evolving standards of decency. Justices Brennan, Marshall, Stevens, and Blackmun dissented.

In *Furman* and *Gregg*, the Court had sought to remove arbitrary and capricious factors, presumably including racial prejudice, from the application of the death penalty in the United States. However, with *McCleskey,* the Court appeared to be turning its back on that promise by foreclosing the last avenue for arguing for the per se unconstitutionality of capital punishment. It did find in the Eighth Amendment limits to the kinds of crimes that could be deemed capital offenses. In *Coker v. Georgia* (1977), the Court found a capital sentence disproportionate to the crime of rape and therefore barred by the Eighth Amendment. Similarly, *Enmund v. Florida* (1982) barred the death penalty for a felony murder in which the defendant did not commit, nor intend or contemplate, the killing. However, this ruling was modified in *Tison v. Arizona* (1987) to permit sentencing to death of a codefendant in a felony murder in which there was major participation in the felony combined with reckless indifference to human life. These rulings indicate that the Court views the Eighth Amend-

ment as imposing substantive limits on the death penalty, at least concerning the issue of proportionality.

At the end of the twentieth century, thirty-eight states authorized the death penalty for first-degree murder. The federal government also authorized death for certain homicides, as well as for espionage, treason, or running a large-scale drug enterprise, but has not carried out a single capital sentence since 1963. As of April, 1999, 3,565 prisoners were on death row in the United States, while only 580 prisoners had been executed since 1977. Death row inmates are overwhelmingly poor and uneducated and disproportionately African American and southern. Many have suffered from inadequate assistance of counsel at trial. The most significant innovation by the Court in recent years has been the increasing of restrictions on the availability of federal *habeas corpus* review of state death penalty convictions and sentences. The apparent goal of the Court is to permit the states to apply post-*Gregg* death penalty law, largely absent federal judicial supervision.

FURTHER READING

Bedau, Hugo Adam, ed. *The Death Penalty in America: Current Controversies.* New York: Oxford University Press, 1997.

Cole, David. *No Equal Justice: Race and Class in the American Criminal Justice System.* New York: New Press, 1998.

Constanzo, Mark. *Just Revenge: Costs and Consequences of the Death Penalty.* New York: St. Martin's Press, 1997.

Haines, Herbert H. *Against Capital Punishment: The Anti-Death Penalty Movement in America, 1972-1994.* New York: Oxford University Press, 1999.

Hanks, Gardner C. *Against the Death Penalty: Christian and Secular Arguments Against Capital Punishment.* Scottsdale, Pa.: Herald Press, 1977.

Latzer, Barry. *Death Penalty Cases: Leading U.S. Supreme Court Cases on Capital Punishment.* Boston: Butterworth-Heinemann, 1998.

Mello, Michael A. *Dead Wrong: A Death Row Lawyer Speaks Out Against Capital Punishment.* Madison: University of Wisconsin Press, 1997.

Protess, David. *A Promise of Justice: The Eighteen-Year Fight to Save Four Innocent Men.* New York: Hyperion, 1998.

John C. Hughes

See also *Coker v. Georgia*; Constitutional interpretation; Cruel and unusual punishment; Due process, procedural; Eighth Amendment; *Furman v. Georgia*; *Gregg v. Georgia*; Habeas corpus; Legal Defense Fund, NAACP; *Louisiana ex rel. Francis v. Resweber*; *McCleskey v. Kemp*; Plea bargaining; Race and discrimination; *Weems v. United States*.

Capitalism

Description: Economic system based on private property, competition, and the production of goods for profit, with the market rather than a central government making decisions about production and distribution.

Significance: The Supreme Court's responsibility is to weigh the constitutional limits of governmental interference against the market's free operation. The Court defines the rules governing the market's operation, adjusts market mechanisms that are not functioning properly, and considers the claims of the many groups involved.

In a basically free-market economic system, the Supreme Court has been obligated to set restrictions on the power of the states and the federal government to intervene in the market's growth and direction. In the nineteenth century, the Court frequently cited substantive due process in rebuffing state proposals to regulate wages or free trade. It upheld freedom of contract, encouraged corporations, and regulated competition.

The Court tried to minimize political interference with capitalism by restricting state authority to the state's own borders and by limiting federal powers to the area of interstate commerce. *Swift v. Tyson* (1842) allowed federal judges to bypass state law in cases between citizens of different states, a decision extended in *Watson v. Tarpley* (1855) to cover not only common-law rules but also state statutes. In *Chicago, Milwaukee, and St. Paul Railway Co. v. Minnesota* (1890), a state regulatory agency was forbidden to set railroad rates. A change of philosophy occurred during the administration of President Franklin D. Roosevelt, when *Swift* was overturned by *Erie Railroad Co. v. Tompkins* (1938) and a general turn toward acceptance of regulation took place on the Court.

Freedom of Contract. In the nineteenth cen-

tury, the Court's preference for an unregulated market contributed to several important decisions involving freedom of contract. The contracts clause (Article I, section 10, clause 1, of the Constitution) says that "No State shall . . . pass any Law impairing the Obligation of Contracts," and its interpretation featured in several early Court decisions opposing actions by states. The private branch of contracts clause jurisprudence dealt mostly with state attempts to weaken contracts between private parties, usually to effect debtor relief. In *Sturges v. Crowninshield* (1819), the Court allowed creditors to attach a debtor's wages, and in *Bronson v. Kinzie* (1843), the Court denied mortgagors additional redemption rights on foreclosed property, a ruling nullified by *Home Building and Loan Association v. Blaisdell* (1934), in which contracts were made subject to reasonable policing by states. In *Gelpcke v. Dubuque* (1864), the Court ruled against the claim that final authority in interpreting the state's laws lay with the state judges, overturning the Iowa supreme court's decision that Dubuque could invalidate its own municipal bonds.

The public branch of contracts clause jurisprudence forced the states to uphold their contracts faithfully. In *Fletcher v. Peck* (1810), the Court, led by Chief Justice John Marshall, forbade the state of Georgia from rescinding a land grant even though the transaction had been shot through with bribery. When the New Hampshire legislature moved to revise the Dartmouth College charter, the Court held in *Dartmouth College v. Woodward* (1819) that Dartmouth's contract was a charter and that the college was a private corporation not subject to state interference. In *Charles River Bridge v. Warren Bridge* (1837), the proprietors of the Charles River Bridge sought to halt construction of an adjacent bridge, arguing that the contracts clause protected them from a new bridge that would lessen their toll income. Chief Justice Roger Brooke Taney's opinion for the 4-3 majority stated that the rights and needs of the community overrode the rights of private property. The bridge case illustrates well how the principle of contract often clashed with the vision of those like Taney who realized how regressive it could be, and from then on, the states were allowed greater freedom in regulating their corporations. Part of this change resulted from the dilemma confronting early jurists who were caught between their devotion to contracts and their contempt for the many privileges the states had conferred on corporations in the early nineteenth century.

Substantive Due Process. Whereas procedural due process ensures fair procedures, the doctrine of substantive due process derived from the Fourteenth Amendment and enabled the Court to judge the substance of legislation. It evolved from American reverence for a free market and assumed tremendous importance in the late nineteenth century. Justice Stephen J. Field's dissent in the *Slaughterhouse Cases* (1873) and his concurrence in *Butchers' Union Co. v. Crescent City Co.* (1884) stressed the "liberty of the individual to pursue a lawful trade or employment." With this new doctrine, the Court was able to judge all state regulatory statutes. In *Allgeyer v. Louisiana* (1897), the Court struck down a Louisiana law forcing corporations trading with Louisiana residents to pay fees to the state. In *Lochner v. New York* (1905), a statute governing maximum work hours for bakers was found unconstitutional. In *Coppage v. Kansas* (1915), a state law forbidding yellow dog contracts (contracts in which employees agreed not to join a union) was overturned, and in *Adkins v. Children's Hospital* (1923), the Court invalidated the District of Columbia's employment commission's minimum-wage-setting authority.

Even in its period of strongest support of substantive due process, however, the Court took a generally broad view of issues. State regulation of railroad rates, for example, was accepted with the understanding that investors must be allowed reasonable competitive profits. In *Muller v. Oregon* (1908), a ten-hour workday law like that in *Lochner* was upheld because it applied only to women, who were thought to have special needs. In *Euclid v. Ambler Realty Co.* (1926), the Court demonstrated a sensitivity to community welfare by upholding broad land-use and zoning statutes. Probusiness regulatory legislation suffered the same disfavor accorded wage and hour legislation, as shown by the Court's decision in *Liggett v. Baldridge* (1928), in which a statute calling for licensing of pharmacists was struck down as an attempt to discourage competition. In *New State Ice Co. v. Liebmann* (1932), ice makers lost their bid to force potential competitors to demonstrate a need for more ice manufacturers.

Criticism by Progressives combined with the New Deal to end the dominance of substantive due process in economic affairs. In *Nebbia v. New York* (1934), the Court accepted the formation of a New York commission to regulate milk prices on the grounds of health concerns. In *West Coast Hotel Co. v. Parrish* (1937), a divided Court approved a Washington state minimum-wage law for women. In a reversal of Justice Field's earlier argument for free labor, Chief Justice Charles Evans Hughes stated in *West Coast Hotel* that the due process clause entailed "the protection of law against the evils which menace the health, safety, morals, and welfare of the people." After these rulings, substantive due process has shifted in emphasis from economics to social issues regarding various manifestations of discrimination.

Corporations. The Court handed down several important decisions in the nineteenth century establishing corporations as individuals. The old view that shareholders had to be named separately in any suit was overthrown in *Bank of the United States v. Dandridge* (1827). In *Bank of the United States v. Deveaux* (1809), the Court ruled that corporations were collections of individual shareholders and that in any suit each shareholder had to come from a different state than its disputants, making federal jurisdiction difficult to claim. However, *Deveaux* was invalidated by *Louisville, Cincinnati, and Charleston Railroad Co. v. Letson* (1844), which held that corporations were citizens of their incorporating states, thus enabling federal court jurisdiction over suits between corporations and out-of-state parties. In *Santa Clara County v. Southern Pacific Railroad Co.* (1886), the Court defined a corporation as a "person" under the Constitution, with the effect that only the corporation, not its individual shareholders, could make constitutional claims on behalf of the corporation.

In *Welton v. Missouri* (1876), the Court abandoned the traditional understanding that corporations could not do business directly outside their own states. *Welton* held that a corporation could not build a plant outside its own state but that its products could not be barred from sale in other states. However, in *Western Union Telegraph Co. v. Kansas* (1910), the Court held that as a person, a corporation could not be prevented from doing any legal business in a given state. In another important case, *Sawyer v. Hoag* (1873), the Court established the trust fund doctrine to safeguard against watered stock by demanding that shareholders had to make up any difference between what they had actually paid in and what the corporation claimed. The Court in these years frequently ruled that a corporate action was *ultra vires*, or beyond the limits of the corporate charter, holding, for example, in *Thomas v. West Jersey Railroad* (1979), that for one railroad to lease its track to another would create a de facto merger. Ironically, a corporate merger with a competitor, despite its potential dampening of competition, was safe because it did not result in business beyond the corporate charter; however, the relatively innocuous conglomerate merger could be forbidden as *ultra vires*. The practice of invoking actions as *ultra vires* soon waned, however, as the Court ruled in *Jacksonville, Mayport, Pablo Railway and Navigation Co. v. Hooper* (1896) that a railroad could purchase a hotel for its passengers. This kind of integration aided corporate growth. In *Briggs v. Spaulding* (1891), the Court relaxed its restraints even further, allowing corporate directors broad authority to make decisions without a threat of stockholders filing liability suits.

Beginning with the New Deal in the 1930's, the Court allowed more state and federal regulation of corporations, as in *Federal Trade Commission v. F. R. Keppel and Bros.* (1934), which gave the Federal Trade Commission increased oversight of business practices. Several later decisions gave more freedom to the market. In *Chiarella v. United States* (1980) and *Basic v. Levinson* (1988), the market for corporate securities was judged efficient enough to relieve corporate managers of the responsibility to provide information about their corporation's securities to buyers and sellers. In *Dirks v. Securities and Exchange Commission* (1983), the Court allowed buying and selling corporate stock on the basis of secret information about corporate wrongdoing as a practice that encouraged market efficiency.

Regulation of Competition. Before the passage of the Sherman Antitrust Act in 1890, the Court relied on the common law of trade restraint in making decisions, but a series of rulings after the act's passage disallowed price fixing and anticompetitive mergers. In *United States v. Trans-Missouri Freight Association* (1897), the Court rejected the argument that railroads were a unique industry that needed an industrywide plan for rate scheduling. In *Loewe v. Lawlor* (1908), agreements by workers on the wage they could demand were outlawed, although laborers were to receive expanded bargain-

ing rights in *National Labor Relations Board v. Jones and Laughlin Steel Corp.* (1937). In *Northern Securities Co. v. United States* (1904), the Court forbade an anticompetitive merger between two transcontinental railroads, and the Court has commonly applied the rule of reason to judge the effects of mergers. The rule of reason remains controversial, largely because one person's reason can be another's prejudice.

FURTHER READING

Two books that focus on capitalism and the law are Herbert Hovencamp's *Enterprise and American Law, 1836-1937* (Cambridge, Mass.: Harvard University Press, 1991) and Arthur Selwyn Miller's *The Supreme Court and American Capitalism* (Westport, Conn.: Greenwood Press, 1968). An excellent study is Kermit L. Hall's *The Magic Mirror: Law in American History* (New York: Oxford University Press, 1989). Among the topics that Hall treats in his bibliographical essay on "Law and the Economy" is the controversy prompted by Morton J. Horwitz in *The Transformation of American Law, 1780-1860* (New York: Oxford University Press, 1977), in which Horwitz argued that the body of common law developed in the nineteenth century worked for entrepreneurs against laborers and farmers. James Willard Hurst is the author of several important books, including *The Legitimacy of the Business Corporation in the Law of the United States, 1780-1970* (Charlottesville: University Press of Virginia, 1970) and *Law and Markets in United States History: Different Modes of Bargaining Among Interests* (Madison: University of Wisconsin Press, 1982). Lawrence M. Friedman's *A History of American Law* (2d ed., New York: Simon & Schuster, 1985) has important chapters on law and the economy: 1776-1850, corporation law, and commerce, labor, and taxation. Charles R. Geisst's *Wall Street: A History* (New York: Oxford University Press, 1997) details the struggles between financial institutions and the Court.

Frank Day

SEE ALSO *Charles River Bridge v. Warren Bridge*; Contract, freedom of; Contracts clause; Corporations; *Dartmouth College v. Woodward*; Due process, substantive; Field, Stephen J.; Fourteenth Amendment; *Home Building and Loan Association v. Blaisdell*; *Lochner v. New York*; *Nebbia v. New York*; *Slaughterhouse Cases*.

Cardozo, Benjamin N.

IDENTIFICATION: Associate justice (March 14, 1932-July 9, 1938)

NOMINATED BY: Herbert Hoover

BORN: May 24, 1870, New York, New York

DIED: July 9, 1938, Port Chester, New York

SIGNIFICANCE: As Supreme Court justice, Cardozo advocated a philosophy of law based on life experience and a theory of justice that needs to account for a changing social, economic, and technological reality.

Cardozo's father, Albert Cardozo, was a successful lawyer elected to the New York state supreme court. However, he was forced to resign in response to charges of undue favors toward Tammany Hall cohorts. The younger Cardozo lived much of his judicial and personal life attempting to whitewash that family stain. His was a life of extreme probity and personal puritanism. For example, Cardozo conscientiously avoided owning stock shares in any company for fear that it might bias him in some case, even indirectly. Cardozo entered Columbia

Benjamin N. Cardozo. (Harris and Ewing/Collection of the Supreme Court of the United States)

College at age fifteen, then attended Columbia University Law School.

Judicial Career. For twenty-two years, Cardozo practiced business law, becoming a highly successful trial lawyer who specialized in appellate litigation. Although not involved in partisan politics, he was a progressive Democrat who was nominated by an anti-Tammany Fusion coalition, winning election to the New York supreme court in 1913. Almost immediately afterward, he was shifted to the court of appeals, to which he was elected in 1917.

In 1927 Cardozo was elected chief judge of the court of appeals, with strong bipartisan support. Because New York state was the commercial hub and the court was staffed with generally outstanding jurists, the court of appeals was widely recognized as the most distinguished common-law tribunal in the nation. Cardozo was one of the founders and an active member of the prestigious American Law Institute. He lectured and published extensively.

Cardozo was so well regarded that in 1932 he was recommended to President Herbert Hoover for appointment to the Supreme Court. Politically, his selection was highly unusual in that the Court already had two New Yorkers and one Jew; and on top of that, Hoover was a Republican. However, based on his outstanding reputation, Cardozo won unanimous approval.

Judicial Philosophy and Impact. In both style and process, Cardozo was like his personal hero, Oliver Wendell Holmes, whom he replaced on the bench. Although politically he was the darling of the Progressives—for challenging the imperialistic power of the big corporations—judicially Cardozo was a pragmatist. He was skeptical of broad abstract principles and law as simply logical deduction from previous cases; rather, he thought that each case had to be judged in light of the particular circumstances. Cardozo argued that judges should look at the realities of the world—economic, political, and social—and not impose their own abstract ideas of justice. In general, Cardozo attempted to make the law adapt to what reasonable people would expect from a contract, thus making the law fit human needs and not imposing alien concepts.

Substantively, he is most noted for his decisions in the area of torts—specifically, liability, negligence, and contracts. Generally, he expanded the sphere of liability and made the process easier for injured parties. In contract law, he helped instill fairness into ambiguous contracts. Cardozo generally believed in allowing the legislature discretion in economic regulation. He was a mainstay in supporting the constitutionality of New Deal legislation. He wrote the majority opinion in the seminal Social Security decisions that turned the Court around, *Helvering v. Davis* (1937) and *Steward Machine Co. v. Davis* (1937). In civil liberties, especially their applicability to states, Cardozo believed in selective incorporation. Those rights that were fundamental, such as free speech, were imposed on the states. In *Palko v. Connecticut* (1937), he ruled that a second trial in the state, free of errors, did not deny due process.

Cardozo wrote five books, two of which became standards. The most enduring, *The Nature of the Judicial Process* (1921), was the first and arguably still the best book written on how judges actually make decisions. The respect and admiration for Cardozo—both personal and intellectual—helped translate his ideas, including the emphasis on case studies rather than abstract textbook concepts, into dominant trends. Sixty years after his death, Cardozo was still one of the most frequently cited justices, his decisions regularly used in law texts, especially in torts.

FURTHER READING

Cardozo, Benjamin N. *The Nature of the Judicial Process*. New Haven, Conn.: Yale University Press, 1921.

Hellman, George S. *Benjamin N. Cardozo: American Judge*. New York: Russell & Russell, 1940.

Kaufman, Andrew L. *Cardozo*. Cambridge, Mass.: Harvard University Press, 1998.

Polenberg, Richard. *The World of Benjamin Cardozo: Personal Values and the Judicial Process*. Cambridge, Mass.: Harvard University Press, 1997.

Posner, Richard A. *Cardozo: A Study in Reputation*. Chicago: University of Chicago Press, 1990.

Alan M. Fisher

SEE ALSO Contracts clause; *Helvering v. Davis*; Holmes, Oliver Wendell; Hughes, Charles Evans; New Deal; *Palko v. Connecticut*; *Steward Machine Co. v. Davis*.

Carolene Products Co., United States v.

CITATION: 304 U.S. 144
DATE: April 25, 1938

ISSUE: Judicial scrutiny

SIGNIFICANCE: The fourth footnote to this case, which described the standards of judicial scrutiny and the appropriateness of their use, became the basis of judicial activism on the part of the Supreme Court.

Although this case is unimportant otherwise, its fourth footnote is regarded as the most important in Supreme Court history because it became the basis for judicial activism in the defense of powerless minorities who were likely to have their Fourteenth Amendment rights denied by state or local governments. The majority opinion in the 5-2 decision was written by Justice Harlan Fiske Stone, who was joined by Chief Justice Charles Evans Hughes and Justices Louis D. Brandeis and Owen J. Roberts. Justice Hugo L. Black concurred but dissented in the portion containing the footnote. Justices James C. McReynolds and Pierce Butler dissented; Justices Benjamin N. Cardozo and Stanley F. Reed did not participate.

In essence, the footnote set out the appropriateness of using different standards of judicial scrutiny for different kinds of legislation. The Court's basic presumption is that all laws are constitutional. If unconstitutional laws are passed under ordinary circumstances, the majority of citizens have the option of electing new legislators and repealing the legislation, but this is not true if there are groups of people who are unable to avail themselves of the political process. The Court must use greater scrutiny when dealing with cases involving these groups because the democratic process can be frustrated by laws limiting the right to vote or preventing free expression. Such laws are suspect when they involve groups that are likely to be unable to use the political process to correct bad legislation. Still more important from the Court's point of view are laws that affect discrete and insular minorities despised and feared by the overwhelming majority in society. Prejudice against these groups may prevent normal processes and result in the loss of constitutional protection.

Richard L. Wilson

SEE ALSO Bill of Rights; Due process, procedural; Due process, substantive; Fourteenth Amendment; Incorporation doctrine; Judicial scrutiny; Preferred freedoms doctrine; Suspect classifications.

Carroll v. United States

CITATION: 267 U.S. 132
DATE: March 2, 1925
ISSUE: Automobile searches
SIGNIFICANCE: The Supreme Court held that the Fourth Amendment permits the police to stop and search a vehicle without a warrant when there is probable cause that it contains illegal contraband.

Based on a combination of circumstances, federal agents had reason to think that George Carroll was illegally transporting liquor in his automobile. Following a chase, the agents searched his automobile without a warrant and found bottles of liquor concealed in the back seat. After Carroll's conviction, his lawyers argued that the evidence should have been excluded from his trial because it violated the requirements of the Fourth Amendment.

By a 6-2 margin, the Supreme Court rejected the claim. Speaking for the majority, Chief Justice William H. Taft wrote that the U.S. legal tradition had long accepted a distinction between stationary buildings and means of transportation such as boats or automobiles, in which mobility often made it impractical for the police to secure a warrant. At the same time, Taft insisted that the Fourth Amendment prohibited all "unreasonable searches and seizures." Trying to reconcile these two considerations, he wrote that the police must not stop and search highway travelers unless there is probable cause that the vehicles are carrying contraband.

Carroll's so-called "automobile exception" is well established. Since the 1970's, however, the Court had to decide many difficult questions about the implications and limits of the decision. In *California v. Carney* (1985), for example, the Court held that a motor home, unless situated in a residential location, falls under the *Carroll* ruling.

Thomas T. Lewis

SEE ALSO Automobile searches; *California v. Acevedo*; Exclusionary rule; Fourth Amendment; Search warrant requirement; Standing.

Carswell, G. Harrold

IDENTIFICATION: Supreme Court nominee (1970)
NOMINATED BY: Richard M. Nixon

G. Harrold Carswell. (Archive Photos)

BORN: December 22, 1919, Irwinton, Georgia
DIED: July 31, 1992, Tallahassee, Florida
SIGNIFICANCE: Carswell's mediocre judicial record and prosegregation stance resulted in his nomination to the Supreme Court being rejected by the Senate.

President Richard M. Nixon appointed Carswell to the Fifth Circuit Court of Appeals in 1969, and Carswell was his choice to fill the Supreme Court seat left vacant when Abe Fortas resigned in 1969. Nixon selected Carswell after the Senate rejected his first nominee, Clement Haynsworth, Jr.

Nixon erred politically in nominating Carswell. As a candidate for the Georgia legislature in 1948, Carswell had supported racial segregation. Moreover, his record as a jurist was unimpressive; his decisions as a district judge had a high reversal rate. Nebraska senator Roman Hruska drew attention to Carswell's deficiencies when he declared, without any sense of irony, that mediocre Americans also deserved representation on the Supreme Court.

Nixon aides informed the president that Carswell had no chance of receiving Senate confirmation. Nevertheless, Nixon ordered his staff to continue their efforts to garner support for the nominee. Despite their efforts, on April 8, 1970, the Senate rejected Carswell by a vote of fifty-one to forty-five. Nixon attacked Congress for what he termed its opposition to any southern nominee. Carswell resigned from the bench, lost a 1970 bid to become the Republican candidate for the Senate, and returned to his private law practice.

Thomas Clarkin

SEE ALSO Haynsworth, Clement, Jr.; Nixon, Richard M.; Nominations to the Court; Segregation, de facto; Segregation, de jure.

Carter v. Carter Coal Co.

CITATION: 298 U.S. 238
DATE: March 18, 1936
ISSUE: Regulation of commerce
SIGNIFICANCE: The Supreme Court overturned a 1935 coal act that set up local boards to regulate coal prices and help workers negotiate wages and hours, holding that only the states had the right to regulate coal mining. Although widely ignored, the ruling was never overturned.

With a 5-4 vote, the Supreme Court overturned the Bituminous Coal Conservation Act of 1935, which attempted to stop strikes and dislocation in the coal industry by creating local boards that set the minimum price for local coal and also provided wage and hour agreements through collective bargaining. In the opinion for the Court, Justice George Sutherland reiterated his view that the Tenth Amendment and the commerce clause placed restrictions on how Congress dealt with economic matters, in particular, limiting its ability to delegate its lawmaking power, whether to executive branch bureaucrats or to private groups such as the coal boards.

In setting up local coal boards, Congress relied on its power to regulate interstate commerce, but Sutherland used the prevailing distinction that Congress could regulate only direct interstate commerce. Indirect intrastate commerce was for states, not the federal government, to control. Justices Benjamin N. Cardozo, Louis D. Brandeis, and Harlan Fiske Stone dissented, objecting to the weakness of the direct-indirect distinction. Only a year later, the dissenters prevailed in *National Labor Relations Board v. Jones and Laughlin Steel Corp.* (1937).

Richard L. Wilson

SEE ALSO Cold War; Delegation of powers; General welfare clause; *National Labor Relations Board v. Jones and Laughlin Steel Corp.*; *Panama Refining Co. v. Ryan*; Rule of law; *Schechter Poultry Corp. v. United States*; Sutherland, George.

Catron, John

IDENTIFICATION: Associate justice (May 1, 1837-May 30, 1865)
NOMINATED BY: Andrew Jackson
BORN: about 1786, probably in Pennsylvania
DIED: May 30, 1865, Nashville, Tennessee
SIGNIFICANCE: While on the Supreme Court, Catron guarded the rights of states and opposed the accumulation of wealth and power within institutions and corporations. During the Civil War, he worked to preserve the union at great cost to himself.

Though little is known of Catron's early years, his background probably was marked by poverty. After serving under General Andrew Jackson in the War of 1812, he was admitted to the bar in 1815 in Ten-

John Catron. (Handy Studios/Collection of the Supreme Court of the United States)

nessee. While practicing and serving as a prosecuting attorney in a regional circuit court, he became knowledgeable in issues of land litigation. Because of his reputation, he was appointed to the Tennessee supreme court (then called the Supreme Court of Errors and Appeals) in 1818. He became its chief justice in 1831, a post he retained until the abolition of the court in 1834.

After he returned to private practice, Catron became more active on the political front, emerging as one of the leading supporters of Jackson's campaign for president. Like Jackson, Catron denounced many practices of the Bank of the United States, especially its loan practices and alleged usury. During the 1836 presidential election, he successfully managed Martin Van Buren's campaign in Tennessee. In recognition of his party loyalty, Jackson nominated him to the Supreme Court on March 3, 1837, the last day of his administration.

Catron's advocacy of states' rights influenced many of his Court decisions. In *License Cases* (1847), for example, he ruled that the Constitution's provision for federal supervision of interstate commerce did not exclude a state's right to enforce state regulations. In *Cooley v. Board of Wardens of the Port of Philadelphia* (1852), he argued that states could legislate even if regulations were incidentally applied to foreign or interstate commerce. Corporate power was another area important to Catron. In *Marshall v. Baltimore and Ohio Railroad Co.* (1853), for example, he rejected the notion that all stockholders of a corporation could be regarded as a collective citizen and, instead, held that its officers should be responsible for the acts of a corporation.

Catron was also involved in judicial issues arising from the apprehension of fugitive slaves. In *Scott v. Sandford* (1857), Catron held that Dred Scott was a slave when he filed the suit and a slave when the case was decided. In the crucial period preceding succession, Catron believed that the maintenance of federal judicial power in the disaffected states was of historic importance. In St. Louis, he denounced secessionists as rebels and, as a result of his strong Unionist stand, was forced to leave his home in Nashville and his property was confiscated. He died shortly after the Confederate surrender assured the preservation of the Union to which he was devoted.

FURTHER READING

Cushman, Clare, ed. *The Supreme Court Justices: Illustrated Biographies, 1789-1995.* 2d ed. Washington, D.C.: Congressional Quarterly, 1995.

Friedman, Leon, and Fred L. Israel, eds. *The Justices of the United States Supreme Court: Their Lives and Major Opinions.* 5 vols. New York: Chelsea House, 1997.

Christine R. Catron

SEE ALSO *Cooley v. Board of Wardens of the Port of Philadelphia*; Fugitive slaves; Jackson, Andrew; *Scott v. Sandford*; Taney, Roger Brooke.

Censorship

DESCRIPTION: Investigation of any material before its publication, performance, or broadcast with the aim of preventing materials the investigator finds objectionable from being disseminated.

SIGNIFICANCE: Although the Supreme Court countenanced significant restrictions on freedom of speech and of the press during the nineteenth and early twentieth centuries, after 1931, it tended to view censorship as an infringement of the First Amendment.

For freedom of speech and press to exist, there must be no prior restraint—no restrictions on expression before utterances are made. During the nineteenth century, the First Amendment was regarded as prohibiting the federal government from passing legislation that restricted freedom of the press or of speech. However, state and local governments were not bound by First Amendment prohibitions, and many enacted censorship statutes, often in the form of sedition acts.

In 1925, in *Gitlow v. New York*, the Supreme Court ruled that the prohibitions of the First Amendment were applicable to state and local governments through the Fourteenth Amendment, thus opening the door to challenges to state censorship statutes. The Court, however, rejected Gitlow's claim that his freedom of speech rights had been violated and upheld his conviction under a New York criminal anarchy statute for the distribution of pamphlets advocating the establishment of socialism.

Prior Restraint. The landmark case for censorship was *Near v. Minnesota* (1931). Minnesota had passed a law intended primarily to stop publication of an anti-Semitic periodical sheet that accused many public officials of improprieties, generally in rather offensive terms. The Court ruled that this was a "gag law" that constituted the "essence" of censorship. *Near v. Minnesota* was for many years the measure of whether state and local legislation constituted impermissible restriction on freedom of speech and press.

Following *Near,* the Court gradually took the position that prior restraint, or any attempt to prevent the circulation of material or suppress part of its content before it reaches the public, is presumptively unconstitutional, a violation of the First Amendment. The Court prefers to determine whether materials are possibly seditious or obscene through criminal prosecution after publication or broadcast because this ensures a jury trial, which will bring "community standards" to bear, and conviction beyond a reasonable doubt. Civil actions do not require such a high standard of proof; therefore, those who wish to restrain publication have employed the injunction, a court order banning the publication or circulation of the material in question. This was the methodology used in *New York Times Co. v. United States* (1971), the famous case of the Pentagon Papers, top-secret government documents regarding the Vietnam War that were leaked by a government employee who opposed the war and were published by *The New York Times.*

On June 15, 1971, the U.S. District Court in New York issued a temporary restraining order preventing *The New York Times* from further publication of the Pentagon Papers pending a decision on the government's application for an injunction. The case went to trial in the district court on June 18, under Judge Murray R. Gurfein. Although Gurfein was initially disposed to favor the government's position, he changed his view during the course of this first trial and denied the government's application for an injunction but kept the restraining order in place long enough for the government to appeal. Gurfein, in his decision, said that while "prior restraint" might be possible in this case, the evidence adduced in the trial by the government did

In 1996 a member of the National Political Congress of Black Women cites rapper Tupac Shakur's album Makaveli *as an example of the failure of the album's distributor, Universal Studios, not to distribute profane or violent music. One of the roles of the Supreme Court is to determine what kinds of expression are subject to censorship.* (AP/Wide World Photos)

not support it, and hence the presumption against prior restraint prevailed.

Meanwhile, the *Washington Post* had also acquired a copy of the Pentagon Papers, though it is not clear if the *Post*'s copy was identical to that at the *Times.* The *Post,* eager to establish its reputation as a national newspaper, decided to publish an article based on the papers, despite requests from the government to refrain. Accordingly, the government also applied for a restraining order, preliminary to an injunction, against the *Post.* However, when the *Post* case went to trial before District Judge Gerhard Gesell, he too denied the government's application, though he also permitted further temporary restraint to give the government time to appeal.

On the appeals level, the courts divided. The federal Appeals Court in the Second District (New York) reversed Judge Gurfein, while the Appeals Court in the District of Columbia upheld Judge Gesell. Both courts knew that this was preliminary to an appeal to the Supreme Court, though haste was necessary as the Court was about to adjourn for the summer. The Court agreed to hear the case on an expedited basis, and on June 30, the Court issued a *per curiam* judgment stating that the government had not met the stringent requirements needed to justify a prior restraint. The point argued by the government, that this material should not be published because it was classified, was not accepted by the Court.

The general position adopted by the Court was that political speech was fully protected, unless it would result in clear and immediate harm, such as an incitement to revolt. The Court had first taken this position in an earlier decision, *Brandenburg v. Ohio* (1969). The Court had already ruled out the use of libel action as a way of imposing financial burdens that would effectively constrain publication in *New York Times Co. v. Sullivan* (1964), when an Alabama official had sued the newspaper over an advertisement critical of Alabama officials in their handling of civil rights demonstrations.

Obscenity. Restrictions on the publication and circulation of what many people considered obscenity presented problems for the Court. Two of the most liberal justices appointed by President Franklin D. Roosevelt, William O. Douglas and Hugo L. Black, took the position that *any* restriction on freedom of speech or of the press was unconstitutional, but they never won over a majority of their colleagues. Consequently, during the last half of the twentieth century, the Court was engaged in the difficult task of balancing the rights of free expression against the rights of people who do not wish to be exposed to materials they find offensive and against the need to protect children from the negative effects of pornographic materials.

The Court regards prior restraint as permissible for pornographic materials that portray children involved in sexual acts, as it ruled in *New York v. Ferber* (1982). However, the Court had more difficulty providing the grounds for prior restraint for pornographic materials involving adults and made for adults to use in the privacy of their own homes. Also, although the First Amendment does not protect obscene materials, a clear definition of obscenity has been hard to develop.

In *Roth v. United States* (1957), the Court reversed the conviction of a bookseller under Michigan law for selling material that would be likely to motivate children to engage in "immoral behavior." In this case, Justice William J. Brennan, Jr., defined obscenity as sexual material appealing to a prurient interest, as understood by the average person in the community. Thus, community standards were introduced into the decision as to what constituted obscenity.

The *Roth* standard was unclear, however, and from 1967 to 1973, the Court decided obscenity cases largely on an individual and retroactive basis, providing no guidelines for lower courts and attorneys. In 1973, in *Miller v. California* and its companion case, *Paris Adult Theatre v. Slaton*, the Court created a new definition of obscenity. An obscene work, it ruled, "taken as a whole, appeals to the prurient interest," depicts sexual acts in a "patently offensive way," and lacks "serious literary, artistic, political, or scientific value." It also decided that local community standards, not national, were to be used in determining obscenity.

Films. The emergence of new communication technologies has also raised the issue of censorship. The problem first appeared in the 1930's, when films began to reach a mass audience. In 1915 the Court permitted film censorship, and in the 1930's the film industry had adopted some forms of self-censorship. However, in 1952, in *Burstyn v. Wilson*, the Court struck down a New York state court ruling intended to ban the showing of *The Miracle*, opposed by elements of the Roman Catholic Church. In the 1960's, in an attempt to avoid governmental censorship, the film industry adopted a ratings guide, designed to warn potential audiences and parents of any possibly objectionable material. Concern about the content of movies continued to alarm important groups, however, and Congress attempted to deal with it in the Communications Decency Act of 1996, making it a criminal offense to "knowingly" transmit obscene or indecent material to anyone under the age of eighteen. In 1996 in *Reno v. American Civil Liberties Union*, the Court struck down the act as too vague as to what constituted obscene or indecent material. Such a broad categorization would also limit adult freedom of speech. The Court appeared to be trying to differentiate between content and viewpoint; the former may to some extent be regulated, but the latter may not.

FURTHER READING

The early history of federal censorship is detailed in James C. N. Paul and Murray L. Schwartz's *Federal Censorship: Obscenity in the Mail* (New York: Free Press of Glencoe, 1961). Morris L. Ernst and Alan U. Schwartz also provide much useful information on censorship issues in *Censorship: The Search for the Obscene* (London: Collier-Macmillan, 1964). Recent issues are included in Herbert Foerstel's *Free Expression and Censorship in America* (Westport, Conn.: Greenwood Press, 1997), which also includes a table of cases. Cass R. Sunstein's *One Case at a Time: Judicial Minimalism on the Supreme Court* (Cambridge, Mass.: Harvard University Press, 1999) argues that in recent years the Court has tried to avoid sweeping judgments. David Rudenstine's *The Day the Presses Stopped: A History of the Pentagon Papers Case* (Berkeley: University of California Press, 1996) is a comprehensive account of the case. *Anatomy of Censorship: Why the Censors Have It Wrong*, by Harry White (Lanham, Md.: University Press of America, 1997), is a polemic but provides some useful information.

Nancy M. Gordon

SEE ALSO *Brandenburg v. Ohio*; *Burstyn v. Wilson*; First Amendment; *Gitlow v. New York*; *Miller v. California*; *Near v. Minnesota*; *New York Times Co. v. United States*; Obscenity and pornography; Pretrial publicity and gag rule; Prior restraint; *Reno v. American Civil Liberties Union*; *Roth v. United States*; Speech and press, freedom of; Unprotected speech.

Cert pool

DESCRIPTION: Process wherein law clerks from different chambers collaborate in the screening of petitions for certiorari for inclusion on the plenary docket.

SIGNIFICANCE: The cert pool has proven to be a useful entity for reducing the caseload crisis faced by the Supreme Court.

In 1970 E. Robert Seaver, clerk of the Supreme Court, examines the docketed cases for the week. The growing caseload led to the creation of the cert pool in 1972. (Library of Congress)

Because thousands of certiorari petitions and appeals are filed each term with the Supreme Court, its justices have come to rely on their law clerks to help determine which cases the increasingly overburdened Court should review. Before the cert pool system, each justice received the briefs for all cases, and each clerk read each petition. In 1972 Justice Lewis F. Powell, Jr., suggested, and a majority of justices agreed, that the justices "pool" their law clerks and have them write memos on incoming certiorari petitions and appeals. Each petition is read and summarized by only one clerk from the pool, who writes a single case memo for all the participating justices. The participating justices agree to abide by the recommendations prepared by the member of the pool. A justice's clerk reviews each incoming pool memo. The clerk may agree with the memo's recommendation or may research and write a separate memo for his own justice.

Critics claim that the cert pool reduces the number of people who screen each case and that screening done by mere clerks increases the risk that important case issues will be overlooked or mischaracterized. Supporters claim that clerks writing pool memos are better able to take a close look at each assigned case, unlike the cursory reviews conducted under the old system.

C. Morin

SEE ALSO Certiorari, writ of; Clerks of the justices; Workload.

Certiorari, writ of

DESCRIPTION: Written order issued by the Supreme Court exercising discretionary power to direct a state supreme court or court of appeals to deliver the record in a case for review. If the Court grants a writ to a petitioner, the case comes before the Court.

SIGNIFICANCE: The Court determines which cases it will hear—and thus what legal issues it will review—through the issuance of writs of certiorari.

The U.S. Constitution and Congress determine the Supreme Court's jurisdiction to review cases. Article III of the Constitution and various congressional statutes grant the Court two main areas of jurisdiction: original and appellate. To relieve the Court of its rapidly growing caseload burden, Congress established the federal circuit court of appeals with the Judiciary Act of 1891. The act also authorized the Court to review final decisions in certain categories of cases through the issuance of writs of certiorari.

Although the Constitution does not expressly grant the Court certiorari jurisdiction in the state courts, the Court may grant certiorari for those state court decisions that implicate federal law. Statutes limit certiorari jurisdiction to federal questions that have been decided in final judgments of the states' highest courts. The Court may review final judgments or decrees of the states' highest court if the validity of a treaty or statute of the United States is questioned. It may also review a state court decision if a state statute is viewed as violating the Constitution, treaties, or laws of the United States. The Court may not review a case involving federal law if the state court's decision can be upheld purely on state law.

The Court reviews the majority of its cases through appellate jurisdiction. Within its appellate jurisdiction, the power to grant or deny certiorari gives the Court discretion in determining which cases it will review. The passage of the Judiciary Act of 1925 greatly expanded the Court's certiorari jurisdiction in an effort to reduce its overwhelming docket of cases. The act also enhanced the Court's status and power by largely allowing it to set its own agenda. Since the act's passage, the number of certiorari petitions greatly expanded, and by the 1970's, writs of certiorari were responsible for 90 percent of the Court's caseload.

The Court reviews petitions for writs of certiorari solely at its discretion. If the Court grants certiorari, it agrees to review the judgments in question in that case. It will generally simply issue its decision to either grant or deny certiorari without giving any explanations for the decision. Certiorari is essential to the Court's functioning because of the high number of cases brought to it each year. In the late twentieth century, the Court granted full review to about 160, or 6 percent, of the nearly 5,000 cases submitted through petitions for writs of certiorari each year. If the Court decides not to hear a particular case by denying the petition for a writ of certiorari, there are almost no other avenues that the petitioner can pursue to have the lower court's judgment reviewed.

The Court grants writs of certiorari only for compelling reasons. It pays special attention to resolving conflicts among the federal courts of appeals, the federal district courts, and the state courts on important legal principles or issues of law.

Petitions. A party to any civil or criminal case in which a judgment was entered by a state court of last resort or a U.S. court of appeals may petition for a writ of certiorari requesting the Supreme Court to review the lower court's judgment. A party may also petition the Court for a writ of certiorari in a case in which a judgment was entered by a lower state court if the state court of last resort has issued an order denying its discretionary review. Parties involved in the same judgment may file a petition jointly or separately. The person petitioning the Court for a writ of certiorari is known as the "petitioner" and the opposing party as the "respondent."

The petition must be accurate, brief, and clear in its presentation of the information necessary for the Court to review the case. The petition contains the questions the petitioner wishes the Court to review, when and how these questions were raised, and the names of the parties involved in the proceeding of the court that rendered the judgment in question. It also includes citations of the courts' and administrative agencies' opinions and orders issued in the case, the basis for the Court's jurisdiction, and the constitutional provisions, treaties, statutes, ordinances, and regulations involved in the case. All this information is necessary for the justices to review the petition and make a sound judgment on whether the Court should review the case.

Review of Petitions. The Court may review cases on appeal, by certification, by an extraordinary writ, or by certiorari. The Court must review cases on appeal, meaning that Congress has mandated review of that type of case, whereas the Court may grant or deny certiorari at its discretion. Because Congress eliminated most categories of appeals in 1988 and original jurisdiction represents only one or two cases a year, the majority of the cases the Court hears are those granted certiorari.

Each justice handles the petitions for certiorari sent to the Court differently; however, justices generally either depend on memos written by their own law clerks or those prepared by clerks in the certiorari pool. Some justices have one of their law clerks read the petition and prepare a memo for them recommending what action the Court should take. Other justices use the certiorari pool that began in 1972 at the behest of several justices. In the pool, the petitions are divided randomly among the clerks, and the clerks read each petition assigned to them and prepare a single memo for all the justices. The justices' individual clerks then receive the memos and may mark them for their particular justice. These memos contain a brief summary of the case, the relevant facts, the lower court's decision, the parties' contentions, an evaluation of the petition, a recommendation for action, and any additional information necessary to an understanding of the case.

Cases the justice feels are worthy of review are added to the Court's list of petitions to be voted on by all the justices. The justices then discuss these cases at their twice-weekly conferences. The Court also schedules several daylong conferences in September to discuss those petitions that have accumulated over the Court's summer recess. About 70 percent of the petitions for certiorari do not make the discussion list and are automatically denied certiorari. The chief justice announces those cases that the justices will discuss, and the justices then vote in order of seniority on whether to grant or deny certiorari. The justices may speak on an individual case if they feel it merits discussion rather than simply a vote. The Court will grant certiorari if four of the nine justices are in favor of the petition. The justices developed this informal rule of four after the 1891 Judiciary Act broadened the Court's discretionary jurisdiction. The rule became public knowledge in 1924. Clerks, secretaries, and visitors may not be present at these conferences, and the Court does not release its votes on certiorari petitions to the public. Justices who dissent from the decision to either grant or deny certiorari rarely publish their dissent or their reasons for dissenting.

If the Court grants the petition for a writ of certiorari, the Court clerk will prepare, sign, and enter the order and notify the council of record and the court whose judgment is in question. The clerk will also schedule the case for briefing and oral argument before the Court. A formal writ of certiorari will not be issued unless specially directed. If the Court denies certiorari, the clerk will prepare, sign, and enter the order and notify the counsel of record and the court whose judgment was in question. A denial of certiorari simply means that the Court

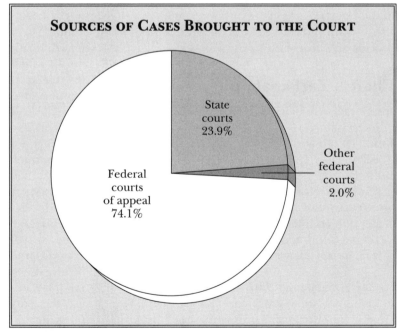

SOURCES OF CASES BROUGHT TO THE COURT

State courts
23.9%

Other federal courts
2.0%

Federal courts of appeal
74.1%

Note: Figures, which do not include original jurisdiction cases, apply to cases in which the Court granted or denied hearings in October, 1996.
Source: Lawrence Baum, *The Supreme Court* (6th ed. Washington, D.C.: Congressional Quarterly, 1998), p. 13.

will not review the case. It does not mean that the Court agrees with the lower court's ruling although that ruling will stand. The denial of certiorari does not constitute a ruling on any legal issues raised by the case although some scholars would argue that it is an informal indication of the Court's position.

FURTHER READING

Robert G. McCloskey's *The American Supreme Court* (Chicago: University of Chicago Press, 1994) offers a good general introduction to the Supreme Court and its jurisdiction. Doris Marie Provine's *Case Selection in the Supreme Court* (Chicago: University of Chicago Press, 1980) and Lee Epstein and Jack Knight's *The Choices Justices Make* (Washington, D.C.: Congressional Quarterly, 1998) both offer an overview of the Court's vital process of deciding which cases it will review. Peter Linzer offers a view on whether the Court's denial to review cases informally constitutes a decision on the merits of the case in his article "The Meaning of Certiorari Denials" in the *Columbia Law Review* 79, no. 7 (November, 1979): 1227-1305.

David Trevino

SEE ALSO Appellate jurisdiction; Cert pool; Clerk of the Court; Clerks of the justices; Conference of the justices; Judiciary Acts of 1801-1925; Review, process of; Rules of the Court; Workload.

Chafee, Zechariah, Jr.

IDENTIFICATION: Law professor and civil libertarian

BORN: December 7, 1885, Providence, Rhode Island

DIED: February 8, 1957, Cambridge, Massachusetts

SIGNIFICANCE: Chafee's expertise on free speech law guided and influenced justices on the Supreme Court and helped define free speech in U.S. jurisprudence.

Chafee graduated in 1907 from Brown University in his hometown of Providence, Rhode Island. He entered into his father's prosperous iron business, but after three years he realized that his calling lay elsewhere. He began his lifelong connection with the Harvard Law School as a student, graduating in 1913. After three years of practicing law back in Providence, Chafee accepted an invitation to teach law at Harvard and returned there in 1916.

He first became interested in free speech through a study of the law of libel. It was, however, the cases that arose out of World War I sedition and espionage legislation that set him on his most important work. His book *Freedom of Speech* (1920) caused wide discussion. Chafee argued for very wide tolerance of speech, even when the message being spoken was unpopular. He acknowledged that when the safety of the public was "really imperiled," free speech could be abridged, but that mere suspicion of future harm from speech was not a sufficient reason to do so. Even during wartime, the society had an interest in maintaining the widest possible liberty consistent with preventing actual and concrete dangers. In general, Chafee thought, the marketplace of ideas in a free society would be a sufficient safeguard against dangerous, unjust, or intemperate speech. His views are credited with liberalizing the important dissenting and concurring opinions of Justices Oliver Wendell Holmes and Louis D. Brandeis during the 1920's.

Although Chafee himself was a rather conservative patrician, his spirited defense of free speech seemed to ally him with American radicals. As a result, a group of Harvard Law School alumni attempted to have him fired in the spring of 1921. After a dramatic hearing at the Boston Harvard Club, during which Chafee made an eloquent defense of the freedom of speech, even of detestable and unpopular speech, all charges against him were dismissed. He was to teach at the Harvard Law School for thirty-six years.

Chafee was by the mid-1920's a leading figure among American civil libertarians, and he enlisted in many battles to preserve basic constitutional freedoms, particularly those under the First Amendment. In the late 1920's he investigated the use of "third-degree" techniques by the police. He became, in 1938, chair of the American Bar Association's Commission on the Bill of Rights. He helped reverse the Supreme Court's earlier ruling against the Jehovah's Witnesses who refused to salute the U.S. flag. He was active in preserving freedom of the press during World War II, and in the late 1940's, he worked for the United Nations Subcommission on Freedom of Information and the Press. He was a prolific author of books and articles.

David W. Levy

SEE ALSO Bill of Rights; First Amendment; First Amendment speech tests; Holmes, Oliver Wendell; Speech and press, freedom of; *West Virginia State Board of Education v. Barnette*; *Whitney v. California*.

Champion v. Ames

CITATION: 188 U.S. 321
DATE: February 23, 1903
ISSUES: Definition of interstate commerce; federal police powers
SIGNIFICANCE: In upholding a federal statute that prohibited the transportation of lottery tickets in interstate commerce, the Supreme Court defined commerce broadly and authorized the development of a federal police power.

Although the U.S. Constitution contains no federal police power, a broad interpretation of the commerce clause allowed the federal government to become involved with the public's safety, health, morality, and welfare. In the late nineteenth century, Congress began to enact commerce-based police power legislation. For example, the Federal Lottery Act of 1895 had the goal of attacking gambling activities rather than regulating an object of commerce. When C. F. Champion was convicted of disobeying the statute, he asserted that the act was unconstitutional for three reasons: First, lottery tickets, as such, were not objects of commerce; second, even if they were objects of commerce, the word "regulate" in the commerce clause did not include the power to prohibit; and third, only the states, according to the Tenth Amendment, could exercise the police power.

Speaking for a 5-4 majority, Justice John Marshall Harlan emphasized the plenary nature of congressional power over interstate commerce. Lottery tickets were objects of real value and therefore items of commerce. The power to regulate commerce, moreover, encompassed the power to prohibit any products considered intrinsically harmful to the public. The effect of the so-called *Lottery Case* was to recognize that Congress might exercise a de facto police power, as desired by Progressives of the era. Based on the precedent, the Court upheld the Pure Food and Drug Act of 1906 in *Hipolite Egg Co. v. United States* (1911), and it upheld the Mann Act of 1910 (involving white slavery) in *Hoke v. United States* (1913). During this era, the Court's acceptance of a federal police power was limited to regulation of criminal or "sinful" activities and did not extend to most economic regulations.

Thomas T. Lewis

SEE ALSO Commerce, regulation of; Federalism; *Hammer v. Dagenhart*; Mann Act; Police powers; Progressivism.

Chaplinsky v. New Hampshire

CITATION: 315 U.S. 568
DATE: March 9, 1942
ISSUE: Freedom of speech
SIGNIFICANCE: The Supreme Court upheld a man's conviction for derisive speech of name calling in public, reasoning that "fighting words" were not subject to First Amendment protection.

Writing for a unanimous Supreme Court, Justice Frank Murphy upheld a state statute under which the defendant was convicted for calling a city marshal a "racketeer" and "fascist" and referring to other officials as "agents of fascists." The relevant state law prohibited derisive speech or name calling in public. Murphy created a two-tier theory of free speech protection in which certain "well-defined and narrowly limited" types of speech do not have First Amendment protection. "Fighting words" as well as lewd, profane, obscene, and libelous words fell outside the boundaries of constitutional protection because they did not represent a free speech value such as the search for truth.

Although *Chaplinsky* was never overturned and the two-tier theory remains valid regarding business advertising, public swearing, and pornography, the thrust of this decision was considerably narrowed. Libelous publications are judged by the standards set in *New York Times Co. v. Sullivan* (1964), and verbal challenges to police officers enjoy constitutional protection, so *Chaplinsky* is only a shell of its former self.

Richard L. Wilson

SEE ALSO *Brandenburg v. Ohio*; *Cohen v. California*; First Amendment speech tests; *O'Brien, United States v.*; Symbolic speech; *Tinker v. Des Moines Independent Community School District*; *Whitney v. California*.

Charles River Bridge v. Warren Bridge

CITATION: 11 Pet. (36 U.S.) 420
DATE: February 12, 1837
ISSUES: Contracts clause; property rights
SIGNIFICANCE: In holding that only clear and explicit terms of contracts were legally binding, the Supreme Court increased the power of state legislatures to regulate private corporations.

Under Chief Justice John Marshall's leadership, the Supreme Court had used a broad construction of the contract clause to protect vested rights in private property. *Charles River Bridge v. Warren Bridge* demonstrated that Chief Justice Roger Brooke Taney and his colleagues wanted to give state legislatures greater latitude in formulating economic policy.

In 1785 the Massachusetts legislature had granted the Charles River Bridge Company a charter to build and operate a toll bridge between Boston and Cambridge. In 1828 the legislature authorized the Warren River Bridge Company to erect a second bridge that would eventually become toll-free. The Charles River Bridge Company sought an injunction against construction of the new bridge on the grounds that the older charter implied the company's exclusive right to operate a bridge at that location during the life of the charter. The issue was whether the Court would make a broad or a narrow interpretation of the charter under the contract clause.

By a 4-3 margin, the Court rejected the company's claim. Writing for the Court, Taney held that legislative charters must be interpreted literally and that charters did not convey any implied corporate privileges. Unless restrained by explicit language in a charter, state legislatures were free to make reasonable regulations and to authorize new projects for the public good. With his distrust of monopolistic power, Taney did not want vested property rights to get in the way of innovation and progress. However, he did not reject the idea that the contract clause required legislatures to honor the explicit terms of their charters. In a strongly worded dissent, Justice Joseph Story accused the majority of diminishing protection for property rights and contended that lawmakers should be required to respect implied promises in charters.

The *Charles River Bridge* decision reflected and encouraged a new emphasis on competition within the capitalistic system. Under Taney, however, the Court did not at all abandon the contract clause. In *Bronson v. Kinzie* (1843), for instance, the Court overturned debtor-relief legislation as an unconstitutional abrogation of contracts.

Thomas T. Lewis

SEE ALSO *Bronson v. Kinzie*; Contracts clause; Ex post facto laws; *Fletcher v. Peck*; *Home Building and Loan Association v. Blaisdell*; *Powell v. Alabama*; Private corporation charters.

Chase, Salmon P.

IDENTIFICATION: Chief justice (December 15, 1864-May 7, 1873)
NOMINATED BY: Abraham Lincoln
BORN: January 13, 1808, Cornish, New Hampshire
DIED: May 7, 1873, New York, New York
SIGNIFICANCE: Presiding over the first impeachment trial of an U.S. president, Chief Justice Chase exercised judicial restraint in a highly partisan atmosphere. As an influential national figure, he brought political wisdom and moderation to the constitutional issues raised by the Reconstruction of the South after the Civil War.

Chase was the eighth child of a Cornish, New Hampshire, couple. His father was a farmer, but several of his uncles were well-educated professionals. One uncle supervised his early education, and an aunt assisted the hard-pressed family by financing further study at Dartmouth College. Young Chase studied law under U.S. attorney general William Wirt, passed his bar examination in 1829, and began practicing law the next year in Cincinnati, Ohio, where interest in the plight of fugitive slaves ran high.

In an early indication of a compelling interest, Chase defended in 1837 a black woman employed by abolitionist James G. Birney but arrested under provisions of the Fugitive Slave Act of 1793. Chase lost the case but impressed observers by his argument that the United States and state governments were mutually independent entities, neither of which could regulate the other. An intensely ambitious man, Chase led the Liberty Party in Ohio in the 1840's and, as a United States senator from

1849 to 1855, spearheaded opposition to the extension of slavery into the territories.

After contributing to the formation of the Republican Party and serving as the first Republican governor of Ohio (1855-1859), he failed in 1856 and 1860 to gain his party's nomination for president but served ably as Abraham Lincoln's secretary of the treasury from 1861 to 1864. Lincoln saw in Chase a person whose antislavery reputation would appease radicals but who could be expected to promote moderation in the difficult post-Civil War Reconstruction. On December 6, 1864, a month after Lincoln won reelection with support from Chase, the Senate confirmed Lincoln's appointment of Chase as chief justice. After taking the oath of office nine days later, Chase twice swore in presidents: Lincoln, on March 4, 1865, and, six weeks afterwards, Andrew Johnson, following Lincoln's assassination.

Reconstruction. Chase's reputation as a leader added greatly to the Court's prestige, then at low ebb. He regarded universal male suffrage as the key to Reconstruction, but he hoped that the states would take the lead in granting the vote to African American men. Quietly he deflected efforts to try Jefferson Davis, the president of the Confederacy, as a war criminal, for several reasons, one of them constitutional. Article III, he pointed out, provides that trials for crimes other than impeachment take place in the state where the crimes were committed. Not only did he consider such a determination impossible to make, he doubted that an impartial jury of Davis's peers could be found in any state. Chase prudently discouraged such action until postwar tempers had cooled, and Davis was never tried.

Reconstruction challenged the Court with a series of thorny jurisdictional problems. In *Ex parte Milligan* (1866), the justices heard the case of a man charged with organizing a rebellion in Indiana for attempting to free Confederate prisoners in the Midwest and subsequently condemned to death by one of the military courts then operating in some Northern as well as Southern states. The Court ruled that the military commission had no jurisdiction. In another conflict of this type, counsel for a southern newspaper editor arrested by military authorities for libel petitioned unsuccessfully in a district court for a writ of *habeas corpus*. In 1868 when it appeared to Chase that a Court ruling for the defendant upon appeal might well jeopardize

Salmon P. Chase. (William F. Cogswell/Collection of the Supreme Court of the United States)

the Reconstruction Act (1867), Chase persuaded his colleagues to postpone a decision. He was much criticized for his seeming to bow to congressional pressure in the earlier phase of Reconstruction, but when political pressure had eased in 1869, the Court, in *Ex parte McCardle*, again ruled this action of a military court to be unconstitutional.

Late in Chase's term as chief justice, *Collector v. Day* (1871) attested his continuing interest in preserving the boundaries between federal and state power. Associate Justice Samuel Nelson, in delivering the majority opinion that the federal government exceeded its authority in levying an income tax on the salary of a state judge, drew heavily upon arguments Chase had previously employed in conflicts between state and federal authority.

Impeachment Trial. Chase presided at the first impeachment trial of a U.S. president in the Senate chamber, a venue otherwise outside the authority of a Supreme Court justice. President Andrew Johnson had been charged with several offenses, the most significant being violation of the recently enacted Tenure of Office Act (1867) by removing Secretary of War Edwin M. Stanton without congressional approval. Without precedents to go by but equipped with a keen awareness of the extent to which partisan opposition to Johnson was operating in the charges against the president, Chase managed to inject elements of judicial procedure into a trial that he knew would inevitably be governed mainly by Senate rules. He also forced the Senate to grant him a vote to decide the matter in the case of a tie. As it turned out, however, the effort to remove Johnson lost by one vote. Both in this trial and in Chase's more usual judicial duties, his commanding presence and keen understanding of the art of politics, rather than pure legal scholarship, were his distinguishing assets.

FURTHER READING

Blue, Frederick. *Salmon P. Chase: A Life in Politics.* Kent, Ohio: Kent State University Press, 1987.

Fairman, Charles. *Reconstruction and Reunion, 1864-1888.* New York: Macmillan, 1971.

Kutler, Stanley I. *Judicial Power and Reconstruction Politics.* Chicago: University of Chicago Press, 1968.

Niven, John. *Salmon P. Chase: A Biography.* New York: Oxford University Press, 1995.

Robert P. Ellis

SEE ALSO *Collector v. Day*; *Habeas corpus*; Impeachment of presidents; *McCardle, Ex parte*; *Milligan, Ex parte*; Reconstruction; Wirt, William.

Chase, Samuel

IDENTIFICATION: Associate justice (February 4, 1796-June 19, 1811)

NOMINATED BY: George Washington

BORN: April 17, 1741, Somerset County, Maryland

DIED: June 19, 1811, Baltimore, Maryland

SIGNIFICANCE: Chase was the only Supreme Court justice impeached for misconduct on the bench. During the Court's early years, he was an influential justice whose opinions established enduring constitutional interpretations.

Chase was admitted to the bar in 1761. From 1764 to 1788 he was a member of the Maryland assembly and a vigorous supporter of U.S. rights. In 1774 the assembly sent him to the Continental Congress in Philadelphia where he became a prominent member, serving on thirty different committees. When

Maryland instructed its delegates to vote against independence in 1776, Chase returned home and conducted a vigorous campaign that led the state to reverse its position. He returned to Philadelphia on July 1, cast the state's vote for independence, and signed the Declaration of Independence. In 1778 Chase left Congress after Alexander Hamilton denounced him for using secret information to speculate on the price of flour.

Chase vigorously criticized the new Constitution during the Maryland ratifying convention in 1787 and voted against its adoption. In 1788 he had become chief judge of the Baltimore city court and in 1791 chief judge of Maryland's general court. By 1795 he had become a Federalist, supporting a strong central government. That year Chase resigned his Maryland position, accepting President George Washington's nomination to the Supreme Court

Interpreting the Constitution. During the 1790's each justice read his opinion in turn, with the most recent appointee, in this case Chase, speaking first. In several precedent-setting cases, Chase's powerfully written opinions were so persuasive that the justices who followed did little more than agree with his views. The newest justice on the bench thus became the formulator of significant constitutional doctrine.

Chase's opinion in *Hylton v. United States* (1796) ruled that a federal tax on carriages was an excise tax, not a direct tax subject to constitutional limitations. Chase defined federal direct taxes as either poll or land taxes, a definition that held as constitutional law until overturned in an 1895 income tax ruling. In *Ware v. Hylton* (1796), Chase vigorously asserted the supremacy of national treaties over state laws, setting an enduring principle of constitutional law.

In *Calder v. Bull* (1798), Chase ruled that the ex post facto clause of the Constitution applied to criminal, not civil, cases. Chase also asserted that natural law principles, even if not spelled out in the Constitution, limited legislative actions. Commentators have viewed Chase's opinion as establishing the basis for interpreting the Fifth and Fourteenth amendments as guaranteeing extensive civil rights not mentioned in the Constitution. Although Chase's opinion in *Calder* supports a "loose construction" of the Constitution, a circuit court opinion by Chase points toward a "strict constructionist" view. In *United States v. Worrall* (1798), Chase (dissenting from the opinion held by other federal judges) asserted that the federal courts did not have jurisdiction over common law crimes, but could act only when Congress passed specific legislation. The Supreme Court adopted his view in 1812.

Impeachment. In the early nineteenth century, Supreme Court justices were required to regularly "ride the circuit" and join lower court judges in conducting trials. A passionate supporter of the Federalist Party, Chase's domineering and highly partisan behavior when conducting politically significant trials infuriated Jeffersonian Republicans who tried to remove him from office.

When presiding over the treason trial of John Fries in 1800, Chase prevented Fries's lawyers from using their planned defense. Fries had led a mob that freed a group of Pennsylvanians held by a federal marshal. His attorneys wanted to argue that the action of the mob did not meet the constitutional definition of treason—levying war against the United States. When Chase prevented them from raising this issue, the lawyers withdrew. The jury convicted Fries, and Chase sentenced him to death, but President John Quincy Adams pardoned him.

Chase's conduct was even more aggressive and partisan in the May, 1800, trial of James Callender for violating the Sedition Act of 1798 by his abusive criticisms of President Adams. Chase refused to excuse a juror who said he had already decided that Callender was guilty. Chase required the defense attorneys to submit in writing the questions they intended to ask their main witness, then refused to let the witness testify. At Chase's Senate trial, Chief Justice John Marshall, who had been in the audience during the Callender trial, admitted that he had never known another judge to act in this manner. Chase proceeded to interrupt and insult defense counsel until they withdrew from the case.

The immediate occasion of Chase's impeachment was his charge to a Baltimore grand jury on May 2, 1803, attacking the leading ideas of the Jeffersonian Republicans. He criticized the recent adoption of universal manhood suffrage in Maryland as preparing the way for a mobocracy and asserted that the idea that "all men in a state of society are entitled to equal liberty and equal rights . . . will rapidly progress until peace and order, freedom and property, will be destroyed."

Samuel Chase. (H. B. Hall/Collection of the Supreme Court of the United States)

On March 12, 1804, the House of Representatives impeached Chase. His attorneys argued that only indictable offenses met the constitutional standard of "high crimes and misdemeanors," insisting that Chase had not violated any laws. All nine Federalist senators voted to acquit Chase. When six Republican senators agreed with the Federalists, the vote to convict fell four votes short of the required two-thirds majority. Most commentators view the failure to remove Chase as affirming the independence of the judiciary against partisan attack. Others disagree, arguing the lesson learned was that judges should avoid partisan behavior on the bench.

After the acquittal, Chase played only a minor role on the Court, writing few opinions and deferring to Chief Justice Marshall, until his death in 1811. His decisions during the 1790's, however, established Chase as the most influential justice of the early Court.

FURTHER READING

Ellis, Richard E. *The Jeffersonian Crisis: Courts and Politics in the Young Republic.* New York: Oxford University Press, 1971.

Haw, James A., Francis F. Beirne, Rosamond R. Beirne, and R. Samuel Jett. *Stormy Patriot: The Life of Samuel Chase.* Baltimore: Maryland Historical Society, 1980.

Rehnquist, William H. *Grand Inquests: The Historic Impeachments of Justice Samuel Chase and President Andrew Johnson.* New York: William Morrow, 1992.

Milton Berman

SEE ALSO *Calder v. Bull; Hylton v. United States;* Impeachment of judges; Sedition Act of 1798; *Ware v. Hylton.*

Cherokee Nation v. Georgia

CITATION: 5 Pet. (30 U.S.) 1
DATE: March 18, 1831
ISSUE: Native American sovereignty
SIGNIFICANCE: The Supreme Court declared that the Cherokee Nation was not a sovereign, independent country and defined the Cherokee as a "domestic dependent nation."

When the Cherokee adopted a constitution and declared themselves an independent state, the Georgia legislature counteracted by annulling all American Indian laws and dividing their land into counties under state jurisdiction. The U.S. Congress and the president were sympathetic to Georgia's position. Because the Cherokee were not citizens of Georgia, they were unable to sue the state in federal court. Therefore, the lawyer for the tribe went directly to the Supreme Court, invoking original jurisdiction as a "foreign state" under Article III of the U.S. Constitution.

By a 4-2 margin, the Court rejected the tribe's claim for independent statehood; the suit was therefore dismissed for a lack of jurisdiction. Discussing the "peculiar" status of the tribes, Chief Justice John Marshall emphasized that they were "under the sovereignty and dominion of the United States." The language of Marshall and other justices suggested that they might, if given a "proper case with proper parties," be prepared to restrain the states from interfering with Indian lands.

Thomas T. Lewis

SEE ALSO *Benton v. Maryland;* Jackson, Andrew; *Johnson and Graham's Lessee v. McIntosh;* Marshall, John; Native American law; Native American sover-

eignty; Native American treaties; States' rights; *Worcester v. Georgia.*

Chicago, Burlington, and Quincy Railroad Co. v. Chicago

CITATION: 166 U.S. 226
DATE: March 1, 1897
ISSUES: Incorporation doctrine; substantive due process
SIGNIFICANCE: The Supreme Court held that the due process clause of the Fourteenth Amendment applied to the states and that, therefore, the state needed to compensate a railroad adequately when it converted private property to a public purpose.

Justice John Marshall Harlan wrote the 7-1 majority opinion with Justice David J. Brewer dissenting in part and Justice Melville W. Fuller not participating. The Supreme Court unanimously held that the Fourteenth Amendment's due process clause required the states to grant just compensation when it took private property for a public purpose. The ruling was unanimous because Justice Brewer concurred on this point even though he dissented on other issues.

The Illinois supreme court had upheld a jury verdict of one dollar awarded to the Chicago, Burlington, and Quincy Railroad for loss of its money-making ability when the city of Chicago created a street across its railroad track. *Chicago, Burlington, and Quincy Railroad Co.* was one of the earliest attempts to use the right of substantive due process to control a state's attempt to regulate economic behavior. Although this latter purpose has been set aside by other decisions, this case remains valid law for the proposition that the Fourteenth Amendment due process clause incorporates specific guarantees for the Bill of Rights. In this case, the Fifth Amendment's guarantee of just compensation when private property is taken for public purpose was incorporated and applied to the states.

Richard L. Wilson

SEE ALSO Bill of Rights; *Chicago, Milwaukee, and St. Paul Railway Co. v. Minnesota;* Due process, procedural; Due process, substantive; Fourteenth Amendment; Incorporation doctrine; Takings clause.

Chicago, Milwaukee, and St. Paul Railway Co. v. Minnesota

CITATION: 134 U.S. 418
DATE: March 24, 1890
ISSUES: Substantive due process; takings clause
SIGNIFICANCE: The Supreme Court, in holding that the courts had the power to review utility rates, incorporated part of the due process clause of the Fourteenth Amendment and applied it to the states.

Justice Samuel Blatchford wrote the 6-3 majority opinion in this case, which struck down a statute forbidding judicial review of railroad shipping rates set by a state commission. The case laid the foundation for the modern regulatory state by departing from the Supreme Court's ruling in *Munn v. Illinois* (1877). Although the decision was vague, the general direction was to break away from the Court's past constitutional standard in which the Court was able to judge only whether a particular branch could act in an area, not whether it acted reasonably in doing so. One basic modern administrative law principle is that due process requires judicial review of bureaucratic decisions to determine compatibility with constitutional standards. The Court stated that courts had the authority to judge the reasonableness of utility rates set by other branches of government. After this decision, the Court began to review not only whether one of the three branches had the authority to act but also whether the government procedures arrived at reasonable decisions.

Richard L. Wilson

SEE ALSO Bill of Rights; *Chicago, Burlington, and Quincy Railroad Co. v. Chicago*; Due process, procedural; Due process, substantive; Fourteenth Amendment; Incorporation doctrine.

Chicago v. Morales

CITATION: No. 97-1121
DATE: June 10, 1999
ISSUE: Procedural due process
SIGNIFICANCE: The Supreme Court held that an antiloitering ordinance was unconstitutionally vague, failing to give ordinary citizens fair notice about the kinds of conduct that are prohibited and allowing the police too much unguided discretion.

Luis Gutierrez, who was arrested on a Chicago antiloitering law designed to prevent gang activity, addresses reporters outside the Supreme Court in 1998. The following year, the Court overturned the Chicago law. (AP/Wide World Photos)

In 1992 the Chicago city council enacted a law making it a misdemeanor to remain in one place with "no apparent purpose" in the presence of a suspected gang member when ordered to move by a police officer. During its three years of application, forty-two thousand people were arrested under the law. Many cities looked to the law as a model for reclaiming streets from gangs that used loitering as a strategy to control territory. A 6-3 majority of the justices found that the law violated due process standards because of the vagueness issue. Three members of the majority wanted to rule that the freedom to loiter for innocent purposes was part of the "liberty" protected by the Fourteenth Amendment. In a strong dissent, Justice Clarence Thomas accused the majority of sentencing "law-abiding citizens to lives of terror and misery." The justices appeared to agree that a law narrowly worded to prohibit intimidating conduct on the streets would be constitutional.

Because the Supreme Court recognized the problems associated with city gangs, the tone of the *Chicago* decision was quite different from *Papachristou v. City of Jacksonville* (1972), in which the Court, in an opinion written by Justice William O. Douglas, struck down a vagrancy law by referring to the values of nonconformity and the open road as extolled by poets Walt Whitman and Vachel Lindsay.

Thomas T. Lewis

See also Black Monday; Douglas, William O.; Due process, procedural; Police powers.

Chief justice

Description: Justice designated as administrator of the Supreme Court. Duties include distributing the workload among the other justices, assigning, and often writing opinions.

Significance: The chief justice leads the eight other justices, assigning the writing of opinions and often casting the deciding vote in split decisions.

Before the Supreme Court was instituted in 1789, Congress decreed that the Court would have five associate justices and a chief justice. The six justices were viewed as being essentially equal, although the chief justice had certain specific, additional duties. Accordingly, the chief justice was paid more than the associate justices, but the salary disparity was never substantial. In 1988 the chief justice received $115,000, just $5,000 more than the associate justices.

The first person President George Washington appointed to the Court was John Jay of New York, who served from 1789 to 1795 as chief justice. The early court, which first met officially in 1790, dealt with an average of five cases a year during its first five years. This caseload was light and manageable compared with the more than two hundred cases a year handled by the Court in the twentieth century. Five associate justices and the chief justice were able to handle such a caseload easily.

Qualifications. The Constitution does not specify qualifications for the position of Supreme Court justice. Although justices articulate the most significant legal decisions made in the country, they need not be lawyers, although most of them are. The only requirement for a person to become a chief justice is that he or she be a citizen nominated by the president of the United States. This nomination must be confirmed by the Senate. Chief justices need not have served as associate justices, although usually they have.

Some chief justices have been consummate legal scholars, but experience has proved that the best legal scholars do not necessarily make the best chief justices and the best chief justices are often not the best legal scholars. Justices, including the chief justice, are served by cadres of well-trained law clerks, many of whom have more specific knowledge of the law than the people for whom they work. The law clerks often research and write the first drafts of the justice's opinions.

Most Important Characteristics. The greatest responsibility of chief justices is leadership. They call the other justices into conference to discuss cases and are the first to speak. In doing so, they become the person best able to direct the course of the court's actions, although each justice acts independently and is not beholden to the chief justice.

The individual justices must work autonomously. Disagreement over the interpretation of the Constitution and over individual decisions does not evoke charges of disloyalty and, ideally at least, does not invite retaliation. People appointed chief justice are generally selected because they can remain dispassionate and disinterested in matters before the Court. To function effectively, chief justices must deal with the other justices and their clerks diplomatically, in nonconfrontational ways. Their major functions are to clarify and persuade rather than to direct and confront.

Ironically, although legal scholars often make excellent associate justices because they become deeply involved in the details of law and of the Constitution, those who have become the most effective chief justices are noted more for their administrative skills than for their legal scholarship. The office of chief justice has, through the years, been affected most significantly by the personalities of the justices themselves.

Specific Duties. Aside from writing opinions, which is one of their major functions, chief justices have substantial power because they preside over the Court in oral arguments and in conference. In conference, a chief justice can channel discussions into important areas and can suggest alternatives.

Chief justices also create the discuss list, or the list of cases to be considered for adjudication. They cannot act unilaterally to exclude petitions for hearings, but they substantially influence the decisions of their colleagues. The chief justices, with the assistance of legal clerks, draw up the discuss list, which gives them the greatest role in determining which cases come before the Court.

The chief justice is also responsible for assigning to the associate justices the cases for which they will write opinions. Some chief justices have themselves written a huge number of opinions, and others delegate a great deal of this important work. The opinions chief justices and associates are required to write involve the legal analysis of extremely complex issues that, in recent times, have become increasingly technological in nature. The written opinions must be buttressed by a full discussion of legal precedents and by references to past cases and to legal protocol.

Usually draft opinions are prepared by bright young assistants, usually newly graduated from law school and recently admitted to the bar. Many of them were editors of their universities' law reviews. They research legal documents extensively to write opinions that they then pass on for revision, emendation, and review by the justices, including the chief justice. In the final analysis, however, the justices rewrite the opinions, putting them into their final form, which is the official form that enters the Court's records.

The chief justice is also specifically designated as the person who will preside over impeachment hearings brought against a president of the United States. William H. Rehnquist served in this capacity during the impeachment hearings of President Bill Clinton early in 1999.

The chief justice has various Court management duties, which include tasks such as administration of the Court's bureaucracy and preparation of budget estimates. He or she also chairs the Judicial Conference of the United States, composed of lower federal court judges. This conference meets and makes recommendations to Congress.

John Marshall's Model. Among the most important decisions of the early Court was *Marbury v. Madison* (1803), which, under the leadership of Chief Justice John Marshall, who served as chief justice for thirty-four years, scored a double victory and set important precedents. Outgoing President John Quincy Adams, under the Judiciary Act of 1801, attempted to pack the courts with Federalist jurists, among them William Marbury, who was to serve as a justice of the peace for the District of Columbia. Adams's term ended at midnight on March 3, 1801. Thomas Jefferson was inaugurated the next day, but the appointment papers for Marbury and several others were still on Adams's desk. James Madison, Jefferson's secretary of state, refused to receive these papers. When Marbury's promised appointment was held up, he took his case to the Court. President Adams had appointed Marshall to the Court as chief justice only weeks before. It was expected that Marshall would support Adams's efforts to pack the courts with "midnight judges," as these last-minute appointments were called. If Marshall supported Marbury in this case, the judiciary would remain in the hands of the Federalists.

CHIEF JUSTICES OF THE UNITED STATES, 1789 TO 2000

Name	Term	Appointed by
John Jay	1789-1795	George Washington
John Rutledge[1]	1795	George Washington
William Cushing[2]	1796	George Washington
Oliver Ellsworth	1796-1800	George Washington
John Marshall	1801-1835	John Adams
Roger B. Taney	1836-1864	Andrew Jackson
Salmon P. Chase	1864-1873	Abraham Lincoln
Morrison R. Waite	1874-1888	Ulysses S. Grant
Melville W. Fuller	1888-1910	Grover Cleveland
Edward D. White	1910-1921	William H. Taft
William H. Taft	1921-1930	Warren G. Harding
Charles E. Hughes	1930-1941	Herbert Hoover
Harlan F. Stone	1941-1946	Franklin D. Roosevelt
Frederick M. Vinson	1946-1953	Harry S Truman
Earl Warren	1953-1969	Dwight D. Eisenhower
Warren E. Burger	1969-1986	Richard M. Nixon
William H. Rehnquist	1986-	Ronald W. Reagan

1. Rutledge was not confirmed by Congress.
2. Cushing sat as chief justice for one week in January, 1796, and then declined the appointment and returned to serving as associate justice.

JUSTICES WHO SERVED AS BOTH ASSOCIATE AND CHIEF JUSTICES			
Justice	*Associate Tenure*	*Chief justice tenure*	*Years on Court*
John Rutledge	Feb., 1790-Mar. 1791	Aug.-Dec. 1795	1
William Cushing	Feb., 1790-Sept., 1810	Jan., 1796[1]	20
Edward D. White	Mar., 1894-Dec., 1910	Dec., 1910-May, 1922[2]	27
Charles Evans Hughes	Oct., 1910-June, 1916	Feb., 1930-July, 1941	17
Harlan F. Stone	Mar., 1925-July, 1941	July, 1941-Apr., 1946[2]	21
William H. Rehnquist	Jan., 1972-Sept., 1986	Sept., 1986-	28[3]

1. Cushing served as chief justice for one week.
2. Died in office.
3. As of early 2000.

In the end, however, newly elected Democratic-Republicans, who now controlled Congress, repealed the Judiciary Act of 1801 under which the judgeships Adams sought to fill in his last hours as president were created. With this repeal, Congress forbid the Court to convene for fourteen months, which meant that the legislative branch sought to control the judicial branch, clearly in violation of the separation of powers that the founding fathers envisioned.

The Court did not meet during 1802, acceding to the congressional mandate. When it met in February, 1803, however, the case of *Marbury v. Madison* was on the docket. For this complicated case, Chief Justice Marshall wrote the opinion in two parts. In the first part, he found that Marbury had every right to the position he had been promised. He added, however, that the Court had no power to force Madison to deliver it. The Judiciary Act of 1789 gave that power to the Court, but in doing so, Marshall found, it was giving a power that, under the Constitution, it could not bestow. Congress had overstepped its authority, thereby failing to follow the mandates of the Constitution.

It was the force of Marshall's leadership that resulted in bringing about a landmark decision that assured the separation of powers that has been a cornerstone of the political strength of the United States. *Marbury v. Madison* established for all time the concept of judicial review, which was perhaps the greatest single contribution of the Marshall Court.

During Marshall's long tenure as chief justice, the size of the Court changed, being reduced in 1801 from six to five, then, in 1807, being increased to seven. (In 1869 it grew to nine justices.) Having an odd number of people on the court prevents split votes. With an odd number of justices, it is usually the chief justice who casts the deciding vote. Marshall, more than any other chief justice, imposed his beliefs on the other justices. A staunch Federalist, he nearly always found in favor of the national government in cases that involved actions against it. Late twentieth century chief justices have found it much more difficult to impose their wills on their colleagues, who accord them little deference.

The Importance of Opinion Assignment. Customarily, chief justices have assigned the writing of the Court's opinions at times when they are in the majority on the initial vote in conference, which is most of the time. In instances where this is not the case, the senior justice in the majority makes the assignment.

The selection of the writer of an opinion will often determine whether the initial majority is retained and how large it will be. Chief justices who know their associate justices well will assign the writing of opinions to those who are most likely to achieve the ends they have in mind. Chief justices can also exercise their power by assigning the writing of opinions to themselves. Most chief justices assign the writing of opinions to those in their own ideological camps.

FURTHER READING
Bernard Schwartz's *A History of the Supreme Court* (New York: Oxford University Press, 1993) pre-

sents a comprehensive history of the Court and its justices. Briefer, but also useful, is Lawrence Baum's *The Supreme Court* (3d ed., Washington, D.C.: Congressional Quarterly, 1989), whose chapters on decision making and on policy outputs are fresh and incisive. Henry J. Abraham, in *Justices and Presidents: A Political History of the Supreme Court* (3d ed., New York: Oxford University Press, 1992), examines the political implications of appointments to the Court, including those involving chief justices. This book is significant and is well presented. Juvenile readers will find Ann E. Weiss's *The Supreme Court* (Hillside, N.J.: Enslow, 1987), Catherine Reef's *The Supreme Court* (New York: Dillon Press, 1994), and Barbara Aria's *The Supreme Court* (New York: Franklin Watts, 1994) useful.

R. Baird Shuman

SEE ALSO Administrative assistant to chief justice; Burger, Warren E.; Collegiality; Judiciary Act of 1789; Judiciary Acts of 1801-1925; *Marbury v. Madison*; Marshall, John; Rehnquist, William H.; Warren, Earl.

Chimel v. California

CITATION: 395 U.S. 752
DATE: June 23, 1969
ISSUE: Search and seizure
SIGNIFICANCE: The Supreme Court held that when a valid arrest is made, the Fourth Amendment permits the police to search the arrested person and the area "within his immediate control," but not any additional area.

Using an arrest warrant, the police arrested Ted Chimel at his home on burglary charges. Ignoring Chimel's objections, the police then conducted a search of the entire house and discovered stolen property that provided the basis for Chimel's conviction. Rejecting Chimel's appeal, the California courts noted that the Supreme Court had upheld a similar warrantless search incident to an arrest in *United States v. Rabinowitz* (1950).

By a 6-2 vote, the Court ruled Chimel's trial unconstitutional and overruled *Rabinowitz*. Speaking for the majority, Justice Potter Stewart recognized that it was reasonable for the police to search the person arrested in order to remove any concealed weapons and to prevent the concealment or destruction of evidence. Likewise, the police had a le-

gitimate reason to search the area into which an arrestee might reach for a weapon.

The Court applied the *Chimel* rationale to allow more extensive searches during arrests when justified by exigent circumstances. In *Maryland v. Buie* (1990), for instance, the Court approved of a protective sweep of a home believed to harbor an individual posing a danger to the arrest scene.

Thomas T. Lewis

SEE ALSO Automobile searches; Exclusionary rule; Fourth Amendment; Search warrant requirement; *Terry v. Ohio.*

Chinese Exclusion Cases

Chew Heong v. United States; United States v. Jung Ah Lung; Chae Chan Ping v. United States; Fong Yue Ting v. United States; Wong Quan v. United States; **and** *Lee Joe v. United States*

CITATIONS: 112 U.S. 536; 124 U.S. 621; 130 U.S. 581; 149 U.S. 698 (three cases)
DATES: December 8, 1884; February 13, 1888; May 13, 1889; May 15, 1893 (three cases)
ISSUE: Immigration
SIGNIFICANCE: Using the Fourteenth Amendment, the Supreme Court first ruled in favor of challenges to laws excluding the Chinese from immigrating and becoming U.S. citizens, then succumbed to popular sentiment and upheld exclusionary statutes.

In 1882 Congress enacted the first Chinese Exclusion Act, prohibiting Chinese laborers and miners from entering the United States. An 1884 amendment required resident Chinese laborers to have reentry certificates if they traveled outside the United States and planned to return. The 1888 Scott Act prohibited Chinese laborers temporarily abroad from returning, thereby stranding thousands of Chinese. Merchants and teachers were exempted from the Scott Act if they had "proper papers," thereby beginning the practice of using "paper names" to create new identities so that Chinese could return. The 1892 Geary Act banned all future Chinese laborers from entry and denied bail to Chinese in judicial proceedings. All Chinese faced deportation if they did not carry identification papers. The 1893 McCreary Act further extended the definition of laborers to include fishermen, miners, laundry owners, and merchants. The 1902 Chinese Exclusion Act permanently banned all the Chinese immigration.

The Supreme Court initially attempted to defend Chinese rights under the Fourteenth Amendment; however, as anti-Chinese sentiment grew more pronounced, it withdrew even its limited protections from Chinese immigrants. The Court defended the right of Chinese to reenter the United States in *Chew Heong* and *Jung Ah Lung.* In *Chae Chan Ping,* it found the Scott Act unconstitutional. However, in the three 1893 cases, it upheld a law retroactively requiring that Chinese laborers have certificates of residence or be deported.

Richard L. Wilson

See also Alien rights and naturalization; Bill of Rights; Citizenship; Due process, procedural; Due process, substantive; Fourteenth Amendment; Immigration law; Incorporation doctrine; Japanese American relocation; *Wong Kim Ark, United States v.*; *Yick Wo v. Hopkins.*

Chisholm v. Georgia

Citation: 2 Dall. (2 U.S.) 419
Date: February 18, 1793
Issue: State sovereignty
Significance: In its first major decision, the Supreme Court held that the U.S. Constitution allowed a citizen of one state to sue another state in federal court.

Article III of the U.S. Constitution granted federal jurisdiction over "controversies between a state and citizens of another state." During ratification of the Constitution, Federalists asserted that this provision would not override the doctrine of sovereign immunity, which meant that the government may be sued only with its consent. Two South Carolina citizens, executors of an estate of a British decedent, attempted to recover property that Georgia had confiscated during the American Revolution. Georgia refused to appear, claiming immunity as a sovereign state.

By a 4-1 vote, the Supreme Court ruled against the state and endorsed the authority of the federal judiciary over the states. In seriatim opinions, Justices John Jay and James Wilson emphasized strong nationalistic views. They declared that the people of the United States had acted "as sovereigns" in establishing the Constitution and that the states, by virtue of membership in a "national compact," could be sued by citizens throughout the nation. In dissent, Justice James Iredell, a southerner who had participated in a ratifying convention, argued that the English common law doctrine of sovereign immunity had not been superseded by constitutional provision or by statute.

The *Chisholm* decision was bitterly denounced by partisans of states' rights. The controversy resulted in the drafting and ratification of the Eleventh Amendment, the first of four amendments to directly overrule a decision of the Court.

Thomas T. Lewis

See also Eleventh Amendment; Federalism; Reversals of Court decisions by amendment; Seriatim opinions; States' rights.

Choate, Joseph H.

Identification: Trial lawyer and diplomat
Born: January 24, 1832, Salem, Massachusetts
Died: May 14, 1917, New York, New York
Significance: Choate argued in several well-known cases before the Supreme Court. In his

Joseph Hodges Choate. (Library of Congress)

most noted case, he successfully argued that the 1894 income tax law was unconstitutional.

After graduating from Harvard Law School in 1854, Choate was admitted to the bar in Massachusetts in 1855 and New York in 1856. He was called on to perform important legal work in connection with the Standard Oil antitrust case, the Chinese Exclusion Acts, and railroad suits. As a Republican, he helped organize the Committee of Seventy that investigated graft in New York City finances, an investigation that led to the disclosure and destruction of the Tweed Ring. A gifted speaker, he was often called on to deliver major speeches for Republican candidates.

Choate made a number of arguments before the U.S. Supreme Court. The most famous was the case of *Pollock v. Farmers' Loan and Trust Co.* (1895), in which Choate established the unconstitutionality of the 1894 income tax law. From 1899 to 1905, he served as U.S. ambassador to Great Britain, settling the Alaskan boundary dispute between Canada and the United States. Choate also secured the abrogation of the 1850 Clayton-Bulwer Treaty by means of the 1901 Hay-Pauncefote Treaty, which opened the way for U.S. construction of the Panama Canal.

Alvin K. Benson

SEE ALSO Antitrust law; Income tax; *Pollock v. Farmers' Loan and Trust Co.*; Sixteenth Amendment.

Church of Lukumi Babalu Aye v. Hialeah

CITATION: 508 U.S. 520
DATE: June 11, 1993
ISSUE: Freedom of religion
SIGNIFICANCE: Overturning a local ban on animal sacrifices, the Supreme Court announced that it would use the strict scrutiny test in examining any law targeting religious conduct for special restrictions.

Believers in the Santería religion, which combines African and Roman Catholic traditions, practice animal sacrifices in order to appeal to benevolent spirits to heal the sick and promote good fortune. Many other people in the United States, however, find such ceremonies to be highly offensive. In 1987 a Santería congregation announced plans to

establish a house of worship in the city of Hialeah, Florida. Responding to a public outcry, the Hialeah city council passed several ordinances that made it illegal to kill animals in religious ceremonies, while still allowing the killing of animals for human consumption.

After federal district and appellate courts upheld the ordinances, the justices of the Supreme Court ruled they were unconstitutional. Speaking for a unanimous Court, Justice Anthony M. Kennedy explained that when a law is plainly directed at restricting a religious practice, it must satisfy two tests: The restriction must be justified by a compelling state interest, and the restriction must be narrowly tailored to advance that interest. General and neutral laws may proscribe cruelty to animals or require the safe disposal of animal wastes; however, a community may not place a direct burden on an unpopular religious practice without a strong secular justification.

Justice Kennedy's opinion did not entirely please libertarians because it did not overturn *Employment Division, Department of Human Resources v. Smith* (1990), which allowed for the more lenient test of rationality in examining laws putting an incidental burden on a religious practice. Three justices—David H. Souter, Harry A. Blackmun, and Sandra Day O'Connor—concurred with the ruling but expressed disagreement with the *Smith* precedent.

Thomas T. Lewis

SEE ALSO *Employment Division, Department of Human Resources v. Smith*; Judicial scrutiny; Religion, freedom of; *Sherbert v. Verner.*

Circuit courts of appeals

DESCRIPTION: Courts exercising varied original and appellate jurisdiction in several circuits at an intermediate level between the federal district courts and the Supreme Court from 1789 to 1911.
SIGNIFICANCE: Supreme Court justices "riding circuit" from 1789 until the 1840's enhanced the presence of the federal judiciary in the states and uniformity in the national law.

With the Judiciary Act of 1789, Congress created a three-tiered federal court system with district courts at the base, circuit courts of appeals at an intermediate level, and the Supreme Court at the

CIRCUITS OF THE COURTS OF APPEALS

Circuit	Covered Areas
First	Maine, New Hampshire, Massachusetts, Rhode Island, Puerto Rico
Second	New York, Vermont, Connecticut
Third	Pennsylvania, New Jersey, Delaware, Virgin Islands
Fourth	West Virginia, Maryland, Virginia, North Carolina, South Carolina
Fifth	Texas, Louisiana, Mississippi
Sixth	Ohio, Michigan, Kentucky, Tennessee
Seventh	Wisconsin, Illinois, Indiana
Eighth	Minnesota, North Dakota, South Dakota, Nebraska, Iowa, Missouri, Arkansas
Ninth	Washington, Montana, Idaho, Oregon, Nevada, California, Arizona, Alaska, Hawaii, Northern Marianas, Guam
Tenth	Wyoming, Utah, Colorado, Kansas, Oklahoma, New Mexico
Eleventh	Florida, Georgia, Alabama
D.C.	District of Columbia

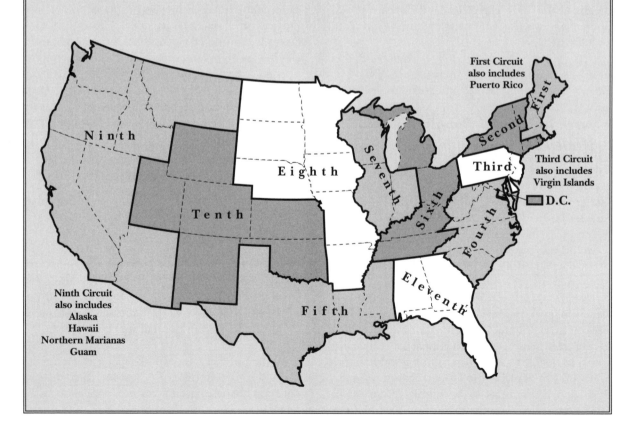

top. Circuit courts had trial and appellate jurisdiction in multistate circuits and originally were staffed by federal district judges and Supreme Court justices riding circuit, traveling from the capital to the court's location. The first Congress established three geographical circuits encompassing the thirteen district courts. As the jurisdiction and number of federal courts expanded, circuit courts became the primary federal trial courts. Supreme Court justices found circuit riding a hardship, and by the 1840's the practice had ended, leaving the district judges to decide cases at the district and circuit court levels.

The Supreme Court became the principal appellate court because appellate review was not available in the circuit courts or judges were reviewing their own district court work. The Judiciary Act of 1869 remedied this by establishing circuit judgeships in each of the then nine circuits. In the 1870's Congress extended federal question jurisdiction to federal courts and dramatically increased their workload. Congress sought to provide relief for the overburdened Court with the Judiciary Act of 1891, which established U.S. circuit courts of appeals and channeled all appellate work through them. With their appellate jurisdiction removed, the old circuit courts continued to try capital cases, tax cases, and some diversity cases. In 1911 Congress made district courts the exclusive federal trial courts, and the circuit courts ceased to exist after December 31 of that year. The U.S. circuit courts of appeal were renamed courts of appeals in 1948.

Theodore M. Vestal

SEE ALSO Appellate jurisdiction; Circuit riding; Courts of appeals; Judiciary Act of 1789; Judiciary Acts of 1801-1925; Lower federal courts; Workload.

Circuit riding

DESCRIPTION: Supreme Court justices traveled hundreds, even thousands, of miles as members of a circuit court designed to bring the federal judiciary system to the people.

SIGNIFICANCE: Direct involvement in jurisdictions outside the nation's capital enabled Supreme Court justices to stay attuned to local law as they contributed to the formation of national law.

The Judiciary Act of 1789 divided the states into three circuits, the eastern, the middle, and the

DISTANCES RIDDEN BY JUSTICES ON CIRCUIT IN 1839	
Justice	*Miles*
Roger B. Taney	458
Henry Baldwin	2,000
James M. Wayne	2,370
Philip P. Barbour	1,498
Joseph Story	1,896
Smith Thompson	2,590
John McLean	2,500
John Catron	3,464
John McKinley	1,000
Total	17,776

Source: Bernard Schwartz, *A History of the Supreme Court* (New York: Oxford University Press, 1993), page 153.

southern, with a circuit court consisting of two Supreme Court justices and one federal district judge meeting twice a year in each region. In 1793 Congress reduced the number of justices on any circuit court bench from two to one.

Both original and appellate jurisdiction were in the hands of the justices, creating a controversial dual role. In response to potential conflicts of interest for justices and the rigors of circuit travel, circuit riding was eliminated by a section in the Judiciary Act of 1801. However, the Judiciary Act of 1802 repealed the 1801 act, assigning each justice a specific circuit without rotation.

To meet the needs of territorial expansion, the Judiciary Act of 1837 added new circuits and new justices until there were nine of each. In 1869 Congress approved a measure authorizing the appointment of nine new circuit judges, reducing the justices' circuit duties to one term every two years. The Judiciary Act of 1891 lightened the court docket of the justices by creating U.S. circuit courts of appeals and assigning all appellate work to them. However, the original circuit courts were not abolished until 1911.

Kevin Eyster

SEE ALSO Appellate jurisdiction; Circuit courts of appeals; Judiciary Act of 1789; Judiciary Acts of 1801-1925; *Stuart v. Laird.*

Citizenship

DESCRIPTION: Legal membership in a country, attained at birth or through naturalization, that conveys certain rights and requires certain responsibilities.

SIGNIFICANCE: In numerous cases, the Supreme Court generally supported Congress's authority to determine who is eligible to be a U.S. citizen. It also interpreted the rights and responsibilities inherent within citizenship.

Article I, section 8, of the U.S. Constitution gives Congress the right to make laws outlining who is eligible to become a naturalized citizen of the United States and detailing how that eligibility can be established. In January, 1790, President George Washington, in his annual message, expressed his concern over citizenship and naturalization issues, urging Congress to develop naturalization laws. In response to Washington's concerns, Congress passed a law later that year providing for naturalization of free white aliens who had resided in the United States for at least two years and who made application for citizenship. Over the years, Congress adjusted the residency requirement several times, but it was not until 1866, when the Fourteenth Amendment was passed, that people of color were accepted as citizens of the United States.

Congress's Right to Define Citizenship. In various decisions, the Supreme Court supported the right of Congress to define citizenship and to control immigration and naturalization. In *Chy Lung v. Freeman* (1875), the Court held that legislation passed by states to control immigration was illegal, stating that only Congress had the right to pass laws concerning the admission and entry into the United States of foreign nationals.

In 1885 in the *Head Money Cases*, the Court placed Congress's right to control immigration within the commerce clause of the Constitution. Although this right was challenged many times in subsequent years in cases involving the Chinese Exclusion Acts (1882-1902), the Court continued to uphold congressional responsibility for control of issues relating to immigration and naturalization. However, in deciding these cases, the Court did not always base its decisions on the commerce clause.

In the *Chinese Exclusion Cases* (1884-1893), the Court stated that Congress might exclude aliens even if they came from a country at peace with the United States. It said Congress was free to exclude any group that it believed could not assimilate into American culture and, therefore, might affect American peace and security.

In *United States v. Ju Toy* (1904), the Court indicated that Congress had the right to exclude anyone from the United States, even citizens. Ju Toy, returning to the United States from China, claimed that he was a naturalized citizen. However, the secretary of labor and commerce agreed with a lower court that Toy was not eligible for entry to the United States under the Chinese Exclusion Act. The Court decision supported the secretary's actions. However, naturalized citizens' rights were somewhat protected in *Quon Quon Poy v. Johnson* (1926), in which the Court stated that, when

During a ceremony in San Francisco, Mexican-born Audelia Ordaz (right front) takes the oath of allegiance. Immigration and naturalization are largely the province of Congress; however, the Supreme Court is sometimes called on to interpret citizenship laws. (Reuters/Blake Sell/Archive Photos)

citizenship was challenged, the person claiming citizenship had the right to a fair and thorough administrative hearing. The 1933 decision in *Volpe v. Smith* confirmed Congress's right to control immigration and naturalization, stating that its right to determine who could enter the United States was "no longer open to question."

In *Trop v. Dulles* (1958), the Court affirmed that only Congress had the authority to decide citizenship matters. Trop, who had been stripped of his citizenship rights by a military court, sued to regain those rights. The Court ruled that only Congress, and not the military courts, could deprive citizens of their citizenship rights. However, in 1967, in *Afroyim v. Rusk*, it was held that not even Congress could strip a citizen of the right to citizenship. Citizenship was held to be a constitutionally protected right that could not be taken away without the assent of the citizen.

Eligibility for Citizenship. In answering the question of who is eligible for citizenship, the Court made interpretations based on the 1790 law. One of the Court's most famous statements on eligibility for citizenship was made in *Scott v. Sandford* (1857), also known as the *Dred Scott Case*. Dred Scott, a slave who had been taken into the free states of Illinois and Wisconsin, sued for his freedom. Justice Roger Brooke Taney, speaking for the court majority, said that the suit would have to be dismissed because no black person, free or slave, could ever be a citizen and, therefore, was not eligible to bring suit in court. The decision was based on the 1790 act in which Congress gave the right to naturalization to free, white aliens.

The Dred Scott decision was the not the only one in which race or color was held as an appropriate test for citizenship. In *Elk v. Wilkins* (1884), the Court ruled that Elk, who had left his Native American tribe to live among white people in Omaha, Nebraska, could not be considered a citizen because Native Americans were dependents of the state, in a ward-guardian relationship with the federal government. Native Americans were granted citizenship by Congress in 1924. This right to citizenship was affirmed by the Nationality Code of 1940.

The case of *Toyota v. the United States* (1924) also illustrated the Court's adherence to the principles of the 1790 law. Toyota had served in the U.S. Coast Guard and had even fought for the United States during World War I. When a 1918 act of Congress gave alien veterans permission to apply for citizenship, Toyota took advantage of the law and applied for and received a certificate of naturalization. However, the Court revoked his certificate, indicating that the 1918 law did not eliminate the 1790 requirement that naturalized citizens be free whites.

In the 1922 *Ozawa v. United States*, the Court ruled that people who were born in Japan could never become citizens of the United States because they were not free, white aliens. In this case the Court defined white as "Caucasian." In *Morrison v. California* (1934), the Court again ruled that a person born in Japan could not become a U.S. citizen. Before the *Ozawa* case, a number of Chinese and Japanese people had become naturalized U.S. citizens. In the *United States v. Thind* (1922), a native of India who had been granted citizenship by an Oregon court was deemed ineligible for citizenship because he did not meet the definition of white. In this case white was defined not as "Caucasian" but as being of European stock.

In 1943 an act of Congress expressly granted Chinese the right to naturalization. In 1945 people from India and the Philippines became eligible for U.S. citizenship. In 1952 the Immigration and Naturalization Act lifted all racial bars to naturalization.

Although in the 1800's and early 1900's the Court often ruled that foreign nationals of color could not become naturalized citizens, it was willing to accept the citizenship of people of African or Asian heritage who were born in the United States. The 1898 decision in *United States v. Wong Kim Ark* established the citizenship of a child born in the United States of Chinese parents. The Court held that this child's citizenship was guaranteed under the provisions of the Fourteenth Amendment.

However, in 1998, when a petitioner attempted to use *Wong Kim Ark* to establish her citizenship in *Miller v. Albright*, the petitioner's right to citizenship was denied. The petitioner was born in the Philippines to an American father and a Filipino mother. Although the father acknowledged paternity, he did not know of his daughter's existence until she was twenty-one years old. The Court ruled that if a child wishes to claim U.S. citizenship, paternity must be established or acknowledged by the time the child is eighteen years old.

Citizenship Rights. The Court ruled on the nature of citizens' rights and responsibilities as well as on the nature of citizenship itself. In ruling on cases involving who can be naturalized, the Court often helped all citizens understand what it means to be a U.S. citizen.

In the *Slaughterhouse Cases* (1873), the Court ruled that all citizens have both national citizenship and state citizenship. The bulk of citizens' rights are regulated by the states; national citizenship rights are outlined by the Constitution. For example, in *Edwards v. California* (1941), the Court ruled that a citizen's right to move from state to state is a national right that is protected by the Constitution.

The Court examined various requirements of U.S. citizenship in cases involving naturalized citizens. In *Girouard v. United States* (1946), the Court ruled that Girouard, who had refused to swear to defend the country, could become a naturalized citizen. In the opinion, Justice William O. Douglas wrote that taking up arms to defend the country is not a specific requirement of U.S. citizenship. In *Schneiderman v. United States* (1939), the Court refused to revoke Schneiderman's certificate of naturalization because he was a member of the Communist Party when he took the oath of citizenship. The Court said citizens should not be subjected to the idea of guilt by association. The Court also refused to revoke the citizenship of pro-Nazi Baumgartner in *Baumgartner v. United States* (1944), ruling that naturalized citizens had as much right to association as citizens born in the United States. This was a very important statement for the rights of naturalized citizens.

In *Mandoli v. Acheson* (1952), the Court ruled that a native-born citizen cannot lose citizenship for not returning to the United States during adulthood. Similarly, in *Schneider v. Rusk* (1964), the Court ruled that a naturalized citizen can retain U.S. citizenship even if that citizen is out of the country for a long time. A native-born citizen would not lose citizenship for an extended stay outside the country, and a naturalized citizen has the same rights as a citizen born in the United States. Also, in *Perkins v. Elg* (1939), the Court ruled that a child who acquires U.S. citizenship at birth does not automatically lose that citizenship if her parents take her abroad to live in another country.

Japanese Americans and World War II. During the administration of President George Bush, the U.S. government apologized to Japanese Americans for its treatment of them during World War II.

Part of this treatment consisted of rulings made by the Court. In *Hirabayashi v. United States* (1943), the Court declared that the March 21, 1942, act of Congress placing a curfew on people of Japanese ancestry was legal even though many of the people who were subjected to the curfew were U.S. citizens. In *Korematsu v. United States* (1944), the Court held that the internment of Japanese Americans was legal and necessary for national security. This decision was reached in spite of the fact that many of those interred were native-born citizens.

FURTHER READING

D. J. Herda thoroughly examines *Scott v. Sandford* in *The Dred Scott Case: Slavery and Citizenship* (Springfield, N.J.: Enslow, 1994). Thomas Janoski's *Citizenship and Society: A Framework of Rights and Obligations in Liberal, Traditional, and Social Democratic Regimes* (London: Cambridge University Press, 1998) introduces and explains the concept of citizenship, discusses the balance between citizenship rights and obligations, and traces changes in citizenship rights over several centuries. Early historical developments related to U.S. citizenship are examined by J. H. Kettner in *The Development of American Citizenship, 1608-1870* (Chapel Hill: University of North Carolina Press, 1978). Issues that historically affected the Asian immigrant's ability to become naturalized were explored by M. R. Konvitz in *The Alien and the Asiatic in American Law* (Ithaca, N.Y.: Cornell University Press, 1946). Richard Sinopoli discusses the values associated with U.S. citizenship in *The Foundations of American Citizenship: Liberalism, the Constitution, and Civic Virtue* (New York: Oxford University Press, 1992). Eve P. Steinberg's *How to Become a U.S. Citizen* (New York: Macmillan General References, 1998) explains what steps an immigrant must take to become a naturalized citizen. Aliza Becker, Laurie Edwards, and the Travelers and Immigrants Aid of Chicago also describe the steps in the naturalization process in *Citizenship Now: A Guide for Naturalization* (Lincolnwood, Ill.: NTC, 1990).

Annita Marie Ward

SEE ALSO Alien rights and naturalization; *Chinese Exclusion Cases*; *Edwards v. California*; Fourteenth Amendment; *Head Money Cases*; *Hirabayashi v. United States*; Immigration law; *Korematsu v. United States*; *Scott v. Sandford*; *Trop v. Dulles*; *Wong Kim Ark, United States v.*

Civil law

DESCRIPTION: Body of law that deals primarily with relationships between individuals; it is distinct from criminal law, which deals with offenses against the state.

SIGNIFICANCE: As the federal government began to play a larger role in commercial and environmental regulation, the Supreme Court had to rule on many new civil issues and the complex jurisdictional issues resulting from commercial and property litigation in a federal system.

The term "civil law" originally referred to the system of Roman jurisprudence and was used to distinguish it from natural and international law. In the United States, the term distinguishes between the legal relationships of individuals—normally property relationships—and crimes, which are established by either federal or state penal statutes. Civil law covers nearly every important human relationship: property ownership, torts, land titles, making and enforcing contracts, buying and selling, employment of labor, business regulation, environmental and workplace safety, marriage and divorce, responsibility for children, and inheritance.

The common-law tradition, which was brought to North America by English settlers, established a complex system of judge-made rules to regulate individual relationships. So complicated had the rules of practice as well as the substance of the law become that a movement to simplify and "codify" the law sprang up in the middle of the nineteenth century. David D. Field, brother to Supreme Court Justice Stephen J. Field, drafted such a code and campaigned vigorously for its adoption in New York state. In 1846 the Field Code was enacted by the New York legislature. It became the prototype for civil codes in all states within the United States except Louisiana. It is also the historical root of the modern Uniform Commercial Code and the rules of civil procedure that exist all over the country.

The Supreme Court's involvement with civil law is primarily in two areas: procedures and content or substance. In 1934 Congress passed the Rules Enabling Act, which authorized the Court to establish rules for lower federal courts. In 1938 the Court promulgated the Federal Rules of Civil Procedure for the first time. These were widely acclaimed for their simplicity and clarity. Most states have adopted some or all of these rules.

Regarding the content or substance of civil law, there are two major issues: the federal government's diversity jurisdiction and the content of civil laws. The diversity referred to is diversity of state citizenship. When litigants are from different states, they have the choice of having their case heard in state or federal courts. However, most commercial and property rules in the United States are state law rather than federal law, so the question arises of what law should be applied. In *Erie Railroad Co. v. Tompkins* (1938), the Court held that unless federal law or the constitution directly applies to a case, the federal courts must apply state case law, usually that of the state of the defendant in the suit. These issues may be particularly complex when there are multiple plaintiffs and defendants, for example in a case that might involve airline negligence. Because of the proliferation of diversity cases, Congress in 1958 established ten thousand dollars as the minimum amount being litigated before a federal court may take jurisdiction. The amount was raised to eighty thousand dollars in 1988. Even with that increase, the principal effect of diversity jurisdiction is to allow large corporations that are sued in state courts to get their cases into federal courts. Such cases now make up one-quarter of the workload of the federal courts.

The Court's role in the content of civil law results from the increased regulatory activity of the federal government. After 1933, primarily using the power to regulate interstate commerce, Congress immensely expanded the scope of federal law. National laws touch on business issues, the environment, product safety, medicine, civil rights, taxation, and workplace safety. These all raise civil law issues. When questions arise, whether of constitutional or statutory interpretation, the Court is the final arbiter. Most of the Court's workload is made up of civil rather than criminal or constitutional cases.

FURTHER READING

Abadinsky, Howard. *Law and Justice: An Introduction to the American Legal System.* 4th ed. Chicago: Nelson-Hall, 1998.

Carter, Lief, Austin Sarat, Mark Silverstein, and William Weaver. *New Perspectives on American Law: An Introduction to Private Law in Politics and Society.*

Durham, N.C.: Carolina Academic Press, 1997.

Field, David Dudley. "The Index of Civilization." In *The Golden Age of American Law,* edited by Charles Haar. New York: George Braziller, 1965.

Friedman, Lawrence M. *A History of American Law.* New York: Simon & Schuster, 1973.

Holmes, Oliver Wendell, Jr. *The Common Law.* Boston: Little, Brown, 1964.

Llewellyn, Karl. *The Common Law Tradition.* Boston: Little, Brown, 1960.

Pound, Roscoe. *Jurisprudence.* St. Paul, Minn.: West Publishing, 1959.

Robert Jacobs

SEE ALSO Commerce, regulation of; Common law; Common law, federal; Diversity jurisdiction; *Erie Railroad Co. v. Tompkins*; Federalism; Natural law; Police powers; Roman law; State courts.

Civil Rights Acts

DATE: 1866-1991

DESCRIPTION: A series of federal laws to ensure equal treatment of citizens who, because of membership in a particular group, suffered unequal treatment at the hands of the various states or individuals.

SIGNIFICANCE: These laws, which were often the focus of challenges before the Supreme Court, attempted to protect the rights of African Americans, women, and other disadvantaged minorities from public and private discrimination.

Following the Civil War (1861-1865), Congress approved the Civil Rights Act of 1866 to ensure that former slaves were treated as U.S. citizens and possessed various rights commonly associated with freedom. Among these were the rights "to make and enforce contracts, to sue, be parties, and give evidence, to inherit, purchase, lease, sell, hold, and convey real and personal property." Former slaves were to enjoy "full and equal benefits of the laws," the same standards enjoyed by whites. In 1870 Congress outlawed conspiracies to deprive persons of their civil rights. In 1871 Congress prohibited individuals acting under the color of law to deprive persons of their civil rights and permitted aggrieved parties to sue for damages. Although southern states found many formal and informal ways to blunt the intent of Congress, parts of these statutes, codified as Title 42, sections 1981-1983, of the U.S.

Code remain good law, and the Supreme Court upheld them during the 1960's.

For example, in *Monroe v. Pape* (1961), the court relied on section 1983 to endorse a damage suit filed against police officers who unlawfully invaded a private home and subjected it to an illegal search. In *United States v. Price* (1966), the Court affirmed the use of sections 1981 and 1982 to prosecute private citizens who conspired to murder three civil rights workers in Mississippi, not only because public officials actively involved themselves in the conspiracy, but also because the conspiracy interfered with rights secured by the Constitution. That same day, the Court broadened the scope of these statutes to reach actions by private citizens, in *United States v. Guest*, a case that involved the murder of civil rights worker Lemuel Penn, because the conspiracy to murder Penn interfered with his right to interstate travel, secured by the Constitution.

The Court also affirmed basic provisions of liberty mandated by the Civil Rights Act of 1866. In *Buchanan v. Warley* (1917), the Court struck down a residential segregation ordinance passed by Louisville, Kentucky, because it violated the right of a black homeowner to make a contract to purchase a home in a white neighborhood, a contractual right explicitly guaranteed by the Civil Rights Act. However, the court refused to extend this right to purely private actions between individuals in *Corrigan v. Buckley* (1926), because the reach of federal civil rights laws to acts of discrimination by private individuals was limited.

Although Reconstruction era statutes could and did protect minorities to some degree from discrimination by municipal and state governments, discriminatory actions by private citizens remained outside the scope of federal law and the enforcement power of the federal courts into the 1960's. Congress had passed the Civil Rights Act of 1875, which prohibited racial discrimination in privately owned places of public accommodation such as hotels, amusement parks, and trains. In the *Civil Rights Cases* (1883), the Court held that Congress had no constitutional authority to regulate the owners of private property in such a manner. The Fourteenth Amendment, for example, forbade discrimination by state laws, not acts of discrimination by private citizens.

The result of this decision and others, such as *Plessy v. Ferguson* (1896), which allowed state governments to use race to classify and regulate their citizens, permitted southern states to craft a legal system of racial apartheid enforced by law, augmented by customary private racial discrimination beyond the reach of federal law. Not until the Civil Rights movement of the 1950's and 1960's did Congress successfully pass further civil rights legislation.

Civil Rights Laws in the Civil Rights Era. Congress enacted the Civil Rights Act of 1957 and the Civil Rights Act of 1960 to deal with deprivation of voting rights of blacks by southern states and their white citizens.

This Harper's Weekly *illustration depicts the response of people gathered outside the galleries of the House of Representatives after the passage of the Civil Rights Act of 1866.* (Library of Congress)

However, the major piece of legislation came in 1964. The Civil Rights Act of 1964, the cornerstone of modern federal civil rights law, contained a number of major provisions, including one outlawing acts of private discrimination by property owners whose businesses are associated with interstate commerce. In *Heart of Atlanta Motel v. United States* (1964), the Court affirmed this provision and forbade a hotel owner to deny African Americans accommodation at his facility. In *Katzenbach v. McClung* (1964), the Court extended this provision to restaurant owners, who could no longer lawfully refuse service to persons because of their race.

The Civil Rights Act of 1964 also overturned the practice of racially segregating public facilities, such as swimming pools and public restrooms. States and municipalities could lose their federal funding for failure to desegregate their public accommodations. The Court affirmed the power of Congress to compel desegregation of public facilities in *Daniel v. Paul* (1969) and *Tillman v. Wheaton-Haven Recreation Association* (1973).

The Civil Rights Act of 1964 also broadened the federal approach to civil rights. Race, color, religion, and national origin appear among the enumerated list of classifications that cannot be used for discriminatory purposes. In matters of employment, sex became a suspect category under federal law. Title VII of the act also authorizes remedial policies in employment, commonly called affirmative action, and brought Court scrutiny to practices that led to gender and racial exclusion from employment opportunities.

For example, in *Griggs v. Duke Power Co.* (1971), the Court challenged practices in hiring and promoting workers that had the effect (disparate impact) of placing black workers in lower-paying, racially segregated job categories. Otherwise race-neutral hiring and promotion practices were unlawful if they result in the continuation of practices rooted in historic discrimination. Indeed, in *United States v. Paradise* (1987), the Court extended this reasoning to its broadest conclusion. Where the evidence of past discrimination was so severe, and especially where state government was the author of the discrimination, the Court held that racially defined numerical goals (quotas) and adjustments in hiring and promotional exams could be employed as a temporary remedy to past race discrimination in hiring.

Typically, however, the Court has been loathe to order promotional quotas and modify hiring practices. In *Washington v. Davis* (1976), the Court distinguished between the discriminatory result of a policy, which may violate Title VII of the Civil Rights Act of 1964 and be subject to judicial remedy, and discriminatory intent, which must be present to violate the Constitution and is much more difficult to prove. This hair-splitting made employment discrimination suits more difficult to bring. In *Regents of the University of California v. Bakke* (1978), the Court affirmed Alan Bakke's claim that the affirmative action program for admission into a university program violated Section VI of the Civil Rights Act of 1964 (which prohibited racial and ethnic preferences in programs receiving federal funds), because it did establish numerical quotas, thus violating Bakke's right to equal protection of the laws.

Indeed, in *Wards Cove Packing Co. v. Atonio* (1989) and *Price Waterhouse v. Hopkins* (1989), the Court limited the application of statistical disparity (more whites or more men in high-paying positions) in bringing a Title VII case. The plaintiff had to account for size of the applicant pool, for example, and establish that the alleged discrimination occurred in the specific case, rather than infer it from a statistical pattern. In *Martin v. Wilks* (1989), the Court required parties bringing class-action suits challenging discriminatory hiring practices to identify those parties that might be injured by the Court's endorsing the plaintiff claims and join them to the suit. This procedure made challenging systematic employment discrimination more difficult. To instruct the Court, Congress passed the Civil Rights Act of 1991, which shifted the burden of proof back to the employer to show that patterns of discrimination were not caused by unlawful practices and eliminated the defense of "business necessity." The overall thrust of the law was to ensure a broader, rather than a narrower, interpretation of the Civil Rights Act of 1964.

The relationship between sex discrimination and the Civil Rights Act of 1964 has proven more elusive. Most plaintiffs bringing cases alleging unlawful or unconstitutional gender discrimination have used the equal protection clause of the Fourteenth Amendment. However, the Court has defined sexual harassment in the workplace as a violation of Title VII. In *Meritor Savings Bank v. Vinson* (1986), the Court held that *quid pro quo* sexual harassment violates the law and can occur even if the employee ultimately "submits" to sexual activity, in order to keep a job. Employees have a right to be free from a hostile workplace environment. In *Harris v. Forklift Systems* (1993), the Court defined hostile workplace environment to include a totality of circumstances including frequency and severity of offensive behavior. Women alleging a hostile workplace environment did not need to show that they were psychologically damaged by the offensive behavior or that it adversely affected their job performance. This ruling made it easier for women to bring harassment cases under Title VII because they do not have to humiliate themselves as psychologically damaged or incompetent to prevail in court.

Private and Housing Discrimination. Congress, the Constitution, and the Supreme Court have eliminated the legal basis for racial and gender discrimination in federal and state law. Because businesses operate in interstate commerce and are chartered under state law, they too have been brought under the scope of federal civil rights laws. Actions by private individuals in purely private situations have been harder to regulate. Groups of individuals, for example, seeking to preserve the racial uniformity of a neighborhood, created restrictive covenants, private contracts by which they agreed not to sell to certain people, typically blacks. Although the covenants themselves were "legal," the court held in *Shelley v. Kraemer* (1948) that they could not be enforced in court. If groups of private individuals, however, refused to sell or rent to insular minorities, current legal thinking placed their behavior beyond the scope of federal civil rights laws.

That changed significantly in *Jones v. Alfred H. Mayer Co.* (1968), in which the court nearly overturned the *Civil Rights Cases* by extending the Civil Rights Act of 1866 to cover the sale of a private home. An individual may not refuse to sell a home to a buyer because the buyer is black. In *Runyon v. McCrary* (1976), the power to regulate private contracts was extended to private schools, breathing new life into the 1866 Civil Rights Act. The Court, however, revisited this broadened interpretation in *Patterson v. McLean Credit Union* (1989) and severely limited the judicial enforcement, by holding that the Civil Rights Act ensures broad contract-making power but does not create an equally broad right of remedy if the contract is then abrogated. Along with the employment decisions that same term, the *Patterson* decision led Congress to pass the Civil Rights Act of 1991.

In keeping with the judicial spirit of the *Jones* decision, Congress further strengthened its claim to regulate private contracts in housing by passing the Civil Rights Act of 1968. This act prohibited discrimination in advertising, financing, selling, or renting a house on the grounds of race, religion, or national origin. Amended in 1974 to include sex, this fair housing law primarily affects owners of apartment complexes and anyone buying or selling through a realtor.

The Court has given the Civil Rights Act of 1968 a broad reading. In *Trafficante v. Metropolitan Life Insurance Co.* (1972), it held that tenants in an apartment complex could sue owners who practiced racial discrimination in behalf of those who were denied leases. In *Gladstone v. Village of Bellwood* (1979), the Court held that a municipality could sue realtors who directed minorities to certain parts of town to buy or rent.

FURTHER READING

Henry J. Abraham and Barbara Perry's *Freedom and the Court* (7th ed., New York: Oxford University Press, 1994) and Lee Epstein and Thomas Walker's *Constitutional Law for a Changing America: Rights, Liberties, and Justice* (3d ed., Washington, D.C.: Congressional Quarterly, 1998) provide context for and analysis of the Court's use of civil rights acts. More focused studies include John R. Howard's *The Shifting Wind: The Supreme Court and Civil Rights from Reconstruction to Brown* (Albany: State University of New York Press, 1999), which examines the fate of early civil rights acts, and Abraham Davis and Barbara Luck Graham's *The Supreme Court, Race, and Civil Rights: From Marshall to Rehnquist* (Thousand Oaks, Calif.: Sage, 1995), which examines the apparent retreat on broadly interpreting civil rights laws in 1989, which led to the Civil Rights Act of 1991. Cass R. Sunstein's *One Case at a Time: Judicial Minimalism and the Supreme Court* (Cambridge, Mass.: Harvard University Press, 1999) offers a scathing critique of the Court for deciding civil rights cases too narrowly. Robert H. Birkby's *The Court and Public Policy* (Washington, D.C.: Congressional Quarterly, 1983) examines the intersection of the court, laws, and bureaucracy. R. J. Johnston's *Residential Segregation: The State and Constitutional Conflict in American Urban Areas* (London: Academic Press, 1984) highlights how intentional and unintentional policies lead to racially defined housing patterns. Harold Hyman and William Wiecek's *Equal Justice Under Law: Constitutional*

Development, 1835-1875 (New York: Harper & Row, 1982) remains the best overview of Reconstruction era civil rights laws.

Edward R. Crowther

SEE ALSO *Barron v. Baltimore*; Bill of Rights; Civil Rights acts; *Civil Rights Cases*; Congressional power to enforce amendments; Fourteenth Amendment; Fundamental rights; *Gitlow v. New York*; Harlan, John Marshall; Incorporation doctrine; Madison, James; Private discrimination; *South Carolina v. Katzenbach*; War and civil liberties.

Civil rights and liberties

DESCRIPTION: The phrase "civil liberties" refers to the personal freedoms that are guaranteed against government infringement. "Civil rights" refers to the rights of minority groups whose protection is understood to require positive government action.

SIGNIFICANCE: The words "liberty" and "right" can be used interchangeably to some extent, without doing violence to the meaning they have acquired over the ages. The "Bill of Rights" in the U.S. Constitution is, in fact, a list of liberties. However, the phrases "civil liberties" and "civil rights" have now acquired sufficiently distinctive meanings, each with a history of its own. They should be treated as discrete concepts.

"Congress shall make no law respecting an establishment of religion." So begins the First Amendment. The Bill of Rights is a repository of people's liberties in that it defines the areas where people are to be left alone to live their lives free of impediments. The word "Congress" is never again mentioned in this document, but neither is there any reference to any other legislative power. Writing in *Barron v. Baltimore* in 1833, Chief Justice John Marshall observed that there was a unity of purpose in these amendments, for they were proposed and ratified at the same time. As such, the rights guaranteed in these amendments were all to be "understood as restraining the power of the general government, not as applicable to the States." In short, these freedoms did not provide any protection against state and local abuses.

The person who gave us the Bill of Rights had warned us that the principal source of mischief against personal liberties would be the states and their local communities, and not the national majority. If James Madison could have had his way, the Bill of Rights would have applied to the states as well. His original draft had an amendment that had the following words: "No state shall infringe the equal rights of conscience, nor the freedom of speech, or of the press, nor of the right of trial by jury in criminal cases." Madison conceived this paragraph to be "the most valuable amendment on the whole list." However, the conservatives in the Senate were afraid of what the new central government might do someday to undermine the sovereignty of the states which they represented. Madison's favorite amendment was rejected decisively.

Eventually, the nation came around to embracing Madison's vision, though more out of desperation in the wake of the Civil War than as a concession to his argument. Not only did the Fourteenth Amendment define U.S. citizenship, with a view to protecting the rights of individuals from abuse by local majorities, it also contained this critical language, which would have pleased the Father of the Bill of Rights: "No State shall make or enforce any law which shall abridge . . ." Nevertheless, the actual use of the Bill of Rights against state and local abuses was not to materialize until 1925, when, in *Gitlow v. New York*, the Supreme Court began to read, in earnest, certain provisions of that document into the due process clause of the Fourteenth Amendment in a series of actions which would come to be known as "selective incorporation."

The Fourteenth Amendment, ratified in 1868, did more than pave the way for the "nationalization of the Bill of Rights." Like the other two Civil War amendments—the Thirteenth (1865), banning slavery, and the Fifteenth (1870), prohibiting the denial of the right to vote for reasons of "race, color, or previous condition of servitude"—the Fourteenth called the nation's attention to a whole new problem known as "civil rights." The blacks were no longer slaves, but they were not yet free, certainly not equal with the whites. They were entitled to their rights. However, who was to deliver to them those rights?

Congress responded to this challenge with a series of legislative enactments, all under the fitting name of "Civil Rights Act," beginning with the bold, sweeping and highly controversial Civil Rights Act of 1866, which defined citizenship and guaranteed rights related to contracts and property own-ership. The fierce debate over the constitutionality of this law did not end until Congress passed a constitutional amendment which included some of these controversial provisions. The Fourteenth Amendment became the basis for Congress's second major assault upon racial injustice. Enacted in the name of the amendment's equal protection clause, the 1875 Civil Rights Act banned all discrimination in public facilities and accommodations owned and operated by corporations and private individuals. However, the Supreme Court declared the law unconstitutional in the *Civil Rights Cases* of 1883, on the grounds that the amendment's prohibitions were aimed at the states, not corporations and private individuals. Congress had no power to prescribe criminal penalties for private acts of discrimination under this amendment, said the Court, against a bitter dissent from Justice John Harlan, who read the three Civil War amendments far more broadly than his brethren.

Congress did not enact another civil rights law until 1957. The 1957 and 1960 Civil Rights Acts made the Justice Department the command post in the war on racial discrimination. Then came the historic Civil Rights Act of 1964, by far the most comprehensive civil rights law in the nation's history. Although it was intended on the whole as an enforcement of the Fourteenth Amendment's equal protection mandate, its sweeping public accommodations provisions in Title II had to be given some other justification so as not to repeat the mistake of 1875. Congress this time decided to rely on the commerce clause, and later that year, in two separate cases, Title II of the 1964 Civil Rights Act was handily upheld by the Supreme Court as an exercise of Congress's commerce power. With that ruling, the Supreme Court left the 1883 precedent undisturbed, merely noting that it was not "apposite" here. The 1964 Civil Rights Act was followed a year later by another monumental statute, the Voting Rights Act, whose contested provisions, dealing with literacy devices and federal examiners, were upheld by the Supreme Court in 1966, in *South Carolina v. Katzenbach*, as a "valid" exercise of the federal government's power under the Fifteenth Amendment.

FURTHER READING

Curtis, Michael Kent. *No State Shall Abridge: The Fourteenth Amendment and the Bill of Rights.* Durham, N.C.: Duke University Press, 1986.

Hall, Kermit L., et al. *American Legal History: Cases and Materials.* New York: Oxford University Press, 1991.

Karst, Kenneth. *Belonging to America: Equal Citizenship and the Constitution.* New Haven, Conn.: Yale University Press, 1989.

Veit, Helen E., et al., eds. *Creating the Bill of Rights: The Documentary Record from the First Federal Congress.* Baltimore, Md.: Johns Hopkins University Press, 1991.

Sugwon Kang

See also Affirmative action; Civil rights and liberties; Civil Rights movement; Commerce, regulation of; Contract, freedom of; Equal protection clause; Fifteenth Amendment; Fourteenth Amendment; Housing discrimination; Private discrimination; Race and discrimination; Thirteenth Amendment.

Civil Rights Cases

Citation: 109 U.S. 3
Date: October 15, 1883
Issues: Race discrimination; state action
Significance: Ruling that key provisions in a federal civil rights law were unconstitutional, the Supreme Court held that the Fourteenth Amendment applied to state action only and that Congress lacked authority to prohibit discrimination by private individuals.

The Civil Rights Act of 1875 outlawed racial discrimination in public accommodations, or privately owned businesses such as hotels, places of entertainment, and railroad cars. Five cases arising under the act were consolidated for argument before the Supreme Court. Speaking for an 8-1 majority, Justice Joseph P. Bradley narrowly interpreted the Fourteenth Amendment to mean that Congress could forbid only abridgment of civil rights by state government officials. Individual citizens, therefore, must look to state governments for protection against discrimination by privately owned businesses. Looking at the Thirteenth Amendment, Bradley conceded that Congress had the power to obliterate the badges and incidents of slavery, but he argued that elimination of these badges and incidents did not guarantee access to private businesses. Free blacks in the North had often faced private acts of discrimination, but they were still free citizens.

In a vigorous dissent, Justice John Marshall Harlan wrote that the majority was using a "narrow and artificial" interpretation of the Constitution. He emphasized that inequality in civil rights was one of the badges and incidents of slavery that Congress might forbid under the Thirteenth Amendment. Seventy-nine years later, the Court reversed the majority's decision in *Heart of Atlanta Motel v. United States* (1964), relying on congressional authority to regulate interstate commerce. The Court accepted much of Harlan's broad interpretation of the Thirteenth Amendment in *Jones v. Alfred H. Mayer Co.* (1968).

Thomas T. Lewis

See also Civil Rights acts; Equal protection clause; Fourteenth Amendment; *Heart of Atlanta Motel v. United States*; *Jones v. Alfred H. Mayer Co.*; *Moose Lodge v. Irvis*; Private discrimination; Race and discrimination; State action; Thirteenth Amendment.

Civil Rights movement

Date: 1950's-1970's
Description: Demonstrations, debates, boycotts, legislation, and litigation that attempted to secure the political, social, and economic rights of African Americans and all other U.S. citizens.
Significance: The efforts of African Americans to secure their civil rights led to numerous challenges before the Supreme Court. The movement's ideologies and styles were adopted by other ethnic communities and minorities, including women and homosexuals, in their struggles to obtain their rights.

In the 1960's and early 1970's, the Civil Rights movement led by African Americans was most effective in altering the politics, culture, and mores of American society. The movement is often regarded as beginning with *Brown v. Board of Education* (1954), a Supreme Court decision that struck down racially segregated education; however, its roots can be traced back to the post-Civil War era.

The Civil War (1861-1865) resulted in the preservation of the union of states and in the freeing of the bulk of the black labor force in the South's cotton economy. It did not, however, provide the freed slaves with the rights of citizenship. The Republican Congress passed the Fourteenth and Fifteenth Amendments to the Constitution (ratified 1868 and 1870 respectively) to provide equal citizenship for the former slaves. However, after the end of Reconstruction, most southern states passed black codes that effectively kept African Americans from voting, segregated them by law in many areas of public life, and maintained their subservience. By the early 1900's, social historian W. E. B. Du Bois wrote in his classic book *The Souls of Black Folk* (1903) that African Americans felt a sense of "twoness": They were Americans but also blacks who were not fully allowed the civil rights all Americans were guaranteed. Early civil rights efforts were initially quite successful, but when poised against entrenched racist institutions, these successes were often reversed.

A Modern Challenge. The Civil Rights movement that began in the mid-1950's differed from earlier civil rights efforts in that its successes had far more lasting consequences. Its approach to the problem of a lack of rights was multifaceted, including legal challenges, economic boycotts, political empowerment, and even efforts to influence the arts and media. The National Association for the Advancement of Colored People (NAACP), through its Legal Defense Fund, offered up numerous legal challenges against segregation, voting restrictions, and other civil rights violations, many of which reached the Supreme Court.

Three events between the years 1954 and 1960 shaped the Civil Rights movement. The first was the historical Supreme Court decision in *Brown v. Board of Education* in which Chief Justice Earl Warren, in his opinion for the Court, ruled that the separate but equal doctrine had no place in the field of public education. This decision, a major victory for the NAACP, had the profound consequence of placing the federal government officially on the side of desegregation. The implication was that the U.S. government would support the demise of segregation in more than education—that is, that separate but equal facilities generally might not be lawful. This single legal decision by the Court emboldened blacks to challenge segregation and encouraged whites who supported them to participate in this growing movement.

The second critical event was the Montgomery, Alabama, bus boycott. In 1955 Rosa Parks, an African American bus rider, refused to relinquish her seat to a white man as required by the bus company. Black clergy united in support of Parks and organized a boycott of the bus company. The Reverend Martin Luther King, Jr., became the group's primary spokesperson. A previous incident in Baton Rouge, Louisiana, was as successful as the Montgomery boycott but was not well publicized. In both instances, African Americans gained the right to equal access and could sit where they chose on public transportation.

The third event was a series of demonstrations that began in Greensboro, North Carolina, in 1960, when black students from a local historically black university participated in a sit-in demonstration in which they occupied seats at a local segregated lunch counter and refused to leave until they were served. The sit-in was successful, and similar demonstrations were held in many other areas in the South. Some demonstrators were arrested for disturbing the peace or trespassing, and these cases were appealed to the Supreme Court. In *Garner v. Louisiana* (1961), the Court overturned the convictions of sixteen African

The National Association for the Advancement of Colored People holds a civil rights demonstration outside the Democratic Party National Convention in Atlantic City, New Jersey, in 1964. (Library of Congress)

Americans who had participated in a lunch counter sit-in, and in *Peterson v. City of Greenville* (1963), it reversed additional sit-in cases, applying the state action doctrine to rule that the refusal to serve African Americans was not simply private discrimination.

The Court continued to expand its definition of state action to include what had been thought of as private conduct through most of the 1960's. For example, in *Burton v. Wilmington Parking Authority* (1961), the Court ruled against a restaurant that had refused to serve an African American because it was located in a parking garage owned by a government agency and the leasing arrangement allowed the agency to profit from the restaurant. The Court also supported the efforts of the Legal Defense Fund of the NAACP. In *National Association for the Advancement of Colored People v. Button* (1963), it blocked the Virginia legislature's attempt to stop the Legal Defense Fund by claiming its efforts were a solicitation of legal business, then prohibited by law.

Internal Conflict. By the mid-1960's, groups within the Civil Rights movement, including the Student Nonviolent Coordinating Committee (SNCC) and the Congress of Racial Equality (CORE), began to question the fundamental strategies of more traditional groups, including the NAACP's emphasis on litigation and nonviolence. The passage of the Civil Rights Act of 1964 and the Voting Rights Act of 1965 also changed the movement's focus. SNCC, CORE, and other groups debated the value of nonviolence as a tactic, argued about whether blacks and whites should be working together in the Civil Rights movement, and asked whether the movement should be attempting reform or revolution. In the second half of the 1960's, some African American civil rights leaders began talking about "black power," the achievement of rights for blacks by blacks within the American sociopolitical system.

By the mid-1970's, the Civil Rights movement had largely ended, although many African Americans continued to work to improve their status and safeguard their civil rights. The focus and emphasis of these efforts changed, however. The first African American mayor of Atlanta claimed that politics were the substitute for civil rights activism. The Reverend Jesse Jackson, by contrast, claimed that ownership and managerial power in the economy

was the substitute. The Civil Rights movement was successful in gaining political and economic rights for African Americans, opening public facilities to them, and influencing American culture through the arts and the media. After it ended, however, an increasing gap emerged between those African Americans who had succeeded in the economy and those who remained part of an underclass. The movement, although it ended legal segregation and overt discrimination, could not eliminate all prejudice and discrimination, nor could it address all the social and economic needs of African Americans.

FURTHER READING

Belfrage, Sally. *Freedom Summer.* New York: New York University Press, 1965.

Boxill, Bernard. *Blacks and Social Justice.* Totowa, N.J.: Rowman & Allanheld, 1984.

Broderick, Francis L. *W. E. B. Du Bois: Negro Leader in a Time of Crisis.* Reprint. Stanford, Calif.: Stanford University Press, 1966.

Carnoy, Martin. *Faded Dreams: The Politics and Economics of Race in America.* Cambridge, England: Cambridge University Press, 1994.

Cashman, Sean Dennis. *African Americans and the Quest for Civil Rights, 1900-1990.* New York: New York University Press, 1991.

Feagin, Joe R., and Melvin P. Sikes. *Living with Racism: The Black Middle-Class Experience.* Boston: Beacon Press, 1991.

William Osborne and Dean Wagstaffe

SEE ALSO Affirmative action; *Brown v. Board of Education*; Civil Rights Acts; Legal Defense Fund, NAACP; National Association for the Advancement of Colored People (NAACP); *National Association for the Advancement of Colored People v. Button*; Private discrimination; Race and discrimination; School integration and busing; Separate but equal doctrine; Sit-in demonstrations; State action; Vote, right to.

Civil War

DATE: 1861-1865

DESCRIPTION: Also known as the War Between the States, the U.S. Civil War pitted eleven Southern states—which seceded to form the Confederate States of America—against the rest of the Union.

SIGNIFICANCE: The Civil War was a profound threat to the stability of the U.S. constitutional order. The Supreme Court played a role in the war's inception, the response by President Abraham Lincoln and Congress, and the war's conclusion and aftermath. Except for a few important and controversial decisions, however, the Court had limited significance during the Civil War.

The Civil War raised questions of fundamental importance to the U.S. constitutional order. Among these were questions about whether a state could secede from the Union, the distribution of the war-making powers between the president and Congress, and the authority of the Supreme Court to review those powers. What was undoubtedly a crisis for the country was no less a crisis for the Court. In the end, these fundamental constitutional issues were decided and resolved, not through appeals to the law or to the Supreme Court, but through political force.

The Road to War. A number of factors led to the war. Prominent among them was the issue of slavery, left unresolved at the nation's founding. Congress formally prohibited the slave trade in 1808 and tried to end the debate with the Missouri Compromise of 1820, but the problems slavery raised for the Union did not dissipate. The Court took up the issue in the case of *Scott v. Sandford* (1857). Dred Scott, a slave, claimed that he had become a free man because he had resided in areas where slavery was illegal under the Missouri Compromise. Writing for the Court, Chief Justice Roger Brooke Taney held that persons of African American descent, whether slaves or emancipated, were not citizens of the United States. For "more than a century," Taney wrote, African Americans had "been regarded as beings of an inferior order, and altogether unfit to associate with the white race . . . and so far inferior, that they had no rights which the white man was bound to respect."

The chief justice also ruled that the Missouri Compromise was unconstitutional because Congress had no constitutional authority to regulate slavery in the territories. Some critics of the Court complain that it should not have tried to resolve a divisive political issue through a legal decision. On the other hand, the Court had not come to the issue uninvited. President James Buchanan, for ex-

ample, had encouraged the Court to rule on the issue, stating in his inaugural speech that slavery "was a judicial question, which legitimately belongs to the Supreme Court, before whom it is now pending and will . . . be speedily settled." The Court's controversial ruling, far from settling the matter, galvanized forces on both sides of the slavery question. Just four years later, the country was at war with itself.

Secession and the Constitution. In late 1860 South Carolina and several other states sought to secede from the Union. Such claims were not novel, at least as a matter of constitutional theory. The nullification controversy of 1832-1833 had involved similar claims. During that controversy, South Carolina had argued "that each state of the Union has the right, whenever it may deem such a course necessary . . . to secede peaceably from the Union, and that there is no constitutional power in the general government . . . to retain by force such stake in the Union." President Buchanan thought secession illegal, but he agreed that the federal government lacked the authority to prevent states from leaving. In *Kentucky v. Dennison* (1861), the Court sanctioned this understanding of the limits of federal power. The case involved a fugitive who had helped a slave escape from Kentucky. The fugitive ran to Ohio, and the Ohio governor refused to return him to Kentucky. Ruling for the Court, Chief Justice Taney refused to order the governor to turn over the fugitive, stating that criminal extradition clause of the Constitution depended on the states for its enforcement. There is, he argued, "no power delegated to the General Government . . . to use any coercive means" to force a governor to act. Implicit in this opinion is the clear sense that President Abraham Lincoln lacked any constitutional authority to keep the states in the Union.

In his inaugural address, President Lincoln argued instead that "the Union of these States is perpetual. Perpetuity is implied, if not expressed, in the fundamental law of all national governments." Lincoln thus concluded that the Union, older than the Constitution, authorized him to prevent states from dissolving the bonds of the Union. One of his first actions was to resupply the Union troops at Fort Sumter. Forces in Charleston fired upon the fort, and the constitutional nature of the Union was left to be decided by military force and not by the Supreme Court.

Presidential Authority to Make War. When he assumed office, President Lincoln was faced with the prospect of war. In his first inaugural address, he responded directly to the Court's decision in *Scott.* "I do not forget the position assumed by some, that constitutional questions are to be decided by the Supreme Court.... At the same time the candid citizen must confess that if the policy of the government, upon vital questions, affecting the whole people, is to be irrevocably fixed by decisions of the Supreme Court. . . . the people will have ceased, to be their own rulers." Lincoln's insistence upon his own authority to interpret the Constitution foreshadowed his interaction with the Court throughout the Civil War.

The first significant issue concerned the president's authority to conduct war without prior congressional approval. The issue was raised when Lincoln, responding to the South's declaration of independence from the Union, ordered a naval blockade of Southern ports in April, 1961. Acting pursuant to Lincoln's order, Union warships seized a number of Southern and foreign ships and put them and their cargoes up for sale. In the *Prize Cases* (1863), the owners of four such ships argued that the president had no constitutional authority to order the blockade, for the power "to declare war [and] make rules concerning captures on land and water" was given by the Constitution to Congress, not the president. Congress did not ratify the president's decision until July, 1861.

In a 5-4 decision, the Court ruled for Lincoln. Writing for the majority, Justice Robert C. Grier admitted that the Constitution gave to Congress alone the power to declare a national or foreign war. He noted also that the Constitution entrusts the position of commander-in-chief to the presidency. "If a war be made by invasion of a foreign nation," Grier continued, "the President is not only authorized but bound to resist by force." In this case, "the President was bound to meet [the war] in the shape it presented itself, without waiting for Congress to baptize it with a name." The Court further underscored the president's autonomy by declaring that "whether the President, in fulfilling his duties, as Commander-in-Chief, in suppressing an insurrection, has met with such armed resistance, and a civil war of such alarming proportions as will compel him to accord to them the character of belligerents, is a question to be decided *by him*, and

this Court must be governed by the decisions and acts of the political department of the Government to which this power was entrusted."

In dissent, Justice Samuel Nelson agreed that "in one sense, no doubt this is war, but it is a statement simply of its existence in a material sense, and has no relevancy or weight when the question is what constitutes war in a legal sense . . . and of the Constitution of the United States." The Court's deference to the president's decision about when the war began was mirrored at war's end by its decision in *Freeborn v. the "Protector,"* (1872), which held that the war was formally concluded when the president said so. Together, these cases have provided strong support for presidential decisions to initiate military actions without first seeking congressional authorization.

The Court and Civil Liberties. President Lincoln's decision to impose a naval blockade on Southern ports was just one part of a larger war effort. In addition to the blockade, Lincoln undertook a series of actions that amounted to the imposition of martial law. Among these were orders directing military authorities to search homes without warrants, imprisonment without charge or trial in civilian or in military courts, and suspension of the writ of *habeas corpus.* The most expansive order suspending the writ was issued in September, 1862; Lincoln did not seek congressional authorization for this order, and Congress did not finally authorize the president to suspend *habeas corpus* until the following March. Thousands of citizens were detained by the military and held without charge and without trial in either a civilian or a military court.

The constitutionality of Lincoln's decision to suspend the writ was first tested in a federal circuit court in Baltimore, Maryland, in 1861. The military had arrested John Merryman for his participation in an attack on Union forces. Merryman petitioned the court for a writ of *habeas corpus.* Chief Justice Taney, riding circuit, granted the writ and had it sent to the general in command of the fort where Merryman was detained. Sending an aide in his place, the general replied that he would not obey the writ because Lincoln had suspended its operation. In response, Chief Justice Taney found the general in contempt of court, an action with little practical effect, and issued an opinion that directly addressed the constitutionality of Lincoln's decision. Taney held that Lincoln had no authority

President Abraham Lincoln (third from left) signs the Emancipation Proclamation during the Civil War. (Archive Photos)

to suspend the writ because Article I of the Constitution entrusted that authority to Congress "in language too clear to be misunderstood by anyone." Taney ordered a copy of the opinion sent to Lincoln. Lincoln failed to respond directly, instead stating in a later special session of Congress: "Now it is insisted that Congress, and not the Executive, is vested with [the power]. But the Constitution itself, is silent as to which, or who, is to exercise the power." In the same speech, Lincoln offered a more fundamental objection: "Are all the laws, *but one*, to go unexecuted, and the government itself go to pieces, lest that one be violated?"

The Supreme Court was presented with another claim concerning *habeas corpus* just two years later, in the case of *Ex parte Vallandigham* (1864). Vallandigham was arrested and tried by the military. He sought a writ of *habeas corpus*, but the Court dismissed his case, claiming that it had no authority over a military court. The Court's reluctance to entertain the case was symbolic of its silent posture on military interferences with civil liberties throughout the Civil War. Moreover, the Court would not again consider the constitutionality of Lincoln's wartime suspensions until well after the war was over, in the case of *Ex parte Milligan* (1866).

Reconstruction. The end of the Civil War left the Union with difficult questions about how to bring the Southern states back into the fold. Congressional representatives from the Northern states

had denied that the Southern states could validly leave the Union, but a return to the status quo that had existed before the hostilities was unlikely. Some congressional representatives and President Andrew Johnson, Lincoln's successor, favored a policy of accelerated reconstruction that included provisional state governments. However, so-called Radical Republicans in Congress insisted that the Southern states could be readmitted only on whatever terms Congress imposed. What followed was the imposition of military rule, which included trials in military courts and the use of federal troops to maintain order. The result was a great contest between the president and Congress, a contest that revolved around the question of how the South should be "reconstructed" and about which branch of government would be responsible for the process. The Supreme Court played a small, but nonetheless significant, part in this contest.

Initially the Court cast some doubt on the constitutionality of various Reconstruction measures. In the *Test Oath Cases* (1867, *Cummings v. Missouri* and *Ex parte Garland*), for example, the Court found the loyalty oaths required of voters, attorneys, and others in the Southern states a violation of the ex post facto clause. In the well-known *Milligan* case, the Court seemed to cast further doubt on the constitutionality of congressional reconstruction by holding that military courts could not try civilians in those areas in which the civilian courts were functioning. In this case, the military had arrested Milligan, and he was convicted and sentenced to be hanged by a military commission. He sought a writ of *habeas corpus*. Notwithstanding its earlier decision in *Vallandigham*, the Court ruled for Milligan. In his opinion for the Court, Justice David Davis wrote

The Constitution of the United States is a law for rulers and for people, equally in war and in peace, and covers with the shield of its protection all classes of men, at all times, and under all circumstances. No doctrine, involving more pernicious consequences, was ever invented by the wit of man than that any of its provisions can be suspended during any of the great exigencies of government."

The Court did agree, though, "that there are occasions when martial law can be properly applied." If civilian courts are "actually closed" and it is "impossible to administer criminal justice according to law," then the military may supply a substitute for civilian authority. In Milligan's case, the courts had been open and functioning; consequently, Milligan's arrest by military authorities had been unconstitutional.

Although the Court did not fervently protect civil liberties until the war was over—in stark contrast to its behavior during the war—many congressional leaders saw in the case a more general threat to Reconstruction policy, which included military governments and tribunals. Thaddeaus Stevens, for example, complained that the decision "although in terms not as infamous as the Dred Scott decision, is yet far more dangerous in its operation." Several bills were introduced in Congress to curb the Court, including one by Representative John Bingham of Ohio, who warned ominously of a constitutional amendment that could result "in the abolition of the tribunal itself."

Opposition to Reconstruction. Many congressional leaders believed that a case then working its way through the federal courts would give the Court a chance to declare much of the Reconstruction effort unconstitutional. The case, *Ex parte McCardle* (1869), concerned a newspaper editor in Mississippi who had been arrested and tried by a military commission. McCardle petitioned for a writ of *habeas corpus*, arguing that the Reconstruction statute that had authorized his trial was unconstitutional. An appellate court denied the writ, whereupon McCardle appealed to the Supreme Court under an 1867 statute that governed such appeals. The Court accepted the appeal and heard arguments on the case. Fearful of the ruling, Congress reacted by passing a new law repealing the 1867 statute. This led the Court to reschedule oral argument, this time focusing on the question of whether Congress could withdraw jurisdiction from the Court in a pending case. A unanimous Court concluded that the statute withdrawing its jurisdiction in *McCardle* was constitutionally per-

missible. No longer having jurisdiction, the Court dismissed McCardle's appeal.

Milligan aside, the Court generally refrained from inquiring into the constitutionality of Reconstruction. Thus, in *Mississippi v. Johnson* (1867), the Court ruled that a president is immune from an injunction by a court to restrain enforcement of Reconstruction legislation. Mississippi had asked the Court to enjoin President Johnson from executing the Reconstruction acts because they were, according to Mississippi, unconstitutional. The Court declined to intervene, finding that such interference would be "an absurd and excessive extravagance." One year later, in a similar case (*Georgia v. Stanton*, 1868), the Court again indicated that it was unwilling to inquire into the details of Reconstruction policy by refusing to enjoin enforcement of the Reconstruction acts by the secretary of war.

In 1869 the Court put its imprimatur on Reconstruction—and on Lincoln's insistence that the Union was perpetual—in *Texas v. White*. The Court ruled, first, that Texas's decision to leave the Union was invalid because Texas "became one of the United States, she entered into an indissoluble relation. . . . There was no place for reconsideration, or revocation." Therefore, Texas had remained a "state" in the Union throughout the war. In some ways, the Court simply reaffirmed the result of the war, but the opinion is also an important statement of constitutional principle, for it held that the Union was not a mere "compact of states." The case is also important for a second reason: The Court conceded that the initial responsibility for Reconstruction rested with the president in his capacity as commander-in-chief; however, that authority "must be considered as provisional" to the greater authority of Congress to "guarantee to every state in the Union a republican form of government."

FURTHER READING

For a detailed study of Lincoln and the Civil War, see Herman Belz's *Abraham Lincoln, Constitutionalism, and Equal Rights in the Civil War Era* (New York: Fordham University Press, 1998). Still useful is James G. Randall's earlier study, *Constitutional Problems Under Lincoln* (Urbana: University of Illinois Press, 1964). Charles Fairman's *History of the Supreme Court of the United States: Reconstruction and Reunion 1864-88* (2 vols., New York: Macmillan,

1971) is a comprehensive account of the Court during the Reconstruction era. Harold Hyman's *A More Perfect Union: The Impact of the Civil War and Reconstruction upon the Constitution* (New York: Alfred A. Knopf, 1973) is still among the best treatments of the Civil War and the Constitution. Stanley Kutler, *Judicial Power and Reconstruction Politics* (Chicago: University of Chicago Press, 1968) examines the Reconstruction's effect on the judiciary. For a later study of *Texas v. White* and Justice Salmon P. Chase, see Harold Hyman's *The Reconstruction Justice of Salmon P. Chase: "In Re Turner" and "Texas v. White"* (Lawrence: University Press of Kansas, 1997).

John E. Finn

SEE ALSO *Habeas corpus*; Lincoln, Abraham; Martial law; Military justice; *Milligan, Ex parte*; *Mississippi v. Johnson*; Presidential powers; *Prize Cases*; Reconstruction; States' rights; *Texas v. White*; War and civil liberties.

Clark, Tom C.

IDENTIFICATION: Associate justice (August 24, 1949-June 12, 1967)

NOMINATED BY: Harry S Truman

BORN: September 23, 1899, Dallas, Texas

DIED: June 13, 1977, New York, New York

SIGNIFICANCE: As attorney general, Clark designed and defended much of President Harry S Truman's domestic anticommunism program. As a Supreme Court justice, he supported these and similar state-level loyalty programs and, in the Warren Court, opposed efforts to curb those programs.

Born into a family of Texas lawyers, Clark served in World War I and received a bachelor's degree in 1921 from the University of Texas at Austin and a law degree from the same school in 1922. He practiced law in his father's Dallas firm, served as the civil district attorney for Dallas County, and gained the respect and friendship of leading Texas Democratic politicians including Senator Tom Connally and Congressman Sam Rayburn.

The election of Franklin D. Roosevelt in 1936 brought young Clark the opportunity to work for the Department of Justice in Washington, D.C. While at the department, Clark worked on wartime claims and the evacuation of Japanese Americans

Tom C. Clark. (Harris and Ewing/Collection of the Supreme Court of the United States)

from the West Coast. In 1943 he was promoted to assistant attorney general to head the antitrust division and later the criminal division.

Clark's service in the Justice Department laid the groundwork for his later career. Then Missouri senator Harry S Truman led an investigation of wartime fraud. Findings were submitted to Clark, who ably prosecuted those accused. Clark worked to secure the 1944 Democratic vice presidential nomination for Truman. When Truman assumed the presidency at Roosevelt's death, Clark's appointment as attorney general was one of Truman's important early appointments. As attorney general, Clark spoke for the Truman administration before congressional committees and personally argued several cases before the Supreme Court. However, Attorney General Clark was best known as one of the main designers of Truman's domestic anticommunism program, including the preparation of the first attorney general's list of dangerous political organizations.

Preparing for the 1948 presidential election, Clark successfully and accurately refuted claims that the Truman administration was "soft on communism." His reward came one year after Truman's 1948 victory when Truman nominated him to the Supreme Court. Clark served Truman well as attorney general, and many believed the nominee would likely support then Chief Justice Fred M. Vinson's strong anticommunist views. Texas Democratic Party leaders and bar associations supported Clark's nomination. The Senate confirmed the nomination by a vote of seventy-three to eight.

Associate Justice Clark supported the anticommunist views of the chief justice, usually voting to uphold anticommunist and loyalty programs, including those established by state and local governments. However, he wrote for a unanimous court in *Wieman v. Epdegraff* (1952) that mere membership of the accused in an organization on the attorney general's list did not prove disloyalty. As a judge, Clark ruled that prosecutors misused the list he drew up years before as attorney general.

In 1953 President Dwight D. Eisenhower's selection of Earl Warren to succeed Vinson as chief justice changed Clark's role on the Court. During the early years of the Warren Court, Clark wrote a series of noncontroversial antitrust majority opinions and was moved by Warren to join a unanimous Court seeking to end racially segregated public schooling and other early Warren Court civil rights decisions.

The appointment of William J. Brennan, Jr., in 1956 signaled the start of liberal dominance of the Court, led by Warren, Hugo L. Black, and William O. Douglas. Clark's long-held anticommunist views and his willingness to support police and prosecutorial powers of the state contrasted with the views of more liberal Court members. Clark dissented again and again as the Court moved to expand the rights of the accused. Regarding loyalty-security decisions, he was usually in the minority, upholding government power while the majority supported the claims of individuals alleging governmental abuses.

With the arrival of the 1960's, Clark turned to other matters. He led the Court in deciding *Mapp v. Ohio* (1961), which required police and prosecutors not to use illegally obtained evidence to get a conviction. He also concurred in a historic decision, *Baker v. Carr* (1962), which effectively required state legislatures to redraw electoral district boundaries to accommodate population shifts. Also, in *Abington School District v. Schempp* (1963),

Clark held that state and local governments violated the First Amendment establishment clause when they required schoolchildren to open the school day by saying officially prescribed prayers or reading from the Bible. Even as the Court's concerns turned away from loyalty tests and related matters, Clark continued to resist challenges to state and local loyalty programs.

Family loyalty motivated Clark's retirement from the Court. In February, 1967, President Lyndon B. Johnson announced the appointment of Clark's son, Ramsey, as attorney general of the United States. Knowing that his son would be presenting cases to the Court, Tom Clark retired in June, 1967, completing eighteen years of service on the Court.

FURTHER READING

Commission on the Bicentennial of the United States. *The Supreme Court of the United States: Its Beginnings and Its Justices, 1790-1991*. Washington, D.C.: Author, 1992.

Kirkendall, Richard. "Tom C. Clark." In *The Justices of the United States Supreme Court: Their Lives and Major Opinions*, edited by Leon Friedman and Fred L. Israel. New York: Chelsea House, 1997.

Gayle R. Avant

SEE ALSO *Abington School District v. Schempp*; *Baker v. Carr*; *Brown v. Board of Education*; Civil rights and liberties; Cold War; New Deal; Vinson, Fred M.; Warren, Earl.

Clark Distilling Co. v. Western Maryland Railway Co.

CITATION: 242 U.S. 311
DATE: January 8, 1917
ISSUE: Commerce clause
SIGNIFICANCE: The Supreme Court upheld the constitutionality of the Webb-Kenyon Act of 1913, forbidding the shipment of alcoholic beverages into a state in violation of its laws.

The Webb-Kenyon Act, passed in 1913 over President William H. Taft's veto, assisted the Prohibition states in enforcing their laws against the sale or shipment of intoxicating liquors to customers within their borders. By a 7-2 vote, the Supreme Court upheld the law, recognizing that Congress had broad discretion in choosing how to regulate interstate commerce. Speaking for the Court, Justice Edward D. White argued that the law applied uniformly throughout the nation and that it did not delegate the commerce power to the states.

Thomas T. Lewis

SEE ALSO Commerce, regulation of; Eighteenth Amendment; Federalism; States' rights.

Clarke, John H.

IDENTIFICATION: Associate justice (August 1, 1916-September 18, 1922)
NOMINATED BY: Woodrow Wilson
BORN: September 18, 1857, New Lisbon, Ohio
DIED: March 22, 1945, San Diego, California
SIGNIFICANCE: During his short tenure on the Supreme Court, Clarke opposed the Court's nullification of social and economic regulatory legislation.

The son of a prominent Ohio attorney, Clarke graduated from Western Reserve College in 1877 and was admitted to the Ohio bar in 1878 after studying law at Western Reserve and with his fa-

John H. Clarke. (Harris and Ewing/Collection of the Supreme Court of the United States)

ther. Clarke practiced law for nearly twenty years in Youngstown, where he was part owner of the *Youngstown Vindicator* and was active in state Democratic politics. Clarke moved to Cleveland in 1897, where he served as counsel for railroads. Meanwhile, Clarke became an outspoken advocate of such progressive measures as the initiative and referendum, the recall of public officials other than judges, regulations of the hours and conditions of labor, woman suffrage, and civil service reform. Clarke made unsuccessful bids for the U.S. Senate in 1904 and 1914.

Clarke's Progressive leanings, his Democratic loyalties and connections, his widely recognized legal abilities, and his dedication to vigorous prosecution of companies under the federal antitrust laws led to his appointment by President Woodrow Wilson in 1914 as a judge of the U.S. District Court for the northern district of Ohio. The same considerations resulted in Wilson's appointment of Clarke to the Supreme Court in 1916 after the resignation of Charles Evans Hughes.

Clarke's record on the Court was consistent with Wilson's expectations. During his six years on the Court, Clarke regularly voted with the Court's Progressive bloc to sustain the constitutionality of social and economic regulatory legislation and to support vigorous enforcement of the antitrust laws. In some cases, Clarke cast the swing vote to sustain regulatory legislation. Clarke dissented in various cases in which the Court struck down such laws. In *Hammer v. Dagenhart* (1918), Clarke joined Justices Joseph McKenna, Louis D. Brandeis, and Oliver Wendell Holmes in dissenting from the Court's decision that a federal child labor law exceeded Congress's power to regulate interstate commerce. In *Bailey v. Drexel Furniture Co.* (1922), Clarke entered a sole dissent, without opinion, from the Court's decision that a reenacted child labor law that taxed goods produced by children was not within the congressional power to levy taxes.

In cases involving free speech, Clarke espoused the same broad view of state power that he expressed in cases involving social and economic regulations. Most notably, Clarke broke with Holmes and Brandeis to write the majority opinion in *Abrams v. United States* (1919), upholding the espionage convictions of political dissidents whose primary offense was to distribute written criticisms of the government's military policies.

Increasingly bored by what he perceived as the triviality of much of the Court's work and frustrated by what he perceived as his inability to promote his progressive philosophy on an increasingly conservative Court, Clarke resigned from the Court after only six years in order to work for world peace. After retiring from the Court, Clarke spoke and wrote widely on behalf of U.S. entry into the League of Nations and served as a trustee of the World Peace Foundation. He also became an outspoken critic of judicial activism by the Supreme Court and publicly supported Franklin D. Roosevelt's Court-packing plan in 1937.

FURTHER READING

Warner, Hoyt Landon. *The Life of Mr. Justice Clarke: A Testament to the Power of Liberal Dissent in America.* Cleveland, Ohio: Western Reserve University Press, 1959.

William G. Ross

SEE ALSO *Abrams v. United States; Bailey v. Drexel Furniture Co.*; Court-packing plan; *Hammer v. Dagenhart*; Progressivism; Resignation and retirement; Wilson, Woodrow.

Classic, United States v.

CITATION: 313 U.S. 299
DATE: May 26, 1941
ISSUE: White primaries
SIGNIFICANCE: Overturning its 1921 decision, the Supreme Court held that Congress has the power to regulate primaries whenever state law makes them an integral part of the process for electing candidates to federal office.

The precedent set in *Newberry v. United States* (1921), which prevented Congress from regulating party primaries, was one of the foundation blocks for the whites-only primaries of the South. The Supreme Court partially overruled *Newberry* in the *Classic* case, which involved charges against a Louisiana election commissioner for deliberately changing the ballots in a congressional primary. Speaking for a 5-3 majority, Chief Justice Harlan Fiske Stone ruled that the federal government, based on Article I of the U.S. Constitution, had the right to ensure the integrity of primary elections if they had a clear relationship to the determination of who would be elected to Congress. *Classic* pre-

pared the way for the landmark case *Smith v. Allwright* (1944).

Thomas T. Lewis

SEE ALSO *Grovey v. Townsend*; Race and discrimination; *Smith v. Allwright*; State action; White primaries.

Clear and present danger test

DESCRIPTION: First legal standard established by the Supreme Court in 1919 to determine whether speech posed such a direct and imminent threat to society that it could be punished without violating the free speech guarantees of the First Amendment to the U.S. Constitution.
SIGNIFICANCE: Originally adopted to uphold the convictions of radicals during World War I, the clear and present danger test was transformed into a standard protecting a wide spectrum of controversial, offensive, and even hateful speech.

Although the First Amendment was ratified in 1791, thereby guaranteeing that Congress could make no law abridging freedom of speech, freedom of the press, or other personal rights, it was not until 1919 that the Supreme Court squarely addressed the limits of free speech.

Fearing the impact of disloyal speeches, leaflets, and newspaper articles during World War I, Congress passed the Espionage Act of 1917, which prohibited obstruction of the war effort. By 1919 three separate cases had reached the Court in which Eugene Debs, leader of the Socialist Party; Charles Schenck, an official of the Socialist Party; and Jacob Frohwerk, the publisher of a socialist newspaper, had all been convicted of violating the Espionage Act and sentenced to jail. In each case, the Court voted unanimously to uphold the convictions, despite arguments that the antiwar activists' statements and publications were constitutionally protected under the First Amendment.

The task fell to Justice Oliver Wendell Holmes to write the opinions explaining the Court's decisions. By 1919, Holmes, at age seventy-six, had served on the Court for seventeen years and had acquired a reputation as one of the finest legal minds in the country. In *Schenck v. United States*, Holmes wrote that the "question in every case is whether the words are used in such circumstances and are of such a nature as to create a clear and present danger that they will bring about the substantive evils that Congress has a right to prevent." Without using the words "clear and present danger," the companion opinions in *Debs v. United States* and *Frohwerk v. United States*, also written by Holmes, upheld the convictions.

A Reconsideration. In the coming months, however, Holmes and his friend and colleague, Justice Louis D. Brandeis, seriously reconsidered the importance of free speech in a democratic society, even in times of war. In *Abrams v. United States* (1919), while the majority of the Court upheld the convictions of a group of Russian immigrants for distributing pamphlets condemning President Woodrow Wilson for sending U.S. troops to fight against the Bolshevik Revolution in Russia, Holmes and Brandeis joined in a vigorous dissent.

Speaking for the Court, Justice John H. Clarke relied on Holmes's own clear and present danger test. The leaflets violated the law because they had been distributed "at the supreme crisis of the war" and amounted to "an attempt to defeat the war plans of the Government." Moreover, the general strike advocated by the *Abrams* defendants would have necessarily hampered prosecution of the war with Germany.

In dissent, Holmes did not repudiate his earlier opinions. Instead, he denied that "the surreptitious publishing of a silly leaflet by an unknown man" created "a clear and imminent danger that will bring about forthwith certain substantial evils that the United States constitutionally may seek to prevent." Tilting the clear and present danger test away from an instrument in service of restricting speech and toward a shield protecting speech, Holmes argued that the First Amendment protected the expression of all opinions "unless they so imminently threatened immediate interference with the lawful and pressing purposes of the law that an immediate check is required to save the country."

A Tool for Protection. The clear and present danger test fell out of favor until the late 1930's when for more than a decade the Court used it to protect speech in a wide array of situations. However, in the midst of the Cold War and the mounting fear of communism, in *Dennis v. United States* (1951), the Court ignored the immediacy requirement of the clear and present danger test and upheld the convictions of eleven Communist Party leaders for conspiring to advocate the violent overthrow of the government.

In 1969 the Supreme Court adopted the Holmes-Brandeis dissent in *Abrams*. In *Brandenburg v. Ohio*, the Court reversed the conviction of a Ku Klux Klan leader under a state statute prohibiting criminal syndicalism. Consequently, a half century after it was first articulated, the clear and present danger test matured into a modern barrier to censorship, setting a high threshold protecting a wide spectrum of diverse and controversial speech. The Court held that the guarantees of the First Amendment "do not permit a State to forbid or proscribe advocacy of the use of force or of law violation except where such advocacy is directed to inciting or producing imminent lawless action and is likely to incite or produce such action." In words reminiscent of Holmes's prescient dissent in *Abrams*, the Court significantly strengthened constitutional protection for freedom of expression.

Stephen F. Rohde

SEE ALSO *Abrams v. United States*; Bad tendency test; Brandeis, Louis D.; *Brandenburg v. Ohio*; Censorship; Criminal syndicalism; Dissents; First Amendment; Holmes, Oliver Wendell; *Schenck v. United States*; *Tennessee v. Garner.*

Clerk of the Court

DESCRIPTION: Individual responsible for the administrative management of the Supreme Court's docket.

SIGNIFICANCE: The clerk of the Court serves as the primary liaison between attorneys practicing before the Court and the Court itself.

The Supreme Court has five statutory officers: the clerk of the Court, the reporter of decisions, the marshal, the librarian, and the administrative assistant to the chief justice. Created in February, 1790, the office of the clerk of the Court was the first of the Court's nonjudicial staff. The clerk's duties have changed considerably since the late eighteenth century. The first clerk, John Tucker, for example, was singularly responsible for maintaining the library, enforcing courtroom etiquette, collecting justices' salaries, and even securing lodgings for the justices during the Court's term. Many of these initial obligations have become the responsibility of other nonjudicial staff. Over the centuries, the clerk's office has grown considerably—to a staff of twenty-six.

For longer than one hundred years, the clerk, who is appointed by the chief justice, received no salary for his services. In lieu of salaries, clerks pocketed filing and attorneys' admission fees. For most of the nineteenth century, their compensation exceeded that of the justices. In 1921 clerks became salaried employees. In 1988 Congress set their annual compensation at $75,000. Only nineteen people have served as a clerk of the Court.

The primary responsibility of the clerk is to manage the Court's docket. The clerk receives and records all motions, petitions, jurisdictional statements, briefs, and other documents and has the authority to reject any submitted filing that does not comply with the rules of the Supreme Court (such as fees, forms and lengths of filings, and timeliness). In the case of an appeal or petition for certiorari, the clerk notifies the adverse party, the respondent, that he or she has thirty days to file a brief in response. After the respondent's brief is received, the clerk circulates a set of briefs for each case to each judicial chamber for consideration. Following judicial consideration, the clerk notifies the parties as to the status of the petition. Assuming that the justices grant certiorari, the clerk requests that attorneys submit briefs setting forth their arguments and how they think the case should be decided. Upon receipt, the clerk distributes these briefs to each judicial chamber and schedules a date for oral argument. The clerk also obtains the case records from lower federal courts.

In addition to these duties, the clerk collects filing and admissions fees, supervises admission to (and disbarment from) the Supreme Court bar, and advises attorneys practicing before the Court on rules and procedures. The clerk also prepares and maintains the order list, which summarizes the Court's action in cases under review, and the *Supreme Court Journal*, which contains the minutes of the Court's sessions.

In 1975 a computer system was installed to assist the clerk in the execution of formal responsibilities. The system helps monitor the clerk's records and automatically notifies counsel as to the disposition of their filings. In spite of this assistance, each motion, petition, jurisdictional statement, brief, and other document must still be processed and entered by hand. This task necessitates voluminous

CLERKS OF THE COURT

1790-1791	John Tucker
1791-1800	Samuel Bayard
1800-1825	Elias B. Caldwell
1826-1827	William Griffith
1827-1863	William T. Carroll
1863-1880	D. W. Middleton
1880-1913	J. H. McKenney
1913-1921	James D. Maher
1921-1927	William R. Stansbury
1927-1952	C. Elmore Cropley
1952-1956	Harold B. Willey
1956-1958	John T. Fey
1958-1961	James R. Browning
1961-1970	John F. Davis
1970-1972	E. Robert Seaver
1972-1981	Michael Rodak, Jr.
1981-1985	Alexander Stevas
1985-1991	Joseph F. Spaniol, Jr.
1991-	William K. Suter

paperwork. In 1998, for example, the Court had 7,692 cases on its docket. Each case on the docket has, at a minimum, one jurisdictional statement and two briefs. Those cases accepted for oral argument have, at a minimum, two additional briefs. Assuming that the Court schedules oral argument for ninety-three cases, as it did in 1998, that brings the total number of "documents" received by the clerk in one term to more than twenty-three thousand.

FURTHER READING

Biskupic, Joan, and Elder Witt. *The Supreme Court at Work*. Washington, D.C.: Congressional Quarterly, 1997.

Epstein, Lee, Jeffrey A. Segal, Harold J. Spaeth, and Thomas G. Walker. *The Supreme Court Compendium: Data, Decisions, and Developments*. Washington, D.C.: Congressional Quarterly, 1996.

O'Brien, David M. *Storm Center: The Supreme Court in American Politics*. New York: W. W. Norton, 1996.

Rehnquist, William H. *The Supreme Court: How It Was, How It Is*. New York: Morrow, William, 1989.

Richard A. Glenn

SEE ALSO Administrative assistant to chief justice; Bureaucratization of the judiciary; Certiorari, writ of; Marshals of the Courts; Reporters, Supreme Court; Rules of the Court; Staff of the Court; Workload.

Clerks of the justices

DESCRIPTION: Employees of the Supreme Court who assist the justices in research, selecting the petitions for certiorari worthy of review and writing the opinions at the decision-on-the-merits stage.

SIGNIFICANCE: Although controversy continues surrounding the extent of influence that clerks wield in the Supreme Court's decision-making and opinion-writing processes, there is little debate regarding the role they play in screening the more than eight thousand petitions for writs of certiorari filed each October term.

Associate Justice Horace Gray was the first justice to employ a full-time clerk in 1882. His clerk's responsibilities included being his personal barber and fulfilling basic secretarial duties. In 1886 Congress permitted each justice to hire a stenographic clerk. Four of the justices of the Supreme Court hired personal clerks, whose responsibilities ranged from running personal errands to conducting basic legal research. During the 1946 to 1969 October terms, most of the associate justices employed two law clerks. In 1970 most of the justices hired three clerks and, in 1980, Congress authorized all the justices to employ as many as four clerks. Scholars found that as the numbers of clerks increased, so did the number of words in decisions, footnotes, and citations to other cases.

Although most law clerks serve only one term on the Court, some have stayed longer. Some clerks have worked for more than one justice, and others have become virtually permanent fixtures in the Court. A clerk for associate justice Pierce Butler, for example, served sixteen terms. It is also common for clerks to stay on a few weeks after the term has expired to train their replacements.

Criteria for Selection. The individual justices have complete discretion in choosing their clerks, although most of those selected have graduated near the top of their law school class and have served in an editorial position on their school's law journal. Researcher David M. O'Brien found that four basic factors appear to be central in the law

clerk selection process: particular law schools, particular geographic regions, prior clerking experience on particular lower courts for certain judges, and personal compatibility. Although justices traditionally select law clerks from Ivy League law schools such as Yale and Harvard, they also draw from other schools, including their alma maters. Justices Sandra Day O'Connor and William H. Rehnquist, for example, are well known for choosing law clerks from their alma mater, Stanford Law School. Geographic region is also a prominent factor in the justices' law clerk selection process. For example, justice Hugo L. Black, an Alabaman, preferred clerks who grew up and attended law school in his home state.

Several justices regularly selected individuals who clerked in the chambers of certain lower court judges. For example, District of Columbia circuit court judge Skelley Wright's chambers often served as a breeding ground for future Supreme Court law clerks. Personal compatibility, moreover, is valued by the justices when searching for law clerks. Given the intimate working relations that a justice has with his or her clerks, the personal habits of an individual can be instrumental in his or her effectiveness. Personal compatibility can be related to similarities or differences in the ideological proclivities between the law clerk and the justice. Although some justices want clerks with similar policy preferences, others choose individuals with different views to get an insider's view of the adversary's position.

Functions of Clerks. The practice of clerks reviewing petitions for certiorari (discretionary appeals filed by the losing party in lower court to the Supreme Court) began during Chief Justice Charles Evans Hughes's tenure on the Court. Hughes used his clerks to review the *in forma pauperis* petitions (petitions to allow an indigent person to bypass the costs of filing a discretionary appeal to the Court) that should be granted or denied by the Court. From the Hughes Court (1930-1941) to the Warren Court (1953-1968), the chief justices' clerks were responsible for reviewing *in forma pauperis* petitions and preparing short memorandums.

A cert pool was created in 1972. The cert pool process begins when an administrator in the chief justice's chambers divides the petitions for certiorari among the eight justices in the pool. A law clerk writes a memorandum (often called a pool memo) to the other justices regarding the lower court and the judges participating in the decision. The facts and contentions of all the parties are presented along with an analysis of the case, such as conflicts among lower court decisions on the issue before the Court. Section 5 of the memo includes a recommendation on the disposition of the case and other relevant information, including the name of the clerk writing the memo. When a pool memo arrives in the justices' chambers, each justice has one of his or her own law clerks review it. In most cases, the law clerk reviewing the memo echoes the initial recommendation, but in some situations, the clerk will do additional research and write an additional memo. All the petitions for certiorari are reviewed by the single justice who does not belong to the pool.

Although the role that law clerks play in reviewing petitions for certiorari is well established, their influence in the Court's decision making and opinion writing is less certain. Certain law clerks have claimed to author most of the justices' written decisions. Conversely, other law clerks claim that they were responsible only for the footnotes or citation checking in the justices' decisions. In all likelihood, the clerks' responsibilities fall somewhere in between these extremes and vary with each individual justice. Nonetheless, the power that law clerks have over the Court's decision making has sparked a contentious debate among the scholarly community. Given that law clerks are not presidential appointees, many scholars argue that they should not play such a principal part in the Court's decision-making and opinion-writing process.

Former Clerks as Future Litigators. Law clerks' experience reviewing petitions for certiorari and assisting the justices in writing their final decisions offers them an invaluable opportunity to see at first hand the internal decision-making dynamics of the Court. Researchers found that more than 51 percent of individuals who clerked between the 1958 and 1985 October terms later participated as direct or third parties before the Court. This percentage was much higher for law clerks than for those individuals with similar educational backgrounds who did not serve as law clerks. One of the reasons for this high participation rate is that the solicitor general's office, the body that represents the United States before the Supreme Court, actively hires former law clerks. In 1992 for example, approximately half of the lawyers in the office were former law clerks.

Because former law clerks have a potential advantage as litigators before the justices, Court rules stipulate that former law clerks cannot appear as counsel for two years after they leave. Law firms also recognize this unique experience, offering former law clerks as much as a $35,000 bonus in addition to their salaries.

FURTHER READING

Two works that provide excellent summaries of the functions of law clerks of the justices are David M. O'Brien's *Storm Center: The Supreme Court in American Politics* (4th ed., New York: W. W. Norton, 1996) and William H. Rehnquist's *The Supreme Court: How It Was, How It Is* (New York: William Morrow, 1983). For a historical perspective on law clerks, see Chester A. Newland's "Personal Assistants to Supreme Court Justices: The Law Clerks," *Oregon Law Review* 40 (1961): 299-317. For the debate regarding how much justices rely on their law clerks and its ramifications on the democratic process, see David Crump's "Law Clerks: Their Roles and Relationships with Their Judges," *Judicature* (December/ January, 1986): 236-240; John P. Frank's "The Supreme Court: The Muckrakers Return," *American Bar Association Journal* (February, 1980): 160-164; Richard A. Posner's *The Federal Courts: Crisis and Reform* (Cambridge, Mass.: Harvard University Press, 1985); and Joseph Vining's "Justice, Bureaucracy, and Legal Method," *Michigan Law* 80: 252-270. The frequent presence of former law clerks turned litigators before the Supreme Court is the subject of Kevin T. McGuire's *Supreme Court Practice: Legal Elites in the Washington Community* (Charlottesville: University Press of Virginia, 1993) and Karen O'Connor and John R. Hermann's "The Clerk Connection: Appearances Before the Supreme Court by Former Law Clerks," *Judicature* (March/ April, 1995): 247-249.

John R. Hermann

SEE ALSO Cert pool; Certiorari, writ of; Decision making; Gray, Horace; Judiciary Acts of 1801-1925; Workload.

Clifford, Nathan

IDENTIFICATION: Associate justice (January 21, 1858-July 25, 1881)

Nathan Clifford. (Library of Congress)

NOMINATED BY: James Buchanan
BORN: August 18, 1803, Rumney, New Hampshire
DIED: July 25, 1881, Cornish, Maine
SIGNIFICANCE: Clifford spoke for the Supreme Court in nearly four hundred cases and presided over the commission that decided the disputed 1876 presidential election. He consistently dissented from Court opinions upholding federal power to confiscate property during wartime.

Clifford studied law under Josiah Quincy and was admitted to the New Hampshire bar in 1827. He served three terms in the Maine legislature and two terms in the U.S. House of Representatives. In 1846 he was appointed attorney general by President James K. Polk, and while serving as special commissioner to Mexico, he arranged the Treaty of Guadalupe Hidalgo that ended the Mexican-American War in 1848. After being nominated by President James Buchanan, Clifford took his seat on the Supreme Court in 1858.

Clifford concurred in the first of the *Legal Tender Cases*, *Hepburn v. Griswold* (1870) but dissented in *Knox v. Lee* (1871), declaring Congress's issuing of treasury notes to pay earlier debts to be constitutional. In *Loan Association v. Topeka* (1874), Clifford stated that state legislative power was almost absolute, subject only to specific state and federal constitutional provisions. Despite his proslavery views, he generally supported the government during the Civil War. Clifford argued in nearly four hundred Court cases, with most involving maritime and commercial law and laws affecting Mexican land grants.

Alvin K. Benson

SEE ALSO Civil War; Dissents; Land grants; *Legal Tender Cases*; *Slaughterhouse Cases*.

Clinton, Bill

IDENTIFICATION: Forty-second president of the United States (1993-   )
NOMINATIONS TO THE COURT: Through 1999, two nominations, both confirmed
BORN: August 19, 1946, Hope, Arkansas
SIGNIFICANCE: Clinton appointed two centrist-liberal justices to the Supreme Court. The attempt by the conservative-dominated Republican majority in Congress to impeach Clinton prompted appeals to the Court that determined more limited interpretations for immunity from testifying.

Born William Jefferson Blythe IV, Clinton began life in a small town in the South three months after the death of his father in an automobile accident. As a teenager, he changed his surname to that of his stepfather, Roger Clinton. At the start of his political career, he came to be widely known as Bill Clinton.

He studied at Georgetown University and from there went to Oxford University on a Rhodes Scholarship. In 1970 he enrolled in Yale Law School, graduating in 1973. At Yale, he met Hillary Diane Rodham, whom he married in 1975.

Clinton began his professional career as a professor at the law school of the University of Arkansas, Fayetteville. His life, however, was to be neither that of a legal scholar nor a practicing lawyer. In 1976 he was successful in his Democratic bid to become Arkansas attorney general. Two years later he was elected to a two-year term as governor. However, the liberal nature of his administration and its challenges to vested interests caused him to lose his reelection bid in 1980. Toning down his radical stances, he was continuously reelected governor from 1982 until he became president a decade later.

As a successful Democratic governor, Clinton was chosen to head the Democratic Leadership Council, where he emphasized his position as a "New Democrat." In the light of conservative political advances during the 1980's, these Democrats modified some of the traditional liberal tenets of the party by advocating a reduced role for big government and an increased one for the private sector.

Based on this political alignment and his decade-long success as governor, Clinton challenged incumbent George Bush in 1992 for the presidency. Clinton defeated a large field of Democratic candidates for the party's presidential nomination. However, both in campaigning for the nomination and after obtaining it, Clinton had to fend off numerous allegations regarding his character, especially in relation to financial dealings and extramarital affairs. Nevertheless, he was elected president.

Judicial Changes. In forming his cabinet in early 1993, Clinton vowed it would represent the diversity of the United States in terms of race, ethnic background, and gender. He insisted that his attorney general be the first woman nominated to that post. Such an appointment was considered important in relation to Clinton policy for defending a woman's right to abortion. After going through several candidates, he was able to obtain Senate approval of Janet Reno, who came to be the longest-serving attorney general in U.S. history.

In the summer of the following year, Justice Byron R. White announced his retirement, providing Clinton with his first opportunity to make a Supreme Court appointment. He chose Ruth Bader Ginsburg, a federal appeals court judge in Washington, D.C. A centrist-liberal, Ginsburg was distinguished for her career in advancing women's rights. She was the first woman to obtain a tenured position at the law school of Columbia University, from which she graduated. Moreover, she headed the American Civil Liberties Union (ACLU) Women's Rights Project and was thereby in charge of several cases regarding bias that went to the Supreme Court. On August 3, 1993, the Senate approved her appointment ninety-six to three. Her most important early opinion was to require that the all-male, publicly funded Virginia Military Academy admit women.

Soon after the Ginsburg appointment, Clinton had another opportunity to appoint a member of the Court. Early in 1994 Justice Harry A. Blackmun announced his retirement. To succeed him, Clinton nominated Stephen G. Breyer, a federal appeals court judge in Boston. A graduate of the Harvard Law School and a former professor there, Breyer was a centrist who held conservative positions on economic issues but more liberal ones regarding social questions. Well connected to political and social elites along a wide ideological spectrum, he was respected among both Democrats and Republicans for his scholarly, judicious character. He especially was noted for his expertise in antitrust legislation and government regulation. On May 13, 1994, the Senate approved his appointment eighty-seven to nine.

The Clinton appointees joined justices Sandra Day O'Connor, Antonin Scalia, and Anthony M. Kennedy, appointed by Ronald Reagan; David H. Souter and Clarence Thomas, by George Bush;

In response to attempts to impeach him, President Bill Clinton made appeals to the Supreme Court that resulted in a reduction in presidential immunity. (Reuters/Win McNamee/Archive Photos)

and John Paul Stevens, by Gerald R. Ford. President Nixon had appointed William H. Rehnquist, and Reagan had named him chief justice. The Clinton appointees established a centrist majority, often voting with moderates such as O'Connor, Souter, Kennedy, and even occasionally Rehnquist. Stevens was the most liberal of the justices; Thomas and Scalia, the most conservative.

Court Issues. Numerous Court cases were argued under the Clinton administration, many of which dealt with issues related to the rights of individuals and of various levels or agencies of government. In *Shaw v. Reno*, during the last part of the 1992-1993 Court year, the justices ruled five to four that white voters in the twelfth congressional district of North Carolina were justified in their charge that the area had been irregularly redistricted, or gerrymandered, to form a black racial majority, contrary to the equal protection clause of the Fourteenth Amendment of the constitution.

During 1995, in the *National Organization of Women. v. Scheidler,* justices voted unanimously to allow abortion rights advocates to interpret the Racketeer Influenced and Corrupt Organizations Act of 1970 against the activities of antiabortion groups. In several cases regarding relations between the federal government and the states, the Court favored the states concerning authority for setting the death penalty, defining conditions of interstate commerce, and state desegregation plans. It struck down a Colorado measure that would have denied equal protection under the law to gays.

The Court made some exceptionally controversial decisions during the first half of 1997. In *Reno v. American Civil Liberties Union,* for example, the Court struck down arguments of the Clinton administration supporting the 1996 Communications Decency Act. The law criminalized the transmission of indecent material via computer networks that juveniles might access. The Court considered parts of the law to be violations of the First Amendment, and by striking these down, it supported free speech on the Internet. It upheld the right of states to prohibit physician-assisted suicide and struck down federal legislation that attempted to regulate how state and local government agencies could deal with religious practices. It also struck down measures of the Brady Gun Control Law (1995) requiring states and local governments to conduct background checks on prospective gun buyers.

CLINTON'S APPOINTMENTS TO THE COURT		
Year	*Nominee*	*Result*
1993	Ruth Bader Ginsburg	confirmed
1994	Steven Gerald Breyer	confirmed

The following year, in *Clinton v. City of New York,* the Court denied that the president could exercise a line-item veto. This power had been given to him by Congress through the 1996 Line-Item Veto Act. The Court held that Congress acted unconstitutionally by giving the president "unilateral power to change the text of duly enacted statutes." The Court also ruled on a record number of sexual harassment cases. Regarding the decennial national census, which determines the population basis for congressional districts, it ruled in 1999 that the census could not be conducted based on sampling, a position supported by the Clinton administration and the Democratic Party.

President Clinton as Defendant. An unprecedented historical event during the first half of President Clinton's second term was his impeachment by a Republican majority in the House of Representatives. This was followed by his trial for perjury and conspiracy in the Senate. The Supreme Court made crucial decisions in cases leading up to this trial and in respect to other legal situations of the president.

During the first Clinton administration, a former Arkansas state employee, Paula Jones, alleged that she had been sexually harassed by the president when he was governor. Since 1994 Clinton had been under investigation by a special counsel, Kenneth Starr, a conservative Republican charged with investigating potential legal irregularities in Clinton's gubernatorial administration in Arkansas. In more than four years of relentless investigation costing more than $40 million, Starr could find no criminal charges to file against the president.

When Clinton testified in depositions taken preparatory to the Jones suit, he swore that he had not sexually harassed Jones, nor had he had sexual relations with a White House intern, Monica Lewinsky. Clinton considered the meaning of sexual relations to be ambiguous, and many jurists questioned the relevance of the testimony to the Jones case. Nonetheless, Starr delivered charges against Clinton to the House of Representatives, maintaining that the president had committed perjury in his testimony and had conspired for others to also commit perjury. Further, he considered these charges high crimes and misdemeanors, thereby worthy of impeachment and removal from office.

In early 1997 the Supreme Court ruled that Jones had the right to pursue her case against Clinton despite the fact that he was a sitting president. She did not have to wait until after he had left office in order to pursue her case. The following year, court rulings supported Starr's argument that the president's attorneys and his Secret Service guards were not immune from testifying against him, rulings with extraordinary historical consequences for the presidency.

Just before Christmas of 1998 the Republican-dominated House impeached Clinton. With this indictment, the Constitution required that the Senate become court and jury for the trial of the president. The chief justice of the United States became the presiding judge. For the first time in U.S. history, the chief justice sat in judgment in an impeachment trial of an elected president. There was overwhelming popular opposition to the impeachment, perceived as no more than an almost grotesque charade of justice, motivated solely by politics and malice. The Senate, its Republican majority decomposing, acquitted the president in January of 1999.

FURTHER READING

A complete, let alone a conclusive, assessment of Clinton and the Court cannot yet be made. Few scholarly, objective studies exist, and the events have been of an exceptional and extraordinary nature. Nevertheless, a number of works provide some information and analysis. Joan Biskupic and Elder Witt give a concise overview of the Supreme Court for the period from 1989 to 1996 in chapter 3 of volume 1 of the *Guide to the U.S. Supreme Court* (Washington, D.C.: Congressional Quarterly, 1997). George E. Curry has put together a collection of essays on one of the most controversial court issues of the Clinton years, affirmative action, in *The Affirmative Action Debate* (Reading, Mass.: Addison-Wesley, 1996). Alan M. Dershowitz points

out the extraordinary legal and constitutional consequences of the indictment and trial of Clinton, based on the Starr investigation, in *Sexual McCarthyism: Clinton, Starr, and the Constitutional Crisis* (New York: Basic Books, 1998). In volume 6 of *Landmark Decisions of the Supreme Court* (San Diego: Excellent Books, 1999), the case of *Clinton v. the City of New York* is reviewed as one of the most significant of the Clinton presidency. Robert J. McKeever offers an overseas perspective on the contemporary Supreme Court in the first section of his work, *The United States Supreme Court: A Political and Legal Analysis* (Manchester, England: Manchester University Press, 1997). David Maraniss analyses the education and legal and political career of Clinton in *First in His Class* (New York: Simon & Schuster, 1995) as does Meredith L. Oakley in *On the Make: The Rise of Bill Clinton* (Washington, D.C.: Regency, 1994).

Edward A. Riedinger

SEE ALSO Breyer, Stephen G.; *Clinton v. City of New York*; *Clinton v. Jones*; Executive privilege; *Gompers v. Buck's Stove & Range Co.*; *Hurley v. Irish-American Gay, Lesbian, and Bisexual Group of Boston*; Impeachment of presidents; Presidential powers; Privileges and immunities; Rehnquist, William H.; *Reno v. American Civil Liberties Union*; *Romer v. Evans*.

Clinton v. City of New York

CITATION: 117 S.Ct. 2312
DATE: June 25, 1998
ISSUES: Presidential powers; separation of powers
SIGNIFICANCE: The Supreme Court ruled the line-item veto was unconstitutional because it allowed the president to amend legislation passed by Congress.

The Line-Item Veto Act of 1996 authorized the president to veto fiscal portions of a bill, with the goal of putting a limit on federal spending. In *Raines v. Byrd* (1997), the Supreme Court ruled that members of Congress had no standing to oppose the law in court. After President Bill Clinton vetoed several spending measures, however, the city of New York and other plaintiffs were adversely affected by the vetoes and were granted standing.

By a 6-3 vote, the Court struck down the veto law. In his opinion for the Court, Justice John Paul Stevens wrote that the Constitution did not authorize the president to enact, to amend, or to repeal statutes. Beginning with George Washington, presidents had recognized that the Constitution required them to "approve all the parts of a bill, or reject it in toto." To make such a change in the legislative process would require a constitutional amendment. The three dissenters believed that the line-item veto violated neither a textual constitutional command nor any implicit principle of the separation of powers doctrine.

Thomas T. Lewis

SEE ALSO Presidential powers; Separation of powers; Standing.

Clinton v. Jones

CITATION: 117 S.Ct. 1636
DATE: May 27, 1997
ISSUE: Executive immunity
SIGNIFICANCE: The Supreme Court unanimously rejected President Bill Clinton's claim of immunity from a civil suit while in office.

In 1994 Paula Jones brought a sexual harassment suit against President Bill Clinton. She alleged that an incident had taken place in 1991, when he was

Paula Jones, pictured during a 1998 news conference, sought to have President Bill Clinton stand trial on charges of sexual harassment. (AP/Wide World Photos)

governor of Arkansas and she a state employee. President Clinton asserted that the suit should be postponed until after his term of office expired. He argued that the separation of powers doctrine places limits on the authority of the judiciary over the executive branch, and he also referred to *Nixon v. Fitzgerald* (1982), which provided presidents with absolute immunity from suits arising from their official duties of office.

Writing for the Supreme Court, Justice John Paul Stevens reasoned that a president was not totally immune from the jurisdiction of the federal courts and that it was appropriate for the courts to determine the legality of a president's conduct, both official and unofficial. Stevens suggested that the suit should not be especially "onerous" in time and efforts. A delay in the trial, he argued, would be unfair to Jones because it would increase the danger of prejudice from lost evidence.

Thomas T. Lewis

SEE ALSO Clinton, Bill; Executive immunity; Presidential powers; Separation of powers.

Cohen v. California

CITATION: 403 U.S. 15
DATE: June 7, 1971
ISSUE: Symbolic speech
SIGNIFICANCE: The Supreme Court overturned the conviction of a man for wearing a jacket emblazoned with a profanity in a courthouse, thereby establishing the concept of symbolic speech and limiting the concept of fighting words.

By a 5-4 vote, the Court overturned the conviction of a defendant who wore a jacket with the words "Fuck the draft" emblazoned across its front into a Los Angeles courthouse, where profanity was prohibited. Justice John M. Harlan II, a generally conservative justice, wrote the opinion for the 5-4 majority, which held that symbolic speech, even if provocative in nature, was protected by the First Amendment.

Although the Court substantially broadened the range of provocative speech under First Amendment protection, it left limits. For example, when young men protested the Vietnam War by burning their draft cards, the Court upheld their conviction in *United States v. O'Brien* (1968). In that case, the protection extended to symbolic speech was judged not to extend to violations of otherwise valid laws. In *Tinker v. Des Moines Independent Community School District* (1969), the Court ruled that schools cannot stop students from protesting by wearing black arm bands. In *Texas v. Johnson* (1989), the Court voided a Texas law that banned the burning of the U.S. flag, finding the act to be protected symbolic speech because it was a form of political protest.

Richard L. Wilson

SEE ALSO *Brandenburg v. Ohio*; First Amendment; *O'Brien, United States v.*; Symbolic speech; *Texas v. Johnson*; *Tinker v. Des Moines Independent Community School District*.

Cohen v. Cowles Media Co.

CITATION: 501 U.S. 663
DATE: June 24, 1991
ISSUE: Freedom of the press
SIGNIFICANCE: The Supreme Court held that the First Amendment does not protect newspapers from civil suits for breaking a promise of confidentiality.

Dan Cohen, a political consultant, was fired from his job after two newspapers identified him as the source of information about a political candidate. Having been promised confidentiality, he sued for breach of contract. Based on the state's contract law, the jury awarded him $200,000 in compensatory damages. The Minnesota supreme court, however, overturned the award, concluding that protection for the First Amendment's freedom of the press outweighed the state's interest in enforcing contractual obligations.

By a 5-4 margin, the Supreme Court directed Minnesota's high court to reconsider the judgment according to the relevant state laws. Speaking for the majority, Justice Byron R. White reasoned that the First Amendment did not give the publisher of a newspaper any special immunity from the enforcement of general laws and that the application of a general law against the press is not subject to any heightened scrutiny simply because its incidental effect is to make it more difficult for the press to gather and report the news. In contrast, the dissenters argued that an indirect restraint on the truthful reporting of political

speech should be judged by the compelling state interest test.

Thomas T. Lewis

SEE ALSO *Branzburg v. Hayes*; First Amendment balancing; Judicial scrutiny; Speech and press, freedom of.

Cohens v. Virginia

CITATION: 6 Wheat. (19 U.S.) 264
DATE: March 3, 1821
ISSUES: Judicial federalism; Eleventh Amendment
SIGNIFICANCE: Chief Justice John Marshall used a minor dispute over the sale of lottery tickets in Virginia to assert the Supreme Court's jurisdiction over state court decisions.

After Congress authorized a lottery sale for the District of Columbia, a Virginia court fined the Cohen brothers one hundred dollars for selling tickets in Virginia in violation of a state statute. The two brothers appealed their fine to the Supreme Court, asserting that the Virginia court had acted unconstitutionally. Virginia claimed immunity from review, based on the Eleventh Amendment as well as principles of state sovereignty. Speaking for a unanimous Court, John Marshall made a narrow ruling in favor of Virginia, with the rationale that Congress had not intended lottery tickets to be sold in states where they were illegal.

Marshall's opinion in *Cohens v. Virginia* is memorable because of its vigorous defense of the Court's broad jurisdiction and the principle of national supremacy. In regard to states' rights, Marshall argued that the states had surrendered much of their sovereignty when they joined a national union. Taking a narrow reading of the Eleventh Amendment, Marshall wrote that the amendment did not apply when the sole purpose of a suit was to inquire about whether a state court had violated the U.S. Constitution or federal law. Marshall's lengthy opinion presented a sweeping interpretation of the Court's appellate jurisdiction over all state court decisions involving issues of national authority. Defenders of states' rights, including Thomas Jefferson, denounced *Cohens* as an extreme step toward the consolidation of federal power.

Thomas T. Lewis

SEE ALSO Eleventh Amendment; Federalism; Judicial powers; *McCulloch v. Maryland*; States' rights.

Coker v. Georgia

CITATION: 433 U.S. 584
DATE: June 29, 1977
ISSUES: Capital punishment; substantive due process
SIGNIFICANCE: The Supreme Court held that capital punishment for the crime of rape is an excessive and disproportionate penalty, and therefore contrary to the prohibition against cruel and unusual punishments in the Eighth and Fourteenth Amendments.

While serving sentences for murder, rape, and other crimes, Ehrlich Anthony Coker escaped from a Georgia prison. That same evening he raped a woman in her home and then forced the woman to leave with him. When apprehended, he was tried on charges of rape, armed robbery, and kidnapping. Using procedures that had been approved by the Supreme Court in *Gregg v. Georgia* (1976), the jury found Coker guilty of rape with aggravating circumstances and sentenced him to death.

By a 7-2 vote, the Court reversed the death sentence and remanded the case to the trial court for new sentencing. Writing for a plurality, Justice Byron R. White argued that the state could not sentence a defendant to a punishment disproportionate to the harm that he had inflicted on the victim. White also noted that Georgia did not apply the death penalty in cases of deliberate murder without aggravating circumstances, and he found that the disproportionality principle meant that a rapist should not be punished more severely than a deliberate murderer. Finally, observing that the Court's precedents defined the term "cruel and unusual" according to the "evolving standards of decency that mark the progress of a maturing society," White pointed to the fact that Georgia was the only state to authorize the death penalty for the rape of an adult woman.

The *Coker* decision suggested that the Court would probably not approve of capital punishment for any crime less than intentional murder. The majority of the justices have usually rejected the disproportionality principle in noncapital cases, as in *Rummel v. Estelle* (1980), but an important exception is *Solem v. Helm* (1983).

Thomas T. Lewis

SEE ALSO Capital punishment; Cruel and unusual punishment; Due process, substantive; Eighth Amendment; *Gregg v. Georgia*; *Quirin, Ex parte*; *Rummel v. Estelle*; *Solem v. Helm*.

Cold War

DATE: Mid-1940's to late 1980's
DESCRIPTION: Nonviolent conflict between the United States and other Western nations and the Soviet Bloc. The efforts of the United States to combat communist ideology raised a number of constitutional issues that were addressed by the Supreme Court.
SIGNIFICANCE: Legal challenges to the laws and policies enacted to fight the Cold War reaching the Supreme Court involved fundamental civil rights, including freedom of speech and freedom of association, and the apportionment of war powers between Congress and the president.

Shortly after the end of World War II (1941-1945), the United States and the Soviet Union became engaged in a military, economic, and ideological rivalry known as the Cold War. For more than four decades, the United States carried out a foreign policy aimed at halting the spread of Soviet influence abroad. This "containment" strategy had a domestic counterpart: preventing the infiltration of Soviet agents and the spread of communist ideology in the United States.

After World War II, successive presidential administrations and congressional leaders were concerned that Soviet agents and communist sympathizers were attempting to convert American public opinion toward their cause. Many leaders worried that the Soviets had already infiltrated some media outlets, the film industry, various universities, and even certain departments of the U.S. government. In response, the U.S. government enacted laws, executive orders, and policies to reduce or eliminate these threats. The enactment of these laws and policies brought up various constitutional issues—most of which were addressed in some way by the Supreme Court. Among these issues were freedom of speech, freedom of association, and freedom of assembly.

Loyalty Oaths and Boards. In 1947 President Harry S Truman issued Executive Order 9835, which established loyalty boards in each state department to adjudicate cases of alleged disloyalty to the state. Suspect federal employees would be removed from their positions if "reasonable grounds" were found to exist for a "belief" of disloyalty. President Dwight D. Eisenhower issued his own version of that policy in 1951, requiring only "reasonable doubt as to the loyalty" of a federal employee in order to trigger removal. Various states, school districts, and other government entities began to require loyalty oaths as a requirement for employment.

Loyalty oaths survived various legal challenges for most of the 1950's. However, in *Kent v. Dulles* (1958), the Court ruled that the State Department's requirement that a traveler sign a "noncommunist affidavit" to receive permission to travel violated the due process clause of the Fifth Amendment. Then, in a landmark decision, the Court ruled in *Keyishian v. Board of Regents* (1967) that a law requiring public school teachers in New York to sign a loyalty oath violated the First Amendment.

Censorship. Many domestic efforts during the Cold War sought to censor publications and speech that were deemed dangerous for various reasons. Some censorship laws, such as the Smith Act of 1940, targeted advocacy of violence against the government. Other efforts centered on sensitive military data and other information that could harm American security if released. In general, the Court upheld such efforts when it could be demonstrated that particular forms of speech posed a distinct and immediate danger to the state.

In other cases, however, the Court rejected efforts to censor putatively dangerous publications and speech. In *Lamont v. Postmaster General* (1965), for example, the Court ruled unanimously against a law requiring the Postmaster General to seize and destroy all unsealed mail from abroad deemed to be "communist political propaganda" because such an act violated the First Amendment.

Guilt by Association. Some laws enacted during the Cold War attempted to eradicate communist "cells," which allegedly existed in a secret network directed by Moscow and intended to overthrow the U.S. government. The McCarran Act of 1950 and the Communist Control Act of 1954, for example, placed restrictions on communist organizations by requiring registration, excluding their members from certain posts, and even providing for the in-

The attempts of Senator Joe McCarthy, pictured here in 1954, and others to eradicate communism in the United States raised constitutional questions that were brought before the Supreme Court. (AP/Wide World Photos)

ternment of communists during a national emergency.

Though these acts represent the height of anticommunist fervor in the United States, the Court did not rule on their constitutionality for a number of years. Eventually, though, major provisions of the acts were deemed to be unconstitutional.

The Vietnam War. The Vietnam War brought a host of occasions for the Court to rule on constitutional issues. In *United States v. Seeger* (1965), for example, the Court effectively extended the military exclusion for "conscientious objectors" to those who oppose war on the basis of sincere moral beliefs that are not part of a particular religious doctrine. In *Bond v. Floyd* (1966), the Court ruled against the Georgia legislature's refusal to seat a duly elected legislator, Julian Bond, because he had supported opponents of the draft. In *Tinker v. Des Moines Independent Community School District* (1969), the Court ruled against a public school that suspended students for wearing black armbands to protest the Vietnam War. The Court thus upheld the protection of "symbolic speech" under the First Amendment, even in schools.

The Court reined in the government's use of the national security argument for censoring factual military information in *New York Times Co. v. United States* (1971). In this case, a former official of the Department of Defense had leaked the Pentagon Papers (a study of the Vietnam War produced by the department) to *The New York Times*. The federal government attempted to halt the publication, but the Court held this case of prior restraint to be unconstitutional.

War Powers. In addition to matters of civil rights and liberties, the Cold War raises constitutional questions about the apportionment of war powers between the president and Congress. The Vietnam War especially focused attention on this question, particularly as public sentiment turned against the war in the late 1960's. Congress had effectively delegated its power to declare war in the Tonkin Gulf Resolution of 1964 but attempted to regain those powers through the War Powers Act of 1973. Though the Court did not rule directly on the War Powers Act, other decisions by the Court, such as *Immigration and Naturalization Service v. Chadha* (1983), suggest that provisions of the act amount to an unconstitutional legislative veto.

The continuous sense of threat to the United States that existed during the Cold War, due in large part to the two superpowers' nuclear arsenals, spawned the idea that the president should have enormous discretion in military deployments and war making, although this ability was not consistent with the Constitution. In retrospect, the Cold War was an almost surreal period in which the Court faced the difficult task of preserving the ideals of the Constitution in a global environment that threatened the country, its ideological values, and its population.

FURTHER READING

Hogan, Michael J. *A Cross of Iron: Harry S Truman and the Origins of the National Security State, 1945-1954.* New York: Cambridge University Press, 1998.

Neville, John F. *The Press, the Rosenbergs, and the Cold War.* Westport, Conn.: Praeger, 1995.

Urofsky, Melvin I. *Division and Discord: The Supreme Court Under Stone and Vinson, 1941-1953.* Columbia: University of South Carolina Press, 1997.

Zeinert, Karen. *McCarthy and the Fear of Communism in American History.* Springfield, N.J.: Enslow, 1998.

Steve D. Boilard

SEE ALSO Censorship; Conscientious objection; McCarran Act; Smith Act; Subversion; Vietnam War; War and civil liberties; War powers.

Colegrove v. Green

CITATION: 328 U.S. 549
DATE: June 10, 1946
ISSUE: Reapportionment
SIGNIFICANCE: The Supreme Court declared reapportionment to be a political question and therefore not justiciable. This decision blocked all judicial efforts to correct malapportionment of legislative district boundaries until it was overturned in 1962.

Qualified Illinois voters challenged their state's U.S. congressional districts, alleging a lack of compactness and equality. Following prevailing precedents, a three-judge district panel dismissed the case, and the Supreme Court affirmed the lower court's decision by a 4-3 vote. Only seven justices participated in this case because Harlan Fiske Stone had died recently and Robert H. Jackson was at the Nuremberg trials. Justice Felix Frankfurter, in his majority opinion, argued that reapportionment was a political question best left to state legislatures under congressional oversight if necessary. Given the division within the Court, the issue was certain to be revisited, but it was sixteen years before the Court allowed the justiciability of reapportionment in *Baker v. Carr* (1962), justifying its decision with the Fourteenth Amendment's equal protection clause.

Richard L. Wilson

SEE ALSO *Baker v. Carr*; Political questions; *Reapportionment Cases*; Representation, fairness of; *Reynolds v. Sims*; *Wesberry v. Sanders*.

Coleman v. Miller

CITATION: 307 U.S. 433
DATE: June 5, 1939
ISSUE: Constitutional amendment process
SIGNIFICANCE: In deciding three issues regarding the ratification of a child labor constitutional

amendment, the Supreme Court introduced the Fourteenth Amendment, adding considerable confusion to the process.

Chief Justice Charles Evans Hughes wrote the opinion for the 7-2 majority with Justices Pierce Butler and James C. McReynolds dissenting. The Court left standing a lower court's decision that the lieutenant-governor of Kansas could cast a tie-breaking vote in the constitutional amendment ratification process. It also found the state's ratification of an amendment it had previously rejected and the issue of whether time limits should exist for ratification of amendments to be political questions for Congress to resolve. Congress later began to add time limits to all proposed constitutional amendments. The vagueness of *Coleman* confused the ratification process for amendments to the U.S. Constitution by introducing Fourteenth Amendment considerations. Subsequently, *Coleman* was limited by *Idaho v. Freeman* (1981), in which the Court allowed a state to rescind its ratification of the Equal Rights Amendment after the original deadline was extended by Congress.

Richard L. Wilson

SEE ALSO Constitutional amendment process; Judicial powers; Political questions.

Collector v. Day

CITATION: 78 U.S. 113
DATE: April 3, 1871
ISSUE: Federalism
SIGNIFICANCE: In a series of decisions on tax immunities, the Supreme Court held that the federal government could not tax the income of a state judge, based on dual sovereignty of the state and the federal government.

Collector is of historical interest for its place in a line of opinions on tax immunities that began with Chief Justice John Marshall's opinion in *McCulloch v. Maryland* (1819). Marshall held that the state could not impose a tax on an institution created by the federal government. Following this line, the Court held in *Dobbins v. Erie County* (1842) that the state could not tax the income of a federal official.

In *Collector*, the opposite situation from *Dobbins*, the Court held that the federal government could not tax the income of a state judge. Justice Samuel

Nelson wrote the 8-1 majority opinion; only Justice Joseph P. Bradley dissented. Nelson relied on the Tenth Amendment and on the theory of dual sovereignty to hold that both the state and federal governments were independent of each other and states retain all aspects of sovereignty not delegated to the national government. This was the strongest view of dual sovereignty presented by the Court, but it could not be sustained over time. *Collector* was substantially weakened by *Helvering v. Gerhardt* (1938) and directly overturned in *Graves v. New York ex rel. O'Keefe* (1939).

Richard L. Wilson

SEE ALSO *Dobbins v. Erie County*; *Graves v. New York ex rel. O'Keefe*; *McCulloch v. Maryland*; Separation of powers.

Collegiality

DESCRIPTION: The practice of cooperation, solidarity, equality, fraternity, shared responsibility, and *esprit de corps* among Supreme Court justices.
SIGNIFICANCE: Collegiality limits procedural and policy divisiveness within the Court, increases administrative efficiency, allows for a close proximate working environment, and allows the Court to present a united front to the public and the other branches of government, thus increasing its power and prestige.

The chief justice provides leadership in maintaining a collegial working relationship among the justices and their staffs. John Marshall, chief justice from 1801 to 1835, fostered fellowship among the justices by arranging shared accommodations in a single boarding house. Marshall also fostered cooperation among the justices by developing the concept of a single opinion of the Court as a symbol of judicial solidarity. The majority opinion is published as the opinion of the entire Court. Concurring and dissenting opinions are permitted as attachments but are not required and are often forgone to decrease any perception of divisiveness within the Court and to increase the perception of judicial solidarity.

Court protocol does not require unanimity but does require deliberation of the cases with mutual respect for the individuality and decision-making ability of each justice, loyalty to the Court as an institution, civil treatment and cordial relations with fellow justices, sharing of opinion writing and other judicial duties, sharing the burden of incapacitated justices in order to shield them from public notice, resolution of internal disputes within the Court and without appeal to outside authorities, and withholding announcement of case decisions until each justice has determined his or her vote on the case.

Collegiality encouraged long tenure for members of the Court, unanimity in cases where the institutional integrity of the Court was threatened, and the development of warm personal friendships among the justices. The ongoing spirit of collegiality also helped the Court resist political pressures from the other branches of government, most notably the Depression era Court-packing plan of President Franklin D. Roosevelt. The Court's collegiality was broken only a few times in the Court's history, most notably in the feuds involving Justices Robert H. Jackson, Hugo L. Black, and James C. McReynolds.

Gordon Neal Diem

SEE ALSO Black, Hugo L.; Chief justice; Concurring opinions; Court-packing plan; Decision making; Disability of justices; Housing of the Court; Jackson, Robert H.; Judicial codes and rules; McReynolds, James C.; Marshall, John; Opinions, writing of; Seniority within the Court; Seriatim opinions.

Columbus Board of Education v. Penick

CITATION: 443 U.S. 449
DATE: July 2, 1979
ISSUE: School integration and busing
SIGNIFICANCE: The Supreme Court supported the use of a districtwide urban desegregation plan at a time when many observers thought the Court was unwilling to uphold the use of busing to correct de facto school segregation.

By 1979 the Supreme Court appeared no longer willing to impose large, complicated school desegregation plans involving busing on urban districts as the result of *Milliken v. Bradley* (1974) and *Pasadena Board of Education v. Spangler* (1976). However, in a 7-2 vote, the Court supported such a system in Columbus, Ohio. It reaffirmed the basic principles

it announced in *Swann v. Charlotte-Mecklenburg Board of Education* (1971). The Court insisted that purposeful segregation in a substantial portion of a metropolitan school district created a strong presumption that the board or system had practiced systemwide segregation or tolerated its existence, thereby mandating widespread extraordinary relief. It ruled that as long as a system seemed infected with segregative intent when *Brown v. Board of Education* (1954) was decided, that school board remained under an obligation to dismantle the segregated system if it had not already done so. This was true even if innocent behavior had produced segregated results. In dissent, Justice Lewis F. Powell, Jr., restated his belief that the de facto/de jure distinction made no sense, and Justice William H. Rehnquist objected to making an improper intrusion into local education decision making.

Richard L. Wilson

SEE ALSO *Brown v. Board of Education*; Desegregation; *Milliken v. Bradley*; *Pasadena Board of Education v. Spangler*; School integration and busing; Segregation, de facto; Segregation, de jure; *Swann v. Charlotte-Mecklenburg Board of Education*.

Comity clause

DATE: 1791
DESCRIPTION: Article IV of the U.S. Constitution, providing a foundation for a state to give the courtesy of enforcing the laws of another state. This courtesy is afforded out of respect and friendship and not out of obligation.
SIGNIFICANCE: Comity clause cases that come before the Supreme Court often involve the extent to which one state court's judgment is enforceable in another state or the unequal treatment of residents and nonresidents.

The Articles of Confederation specifically mentioned interstate relations premised on the concept of comity. Article IV, sections 1 and 2, of the U.S. Constitution provide for comity and facilitate interstate relations through the full faith and credit, rendition, and privileges and immunities provisions. The full faith and credit provision requires that each state recognize and enforce the "public acts, records, and judicial proceedings of every other state." Congress first enacted implementation legislation for the full faith and credit provision, which has become a significant component of the U.S. legal system. The most significant issue arising under this provision entails the extent to which a valid final judgment of one state's court is enforceable in another state. In *Estin v. Estin* (1948), the Supreme Court determined that one state must honor the validity of a divorce decree granted by another state; however, it is not bound by the other state's court decision regarding alimony, child custody, and division of liabilities and assets.

The full faith and credit provision is inapplicable to criminal jurisprudence. The rendition provision, also known as the fugitive from justice clause and extradition, calls on one state to surrender to another state a fugitive from justice. In 1793 Congress enacted implementation legislation. In *Kentucky v. Dennison* (1861), the governor of Ohio refused to comply with Kentucky's demand to surrender a defendant charged in Kentucky with aiding the escape of a slave. The Court held that Ohio's governor had a moral, but unenforceable, duty to comply with Kentucky's extradition demand. In *Puerto Rico v. Branstad* (1987), the Court overruled a portion of *Dennison* and held that federal courts have the authority to require a governor to perform his ministerial duty by delivering a fugitive upon a proper demand from another state.

The privileges and immunities provision, also known as the comity clause, provides that the "citizens of each state shall be entitled to all of the privileges and immunities of citizens in the several states." The Court in the *Slaughterhouse Cases* (1873) ruled that Article IV privileges and immunities addressed state citizenship; however, the Fourteenth Amendment protected only national citizenship. The Court has upheld the differential treatment of out-of-state citizens when a state has enacted a state citizenship or state residency classification. State laws differentiating between residents and nonresidents have been upheld by the Court regarding commercial fishing licenses, recreational fishing licenses, recreational hunting licenses, business licenses, the right to practice a profession, the privilege of voting in state elections, and running for state office. Presently the Court relies more heavily upon the equal protection and commerce clauses in order to facilitate interstate comity than the Article IV privileges and immunities provision.

FURTHER READING

Corwin, Edward S. *The Constitution and What It Means Today.* 12th ed. Princeton, N.J.: Princeton University Press, 1958.

Levy, Leonard W., Kenneth L. Karst, and Dennis J. Mahoney. *Encyclopedia of the American Constitution.* New York: Macmillan, 1986.

Robert P. Morin

SEE ALSO Finality of decision; Fugitives from justice; Full faith and credit; *Kentucky v. Dennison*; Privileges and immunities; *Slaughterhouse Cases*.

Commerce, regulation of

DESCRIPTION: Control, through laws, licenses, and other means, of the buying and selling of goods and services of all kinds, the related transportation of goods, and business and employment practices.

SIGNIFICANCE: The commerce clause, Article I, section 8, gives Congress plenary power to regulate commerce with foreign nations, among the states, and with the Indian tribes. The Supreme Court, in defining the boundaries of authority between the national and state governments, authorized Congress to regulate almost every aspect of business and the economy and to enact laws protecting the civil rights of citizens.

In the early 1800's New York granted a monopoly to a steamboat operating in New York waters, which conflicted with a congressional coastal license given to another person operating in waters between New York and New Jersey. In *Gibbons v. Ogden* (1824), Chief Justice John Marshall, writing the majority opinion for the Supreme Court, enunciated the fundamental principles of the power of Congress to regulate commerce in the face of contrary state action. He held that commerce is intercourse between nations and parts of nations in all its branches and that Congress has plenary power to prescribe rules to carry out that intercourse. Navigation is part of commerce and the power of Congress to regulate such activity cannot stop at the state boundaries because the power to regulate "among the states" means intermingled with traffic in the interior of states. Nonetheless, Marshall ruled that commerce that is completely within a state is reserved for state regulation.

Absence of Federal Regulation. In *Cooley v. Board of Wardens of the Port of Philadelphia* (1852), the Court held that if Congress manifests a clear intent to leave the matter of commerce regulation to the states, it may do so. In subsequent decisions, the Court found that states might regulate commerce in the absence of congressional regulation if the regulation is wholly local and does not create uniform national standards. The rule in *Cooley* was supplemented with a balancing of interests test designed to ascertain whether litigated state regulation creates an undue burden on interstate commerce. Therefore, for example, in *South Carolina State Highway Department v. Barnwell* (1938), the Court found that a width and weight limitation on trucks driving through South Carolina was a reasonable safety limitation when balanced against the national interest in the free flow of interstate commerce. Interest balancing, however, does not automatically result in upholding the state regulation, as was the case for Arizona's attempt to limit the length of freight trains traveling through that state in *Southern Pacific Co. v. Arizona* (1945).

The Court's decision in *Philadelphia v. New Jersey* (1978) illustrates how the Court adjudicates a classic federalism issue caused by a modern problem. To protect the quality of the state environment, the New Jersey state legislature enacted a law prohibiting the importation of most solid or liquid wastes that originated or were collected outside the state. Though waste by definition seems valueless, the Court ruled that it is, nonetheless, commerce. It then determined that New Jersey was trying to burden out-of-state companies by slowing the filling of its landfills. The basic principle of federalism is that one state in its dealings with another may not place itself in a position of economic isolation. Earlier the Court had occasion in *Edwards v. California* (1941) to emphatically assert this same principle when California attempted to keep poor residents of other states from migrating to that state.

Penetration of Federal Regulation. The question of how far within the confines of state boundaries federal legislation may penetrate to regulate commerce is answered by two Court decisions during the first quarter of the twentieth century. In the first instance, the Interstate Commerce Commission responded to the discriminatory practices of a railway company in charging lower rates for intrastate shipments among east Texas locations than for interstate shipments over similar distances. The Court, in the *Shreveport Rate Cases* (1914), held that although the rate fixing was completely intrastate, Congress may regulate intrastate carriers in all matters that have a "close and substantial relation" to interstate commerce. In *Stafford v. Wallace* (1922), the Court decided that Congress could authorize the secretary of agriculture to regulate the business conducted in stockyards although cattle in stockyards are not in transit. Chief Justice William H. Taft concluded that "the stockyards are but a throat through which the current flows, and the transactions which occur therein are only incident to this current from the West to the East, and from one state to another."

Although matters affecting transportation were found to be firmly within the regulatory power of Congress, the Court limited the power of Congress under the commerce clause by creating a sharp distinction between commerce and manufacturing. Chief Justice Melville W. Fuller, writing for a 8-1 majority in *United States v. E. C. Knight Co.* (1895), held that the Sherman Antitrust Act (1890) is not applicable to monopolies in manufacturing or production because they have only an incidental or indirect relationship to commerce. Consequently, as applied in this case, the Sherman Antitrust Act represents an intrusion into the reserve power of the states under the Tenth Amendment. The Court used similar reasoning to strike down congressional attempts to regulate child labor (*Hammer v. Dagenhart*, 1918), codes of fair competition (*Schechter Poultry Corp. v. United States*, 1935), wages and hours of workers in mining (*Carter v. Carter Coal Co.*, 1936), and even agricultural subsidies, although not as a violation of the commerce clause (*United States v. Butler*, 1936). These and other Court decisions represented a serious threat to President Franklin D. Roosevelt's New Deal. Consequently, the Court was subjected to considerable pressure that no doubt led to the alteration in the Court's commerce clause interpretation.

By 1937 the Court changed its antifederal government interpretations. The transition to a cooperative view of federalism as opposed to the dualistic and antagonist view of federal-state relations occurs with the 5-4 decision in *National Labor Relations Board v. Jones and Laughlin Steel Corp.* (1937). The Court found the act establishing the right of organized labor to bargain collectively was a valid regulation of commerce. Although labor-management relations are intrastate in character when they are considered separately, these relationships have a "close and substantial relation" to interstate commerce as part of the "stream of commerce." Therefore, the Court discarded its previous direct-indirect decision rule. In subsequent decisions pertaining to maximum-hour and minimum-wage laws (*United States v. Darby Lumber Co.*, 1941) and the regulation of farm acreage allotments (*Wickard v. Filburn*, 1942), the Court upheld the power of Congress to regulate commerce. Virtually any amount of economic activity in one place affects activity elsewhere, and consequently there seemed no limit to the power of the national government.

Civil Rights and Commerce. The Court opted to base its interpretation of the 1964 Civil Rights Act on the commerce clause alone and not on the more obvious equal protection clause and its enforcement provision found in the Fourteenth Amendment. The Court found an interstate commerce link in cases involving hotels because of their role in interstate travel (*Heart of Atlanta Motel v. United States*, 1964), service at restaurants because foodstuffs are shipped via interstate carriers (*Katzenbach v. McClung*, 1964), and a resort located many miles from an interstate highway because the private park leased equipment from an out-of-state supplier (*Daniel v. Paul*, 1969). Conceding that when Congress enacted the 1964 Civil Rights Act it may have been addressing a moral wrong, Justice Tom C. Clark in *Heart of Atlanta* concluded that the act is nonetheless constitutional. The congressional power extends to local activity in the states of both origin and destination when the activity in question has a substantial and harmful effect upon commerce. The only restriction of congressional power is that it must be "reasonably adapted to the end permitted by the Constitution."

States' Rights Reaction. Although a temporary setback for national power, Justice William H. Rehnquist's majority opinion in *National League of Cities v. Usery* (1976) represented a stunning victory for state power. He held when dealing with their own employees, cities need not abide by the minimum-wage and maximum-hour provisions of federal law. Rehnquist argued that the law impaired the integrity and ability of the states to perform their traditional government functions, thereby invading the

Tenth Amendment power reserved to the states. Rehnquist effectively reversed the logic of a long line of cases beginning with *Gibbons* that held that if a federal law is within the congressional commerce power, then by definition there can be no violation of the Tenth Amendment. Ten years later, however, the Court specifically overruled its earlier 6-3 decision with a 5-4 majority in *Garcia v. San Antonio Metropolitan Transit Authority* (1985). Writing for the majority, Harry A. Blackmun expressed frustration with the Court's inability to draw a workable line defining what is and what is not a traditional governmental function. He found that wage and working conditions have an impact on interstate commerce and therefore may be regulated by Congress.

In *United States v. Lopez* (1995), the conservative majority of the Rehnquist Court concluded that the Gun Free School Zones Act of 1990 violated the reserved power of the states because the statute was a criminal statute that had little to do with "commerce" or any type of economic activity. In his opinion, Rehnquist wrote that Congress may regulate the channels of interstate commerce; regulate and protect the instrumentalities of interstate commerce, even though the threat may come only from intrastate activities; and regulate those activities that substantially affect interstate commerce. He found that the law in question did not involve the channels or instrumentalities of interstate commerce and that the activity involved did not substantially affect interstate commerce. He rejected the view of the Justice Department and the four-member Court minority that a violent atmosphere in schools adversely affects the learning environment, which in turn ultimately substantially affects the economy. If the federal law against the carrying of weapons near and on school grounds was constitutionally permissible, then, Rehnquist stated, the Court could find no reason why Congress could not, for example, enact laws prescribing curriculum for local elementary and secondary schools.

Preemption, Indians, and Foreign Commerce. Much of contemporary commerce clause litigation involves the federal preemption doctrine. If a state law conflicts with a federal law, the national law supersedes it. The Court must determine whether Congress intended, either explicitly or implicitly, by its extensive regulation to take over a field such as nuclear power (*Pacific Gas and Electric Co. v. State Energy Resources Conservation and Development Commission*, 1983). The commerce clause is also the primary constitutional tool that Congress possesses when legislating in the field of Indian affairs. This is especially the case after 1871 when Congress declared that there would be no more treaties with Native Americans. Finally, the Court consistently held that the congressional right to regulate commerce with foreign nations is quite extensive (especially in the light of state attempts to tax foreign products) because it is important for the nation to speak with one voice. However, that voice is Congress and not the president (*Barclays Bank v. Franchise Tax Board of California*, 1994).

FURTHER READING

Maurice G. Baxter's *The Steamboat Monopoly: "Gibbons v. Ogden," 1824* (New York: Alfred A. Knopf, 1972) is a good case study of Marshall's seminal opinion and a useful history of the commerce clause in the pre-Civil War years. Another work on this subject is Felix Frankfurter's *The Commerce Power Under Marshall, Taney, and Waite* (Chapel Hill: University of North Carolina, 1937). Edward S. Corwin's *The Commerce Power Versus States Rights* (London: Oxford University Press, 1936) treats competing Court interpretations of the commerce clause that preceded the conflict with the New Deal. Because the case in question is essential to understanding the history of the commerce clause, Richard C. Cortner's *The "Jones and Laughlin" Case* (New York: Alfred A. Knopf, 1970) is essential reading. Paul R. Benson, Jr.'s *The Supreme Court and the Commerce Clause, 1937-70* (New York: Dunellen, 1970) also provides a good historical account for the period covered. For a modern conservative and restrictive view of the commerce clause see Thomas W. Merrill's " Toward a Principled Interpretation of the Commerce Clause," *Harvard Journal of Law and Public Policy* 22 (1998): 31-43. A searching analysis of the modern conservative agenda with respect to federalism is found in Peter A. Lauricella's "The Real 'Contract with America': The Original Intent of the Tenth Amendment and the Commerce Clause," *Albany Law Review* 60 (1997): 1377-1408.

Albert P. Melone

SEE ALSO Agricultural issues; Capitalism; Constitutional interpretation; *Cooley v. Board of Wardens of the Port of Philadelphia*; Federalism; *Gibbons v. Ogden*; Interstate Commerce Commission (ICC); *Lopez, United States v.*; *National Labor Relations Board v. Jones and Laughlin Steel Corp.*; Private corporation charters; Race and discrimination; *Shreveport Rate Cases*; States' rights; Travel, right to.

Commercial speech

DESCRIPTION: Communication involving the sale of products or services to a consumer.

SIGNIFICANCE: In 1975 the Supreme Court declared that commercial speech is protected under the First Amendment's free speech clause, thus protecting consumers from excessive government interference in their right to know about products and services.

Beginning in the 1970's the Supreme Court recognized that commercial speech was protected under the U.S. Constitution. Declaring that the First Amendment's speech clause included commercial speech, the Court created a systematic approach to commercial speech cases and aggressively used it to overturn federal and state regulations.

The Court first recognized commercial speech as protected under the First Amendment in *Bigelow v. Virginia* (1975). In *Bigelow*, the Court struck down a state ban on advertising for abortion services. The justices asserted that speech involving the marketplace deserved some protection under the First Amendment.

The Court extended its reasoning in *Virginia State Board of Pharmacy v. Virginia Citizens Consumer Council* (1976). It struck down a state ban on advertising prescription drug prices. The justices reasoned that consumers had a constitutional right to receive information on products and that commercial speech provided a basis for the flow of information necessary for an open economy. Consumers had a strong interest in receiving correct information about products and services. That information would allow them to make economic decisions critical to their personal survival. The Court recognized that misleading or untruthful speech would not aid consumers and thus would not be covered under commercial speech protections.

A Standard Test. The commercial speech doctrine remained undeveloped until 1980. Then in

Central Hudson Gas and Electric Corp. v. Public Service Commission of New York, the Court developed a systematic approach to commercial speech cases. In *Central Hudson*, the Court struck down a ban on utility advertising as a violation of the utility's commercial speech rights. In arriving at this conclusion, the justices used a four-part test. The *Central Hudson* test requires the justices to determine whether the advertising is misleading or involves an illegal product or service, whether there is a substantial governmental interest in regulating the speech, whether that substantial interest is advanced by the regulation, and whether less restrictive means exist. The justices in *Central Hudson* found that the state's substantial interest in promoting energy efficiency was not advanced by the advertising ban.

With the development of the *Central Hudson* test, commercial speech was protected under intermediate scrutiny rather than strict scrutiny. Under strict scrutiny, the government must show a compelling interest for limiting speech rights and the law must be narrowly tailored to meet that interest. Intermediate scrutiny requires the government to show a substantial interest in regulating speech. Eventually, though, the test came closer to strict scrutiny.

Liquor and Gambling. After *Central Hudson* was decided, the justices began looking carefully at two areas of commercial speech restrictions, liquor advertisements and gambling. In *Rubin v. Coors* (1995), the Court struck down a federal ban on displaying alcohol content on the packaging of certain high-alcohol-content beers. The justices dismissed the government's contention that the ban was linked to limiting strength wars among beer producers and found that consumer information was restricted without advancing the government's interest.

In *Forty-four Liquormart v. Rhode Island* (1996), the justices overturned a forty-year-old state ban on the advertising of liquor prices. Again a restriction on commercial speech ran afoul of the *Central Hudson* requirement that regulations be related to a substantial state interest, in this case promoting temperance. According to the Court, the ban on price advertising would not necessarily prevent excessive alcohol sales because there was no link between the price of alcohol and the amount consumed.

In both cases, the justices warily eyed the ban on consumer information, demanding the government meet a high standard of showing that its regulation advanced its interest. The justices would lower that standard in cases involving gambling advertising.

The increasing popularity of state-run gambling presented several cases to the justices involving commercial advertisements for casinos and lotteries. In *Posados de Puerto Rico v. Tourism Co. of Puerto Rico* (1986), the Court upheld a ban on gambling advertising in Puerto Rico, which allowed legalized gambling. The justices determined that the ban did advance the governmental interest in preventing compulsive gambling among the island's residents and that there were no alternative means to accomplish this end.

Likewise in *United States v. Edge Broadcasting* (1993), the justices upheld a federal ban on advertising gambling in states where gambling was illegal. The Court ignored the third part of the *Central Hudson* test in stating that the federal interest in protecting nongambling states from such advertising was constitutional and that there was no alternative to the ban.

However, in *Greater New Orleans Broadcasting Association v. United States* (1998), the justices struck down a ban when it applied to states where gambling was legal. The Court noted the exceptions to law including the exemption from the ban for state-run casinos and lotteries that undermined the effort of the federal government to prevent compulsive gambling. This decision called into question the viability of the decision in *Edge Broadcasting*.

The Court's inconsistency in the gambling cases reflected the subjectivity of the *Central Hudson* test. Whether a restriction on commercial speech advanced a substantial interest required a judgment by justices based on subjective criteria. Under the *Rubin*, *Liquormart*, and *Greater New Orleans* cases, the Court used a stringent definition of whether the government regulation advanced its interest. A less stringent standard was used to uphold speech restrictions in *Posados* and *Edge Broadcasting*. The continued use of the *Central Hudson* test indicates the Court's intention to move it from an intermediate scrutiny type of test to one closer to strict scrutiny and placing commercial speech on par with political speech.

FURTHER READING

Baldwin, Jo Jo. "No Longer the Crazy Aunt in the Basement: Commercial Speech Joins the Family." *University of Arkansas Little Rock Law Review* (Fall, 1997).

Oliphant, Richard Shawn. "Prohibiting Casinos from Advertising." *Arizona Law Review* (Winter, 1996).

Siegan, Bernard. *Economic Liberties and the Constitution.* Chicago: University of Chicago Press, 1980.

Douglas Clouatre

SEE ALSO First Amendment; First Amendment speech tests; Judicial scrutiny; Speech and press, freedom of; Unprotected speech.

Common carriers

DESCRIPTION: Legally, all businesses involved in public transportation are designated common carriers.

SIGNIFICANCE: In the United States, after the establishment of the Interstate Commerce Commission (ICC) in 1887, the Supreme Court became the arbiter in regulatory matters affecting national transportation that previously had been adjudicated by state judges.

In the eyes of the law in both the United States and Great Britain, a distinction is made between ordinary businesses and those that have a special obligation to the public. In the case of common carriers, in British common law (a subcategory of "common callings"), the latter are distinguished from the former by the fact that their services are available to the general public. The social and economic welfare of the community is much affected by the quality and cost of such services.

The Obligations of Common Carriers. Because of their intimate involvement with the community good, common carriers in Great Britain were charged with three specific obligations. First, they could not discriminate among those who sought their services. They were compelled by law to make these services available to all who applied for them. Second, common carriers were prohibited from assessing unreasonable rates or conditions on those who wanted and needed their services. Third, the liability standards applied to them were much more stringent than those applied to ordinary businesses. Regulation was imposed upon common carriers strictly for the good of the entire community they served.

In the United States, before the Interstate Commerce Commission (ICC) was established in 1887, the obligations that had long been a part of British common law were essentially observed and enforced. In the first century of U.S. independence, the laws regarding interstate commerce, which under Article I, section 8, of the U.S. Constitution bestowed the power of regulation on Congress, were enforced by individual judges who adjudicated the cases that came before them. This created a chaotic situation often marked by inequities, favoritism, and, in some cases, graft and corruption.

The Court and Common Carriers. In *New Jersey Steam Navigation Co. v. Merchants' Bank of Boston* (1848), the Supreme Court established the rules governing whether a common carrier might contract its liability for negligence to another company. This decision was followed by *Parrot v. Wells Fargo* (1872), in which the question was whether a common carrier, in this case Wells Fargo, had a duty to serve, as stipulated by common law, if what it was called on to do involved the transportation of dangerous cargo. In this instance, the Court found valid cause for making an exception to the rule that common carriers had a duty to serve all who applied for their services.

It was not until *Munn v. Illinois* (1877), however, that the Court categorically introduced into constitutional law the distinction that British common law had made between ordinary businesses and those that had a special obligation to serve the public. The *Munn* decision was concerned with grain elevators and railroads, both considered essential in serving the public interest. It had been a common practice at that time for rates to be set for both grain storage facilities and the railroad transportation of grain to market centers and increased substantially as the fall harvest approached. Under newly enacted statutes, the railroads were forced to offer equal rates to all shippers of freight related only to what the cargo was, rather than to when it was being shipped, to how much was being shipped, or to how far it was being shipped. The Court upheld the constitutionality of these statutes. After *Munn*, the excessive rates the railroads had been charging for short hauls and small shipments began to be equalized, much to the benefit of small farmers.

The Effects of the *Munn* Decision. The *Munn* decision established clearly the difference between ordinary businesses and those that had a profound effect on the social and economic welfare of American society. This doctrine established that grain storage facilities and railroads were businesses "affected with a public interest." The Court further ruled that in the absence of federal mandates regarding the rates charged by businesses with special obligations to the public, the responsibility for regulating interstate transportation would fall to state legislatures. This solution created more problems than it solved and resulted in a chaotic network of railroad charges from one state to another.

The Court sought to remedy this situation in its decision in *Wabash, St. Louis, and Pacific Railway Co. v. Illinois* (1886). This case was brought before the Court because of the inequities that existed among various states in the regulation of interstate commerce, notably the regulation of railroads. The Court found that the only agency that could reasonably regulate interstate commerce charges was Congress, which had been given the authority to do so in Article I, section 8, of the Constitution but had never exercised this prerogative. Out of this decision grew the creation of the ICC the following year.

FURTHER READING

Blandford, Linda A. *Supreme Court of the United States, 1789-1980: An Index to Opinions Arranged by Justice*. 2 vols. Millwood, N.Y.: Kraus International, 1983.

Friedman, Leon, and Fred L. Israel, eds. *The Justices of the United States Supreme Court: Their Lives and Major Opinions*. 5 vols. New York: Chelsea House, 1997.

Galloway, Russell. *Justice for All? Rich and Poor in Supreme Court History, 1790-1990*. Durham, N.C.: Carolina Academic Press, 1991.

Hoogenboom, Ari, and Olive Hoogenboom. *A History of the ICC: From Panacea to Palliative*. New York: Norton, 1976.

Wright, Charles Alan. *The Law of Federal Courts*. 5th ed. St. Paul, Minn.: West Publishing, 1994.

R. Baird Shuman

SEE ALSO Interstate Commerce Commission (ICC); Interstate compacts; *Munn v. Illinois*; *Wabash, St. Louis, and Pacific Railway Co. v. Illinois*.

Common law

DESCRIPTION: Law generated from court cases and judicial decisions.

SIGNIFICANCE: The Supreme Court is a common-law court in that it generally follows earlier decisions made by judges.

Common law, or judge-made law, is generated from a succession of judicial decisions or precedents. In common-law systems, courts are bound by the rule called *stare decisis*, or "let the precedent stand." In the United States, common law is distinguished from equity law, which is based on reasoning about what is fair or equitable. It also differs from law based on statutes enacted by legislatures.

Common-law systems are contrasted with civil-law systems found on the continent of Europe and elsewhere, which are based on legal codes. Some of these systems are based on the Code Civil ("civil law") drafted in Napoleonic France, derived partially from Roman law. By contrast, the common-law system was developed in England and brought to the American colonies. By 1776 the colonial courts used common law as a matter of course. After the American Revolution, decisions made in U.S. courts added to the body of common law.

The Supreme Court is a common-law court. Its decisions are the basis of constitutional law and it generally adheres, except when changing circumstances warrant creation of new rules, to *stare decisis*. When government under the Constitution began in 1789, questions arose as to whether federal courts had jurisdiction over common law cases. The question also arose as to whether federal cases would themselves become a kind of common law in civil or criminal cases. The Court's decisions regarding these questions had far-reaching consequences.

In *United States v. Hudson and Goodwin* (1812), the Court ruled that no federal court could exercise common-law jurisdiction in criminal cases. It therefore denied the existence of a federal common law of crimes. Whether a federal common law of civil cases exists, however, was another matter. In 1842 in *Swift v. Tyson*, the Court ruled that there is federal common law in commercial cases. This ruling prevailed for nearly a century; then the Court, departing from *stare decisis*, reversed itself, ruling in *Erie Railroad Co. v. Tompkins* (1938) that one of its own decisions—*Swift*—was unconstitutional.

Speaking for the majority, Justice Louis D. Brandeis wrote: "There is no federal common law." Nevertheless, this ruling did not completely eliminate the idea of federal common law, though today it is limited to specialized subjects.

The common-law process of following precedent in making decisions has allowed the federal judiciary to assume the position it holds in the U.S. constitutional plan. When Chief Justice John Marshall rendered the key decision in *Marbury v. Madison* (1803) that established the federal courts' power to declare laws void, he was following the common law obligation to apply all relevant law. Because of the force of precedent in common law procedure, the Court's action in *Marbury* has reverberated through two centuries of legal tradition, helping to shape the theory and practice of U.S. government.

FURTHER READING

Farnsworth, E. Allan. *An Introduction to the Legal System of the United States.* 3d ed. Dobbs Ferry, N.Y.: Oceana Publications, 1996.

Friedman, Lawrence M. *A History of American Law.* 2d ed. New York: Simon & Schuster, 1985.

Plucknett, Theodore F. T. *A Concise History of the Common Law.* 5th ed. London: Butterworth, 1956.

Charles F. Bahmueller

SEE ALSO British background to U.S. judiciary; Civil law; Common law, federal; Constitutional law; *Erie Railroad Co. v. Tompkins*; *Hudson and Goodwin, United States v.*; *Marbury v. Madison*; Roman law; Rule of law; *Swift v. Tyson.*

Common law, federal

DESCRIPTION: Body of decisional, or judge-made, laws applied by federal courts.

SIGNIFICANCE: For nearly a century, until a 1938 Supreme Court ruling, federal common law abridged the power of the states to control their internal legal affairs.

The Supreme Court holding, in *United States v. Hudson and Goodwin* (1812), that no federal common law existed with regard to criminal matters, did not prevent the federal courts from developing a substantial body of civil common law. Federal common law development was abetted by the Court's interpretation of section 34 of the Judiciary Act of 1789. Justice Joseph Story, speaking for a unanimous Court in *Swift v. Tyson* (1842), held that section 34 required federal courts exercising diversity of citizenship jurisdiction (cases involving citizens of different states) to follow only the statutory law of the states in which they sat; they were not bound by state common law. The decision freed the federal courts from the constraints of state common law, enabling them to develop a coherent body of federal common law that the states in turn were expected to adopt for the sake of uniformity.

However, the expected uniformity was never achieved. The failure of the states to adopt the federal models led to competing systems of state and federal common law. Far from promoting uniformity among the states, *Swift* caused confusion and uncertainty within the states. In *Erie Railroad Co. v. Tompkins* (1938), a unanimous Court overruled *Swift*, holding that federal courts exercising diversity jurisdiction must follow both the statutes and common law of the states in which they sit. The decision voided nearly a century of federal common law, returning to the states full control of their internal legal affairs.

Edgar J. McManus

SEE ALSO Civil law; Common law; Diversity jurisdiction; *Erie Railroad Co. v. Tompkins*; *Hudson and Goodwin, United States v.*; Judiciary Act of 1789; *Swift v. Tyson.*

Communist Party v. Subversive Activities Control Board

CITATION: 367 U.S. 1

DATE: June 5, 1961

ISSUE: Freedom of assembly and association

SIGNIFICANCE: The Supreme Court upheld the registration provisions of the McCarran Act of 1950, although it declined to rule on the constitutionality of sanctions written into the act.

A five-member majority of the Supreme Court upheld the McCarran Act of 1950, which required members of the Communist Party to register and file financial statements with the Subversive Activities Control Board, which made them subject to sanctions such as being banned from work in the defense industry. Felix Frankfurter wrote the opinion for the Court and Chief Justice Earl Warren and Justices Hugo L. Black, William J. Brennan, Jr., and William O. Douglas dissented. Although the Court upheld the act's registration provisions, it declined to rule on enforcement until enforcement was attempted. This led some observers to believe that the Court might rule against the McCarran Act. In *Aptheker v. Secretary of State* (1964), the Court ruled the denial of passports to Communist Party members to be an unconstitutional violation of the right to travel. The next year, the Court struck down the registration provisions in *Albertson v. Subversive Activities Control Board* (1965), calling them a violation of Fifth Amendment rights as registration led to sanctions. These decisions destroyed the effectiveness of the Subversive Activities Control Board, and Congress allowed the board to expire in the early 1970's.

Richard L. Wilson

SEE ALSO *Albertson v. Subversive Activities Control Board*; *Aptheker v. Secretary of State*; Assembly and association, freedom of; Cold War; *Dennis v. United States*; *Scales v. United States*; Subversion; Travel, right to; *Yates v. United States*.

Concurring opinions

DESCRIPTION: Opinions in which a Supreme Court justice agrees with the decision that a majority or plurality of justices reached in the opinion for the Court but sets forth different reasoning in support of the decision.

SIGNIFICANCE: Concurring opinions often alert the legal community to the significance of the opinion for the Court or to nuances in that opinion and can be particularly significant when only a plurality joins the opinion of the Court.

The Supreme Court produces an opinion for the Court in each case it resolves, but individual justices or groups of justices may file separately, setting forth the differences between their views and those stated in the opinion for the Court. The opinion written by a justice who agrees with the result reached in the opinion for the Court but disagrees on some other point is a concurring opinion. That written by a justice who disagrees with the Court's decision is a dissenting opinion. If the case raises several issues, a separate opinion can concur in part and dissent in part. A concurring opinion's author may join the opinion of the Court but often either joins only part of it or does not join it at all.

Concurring opinions can serve many purposes. A justice may write one to influence the legal community's interpretation of the opinion for the Court. A concurring justice may seek to limit the implications or reach of the Court's decision or, conversely, may suggest that the opinion of the Court states too limited a rule of decision. Justices

	CONCURRING OPINIONS AMONG JUSTICES IN 1994 AND 1995								
	Percentage of cases in which pairs of justices supported the same opinions								
	Stevens	Ginsburg	Breyer	Souter	O'Connor	Kennedy	Rehnquist	Scalia	Thomas
Stevens	—	74	72	70	58	63	50	45	44
Ginsburg	74	—	79	82	67	76	66	59	55
Breyer	72	79	—	86	75	70	63	57	54
Souter	70	82	86	—	78	74	68	60	57
O'Connor	58	67	75	78	—	77	78	70	70
Kennedy	63	76	70	74	77	—	81	74	71
Rehnquist	50	66	63	68	78	81	—	81	82
Scalia	45	59	57	60	70	74	81	—	88
Thomas	44	55	54	57	70	71	82	88	—

Note: Numbers are averages, for the two terms, of the percentages of cases in each term in which a pair of justices agreed on an opinion. Both unanimous and nonunanimous cases are included.

Source: Lawrence Baum, *The Supreme Court* (6th ed. 1998), p. 156.

also write concurring opinions for more personal reasons, such as the desire to create a unique philosophy over the course of several cases. For example, in the 1990's Justice Antonin Scalia regularly wrote concurrences arguing that courts should not use legislative history when interpreting statutes. A concurring opinion may also simply state the justice's alternative reason for coming to the decision the Court reached.

Concurring opinions have special significance when fewer than five justices join the opinion of the Court (making the decision a plurality decision) or when the votes of the concurring justices are necessary for the Court's opinion to have the support of five justices. Some concurring opinions, such as those by Justice Lewis F. Powell, Jr., in *Regents of the University of California v. Bakke* (1978) and *Branzburg v. Hayes* (1972), profoundly affect the development of the law because they are issued in the absence of a clear majority. When five justices (or more) join the opinion of the Court, any concurring opinion will probably carry less weight. Nevertheless, some such concurring opinions gain significance because they set forth a cogent approach that can be applied to other cases or because they may indicate the Court's future direction.

FURTHER READING

Flanders, Robert G. "The Utility of Separate Judicial Opinions in Appellate Courts of Last Resort: Why Dissents Are Valuable." *Roger Williams University Law Review* 4 (Spring, 1999): 401.

Stephens, Richard B. "The Function of Concurring and Dissenting Opinions in Courts of Last Resort." *University of Florida Law Review* 5 (Winter, 1952): 394-410.

Bernard W. Bell

SEE ALSO *Branzburg v. Hayes*; Collegiality; Dissents; *Edwards v. Aguillard*; Opinions, writing of; *Regents of the University of California v. Bakke*; Reporting of opinions; Seriatim opinions; Statutory interpretation; Workload.

Conference of the justices

DESCRIPTION: Formal meeting of the justices to conduct Supreme Court business, including the selection of cases to hear, votes on cases already argued, and the issuance of miscellaneous orders.

SIGNIFICANCE: The opportunity for face-to-face deliberation is an important component in the promotion of collegiality, enabling the justices to speak in a unified institutional voice. In the contemporary period, however, the conference is of declining significance.

The nature of the conference of the justices has evolved over time, reflecting the changing environment and developing role of the Supreme Court. During its first decade, the Court followed the English practice of issuing seriatim opinions, each justice writing a separate opinion for each case. Among the innovations of Chief Justice John Marshall, in 1801, was the adoption of the opinion of the Court. This permitted the Court to speak in a singular, unified voice, thus enhancing its prestige and promoting greater clarity in its legal pronouncements. Achieving this unity required the justices to negotiate a compromise among their individual opinions. Marshall's practice, followed through much of the nineteenth century, was to conduct conferences during the evening to deliberate cases argued each day. This was facilitated by the fact that Court sessions were then of short duration, the justices having circuit duties during the rest of the year. Residing in a common boarding house, the justices dined together and had ample time to reach a common result and a common rationale for the Court's decision. Dissents were relatively few, and concurring opinions were rare.

For much of the early twentieth century, conferences were held on Saturday during the Court's term. Chief Justice Earl Warren moved the conference to Friday in 1955. The justices usually spend the morning voting on writs of certiorari to choose the cases the Court will later hear from among those petitions on the discuss list. Typically, some attention is also given to routine orders, such as stays to delay action by the parties of a suit until the Court can resolve their dispute. The remainder of the conference is devoted to deciding the twelve cases argued the previous week. During the 1970's and 1980's an additional conference was introduced on Wednesday afternoon, to discuss the four cases argued the previous Monday, leaving the eight cases argued on Tuesday and Wednesday for the Friday conference. A reduction in the number of cases heard by the Court has eliminated the need for this supplementary conference in recent years. All cases are now discussed on Friday. However, during May and June, when the Court is not hearing oral arguments, the conference is moved to Thursday. In late September, the justices meet in special daylong conferences to discuss the certiorari petitions that have arrived over the summer. Additional conferences might be called to meet special needs.

Conference Procedure. All conferences are held in the conference room, adjacent to the chief justice's chambers. After a ceremonial handshake among all the justices, the chief justice presides over the conference from the head of a long conference table. The senior associate justice sits at the opposite end, and the remaining justices sit around the table, usually in order of seniority. Absolute confidentiality is observed, and no outsider—not even the justice's clerks—may enter the room while the justices are meeting. If messages or items must be delivered to the conference room, a knock on the door will be answered by the most junior justice. Because of this secrecy, the conference is difficult to study. Knowledge of the proceeding comes from docket books and assorted notes by individual justices that have been saved and have become available to the public, often years after the justice's death. Occasional published reflections by justices also shed light on the subject. No doubt the tenor of the conference varies according to the personalities of the justices, the skills of the chief justice, the ideological divisions on the Court, and the contentiousness of the issues under discussion.

Conference discussion tends to be candid, even blunt, but brief. The chief justice speaks first, outlining the issues of the case and stating his or her views. Other justices speak in order of seniority and may disagree with the chief justice's understanding of the case or its proper resolution. Previously, after every justice spoke, the justices voted in ascending order of seniority, but this practice has been discontinued. The position of each justice is implicit in his or her comments and an apparent majority can usually be discerned without an actual vote. Discussion will then move on to another matter. The assignment of opinion writing occurs soon after the conference. If in the majority, the chief justice assigns the opinion; if not, that task falls to the most senior member of the majority.

In the latter part of the twentieth century, the opportunity for face-to-face deliberation became a scarce luxury, sacrificed to burgeoning caseloads. No longer an instrument for building consensus, the modern conference is mainly an occasion for the justices to state their individual views, make a tentative vote, and gain a sense of the majority. Discussion on each case is perfunctory, with little attempt made to persuade or to negotiate a consensus. A justice might occasionally change his or her opinion on some matter as a result of conference discussion, but this appears to be the exception, not the rule. After many years of working together, the justices rarely surprise their colleagues, and time for extended discussion simply does not exist. The deliberative process continues, but the negotiation of common ground in support of the Court's pronouncements now occurs primarily through the process of drafting and circulating opinions. The pressure of the workload, the growth of the role of clerks, and modern office technology have isolated the justices from one another, as captured in Justice Lewis F. Powell, Jr.'s description of the modern Court as "nine small, independent law firms." Collegiality remains only to the degree that these separate firms come together to criticize each other's work. With this decline in collegiality, the Court has seen a rise in the number of concurrences and dissents filed. The result is that the Court now speaks in a less clear voice.

FURTHER READING

Epstein, Lee, and Jack Knight. *The Choices Justices Make.* Washington, D.C.: Congressional Quarterly, 1998.

Lazarus, Edward. *Closed Chambers: The Rise, Fall, and Future of the Modern Supreme Court.* New York: Penguin Books, 1999.

O'Brien, David. *Storm Center.* 4th ed. New York: W. W. Norton, 1996.

Perry, H. W. *Deciding to Decide: Agenda Setting in the United States Supreme Court.* Cambridge, Mass.: Harvard University Press, 1991.

Rehnquist, William H. *The Supreme Court: How It Was, How It Is.* New York: Oxford University Press, 1987.

Schwartz, Bernard. *A History of the Supreme Court.* New York: Oxford University Press, 1993.

John C. Hughes

SEE ALSO Briefs; Bureaucratization of the judiciary; Certiorari, writ of; Chief justice; Clerks of the justices; Collegiality; Decision making; First Monday in October; Opinions, writing of; Seriatim opinions.

Congress, arrest and immunity of members of

DESCRIPTION: Protection from legal actions given to members of Congress by the speech and debate clause of Article I, section 6, of the U.S. Constitution.

SIGNIFICANCE: The primary purpose of the speech and debate clause is to preserve the notion of separation of powers by protecting the legislative branch from interference by the executive and judicial branches.

The speech and debate clause was originally intended to protect Congress and its members from attempts by other branches of government to interfere with and disrupt Congress's ability to do its work. Although the clause appears to offer absolute immunity, the Supreme Court has narrowed its scope through a series of rulings.

In *Kilbourn v. Thompson* (1881), the Court provided a broad interpretation of the clause and held that its protection extended to activity generally engaged in during a House session by its members in relation to the business before the House. Subsequent Court decisions determined that the clause may be asserted in both civil and criminal actions. However, the clause protects only legislative activities, not political matters. In *Gravel v. United States* (1972), the Court held that only those acts that are integral parts of the legislative process receive protection. Protected legislative activities include voting, speaking, debating, preparing committee reports, and conducting committee hearings. Unprotected political activities include publishing books, distributing press releases, creating constituent newsletters, delivering speeches outside Congress, and providing constituent services. In *Gravel*, the Court further held that the clause's protection extends to a member's aide, as long as the services the aide performs would be immune legislative conduct if performed by a member.

Robert P. Morin

SEE ALSO Congress, qualifications for; Executive immunity; Federalism; *Kilbourn v. Thompson*; Separation of powers; Speech and debate clause.

Congress, qualifications for

DESCRIPTION: The citizenship, age, and residence requirements for senators and representatives set out in Article I, sections 2 and 3, of the U.S. Constitution.

SIGNIFICANCE: Although each house of Congress judges the qualifications of its members in the first instance, the Supreme Court has decided some important cases regarding congressional membership.

The U.S. Constitution establishes the qualifications for members of Congress. Representatives must be inhabitants of the state from which they are elected, must be at least twenty-five years of age, and must have been citizens of the United States for at least seven years. Senators must be inhabitants of their state at the time of election, must be at least thirty years old, and must have been citizens for at least nine years.

Article I, section 5, of the Constitution gives each house of Congress the power to "be the Judge of the Elections, Returns and Qualifications of its own members." Should a dispute about citizenship, age, residence, or election returns arise, the matter would be decided in the Senate or House of Representatives. However, when one of the houses of Congress goes beyond the constitutionally stated criteria, the Supreme Court's judgment comes into play. In 1967 the House of Representatives refused to seat Representative Adam Clayton Powell because he had misused House funds. Powell brought suit, arguing that the only role the House could play was to judge age, residence, and citizenship. In *Powell v. McCormick* (1969), Chief Justice Earl Warren, for a majority of the Court, held that Congress's power was limited to the constitutionally stated criteria, and that Congressman Powell was entitled to his seat.

Robert Jacobs

SEE ALSO *Goldwater v. Carter; Luther v. Borden*; Political questions; *Powell v. McCormick*; Separation of powers.

Congressional power of investigation

DESCRIPTION: Power of Congress to demand information from people, orally or in writing, and to punish those who refuse to cooperate.

SIGNIFICANCE: The Supreme Court ruled in a series of cases on the extent of Congress's power, focusing on questions of congressional intent in investigations and the rights of witnesses.

Congressional committees usually secure information by summoning individuals to testify orally at hearings and to provide necessary documents. Most of those summoned want to testify and thereby have input into the legislative process, but some refuse to cooperate. Congress has always acted on the assumption that it has the power to punish these people for contempt. In the nineteenth century, several hostile witnesses were arrested and confined in the basement of the Capitol or in the District of Columbia jail. Because these arrangements were awkward, Congress created a court procedure to punish contempt of Congress as a federal crime in 1857. In *McGrain v. Daugherty* (1927), the Supreme Court held that the contempt power in such cases was inherent in the legislative process and was therefore an implied power of Congress.

Most of the Court's pronouncements on Congress's investigative power were made during the Cold War. As part of efforts to prevent communist spying and subversion in the United States, congressional committees used hearings to expose people who might have procommunist sympathies. Because Congress did not use this information to pass anticommunist legislation, these hearings were denounced as "exposure for the sake of exposure." The exposed witnesses and the people they were forced to denounce in their testimony were sometimes denied employment or otherwise harmed although they were not accused of committing any crimes.

Limits on Congress's Power. In several rulings in the 1950's, the Court made it clear that the power of Congress to investigate, while broad, is not unlimited. In *Watkins v. United States* (1957), the Court held that Congress cannot compel testimony unless it is pursuing a legitimate legislative goal, a goal within the scope of its constitutionally enumerated powers. Most hearings are intended to help Congress write laws. However, the Court also held that Congress can collect whatever information it needs to exercise its oversight function, expose corruption, judge the validity of an election, or determine whether to expel a member. Although the Court usually presumed that a congressional investigation had a valid purpose, it occasionally required Congress to specify that purpose. Federal courts examined a number of congressional debates and authorizing resolutions to find congressional intent.

In the process of pursuing a valid legislative goal, Congress may demand only information relevant to that goal. An investigative committee does not have the power to ask vague or leading questions in the hope that something interesting will develop. Nor does it have the power to question witnesses simply to expose them to shame or humiliation. Before a person can be punished for refusing to answer a question, Congress must prove its pertinence to the legislative goal. The Court looked for evidence of pertinence in a number of legislative debates and in the statements of the chairperson of the committee holding the hearing.

The Bill of Rights. Because congressional investigations are government actions, they are limited by the relevant rights of individuals. The Court held that witnesses, under the Bill of Rights, are entitled to timely notification to appear, to know the goal of Congress, to have their testimony recorded exactly in writing, and to have counsel. They cannot, however, demand that closed hearings be open to the public.

Because the questions and answers in a congressional hearing are recorded, they can be used as evidence in a criminal proceeding. In particular, witnesses during the communist witch-hunts were afraid that their testimony could be used against them in Smith Act (1940) prosecutions meant to limit the political activities of the Communist Party. In *Quinn v. United States* (1955) and other cases, the Court held that the Fifth Amendment privilege against compulsory self-incrimination is available during congressional hearings. Witnesses can invoke this privilege and refuse to answer questions if the answers could be used as evidence by the prosecution in a criminal proceeding. However, this protection is limited. Witnesses can use it to protect only themselves, not other people or organizations. If witnesses begin answering questions, the Fifth Amendment is considered waived, and they cannot refuse to answer subsequent questions on the same subject. Finally, witnesses cannot refuse to answer questions if Congress has conferred immunity from prosecution.

In *Watkins*, the Court ruled that the First Amendment protection of freedom of speech is available in congressional investigations. Its intent was to protect witnesses from being exposed to public censure by being forced to admit to holding unpopular political beliefs. However, in *Barenblatt v. United States* (1959), the Court drastically limited the First Amendment protection available in congressional hearings. It ruled that as long as Congress has a valid reason for asking a question, witnesses cannot refuse to answer on the grounds that they will be forced to reveal a political belief. Likewise, journalists cannot refuse to answer questions on the grounds that they will be forced to reveal the sources for their information.

The Fourth Amendment protection against unreasonable searches and seizures may offer congressional witnesses some protection. Congress must provide a clear reason for wanting specific documents or records. It cannot make vague or general requests in hopes that something useful will turn up. Although a subpoena need not be as detailed as a search warrant, Congress must give witnesses a clear idea of the documents and records it is demanding. If Congress violates the Fourth Amendment's requirements, the information it collects, even if made public, cannot be used in subsequent criminal prosecutions.

FURTHER READING

Beck, Carl. *Contempt of Congress: A Study of the Prosecutions Initiated by the Committee on Un-American Activities, 1945-1957.* New Orleans, La.: Hauser Printing, 1959.

Fisher, Louis. *The Politics of Shared Power: Congress and the Executive.* College Station: Texas A&M University Press, 1998.

Goodman, Walter. *The Committee: The Extraordinary Career of the House Committee on Un-American Activities.* New York: Farrar, Straus and Giroux, 1968.

House Committee on the Judiciary. *Clarifying the Investigatory Powers of the United States Congress.* Washington, D.C.: Government Printing Office, 1988.

Landis, James M. "Constitutional Limitations on the Congressional Power of Investigation." *Harvard Law Review* 40, no. 2 (December, 1926): 153-221.

Taylor, Telford. *Grand Inquest: The Story of Congressional Investigations.* New York: Simon and Schuster, 1955.

_____. "Legislative Investigation." In *Encyclopedia of the American Constitution.* New York: Macmillan, 1986.

Paul Lermack

SEE ALSO Cold War; Contempt power of Congress; Self-incrimination, immunity against; Smith Act.

Congressional power to enforce amendments

DESCRIPTION: A power expressly granted to Congress in an amendment to the Constitution to "enforce" provisions of that amendment "by appropriate legislation."

SIGNIFICANCE: The power of enforcement is traditionally associated with the executive branch, not the Supreme Court or Congress. Enforcing an amendment is a concept that came into use only in the aftermath of the Civil War. It came to play a pivotal role in redefining the relationship between the national government and states.

Of the twenty-seven amendments to the Constitution, eight have enforcement clauses at the end, including the now-repealed Eighteenth Amendment. Of the remaining seven, the Thirteenth, Fourteenth and Fifteenth, commonly referred to as the Civil War Amendments, share the purpose of ensuring former slaves equality of opportunity and full citizenship. Despite the obligatory inclusion of the enforcement clause at the end of each, the remaining four amendments—the Nineteenth (female suffrage), Twenty-third (electoral vote for the District of Columbia), Twenty-fourth (elimination of the poll tax in national elections), and Twenty-sixth (lowering of the voting age to eighteen)—have shown little need for congressional enforcement.

The concept central to any discussion of congressional enforcement is discrimination. Where there is no pattern of willful discrimination, there is no issue of denial or abridgment of stated rights or privileges, and, hence, no issue of "enforcing" them. Correctly understood, an enforcement is a congressional remedy for a problem. Congress exercises this power lawfully when it steps in to cure a perceived problem. Congress abuses that power when it merely seeks to embellish upon the provisions of an amendment it does not like.

The remedial or corrective nature of the power of enforcement was underscored by the Supreme Court in its 1883 landmark decision in the *Civil Rights Cases*. Writing for the court, Justice Joseph Bradley wrote that the problem with the 1875 Civil Rights Act was that it made "no reference whatever to any supposed or apprehended violation of the Fourteenth Amendment on the part of the States." The 1875 law was "not corrective" at all but, instead, "primary and direct" in its aim, which was to "supersede" and "displace" existing state laws, in an area traditionally reserved for states' police power. Show proof that the "laws themselves make any unjust discrimination," wrote Bradley; then, "Congress has full power to afford a remedy under that amendment. . . . " In 1997, in *Boerne v. Flores*, which touched upon the same enforcement clause, the Supreme Court's majority stated that the amendment's "history confirms the remedial, rather than substantive, nature of the Enforcement Clause." Justice Anthony M. Kennedy went on to invoke the 1883 precedent as "confirming" the "remedial and preventive nature of Congress's enforcement power, and the limitation inherent in the power."

The first of these "enforcement" amendments, the Thirteenth, was declared ratified in December, 1865, eight months after the surrender of the Confederate states. Then, responding to the alarming spread of black codes in the defeated states, Congress enacted the Civil Rights Act of 1866 under the amendment's enforcement power, granting former slaves U.S. citizenship, armed with the usual rights of free people—to buy, own, inherit, and lease property; to make contracts; to testify in court; and so on. The statute was passed over President Andrew Johnson's veto, but problems lay ahead because of the bitterness generated by the law's sweep and what many regarded as its vindictiveness. Congress undertook to add a new amendment in hopes of validating the controversial law; the Fourteenth Amendment was ratified in 1868.

In 1870 Congress enacted a law to reinforce the prohibitions of the 1866 law while, at the same time, setting out criminal sanctions for interfering with the right to vote, now guaranteed under the Fifteenth Amendment, ratified earlier that year. For a while the 1870 law was called the Enforcement Act. Then, Congress enacted the Civil Rights

Act of 1871 as an amendment to that Enforcement Act, and a year later it enacted the Ku Klux Klan Act as an enforcement of the equal protection provision of the Fourteenth Amendment. The most important civil rights law since 1866, however, was the Civil Rights Act of 1875, sometimes referred to as the Second Civil Rights Act. It was designed to ensure "the full and equal enjoyment of the accommodations," imposing penalties for violations. As noted earlier, the Supreme Court had difficulty with this law as an enforcement of an amendment. It struck it down in 1883, against a bitter dissent from Justice John Marshall Harlan, who argued that private discrimination against blacks could be prohibited by Congress under the Thirteenth Amendment, whose intent he interpreted to be the eradication of slavery, "not simply of the institution, but of its badges and incidents."

No new federal civil rights law was enacted until 1957; the damage of the 1883 ruling had become evident. Emboldened by the eclipse of congressional power of "enforcement," the southern states began enacting Jim Crow laws. Then, segregation received its judicial blessing in 1896 when the Supreme Court declared in *Plessy v. Ferguson*, again against Harlan's lone dissent, that there was no violation of "equal protection of the laws" in public accommodations so long as blacks were given separate but equal facilities.

In 1968, having recently upheld provisions of the 1964 Civil Rights Act as a valid use of Congress's commerce power and provisions of the 1965 Voting Rights Act as an enforcement of the Fifteenth Amendment, the Court under Chief Justice Earl Warren now had an opportunity to revisit the 1866 Civil Rights Act, and in so doing it revived Harlan's expansive interpretation of the Thirteenth Amendment. The court ruled, in the case of *Jones v. Alfred H. Mayer Co.*, that private racial discrimination in the sale and rental of housing was amply prohibited by the 1866 law and that those prohibitions were a valid exercise of the enforcement power under the Thirteenth Amendment. In 1976 *Jones*'s reading of the Thirteenth Amendment was reaffirmed by the Burger Court in *Runyon v. McCrary*. In 1989 the Court under Chief Justice William H. Rehnquist was widely expected to overturn these expansive readings of the Thirteenth Amendment in *Patterson v. McLean Credit Union*. However, the Court chose not to do so. There was "no special justification . . . for overruling *Runyon*," said the Court, for its interpretation of the 1866 law was "not inconsistent with the prevailing sense of justice in this country."

FURTHER READING

Conkle, Daniel O. "The Religious Freedom Restoration Act: The Constitutional Significance of an Unconstitutional Statute." *Montana Law Review* 59 (1995): 39.

Cover, Robert. "The Origins of Judicial Activism in the Protection of Minorities." *Yale Law Journal* 91(1982): 1287.

Hyman, Harold, and William Wiecek. *Equal Justice Under Law: Constitutional Development 1835-1875.* New York: Harper & Row, 1982.

Van Alstyne, William, and Kenneth Karst. "State Action." *Stanford University Law Review* 14 (1961): 3.

Sugwon Kang

SEE ALSO *Boerne v. Flores*; Civil Rights Acts; Civil rights and liberties; *Civil Rights Cases*; Constitutional amendment process; Fifteenth Amendment; Fourteenth Amendment; Harlan, John Marshall; *Jones v. Alfred H. Mayer Co.*; *Patterson v. McLean Credit Union*; *Runyon v. McCrary*; State action; Thirteenth Amendment.

Conkling, Roscoe

IDENTIFICATION: U.S. senator and lawyer
BORN: October 30, 1829, Albany, New York
DIED: April 18, 1888, New York, New York
SIGNIFICANCE: In 1882 Conkling argued before the Supreme Court that the due process clause of the Fourteenth Amendment applied to corporations as well as individuals. He also played a prominent role in bringing impeachment proceedings against President Andrew Johnson.

The son of a New York congressman, Conkling studied law in Utica and was admitted to the New York bar in 1850. A skilled orator, he made campaign speeches for Zachary Taylor and Millard Fillmore. An advocate of vigorous prosecution in Civil War (1861-1865) cases, Conkling promoted a policy for Radical Reconstruction of the South and helped bring impeachment proceedings against President Andrew Johnson. He helped form the Republican party, served in the House of Representatives, and was elected to the Senate in 1867,

Roscoe Conkling. (Archive Photos)

1873, and 1879. In 1873 President Ulysses S. Grant offered him a position on the Supreme Court, but Conkling declined. A presidential hopeful in 1876, he lost the Republican nomination to Rutherford B. Hayes.

In 1882 President Chester A. Arthur offered Conkling a seat on the Supreme Court, but he once again declined. Later in 1882 Conkling argued before the Court that the drafters of the Fourteenth Amendment intended to protect corporations as well as African Americans. However, little positive evidence was or has been discovered for this theory. With politics becoming more issue oriented in the 1880's, Conkling faded from public prominence.

Alvin K. Benson

SEE ALSO Civil War; Fourteenth Amendment; Impeachment of presidents; Reconstruction.

Conscientious objection

DESCRIPTION: Claim of exemption from compulsory military service, or at least from combat, based on ethical, moral, or religious grounds. Only claims based on religious principles raise constitutional issues.

SIGNIFICANCE: Controversies surrounding conscientious objection are most likely to occur when the nation is at war and begins conscription, especially during an unpopular war. The Supreme Court struggled with controversies over how conscientious objector status is to be defined and who is exempted from military obligation.

Conscription to raise an armed force dates to the American Revolution, when some states imposed requirements of military service on their male citizens. Both North and South resorted to a military draft during the Civil War. In the twentieth century, conscription is well established as an efficient means for Congress to carry out its Article I authority "to raise and support armies." Thus far, the requirement to answer the call to arms has been confined to men, and the decision to exempt from obligatory military service on religious grounds has been left to the political discretion of Congress. However, when Congress adopts a policy respecting conscientious objection, the constitutional problems that result are many and complex.

Religious Objectors. Controversies over conscientious objection arise from the unprecedented religious diversity of the American population, including a number of pacifist sects whose adherents avoid all participation in warfare and others permitting their adherents to participate only in "just wars." Quite apart from the practical observation that pacifists make ineffectual soldiers, it might be thought that the First Amendment's free exercise of religion clause would require Congress to exempt religious pacifists from military service, rather than force citizens to act contrary to religious conscience. However, the Supreme Court, in the *Selective Draft Law Cases* (1918), rejected such a claim, calling "its unsoundness . . . too apparent to require us to do more." Even so, it had historically been the practice to grant exemptions to members of specific sects, at least when the latter were sufficiently prominent to secure the respect of the surrounding community. For example, New York's first constitution, adopted in 1777, exempted Quakers from service, although it also authorized the legislature to impose special fees in lieu of service. The Draft Act of 1864 and that of 1917 offered exemptions for members of pacifist sects, although the latter authorized their conscription into noncombat roles.

This deference to religious principle generates its own constitutional problems, however. When membership in a pacifist sect becomes the basis for granting exemption from the draft, Congress would seem to violate the establishment of religion clause. Although the precise meaning of this clause is uncertain, all agree that it requires Congress to avoid discriminating among sects. Identifying Quakers, or any other specific sects, as recipients of conscientious objector status might be viewed as creating a privilege on the basis of religious belief. Even without naming specific sects, Congress faces a dilemma in finding a religiously neutral way of limiting the exemption, lest it become universal. Thus, the crux of the problem is to define a category of persons who might claim exemption from conscription in a way that violates neither the free exercise nor the establishment of religion clauses of the First Amendment. Any attempt to do so exposes the potential conflict between these two clauses.

A Careful Approach. Perhaps in recognition of this dilemma, the Court usually avoided constitutional rulings in conscientious objector cases, purporting to resolve them by statutory interpretation. However, despite its ruling in the 1918 draft law cases, in the twentieth century, the Court clearly attempted to interpret draft statutes in a way that makes them conform to the complex demands of the First Amendment. It is equally clear that Congress struggled with this issue but was less sensitive to the requirements of the establishment of religion clause than the Court.

The Draft Act of 1917, for example, extended conscription to all able-bodied men, exempting members of any "well-recognized religious sect or organization" that forbade its "members to participate in war in any form." This formulation privileged adherents of well-recognized religions, compared with religions lacking such organization or doctrinal clarity, thereby conferring conscientious objector status on Quakers but denying it to equally sincere objectors who did not belong to any such organization. It also denied conscientious objector status to those whose religious principles included distinctions between just and unjust wars, such as Roman Catholics.

The Selective Training and Service Act of 1940 sought to avoid the problem of sectarian discrimination by dropping the requirement that the conscientious objector be a member of a well-recognized sect. An individual had only to object to war in any form based on "religious training and belief." This standard was refined in 1948, when Congress defined religious training and belief to include "an individual's belief in a relation to a Supreme Being involving duties superior to those arising from any human relation, but [excluding] essentially political, sociological, or philosophical views or a merely personal moral code." Even with these enhancements, however, the definition of conscientious objection failed to achieve religious neutrality because it excluded religions that did not include a supreme being (such as Buddhism) and religions that were not monotheistic (such as Hinduism). In *United States v. Seeger* (1965), the Court sought to remedy this problem by interpreting this definition of religious training and belief as including any "sincere and meaningful belief which occupies in the life of its possessor a place parallel to that filled by the God of those admittedly qualifying for the exemption." Although this interpretation sought to eliminate the problem of discrimination among sects, it did so by extending conscientious objector status to many persons holding "political, sociological or philosophical views or merely a personal moral code," people to whom Congress had specifically denied such an exemption, as the Court recognized in *Welsh v. United States* (1970). However, in *Gillette v. United States* (1971), the Court held that exemption from service could still be denied to those whose religiously based objection did not include war in all forms. Thus, those who believed in fighting only just wars still could not qualify for conscientious objector status.

In *Clay v. United States* (1971), the Court established a three-part test by which conscientious objector claims were to be evaluated, requiring that the claim be based on a religious belief as defined in *Seeger*, that the objection is to war in all forms, and that the claim is sincere.

FURTHER READING

Choper, Jesse H. *Securing Religious Liberty: Principles for Judicial Interpretation of the Religion Clauses.* Chicago: University of Chicago Press, 1995.

Morgan, Richard E. *The Supreme Court and Religion.* New York: Free Press, 1972.

Moskos, Charles C., and Whiteslay, eds. *The New Conscientious Objection: From Sacred to Secular Re-*

sistance. New York: Oxford University Press, 1993.

Pfeffer, Leo. *Church, State, and Freedom.* Boston: Beacon Press, 1967.

Tribe, Lawrence. *American Constitutional Law.* 2d ed. Westbury, N.Y.: The Foundation Press, 1990.

John C. Hughes

SEE ALSO Cold War; Conscription; Religion, establishment of; Religion, freedom of; *Selective Draft Law Cases*; Statutory interpretation; Vietnam War.

Conscription

DESCRIPTION: Compulsory induction of persons into military service by the government.

SIGNIFICANCE: The Supreme Court, which traditionally gives deference to the executive and legislative branches in matters relating to war, never invalidated a conscription statute.

Legal challenges brought before the Supreme Court to conscription statutes tend to ebb and flow with U.S. military action. Each new war or conflict, particularly if it is unpopular, brings to the Court a new set of draft cases. The first major test of the constitutionality of conscription occurred in the context of World War I.

In *Arver et al. v. United States* (1918), the Court addressed the constitutionality of the Draft Act of 1917 and unanimously upheld the statute. The Court held that Congress's power to "raise and support armies" included the power to compel military service. The opinion dismissed, as obviously unsound, the argument that the Draft Act violated both the establishment clause and the free exercise clause.

During the Vietnam War, the Court gave more considered treatment to the arguments of religious conscientious objectors, while refusing to be drawn into the national debate over the legitimacy of the war itself. In a series of cases, most notably *Massachusetts v. Laird* (1970), the Court refused to grant certiorari to determine the general legality of drafting persons into the Vietnam War. A majority of the justices, over the strenuous objections of Justice William O. Douglas, believed that the constitutionality of the war, and hence the legality of the draft, was a "political decision" and that the Court should not interfere in matters of foreign policy and national security.

Gillette v. United States (1971) considered the arguments of petitioners who claimed that the Selective Service Act of 1967 violated both of the First Amendment's religion clauses. The act exempted people from military service who, on the basis of a religious belief, are opposed to participating in any war. Petitioners opposed only unjust wars, and they considered the Vietnam War to be unjust. Justice Thurgood Marshall, in an opinion joined by six other justices, rejected the petitioners' First Amendment claims and upheld the constitutionality of the act's exemption clause on the grounds that it promoted a secular purpose (military effectiveness) and did not discriminate on its face against any religion.

With the end of the draft in 1973, the focus of the conscription cases accepted by the Court changed. In *Rostker v. Goldberg* (1981), the Court considered a due process challenge by several men to the exclusion of women from compulsory registration for conscription. The plaintiffs argued that the exemption of women was unlawful gender-based discrimination. The Court upheld the constitutionality of the exemption based on the military policy, then in place, of excluding women from all combat roles. (Since 1993 all combat positions, other than ground combat, are open to women.)

A group of women identifying themselves as American mothers protest against conscription in front of the Supreme Court building in 1940. Beginning with World War I, the Supreme Court has ruled on the constitutionality of the draft and on who can be a conscientious objector. (AP/Wide World Photos)

FURTHER READING

Chambers, John Whiteclay, II. *To Raise an Army: The Draft Comes to Modern America.* New York: Free Press, 1987.

Kohn, Stephen M. *Jailed for Peace: The History of American Draft Law Violators, 1658-1985.* Westport, Conn.: Greenwood, 1986.

Nicholas C. Lund-Molfese

SEE ALSO Conscientious objection; Military and the Court; Political questions; *Rostker v. Goldberg; Selective Draft Law Cases;* Vietnam War; War powers; World War I; World War II.

Constitution, U.S.

DATE: 1789

DESCRIPTION: Document that defined the structure and powers of the U.S. national government.

SIGNIFICANCE: The Supreme Court, which was created by the U.S. Constitution, bears primary responsibility for interpreting that document. By giving meaning to the country's foundational legal document, the Court establishes the extent of both governmental powers and individuals' rights.

The U.S. Constitution was created in an effort to design a workable, strong national government for the American states that had freed themselves from the British Empire through the Revolutionary War. The Constitution replaced the Articles of Confederation, which were regarded as an ineffective basis for a strong national government because they did not grant the federal government sufficient powers with respect to economic and military matters. The Constitution represented a new attempt to design an effective national government for a diverse set of states that expected to retain many powers for themselves.

Article I of the Constitution describes the structure and powers of Congress, the national legislative body. Article II describes the president's role and powers. Article III describes the judicial branch of the national government. Section 1 of Article III established the Supreme Court and describes the protected tenure and compensation provided for Court justices to ensure that they have sufficient insulation from political pressures to be able to make proper decisions. Justices serve "during good Behavior," which can effectively mean for life. Moreover, Congress cannot reduce the justices' salaries; therefore, other branches of government cannot threaten the justices with loss of income to pressure their decisions. In addition, only the Supreme Court is established by Article III. All other federal courts are created by Congress and therefore can be altered or even abolished by Congress.

The Constitution also specifies that Supreme Court justices shall be appointed by the president and confirmed by the Senate. Because justices may serve on the Court for decades, the selection of a Court member is often one of a president's most important decisions. Most presidents are able to appoint at least one justice to the Court, but some presidents, including President Jimmy Carter, are never able to appoint a justice because no one on the Court dies, retires, or resigns during their term in office.

Article IV of the Constitution discusses the obligations of states to each other, such as respecting each other's court judgments. Article V describes the process for amending the Constitution. Article VI declares that the Constitution and laws made under the authority of the Constitution shall be the supreme law of the land and that states shall respect the Constitution and federal laws. This is an important provision because it helped to establish the broad scope of the Court's power. When the Court interprets the Constitution, it is establishing legal rules for the entire nation to follow. Article VII notes that nine states needed to ratify the Constitution in order to give it effect.

The original Constitution was amended twenty-seven times. The first ten amendments, called the Bill of Rights, describe the protections that individuals possess against interference by government. These protections include many familiar rights, such as freedom of speech, freedom of religion, and the right to trial by jury. Although these rights originally protected citizens only against actions by the federal government, the Court subsequently interpreted the Constitution as providing most of these protections against violations by state and local governments. Other amendments have changed the way in which U.S. senators are selected, limited the president to two terms in office, abolished slavery, granted voting rights to women, and announced the plan for who would take charge in the event that the president and vice president should die or become disabled while in office. The Court is frequently asked to interpret the amendments to the Constitution, especially those amendments that grant rights to individuals. The Court's interpretations of these amendments define the extent to which individuals' constitutional rights protect them against actions by government.

Constitutional Interpretation. Because the Constitution was drafted by an assembly of representatives from various states, its wording is the product of negotiation and compromise. Therefore, many of the document's words and phrases are ambiguous. Even those phrases whose meaning appears to be relatively clear may require interpretation when they are applied to unanticipated situations. It falls to the Court to take primary responsibility for interpreting and applying the Constitution. The Court is given opportunities to interpret the Constitution when legal cases are brought forward involving disputes about the Constitution's meaning. Typically these cases involve either a challenge to the exercise of power by a government agency or a claim that a government employee, such as a police officer or prosecutor, has violated the rights of an individual. These questions about the Constitution's meaning are given initial decisions by lower federal courts or by state courts before they reach the Supreme Court. The Court has authority to pick and choose which constitutional issues to decide. If the Court does not wish to decide an issue, it simply leaves intact the prior decision by a lower federal or state court.

Justices often disagree with one another about how the Constitution should be interpreted. Many justices have their own theories about the proper approach to constitutional interpretation. Justice Hugo L. Black often argued that the justices should pay careful attention to the literal meaning of the Constitution's words and not add their own preferred meanings to interpretations of the document's words and phrases. When other justices decided in *Griswold v. Connecticut* (1965) that the Constitution contains a right to privacy that protects married couples' choices about birth control, Black argued that there could be no right to privacy because the word "privacy" did not appear anywhere in the Constitution. Similarly, Justice Clarence Thomas argued that the Constitution must be interpreted according to the meanings originally intended by the people who wrote the document. Therefore, when other justices applied the Eighth Amendment's prohibition against cruel and unusual punishment to protect prisoners from abuse and mistreatment within correctional institutions in *Helling v. McKinney* (1993), Thomas asserted that the people who wrote the Eighth Amendment at the end of the eighteenth century never intended for the provision to protect incarcerated people. Thomas claimed that the Eighth Amendment does not apply to the treatment of convicted offenders in prison.

In contrast, Chief Justice Earl Warren believed that the meaning of the Constitution can change as society changes. Warren and several of his colleagues believed that the Constitution embodies ideals of human dignity that are flexible enough to adapt to new situations that arise in society. Therefore, in *Trop v. Dulles* (1958), Warren declared that the cruel and unusual punishment clause of the Eighth Amendment must be defined according to the evolving standards of decency that develop as society progresses. Critics of Warren's approach to constitutional interpretation complain that such flexible interpretation merely permits justices to say that the Constitution means whatever they want it to mean. Critics of Thomas's approach, in contrast, complain that interpretation by original intent locks society into the rules of the eighteenth century without recognizing that society has changed drastically, with the emergence of new problems and different values. In general, the majority of justices take a flexible approach to constitutional interpretation, but many of them are self-conscious about the risks of interpreting the Constitution inappropriately according to their own personal values and are generally cautious about announcing new meanings for the document's provisions.

The Court and the Constitution. The nature of the constitutional questions brought to the Court

The U.S. Constitution was first printed in The Pennsylvania Packet, *a daily newspaper, on September 19, 1787.* (Library of Congress)

changed along with American society, according to the particular controversies that affected government and society at different moments in history. During the first eighty years of the Constitution's history, the Court faced significant questions about the constitutional provisions defining the powers of government. The constitutional governing system of the United States was, in effect, an experiment. It was uncertain whether the scheme of government established by the Constitution would succeed and endure. The Court helped solidify the success of the Constitution through decisions addressing disputes about governmental powers. In

McCulloch v. Maryland (1819), the Court interpreted the Constitution as barring states from imposing taxes on the federal government and its agencies. Without the Court's decision, the federal government would have been weaker and more vulnerable to assertions of authority by the states. In *Gibbons v. Ogden* (1824), the Court asserted the authority of the federal government to regulate interstate commerce when states had begun to assume such powers for themselves. The Court's decision helped to strengthen the federal government and diminish the risk that states would use economic policies to compete with one another and thereby harm the national economy.

The Court's decision in *Marbury v. Madison* (1803) established judicial review, which is the power of judges to review and invalidate actions by other branches of government. Judicial review is a very significant power that is not expressly stated in the Constitution. The Court asserted the existence of the power and then employed it to strike down a congressional enactment. By establishing and using the power, the Court made the judicial branch a powerful, equal partner with the other branches of government and helped establish a workable balance of power between the three branches of government.

The Court cannot solve all disputes about governmental power through its interpretations of the Constitution. Some disputes are worked out through political conflicts between the legislative and executive branches of government. During the Civil War (1861-1865), these disputes were resolved by warfare. The war served to settle debates about the relationship of the federal government with the states when the states that asserted their independence and autonomy under the Confederate flag lost the war. For the Court, the end of the war simply brought forward new issues about the meaning of the Constitution in a country undergoing the processes of industrialization and urbanization. The Court also faced questions about the legal protections possessed by newly freed slaves.

At the close of the Civil War, the Thirteenth, Fourteenth, and Fifteenth Amendments (the Civil War Amendments) were added to the Constitution. These amendments sought to prohibit slavery, protect people's legal rights from violation by state and local governments, and prevent racial discrimination in voting rights. Between the end of the Civil War and the dawn of the twentieth century, Court decisions affecting racial discrimination did little to improve the lot of African Americans. In the *Slaughterhouse Cases* (1873), the Court declined to identify specific rights protected by the Civil War Amendments. When southern states began enacting extensive, systematic laws to segregate African Americans in schools and other public places and services, the Court endorsed these discriminatory laws in *Plessy v. Ferguson* (1896). These cases in the late nineteenth century demonstrated that the Court's justices have no special capacity to recognize truth and justice. As human beings who happen to have been selected to serve, they are always susceptible to following and reflecting the prevailing attitudes and prejudices of their era. Few whites believed that African Americans were equal to them as human beings during the nineteenth century, and the Court's interpretations of the Constitution reflected this view.

In the late nineteenth century and early twentieth century, the Court faced many issues concerning economic regulation and social welfare. Many new social problems developed as the country experienced significant industrialization, urbanization, and immigration. Federal and state governments responded to these problems by enacting legislation to protect workers. However, the Court used its power of judicial review to systematically invalidate laws mandating minimum wages, laws establishing permissible working hours, and laws intended to limit the exploitation of child laborers. For example, in *Hammer v. Dagenhart* (1918), the Court declared that the federal government lacked the authority under the Constitution to regulate the transport and sale of goods made by child laborers. The Court's decisions impeded governmental regulation of the economy until the 1930's, when the composition of the Court changed significantly and the Court began to defer to legislative and executive decisions about economic regulation.

After the 1930's, the Court took a more active interest in interpreting the constitutional amendments that established rights for individuals. In a series of cases over the course of several decades, the Court applied most of the provisions of the Bill of Rights against the states by declaring that they had been incorporated into the due process clause of the Fourteenth Amendment. Before this time, the Bill of Rights protected citizens against actions by only the federal government. Because the Fourteenth Amendment was intended to give individuals rights against actions by state and local government, it became the vehicle through which the Court's interpretations of the Constitution applied other rights against the states. In the course of broadening the definitions of constitutional rights, the Court moved aggressively against racial discrimination. Using the equal protection clause of the Fourteenth Amendment, the Court prohibited racial discrimination in public schools in *Brown v. Board of Education* (1954). The Court also interpreted constitutional provisions about congressional power to permit the enactment of statutes against discrimination by private businesses and individuals in *Katzenbach v. McClung* (1964). By the end of the 1970's, the Court had identified new rights affecting racial equality, gender equality, protection of defendants in the criminal justice process, freedom of speech and religion, and many other aspects of American life.

In the final decades of the twentieth century, the Court's composition changed in a conservative direction. The new justices reconsidered many of the prior decisions expanding rights for criminal defendants and others. In new decisions interpreting the Bill of Rights, the Court reshaped constitutional law by narrowing the scope of many rights and permitting states to have greater authority over their own affairs. The Court also limited the authority of the federal government to enact legislation under the claim of economic regulation. In *United States v. Lopez* (1995), the Court declared that Congress lacked the authority to create a statute making it a crime to carry a gun in a schoolyard. In a move back toward the nineteenth century decisions that imposed clear limits on federal authority, the Court decided that states should regulate such matters because they were not directly related to interstate commerce and the economic matters that the Constitution clearly placed under federal authority.

The Constitution provided the design for the U.S. system of government. On its own, however, the Constitution could not ensure that the government would be durable and workable. The Court made major contributions to the stability and workability enjoyed by the Constitution through its decisions interpreting the document in order to define the powers of government and clarify the extent to which individuals possess protected constitutional rights.

FURTHER READING

A detailed history of constitutional law is presented in Melvin Urofsky's *A March of Liberty: A Constitutional History of the United States* (New York: Alfred A. Knopf, 1988). Detailed examinations of Court decisions interpreting the Constitution are found in Daniel Farber, William Eskridge, and Philip Frickey's *Constitutional Law: Themes for the Constitution's Third Century* (St. Paul, Minn.: West Publishing, 1993) and Gerald Gunther's *Constitutional Law* (11th ed., Mineola, N.Y.: Foundation Press, 1985). The theories and approaches employed by the Court justices in interpreting the Constitution are discussed in John H. Garvey and T. Alexander Aleinikoff's *Modern Constitutional Theory* (3d ed., St. Paul, Minn.: West Publishing, 1994) and Michael McCann and Gerald Houseman's *Judging the Constitution* (Glenview, Ill.: Scott, Foresman, 1989). The personal stories of individual citizens who took their constitutional claims all the way to the Supreme Court are presented in Peter Irons's *The Courage of Their Convictions* (New York: Free Press, 1988) and Ellen Alderman and Caroline Kennedy's *In Our Defense: The Bill of Rights in Action* (New York: William Morrow, 1991). The procedures and processes used by the Court in interpreting the Constitution are discussed in David O'Brien's *Storm Center: The Supreme Court in American Politics* (2d ed., New York: W. W. Norton, 1990).

Christopher E. Smith

SEE ALSO Articles of Confederation; Bill of Rights; Black, Hugo L.; Constitutional Convention; Constitutional interpretation; Constitutional law; Federalism; Fundamental rights; Judicial review; Race and discrimination; Rule of law; States' rights; Thomas, Clarence; Warren, Earl.

Constitutional amendment process

DESCRIPTION: Procedure by which formal changes are made to the text of the U.S. Constitution.

SIGNIFICANCE: Amendments are the only means by which formal changes may be made to the Constitution. The Supreme Court made several rulings regarding the amendment procedure, including ratification.

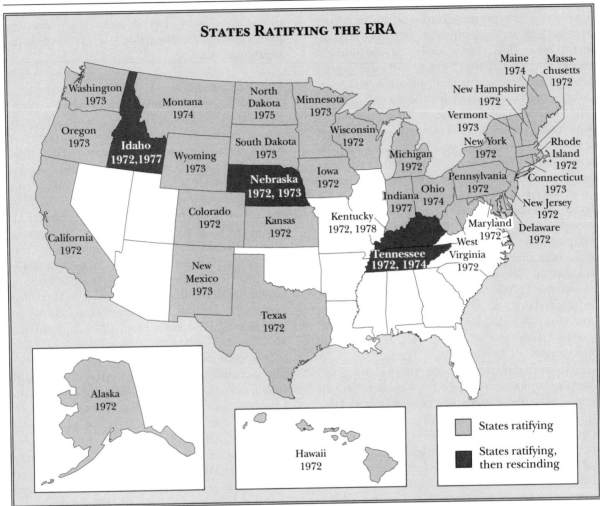

STATES RATIFYING THE ERA

Source: Data are from Janet K. Boles, *The Politics of the Equal Rights Amendment.* New York: Longman, 1979.

Article V of the Constitution specifies the procedures by which the document can be amended. The process has two steps, proposal and ratification, and two methods can be used to carry out each step. Amendments can be proposed by a two-thirds vote of both houses of Congress or by a convention called by Congress at the request of the legislatures of two-thirds of the states. Amendments can be ratified by the legislatures of three-fourths of the states or by conventions in three-fourths of the states. Article V leaves the choice of ratification method to Congress. There are, therefore, four methods of amending the Constitution under Article V: first, proposal by two-thirds vote in both houses of Congress and ratification by the legislatures of three-fourths of the states; second, pro-

posal by two-thirds vote in both houses of Congress and ratification by conventions in three-fourths of the states; third, proposal by a convention called by Congress at the request of the legislatures of two-thirds of the states and ratification by the legislatures of three-fourths of the states; and fourth, proposal by a convention called by Congress at the request of the legislatures of two-thirds of the states and ratification by conventions in three-fourths of the states.

Twenty-six of the twenty-seven amendments to the Constitution have been adopted using the first of these four methods. One, the Twenty-first Amendment (the repeal of Prohibition), was adopted using the second method. Congress used conventions instead of the state legislatures to ratify this amendment because it seemed that conventions would be more likely to ratify than the legislatures.

The third and fourth methods of amending the Constitution have never been used because two-thirds of the states have never petitioned Congress to call a convention on any subject. Thirty-two of the states asked Congress to call a convention to propose a balanced budget amendment, and thirty-three requested a convention to allow one house of state legislatures to be apportioned on the basis of geography or political subdivisions rather than population. These efforts fell two votes and one vote short of two-thirds, respectively.

Because the convention method has never been used, the rules governing the process are unclear. One view is that Congress would have complete control over the process and could make the rules governing the convention's operations as it saw fit. Another view holds that once a convention is called, it may take control of the process and propose whatever changes to the Constitution it might wish. Supporters of conventions have often attempted to get state legislatures to pass resolutions proposing the desired amendment in identical language. This tactic is intended to reassure Congress and the public that any convention called would deal with only one subject and would propose only the amendment contained in the resolutions. Should any convention effort ever gain support from the necessary thirty-four state legislatures, Congress could eliminate any uncertainty by simply proposing the suggested amendment. Given the uncertainties of the convention process, Congress would be tempted to follow this course of action.

Supreme Court Involvement. The constitutional amendment process lies largely within the purview of Congress. As early as 1798, Justice Samuel Chase indicated in *Hollingsworth v. Virginia* that the president played no role in the proposal or ratification of constitutional amendments. Therefore, the president's approval of the resolution proposing an amendment was not needed, and he or she could not veto congressional actions proposing amendments. For a time, the Court involved itself in aspects of the amendment process. In the *National Prohibition Cases* (1920), the Court ruled that the two-thirds requirement of Article V meant two-thirds of those present and voting, not two-thirds of the entire membership of the houses of Congress.

In *Dillon v. Gloss* (1921), the justices said that Congress could impose a time limit on ratification of amendments and that amendments had to be ratified in a reasonable period of time. The Court also held that a state could not impose a popular referendum on the ratification process when Congress specified ratification by state legislatures (*Hawke v. Smith*, 1920) and that states may not impose other requirements that prevent state legislatures from ratifying amendments submitted to them for action by Congress (*Leser v. Garnett*, 1922). In *Coleman v. Miller* (1939), however, the Court seemed to move toward the political question doctrine and greater congressional control over the constitutional amendment process.

In *Coleman*, the Court was asked to decide three issues: first, whether the lieutenant governor of Kansas could vote on ratification to break a tie in the state senate; second, whether a state could ratify a previously rejected amendment; and third, whether ratification of an amendment was valid when it had been proposed thirteen years earlier with no time limit for ratification. The Court divided evenly on the first question, therefore leaving undisturbed the Kansas supreme court decision that participation by the lieutenant governor posed no constitutional problem. The Court held that the second and third questions were political questions for Congress to decide. Four members of the seven-judge majority wanted to hold all amendment process issues to be matters for Congress to decide.

The Court continued its reliance on the political question doctrine after the *Coleman* decision. For example, its handling of the Equal Rights

---

TEXT OF THE EQUAL RIGHTS AMENDMENT

Section 1. Equality of rights under the law shall not be denied or abridged by the United States or by any State on account of sex.

Section 2. The Congress shall have the power to enforce, by appropriate legislation, the provisions of this article.

Section 3. The Amendment shall take effect two years after the date of ratification.

Amendment (ERA) suggests continued reliance on *Coleman*. Stating that "Equality of rights under the law shall not be denied or abridged by the United States or by any State on account of sex," the ERA was proposed by Congress in March, 1972. The deadline for ratification, specified in the resolution accompanying the amendment when it was sent to the state legislatures for ratification, but not in the text of the amendment itself, was seven years. In 1978 when the amendment was three states short of the three-fourths needed for ratification, Congress extended the deadline for approval by thirty-nine months, to June 30, 1982.

When the extension legislation was passed, Congress rejected a proposal that would have allowed states to rescind their prior approvals of the amendment, something that four states had done. Congress has typically allowed states that have rejected amendments to change their minds and ratify them but has not permitted states that have ratified to rescind their ratification. Congressional action in the ERA case was therefore consistent with past practice, but some members argued that because the deadline was being extended, fairness dictated that rescissions be permitted. Idaho, one of the four states that had rescinded, attempted to pursue its change of mind, and the National Organization for Women challenged its attempt. The federal district court in Idaho approved the rescission, and the Supreme Court docketed the case but dismissed the suit as moot after the extended ratification period ran out (*National Organization for Women v. Idaho*, 1982). This action suggests that the Court recognized the authority of Congress to extend the period for ratification and to refuse state recission of ratification. After the ERA controversy, Congress returned to the practice of placing time limits for ratification in the text of amendments they were considering. Supporters of the extension had argued that because the time limit was not in the text of the ERA itself, Congress could extend the deadline for ratification.

The Twenty-seventh Amendment. The adoption of the Twenty-seventh Amendment also suggests that the power of Congress over the amendment process is substantial, if not plenary. This amendment requires an election for members of Congress to intervene between the passage of a congressional pay raise and its effective date. It was proposed by Congress on September 28, 1789, as the second of twelve proposed articles of amendment. Articles three through twelve were ratified in 1791 and became known as the first ten amendments, or the Bill of Rights. The first two articles remained in limbo because Congress had set no time limit for their ratification.

By the latter part of the twentieth century, constitutional commentators generally assumed that these two amendments, along with others submitted later but not ratified, were no longer viable because of the Court's pronouncement in *Dillon* (1921) that amendments had to be ratified within a reasonable period of time. In 1989 a graduate student learned about the long-forgotten proposal while doing research and began an effort to get state legislatures to ratify the amendment. His timing could not have been more opportune. The proposal became a symbol of dissatisfaction with Congress, in particular with congressional pay increases during an economic downturn. The ratification effort was successful. When the thirty-eighth state ratified, Congress decided that 202 years was a reasonable time and declared the amendment to be part of the Constitution on May 7, 1992.

To avoid similar situations in the future, the Senate subsequently declared all other pending constitutional amendments to be "dead." However, because Congress has such extensive power over the process and could change its mind at any time, this declaration may be meaningless. It did not affect very many amendments. Over the years Congress has proposed thirty-three amendments of which twenty-seven have been ratified. It was the remaining six, especially the four proposed without time limits, that the Senate was attempting to put to rest.

The passage of the Twenty-seventh Amendment also demonstrates that the constitutional amendment process is a political one. Had Congress refused to declare the amendment part of the Constitution on the grounds that it had been pending too long, the reaction from the public would have been unfavorable, something Congress was not willing to face. However, while the 202-year interval between proposal and passage of the Twenty-seventh Amendment is not a model of timeliness, it is not likely to be repeated. Today, Congress routinely puts time limits for ratification (usually seven years) on amendments, and as noted previously, the Senate has attempted to eradicate from the record the four remaining amendments still pending without time limits.

FURTHER READING

Two general overviews of the Constitution contain sections on the amendment process. These are Jack W. Peltason's *Corwin and Peltason's Understanding the Constitution* (14th ed., Fort Worth, Tex.: Harcourt Brace Jovanovich, 1997) and *The Constitution of the United States of America: Analysis and Interpretation* (Washington, D.C.: Government Printing Office, 1996). The latter publication is also available on line (http://www.access.gpo.gov/congress/senate/constitution/toc.html). Isobel V. Morin's *Our Changing Constitution: How and Why We Have Amended It* (Brookfield, Conn.: Millbrook Press, 1998) is an overview of the amendment process for younger readers. John R. Vile has written a great deal about the constitutional amendment process. His *The Constitutional Amending Process in American Political Thought* (Westport, Conn.: Praeger, 1992) puts the process into theoretical perspective. His subsequent work *Contemporary Questions Surrounding the Constitutional Amending Process* (Westport, Conn.: Praeger, 1993) discusses in detail the issues surrounding the process. Finally, Vile wrote a very useful and comprehensive *Encyclopedia of Constitutional Amendments, Proposed Amendments and Amending Issues, 1789-1995* (Oxford: ABC-CLIO, 1996). A volume edited by Sanford Levinson, *Responding to Imperfection: The Theory and Practice of Constitutional Amendment* (Princeton, N.J.: Princeton University Press, 1995) is a useful attempt to bridge the gap between principle and political practice. The many books on the Equal Rights Amendment illustrate nicely the pitfalls of the amending process. Two of the better treatments are Jane Mansbridge's *Why We Lost the ERA* (Chicago: University of Chicago Press, 1986) and Gilbert Y. Steiner's *Constitutional Inequality: The Political Fortunes of the Equal Rights Amendment* (Washington, D.C.: Brookings Institution, 1985). Another instructive case study of one amendment is James E. Bond's *No Easy Walk to Freedom: Reconstruction and the Ratification of the Fourteenth Amendment* (Westport, Conn.: Praeger, 1997).

Daryl R. Fair

SEE ALSO Bill of Rights; *Coleman v. Miller*; Congressional power to enforce amendments; *Dillon v. Gloss*; Judicial review; Political questions; Twenty-first Amendment.

Constitutional Convention

DATE: May 25-September 17, 1787
DESCRIPTION: Meeting of delegates from the thirteen original states held in Philadelphia for the purpose of framing the Constitution of the United States and submitting it to the Continental Congress, which subsequently offered it to the states for ratification.
SIGNIFICANCE: The convention delegates wrote the original seven articles of the Constitution, renewing the foundation of U.S. national government. They laid the basis for three separate branches of government—judicial, legislative, and executive—at the national level, each with ability to check the power of the others, while retaining significant power of self-government at the state level.

By 1787 the weaknesses of the new U.S. government under the Articles of Confederation had become sadly evident. Disunity and social unrest prompted nationalist politicians such as James Madison of Virginia and Alexander Hamilton of New York to call for a national convention to revise the old governmental system and form a stronger union among the states. On February 15, 1787, the Continental Congress agreed and asked the states to select delegates to such a convention scheduled for May 14 that same year in Philadelphia. The states gradually responded, but it was not until May 25 that a quorum of state delegations had arrived and the Constitutional Convention, the Grand Convention of 1787, got underway.

The Convention. During the next four months, fifty-five delegates from twelve states (Rhode Island refused to send anyone) attended the convention. Prominent among these delegates were, in addition to Madison and Hamilton, George Washington, Edmund Randolph, and George Mason of Virginia; Benjamin Franklin, James Wilson, and Gouverneur Morris of Pennsylvania; Rufus King, Nathaniel Gorham, and Elbridge Gerry of Massachusetts; John Rutledge of South Carolina; William Paterson of New Jersey; and Roger Sherman of Connecticut. Although they were generally drawn from the educated and propertied elite of the day, they represented different regions and therefore had different interests.

To attenuate conflict, the delegates agreed to

hold deliberations in the strictest secrecy, thus screening out external influences. They also adopted the procedure of parceling out tough issues to committees composed of delegates representing all sides in the hope that compromise could be reached. This worked admirably with regard to the most divisive issue the convention faced, that concerning the basis for representation in the new Congress. Under the Articles of Confederation, each state had one vote in a unicameral Congress, but at the convention, the most populous states sought what was to them a fairer plan: representation in a bicameral legislature based on population size. By mid-June, the smaller states had countered with an alternative plan based on the old system. For a month, this dispute threatened to wreck the convention. In committee, however, the delegates embraced what came to be known as the Great Compromise, proposed by Roger Sherman, under which the new Congress would be bicameral with the seats in one house, the House of Representatives, allocated to the states according to population and the seats in the other, the Senate, allocated equally, two seats for each state. The convention adopted the compromise by the narrowest of possible margins, but the system created survived.

Not all issues were resolved successfully, however. Slavery, for example, was upheld through compromises that were ultimately undone by the Civil War and the Civil War Amendments. The convention also rejected the idea of adding a bill of rights over the strenuous objections of three delegates who later refused to sign the finished document in protest. The series of amendments that have come to be known as the Bill of Rights had to be added later in response to political pressure.

The delegates, however, were of one mind on the need for a national supreme court and an independent national judiciary. No judicial branch existed under the Articles of Confederation, and this was deemed a serious defect. The principal matter of contention concerned who should appoint the court's judges, Congress or the chief executive. Here again the spirit of compromise prevailed. The convention adopted a proposal by Nathaniel Gorham, which was actually the system used in Massachusetts for many years, whereby the judges would be appointed by the executive with the advice and consent of the Senate. The convention defined the court's jurisdiction but created only a court and a chief justice in Article III of the Constitution, leaving the composition of the court and the organization of the lower judiciary to Congress.

The Debates and the Court. The Constitutional Convention itself rarely comes into play in cases where the Supreme Court must interpret constitutional clauses. The most reliable account of the debates, James Madison's *Notes of Debates in the Federal Convention of 1787*, did not even appear publicly until 1840. Furthermore, the Court preferred to interpret the Constitution by defining its terms in the context of a case before it, as it did with the commerce clause in *Gibbons v. Ogden* (1824). The Court, however, made good use of the debates in several important cases. In *Wesberry v. Sanders* (1964), for example, the Court carefully explored the convention debates on the representation controversy to establish the basis for the principle of one person, one vote in congressional district apportionment. The Court also alluded to convention debates regarding qualifications for office in determining that states may not limit the terms of congressional offices in *United States Term Limits v. Thornton* (1995). Both of these decisions were accompanied by strongly written dissenting opinions, illustrating that the debates of the convention have never entirely died out.

After an exhausting and sometimes angry summer of debate, the convention closed on September 17, 1787, with the signing of the Constitution by thirty-four of the thirty-seven delegates present. Mason, Randolph, and Gerry were the three delegates who refused to sign, still holding out for a bill of rights.

FURTHER READING

Barash, Fred. *The Founding: A Dramatic Account of the Writing of the Constitution.* New York: Simon & Schuster, 1987.

Bernstein, Richard B., and K. S. Rice. *Are We to Be a Nation? The Making of the Constitution.* Boston: Harvard University Press, 1987.

Kammen, Michael, ed. *The Origins of the American Constitution: A Documentary History.* New York: Penguin Books, 1986.

Madison, James. *Notes of Debates in the Federal Convention of 1787.* New York: W. W. Norton, 1987.

Rossiter, Clinton. *1787: The Grand Convention.* New York: W. W. Norton, 1987.

John R. Rink

SEE ALSO Articles of Confederation; British background to U.S. judiciary; Civil War; Constitution, U.S.; Constitutional interpretation; *Federalist, The*; *Gibbons v. Ogden*; Hamilton, Alexander; Madison, James; Paterson, William; Rutledge, John; *United States Term Limits v. Thornton*; Washington, George; *Wesberry v. Sanders*.

Constitutional interpretation

DESCRIPTION: Process by which general principles of a constitution are applied by officials to individual laws or actions.

SIGNIFICANCE: The Supreme Court has traditionally had the last word on constitutional interpretation, which can change the powers of government and alter the degree of protection that individuals have from government action. In turn, the permissible scope of interpretation has been determined by what the Court did as it decided cases through its existence.

Chief Justice John Marshall noted, in *Marbury v. Madison* (1803), that the U.S. Constitution requires extensive interpretation. Although it was written and put into effect in the eighteenth century, its creators expected it to last for a long time and assumed that the three branches of the federal government it established would do different things at different times. Although the Constitution purports to control government action, the limits it creates are phrased in broad, general terms and are often vague. Therefore, questions about what each branch is constitutionally allowed to do and the rights of individuals are constantly recurring.

The Need for Finality. Of necessity, all three branches of the federal government, as well as state governments, must sometimes interpret the Constitution. A tacit part of the creation of any law is the assertion that the legislature has the power to pass it. Before the Civil War (1861-1865), when government exercised only traditional and well-explored functions, these interpretations were rarely controversial. After the war, however, because of national expansion and the Industrial Revolution, governments began to legislate in new areas, to impose new taxes, and in general to be more energetic. These new actions often raised questions over whether legislatures or the president

had the constitutional power to make them. In the twentieth century, large businesses, political pressure groups, and litigious cranks often have incentives (and money) to file lawsuits to challenge interpretations with which they disagree.

If there is a question over what the Constitution means and it is properly raised in a federal lawsuit, usually the Supreme Court's interpretation prevails. As part of its power, the Court can declare that an action of another branch of government violates some limit on the power of that branch and is therefore void, or unconstitutional. This power of judicial review is the most important of the Court's powers. The Court thus serves as the "umpire" of the political game, telling the various elected "players"—Congress, the president, and the states—what they can and cannot do. Through the late 1990's, the Court declared more than two hundred acts of Congress unconstitutional and invalidated a much larger number of state laws. It is also the guarantor of individual rights, determining how much protection Americans enjoy from government action.

The Constitution does not explicitly grant the Court this interpretive finality, and it is by no means clear why the Court should have it. Marshall himself argued that if interpretation is needed, courts are best suited to the task because they have extensive experience interpreting written documents and because they are sworn to give the Constitution priority over ordinary legislation. Scholars have argued that because federal judges have lifetime appointments and are insulated from political pressure, they can interpret the Constitution relatively free of ambition and political bias. Further, because judges are trained in the law, they are more likely to base their interpretations on legal or moral principles than Congress or the president (who are more likely to be swayed by transitory political concerns). Finally, because courts are weaker than Congress or the president, they pose less danger of becoming tyrannical. If nothing else, a final arbiter is needed in a government with a separation of powers, and public opinion seems comfortable with the Court serving as that arbiter.

Judicial Restraint. However, the actions of elected presidents and legislators—who presumably try to do what the public wants in order to be reelected—can be set aside by the undemocratic decisions of nonelected judges. For this reason, most Court justices believe that they must restrain themselves to avoid coming into conflict with the elected branches too often. Justice Felix Frankfurter argued for this philosophy of judicial self-restraint in numerous texts between 1939 and 1962. He pointed out that courts have no financial or military power and depend on broad support from the public to persuade the other branches to enforce court decisions. If they set aside the democratic decisions of legislatures or presidents too often, this public support will evaporate. Moreover, judges typically have less education in the details of policy and taxation than legislators do.

Justices who follow the philosophy of restraint try to avoid or at least delay interpreting the Constitution. They raise procedural obstacles to prevent lawsuits from being brought or decide cases on nonconstitutional grounds. If interpretation cannot be avoided, they try to make their interpretations as narrow and case-bound as possible. Above all, they presume that the actions of other branches are valid and do not declare them unconstitutional unless absolutely necessary.

Judicial Activism. Justices who follow the philosophy of judicial activism have strong political preferences and believe that they should use constitutional interpretation to write these preferences into law, even if the elected branches disagree. Consequently, they are much more willing to invalidate actions of the other branches.

Activists who supported the economic ideology of laissez-faire controlled the Court between 1895 and 1936. Because they believed that business should be allowed to operate as free of government regulation as possible, they interpreted the commerce clause and other parts of the Constitution very narrowly. They struck down many laws designed to protect worker health and safety or to otherwise limit how businesses were allowed to operate. By 1936, neither the states nor the federal government had much economic regulatory power left; consequently, neither was able to deal with the Great Depression. Public opinion turned against the Court, and the activist position was discredited. Judicial restraint justices, who became a majority after 1936, overturned many of the activist economic rulings, leaving it to legislatures to determine how extensively they could regulate the economy.

After 1936, most justices have been suspicious of activism. However, that stance enjoyed a resur-

gence between 1954 and 1969, when activist justices struck down state laws mandating racially segregated public schools and created new court procedures designed to protect the constitutional rights of people accused of crimes. Professor John Hart Ely argued that although elected branches usually can be trusted to operate constitutionally when they deal with economic issues, they can sometimes be perverted by improper election procedures or other structural flaws. If legislatures are malapportioned or voting registration procedures are corrupted so that some people cannot register to vote, the public may not be able to make its wishes known at elections. Majority rule and democracy will not occur. Ely argued that judicial activism is needed to correct these structural flaws when legislatures are unable or unwilling to do so. Following *Baker v. Carr* (1962), the Court ordered legislative reapportionment in many states to ensure that each person's vote counted equally in choosing legislators.

Some justices take compromise positions between activism and restraint. Justice Harlan Fiske Stone argued that courts can defer to legislatures when economics is involved but need to be especially vigilant when legislatures act to limit freedom of speech, press, or religion because these rights are fragile and easily lost. The Court must, in his words, give these political rights a preferred position. In the 1970's the Court used Stone's view as the basis for the strict scrutiny principle: Unlike economic legislation, laws that limit basic rights or that operate to harm politically weak minorities are presumed to be invalid unless they are indispensable to achieving some extremely important government goal. Through the 1990's, the Court continued to construe legislative power very narrowly in such cases.

Interpretivism. The dispute between judicial activists and restraintists is largely a dispute about when, or how often, the Court should interpret the Constitution. Justices are also divided over how the job should be done. Supreme Court justices have always assumed that they should function as a court of law, by applying principles of interpretation to individual cases in an objective and disinterested way and by treating like cases alike.

However, the Constitution does not contain principles for its own interpretation. These have to be discovered elsewhere, and justices and scholars disagree over the method. Interpretivists, sometimes called originalists, believe that the Constitution should be interpreted as intended by the people who wrote and ratified the Constitution—the Founders. Interpretivists typically believe that there are eternal political principles, such as the belief that power corrupts, which must be controlled if government is to operate fairly. The wise Founders knew these principles, embodied them in the Constitution, and expected these principles to control all constitutional interpretation. Thus, interpretivists claim that they are following the path marked out by the Founders.

In addition, as Justice Clarence Thomas and many others argued, the legitimacy of the Constitution depends on its having been accepted by the people in the ratification procedure in 1789. In that "constitution-making moment," a contract was created between the rulers and the ruled. The Constitution, which is the written part of that contract, secured the consent of the governed for the limited government it set up. However, the people accepted the Constitution as the Founders expected it to be interpreted. The interpretations of the Founders, the unwritten part of the agreement, are thus equally binding. If the Court interprets the Constitution in some other way, governments may come to exercise more powers than the people granted.

When controversies arise about what the Constitution means, interpretivists try to determine what the Founders intended. Most try to learn about the values of the Founders by studying their records and papers. Others seek principles in the records of American and British common-law courts because courts discuss and apply the political values of their times. Still others study traditions and customs. For example, the practice of beginning each session of Congress with a prayer, which has existed since the first Congress wrote the First Amendment in 1790, has been cited as proof that the Founders did not intend that Amendment to forbid all ceremonial prayer in government proceedings. Finally, others, called textualists, try to discover principles embedded in the language of the Constitution by studying how its words and phrases were used in the eighteenth century.

Sometimes the interpretive intent of the Founders can easily be discovered. For example, it is clear that the Founders did not intend the prohibition on cruel and unusual punishments to forbid the death penalty as such because they continued to use it. However, many parts of the Constitution remain stubbornly unclear. Sometimes the intent of the Founders cannot be discovered, and sometimes, they disagreed with one another. In more troubling cases, some values of the Founders, including their toleration of slavery, have become outdated or offensive. Professor Ronald Dworkin, for example, has observed that although the Founders overwhelmingly accepted racially segregated schools and many other governmental inequities, any constitutional interpretation that permitted these inequities to exist today would be overwhelmingly rejected by most Americans.

Noninterpretivism. For these reasons, noninterpretivists argue that the intent of the Founders should be given little weight in contemporary constitutional interpretation. Most noninterpretivists either deny that there are political principles of eternal validity or else believe that the few such principles that do exist are of such generality that they offer little guidance to dealing with concrete problems. As Chief Justice Earl Warren observed, the rule to "treat people equally except in exceptional cases" does not help a justice trying to decide whether segregated schools should constitute such an exception.

Nor, as Justice William J. Brennan, Jr., has noted, does the Constitution depend for its binding effect on the consent of people in 1789. Instead, he argues, the people must constantly accept the Constitution as it exists today. They do so tacitly, by obeying its requirements. They will continue to do so as long as the Constitution meets their expectations about what it should be like. If there is any conflict between what the law says the Constitution is and what the people want it to be at any moment, then the job of the Court is to sit as a "permanent constitutional convention" and, by interpretation, to revise the Constitution to fit the public expectations.

This is what the Court did in *Brown v. Board of Education* (1954), when it struck down the segregated schools that had long been legally accepted. Significantly, in *Brown,* the Court ignored the history urged on it by interpretivists, saying only that it could not "turn back the clock" to the Civil War or the colonial period. Instead, Chief Justice Warren emphasized sociology, stressing the importance of contemporary education to the ability of individuals to achieve their goals and function as citizens.

As compared with interpretivists, noninterpretivists assume that change is more rapid and cuts deeper into political values and beliefs. Though they insist that the values of contemporary citizens should be given priority, they offer little guidance on how to discover these values. Nor do they explain how to tell the difference between basic principles and values, which should govern views on many political issues over time, and short-term political principles specific to an issue. Finally, noninterpretivists do not explain the source of the power they claim to continually revise the Constitution. Though that document contains procedures for formal amendment, it nowhere gives the Court the right to serve as a "permanent amending convention."

Other Views. In an influential 1959 article, Professor Herbert Wechsler argued that any constitutional interpretation, to be fair, must be made on the basis of a neutral principle, a rule capable of being applied uniformly to all similar cases without creating an advantage for any particular political force. Neutral principles may be those of the Founders or may be discovered later. His examples are derived from moral principles and relate to controversies of the period: A state cannot escape limits on public action by transferring some government function (such as holding primary elections) to private control, and racial segregation (a denial of equality per se) may constitute a denial of freedom of association. Presumably, the neutrality of such principles can be tested by philosophers who study critical cases.

Neutrality has long been an important consideration in constitutional law. Therefore, the holding that the First Amendment guarantees the right to hold peaceable public parades cannot be considered fair unless it is applied impartially to Republicans and Democrats and civil rights activists and members of the Ku Klux Klan. Professor Wechsler suggests that interpretive principles can be similarly neutral and should not be used by the Court unless they are.

The neutral principles approach seems intuitively fair. In legal proceedings, neutrality seems achievable. Thus, courts insist that laws be knowable in advance, for example, and that lawyers for both sides in a lawsuit have adequate time to prepare their cases. However, it may not be possible to find nontrivial principles that are truly neutral. Wechsler suggests that equality may be such a principle, but others have disagreed.

Most of the individual rights guaranteed by the Constitution are not meant to be absolute. The public is protected, for example, against only unreasonable searches and seizures; the privilege of *habeas corpus* must not be suspended "unless the public safety requires." However, some parts of the Constitution are phrased to suggest that they allow no exceptions. For these, absolutists argue that the Constitution should always be interpreted to forbid government action. For example, absolutists interpret the First Amendment statement that Congress shall make no law abridging freedom of speech as meaning that Congress cannot regulate sedition, the utterance of threats, or the publishing of obscene literature.

Absolutists make it unnecessary to draw precise legal lines between things that may be vague and subjective. If they prevailed, it would be unnecessary, for example, for justices to distinguish between obscene material, which legislatures could ban, and nonobscene pornography, which is protected under the First Amendment. However, this would require the acceptance of extremes of behavior offensive to both Founders and contemporary Americans. In practice, absolutists tend to allow exceptions by casuistry. Uttering a threat, for example, is said to be a form of action, not speech. The publication of obscene material is seen as an incitement of violence against women, rather than as freedom of the press.

Finally, in cases in which rights conflict, the Court has created legal rules, or doctrines, for handling the conflict. Sometimes rights are placed in a hierarchy. Those rights of criminally accused persons that are necessary for courts to hold fair criminal trials, for example, have been preferred to individual rights to speak or publish. The latter, in turn, have been preferred to the rights of political leaders and bureaucrats to act with "administrative efficiency."

In other cases, rights have been balanced against one another. In *United States v. Nixon* (1974), for example, in which the president unsuccessfully sought to keep secret audiotapes that had been requested by former aides who needed them to defend themselves against criminal charges, the Court balanced the need of the president to keep information confidential against the constitutional rights of the defendants in a criminal court.

FURTHER READING

Lee Epstein and Jack Knight have described how the Court goes about its work in *The Choices Justices Make* (Washington, D.C.: Congressional Quarterly, 1998). The most comprehensive presentation of the various approaches to interpretation is Craig Ducat, *Modes of Constitutional Interpretation* (St. Paul, Minn.: West Publishing, 1978). Activism and restraint are examined in *Supreme Court Activism and Restraint* (Lexington, Mass.: Lexington Books, 1982), edited by Stephen C. Halpern and Charles M. Lamb, and Christopher Wolfe's *Judicial Activism: Bulwark of Liberty or Precarious Security?* (rev. ed., Lanham, Md.: Rowman & Littlefield, 1997). Leif Carter has written an accessible introduction to the problem of original intent, *Contemporary Constitutional Lawmaking* (New York: Pergamon, 1986). Judge Robert H. Bork argues for one form of interpretivism in *The Tempting of America* (New York: Simon & Schuster, 1990), and scholar Michael Perry examines noninterpretivism in *The Constitution, the Courts, and Human Rights* (New Haven, Conn.: Yale University Press, 1982) and interpretivism in *The Constitution in the Courts: Law or Politics?* (New York: Oxford University Press, 1994). Herbert Wechsler's views are best described in his own article, "Toward Neutral Principles of Constitutional Law," *Harvard Law Review* 73 (1959). Mark Tushnet demonstrates the difficulty of applying such an approach in practice in "Following the Rules Laid Down: A Critique of Interpretivism and Neutral Principles," *Harvard Law Review* 96 (1983): 781. Finally, the Court's traditional control of interpretation has not gone unchallenged. Tushnet takes a critical perspective in *Taking the Constitution Away from the Courts* (Princeton, N.J.: Princeton University Press, 1999).

Paul Lermack

SEE ALSO *Baker v. Carr*, Constitutional law; Judicial activism; Judicial review; Judicial self-restraint; *Marbury v. Madison*; Original intent.

Constitutional law

DESCRIPTION: Dynamic body of law that defines and limits the powers of government and sets out its organizational structure.

SIGNIFICANCE: As the fundamental law contained in the U.S. Constitution and in Supreme Court decisions interpreting that document, constitutional law blends legal decisions with elements of politics and political theory, history, economics, public policy, philosophy, and ethics.

A resilient document, the U.S. Constitution has endured with only twenty-seven amendments since its formulation in 1787. Its sweeping language and generalities allow change and interpretation in the face of altered circumstances, from the changing human condition to the changing composition of the Supreme Court. The Constitution contains few rules and is not self-explanatory. That lack of specificity was intentional. The Framers outlined their general intent to create the fundamentals of a national government, prescribing how it should operate and limiting its scope of power. The ongoing interpretative process engaged in by the Court allows the provisions of the Constitution to change and adapt over time. The Court refers to the original Constitution because by doing so, it can bring resolution of the new and often divisive issues of each generation. The genius of constitutionalism, therefore, lies in the opportunities provided in the document for change and continuity, the method of judicial interpretation, and the overall skill and sensitivity of the justices. The fact that the justices are lifetime appointees frees them from concerns about approval by political leaders and voters and permits concentration on the issues.

Constitutional Decision Making. Virtually all cases before the Court involve seeking review of a decision by a federal court of appeals or a state supreme court. As the final authority on federal matters and questions dealing with the Constitution and treaties, the Court exercises appellate jurisdiction (appeals) and functions as a trial court (original jurisdiction) only in certain limited situations involving ambassadors or where a state is a party. Most of the cases reach the Court for review by means of a writ of certiorari, or through the exercise of the Court's discretion. This means that the Court has almost complete control of its docket. Of the 7,000 petitions for review annually, only 2 percent are granted. The Court issues an average of 110 opinions per year, permitting a selected group of policy issues to be addressed.

The Court is shrouded in secrecy, assuming

some of the awe and mystery of the document it interprets. Some have criticized the Court for remaining in an "ivory tower" far removed from "we the people" set out in the preamble to the Constitution. Decisions to grant or deny review are made in secret conferences attended only by the nine justices with no support staff. A traditional unwritten rule specifies that a case is accepted for review if four justices feel that it merits the Court's attention (rule of four) and that it would serve the interests of justice. The Court does not have to explain its refusal.

When the Court decides to hear a case, the clerk schedules oral argument during which the justices may interrupt and ask questions of the attorneys to clarify, debate, or explain the written briefs. Cases are discussed in secret conferences following oral argument. It takes a majority vote to decide a case.

Following the conference and ensuing discussion, an opinion or reasoned argument explaining the legal issues in the case and the precedents on which the opinion is based must be drafted. The manner in which a majority opinion is written can have a great impact on Americans. That impact depends in part on who writes the opinion and how it is written, and also on the extent of support or dissent by the remaining justices. A 5-4 plurality opinion does not demonstrate the firm conviction of the Court that is present in a unanimous or 8-1 decision.

Any justice can write a separate opinion. If justices agree with the majority's decision but disagree with its reasoning, they may write a concurring opinion. If they disagree with both the result and reasoning contained in the majority opinion, they may write a dissenting opinion or simply go on the record as dissenting without an opinion. More than one justice can join in a concurring or dissenting opinion.

Decision making or opinion writing is a painstaking and laborious process. The time involved varies from one justice to another depending on the complexity of the issues in the case. The actual reporting of decisions has changed from the days in which members of the Court read long opinions aloud, sometimes taking days to do so. When Charles Evans Hughes became chief justice in 1930, he encouraged the delivery of summaries of opinions. That practice has continued, and the justice writing the majority opinion delivers the sum-

mary. Dissenting justices deliver their own opinions. Computerization and Lexis and Westlaw legal databases have made newly decided opinions accessible to all within hours of their release.

The Highest Court. Decisions of the Court are final because there is no higher court to which to appeal. Its interpretation of statutes can be reversed only by congressional legislation, and its constitutional rulings overturned only by constitutional amendment. Absent these remedies, all courts are obliged to follow the Supreme Court in matters of federal law. In its decisions, the Court attempts to adhere to precedent, or *stare decisis*, and in that capacity serves as final authority in constitutional matters, thereby providing a uniform interpretation of the law, historical continuity, stability, and predictability. Just as the Court sets its own agenda and controls what it hears, accepting or rejecting cases according to individual and collective goals such as avoiding troublesome issues, resolving legal conflicts, and establishing policies favored by the justices, Court decisions are group products shaped by the law, the Court and the country's environment, and the personal value systems of and interactions among the justices.

The power to define the Constitution makes the Court unique among government institutions. Through the exercise of its constitutional role together with the rule of law, the Court has wielded far-reaching power. The proper functioning of federalism and the scope of the rights of the individual depend on the actions of the Court, whose words mark the boundaries of the branches and departments of government.

The justices function as "nine little law firms," autonomous but working as a collegial body to decide a case. In important cases, the opinions issued by the Court are often negotiated among the members, the result of a cooperative collaboration in which the end product is the joint work of all rather than the product of the named author alone.

Self-Imposed Limitations. The Court imposes certain limitations or barriers before accepting a case for review. It poses certain threshold questions to deal with tactical issues that must be resolved before the Court reaches the substance of the controversy. Referred to as "judicial restraint," if these elements are not overcome, the Court will not exercise jurisdiction over a case. Article III, section 2, of the Constitution requires that there exist an ongoing "case or controversy" at all stages of the proceedings, including appeal. As interpreted by the Court, these words limit the power of federal courts to resolving disputes between adversaries whose rights are truly in collision. Often called "justiciability," the requirement provides concreteness when a question is precisely framed. The case, therefore, must present a live dispute.

Precluded are advisory opinions, or giving advice on abstract or hypothetical situations, as the Court ruled in *Muskrat v. United States* (1911), and moot cases, or those that have already been resolved, settled, or feigned, or those in which circumstances or time have removed the dispute or conflict because there is nothing for a court to decide, as it ruled in *DeFunis v. Odegaard* (1974). Several narrow exceptions to the mootness rule exist where conduct is of short duration but capable of repetition such as election disputes or abortion cases such as *Roe v. Wade* and its companion case *Doe v. Bolton* (1973). In *Baker v. Carr* (1962), the Court determined that political questions or those matters more properly applicable to another branch of government will not be accepted, nor will friendly or collusive suits and test cases. Standing to sue requires that the litigants have a personal stake in the outcome of the case, having suffered an actual injury, in order to assure concrete adverseness. Ripeness requires the issues in the case to be clearly delineated and sharply outlined, not premature, in flux, or abstract. Moreover, the Court will not engage in speculation, contingencies, or predictions or issue extrajudicial advice.

Judicial Review. Courts participate in the development of constitutional law through judicial review. In the landmark case *Marbury v. Madison* (1803), considered to be the point at which constitutional law begins, the Court held that Article III empowers courts to review government actions and invalidate those found to be repugnant to the Constitution by declaring them unconstitutional. The supremacy clause of Article IV states that no provision of state law and no legislative enactment may conflict with the national Constitution, which is the supreme law of the land.

The Framers of the Constitution decentralized control through federalism, considered one of the most important contributions to government. Federalism is a dual system in which powers are divided between national and state authorities.

Bill of Rights. Protecting the fundamental rights of individuals was considered of the utmost importance. The Framers believed that explicit enumeration of those rights would make the rights more secure. In order to achieve ratification of the main body of the Constitution, therefore, in 1791 the Framers appended to it a Bill of Rights, consisting of the first ten amendments of the present document. While the body of the main Constitution concerns government, the Bill of Rights represents the popular perception of constitutional guarantees.

Basic to American identity is the First Amendment and its central guarantees of freedom of speech, press, religion, assembly, and right to petition for redress of grievances. Despite language to the contrary, the rights contained in the Bill of Rights are not absolute. In the speech area, for example, certain categories of expression can be regulated; others are not protected at all. "Pure" speech that creates no danger to the public is protected. However, if speech advocates an imminent lawless action that presents a "clear and present danger," the speech loses its protection, as the Court ruled in *Schenck v. United States* (1919). In *Texas v. Johnson* (1989), the Court found that symbolic speech or use of actions as a substitute for words is generally protected, such as flag burning as a controversial but valid expression of political views. Obscenity or pornography, defamatory communications (libel and slander), and "fighting words" that provoke an immediate breach of the peace do not receive First Amendment protection.

Some rights that Americans consider basic to their fundamental freedoms are not mentioned specifically in the Constitution. Among these are the right of personal privacy, which protects the individual from state interference. The Court struggled with the constitutional foundation of the right, suggesting various sources: the due process guarantee of the Fourteenth Amendment and the penumbras or emanations from the interests protected by the First, Third, Fourth, Fifth, and Ninth Amendments (*Griswold v. Connecticut*, 1965).

FURTHER READING

Two well-written works containing detailed treatment with case references and quotations are Joan Biskupic and Elder Witt's *The Supreme Court and the Powers of the American Government* (Washington, D.C.: Congressional Quarterly, 1997) and *The Su-*

preme Court at Work (2d ed., Washington, D.C.: Congressional Quarterly, 1997), with biographical sketches of the justices and illustrations. Lawrence Baum's *The Supreme Court* (5th ed., Washington, D.C.: Congressional Quarterly, 1995) examines the role of the Court, the justices, the decision-making process, factors that influence the Court, activism in policy making, and the Court's significance. Organized by case themes, *Decision: How the Supreme Court Decides Cases* (New York: Oxford University Press, 1996) by Bernard Schwartz offers a behind-the-scenes look at how the Court decides cases. Archibald Cox's *The Court and the Constitution* (Boston: Houghton Mifflin, 1987) is a readable yet scholarly account of how the Court shaped constitutional law. Peter G. Renstrom's *Constitutional Law and Young Adults* (Santa Barbara, Calif.: ABC-CLIO, 1992) is a guide to the Constitution, the court system, and key provisions of the Bill of Rights and Fourteenth Amendment with case references. It is comprehensive in scope and comprehensible to the general reader. David P. Currie's *The Constitution of the United States: A Primer for the People* (Chicago: University of Chicago Press, 1988) contains an overview of the document and the major concepts contained in it in language intended for the general reader.

Marcia J. Weiss

SEE ALSO Bill of Rights; Constitution, U.S.; Constitutional interpretation; Federalism; Judicial activism; *Marbury v. Madison*; Rule of law; Separation of powers.

Constitutionalism

DESCRIPTION: Idea that political power can and should be limited so as to prevent the possibility of tyranny. Typically, but certainly not always, the concept is supported by the presence of an actual written constitution.

SIGNIFICANCE: To restrain political authority and ensure the rights and freedom of the sovereign people, the Framers of the U.S. Constitution constructed an impartial text that delegated specific powers to various governmental institutions.

At the center of the idea of constitutionalism is the fear that if given the chance, government officials will somehow abuse or oppress the people. There-

fore, constitutionalism requires that governmental rules and conduct be objective or impartial and that the human tendency to be guided by passion, ambition, and self-interest rather than reason be curtailed by formal, institutional means. In practice, constitutionalism addresses the question of how to balance the will of the community with the need to control and prevent tyranny. In political regimes that are organized around the principle of majority rule, including that of the United States, the majority should get its way more often than not in the policy-making process. However, minorities in these regimes require some protection from the oppressive tendencies of majorities. Constitutionalism mandates that certain principles, mechanisms, and procedures are instituted so as to ensure that the majority prevails in all public decisions except those that interfere with the rights and freedoms of those in the minority.

Origins of Constitutionalism. Constitutionalism began in America in the seventeenth century when the colonists formed voluntary associations and compacts through which they formed a community and ordered the political institutions in a very precise way. These compacts were based on the principle of consent. Citizens agreed to give up some of their natural freedom in exchange for the security and protection of the entire community. They consented to follow the rules laid down by the community, even if those rules impinged on their individual freedoms, so that they could enjoy the enhanced protection of the collective group. In giving the majority the power to make political decisions for the entire community, the colonists were understandably wary of the potential for abuse. They took seriously the need for a limited government that also reflected the general will of the people. Their attitudes were shared by the writers of the Declaration of Independence, the Articles of Confederation, and the Constitution, who chose to express both the ideal of government by consent and the principle of limited power in these fundamental documents.

To guarantee the principle of limited government, the U.S. Constitution distributes power between the states and the federal government and between the specific institutions within each level of government. The Constitution further sets up a system of checks and balances in which each branch becomes both a check on the other branches and an institution that is partially responsible for the overall success of the government itself. However, what has become the most powerful symbol of constitutionalism in the modern era is the existence of a list of rights and liberties that identifies certain freedoms retained by the people. In particular, those guarantees found in the Bill of Rights and the Fourteenth Amendment of the U.S. Constitution have been used since the founding of the nation by individuals and groups to limit the power of the majority and to forestall the possibility of tyranny.

The Supreme Court's Role. Since its creation, the Supreme Court has been devoted to preserving and protecting the idea of constitutionalism. The unique position of the members of the Court—isolated from the political process through their lifetime tenure and fixed salaries—enables them to review the decisions of the community while also protecting minorities from the abuses of the majority. In fact, judicial review has become one of the most powerful weapons in the fight against the tyranny of the majority. The Court, in an opinion written by Chief Justice John Marshall, established the power of judicial review in *Marbury v. Madison* (1803). The power of judicial review permits the judiciary to refuse to enforce any governmental action that contradicts the Constitution.

In the twentieth century the Court continued to preserve the principle of constitutionalism by using its power of judicial review. After the mid-1920's, the Court engaged in a number of cases involving consideration of some very important civil rights and liberties. The Court's willingness to protect minority interests is demonstrated in cases such as *Brown v. Board of Education* (1954), in which the Court ruled that segregation of public schools violated the Fourteenth Amendment, and *Brandenburg v. Ohio* (1969), in which the Court used the First Amendment to protect speech meant to incite violence. Later, the Court concluded that legislation preventing the desecration of the flag (*Texas v. Johnson*, 1989) and policies permitting prayer at public school ceremonies (*Lee v. Weisman*, 1992) cannot withstand judicial scrutiny because they interfere with some vital freedoms. In these and similar cases, the Court has adhered faithfully to the principle of constitutionalism by limiting the will of the majority and preserving the delicate balance between progress and freedom.

FURTHER READING

Gordon, Scott. *Controlling the State: Constitutionalism from Ancient Athens to Today.* Cambridge, Mass.: Harvard University Press, 1999.

Thompson, Kenneth W., ed. *The Political Theory of the Constitution.* Lanham, Md.: University Press of America, 1990.

Thurow, Sarah Baumgartner, ed. *Constitutionalism in America.* Lanham, Md.: University Press of America, 1988.

Beau Breslin

SEE ALSO *Brandenburg v. Ohio*; *Brown v. Board of Education*; Constitution, U.S.; Constitutional interpretation; Judicial review; *Lee v. Weisman*; *Marbury v. Madison*; Rule of law; *Texas v. Johnson*.

Contempt power of Congress

DESCRIPTION: Power of Congress to punish those persons who refuse to cooperate in its investigations by jailing them.

SIGNIFICANCE: The Supreme Court recognized the contempt power of Congress as inherent in its investigatory powers. In 1857 Congress enacted a statute making it a criminal offense to refuse to provide information to the House or the Senate.

In *Anderson v. Dunn* (1821), the Supreme Court recognized the inherent contempt power of Congress. The power included the ability of the House of Representatives and the Senate to punish contempt, or failure to cooperate with an investigation, by jailing the offender. The Court limited the contempt power by specifying that imprisonment could not extend beyond the adjournment of Congress.

Congress removed the limitations on its contempt power by enacting a law in 1857 that made it a criminal offense to refuse to provide information to either chamber. During the Cold War and congressional investigations of communism in the United States, the Court changed its position on the ability of Congress to force witnesses to testify. In *Watkins v. United States* (1957), the Court stated that a witness could be held in contempt only for not answering questions that were relevant to the investigation. The Court moved away from this position in *Barenblatt v. United States* (1959), stating that Congress had a significant interest in learning about Barenblatt's activities as an alleged communist.

John David Rausch, Jr.

SEE ALSO *Barenblatt v. United States*; Congressional power of investigation; Contempt power of courts; *Watkins v. United States*.

Contempt power of courts

DESCRIPTION: Mechanism by which courts punish those who disobey their orders or disrespect their authority, in and out of court.

SIGNIFICANCE: The Supreme Court has acted to place limits on this power, which is not mentioned in the Constitution but is deemed inherent.

The contempt power of the courts, derived from common law, was directly conferred on federal courts by the Judiciary Act of 1789. It was broadly interpreted until 1830 when Judge James H. Peck used the power to disbar and imprison a man who published an article critical of him. In 1831 a statute was enacted limiting the contempt power to three situations: misbehavior in the court's presence or so near as to cause disruption of the court's

Passmore Williamson, an abolitionist, was jailed for contempt of court for giving evasive testimony regarding his part in freeing three slaves. This court power has been limited somewhat by Supreme Court rulings designed to prevent abuses. (Library of Congress)

business, misbehavior of an officer of the court in the conduct of official business, and disobedience or resistance to a court's order by an officer of the court or any other interested party, including jurors and witnesses.

Contempt can be civil or criminal. Civil contempt, disobedience to a court's order, is a summary proceeding, with a sentence imposed immediately. Punishment may be incremental and continue until the wrongdoer complies with the court's order. Criminal contempt, commission of a forbidden act, carries a set, defined punishment. It was not subject to trial until 1966, when the Supreme Court ruled federal courts could not impose a sentence longer than six months without a trial. The Court constitutionally extended the right to trial to state courts in *Duncan v. Louisiana* (1968). On the same day, in *Bloom v. Illinois* (1968), the Court ruled that both state and federal courts must allow a jury trial to persons charged with serious criminal contempt.

A number of Court rulings limited the ability of judges to act summarily by requiring due process safeguards. The Court also limited courts' ability to use contempt in cases involving the First Amendment, such as *Nebraska Press Association v. Stuart* (1976), in which it revoked a gag order placed on the press.

Elizabeth Algren Shaw

SEE ALSO Contempt power of Congress; *Duncan v. Louisiana*; First Amendment; Judiciary Act of 1789; *Nebraska Press Association v. Stuart*; Pretrial publicity and gag rule.

Contract, freedom of

DESCRIPTION: Also known as "liberty of contract," the doctrine that individual persons and business firms should be free to enter into contracts without undue interference from government.

SIGNIFICANCE: From 1897 to 1937, a probusiness Supreme Court used the freedom of contract doctrine to overturn numerous economic regulations designed to protect the interests of workers and the general public.

The Supreme Court recognized that the Fifth Amendment's due process clause protected some substantive rights to property and liberty as early as *Scott v. Sandford* (1857). The drafters of the Fourteenth Amendment, among other goals, wanted to protect the liberty and equality of African Americans to enter into legally binding contracts involving property and employment. With the growth of state regulations in the late nineteenth century, therefore, it was not surprising that proponents of laissez-faire capitalism seized on the Fourteenth Amendment's due process clause as a means of promoting substantive liberties in matters of business and economics. Justice Stephen J. Field and jurist Thomas M. Cooley were among the most influential proponents of this substantive due process approach, which was soon accepted by several state courts.

After debating the concept on numerous occasions, a majority of the Court finally accepted the idea that the Fourteenth Amendment protected a substantive freedom of contract in *Allgeyer v. Louisiana* (1897). In this case, the Court invalidated a Louisiana law that made it illegal for residents of the state to enter into insurance contracts by mail with out-of-state companies. Writing for the majority, Justice Rufus W. Peckham declared that U.S. citizens enjoyed the freedom to make contracts relevant to the pursuit of their economic interests.

The *Lochner* Era. Through the four decades following *Allgeyer,* the Court looked on freedom of contract as a normative ideal and required states to assume a high burden for proving that any restraint on the liberty was justified on the basis of accepted police powers, such as protecting the public's safety, health, or morality. The most prominent cases usually involved legislation regulating terms of employment, such as maximum working hours and minimum wages. In *Lochner v. New York* (1905), for example, a five-member majority overturned a labor law limiting the number of hours that bakers could work each week, and the majority insisted that employees should have the freedom to work as many hours as they wished. In *Adair v. United States* (1908) and *Coppage v. Kansas* (1915), the Court struck down federal and state laws that outlawed yellow dog contracts (employment contracts in which workers agree not to join unions). The majority of the Court was not impressed with the inequality in bargaining positions between employers and workers. Justice Oliver Wendell Holmes wrote vigorous dissents in such cases.

Nevertheless, the freedom of contract doctrine was used in ways that would later be considered progressive. In *Buchanan v. Warley* (1917), for example, the concept was a major reason for the Court's overturning of a St. Louis segregation ordinance that prohibited whites from selling residential housing to African Americans.

The Court often accepted the constitutionality of restraints on the freedom of contract, but only when a majority concluded that a restraint was a reasonable means for enforcing legitimate police powers. For example, the Court in *Holden v. Hardy* (1898) upheld a Utah law that made it illegal for miners to work more than eight hours a day because of the manifest dangers of underground mining. Likewise, in *Muller v. Oregon* (1908), the Court determined that the special health needs of women provided justification for limiting their industrial workday to ten hours. Yet, in *Adkins v. Children's Hospital* (1923), a bare majority overturned a District of Columbia's minimum wage for women. The obvious inconsistency between *Muller* and *Children's Hospital* reflected the inherent subjectivity in all decisions grounded in substantive due process.

Judicial Revolution of 1937. The Court began to moderate its position on freedom of contract after Charles Evans Hughes became chief justice in 1930. During President Franklin D. Roosevelt's first term, nevertheless, four conservative justices—dubbed the "Four Horsemen"—remained firmly committed to the *Lochner/Adair* line of thinking. In *Morehead v. New York ex rel. Tipaldo* (1936), Owen J. Roberts joined the four to overturn New York's minimum-wage law. During the 1936 election, *Morehead* was widely denounced and was one of several cases that led to Roosevelt's Court-packing plan. For several reasons, Roberts abandoned the Four Horsemen in *West Coast Hotel Co. v. Parrish* (1937), which upheld Washington state's minimum-wage law. Speaking for a majority of five, Hughes acknowledged that the Constitution protected liberty, but he defined liberty as the absence of arbitrary restraints. Two weeks later, the Court abandoned its *Adair* precedent in *National Labor Relations Board v. Jones and Laughlin Steel Corp.*, upholding the Wagner Act protections of labor's right to organize and join unions.

After the Court reversed itself in 1937, it never again struck down a public policy based on the freedom of contract doctrine. In effect, it almost entirely abandoned any judicial supervision based on the doctrine—a development that is part of its movement toward exercising only minimal scrutiny of all economic regulations. Since then, the Court has upheld economic regulations only when they have appeared to be rationally related to legitimate governmental interests. The Court might resurrect the freedom of contract doctrine if it were to find some governmental regulation of contracts totally unreasonable or arbitrary. Although the Court lost interest in freedom of contract after 1937, it did not entirely stop reading substantive due process guarantees into the Fifth and Fourteenth Amendments.

FURTHER READING

Corwin, Edward. *Liberty Against Government: The Rise, Flowering, and Decline of a Famous Judicial Concept.* Reprint. Westport, Conn.: Greenwood Press, 1978.

Ely, James, Jr. *The Guardian of Every Other Right: A Constitutional History of Property Rights.* New York: Oxford University Press, 1992.

Seigan, Bernard. *Economic Liberties and the Constitution.* Chicago: University of Chicago Press, 1980.

Thomas T. Lewis

SEE ALSO Agricultural issues; Brandeis Brief; Capitalism; Contracts clause; Corporations; Due process, substantive; Judicial scrutiny; Police powers; Privacy, right to; Private corporation charters.

Contracts clause

DESCRIPTION: Article 1, section 10, of the U.S. Constitution prohibits states from impairing contractual obligations. Through Supreme Court interpretation, the prohibition extends to state impairment of contracts not only among private parties but also between private parties and the states themselves.

SIGNIFICANCE: During the nineteenth century, the contracts clause became a primary constitutional weapon to defend private business from state regulation, but it fell into relative disuse in the 1930's. The Court under Warren E. Burger revived the contracts clause in the late 1970's, although it did not regain its earlier status.

The Framers drafted the contracts clause because they were concerned with various attacks of the debtor class on property interests. In a variety of ways, state legislatures enacted laws that effectively relieved debtors of their contractual obligations. However, the first important Supreme Court interpretations of the contracts clause involved a legislative grant of land and the terms of a corporate charter, not a state impairment of contractual relations between private parties.

Protection from the States. In *Fletcher v. Peck* (1810), Chief Justice John Marshall found that public grants by a sovereign state are subject to the same limitations as are contracts among private parties. Once a contract is granted, the grantors imply they will not reassert their original rights, and therefore, a state does not possess the authority to revoke its own grants. Marshall applied this same absolutist mode of constitutional interpretation to *Dartmouth College v. Woodward* (1819). He held that a charter granted to the trustees of Dartmouth College in 1769 by the British crown could not be amended after the Revolutionary War by the New Hampshire legislature. In *Sturges v. Crowninshield* (1819), the Court held that in the absence of congressional legislation, states may enact bankruptcy laws. If a state bankruptcy law exists at the time when a contract is consummated, the Court held in *Ogden v. Saunders* (1827) that the state bankruptcy provisions are implied, and therefore, the contract is not impaired by the state law. Despite this particular setback for the doctrine of vested property rights, Marshall presided over a Court that created the judicial precedents protecting individual creditors and business organizations from the states' regulatory power.

The Court led by Chief Justice Roger Brooke Taney continued to apply the contracts clause to a wide array of disputes, including debtor-creditor relations, state legislation regulating and taxing banks, and even an agreement between the federal government and the states. The most noteworthy decision of the Taney Court is *Charles River Bridge v. Warren Bridge* (1837). Although the ruling in the case permits the exercise of state power, Taney's decision stands for the proposition that only those rights explicitly spelled out in corporate charters are protected by the contracts clause.

Stronger States. After the Civil War (1861-1865) to the 1880's the Court continued to render decisions generally favorable to propertied interests. For example, during this period municipalities attempted to repudiate their bonded indebtedness.

The Court ruled against them in all but a few of the two hundred cases that came before it. However, late in this period the Court began to recognize the legitimate use of state police powers as a limitation on private power in the economic marketplace. It permitted states to change the terms of bond issues and to regulate the rates railroads charged their customers. The Court also refused to apply the contracts clause to the federal government. The most celebrated pronouncement of this period is found in Chief Justice Morrison R. Waite's opinion in *Stone v. Mississippi* (1880): "No legislature can bargain away the public health or the public morals. The people themselves cannot do it, much less their servants."

Chief Justice Charles Evans Hughes's majority opinion in *Home Building and Loan Association v. Blaisdell* (1934) marks the start of a rapid decline in the Court's willingness to strike down state laws in the name of the contracts clause. Minnesota sought to ease the economic hardships associated with the Great Depression by slowing farm and home foreclosures by temporarily delaying the period of loan repayments. Hughes established criteria for when a state may interfere with the obligation of contracts among private parties. Because the state law did not alter the basic integrity of the contractual obligation and because the alteration was designed to apply in a temporary fashion, the Court's 4-3 majority was able to distinguish this case from the abuses that took place before the 1787 Constitutional Convention.

By the mid-1960's, the Court completed the process of rejecting constitutional absolutism in favor of a balancing-of-interests approach to contract clause interpretation. For example, Texas amended in 1941 a 1910 public land sale law. The original law allowed purchasers who had missed their payments to reinstate their claims at any time upon payment of the missed interest but before a third party obtained title to the land in question. The 1941 amendment limited the repayment option to five years. Upholding the unilateral change, Justice Byron R. White in *El Paso v. Simmons* (1965) explicitly rejects the absolutism of the past with the observation that not every modification of a contractual promise impairs the obligation of contract.

The Resurgence. In a pair of cases, the Burger Court created the necessary precedents for a resur-

gence of the contracts clause. In *United States Trust Co. v. New Jersey* (1977) and *Allied Structural Steel Co. v. Spannaus* (1978), a majority of justices employed a balancing-of-interests approach in a way that favored the interests of private litigants over states' interests. After the contractual impairment in question was demonstrated to be significant and not minor, the Court carefully scrutinized whether the impairment was both necessary and reasonable. Using this version of the balancing test, the Burger Court found in both cases against the state and in favor of private property.

Subsequently, the Court was asked to extend its reasoning to eminent domain and equal protection matters, but it consistently refused to do so. The contracts clause does not appear to be destined to a resurgence reminiscent of the days of John Marshall. However, because the balancing-of-interests test by its nature is highly subjective, a sufficiently property-minded Court may employ it at any time.

FURTHER READING

Ely, James, Jr. *The Guardian of Every Other Right: A Constitutional History of Property Rights.* New York: Oxford University Press, 1992.

Magrath, C. Peter. *Yazoo: The Case of "Fletcher v. Peck."* New York: W. W. Norton, 1966.

Melone, Albert P. "The Contract Clause and Supreme Court Decisionmaking: A Bicentennial Retrospective." *Midsouth Political Science Journal* 9 (1988): 41-63.

_____. *"Mendelson v. Wright*: Understanding the Contract Clause." *Western Political Quarterly* 41 (1988): 791-799.

Wright, Benjamin F., Jr. *The Contract Clause of the Constitution.* Cambridge, Mass.: Harvard University Press, 1938.

Albert P. Melone

SEE ALSO *Charles River Bridge v. Warren Bridge; Dartmouth College v. Woodward; Fletcher v. Peck; Home Building and Loan Association v. Blaisdell; Ogden v. Saunders;* Police powers; *Stone v. Mississippi; Sturges v. Crowninshield.*

Cooley, Thomas M.

IDENTIFICATION: Writer and jurist
BORN: January 6, 1824, near Attica, New York
DIED: September 12, 1898, Ann Arbor, Michigan

SIGNIFICANCE: Cooley's extensive writings on constitutional law influenced and were sometimes cited by Supreme Court justices.

When Cooley was nineteen, he decided to go to Chicago to further his education but ran out of funds in Adrian, Michigan. He finished his law studies there and was admitted to the Michigan bar. Cooley worked at several jobs before he turned to the full-time practice of law. He was an excellent researcher and writer and in 1857 was appointed to compile the legal statutes of the state of Michigan, which were published in multiple volumes. The work took him a year to complete. Officials were so impressed with his hard work and detailed results that he was appointed the official reporter for the Michigan supreme court. Cooley published eight volumes of Michigan supreme court reports during his six years as the official reporter.

In 1864 he was elected a justice of the Michigan supreme court; he was reelected several times but was defeated in 1885. While a judge, he was a prolific evaluator of and writer on constitutional laws. In 1866 he published the *Digest of Michigan Reports*, and in 1868 a *Treatise on Constitutional Limitations of the Legislative Power of the States*. The latter legal work made Cooley famous as a jurist. His discussion of due process in the treatise and his assertion that individuals should not be arbitrarily deprived of liberty in matters that affected their pursuit of happiness are believed to have influenced the doctrine of freedom of contract and protection of property rights developed by the Supreme Court. His reputation spread across the nation, and his opinions were widely cited by lawyers and law students.

Earl R. Andresen

SEE ALSO Constitutional law; Contract, freedom of; Due process, substantive.

Cooley v. Board of Wardens of the Port of Philadelphia

CITATION: 12 How. (53 U.S.) 299
DATE: March 2, 1852
ISSUE: Interstate commerce
SIGNIFICANCE: In upholding a state statute regulating navigation standards for ships, the Supreme Court formulated the doctrine of selective exclusiveness, allowing states to regulate aspects of interstate commerce in the absence of federal laws.

A Pennsylvania law required each ship entering or leaving Philadelphia to hire a local pilot for navigation purposes. When Aaron Cooley was fined for disobeying the law, he argued that it was an unconstitutional regulation of interstate commerce. By a 6-2 vote, the Supreme Court rejected his argument. Speaking for the majority, Justice Benjamin R. Curtis made a distinction between activities needing a single national rule and other activities, such as pilotage laws, that were essentially local in nature. In the latter category, states retained a concurrent authority until Congress exerted its paramount power. The *Cooley* rule was essentially a compromise that allowed states to exercise limited control over interstate commerce, and it operated as a practical formula for nearly a century.

Thomas T. Lewis

SEE ALSO Commerce, regulation of; *Passenger Cases*; *Pennsylvania v. Wheeling and Belmont Bridge Co.*; Police powers.

Cooper v. Aaron

CITATION: 358 U.S. 1
DATE: September 12, 1958
ISSUES: Authority of the Supreme Court; desegregation
SIGNIFICANCE: The Supreme Court held that fear of violence did not provide justification for postponing school desegregation, and it also affirmed that its constitutional interpretations were legally binding on governors and state legislators.

In *Brown v. Board of Education* (1954), the Supreme Court ruled that racial segregation of the public schools violated the equal protection clause of the Fourteenth Amendment. The next year, in *Brown II*, the Court ordered desegregation to proceed "with all deliberate speed." The Little Rock crisis of 1957-1958 occurred after a federal district judge approved a desegregation plan that scheduled nine African American students to enter Little Rock's Central High School in September, 1957. When classes began, Arkansas Governor Orville Faubus and the state legislature acted on the premise that they had no legal obligation to enforce the *Brown* decision. Confronted with an open defiance to federal authority, President Dwight D. Eisenhower dispatched federal troops to restore order and to enforce the desegregation order.

With tensions in Little Rock continuing in 1958, the school board asked the district judge to withdraw the African American students from the school and to postpone desegregation until September, 1960. The judge accepted the proposal. In expedited proceedings, the Supreme Court reversed the judge's ruling. Justice William J. Brennan, Jr., prepared a draft of an opinion, which was then reworked and signed by all nine justices. The joint opinion held that postponement was unacceptable because it would violate the constitutional rights of the African American students. In addition, the Court declared that "the federal judiciary is supreme in the exposition of the law of the Constitution," meaning that state governments must recognize the *Brown* holding as "the supreme law of the land." Never before had the Court expressed the doctrine of judicial supremacy in such strong terms.

Although President Eisenhower personally disagreed with the *Brown* decision, he made it manifestly clear that he would use his executive powers to enforce the decrees and interpretations of the Court. Confident of presidential enforcement, the justices were encouraged to take a firm stand in the *Cooper* ruling. It was not until the Civil Rights Act of 1964 that Congress provided statutory support for the desegregation effort.

Thomas T. Lewis

SEE ALSO *Brown v. Board of Education*; Equal protection clause; Judicial powers; Nullification; Race and discrimination; School integration and busing; States' rights.

Copyright

DESCRIPTION: Protection granted to the creator of an original work of authorship fixed in a tangible medium of expression that confers the exclusive right to make copies, create derivative works, distribute, display, or perform the work publicly.

SIGNIFICANCE: In defining the scope of copyright protection, the Supreme Court attempted to balance the rights of the work's creator against the public interest in the free exchange of ideas.

Concerned that a copyright might perpetuate an undesirable monopoly, the Supreme Court care-

In 1954 poet Carl Sandburg gave his support to a proposed copyright law being examined by a Senate subcommittee. In determining copyright questions, the Supreme Court weighs the rights of the public against those of the creator. (AP/Wide World Photos)

fully interpreted the copyright statute. In *Wheaton v. Peters* (1834), the Court stated that a copyright of limited duration is in the public interest, and in *Baker v. Selden* (1879), it held that only the original expression of an idea is copyrightable, not the idea itself. Likewise, in *Feist Publications v. Rural Telephone Service Co.* (1991), the Court decided that copyright does not protect facts unless their selection or arrangement is original.

Although the statute permits certain fair use without the owner's permission, the tension between the owner's rights and the public interest remains. When an otherwise infringing work is alleged to be a parody of the original work, the Court has sought to ensure that the market for the owner's original work is not displaced by the parody. Similarly, the Court has determined the owner's exclusive right to publish the work may outweigh another's claim of fair use when the part of the work used, even if minimal, is the heart of the entire work.

Kurt M. Saunders

SEE ALSO *Feist Publications v. Rural Telephone Service Co.*; Holmes, Oliver Wendell; McLean, John; Patent; Reporters, Supreme Court.

Corporations

DESCRIPTION: Group of people receiving a government charter permitting activities (primarily business) with certain of the rights and responsibilities of an individual.

SIGNIFICANCE: From the 1880's until the 1930's, many Supreme Court decisions struck down government efforts to regulate business corporations. After 1936, however, the Court accepted most assertions of federal authority and became more involved in monitoring details.

Business corporations developed in the early United States mainly in banking and finance. In *McCulloch v. Maryland* (1819), the Supreme Court upheld the federal government's power to charter the second Bank of the United States. This ruling opened the way for the federal government to create the national banking system (1863), the federal reserve banks (1913), and the Federal Deposit Insurance Corporation (1933).

In *Bank of Augusta v. Earle* (1839), the Court ruled that a corporation chartered in one state was free to operate in another state unless the latter prohibited it. This was immensely valuable in promoting competition and the mobility of capital. In *Santa Clara County v. Southern Pacific Railway Co.* (1886), the Court affirmed that corporations as well as people were protected by the due process and equal protection provisions of the Fourteenth Amendment.

Defining Regulatory Scope. From 1866 to 1875 Congress adopted a series of Civil Rights acts designed to prevent discrimination against African Americans. Although these did not apply to employment, they potentially limited the opportunities for corporations to discriminate in matters relating to property and contract. However, a series of Supreme Court cases beginning in 1876 (including the *Civil Rights Cases,* 1883) denied federal jurisdiction over discrimination by private persons.

The coming of the railroads in the middle of the nineteenth century provided the first major opportunity for use of the corporate form outside of financial business. The inherent monopolistic nature of most railroads soon led to state experiments with rate regulation. In 1877 the Court upheld the authority of states to impose such regulations in *Munn v. Illinois.* However, in *Wabash, St. Louis, and Pacific Railway Co. v. Illinois* (1886), the Court forbade states to set rates for interstate shipments. This case helped persuade Congress to create the Interstate Commerce Commission to regulate rail rates in 1887.

By 1890, corporations had extended into many industries. Allegations of monopolistic practices against such firms as Standard Oil led to the adoption in 1890 of the Sherman Antitrust Act. The Court affirmed that collusion among separate firms was illegal in *United States v. Trans-Missouri Freight Association* (1897) and that the Sherman Antitrust Act could be used to block a corporate merger in *Northern Securities Co. v. United States* (1904). In two landmark cases in 1911, Standard Oil and American Tobacco corporations were broken up.

State regulation of rates charged by public utilities such as water, gas, and electricity suppliers also led to appeals to the Court. In *Smyth v. Ames* (1898), the court held that regulation could not deprive a company of a "fair return on the fair value" of its property used to serve the public.

Freedom of Contract. The early twentieth century brought extensive experimentation with protective labor legislation directed primarily against corporate employers. Until the 1930's the Court was generally unsympathetic. In *Lochner v. New York* (1905), the Court struck down an 1897 New York statute limiting weekly work hours for employees. The Court held the law infringed the freedom of contract between worker and employer. Similar reasoning was used in 1923 to throw out a federal law setting minimum wages for women and children in the District of Columbia in *Adkins v. Children's Hospital.* The Court also struck down a 1916 federal law to curb child labor in *Hammer v. Dagenhart* (1918).

The Supreme Court's anti-interventionist position brought it into conflict with the efforts of President Franklin D. Roosevelt to deal with the economic depression of the 1930's. The National Industrial Recovery Act (NIRA) of 1933 authorized corporations and other business firms to form "codes of fair competition"—collusive arrangements that might reduce output or increase prices—to which all firms would have to adhere. The Court held that the program was unconstitutional in *Schechter Poultry Corp. v. United States* (1935). The Court also struck down the Agricultural Adjustment Act of 1933, the Railway Retirement Act of 1934, and the Guffy Coal Act of 1935, all of which had a powerful potential impact on corporations. The outraged Roosevelt sought legislation to increase the membership of the Court.

However, the Court then shifted to a permissive stance toward interventionist programs. It upheld the first federal minimum-wage law (1935) and the National Labor Relations Act of 1935 (also known as the Wagner Act) and revised agricultural and coal regulatory programs and laws regulating securities, exchanges, and holding companies. All these significantly restricted or mandated corporation actions.

Monitoring Details. In the 1960's, new federal economic interventions further restricted the discretionary management of business corporations. The Civil Rights Acts of 1964 and 1968 outlawed discrimination in employment, public accommodation, and housing. The Court upheld their constitutionality, repudiating the rulings of 1883, but sometimes had to rule on their applications. Therefore, in *Los Angeles v. Manhart* (1978), the Court ruled it was illegal to require women to pay more into an employer's pension fund than males, even though women's life expectancy was longer. It also decided, in *Faragher v. City of Boca Raton* (1998), that damage claims for sexual harassment could be upheld against employers even for conduct of which they were not aware and which was against company policy.

In *Youngstown Sheet and Tube Co. v. Sawyer* (1952), the Court struck down President Harry S Truman's seizure of steel industry plants because of a labor dispute. In this case, the issue was one of proper government procedure. The Court also protected the right of corporations to influence public opinion in *First National Bank of Boston v. Bellotti* (1978). Numerous decisions on details have arisen out of the just compensation clause of the Fifth Amendment, including *Penn Central Transportation Co. v. City of New York* (1978) and *Keystone Bituminous Coal Association v. DeBenedictis* (1987).

FURTHER READING

Cohen, William, and Jonathan D. Varat. *Constitutional Law: Cases and Materials.* 10th ed. Westbury, N.Y.: Foundation Press, 1997.

Galub, Arthur L. *The Burger Court, 1968-1984.* Vol. 9 in *The Supreme Court in American Life.* Millwood, N.Y.: Associated Faculty Press, 1986.

Miller, Arthur Selwyn. *The Supreme Court and American Capitalism.* New York: Free Press, 1968.

Paul B. Trescott

SEE ALSO Antitrust law; Capitalism; Civil Rights Acts; Contract, freedom of; Labor; *McCulloch v. Maryland*; New Deal; Private corporation charters; Private discrimination; *Smyth v. Ames.*

Corrigan v. Buckley

CITATION: 271 U.S. 323
DATE: May 24, 1926
ISSUE: Restrictive covenants
SIGNIFICANCE: The Supreme Court upheld a restrictive covenant in the District of Columbia, a ruling that would stand until 1948, more than twenty years later.

Restrictive covenants blocked the sale of properties owned by whites to members of minority groups and were designed to maintain segregation in an area. When a white owner of property controlled by a restrictive covenant subsequently contracted to sell it to an African American, other white owners asked the District of Columbia federal court to enforce the covenant and block the sale. The district court upheld the covenant. The Supreme Court unanimously affirmed the lower court's decision. Justice Edward T. Sanford, writing the opinion for the Court, disposed of various constitutional provisions. He noted that the Fifth Amendment was limited to the federal government (not individuals), that the Thirteenth Amendment protected African Americans only in their personal liberty (not contracts), and that the Fourteenth Amendment applied to states (not the District of Columbia).

The Court further held that the 1866 Civil Rights Act granted all people the legal authority to contract but did not prohibit or invalidate contracts between private individuals such as restrictive covenants. Sanford also said that judicial enforcement of covenants was not the same as state action denying people their Fourteenth Amendment rights. This decision closed the door to racially integrated housing that had been partially opened by *Buchanan v. Warley* (1917). It lasted more than two decades until *Shelley v. Kraemer* (1948) upheld such covenants but banned judicial enforcement as a form of state action prohibited by the Fourteenth Amendment.

Richard L. Wilson

SEE ALSO *Buchanan v. Warley*; Contract, freedom of; Housing discrimination; Restrictive covenants; *Shelley v. Kraemer*; State action.

Corwin, Edward S.

IDENTIFICATION: Political scientist and constitutional historian
BORN: January 19, 1878, Plymouth, Michigan
DIED: April 29, 1963, Princeton, New Jersey
SIGNIFICANCE: Constitutional law expert Corwin traced the history of due process law and criticized the Supreme Court for creating a twilight zone in which neither state nor federal law applied.

Corwin was the premier constitutional analyst of his time, shaping much of the terminology and style of American discourse in the field of constitutional history. His major contribution was in typifying the history of due process of law, from procedural to substantive. Most of his key articles on this subject are collected in his *Liberty Against Government* (1948). Although historians increasingly find use of substantive due process that predates the Fourteenth Amendment, Corwin's general view still dominates. Corwin also questioned the Supreme Court's crippling of national authority and its creation of a twilight zone where neither state nor federal legislation was possible. Corwin, like the Progressives before him, criticized the Court for holding unconstitutional many statutes designed to protect the health, safety, and welfare of the public.

Corwin's other important works include essays on the higher law basis of judicial review and on the federal courts' use of the doctrine of vested rights in the nineteenth century. He also advanced the study of the presidency, especially concerning war powers and foreign power. His most enduring and popular work was *The Constitution and What It Means Today* (1920), a clause-by-clause terse summary of constitutional law that, modified and revised, remained in print more than eighty years later. His preeminence was acknowledged in many ways. He was asked to supervise expansion of his 1920 work into a guide for Congress on constitutional law,

which was revised and updated many times. He was asked to serve as cochair of an American Bar Association committee to oppose the Bricker Amendment (1953), which aimed to limit the scope of international treaties and the president's power to negotiate them, and he has by far the largest number of articles of any author in *Selected Essays on Constitutional Law, 1938-1962* (1963), collected by the American Association of Law Schools. He was a consultant to the Department of Justice in *Carter v. Carter Coal Co.* (1936). Recruited by Princeton University president Woodrow Wilson, Corwin taught for his entire career at that institution.

Samuel Krislov

SEE ALSO Constitutional law; Due process, procedural; Due process, substantive; Foreign affairs and foreign policy; Presidential powers; War powers.

Counsel, right to

DESCRIPTION: The opportunity for defendants in federal criminal proceedings to be represented by lawyers, as guaranteed by the Sixth Amendment to the U.S. Constitution.
SIGNIFICANCE: The right to legal counsel gives people accused of crimes access to expert help in defending themselves in the complex arena of a criminal trial. In 1963 the Supreme Court interpreted the Fourteenth Amendment as extending this element of due process to defendants in state trials.

Although the Sixth Amendment of the U.S. Constitution appeared to contain the right to legal counsel, the exact meaning of that provision was unclear until interpreted by Congress and the Supreme Court. In 1790, while the Sixth Amendment was still being ratified, Congress passed the Federal Crimes Act, which required that defendants in federal capital cases be provided with legal representation. The Court extended this same protection to all federal criminal cases, regardless of whether they involved the death penalty, in *Johnson v. Zerbst* (1938).

Special Circumstances Doctrine. Although some states required the appointment of lawyers even before the Sixth Amendment was ratified, there was no national code of due process that obligated the states to provide legal help for people accused of crimes. It was not until 1932 that the Court imposed even a limited requirement on state courts to provide legal counsel, and as late as 1963, some states still refused to pay for lawyers for poor defendants.

In *Powell v. Alabama* (1932), the first Scottsboro case, the Court, by a 7-2 majority, overturned Alabama's convictions of nine African American youths for raping two white women. The young men had been given a *pro forma* trial and sentenced to death. Although they had received court-appointed lawyers, the attorneys provided a weak defense. The trial judge behaved in an overtly biased fashion toward the defendants, and evidence that might have cast doubt on Alabama's case was never presented by the young men's lawyers. In his majority opinion, Justice George Sutherland did not extend the right to counsel to all state criminal cases, but he did establish the "special circumstances" doctrine. The Court ruled that in state capital cases where there were special circumstances, such as the illiteracy of the defendant, state trial judges were obligated to appoint competent lawyers to represent the accused. For more than thirty years, the special circumstances doctrine would be the law of the land, requiring state courts to appoint legal counsel in only the most obvious and serious situations of defendant need.

A Reconsideration. Although the Court had the opportunity to apply the right to counsel to all state criminal cases in *Betts v. Brady* (1942), it declined to do so, sticking to the case-by-case scheme it had prescribed in the *Powell* case. It was not until the 1963 case of *Gideon v. Wainwright* that the Court finally retired the special circumstances doctrine. Clarence Gideon was a drifter with a history of committing petty crimes. He was accused of breaking into a pool hall and stealing some money and liquor. Although Gideon asked the trial judge to appoint him a lawyer, the judge, relying on *Betts*, refused to do so. After a failed attempt at defending himself, Gideon was sentenced to a long term in prison. Gideon appealed his conviction on Sixth and Fourteenth Amendment grounds to the Supreme Court.

The Court had been looking for just the right case to overrule what most of them considered a flawed decision in *Betts v. Brady*. To reverse *Betts*, the Court needed a case in which an intelligent person, denied a lawyer, had been unable to successfully defend himself. Because Gideon was an intel-

ligent man, there could be no question that the trial judge might have improperly denied him special circumstances status. Likewise, because Gideon was white, there could be no question of possible racial discrimination to muddy the waters. The charges against Gideon were not complicated. Gideon was an intelligent man, with a sympathetic, even helpful trial judge, who failed miserably to defend himself against noncomplex charges. This made *Gideon* the perfect case to overrule the special circumstances doctrine, and on March 18, 1963, a unanimous Supreme Court, speaking through Justice Hugo L. Black, applied the right to counsel to all state criminal proceedings.

In *Argersinger v. Hamlin* (1972) and *Scott v. Illinois* (1979), the Court extended the right to counsel to misdemeanor trials that resulted in jail sentences but not to those that resulted in fines or lesser punishment.

The Pretrial Period. *Gideon* left many important questions unanswered, including at what point in the criminal investigation a suspect who requested a lawyer had to be provided with one. In *Escobedo v. Illinois* (1964), the Court ruled that a suspect asking for counsel during a police interrogation had to be granted representation.

In *Miranda v. Arizona* (1966), the Court went a step further, requiring the police to advise suspects of their right to a lawyer even if they did not ask to speak with an attorney. According to the Court, a person suspected of committing a crime should be provided with a lawyer at the moment that individual ceases being one of several possible suspects and becomes the principal focus of the criminal investigation. The decisions in these two cases showed that, in the Court's collective mind, the Sixth Amendment right to counsel was firmly connected to the Fifth Amendment's protection from compulsory self-incrimination.

FURTHER READING

Garcia, Alfredo. *The Sixth Amendment in Modern American Jurisprudence.* Westport, Conn.: Greenwood, 1992.

Horne, Gerald. *"Powell v. Alabama": The Scottsboro Boys and American Justice.* New York: Franklin Watts, 1997.

Lewis, Anthony. *Gideon's Trumpet.* New York: Vintage, 1989.

Wice, Paul B. *"Miranda v. Arizona": "You Have the*

Right to Remain Silent . . . " New York: Franklin Watts, 1996.

Marshall R. King

SEE ALSO *Argersinger v. Hamlin; Betts v. Brady; Escobedo v. Illinois; Gideon v. Wainwright;* Indigent criminal defendants; *Johnson v. Zerbst;* Miranda rights; *Miranda v. Arizona; Powell v. Alabama;* Self-incrimination, immunity against; Sixth Amendment.

Counselman v. Hitchcock

CITATION: 142 U.S. 547
DATE: January 11, 1892
ISSUE: Self-incrimination, immunity against
SIGNIFICANCE: The Supreme Court upheld a person's refusal to testify before a grand jury, stating that the privilege against self-incrimination extends beyond criminal trials to investigations such as grand jury proceedings.

In *Counselman v. Hitchcock,* the Court considered a federal statute that granted witnesses immunity from criminal prosecution based on their testimony during judicial proceedings but not on their testimony before a federal grand jury. Charles Counselman asserted his Fifth Amendment privilege against self-incrimination in refusing to answer questions before a federal grand jury and asked for a writ of *habeas corpus* when he was confined for contempt of court for not answering.

The Court unanimously upheld his refusal to testify. In his opinion for the Court, Justice Samuel Blatchford stated that the privilege against self-incrimination could be used by an accused not only in a criminal trial but also in any investigation including grand jury proceedings. Federal immunity law could not compel the appellant to testify because its protective scope was less than the Fifth Amendment guarantee. The statute prohibited the direct use of testimony in subsequent prosecution of the witness but not the testimony's use to search for other evidence. This broad privilege was narrowed substantially in *Kastigar v. United States* (1972) when the Court allowed evidence obtained independently to be used against a person who had testified under an immunity agreement.

Richard L. Wilson

SEE ALSO *Adamson v. California;* Due process, procedural; Fifth Amendment; *Habeas corpus; Kastigar v. United States;* Self-incrimination, immunity against.

Court of Justice of the European Communities

DESCRIPTION: Court with jurisdiction over the European Communities (EC), ruling on questions regarding treaties and other agreements that involve the member states.
SIGNIFICANCE: The Court of Justice has broad jurisdiction to ensure the observance of laws in the interpretation and application of the treaties governing the EC. Disputes before the court may be brought by EC institutions, member states, national tribunals, and individuals.

In May, 1950, the French foreign minister, Robert Schuman, proposed to place the whole of French and German coal and steel production in an organization that would allow participation by other European countries (member states). In his proposal was a court of justice that would subject the authority of the new organization to judicial control. In April, 1951, the treaty establishing the European Coal and Steel Community (ECSC) was signed in Paris. It created, among other institutions, a Court of Justice whose judicial structure was strongly influenced by continental administrative law.

When the two Treaties of Rome were signed in March, 1957, establishing the European Economic Community (EEC) and the European Atomic Energy Community (Euratom) respectively, each was given a Court of Justice and a Council of Ministers. The treaties also authorized the creation of a single Court to serve these two communities and the ECSC. The Convention on Certain Institutions Common to the European Communities and the Court of the ECSC became the Court of Justice of the European Communities, based in Luxembourg, where it is in permanent session.

The great innovation of the Court of Justice, compared with earlier institutions that attempted to unify Europe, was its use of the rule of law. The six founding member states (Belgium, France, Germany, Italy, Luxembourg, and the Netherlands) were aware that unification had to be achieved and maintained through legal means and that the EC should be conceived in a legal instrument (Treaties of Paris and Rome). The judicial institution of the EC, the Court of Justice has fifteen judges and nine advocates general to ensure that EC law is not interpreted and applied differently in each member state. To achieve this, the Court of Justice has jurisdiction to hear disputes to which the member states may be parties. The decisions of the Court of Justice cannot be reversed by an act of the Councils of Ministers; however, any measure of the councils having legal effect can by annulled by the Court of Justice if contrary to the treaties or other provisions of EC law. The Court of Justice plays no direct part in the formal legislative process. To maintain its impartiality, the Court of Justice uses judges from a wide range of nations. It draws one judge from each member state, along with an additional judge drawn in rotation from one of the "big four" (France, Germany, Italy, and the United Kingdom, with Spain added to this group in 1988). Unlike judges, advocates general have an ambivalent role: They are members of the Court of Justice but act as independent advisers and do not attend the judges' deliberations; however, they do vote in parity with them on all procedural issues.

Since the court's founding in 1952 as the Court of Justice of the European Coal and Steel Community, more than eight thousand cases have been brought before it. To handle such a caseload while processing cases with reasonable despatch, the Court of Justice requested the Councils to set up a Court of First Instance in 1989 to try cases not brought by member states or by EC institutions. This new tribunal relieves the Court of Justice from examining questions of fact and improving the quality of judicial review.

Importance of the Court. The Court of Justice plays a crucial role in the institutional system set up by the treaties. In particular, it is responsible for maintaining the balance between the respective powers of the EC institutions and between the powers transferred to the community and those retained by the member states. In exercising its powers of judicial review, the Court of Justice is often called on to settle questions of a constitutional nature or of major economic significance. In a 1971 judgment concerning road transport, the Court of Justice held that the member states no longer had the right to undertake obligations with third countries that affected the community rules, determining that the principle of the community's powers in the field of external relations must be interpreted in line with changing circumstances.

The Court of Justice further defined the EC as a community governed by the rule of law with two essential rules: the direct effect of community law in the member states and the primacy of community law over national law. On the basis of those decisions, European citizens may now rely on the provisions of the treaties and community regulations and directives in proceedings before their national courts and may seek to have a national law disapplied if it is contrary to community law.

Interpretation of European Community Law. The Court has been asked to clarify member states' obligations with regard to the free movement of goods and the establishment of a common market and to secure the removal of barriers protecting national markets and undertakings and, generally, of all hindrances to trade between member states. Following the Cassis de Dijon judgment (1979), European consumers may buy in their own country any food product from a country in the community provided that it is lawfully produced and marketed in that country and that there are no serious grounds related to the protection of health or the environment for preventing its importation into the country of consumption. The Court of Justice held in a case concerning Ireland (1982) that measures having no binding effect, such as a commercial campaign, adopted by a member state could nevertheless influence the conduct of traders and consumers and were thus capable of frustrating the aims of the treaty. In 1997 the Court of Justice found against the French Republic for failing to take the measures necessary to prevent certain French farmers from obstructing the free passage over French territory of agricultural products from other member states. In the van Binsbergen and Reyners cases (1974), the Court of Justice swept away obstacles to the enjoyment of those freedoms by holding that the relevant provisions of the treaty had direct effect and could be relied on in the national courts.

The development of the community legal order has been mostly the result of the dialogue that has built up between the national courts and the Court of Justice through the preliminary ruling procedure. It is through such cooperation that the essential characteristics of the community legal order have been identified, in particular its primacy over the laws of the member states, the direct effect of a whole series of provisions and the right of individuals to obtain redress when their rights are infringed by a breach of community law for which a member state is responsible.

FURTHER READING

Bledsoe, Robert L., and Boleslaw A. Boczek. *The International Law Dictionary*. Santa Barbara, Calif.: ABC-CLIO, 1987.

Brown, L. Neville, and Francis G. Jacobs. *The Court of Justice of the European Communities*. 3d ed. London: Sweet and Maxwell, 1989.

Charpentier, Louis. *The European Court of Justice and the Rhetoric of Affirmative Action*. San Domenico, Italy: European University Institute, Robert Schuman Centre, 1998.

Dehousse, Renaud. *The European Court of Justice: The Politics of Judicial Integration*. Basingstoke, England: Macmillan, 1998.

Kommers, Donald, and John E. Finn. *American Constitutional Law: Essays, Cases, and Comparative Notes*. Belmont, Calif.: West/Wadsworth, 1998.

Slaughter, Anne-Marie, Alec S. Sweet, and J. H. H. Weiler, eds. *The European Court and National Courts: Doctrine and Jurisprudence: Legal Change in Its Social Context*. Oxford, England: Hart Publishing, 1998.

Stone, Peter. *Civil Jurisdiction and Judgments in Europe*. London: Longman, 1998.

Martin J. Manning

SEE ALSO British Law Lords; French Constitutional Council; German Federal Constitutional Court; International perspectives on the Court.

Court-packing plan

DATE: 1937

DESCRIPTION: President Franklin D. Roosevelt's proposal to enlarge the federal judiciary in order to liberalize the Supreme Court and protect New Deal legislation.

SIGNIFICANCE: In the proposal's wake, the Court accepted the New Deal's expansion of government power, but Roosevelt lost congressional support and later New Deal social reform was derailed.

Franklin D. Roosevelt inherited a Republican-dominated federal judiciary when he became president in 1933 and had no opportunity to appoint a new justice during his first term. The Supreme Court then consisted of three liberal justices, two moderates, and four conservatives, with six of these justices over seventy years of age. The nation's economy was still suffering the effects of the Great Depression, and Roosevelt developed a set of New Deal programs designed to boost the economy through legislation and government regulation of business and industry.

In 1935 the Court began to reject New Deal legislation as giving unconstitutional powers to the federal government. These decisions were frequently divided, with moderate Justice Owen J. Roberts creating a majority by voting with the conservatives. In January of 1935, the Court rejected provisions of the National Industrial Recovery Act (NIRA) by an 8-1 vote. In May, the Court ruled five to four that the Railway Retirement Act of 1934 was unconstitutional. On May 27, a day known as Black Monday, the Court unanimously invalidated the code-making and price-fixing powers of Title I of the NIRA in *Schechter Poultry Corp. v. United States*, struck down the Frazier-Lemke Farm Bankruptcy Act of 1934 in *Louisville Joint Stock Land Bank v. Radford*, and voided presidential removal of regulatory commission members in *Humphrey's Executor v. United States*. The Court's 6-3 decision in *United States v. Butler* (1936) revoked the processing tax set up by the Agricultural Adjustment Act of 1933. During the spring of 1936, a divided Court announced its decision in *Carter v. Carter Coal Co.*, declaring the Guffey Coal Act of 1935 unconstitutional, and its decision in *Morehead v. New York ex rel. Tipaldo*, invalidating New York State's minimum-wage law. These rulings appeared to threaten the existence of Social Security, the National Labor Relations Act of 1935 (Wagner Act), and many other New Deal innovations.

Roosevelt's Response. Roosevelt had been considering how to deal with the Court's resistance since January, 1935, when, in the *Gold Clause Cases*, it appeared as if the Court might overturn Congress's voiding of bond clauses pledging redemption in gold, which had provided the basis for devaluation and currency regulation. Immediate response became unnecessary when the Court ruled favorably on February 18, but the idea of restraining the Court took root. After *Schechter*, Roosevelt said, "We have been relegated to the horse-and-buggy definition of interstate commerce," causing a public uproar. He began to consider a constitutional amendment that would either give Congress new powers or limit the Court's power. Attorney General Homer Cummings, however, insisted that the problem lay with the Court's current composition. He suggested an increase in the number of justices to create a favorable majority or an amendment requiring retirement at age seventy. In early 1936, Roosevelt came to agree that an amendment would be too difficult to frame, too slow and difficult to pass, and too open to interpretation by the Court. He also was unwilling to propose a remedy during a presidential election year.

The Plan. After his 1936 electoral landslide, Roosevelt was ready to act. Cummings developed a plan linking the number of justices over age seventy with new appointments to the Court, thus establishing a principle to legitimize Court packing. On February 5, 1937, Roosevelt submitted a judicial reform bill; at its heart was a proposal to give his office power to appoint a new federal judge or justice for every one with ten years' service who did not retire within six months after his seventieth birthday. Up to six new Court positions could be established and forty-four on the lower federal tribunals. Roosevelt justified this measure by arguing that aging judges could not keep up with the workload and that additional appointees would help clear out overcrowded federal court dockets, decreasing delays and expense to litigants. However, his intention to create a pro-New Deal Court majority was obvious. In March, he began instead to emphasize the necessity of bringing in younger justices who understood modern facts and circumstances and who would not undertake to override legislative policy.

The proposal was not unconstitutional; Congress had changed the Court's size several times during the nineteenth century. However, Roosevelt's open grab for power provided an opportunity for closet conservatives, previously afraid to attack the New Deal, to criticize him, charging him with attempting to move toward absolute power. Although moderates and liberals disagreed, many feared the precedent would allow later abuse by a

This editorial cartoon in the March 24, 1937, San Francisco Chronicle *ridiculed President Franklin D. Roosevelt's effort to put into effect his New Deal program.* (FDR Library)

reactionary president. Republicans let the Democrats lead the public opposition, hoping to profit from the split within the president's party.

Despite opposition, the proposal seemed headed for adoption until a series of surprising Court actions. On March 29, in *West Coast Hotel Co. v. Parrish* (1937), the Court announced a 5-4 decision upholding a Washington state minimum-wage law similar to that struck down in *Tipaldo*, Justice Roberts voting with the majority. This decision had been completed before the Court-packing proposal, so Roberts's "switch in time that saved nine" was not a response to the president's threat but an acknowledgment of the election results. The Court upheld the Wagner Act in a series of 5-4 decisions on April 12, including *National Labor Relations Board v. Jones and Laughlin Steel Corp.* (1937). On May 18, conservative Justice Willis Van Devanter announced his intention to retire. The Court's decisions on May 24 in *Helvering v. Davis* (1937) and *Steward Machine Co. v. Davis* (1937) upheld Social Security.

The End and Aftermath. Given the Court's ideological repositioning, many politicians believed the Court-packing proposal was now unnecessary. Roosevelt, however, argued that it was still essential, despite the Senate Judiciary Committee's adverse report on the bill and bitter Senate debate. The bill was revised to authorize the appointment of one additional justice each year for each justice who remained on the Court after age seventy-five. The efforts of majority leader Joseph Robinson, expected to be Roosevelt's first Court appointee, made it appear possible in late June that the bill would pass. However, after Robinson died on July 14, the Senate voted seventy to twenty to send the bill back to the Judiciary Committee for further review. It never reemerged.

The Court-packing issue exacted a huge toll. It weakened the New Deal coalition and helped create a conservative coalition of Republicans and southern Democrats that blocked most liberal legislation from 1937 onward. However, Roosevelt (who ultimately appointed eight new justices) had permanently altered the constitutional interpretation of the Court, which from that time accepted a vast expansion of the power of government in American life.

FURTHER READING

Kyvig, David. "The Road Not Taken: FDR, the Supreme Court, and Constitutional Amendment." *Political Science Quarterly* 104 (Fall, 1989): 463-481.

Leuchtenburg, William E. *The Supreme Court Reborn: The Constitutional Revolution in the Age of Roosevelt.* New York: Oxford University Press, 1995.

McDowell, Gary L. *Curbing the Courts: The Constitution and the Limits of Judicial Power.* Baton Rouge: Louisiana State University Press, 1988.

Nelson, Michael. "The President and the Court: Reinterpreting the Court-Packing Episode of 1937." *Political Science Quarterly* 103 (Summer, 1988): 267-293.

Bethany Andreasen

SEE ALSO *Butler, United States v.*; Constitutional interpretation; *Gold Clause Cases*; *Helvering v. Davis*; *Humphrey's Executor v. United States*; Judicial review; *National Labor Relations Board v. Jones and Laughlin Steel Corp.*; New Deal; Roberts, Owen J.; Roosevelt, Franklin D.; *Schechter Poultry Corp. v. United States.*

Courts of appeals

DESCRIPTION: Intermediate appellate courts situated just below the Supreme Court in the judicial hierarchy. They are the appellate workhorses, hearing the majority of appeals from the federal trial courts and federal regulatory commissions.

SIGNIFICANCE: The twelve courts of appeal must decide all cases that are properly brought to their attention, so they handle a large volume of cases. Because of this and the small percentage of appeals heard by the Supreme Court, the importance of these courts is increasing.

In the late 1700's the Supreme Court was overburdened with cases, so Congress took steps to ease its burden. With the Judiciary Act of 1789, Congress created two lower courts, the circuit courts of appeals and the federal district courts. Initially, Supreme Court justices presided over the courts of appeals, riding from city to city to hear cases and sitting on circuit court panels with one district court judge. Because of the strain this placed on the Supreme Court justices as well as a general dissatisfaction with the way these courts were functioning, Congress passed the Judiciary Act of 1801, which eliminated the circuit riding practice. However, a year later, the practice was restored; it lasted until the 1840's, when it fell into disuse. The 1891 Judiciary Act assigned all appellate functions to the circuit courts of appeals, separating these courts from the old circuit courts, which retained jurisdiction over capital cases, tax cases, and some diversity cases until they were abolished at the end of 1911. In 1948 the circuit courts of appeals were renamed as the courts of appeal.

The Courts' Functions. The twelve circuit courts of appeals serve specific geographical areas. The District of Columbia has its own circuit, which is somewhat different in nature from the others because of the district's wealth of appeals from the decisions of administrative agencies and its lack of cases arising from the states.

The courts of appeals have mandatory jurisdiction, which means that, unlike the Supreme Court, they cannot choose the cases they hear but must hear every appeal that comes to them. This makes for a very large docket, and many legal experts worry about the judges' increasing workload. Although the Supreme Court's decisions are reviewable only by constitutional amendment in constitutional cases and congressional enactment in others, the courts of appeals are subject to overruling by the Supreme Court.

Because the Court tends to reverse the cases it takes, some experts think there is some incentive for the judges on these courts to decide in accordance with the clearest Supreme Court pronouncement on the subject in order to avoid reversal. However, others argue that because the Court very seldom reviews the decisions of these courts, any compliance on the part of the courts of appeals with the Court occurs for other reasons. Lower court judges may simply deem it their duty to comply with the Court because it holds moral authority over them. Lower court judges may comply with the Court because they perceive their role to be one of subordination and obedience or because it is easier to simply cite the Court precedent rather than developing their own sound legal reasoning. They may also be looking to maintain a good reputation so that they might one day be elevated to the Court or to another high post within the government, such as attorney general. Whatever the reason, increasingly, it appears that the decision making in these lower courts is in some ways dependent on the decision making in the Court. Therefore, to understand decision making in the courts of appeals, it is necessary to comprehend the relationship between the courts of appeals and the Supreme Court.

The courts of appeals hear many types of cases and disputes that the Supreme Court deems too inconsequential to consider, and therefore their rulings on those cases are relatively more final. The Court trusts that these lower courts will decide cases as it would if it were able to hear all disputes arising in the United States. However, this is not necessarily the case. Therefore, these lower courts exert some level of influence on the Court because they enact some policies basically on their own.

Internal Reviews. The courts of appeals are also monitored internally. Generally, the circuits split the workload among three-judge panels, the membership of which is under the control of the chief judge of the circuit. Sometimes, because of a shortage of judges, district court judges, senior or retired circuit and district court judges, or retired Supreme Court justices sit on these panels as well.

However, in rare instances, the entire circuit is asked to sit on an appeal, reviewing the decision of one of the three-judge panels. This means that, in some circuits, there will be twenty-eight judges hearing oral arguments in a given case. These reviews are called *en banc* (full-court) hearings. The judges hear arguments, write opinions, and perform an error-correction function. However, on the lower courts, in both regular hearings and *en banc* hearings, separate opinions (concurrences and dissents) are far less frequent than they are on the Supreme Court. In addition, at least on some circuits, the assignment of the majority opinion is random, while on the Supreme Court, it usually is deliberate. This makes for some substantive differences between the two federal appellate courts that manifest themselves in differences in decision making.

FURTHER READING

Carp, Robert A., and Ronald Stidham. *The Federal Courts.* 3d ed. Washington, D.C.: Congressional Quarterly,1998.

Epstein, Lee, ed. *Contemplating Courts.* Washington, D.C.: Congressional Quarterly, 1995.

Howard, J. Woodford, Jr. *Courts of Appeals in the Federal Judicial System.* Princeton, N.J.: Princeton University Press, 1981.

Sara C. Benesh

SEE ALSO Appellate jurisdiction; Circuit courts of appeals; Concurring opinions; Dissents; Judiciary Act of 1789; Judiciary Acts of 1801-1925; Lower federal courts; Opinions, writing of; Workload.

Cox v. Louisiana

CITATION: 379 U.S. 536
DATE: January 18, 1965
ISSUE: Freedom of assembly
SIGNIFICANCE: The Supreme Court overturned the conviction of a group of civil rights demonstrators, arguing that the group had a right to demonstrate peacefully even if local government officials disliked their political views.

By a 7-2 vote, the Supreme Court ruled that the conviction of civil rights demonstrators in Louisiana must be reversed because the state had allowed other approved groups to block traffic in similar ways to those convicted in this case. In *Cox*, it appeared that the state had improperly convicted these demonstrators because of the unpopularity of their views. In its decision, the Court was following the logic of time, place, and manner regulations that allow for safe, orderly streets but require like treatment of all demonstrators. Assembly is not as protected as speech is because the First Amendment qualifies assembly by the use of the word "peaceably." This case should be contrasted with *Adderley v. Florida* (1966), in which the Court upheld the conviction of people who had demonstrated on the grounds of a county jail.

Richard L. Wilson

SEE ALSO *Adderley v. Florida*; Assembly and association, freedom of; *Brandenburg v. Ohio*; *Cox v. New Hampshire*; First Amendment; Symbolic speech; Time, place, and manner regulations; *Whitney v. California*.

Cox v. New Hampshire

CITATION: 312 U.S. 569
DATE: March 31, 1941
ISSUE: Freedom of assembly; time, place, and manner regulations
SIGNIFICANCE: The Supreme Court's decision protected the right of local government officials to place nondiscriminatory time, place, and manner restrictions on demonstrators.

Cox is part of a series of cases establishing the government's right to place reasonable time, place, and manner regulations on assemblies as long as these laws do not prevent people from speaking out or favor some speakers over others. It is also one of a number of cases in which the Jehovah's Witnesses challenged various laws as denials of their free exercise of religion. Although the Jehovah's Witnesses were often successful, they did not prevail in *Cox*.

A Manchester, New Hampshire, city ordinance required groups to have a parade license and pay a fee. Some Jehovah's Witnesses marched single file through city streets carrying placards to advertise a meeting but refused to get a license or pay the fee. Upon their arrest, their leader argued that they were not having a parade. Further, they also asserted that the Manchester ordinance was vague, unreasonable, and arbitrary and deprived them of their First Amendment rights as guaranteed by the

Fourteenth Amendment. In its unanimous decision, the Court upheld the ordinance solely as a means of regulating traffic and reasonably providing for orderly, safe streets.

Richard L. Wilson

SEE ALSO *Adderley v. Florida*; Assembly and association, freedom of; *Brandenburg v. Ohio*; *Cox v. Louisiana*; First Amendment; Jehovah's Witnesses; Symbolic speech; Time, place, and manner regulations; *Whitney v. California*.

Coyle v. Smith

CITATION: 221 U.S. 559
DATE: May 29, 1911
ISSUE: Territories and new states
SIGNIFICANCE: The Supreme Court, citing the equality of states, ruled that Congress could not impose conditions on a territory that remained valid after it had become a state.

When Congress passed legislation admitting Oklahoma as a state, it stipulated that Guthrie was to be the capital until 1913. Oklahoma accepted this provision when it became a state in 1907, but after three years, it decided to move the capital to Oklahoma City. Some citizens asked the Supreme Court to decide if Congress could impose conditions that remained valid after admission. After examining cases relating back to the Northwest Ordinance of 1787, the Court, by a vote of 7-2, found that congressional restrictions were an impermissible infringement that made Oklahoma unequal with other states. Justice Horace H. Lurton, writing for the majority, stated that although the Constitution did not explicitly deal with this issue, the Court viewed state equality as an unwritten tradition.

Richard L. Wilson

SEE ALSO Northwest Ordinance; States' rights; Territories and new states.

Craig v. Boren

CITATION: 429 U.S. 190
DATE: December 20, 1976
ISSUE: Sex discrimination
SIGNIFICANCE: The Supreme Court adopted a heightened level of judicial scrutiny when dealing with gender-based classifications alleged to be discriminatory.

Oklahoma law permitted eighteen-year-old women to purchase beer with 3.2 percent alcohol but required men to be twenty-one years old for the same privilege. Curtis Craig and a licensed vendor challenged the law. The state had statistical evidence demonstrating a reasonable basis for the law. The Supreme Court had recognized since 1971 that the equal protection clause of the Fourteenth Amendment applied to classifications based on sex. The issue in the *Craig* case was whether the law should be evaluated according to the rational basis test or the very demanding standard of strict scrutiny, as used in classifications based on race.

By a vote of seven to two, the Court found that the Oklahoma law was unconstitutional. Writing for the majority, Justice William J. Brennan, Jr., demanded that any statute classifying by gender "must serve important governmental objectives and must be substantially related to these objectives." Although the justices were badly divided, *Craig* established the intermediate level of scrutiny for determining whether particular gender distinctions are constitutional, and the compromise has continued ever since. Apparently, the decision did not apply to cases involving affirmative action programs.

Thomas T. Lewis

SEE ALSO Equal protection clause; *Frontiero v. Richardson*; Gender issues; Judicial scrutiny; *Michael M. v. Superior Court of Sonoma County*; *Reed v. Reed*; *Rostker v. Goldberg*.

Craig v. Missouri

CITATION: 29 U.S. 410
DATE: March 12, 1830
ISSUES: Fiscal and monetary powers; states' rights
SIGNIFICANCE: The Supreme Court's split decision in a case involving loan certificates issued by the state of Missouri showed the beginning of the Court's evolution away from the influence of Chief Justice John Marshall.

Article I, section 10, of the U.S. Constitution bans states from emitting "bills of credits." Nonetheless, Missouri had authorized circulating loan certificates, arguing that they were a legitimate exercise of state sovereignty. The state further challenged the constitutionality of section 25 of the 1789 Judiciary Act. In a 4-3 split decision—unusual for the

Supreme Court at the time—the Court overturned the Missouri law authorizing the certificates. In his opinion for the Court, Chief Justice John Marshall used a historical analysis of paper money in America to explain why the Constitution's prohibition on state bills of credit voided the Missouri statute. In keeping with his *Cohens v. Virginia* (1821) opinion, Marshall also defended section 25 of the 1789 Judiciary Act, which granted nondiscretionary authority to the Court.

The three dissenters—Justices William Johnson, Smith Thompson, and John McLean—believed that there was enough variation in the statutory language to exempt the Missouri law from the constitutional provision. Seven years later, the new chief justice, Roger Brooke Taney, upheld a variant of the Missouri currency arrangement in *Briscoe v. Bank of the Commonwealth of Kentucky* (1837).

Richard L. Wilson

SEE ALSO *Briscoe v. Bank of the Commonwealth of Kentucky*; *Cohens v. Virginia*; Judiciary Act of 1789; Marshall, John; States' rights.

Cranch, William

IDENTIFICATION: Supreme Court reporter (1801-1815)
BORN: July 17, 1769, Weymouth, Massachusetts
DIED: September 1, 1855, Washington, D.C.
SIGNIFICANCE: Cranch's reports covered Supreme Court decisions exclusively. Cranch believed the stability of U.S. national jurisprudence depended on keeping a complete record of Supreme Court cases.

The position of reporter of decisions had informal beginnings. The first two reporters, Alexander J. Dallas and Cranch, were self-appointed. Each was motivated by profit and the desire to perform a public service. Cranch was living in Washington, D.C., when one of his real estate ventures collapsed and ruined him. President John Quincy Adams, Cranch's uncle, appointed him assistant judge of the newly created District of Columbia circuit court in 1801. Cranch escaped the 1802 Republican purge of federal judgeships, became chief judge in 1805, and served on the bench for fifty-four years.

When the Supreme Court moved from Philadelphia to Washington, D.C., Cranch began reporting

William Cranch. (Library of Congress)

its decisions. Cranch emphasized that written reports provided attorneys and judges with accurate records, which acted as U.S. case precedent and thereby reduced arbitrary decision making. Law reporting, a tedious task, was not a particularly lucrative private venture. Assisted by the new trend of justices to provide opinion notes in important cases, Cranch was able to produce reports that were praised for their clarity and accuracy. His later works were criticized as being inaccurate and untimely. Plagued by production costs, the quadrupling of the number of cases to report, and the fact that most of the cases addressed topics of little interest to most prospective purchasers, Cranch fell behind schedule in publishing his reports.

C. Morin

SEE ALSO Dallas, Alexander J.; Judiciary Act of 1789; *Marbury v. Madison*; Reporters, Supreme Court; Reporting of opinions; Staff of the Court; Wheaton, Henry.

Criminal syndicalism

DESCRIPTION: A philosophy calling for workers to organize and seize control of economic organizations and politics through illegal use of force.

SIGNIFICANCE: The Supreme Court's rulings on the constitutionality of laws against syndicalism affected the rights of freedom of speech and association.

Between 1906 and 1916 the Industrial Workers of the World (IWW) embraced syndicalism and conducted a "free speech" campaign to propagate the idea of a worker's rebellion. Although local officials suppressed IWW speakers, between 1917 and 1920, twenty-one state and two territorial legislatures passed laws that criminalized syndicalist associations and the advocacy of syndicalism and other ideologies promoting revolutionary change.

The Supreme Court's opinions on the constitutionality of the state criminal syndicalism laws greatly affected the protection of speech and association. In *Whitney v. California* (1927), the justices sanctioned criminal prosecution of Socialist Party member and activist Charlotte Anita Whitney for association with a syndicalist organization with a program that potentially threatened public order. Dissenting, Justice Louis D. Brandeis argued that Whitney's association with a syndicalist political party fell short of being a clear and present danger to the public because no "immediate serious violence was to be expected or was advocated." In subsequent cases, including *DeJonge v. Oregon* (1937), the justices gradually adopted Brandeis's standard and constricted the circumstances in which criminal syndicalism laws could be used to penalize speech and association. Finally, in *Brandenburg v. Ohio* (1969), the justices overruled the *Whitney* decision to protect advocacy "except where such advocacy is directed to inciting or producing imminent lawless action and is likely to incite or produce such action." By 2000, only six states retained laws against criminal syndicalism.

Richard A. Brisbin, Jr.

SEE ALSO Brandeis, Louis D.; *Brandenburg v. Ohio*; *DeJonge v. Oregon*; First Amendment speech tests; *Whitney v. California*.

Crittenden, John J.

IDENTIFICATION: Supreme Court nominee (1828)
NOMINATED BY: John Quincy Adams
BORN: September 10, 1787, Versailles, Kentucky
DIED: July 26, 1863, Frankfort, Kentucky

SIGNIFICANCE: Crittenden, a U.S. senator who strove to preserve the Union, was nominated as associate justice of the Supreme Court. He served as attorney general under two presidents.

Crittenden, son of a Revolutionary War officer, graduated from the College of William and Mary in 1807 and began practicing law in Kentucky. Appointed attorney general for Illinois in 1809, he returned home for military service during the War of 1812.

Crittenden was elected to the Kentucky state assembly in 1812 and gained an appointment to the U.S. Senate to fill an unexpired term in 1817. He was strongly allied with Henry Clay and John Quincy Adams, who made him U.S. district attorney for Kentucky in 1827. The following year, Adams nominated Crittenden to the Supreme Court, but the Senate declined to consider his appointment as associate justice. President William Henry Harrison chose Crittenden as attorney general in 1841, but after Harrison's death, he resigned.

Crittenden returned to the Senate as a Whig in 1842 and became known as an opponent of the annexation of Texas and war with Mexico. In 1850

John J. Crittenden. (Library of Congress)

President Millard Fillmore named him attorney general.

Returning to the Senate in 1854, Crittenden devoted himself to averting civil war. In 1860 he introduced the Crittenden compromise, banning slavery north of a line 36° 30′ N extending to the Pacific Ocean, while permitting slavery south of the line, thus resolving disputes over the issue in new territories and states. A constitutional amendment was proposed to prohibit Congress from passing further laws concerning slavery. The compromise failed.

Crittenden returned to Kentucky where he worked fervently to save the Union, serving as chairman of a border states convention, fighting for Kentucky's neutrality, and attempting to bring back seceding states, until his death in 1863.

Carol G. Fox

SEE ALSO Civil War; Slavery; Territories and new states.

Crow Dog, Ex parte

CITATION: 109 U.S. 557
DATE: December 17, 1883
ISSUE: Native American sovereignty
SIGNIFICANCE: The Supreme Court held that federal law does not preempt tribal authority unless Congress clearly expressed its intent to do so.

Crow Dog, a Brule Sioux, was convicted and sentenced to death in a Dakota territorial court for the murder of another Sioux. Under tribal law, Crow Dog would not have received a sentence of death but would have been required to support the victim's family. He sought a writ of *habeas corpus*, contending that the federal government had no criminal jurisdiction over disputes among Native Americans in Indian territory. The U.S. government asserted that the Treaty of 1868 implicitly provided for federal jurisdiction over criminal prosecutions.

By a 9-0 vote, the Supreme Court ruled in favor of Crow Dog's claim. In his opinion, Justice Stanley Matthews wrote that although Congress possessed the constitutional authority to determine the scope of Indian self-government, it had not clearly expressed its intent to limit tribal authority in Dakota territory. Unless the legislation was explicit, the Indian tribes retained exclusive jurisdiction over Indian affairs on the reservations. Reacting to the decision, Congress in 1885 passed the Major Crimes Act, which provided federal jurisdiction over seven felonies committed on Indian lands.

The *Crow Dog* precedent, which remains good law, requires that treaties and statutes are normally interpreted in favor of retained Indian sovereignty and treaty rights. This principle is especially important in regard to nineteenth century documents that tend to contain many ambiguities. In areas such as the retained rights to hunt and fish, for example, the *Crow Dog* decision often helped Native American lawyers prevail in court.

Thomas T. Lewis

SEE ALSO Indian Bill of Rights; *Lone Wolf v. Hitchcock*; Native American sovereignty; Native American treaties.

Cruel and unusual punishment

DESCRIPTION: A key provision of the Eighth Amendment to the U.S. Constitution prohibiting the most shockingly barbarous punishments and conditions of incarceration.

SIGNIFICANCE: Although elusive and elastic, the concept of cruel and unusual punishment has

Sister Helen Prejean, author of Dead Man Walking, *a book about a man on death row, is a vocal opponent of capital punishment. Opponents of capital punishment often view it to be cruel and unusual punishment.* (AP/Wide World Photos)

enabled the Supreme Court to adjust criminal punishments according to varying standards of decency and proportionality.

Borrowing from the English Bill of Rights of 1688, the Framers of the U.S. Bill of Rights (1791) included in the Eighth Amendment to the U.S. Constitution a prohibition against "cruel and unusual punishment." Like so much else in the Constitution, and particularly in the Bill of Rights, the meaning, scope, and limitations of these figurative words were left to be determined by the Supreme Court. The results have been inconsistent, conflicting, and enigmatic.

The Court has struggled over whether the prohibition sets absolute and immutable standards that persist over time or instead expresses a goal of proportionality that varies depending on the circumstances. Consequently, the body of Court decisions interpreting the prohibition suffers from a lack of cohesion, allowing succeeding justices to fill the words with their own values and sensibilities.

During its first century, the Court paid scant attention to the prohibition on cruel and unusual punishment. In 1910 the Court held, in *Weems v. United States,* that the crime of being an accessory to the falsification of a public document could not justify a sentence of twelve to twenty years at hard labor in chains and a permanent deprivation of civil rights.

It was not until the 1970's that the Court dwelt seriously on the prohibition, most prominently in the context of the death penalty. In *Furman v. Georgia* (1972), a fractured Court, with all nine justices writing separate opinions, struck down capital punishment with a 5-4 vote. Only Justices William J. Brennan, Jr., and Thurgood Marshall found that the death penalty was categorically unconstitutional based on the prohibition against cruel and unusual punishment, which the two justices construed as a flexible device reflecting "evolving standards of decency" based on public opinion, jury verdicts, and legislative enactments.

However, four years later in *Gregg v. Georgia* (1976), a plurality of the Court found that the prohibition did not invariably preclude capital punishment but only prohibited torture, gratuitously painful methods of execution, or punishments not officially authorized by law.

In noncapital cases, the Court has sent mixed signals. In *Rummel v. Estelle* (1980), a 5-4 majority held that sentencing a man to a life sentence for three felonies committed over nine years for crimes totaling $229.11 was not cruel and unusual. However, in *Solem v. Helm* (1983), again on a 5-4 vote, the Court invalidated a life sentence for a man, with prior nonviolent felony convictions, found guilty of passing a hundred-dollar check on a nonexistent account.

Inevitably, the Court will continue to grapple with the dilemma of giving meaning to one of the most opaque provisions in the Bill of Rights.

Stephen F. Rohde

SEE ALSO Brennan, William J., Jr.; Capital punishment; Eighth Amendment; *Furman v. Georgia*; *Gregg v. Georgia*; Marshall, Thurgood; *Rummel v. Estelle*; *Solem v. Helm*; *Weems v. United States*.

Cruikshank, United States v.

CITATION: 92 U.S. 542
DATE: March 27, 1876
ISSUES: Federal enforcement of civil rights; states' rights
SIGNIFICANCE: Based on narrow interpretations of the Fourteenth and Fifteenth Amendments, the Supreme Court severely limited the authority of the federal government to protect the civil rights of African Americans.

Because state courts rarely prosecuted acts of violence against the freed slaves of the South, the Enforcement Act of 1870 made it a federal crime to engage in a conspiracy to deprive a citizen of constitutional rights. In Colfax, Louisiana, an armed group of white rioters killed about one hundred blacks gathered for a political meeting. Federal prosecutors used the Enforcement Act to prosecute and convict William Cruikshank and two others for participating in the Colfax massacre.

The Supreme Court unanimously held that the indictments were invalid. In a complicated ruling, Chief Justice Morrison R. Waite concentrated on the difference between the rights of state and national citizenship. Any assaults on the rights of state citizenship, which included participation in state politics, were not enforceable in federal courts. In addition, the due process and equal protection clauses of the Fourteenth Amendment authorized federal legislation relating only to actions by state officials, not to acts of private persons. Finally, in charging interference with a Fifteenth Amendment right to vote, the indictments failed to specify that the defendants had been motivated by the race of the victims.

The decision in *United States v. Cruikshank* left protection for most African American rights with the southern states, where few people sympathized with their cause. The decision reflected the national mood, which had become tired of federal intervention in southern politics.

Thomas T. Lewis

SEE ALSO Fourteenth Amendment; Race and discrimination; Reconstruction; *Slaughterhouse Cases*; State action; States' rights.

Cruzan v. Director, Missouri Department of Health

CITATION: 497 U.S. 261
DATE: June 25, 1990
ISSUE: Right to die
SIGNIFICANCE: The Supreme Court ruled that the Fourteenth Amendment protects a competent adult's "liberty interest" in refusing unwanted medical treatment even if the result is death and that the U.S. Constitution permits, but does not require, state courts to demand "clear and convincing" evidence of the person's desire before terminating life support services.

In 1983 Nancy Cruzan suffered brain injuries in an automobile accident that left her in a permanent "vegetative state," with no realistic hope for recovery. An implanted feeding tube provided her body with a constant source of nutrition and water. She was one of approximately ten thousand such cases in the United States. In 1987 Cruzan's parents sought permission to have the feeding tube removed, which would result in her death. Missouri's living will statute, however, required clear and convincing evidence that Nancy Cruzan herself would have wanted to have the tube removed. Because the parents could not produce the necessary evidence, the state courts rejected their request.

By a 5-4 vote, the Supreme Court upheld the constitutionality of the Missouri law. In the majority opinion, Chief Justice William H. Rehnquist wrote that the requirement of clear and convincing evidence of a person's desire was reasonable in view of the state's interest in preserving human life. Not only was it possible for family members to be mistaken about what a person would desire, but there was also the real danger that some families might be motivated by a financial incentive to seek a person's demise. Rehnquist noted that the Court in *Jacobson v. Massachusetts* (1905) had balanced an individual's liberty interest in rejecting a medical procedure with the legitimate interests of the state.

Rehnquist was careful not to define the extent of a person's "right to die." Based on the Court's precedents as well as the common-law doctrine of informed consent, an 8-1 majority of the justices were willing to "assume" that the Constitution grants a competent person the right to refuse life-saving nutrition. Justice Antonin Scalia was the only justice to reject this assumption. Rehnquist's opinion did not attempt to draw a distinction between artificial nutrition and more complex forms of medical procedures, nor did it distinguish between patients facing imminent death and patients whose lives might be preserved for many years. Thus, the decision allowed states a great deal of latitude in making laws about living wills and related matters.

The Missouri courts eventually ruled that new evidence provided enough justification to honor the request of the Cruzan family. In *Washington v. Glucksberg* (1997), the Court unanimously agreed that the Constitution does not guarantee any right to physician assistance in ending one's life.

Thomas T. Lewis

SEE ALSO Due process, substantive; *Jacobson v. Massachusetts*; Right to die; *Roe v. Wade*; *Washington v. Glucksberg*.

Cumming v. Richmond County Board of Education

CITATION: 175 U.S. 528
DATE: December 18, 1899
ISSUE: Separate but equal doctrine
SIGNIFICANCE: The Supreme Court refused to enforce the equal stipulation in the separate but equal doctrine governing segregated schools that had been established in its landmark 1896 decision.

Just three years after announcing the separate but equal doctrine in *Plessy v. Ferguson* (1896), the Supreme Court unanimously refused to take action in a case in which school facilities for blacks and whites were definitely unequal. *Cumming*, which amounted to the Court's first approval of racially segregated public schools, was never overturned. John Marshall Harlan, who wrote the opinion for the Court, had dissented vigorously in *Plessy* but was unable to find a clear, unmistakable disregard of equality in *Cumming*.

In 1879 the Augusta, Georgia, school board had established the first African American public high school in the state. The board closed the school in 1897, claiming that the money was needed for black primary school education. Because a Georgia statute explicitly provided for separate but equal facilities, the local judge did not bother to consider the U.S. Constitution in overturning the board's judgment. Still, the Georgia supreme court, without offering any significant reasons, overturned the local judge's opinion.

African Americans argued that under the Fourteenth Amendment's equal protection clause, they were entitled to a high school if one was provided for white students, but Harlan asserted that the African American plaintiffs had to prove the board decision was motivated exclusively by hostility toward African Americans, which was impossible to prove. To reach his decision, Harlan ignored several lower court precedents that went in the opposite direction.

Richard L. Wilson

SEE ALSO *Brown v. Board of Education*; Equal protection clause; Fourteenth Amendment; Harlan, John Marshall; *Plessy v. Ferguson*.

Cummings v. Missouri

CITATION: 71 U.S. 277
DATE: March 20, 1867
ISSUE: Loyalty oaths
SIGNIFICANCE: The Supreme Court overturned statutes requiring loyalty oaths, viewing them as unconstitutional ex post facto laws and bills of attainder.

Justice Stephen J. Field wrote the opinions for both *Cummings* and its companion case, *Ex parte Garland*, which were decided by 5-4 votes with Justice Samuel F. Miller dissenting. *Cummings* involved a Missouri law that retroactively imposed loyalty oaths requiring people in various jobs to swear that they had not aided or sympathized with the southern cause during the Civil War. *Garland* dealt with a federal law requiring attorneys practicing in federal court to swear that they had not supported the Confederacy.

Field noted that, although these statutes did not impose fines or imprisonment, they were punitive because they banned those who could not take oaths honestly from practicing their professions. Sections 9 and 10 of Article I of the U.S. Constitution ban bills of attainder and ex post facto laws at the state and federal level. Field found the statutes in *Cummings* and *Garland* to be ex post facto retroactive legislation (laws that criminalized acts considered legal when committed) and bills of attainder because they imposed punishment without trial to a designated group of individuals. Miller, in dissent, argued that the statutes were not imposing punishment and therefore could not be either bills of attainder or ex post facto laws. This decision, never repudiated by the Supreme Court, was used in *United States v. Brown* (1965) to void a federal law that banned former communists from serving as labor union officials.

Richard L. Wilson

See also Bill of attainder; *Dennis v. United States*; *Ex post facto laws*; *Scales v. United States*; *Yates v. United States*.

Curator

Description: Position officially created in 1974 by the chief justice to chronicle and maintain the history and memorabilia of the Supreme Court.
Significance: The office is responsible for a multitude of tasks relating to Court documents and presentations.

The office has accrued a vast collection of important films, manuscripts, photographs, prints, videos, and other memorabilia associated with the Court and its justices. Other pieces included in the collection are antique furnishings and artwork. The staff maintains records on hoards of research topics related to the Court and answers numerous informational requests from the justices, the public, and scholars. The office also assists with documentaries and publications.

The curatorial staff presents hourly lectures in the courtroom for the more than 700,000 annual visitors. Congressional and private tours are also offered for interested parties. Twice a year the curator's office displays pieces from its collection in an exhibit held in the lower Great Hall. The exhibit also features a film that examines the history and role of the Court.

The first curator was Catherine Hetos Skefos, who held that position from 1973 to 1976, beginning service before the office was officially established.

Andrea E. Miller

See also Chief justice; Housing of the Court; Public information office; Staff of the Court.

Curtis, Benjamin R.

Identification: Associate justice (December 20, 1851-September 1, 1857)
Nominated by: Millard Fillmore
Born: November 4, 1809, Watertown, Massachusetts
Died: September 15, 1874, Newport, Rhode Island
Significance: Curtis was the major dissenting voice in *Scott v. Sandford* (1857), although he had a reputation as a supporter of slavery. He served as chief counsel defending President Andrew Johnson at his impeachment trial.

When Curtis was a child, his father, an officer in the merchant marines, died, and his widowed mother operated a store and circulating library to send her son to Harvard. Curtis graduated in 1829 and attended Harvard Law School but left to practice law. Gradually gaining respect as a lawyer, Curtis turned to politics and was elected to the Massachusetts legislature in 1849. A dedicated Whig and supporter of Daniel Webster, Curtis was chosen by President Millard Fillmore to fill a vacancy on the Supreme Court in 1851. While on the Court, Curtis usually agreed with the majority, although he was a New England Whig among many southern Democrats.

In *Cooley v. Board of Wardens of the Port of Philadelphia* (1852), a case involving jurisdiction over inter-

Benjamin R. Curtis. (Albert Rosenthal/Collection of the Supreme Court of the United States)

state commerce, Curtis upheld Pennsylvania's right to determine and collect fees for pilotage in the port of Philadelphia. Curtis effected a compromise giving the federal government control over foreign and interstate commerce, while states had authority within their borders.

In 1855 Curtis wrote for a unanimous Court in *Murray's Lessee v. Hoboken Land and Improvement Co.*, defining and limiting the concept of due process of law by upholding the solicitor of the treasury's ability to demand payment of debts from a customs official without obtaining a court order.

Curtis is best remembered for his dissenting opinion in the case of *Scott v. Sandford* (1857). Dred Scott, a slave, had accompanied his surgeon-owner to posts in Illinois and the Minnesota territory. Upon the surgeon's death, Scott maintained that his residency in free lands entitled him to freedom. The Court decided against Scott. The case caused controversy as groups debated the issue of slavery, particularly whether it should be allowed in new territories.

Curtis had a reputation as a supporter of slavery or at least as a defender of the status quo to avoid quarreling among the states. His previous deci-

sions had been instrumental in returning runaways to slavery. However, in the Scott case, Curtis dissented vehemently from the majority opinion, and his reputation gave added weight to his words. He rejected the majority opinion that African Americans were not citizens because in 1787 they were considered citizens eligible to vote in five states, and citizens of states are also citizens of the United States. Curtis added that a slave who had lived in a free territory was entitled to freedom. Relations with the rest of the justices immediately became strained, and Curtis resigned.

When President Andrew Johnson faced impeachment proceedings in 1868, Curtis served as his chief counsel, providing logical, lucid arguments instrumental in Johnson's acquittal.

Curtis turned down offers of political appointments, continued his law practice, and taught at Harvard until his death.

FURTHER READING

Fehrenbacher, Don E. *Slavery, Law, and Politics.* New York: Oxford University Press, 1981.

Friedman, Leon, and Fred L. Israel, eds. *The Justices of the Supreme Court: Their Lives and Major Opinions.* 5 vols. New York: Chelsea House, 1997.

Carol G. Fox

SEE ALSO *Cooley v. Board of Wardens of the Port of Philadelphia;* Fugitive slaves; *Murray's Lessee v. Hoboken Land and Improvement Co.; Scott v. Sandford;* Slavery.

Curtiss-Wright Export Corp., United States v.

CITATION: 299 U.S. 304
DATE: December 21, 1936
ISSUES: Presidential powers; foreign affairs
SIGNIFICANCE: The Supreme Court declared that the federal government possesses broad and inherent powers to deal with other countries and that the president exercises primacy in formulating and conducting foreign policy.

In 1934 Congress passed a joint resolution authorizing the president to prohibit the sale of arms to the warring nations of Bolivia and Paraguay. Congress also provided criminal penalties for violators. President Franklin D. Roosevelt quickly proclaimed an embargo. After the Curtiss-Wright Export Corporation was indicted for disobeying the embargo, it asserted that the congressional resolution was an unconstitutional delegation of legislative power to the president.

By a 7-1 margin, the Supreme Court found nothing unconstitutional about the government's arrangement. Justice George Sutherland distinguished between two kinds of legislation, domestic and foreign, and held that the rule against delegation of duties applied only to the former. He theorized that the powers in foreign affairs derived less from the Constitution than from the inherent attributes of a sovereign country. In the international field, moreover, the president has primacy, and Congress "must often accord to the President a degree of discretion and freedom from statutory restriction which would not be admissible were domestic affairs alone involved."

There has been much controversy concerning *Curtiss-Wright*'s expansive views of inherent presidential powers in foreign affairs. The decision was cited by opponents of the War Powers Act of 1973 and by supporters of executive discretion in the Iran-Contra affair. Probably a majority of legal scholars believe that Sutherland's statements about presidential powers are inconsistent with constitutional principles of separation of powers. In *Regan v. Wald* (1984), the Court recognized that the conduct of foreign affairs is under the domain of both the legislative and executive branches.

Thomas T. Lewis

See also Delegation of powers; Foreign affairs and foreign policy; National security; Presidential powers; Rules of the Court; War powers; War Powers Act of 1973.

Cushing, Caleb

Identification: Supreme Court nominee (1874)
Nominated by: Ulysses S. Grant
Born: January 17, 1800, Salisbury, Massachusetts
Died: January 2, 1879, Newburyport, Massachusetts
Significance: Cushing's changing political party affiliations, which he said were the result of his allegiance to the Union, probably cost him a position on the Supreme Court.

Cushing was an accomplished statesman, lawyer, and diplomat who nevertheless requested to have

his nomination to the Supreme Court withdrawn when it became clear that the Senate would not confirm him. President Ulysses S. Grant nominated Cushing on January 9, 1874, but objections soon arose about Cushing's age—he was soon to be seventy-four—and political record, especially regarding his switch from the Whig to the Democratic to the Republican parties. Cushing defended his changing affiliations as being the result of his staunch devotion to the Union, rather than being for or against slavery, but his detractors accused him of being a political chameleon.

Before being nominated by President Grant, Cushing served President John Tyler as a diplomat to China and served as attorney general under President Franklin Pierce, significantly expanding the role of the office during his tenure. After the failed nomination, Cushing served as ambassador to Spain from 1874 to 1877.

Eric Howard

See also Nominations to the Court; Slavery; Tyler, John.

Cushing, William

Identification: Associate justice (February 2, 1790-September 13, 1810)
Nominated by: George Washington
Born: March 1, 1732, Scituate, Massachusetts
Died: September 13, 1810, Scituate, Massachusetts
Significance: Cushing was the first appointee to the Supreme Court. Serving on the Court for almost twenty-one years, he was adept at disposing of cases quickly and tersely by focusing on one simple issue that could resolve each case.

After graduating from Harvard College in 1751, Cushing taught grammar school for one year in Roxbury, Massachusetts. Turning his interests to law, he began his own law practice in 1755. In 1760 he moved to Maine to become a probate judge and justice of the peace. Cushing returned to Massachusetts in 1771 and was subsequently chosen as a justice in the Massachusetts superior court. After the American Revolutionary War began, he was elected to the Massachusetts superior court of judicature, and in 1779 he was elevated to the position of chief justice to replace John Quincy Adams. In 1786 Cushing maintained order and respect for

William Cushing. (Library of Congress)

the law in western Massachusetts by handling the armed rebels in Shay's Rebellion. Cushing's experience with regional disorders made him a strong supporter of the Constitution. He served as the vice president of the Massachusetts state convention that ratified the Constitution in 1788, presiding over most of the proceedings because the president, John Hancock, was ill.

On September 24, 1789, Cushing was nominated to the Supreme Court by President George Washington. He was confirmed by the Senate two days later. Serving more than twenty years on the Court, Cushing wrote only nineteen opinions. His opinions were brief, careful, and straightforward. Because of his previous experience with the early jurisprudence of the American states, Cushing was chosen to write the decisions on the property rights of colonists who had remained loyal to Great Britain during the Revolutionary War. In 1793 he concurred with the majority in the extremely unpopular decision of the Court in the *Chisholm v. Georgia* case, in which the Court upheld the rights of the citizens of one state to bring original suits in the Court against another state. Due to potential economic damage that might occur, this decision led to the adoption of the Eleventh Amendment in 1798.

In 1796 Cushing demonstrated his support of the Federalist agenda in *Ware v. Hylton.* He voted with the majority in concluding that debts encumbered before the Revolutionary War were still valid and that treaties were the supreme law of the land. As a result, President Washington nominated Cushing as the successor to Chief Justice John Jay. Cushing was confirmed by the Senate but resigned after one week due to declining health. However, he kept his position on the bench as an associate justice. Cushing served on the Court the longest of any of the six original appointees, being the only one to serve under both Jay and Chief Justice John Marshall.

Alvin K. Benson

SEE ALSO *Chisholm v. Georgia*; Constitutional law; Eleventh Amendment; Seniority within the Court; *Ware v. Hylton*; Washington, George.

D

Dallas, Alexander J.

IDENTIFICATION: Supreme Court reporter (1791-1800)

BORN: June 21, 1759, Kingston, Jamaica

DIED: January 16, 1817, Philadelphia, Pennsylvania

SIGNIFICANCE: Dallas published edited reports of the first cases decided in the Supreme Court. He also published a pamphlet expressing opposition to Chief Justice John Jay's Treaty of 1794 with Great Britain.

Educated at Edinburgh University, Dallas migrated to the United States and settled in Philadelphia in 1783. In 1793 he helped found the Pennsylvania Democratic Society and was an active politician, serving three consecutive terms as the secretary of state of Pennsylvania between 1791 and 1801. On March 10, 1801, President Thomas Jefferson appointed Dallas as the U.S. district attorney for the eastern district of Pennsylvania, where he served for thirteen years and handled numerous cases.

While waiting for legal cases, Dallas edited the first reports of the Supreme Court and published four volumes of *Reports of Cases, Adjudged in the Several Courts of the United States and of Pennsylvania Before and Following the Revolution*, during the period from 1790 to 1807. Dallas was a strong opponent of Chief Justice John Jay's Treaty of 1794 and published arguments against it in *Features of Jay's Treaty* (1795). President James Madison appointed Dallas as the secretary of the treasury in 1814 at a critical juncture in government finance. Dallas restored public credit, advocated a national banking institution, which passed in 1816, and promoted a protective tariff.

Alvin K. Benson

SEE ALSO Jay, John; Reporters, Supreme Court; *Supreme Court Reporter, United States Reports*.

Alexander J. Dallas. (Archive Photos)

Dames and Moore v. Regan

CITATION: 453 U.S. 654

DATE: July 2, 1981

ISSUE: Presidential powers

SIGNIFICANCE: The Supreme Court upheld actions taken by President Jimmy Carter during the Iran hostage crisis, expanding the U.S. president's broad power to act in foreign affairs.

U.S. embassy personnel in Iran were taken captive in 1979 and held hostage by Iranians. To resolve the crisis before leaving office in January, 1981, President Jimmy Carter signed several executive orders implementing certain actions that met a number of Iranian conditions in return for release of the hostages. The actions included ending legal actions of U.S. citizens and nationals against Iran, voiding attachments against Iranian property in U.S. courts to satisfy judgments against Iran, and transfer of such claims to a new arbitration panel. The Supreme Court upheld these actions even when it was impossible to show that they were authorized by law. Some actions were covered by the International Emergency Economic Powers Act, but others lacked statutory authority. However, the Court relied on past congressional practice and court decisions granting broad executive authority in foreign affairs. The decision was criticized for granting the executive branch extremely broad powers in foreign affairs.

Richard L. Wilson

SEE ALSO Constitutional law; *Curtiss-Wright Export Corp., United States v.*; Delegation of powers; Foreign affairs and foreign policy; Presidential powers; War Powers Act of 1973.

Daniel, Peter V.

IDENTIFICATION: Associate justice (January 10, 1842-May 31, 1860)
NOMINATED BY: Martin Van Buren
BORN: April 24, 1784, Crows Nest, Virginia
DIED: May 31, 1860, Richmond, Virginia
SIGNIFICANCE: As a Supreme Court justice, Daniel was a defender of slavery and an opponent of corporations and federal authority.

Daniel began practicing law in 1808, was elected to the Virginia house of delegates in 1809, and served

Peter V. Daniel. (Max Rosenthal/Collection of the Supreme Court of the United States)

as lieutenant governor from 1818 to 1835. In 1836 he was appointed a federal judge by President Andrew Jackson. On February 27, 1841, he was nominated to the Supreme Court by President Martin Van Buren. He was confirmed by the Senate on March 2 and took office in January of the next year.

At a time when corporations were asserting their legal rights, Daniel believed that the law should not recognize these rights at all. He also opposed expanding admiralty law, which granted the federal government authority over ocean transport, to include commerce on major rivers and lakes.

Although he opposed federal power, Daniel was a strong advocate of state authority. In *West River Bridge Co. v. Dix* (1848), a case involving the power of a state to purchase ownership of a bridge, he wrote the majority opinion in favor of the state. He was also a strong defender of slavery and its control by the states. In *Scott v. Sandford* (1857), he agreed with the majority that the federal government had no power to outlaw slavery in new territories.

Rose Secrest

SEE ALSO Admiralty and maritime law; Corporations; *Scott v. Sandford*; Slavery; *West River Bridge Co. v. Dix*.

Darby Lumber Co., United States v.

CITATION: 312 U.S. 100
DATE: February 3, 1941
ISSUE: Regulation of manufacturing
SIGNIFICANCE: Using a broad interpretation of the commerce clause, the Supreme Court upheld a federal law mandating minimum wages and maximum hours for employees producing goods for interstate commerce.

The Fair Labor Standards Act of 1938, the last major piece of New Deal legislation, applied to employees engaged "in commerce" and "in the production of goods for commerce." Fred Darby, owner of a Georgia company making goods to be shipped out of state, was indicted for paying his employees less than the minimum wage. In his appeal, Darby referred to the precedent of *Hammer v. Dagenhart* (1918), which had held that the U.S. Congress, under the commerce clause and the Tenth Amendment, had no authority to regulate activities that were only indirectly connected to interstate commerce. By a 9-0 vote, the Court overturned *Hammer* and upheld the 1938 statute. Chief Justice Harlan Fiske Stone wrote that Congress possessed the comprehensive authority to regulate any intrastate activities that had either a direct or indirect effect on interstate commerce. Only the employees of companies engaging in purely local activities remained outside the protection of the federal minimum-wage law. Stone's landmark opinion specifically repudiated the doctrine of dual federalism, so that the Tenth Amendment would no longer serve as a significant restraint on federal supervision of anything relating to interstate commerce.

Thomas T. Lewis

SEE ALSO *Carter v. Carter Coal Co.*; Commerce, regulation of; Federalism; *Hammer v. Dagenhart*; Labor; *Lopez, United States v.*; New Deal; Tenth Amendment.

Dartmouth College v. Woodward

CITATION: 4 Wheat. (17 U.S.) 518
DATE: February 2, 1819
ISSUES: Contracts clause; property rights
SIGNIFICANCE: By deciding that a state charter of a private institution was protected by the contracts clause of the Constitution, the Supreme Court enhanced protection of corporate property from interference by the states.

Early in the nineteenth century, many Republicans wanted the states to exercise more controls over a new form of economic concentration—the corporation. Forces favorable to business usually desired fewer controls. Although privately owned and managed, corporations were created by legislative charters. In 1816 the Republican-dominated legislature of New Hampshire enacted three laws that changed the colonial charter of Dartmouth College and imposed a number of public controls. The Federalist-dominated trustees of the school appealed to the Supreme Court.

By a 5-1 majority, the Court declared the New Hampshire laws void because they were an unconstitutional impairment on the obligations of a contract. Writing for the Court, Chief Justice John Marshall found that the college was a private corporation and that the colonial charter was a contract. The states were required to respect such vested rights of private property. In a concurring opinion, Justice Joseph Story suggested that legis-

latures might retain some degree of control by writing "reservations" into charters, allowing for their modification in the future.

The *Dartmouth College* decision promoted the expansion of business interests when they were vulnerable to attack from state legislatures. In effect, the ruling allowed the contract clause to provide most Fifth Amendment protections for private property, which at that time did not apply to the states. The legislatures, however, managed to diminish the impact of *Dartmouth College* by including reservation clauses, as suggested by Justice Story. Also, in *Charles River Bridge v. Warren Bridge* in 1837, the Court took a more limited view of contracts.

Thomas T. Lewis

SEE ALSO *Charles River Bridge v. Warren Bridge*; Contracts clause; Ex post facto laws; *Fletcher v. Peck*; Private corporation charters; Property rights.

Davis, Bancroft

IDENTIFICATION: Supreme Court reporter (1883-1902)
BORN: December 29, 1822, Worcester, Massachusetts
DIED: December 27, 1907, Washington, D.C.
SIGNIFICANCE: As Supreme Court reporter for nineteen years, Bancroft edited volumes 108-186 of the *United States Reports*.

In 1847 Davis graduated from Harvard, opened an office in New York City, and published *The Massachusetts Justice*. Two years later, he was appointed secretary of the U.S. legation in London, but he resigned in 1852 to practice law.

Despite election to the New York State assembly in 1868, Davis was appointed to the State Department in 1869 to arbitrate the Anglo-Portugal dispute over the status of Bulama and to arbitrate the settlement of the Anglo-American dispute over the Alabama claims for alleged damages to U.S. shipping by Confederate cruisers built in Great Britain.

Davis resigned his State Department post to become the American agent before the Alabama claims arbitration tribunal but was reappointed to the State Department in 1873 and designated as minister to Germany by President Ulysses S. Grant in 1874. He resigned his post at the beginning of the Rutherford B. Hayes administration, but Hayes named him to the U.S. Court of Claims in January, 1878. He returned to the State Department in 1881.

Davis was reappointed to the U.S. Court of Claims in June, 1882, but resigned in November, 1883, to become reporter of the Supreme Court. He was always fascinated by the historical development of the law and probably found his true niche as Supreme Court reporter. He edited volumes 108 (fall term, 1882) through 186 (fall term, 1901) and classified and arranged the historical material in the office of the clerk of the Supreme Court, publishing much of it in the appendix to volume 131 of *United States Reports*. He wrote on a variety of mainly historical legal subjects. He resigned in 1902.

Martin J. Manning

SEE ALSO Reporters, Supreme Court; Reporting of opinions; *United States Reports*.

Davis, David

IDENTIFICATION: Associate justice (December 10, 1862-March 4, 1877)

NOMINATED BY: Abraham Lincoln

BORN: March 9, 1815, Cecil County, Maryland

DIED: June 26, 1886, Bloomington, Illinois

SIGNIFICANCE: Known as one of Abraham Lincoln's best friends, Davis is best known for writing the opinion in an 1866 Supreme Court case that limited the use of military authority over civilians in areas not threatened by military action.

Upon graduation from Kenyon College in Ohio in 1832, Davis moved to Massachusetts and read law with a local judge, Henry W. Bishop. Davis attended Yale Law School and was admitted to the Illinois bar in 1835, establishing a private practice in Pekin. During this time, Davis met Abraham Lincoln, a member of the Illinois legislature, who became a lifelong friend. In 1836 Davis moved to Bloomington, Illinois, where he steadily built a reputable law practice.

In 1844 Davis won a seat in the Illinois legislature and served on the education committee. As an elected member of the Illinois Constitutional Convention in 1847, Davis was instrumental in changing the judicial system by advancing reforms so that judges were elected by the people instead of by the legislature. In 1848 Davis was elected as a circuit judge on the Illinois Eighth Circuit, a position he

David Davis. (Archive Photos)

held for fourteen years. Both Lincoln and Stephen Douglas tried cases in his court.

Davis campaigned for Lincoln in his two losing bids for the U.S. Senate. At the 1860 Republican convention, Davis orchestrated the nomination of Lincoln for president of the United States. Subsequently, he advised Lincoln on campaign strategy. After Lincoln's election, Davis advised him in assembling the cabinet.

In 1862 President Lincoln nominated Davis to the Supreme Court. Davis never demonstrated a strong interest in legal scholarship and wrote few important Court opinions. His most noteworthy decision came in *Ex parte Milligan* (1866). The case involved a civilian, Lambdin P. Milligan, who was tried by an Indiana military court and convicted of conspiracy during the Civil War. Eventually, Milligan appealed his case to the Supreme Court. Davis argued that constitutional rights do not cease to exist during wartime and that Milligan's rights had been violated when he was tried by a court that was not sanctioned by Congress and also when he was denied his right to trial by a jury. Davis concluded that the president of the United States had no power to mandate the trial of civilians by a military commission in areas where civilian courts were operating.

After serving on the Court for fourteen years, Davis became bored and wanted to return to the excitement of the political arena. In 1872 Davis had been an unsuccessful candidate for nomination for the president of the United States on the Liberal-Republican ticket. In 1877 he resigned his position on the Court when he was elected as a U.S. senator from Illinois. From 1881 to 1883 Davis served as president pro tempore of the Senate.

Alvin K. Benson

SEE ALSO Constitutional law; Jury, trial by; Lincoln, Abraham; Military and the Court; *Milligan, Ex parte.*

Davis, John W.

IDENTIFICATION: Lawyer, ambassador, and legislator
BORN: April 13, 1873, Clarksburg, West Virginia
DIED: March 24, 1955, Charleston, South Carolina
SIGNIFICANCE: Davis argued more cases (140) before the Supreme Court than any attorney in

John W. Davis. (Library of Congress)

history, including numerous high-profile cases resulting in decisions that changed U.S. jurisprudence and society.

Born in West Virginia and educated at Washington and Lee University, Davis possessed a stoic conservatism that often created conflicts between his personal beliefs and his professional obligations. A meticulous person with a penchant for elegant oratory, Davis served in the U.S. House of Representatives (1911-1913) before President Woodrow Wilson appointed him solicitor general in 1913. During his tenure as solicitor general (1913-1918), Davis won forty-eight of the sixty-seven cases he argued before the Supreme Court, often championing causes (such as antitrust legislation, fair labor practices, and black voting rights) that he personally opposed. Following a stint as ambassador to Great Britain and an unsuccessful run for president, Davis worked on Wall Street as a corporate attorney, winning several landmark probusiness decisions before the Court.

Davis also established a reputation as a civil liberties attorney, successfully defending conscientious objection to military service in *United States v. Macintosh* (1931) and winning a number of key cases pertaining to free press and association. Yet Davis, an ardent segregationist, demonstrated little concern for the rights of racial minorities. In 1952, at the age of eighty, he led prosegregation attorneys before the Court in the case of *Brown v. Board of Education* (1954), in which plaintiffs petitioned the Court to integrate public schools. In his final appearance before the Court, Davis lost the *Brown* case by unanimous decision.

Michael H. Burchett

SEE ALSO *Brown v. Board of Education*; *Guinn v. United States*; Wilson, Woodrow; *Youngstown Sheet and Tube Co. v. Sawyer.*

Davis v. Bandemer

CITATION: 478 U.S. 109
DATE: June 30, 1986
ISSUE: Gerrymandering
SIGNIFICANCE: The Supreme Court held that a gerrymandering scheme that benefits the dominant political party may be examined by the judiciary, serving notice to legislatures that an extreme partisan use of apportionment powers

might be judged unconstitutional by the federal courts.

Indiana Democrats contended that the Republicans, who were in the majority, had sought and obtained partisan advantage in a 1981 reapportionment plan for the election of the state legislature. Irwin Bandemer and other Democrats filed suit, claiming that the scheme violated the equal protection rights of Democratic voters. By a 6-3 vote, the Supreme Court decided that the political question doctrine does not prevent a political party from making an equal protection challenge of partisan gerrymandering. By a 7-2 vote, however, the Court found that the degree of gerrymandering was not extreme enough to constitute a violation of the constitutional rights of the Democrats. Justice Byron R. White's plurality opinion declared that an apportionment scheme that disadvantaged a political party does not necessarily violate the equal protection clause, but that plaintiffs must show evidence that the will of the majority of voters is continually frustrated. It is important to note that the plaintiffs in *Bandemer* did not make any allegations of discrimination against an identifiable racial or ethnic group.

Thomas T. Lewis

SEE ALSO Gerrymandering; Political questions; Representation, fairness of; *Reynolds v. Sims*; *Shaw v. Hunt*.

Davis v. Beason

CITATION: 133 U.S. 333
DATE: February 3, 1890
ISSUES: Freedom of religion; right to vote
SIGNIFICANCE: The Supreme Court allowed a territory to deny the vote to members of a religious sect that advocated an illegal practice.

In the landmark 1879 case, *Reynolds v. United States*, the Supreme Court upheld a federal ban on polygamy, a religious practice of members of the Church of Jesus Christ of Latter-day Saints (Mormons) at the time. Idaho subsequently enacted a territorial statute that denied the right to vote to anyone who practiced polygamy or who belonged to an organization that advocated polygamy. Samuel Davis and other nonpolygamous Mormons sued after they were not allowed to vote in the election of 1888.

By a 9-0 vote, the Court upheld the statute. Taking a very narrow view of both religion and the free exercise clause, Justice Stephen J. Field construed the statute as simply excluding the privilege of voting from those who encouraged and approved of the commission of "odious" crimes. Although persons could not be punished for their beliefs, membership in a church was considered a conduct; therefore membership itself was not protected by the First Amendment. Few people would defend *Davis* a century later. In *Romer v. Evans* (1996), Justice Anthony M. Kennedy observed that *Davis* was no longer good law to the extent that it held that advocacy of a certain practice could be the basis for denying a person the right to vote.

Thomas T. Lewis

SEE ALSO *Employment Division, Department of Human Resources v. Smith*; First Amendment; Religion, freedom of; *Reynolds v. United States*; *Romer v. Evans*; Vote, right to.

Day, William R.

IDENTIFICATION: Associate justice (March 2, 1903-November 13, 1922)
NOMINATED BY: Theodore Roosevelt
BORN: April 17, 1849, Ravenna, Ohio
DIED: July 9, 1923, Mackinac Island, Michigan
SIGNIFICANCE: The first of President Theodore Roosevelt's Supreme Court appointees, Day supported antitrust regulation and state power to regulate economic rights. In his most important opinion, he struck down the Keating-Owen Child Labor Act (1916).

Born in Ohio in 1849, Day was descended from a family of judges. His grandfather and father served as justices on state supreme courts. Day followed in their footsteps, graduating from law school and running his own law practice. During his law career, he became friends with the Republican governor, William McKinley. When McKinley was elected president, he appointed Day to the State Department. McKinley's successor, Theodore Roosevelt, was soon faced with his first Supreme Court appointment and searched for a judge who would favor his antitrust policies. He settled on Day.

The justice did not disappoint him. In the first important antitrust case for the administration, *Northern Securities Co. v. United States* (1904), Day

William R. Day. (Library of Congress)

provided the critical fifth vote in support of the government's prosecution of the company. Throughout his career, the justice consistently supported government regulation of monopolies.

Day was also a swing vote on the critical legal issue of the day, economic rights. Although he was willing to uphold some state economic regulations, he consistently voted to strike down federal economic regulations. It was these contradictory beliefs that placed Day on different sides of important cases during his Court tenure. For example, Day dissented in *Lochner v. New York* (1905), where the Court struck down a state workday maximum-hour law as a violation of liberty of contract. He also disagreed with the Court's decision in *Coppage v. Kansas* (1915), in which a five-member majority struck down a state law prohibiting antiunion employment contracts.

Day did vote to limit federal power in prosecutions. He authored the Court's opinion in *Weeks v. United States* (1914). In *Weeks*, the Court created the federal exclusionary rule, which prohibited the use of any evidence in trial if that evidence had been obtained in violation of the Fourteenth Amendment. The exclusionary rule was used by subsequent Courts to overturn convictions in federal and state cases.

Day is probably best known for his opinion in *Hammer v. Dagenhart* (1918). In *Hammer*, Day wrote for a narrow majority in striking down the Keating-Owen Child Labor Act of 1916. The act prohibited the shipment across state lines of products made by children under the age of fourteen. Day stated that the regulation intruded upon the state power to regulate labor.

After the *Hammer* decision, Day served as a justice for four more years, but old age and ill health made him a less productive member of the Court. By 1922 he had become unable to complete his duties and, after consultation with his colleagues, decided to resign.

FURTHER READING

Baker, Liva. *The Justice from Beacon Hill.* New York: HarperCollins, 1994.

Bickel, Alexander, and Benno Schmidt. *Judiciary and Responsible Government.* New York: Macmillan Press, 1984.

Friedman, Leon, and Fred L. Israel, eds. *The Justices of the United States Supreme Court: Their Lives and Major Opinions.* 5 vols. New York: Chelsea House, 1997.

Douglas Clouatre

SEE ALSO Antitrust law; Exclusionary rule; *Hammer v. Dagenhart*; *Northern Securities Co. v. United States*; *Weeks v. United States*.

Debs, In re

CITATION: 158 U.S. 564
DATE: May 27, 1895
ISSUES: Injunctions; Sherman Antitrust Act
SIGNIFICANCE: The Supreme Court upheld a federal injunction against a labor union in order to protect the U.S. mails and to preserve the orderly movement of interstate commerce. Also, the Court implicitly permitted lower courts to apply the Sherman Antitrust Act (1890) to labor unions.

During the famous Pullman strike in Chicago, members of the American Railway Union throughout the nation refused to handle trains carrying Pullman cars. When this resulted in firings, the union declared new strikes. President Grover

Cleveland's administration sought and obtained a federal injunction against the strikers. The circuit court justified the injunction under the Sherman Antitrust Act of 1890 and the authority of the federal government to deliver the mails. With the spread of violence, Cleveland sent federal troops to Chicago to preserve order. When Eugene Debs, president of the union, refused to honor the injunction, he was held in contempt and given a sentence of six months in jail. He appealed to the Supreme Court on a writ of *habeas corpus*.

Speaking for a unanimous Court, Justice David J. Brewer upheld the injunction and the contempt citation of Debs. Brewer reasoned that the national government possessed a broad constitutional mandate to remove obstacles to interstate commerce and movement of the mails and that it might choose to use either military power or the equity jurisdiction of the federal courts. By maintaining silence about the lower court's reliance on the Sherman Antitrust Act, Brewer's opinion left the door open for antitrust injunctions against union activities in interstate commerce. In *Loewe v. Lawlor* (1906), the Court explicitly ruled that the Sherman Antitrust Act applied to combinations of workers. The Clayton Act of 1914 exempted labor

Eugene Debs, head of the Pullman union, was jailed for contempt of court when he refused to obey an injunction. (Library of Congress)

unions from antitrust injunctions, but the use of injunctions to stop strikes continued until the New Deal period.

Thomas T. Lewis

SEE ALSO Antitrust law; Commerce, regulation of; Injunctions and equitable remedies; Labor; *Loewe v. Lawlor*; Lower federal courts; Sherman Antitrust Act.

Decision making

DESCRIPTION: The ways in which Supreme Court justices make decisions.

SIGNIFICANCE: Because the Court plays a crucial role in public policy making, understanding its decision-making processes becomes crucial.

The Supreme Court is a powerful institution, and its decision making pervades the state of public policy in key areas such as criminal procedure, abortion, religious freedom, sex discrimination, and race relations. Moreover, this very strong institution is also quite autonomous. Its members are appointed for life by the president (subject to Senate confirmation) and are basically free to vote according to their personal policy preferences. However, some constraints arguably inhibit their decision making, including the law, the Constitution, precedent or *stare decisis*, and the preferences of the president and Congress.

The justices follow some general procedures in deciding cases. First, they hear oral arguments presented by the parties' attorneys. Following the week's oral arguments, they hold a conference in which they take a preliminary vote on the merits of the case and assign the opinion. The author of the opinion then circulates a draft for comments. Based on the draft and any dissents or concurrences that may be circulated, the justices decide whether to join in the opinion or to write separately. Who writes the opinion and what it contains is important because that opinion is the Court's policy prescription, the law of the land.

Two major theories, the legal and attitudinal models, dominate discourse on how the Court makes its decisions. The legal model states that justices decide cases according to precedent, the plain meaning of the statute in question, intent of the framers of the Constitution, or the literal wording of the Constitution. In other words, the legal model

This Currier and Ives print depicts the signing of the Declaration of Independence on July 4, 1776. (Library of Congress)

supposes that the justices behave professionally, deciding cases in accordance with objective standards of review. The attitudinal model, however, treats the justices as human decision makers who hope to enact into law their policy preferences. Those adhering to attitudinal theory suggest that the justices decide cases according to their attitudes; liberal justices vote liberally and conservative justices conservatively. Attitudinalists cite the abundance of precedent on either side of any issue, saying that behavior that appears to be legally motivated is really masked ideological decision making.

Some scholars argue that although Supreme Court justices are policy seekers, they also behave strategically, and that strategic behavior may sometimes cause them to vote against a policy they like in order to achieve a more personally important goal. This strategic model supposes that the justices, because of their substantial interaction, influence one another and use that influence to enact the policies most salient to them. Although some argue that the strategic model refutes the attitudinal model, on many levels they appear to be perfectly compatible.

Sara C. Benesh

SEE ALSO Collegiality; Concurring opinions; Conference of the justices; Dissents; Judicial activism; Judicial self-restraint; Opinions, writing of; Oral argument; Original intent; Seniority within the Court; Workload.

Declaration of Independence

DESCRIPTION: Document that declared the independence of the thirteen colonies in America from England.

SIGNIFICANCE: The Supreme Court has been reluctant to treat the Declaration of Independence as U.S. organic law, although Congress placed the document at the top of the U.S. Code.

The Continental Congress adopted the Declaration of Independence on July 4, 1776. Its adoption and publication changed the struggle between England and the thirteen colonies from a rebellion into a war for independence. The declaration was written in June and July, 1776, mostly by Thomas Jefferson of Virginia, with John Adams, Benjamin Franklin, Robert Livingston, and Roger

Sherman. Richard Henry Lee introduced the initial resolution calling for such a declaration on June 7, 1776.

The motion for independence passed by voice vote on July 2, 1776. The motion declared "that these United Colonies are, and of right should be, free and independent states, that they are absolved from all allegiance to the British Crown, and that all political connection between them and the state of Great Britain is, and should be, totally dissolved." Broadsides of the declaration were read in major American cities and to soldiers in the Continental Army throughout July.

On July 19, 1776, Congress resolved to have the declaration written on parchment and signed by every member. John Hancock signed as president of the Congress. Not all the men who were present on July 2 eventually signed the document; some delegates had opposed independence and were replaced by men more in sympathy with the Patriot cause. However, most of the signatures were included by the end of August, 1776, although Thomas McKean of Delaware claimed not to have signed until 1781. The original parchment document is on public display at the National Archives in Washington, D.C.

The adoption of the Declaration of Independence came after more than a decade of constitutional crises within the British Empire. In April, 1775, open warfare began between colonists and British soldiers. The declaration embodied both specific complaints against royal government in North America and general Enlightenment philosophy. Delegates to the Congress agonized over the wording of the declaration and made many changes to Jefferson's original draft. They deleted his inclusion of the African slave trade as one of the crimes of the British people and crown. They removed 480 words, leaving 1,337.

Although Jefferson railed against any changes, the final document became a masterpiece of English prose and political theory. Its assertion "We hold these Truths to be self-evident, that all Men are created equal, and that they are endowed by their Creator with certain unalienable Rights, that among these are Life, Liberty, and the Pursuit of Happiness," remains a powerful expression of American ideals. The declaration describes government as a mutually agreed upon institution designed by people to protect, not grant, these nat-

ural rights. The bulk of the remainder of the declaration listed the specific charges to support the case that the British government had failed to uphold natural rights in America. The declaration asserted that when government failed to uphold natural rights, people had a natural right to alter their government.

Although the Declaration of Independence contained many of the ideas later expressed in the U.S. Constitution and the Bill of Rights, the document is of uncertain legal and constitutional status. The document was placed at the top of U.S. Code as the organic laws of the United States. The Supreme Court, however, has been reluctant to treat it as part of U.S. organic law. Some early reformers cited the declaration as giving them the constitutionally recognized right of rebellion. Many of the declaration's principles found expression in the amendments to the Constitution, particularly the Thirteenth and Fourteenth Amendments.

Barry M. Stentiford

See also Articles of Confederation; British background to U.S. judiciary; Fundamental rights; Jefferson, Thomas; Natural law.

DeJonge v. Oregon

Citation: 299 U.S. 353
Date: January 4, 1937
Issue: Freedom of assembly and association
Significance: The Supreme Court, in overturning a conviction under a state criminal syndicalism law, incorporated the right of freedom of peaceable assembly and association to the states through the Fourteenth Amendment.

Chief Justice Charles Evans Hughes wrote the Supreme Court's unanimous opinion (Justice Harlan Fiske Stone did not participate) overturning the conviction of Dirk DeJonge under Oregon's criminal syndicalism law. DeJonge had helped run a meeting sponsored by the Communist Party to protest actions taken by police against workers. Although DeJonge, some of the other leaders, and about 15 percent of attendees were affiliated with communists, the meeting was entirely orderly. Minor Communist Party activities may have taken place, but no one advocated violence or criminal syndicalism. The prosecution relied heavily on party literature not used in the meeting but found elsewhere that tangentially associated the Communist Party with syndicalism.

The Oregon supreme court upheld DeJonge's conviction on grounds that merely participating in a totally peaceful meeting called by the Communist Party could still violate the law. The Court reversed the decision, saying lawful discussion in a peaceful assembly is not a crime. This decision first applied the freedom of association to the states under the Fourteenth Amendment's due process clause.

Richard L. Wilson

SEE ALSO *Aptheker v. Secretary of State*; Assembly and association, freedom of; *Brandenburg v. Ohio*; *Communist Party v. Subversive Activities Control Board*; Criminal syndicalism; *Dennis v. United States*; First Amendment; Incorporation doctrine; *Scales v. United States*; *Schenck v. United States*; *Whitney v. California*; *Yates v. United States*.

Delegation of powers

DESCRIPTION: The authorization by Congress of a transfer of its lawmaking power to another branch of government.

SIGNIFICANCE: By validating Congress's transfer of considerable lawmaking authority to executive branch agencies and to the president, the Supreme Court contributed to the growth of the federal government's administrative and regulatory power.

The Supreme Court has been called on several times to address the controversial issue of when, if ever, Congress may transfer, or delegate, legislative power to the executive branch. The controversy is rooted in the text of the Constitution, whereby the people have delegated the authority to Congress to exercise "all legislative powers." According to one view, any subsequent delegation of those powers by Congress is unconstitutional and may lead to undemocratic government by unelected, and unaccountable, administrators. For political and practical reasons, this so-called "nondelegation" view has been generally rejected by the Court. With rare, but notable, exceptions, the Court has allowed Congress to authorize executive branch agencies to make law in the form of rules and regulations and to allow the president to make the rules that the president is constitutionally charged to execute.

Early Rulings. In early cases, the Court attempted to respect the principle of nondelegation even while acknowledging that, for practical reasons, the executive and judicial branches had to be allowed to share some of the federal government's legislative responsibilities. Chief Justice John Marshall, writing for the Court in *Wayman v. Southard* (1825), distinguished powers that are "exclusively" legislative from those that are not and argued that Congress may let executive officials "fill up the details" of the nonexclusive powers. In 1892 the Court was asked to decide whether Congress could authorize the president to suspend trade with foreign countries when, in the president's judgment, it was necessary. Asserting that it is a "universally recognized" principle that Congress cannot delegate legislative power to the president, the Court nevertheless upheld this delegation of legislative responsibility to the president.

This ambivalence of the Court toward delegation continued into the twentieth century. As the responsibilities of the federal government grew, Congress created more administrative agencies and regulatory commissions to perform increasingly specialized tasks. The Federal Trade Commission (FTC), for example, was created by Congress to prohibit "unfair methods of competition." In *Federal Trade Commission v. Gratz* (1920), the Court upheld this broad delegation of rule-making authority, as it did repeatedly in similar cases in this period. However, unwilling to completely abandon the principle that legislative power was not to be delegated, the Court crafted the doctrine that delegation was permitted as long as the Congress provides an "intelligible principle" to guide the exercise of delegated powers.

Rulings After 1930. As part of a wide-ranging attack on the New Deal initiatives of President Franklin D. Roosevelt, the Court ruled in *Schechter Poultry Corp. v. United States* (1935) that Congress had not supplied an intelligible principle when delegating legislative authority to the president and to the National Industrial Recovery Administration. After this exceptional case, however, the Court began to issue a succession of rulings validating the delegation of legislative power. In *United States v. Curtiss-Wright Export Corp.* (1936), the Court held that Congress may delegate very broad foreign policy-making power to the president. By the end of the 1930's, a politically weakened Court retreated from the intelligible principle standard, and Congress proceeded to spawn numerous administrative agencies and commissions to deal with the demands of an increasingly complex industrial nation.

In domestic affairs, the Court ruled in *Yakus v. United States* (1944) that Congress could authorize an executive official, the price administrator, to set maximum prices on goods and services, guided only by the vague standard that the prices be "generally fair and equitable." In *Securities and Exchange Commission v. Chenery Corp.* (1947), the Court diluted the intelligible standard principle further by holding that as long as the administrators made a reasonable effort to acknowledge some limits to their discretionary power, the delegation was allowable. In 1970 Congress granted sweeping powers to the president to impose wage-and-price controls. Challenges to the Economic Stabilization Act of 1970 were rebuffed by the Court, even though the guidelines given by Congress to the president were stated in the most general of terms. By 1974 the Court was ready to declare, in *National Cable Association v. United States*, that the idea that there were meaningful limits on Congress's authority to delegate power has been "virtually abandoned by the Court for all practical purposes."

In the 1980's and 1990's the Court continued to allow the delegation of legislative powers, but it signaled that it would impose some constitutional limits. In 1984 Congress chose to create an independent sentencing commission to generate mandatory sentencing guidelines. This commission was to be composed of seven members, three of whom were federal judges. The commission was challenged as an unconstitutional delegation of legislative power to the judicial branch, but the Court upheld its creation in *Mistretta v. United States* (1989). In *Immigration and Naturalization Service v. Chadha* (1983), however, the Court ruled that the legislative veto, a procedure used by Congress to reassume rule-making authority after its delegation to an executive agency or official, was unconstitutional. In *Bowsher v. Synar* (1986), the Court also denied Congress the ability to delegate *to itself* what the Court considered to be an executive power. In this case, the comptroller general was considered to be a legislative officer charged by Congress to perform an executive function, namely, to execute budget cuts. In *Clinton v. City of New York* (1998), the

Court ruled that Congress could not grant the president a line-item veto power whereby he could cancel selected items in spending bills.

FURTHER READING

Cann, Steven J. *Administrative Law.* 2d ed. Thousand Oaks, Calif.: Sage, 1998.

Lowi, Theodore. *The End of Liberalism.* 2d ed. New York: W. W. Norton, 1979.

Warren, Kenneth F. *Administrative Law in the Political System.* 2d ed. St. Paul, Minn.: West Publishing, 1988.

Philip R. Zampini

SEE ALSO Administrative law; *Clinton v. City of New York*; *Curtiss-Wright Export Corp., United States v.*; Elastic clause; *Immigration and Naturalization Service v. Chadha*; *Mistretta v. United States*; New Deal; *Schechter Poultry Corp. v. United States*; Separation of powers.

Democracy

DESCRIPTION: Rule by the mass of people through institutions, processes, and principles that disperse power from the few to the many.

SIGNIFICANCE: While members of the Supreme Court are generally regarded as working to support democratic values, the question of whether the Court advances or impedes democracy rests on what conceptions of democracy are applied.

In some ways, the Supreme Court is an unlikely focus for a discussion of democracy. Within the Court itself, decisions are made democratically by majority votes. On the other hand, the Court's justices are unelected officers—with lifetime appointments—who can overturn the actions of the elected officers of the executive and legislative branches.

Judicial Review. An established feature of American government is the principle of judicial review. Firmly established in the Supreme Court's *Marbury v. Madison* (1803) decision, this principle gives courts the power to invalidate the actions of the executive and legislative branches on constitutional grounds. This power poses what constitutional authority Alexander Bickel called the "countermajoritarian" difficulty. The ability of a tiny body of appointed officials to strike down acts of popularly elected officials seems more characteristic of aristocracy than democracy.

The Framers of the U.S. Constitution were wary of the danger of granting too much power to the masses because of excesses they associated with the ancient Western democracies. However, their own experiences with authoritarian British government made them committed to popular control of government in some form. They eventually settled on a system of mixed government—one with elements of popular democracy, aristocracy, and even monarchy. They wrote no explicit provision for judicial review in the Constitution. Nevertheless, the principle of judicial review is consistent with the principle of checks and balances they provided in the Constitution.

Variant Conceptions of Democracy. Any considerations of whether the Supreme Court advances or impedes democracy require that careful distinctions be made among basic conceptions of democracy. Under a so-called substantive conception, judicial decisions accord with democracy only to the extent that they uphold principles of liberty and equality. For example, in First Amendment cases on which the Court has ruled, its justices have consistently opposed content-based restrictions on free expression. This tendency appears to advance democracy insofar as it protects individual liberties and favors equality.

By contrast, procedural conceptions of democracy emphasize the *processes* through which public policies are made. This approach recognizes that people often disagree over which policies protect substantive democratic values of liberty and equality. What matters is that law be a product of democratic processes. Under a procedural approach, it is presumed that any federal law that wins majority votes in both houses of Congress and has been signed by the president, or passed over a presidential veto, is constitutional. The Supreme Court's presumptive deference to most laws forged by this process is itself thus consistent with democracy.

The Court's *Brown v. Board of Education* (1954) decision illustrates contrasting views of democracy because it involved education, which is connected with both liberty and equality issues. During the years leading up to the decision, the Topeka, Kansas, board of education operated a system of segregated public schools under the separate but equal principle articulated in the Court's 1896 *Plessy v. Ferguson* decision. In the *Brown* case, no proofs were advanced that there had been defects in the process by which Topeka designed its segregated school system. Nevertheless, the Court unanimously struck down its segregated schools under principles articulated in the equal protection clause of the Fourteenth Amendment. The Court ruled not only that did segregated schools undermine the liberty interests of African American children, but also that the very concept of "separate" is "inherently unequal." In making this ruling, the Court looked past form into substance.

Structural Conceptions of Democracy. Related to procedural understandings of democracy is a structural conception. According to this conception, structural principles of government, such as federalism and separation of powers, advance democracy by distributing power. Under this view, the lawmaking processes, such as those considered above, are legitimate only if the principle of separation of powers is maintained. Bicameralism and presentment embody democratic processes only if Congress and the president are not impermissibly invading each other's powers.

Through the last decades of the twentieth century, the Court wavered between substantive and procedural/structural conceptions of democracy. This tendency is illustrated in two post-*Brown* education cases to which the Court applied the equal protection clause.

In *San Antonio Independent School District v. Rodriguez* (1973), a challenge was brought against the Texas state school-financing scheme that spent nearly twice as much money per pupil in some school districts than in others. Although this disparity was a seeming affront to the democratic principles of liberty and equality, the Court did not overturn the system. Instead, it ruled that there was no basis for "judicial intrusion into otherwise legitimate state activities" in the absence of proof of defects in the process by which the financing scheme was enacted. In that case the democratic principles of separation of powers and presumptive judicial deference to process outweighed the democratic principles of liberty and equality.

The Court's 1982 *Plyler v. Doe* decision produced a different result. In that case, a challenge had been brought against a Texas law allowing local school districts to deny free public education to children not legally admitted into the United States. Although the Court conceded its *Rodriguez* rule that education is not a fundamental interest for equal protection purposes, it rendered the liberty and equality interests of immigrant children so compelling and the state's interest in denying them an education so insubstantial, that it invalidated the Texas law by a 5-4 majority. The *Plyler* decision was later generally considered an anomalous ruling whose authority was limited to its facts. Nevertheless, it was clear that in that case, as in *Brown*—but in contrast to *Rodriguez*—the Court elevated the substantive conception of democracy above procedural/structural concerns.

Federalism and Democracy. In American constitutional law, federalism is rooted largely in the Tenth Amendment, which protects state sovereignty against undue encroachments by the national government. In one sense, this is clearly a democratic impulse, insofar as it checks excessive concentrations of power. On a substantive understanding of democracy, however, protection of state power is viewed as antidemocratic by those who believe that liberty and equality are better served by policymaking at the federal level. During the decades following the New Deal, the Supreme Court routinely deferred to the expansion of congressional power under the Constitution's commerce clause to regulate even local activity. Many saw this as democratic insofar as Congress was the source of progressive legislation, such as the Civil Rights Act of 1964. A major tendency of the Court under Chief Justice William H. Rehnquist, however, has been to reverse this trend by reasserting states' rights.

FURTHER READING

Bessette, Joseph M. *The Mild Voice of Reason: Deliberative Democracy and American National Government.* Chicago: University of Chicago Press, 1994.

Bickel, Alexander. *The Least Dangerous Branch.* New Haven, Conn.: Yale University Press, 1962.

Ely, John Hart. *Democracy and Distrust.* Cambridge, Mass.: Harvard University Press, 1980.

Fernbach, Alfred, and Charles J. Bishko, eds. *Charting Democracy in America: Landmarks from History and Political Thought.* Washington, D.C.: American University Press, 1995.

Mueller, Dennis C. *Constitutional Democracy.* New York: Oxford University Press, 1996.

Martin D. Carcieri

SEE ALSO British background to U.S. judiciary; Education; Federalism; *Pennsylvania Coal Co. v.*

Mahon; Rehnquist, William H.; Separate but equal doctrine; Separation of powers; Tenth Amendment.

Dennis v. United States

CITATION: 341 U.S. 494
DATE: June 4, 1951
ISSUE: Freedom of association
SIGNIFICANCE: The Supreme Court upheld the convictions of Communist Party members under the 1940 Smith Act, which led to more vigorous prosecution of alleged communists in the 1950's.

Chief Justice Fred M. Vinson wrote the 6-2 majority decision (Justice Tom C. Clark did not participate) in which the Supreme Court upheld the convictions of eleven Communist Party leaders for violating the 1940 Smith Act by teaching or advocating the "violent overthrow of the U.S. government." Although the Smith Act had always been aimed at communists, the U.S. government had avoided confrontation with the Soviet Union, a World War II ally. As the Cold War began, Republicans and Democrats began to compete with each other to prove their anticommunist fervor. A seriously flawed trial led to the conviction of the eleven party members. The circuit court of appeals upheld their conviction, and the Court agreed to hear the case solely on the question of the Smith Act's constitutionality, thereby eliminating many grounds for reversal. However, the tenor of the times and recent changes in the composition of the Court largely appointed by Franklin D. Roosevelt made it likely that the anticommunist legislation would have been upheld in any case.

Vinson significantly modified the clear and present danger test so that much less serious threats to public safety could be banned by creating a grave and probable danger standard. This view never actually achieved the status of a legal standard because only a plurality of Vinson and three others subscribed to it. Justice Robert H. Jackson rejected the modification of the clear and present danger rule but would have convicted the Communists for conspiracy anyway. Justice Felix Frankfurter disliked the Smith Act but was constrained by his view of judicial self-restraint.

Justices Hugo L. Black and William O. Douglas wrote strong dissents attacking the majority for seriously misreading the clear and present danger test and damaging freedom of speech in the United States. Because one of the activities for which the convictions were upheld was the defendants' plan to publish a newspaper, these dissents also alleged that freedom of the press was endangered. Freed from the constraints of previous interpretations, the government began a vigorous prosecution of the Communist Party that continued until the Court's decision in *Yates v. United States* (1957) blunted the attack. However, *Yates* did not overturn *Dennis* or invalidate the Smith Act. The holding in *Dennis* is at variance with more recent decisions, but the Court never completely repudiated its grave and probable danger rule.

Richard L. Wilson

SEE ALSO Bad tendency test; *Brandenburg v. Ohio*; Clear and present danger test; *Communist Party v. Subversive Activities Control Board*; Criminal syndicalism; Fifteenth Amendment; *Gitlow v. New York*; *Scales v. United States*; *Schenck v. United States*; Speech and press, freedom of; *Yates v. United States*.

Desegregation

DESCRIPTION: Process of dismantling the legally sanctioned system that separated people according to such characteristics as race, religion, or gender.

SIGNIFICANCE: The trend toward desegregation in the 1950's and 1960's and the subsequent movement away from integration and busing that began in the 1970's reflect the larger social and political power struggles that often determine Supreme Court rulings.

In the United States, mandated racial segregation in housing, education, employment, and public accommodations and facilities was widespread, particularly in the South, before it was prohibited in

Troops escort black students during the 1957 desegregation of Central High School in Little Rock, Arkansas. (Archive Photos)

the 1950's and 1960's. Substantive desegregation began with the 1954 landmark decision *Brown v. Board of Education*, in which the Supreme Court struck down the separate but equal doctrine that had authorized racial and ethnic segregation and masked racist inequality since *Plessy v. Ferguson* (1896). The justices who handed down the *Brown* decision were appointed by presidents Franklin D. Roosevelt, Harry S Truman, and Dwight D. Eisenhower, all of whom had, to some degree, taken on the mantle of civil rights.

In *Brown*, the Court unanimously concluded that segregated public schools were "inherently unequal" and unconstitutional. In the unanimous opinion, Chief Justice Earl Warren argued that education was perhaps the most important function of state and local governments and that it was "doubtful that any child may be reasonably expected to succeed in life if he is denied an education. . . . Such an opportunity is a right which must be available to all on equal terms." In *Brown*, the Court also argued that the dehumanizing effects of mandated racial segregation were such that minority children were deprived of equal educational opportunities even when facilities and other tangible factors are equal.

Further Steps. In the late 1960's and the early 1970's, the Court, which had gained a few pro-civil rights justices appointed by Presidents John F. Kennedy and Lyndon B. Johnson, redoubled its desegregation efforts. It not merely opened schools and facilities to all races; it sought to integrate these facilities and ensure that culture and custom did not result in or perpetuate segregation. In *Green v. County School Board of New Kent County* (1968), the Court declared that segregated school systems must be dismantled "root and branch," desegregating facilities, staff, faculty, extracurricular activities, and transportation. These areas of desegregation became known as "Green factors" and were subsequently used as a guide for crafting desegregation plans and for determining whether school districts had achieved unitary status, or fully integrated schools.

Other major steps toward desegregation were taken by the Court in the *Swann v. Charlotte-Mecklenburg Board of Education* (1971) and *Keyes v. Denver School District No. 1* (1973) decisions. In *Swann*, the Court struck down "racially neutral" student assignment plans that produced segregation by relying on existing racially segregated residential patterns. The Court ruled that desegregation must be achieved in each school in a district to the greatest possible extent and approved busing as a means of accomplishing integration. In *Keyes*, the Court first ruled against segregation policies in schools in the North and West and mandated desegregation in these regions.

Limiting the Scope. Appointments to the Court after 1968 were made by presidents whose campaigns promised a more conservative judiciary and a weakening of civil rights policies. In 1971 President Richard M. Nixon appointed conservative William H. Rehnquist to the Court. Rehnquist, who was later elevated to chief justice by Ronald Reagan, was selected for his belief that the Court should play a more restrained, less activist role. In 1991 President George Bush named Clarence Thomas, a staunch conservative critic of civil rights policy, to replace Thurgood Marshall, the former lawyer of the National Association for the Advancement of Colored People Legal Defense Fund who had argued the *Brown* case. By the 1990's the views of Rehnquist and Thomas had become the majority view of the Court.

Leading decisions made by the Court beginning in 1974 reflect a narrowing of the scope and a partial dismantling of desegregation policy. In *Milliken*

v. Bradley (1974), the Court blocked efforts to integrate city schools through a plan that featured interdistrict, city-suburban busing. In a 5-4 decision, the Court rejected a plan to integrate Detroit, Michigan's predominantly African American central-city schools with students from the predominantly white surrounding suburbs, arguing that this remedy would be unfairly punishing to the suburbs. Chief Justice Warren E. Burger cited the "deeply rooted tradition" of local control of public schools as legal rationale. This decision was particularly devastating to civil rights advocates because only a year before, the Court had ruled in *San Antonio Independent School District v. Rodriguez* (1973) that children had no constitutional right to equality of school expenditures. Taken together, the *Rodriguez* and *Milliken* rulings meant that schools in districts with high numbers of nonwhite students did not have the right to either equalization or integration.

In *Milliken v. Bradley* (1977; also known as *Milliken II*), the Court was faced with providing a remedy for unconstitutional segregation in Detroit schools in the light of *Milliken I*. The Court ruled that a state could be ordered to pay for educational programs to repair the harm done by illegal segregation in the absence of actual desegregation. In so ruling, the Court returned what many viewed as a modern version of the separate but equal standard.

Other leading cases that indicate a dismantling of desegregation policy include *Board of Education of Oklahoma City v. Dowell* (1991), which allowed school boards, after being declared unitary (or integrated) by a federal judge, to be released from any obligation to maintain desegregation, and *Freeman v. Pitts* (1992), in which the Court ruled that school districts could be partially released from their desegregation responsibilities without achieving integration in all the areas outlined in the *Green* decision.

In *Missouri v. Jenkins* (1995), the Court ruled that *Milliken II* equalization remedies (paying for programs to repair the harm of segregation in lieu of actually desegregating) should be limited in duration and extent and that proof of correction of the educational harms of segregation was not necessary. In the *Jenkins* decision, the Court defined rapid restoration of local control of public schools to be a new goal of desegregation cases.

FURTHER READING

Massey, Douglas, and Nancy Denton. *American Apartheid: Segregation and the Making of the Underclass*. Cambridge, Mass.: Harvard University Press, 1993.

Orfield, Gary, and Susan Eatonn. *Dismantling Desegregation: The Quiet Reversal of "Brown v. Board of Education."* New York: New Press, 1996.

Wasby, Stephen, Anthony D'Amato, and Rosemary Metrailer. *Desegregation from "Brown" to "Alexander": An Exploration of Supreme Court Strategies*. Carbondale: Southern Illinois University Press, 1977.

Wicker, Tom. *Tragic Failure: Racial Integration in America*. New York: William Morrow, 1996.

Kelly J. Madison

SEE ALSO *Brown v. Board of Education*; Fourteenth Amendment; Marshall, Thurgood; *Milliken v. Bradley*; National Association for the Advancement of Colored People; *Plessy v. Ferguson*; Race and discrimination; Rehnquist, William H.; School integration and busing; Segregation, de facto; Segregation, de jure; Warren, Earl.

DeShaney v. Winnebago County Department of Social Services

CITATION: 489 U.S. 189
DATE: February 22, 1989
ISSUE: Due process clause
SIGNIFICANCE: The Supreme Court held that a state was not liable if its social workers failed to remove a child from the custody of the father even after reports of serious child abuse.

The Winnebago County Department of Social Services received numerous complaints of serious beatings administered to Joshua DeShaney by his father, Randy DeShaney, who was given custody of the boy in a divorce proceeding. Despite repeated reports from family members, physicians, case workers, and emergency medical personnel that the child had suffered from several beatings to the head, the social workers did not remove the boy from the home. Finally, the boy was beaten so badly that he suffered permanent brain damage. By a 6-3 vote, the Supreme Court ruled that a state had no constitutional obligation to protect a child from his father even though the state's social service workers had received multiple reports of serious

child abuse. In his opinion for the Court, Chief Justice William H. Rehnquist found that the Fourteenth Amendment's due process clause was negatively worded and created no affirmative obligation for the state to act, even in cases when the state had notice and the child was very young. Justices William J. Brennan, Jr., Thurgood Marshall, and Harry A. Blackmun dissented vigorously, and Blackmun filed a separate dissent.

Richard L. Wilson

SEE ALSO Due process, procedural; Due process, substantive; Family and children; Fourteenth Amendment; *Gault, In re*; Juvenile justice.

Dillon v. Gloss

CITATION: 256 U.S. 368
DATE: May 16, 1921
ISSUE: Constitutional amendment process
SIGNIFICANCE: The Supreme Court upheld the conviction of a man accused of illegally transporting liquors, approving time limits for ratification of amendments and determining that their effective date would be based on ratification.

Justice Willis Van Devanter wrote the unanimous decision for the Supreme Court upholding the conviction of defendant Dillon for transporting liquors in violation of the Eighteenth Amendment. The defendant had challenged his conviction on grounds that Congress had—for the first time—added a time limit for ratification of the proposed amendment and that the law under which he had been arrested was not yet in force as his arrest occurred less than one year after the Eighteenth Amendment was proclaimed by the secretary of state (although more than one year after its ratification). The Court concluded the deadline for ratification was reasonably contemporaneous and that the adoption of the amendment and not its announcement was the critical issue in the effective starting date of the provision. Subsequent proposed amendments all carried deadlines for ratification. The proposed Equal Rights Amendment contained a deadline that Congress extended in a manner that aroused controversy.

Richard L. Wilson

SEE ALSO *Coleman v. Miller*; Constitutional amendment process; Eighteenth Amendment.

Disability of justices

DESCRIPTION: Physical or mental impairment that prevents a justice from participating fully in the activities of the Supreme Court.

SIGNIFICANCE: Justices who became disabled, usually through illness, and were no longer able to perform their duties effectively were sometimes encouraged to resign or retire from the Court. No ailing justice was ever removed by impeachment.

One of the earliest cases of disability involved Justice Gabriel Duvall, who became a justice in 1811. By 1834, he had become so deaf that it was virtually impossible for him to converse with others. Duvall could not follow oral arguments and was often absent from the Supreme Court. In 1835 he agreed to resign after being informed that President Andrew Jackson would appoint Roger Brooke Taney, a fellow Marylander, as his successor.

A Pension Plan. Before 1869, there was no provision for justices to receive a pension. In that year, a pension plan was established, allowing justices who had served for ten years and reached the age of seventy to retire with salary. The existence of such a plan served as an incentive for retirement; however, a justice who failed to meet these requirements and became disabled would not be eligible for benefits. For the impecunious justice, this posed a significant problem. In the late 1860's, Justice Robert C. Grier, whose service on the Court dated from 1846, became increasingly infirm, and his behavior on the bench increasingly erratic. When the constitutionality of the Legal Tender Act of 1862 came before the Court in *Hepburn v. Griswold* (1870), Justice Grier initially voted in favor of the act but shortly afterward changed his vote to strike down the act. His colleagues were concerned about his continued participation on the Court, and they dispatched Justice Stephen J. Field, the Court's most junior justice, to encourage Grier to resign. In 1870, after the pension legislation became effective, Grier agreed to step down.

Almost thirty years later, a similar situation existed involving, ironically, Justice Field, the Court's emissary in the Grier case. On this occasion Justice John Marshall Harlan was sent to encourage Field, who had served on the Court since 1863, to retire because of his physical condition. Trying to think of a tactful way to raise the issue, Harlan reminded Field of the Grier resignation, hoping that the message might thus be raised obliquely. Field's response was "Yes, and a dirtier day's work I never did in my life." Nonetheless, the message had been conveyed, and Field tendered his resignation in April, 1897, to become effective on December 1, 1897, thereby ensuring that he would eclipse the record tenure on the Court of the late Chief Justice John Marshall.

Congress acted to extend pension benefits by special legislation to Justice Ward Hunt (1872-1882). Hunt suffered a stroke in 1878 that left him incapacitated. Because he had not served long enough to qualify for a pension, he maintained that he could not afford to resign. For a time the Court simply functioned without him. Finally, in 1882 the impasse was broken when Congress enacted a special retirement act for Hunt conditioned on the requirement that he immediately resign from the Court. The bill was shepherded through the Congress by Senator David Davis, a former justice. However, when the brother of Justice Howell E. Jackson (1893-1895) suggested to Chief Justice Melville W. Fuller in January, 1895, that the justice, who was seriously ill, be accorded the same treatment as that given to Hunt, the justices took no action, and Justice Jackson died a few months later.

The Twentieth Century. William H. Moody (1906-1910) contracted acute rheumatism before he had served a sufficient period of time to qualify for a pension. At the behest of friends, Congress passed a special law making him eligible for benefits. Justice Joseph McKenna (1898-1925) became mentally impaired near the end of his career on the Court. Chief Justice William H. Taft and his colleagues were concerned about McKenna's ability to function. He often missed the point of a case and had to have several of his opinions rewritten. The chief justice secured an agreement from the other members of the Court that decisions would not be rendered in cases in which McKenna's vote decided the case. With gentle nudging from Taft, McKenna agreed to retire in 1925. Chief Justice Charles Evans Hughes informed Justice Oliver Wendell Holmes (1902-1932) that the time had come for him to step down. In 1971 Justices Hugo L. Black (1937-1971) and John M. Harlan II (1955-1971) retired from the Court because of declining health. Both died a short time after leaving the Court.

On December 31, 1975, Justice William O. Douglas (1939-1975) suffered a major stroke and, as a consequence, was left partially paralyzed and in considerable pain. After an absence of some months, he attempted to resume his duties. However, it soon became clear to his colleagues and to his friends that he would no longer be able to shoulder his Court responsibilities. Nevertheless, he was reluctant to end his career. Only with the urging of his wife and friends did he accede to their suggestion that he retire. Ironically, the choice of his successor was made by President Gerald R. Ford, who some years earlier, as a member of the House of Representatives, had advocated Douglas's impeachment.

The justices who have incurred serious disabilities have been few in number. The availability of a generous retirement program obviously has made it easier for justices to take leave of the Court when confronted by a major physical or mental ailment. The timely intervention of colleagues on the Court has usually been the most important factor in influencing the disabled justice to leave the Court.

FURTHER READING

Abraham, Henry. *Justices and Presidents: A Political History of Appointments to the Supreme Court.* New York: Oxford University Press, 1985.

Freidman, Leon, and Israel, Fred, eds. *The Justices of the United States Supreme Court: Their Lives and Opinions.* 5 vols. New York: Chelsea House, 1997.

Hughes, Charles Evans. *The Supreme Court of the United States.* Garden City, N.Y.: Garden City Publishing, 1928.

Warren, Charles. *The Supreme Court in United States History.* 2 vols. Boston: Little, Brown, 1922.

Witt, Elder, ed. *Guide to the United States Supreme Court.* 2d ed. Washington, D.C.: Congressional Quarterly, 1997.

Robert Keele

SEE ALSO Circuit riding; Douglas, William O.; Duvall, Gabriel; Field, Stephen J.; Grier, Robert C.; Hunt, Ward; McKenna, Joseph; Moody, William H.; Nominations to the Court; Resignation and retirement.

Dissents

DESCRIPTION: Disagreements with the outcome of a case before the Supreme Court and the

---

CHIEF JUSTICE CHARLES EVANS HUGHES ON DISSENT

There are some who think it desirable that dissents should not be disclosed as they detract from the force of the judgment. Undoubtedly, they do. When unanimity can be obtained without sacrifice or coercion, it strongly commends the decision to public confidence. . . .

Dissent in a court of last resort is an appeal to the brooding spirit of the law, to the intelligence of a future day, when a later decision may possibly correct the error into which the dissenting judge believes the court to have been betrayed.

—Charles Evans Hughes, *The Supreme Court of the United States* (1928).

---

treatment of the involved parties. These disagreements are usually expressed in the form of a written opinion added to the majority opinion.

SIGNIFICANCE: Although a dissenting opinion has no legal effect, it allows justices to call attention to perceived errors in the majority's reasoning and to suggest to potential opponents strategies for circumventing or overturning the majority result. Dissents may also influence the Court's final majority opinion.

Dissenting opinions were relatively rare in the first one hundred years of the Supreme Court's history and were far from the norm even in the early decades of the twentieth century. After the 1940's the number of dissents increased dramatically. Dissents should be distinguished from concurring opinions, in which a justice supports the majority outcome but offers a different rationale for reaching that outcome. Although dissenting opinions may affect the Court's decision making or the development of a law, they have no legal effect whatsoever. A rather cynical law professor was once asked by a first-year student how important dissents were and whether they should be studied. The professor responded that dissents were the equivalent of "judges baying at the moon." Court justices themselves are divided on the significance and effects of dissents.

History of Supreme Court Dissent. Before elevation of John Marshall to fourth chief justice in 1801, Court opinion procedures followed English practice as represented by the King's Bench. English judges delivered their opinions seriatim—each judge announcing his own opinion and the reasoning behind it. Unlike the King's Bench, Supreme Court justices delivered their opinions in reverse order of seniority, the most junior justice speaking first.

Marshall came to the bench with a powerful concern for the independence and authority of the judiciary, and he believed that the Court would command greater respect if it spoke with a single voice, presenting a united front to its opponents. Marshall therefore instituted the practice of issuing a single opinion and discouraged justices from writing dissenting opinions. Through most of his tenure, Marshall dominated the Court, for example, delivering twenty-four of the twenty-six opinions handed down between 1801 and 1805. Marshall's leadership skills, combined with the relative mediocrity of many of the justices who served with him during his thirty-four years on the Court, ensured that the norm of a single opinion for the Court and its corollary of no dissent became strongly embedded.

Although public regard for the Court increased, Marshall was not without his critics, and none perhaps was more vehement than Marshall's frequent political and personal opponent, his cousin President Thomas Jefferson. In an 1820 letter, Jefferson criticized Marshall's practice of issuing a single opinion and urged a return to seriatim opinions, denouncing the "crafty chief judge, who sophisticates the law to his own mind, by the turn of his own reasoning."

Marshall's dominance was not complete. There were dissents during Marshall's chief justiceship, most coming from Associate Justice William Johnson, characterized by a biographer as "the first dissenter." Johnson's first dissent was in *Huidekoper's Lessee v. Douglas* (1805). During Johnson's service on the Court, seventy dissenting opinions were filed, almost half written by Johnson. Marshall himself filed nine dissents and one special concurrence during his years on the Court.

During the tenure of Marshall's successor, President Andrew Jackson's appointee Roger Brooke Taney, dissents became more frequent. Taney was less obsessed with delivering the opinion of the Court himself than Marshall had been, and there were even instances of seriatim opinions. However, Marshall's norm of unity remained strong throughout the remainder of the nineteenth century, with concurring or dissenting opinions in only about 10 percent of the Court's decisions.

Marshall's norm held sway into the early decades of the twentieth century. Justice Oliver Wendell Holmes, who served on the Court from 1902 to 1932, is often referred to as the "Great Dissenter," but he dissented less frequently than his fellow justices did. Much of his reputation undoubtedly rests on the rhetorical quality of his dissents rather than their quantity, as is true of his frequent ally in dissent, Justice Louis D. Brandeis.

The turning point came in 1941 with the elevation of Associate Justice Harlan Fiske Stone to chief justice. Stone's predecessor, Charles Evans Hughes, was a stern taskmaster, and Stone resented Hughes's approach to presiding over the justices' conferences. Stone reacted by allowing extensive and often rambling discussion at conferences and tolerating dissent far more readily than Hughes. Stone's own rate of dissent was higher than that of any previous chief justice. High rates continued under Stone's successor, Fred M. Vinson. In the 1970's and early 1980's the number of dissenting opinions rose dramatically, but after the departure of Chief Justice Warren E. Burger in 1986, dissenters tended to join in a single dissenting opinion rather than write separate opinions. In the 1990's typically the senior justice in the minority assigned one of the dissenters to write a dissent for all to join.

The profound change in judicial norms regarding dissent is evident from a comparison of rates of dissenting opinions on the Warren E. Burger and William H. Rehnquist Courts with those of some of the most notable dissenters in earlier periods. According to one researcher, Brandeis averaged 2.9 dissents per term and Holmes 2.4. Justice William O. Douglas averaged 38.5 dissents per term during his time on the Burger and Rehnquist Courts. Second in line was Justice John Paul Stevens, who, in the period from 1975 to 1994, averaged 21 per term. Indeed, in the modern era, it is by no means rare for justices to dissent from denials of petitions for hearing and to file an opinion explaining their vote, an action considered unthinkable throughout the nineteenth century and into the early twentieth.

Scholars cite several reasons for the high dissent rates prevalent since the Stone Court. To some extent, the kinds of issues faced by the Court after 1937 may explain the erosion of consensual norms. The Court during the New Deal began to hear difficult cases dealing with the nature and scope of individual liberties. An increase in the number of law clerks assigned to each justice made it easier for justices to prepare separate opinions, while at the same time, the Court's dramatically increased caseload (a thousand cases per term during Stone's chief justiceship versus more than four thousand in the 1980's) heightens dissent because the justices no longer have time to engage in the extended discussions necessary for reaching a compromise opinion. Changes in the Court's jurisdiction during the early decades of the twentieth century also may have had an impact. As the Court gained more and more discretion over the cases it would hear and as its mandatory appellate jurisdiction was diminished, the easy cases that in the past would have produced unanimous decisions disappeared, leaving only the more difficult and divisive cases.

Functions of Dissent. The battles that are fought in the conference room over difficult issues are hard and sometimes bitter. Indeed, in abortion, right-to-die, or capital punishment cases, the issues are quite literally matters of life and death. Not surprisingly therefore, one function of dissent is to allow expression of what a justice believes to be fundamental error by the majority. In the last decade of their tenure on the Court, both Justices William J. Brennan, Jr., and Thurgood Marshall knew that in most death penalty cases, they did not and probably never would have the votes to gain a majority for their view that the death penalty constitutes cruel and unusual punishment in violation of the Eighth Amendment. However, they regularly filed dissents in such cases. An opinion expressing their views was programmed into the Court's computer system and automatically added to every capital punishment case in which review was denied.

A dissent may result from a battle among the justices. In *Bowers v. Hardwick* (1986), five justices upheld the constitutionality of a Georgia antisodomy statute as applied to homosexual sex between consenting adults. The fifth vote in that case was supplied by Justice Lewis F. Powell, Jr., who had initially voted with the four dissenters. Justice Harry A. Blackmun was assigned to write for the majority, but when Powell switched his vote a few days after the conference, what was to have been the majority opinion overturning the Georgia statute became a dissent.

Justice Antonin Scalia argues that a dissent, threatened or actual, may serve to improve the quality of the majority opinion by forcing the author to think carefully about the argument and to remove any dubious assertions or reasoning. Scalia also believes that dissents have several external functions. A dissent may augment rather than diminish the prestige of the Court, particularly if history judges the majority's decision harshly. The damage is mitigated if there is evidence that at least some of the justices saw the danger. In 1896 in *Plessy v. Ferguson*, seven justices voted to uphold separate but equal accommodations for blacks and whites. History's judgment of the Court would likely be much harsher were it not for the lone, eloquent dissent in that case by Justice John Marshall Harlan. In the *Bowers* case, later scholarly commentary was more favorable regarding Blackmun's position than that of the majority. After leaving the Court, Powell claimed that Blackmun's dissent in *Bowers* presented the better argument.

Other external consequences of a dissent, according to Scalia, are that it may help to change the law and to give the general public and the legal profession some sense of how the Court as a body thinks about fundamental issues of constitutional law. In the process, the Court is kept where, according to Scalia, it should be, "in the forefront of the intellectual development of the law."

Impact of Dissents. Assessing the impact of dissenting opinions is even more difficult than determining the impact of Court decisions. Undoubtedly some of the internal and external consequences posited by Scalia do occur in some instances, but judging when and to precisely what effect is problematic. Blackmun's dissent in *Bowers* ultimately persuaded Powell, but only after Powell had left the Court.

Some argue that dissents undermine the legitimacy of the Court and may encourage noncompliance. The dissents by Holmes, Brandeis, and Stone that accompany some of the Court's anti-New Deal decisions in the early 1930's provided additional ammunition to President Franklin D. Roosevelt's supporters in the press and in Congress. In certain obvious landmark cases, the Court has gone to great pains to achieve unanimity. Chief Justice Earl Warren's prodigious efforts to produce a unanimous opinion in *Brown v. Board of Education* (1954) are well documented, but the unanimous opinion did not prevent massive resistance to desegregation in the states affected by the decision. In *United States v. Nixon* (1974), the justices consciously strove to produce a unanimous opinion in the face of suggestions from President Richard M. Nixon's attorney that the president would not comply with a fragmented decision. Ultimately, Nixon released the tapes as the Court ordered.

FURTHER READING

Two excellent studies of the workings of the Court provide detailed treatments of its decision-making process, particularly opinion writing: Lawrence Baum's *The Supreme Court* (5th ed., Washington, D.C.: Congressional Quarterly, 1995) and David M. O'Brien's *Storm Center* (4th ed., New York: W. W. Norton, 1996). O'Brien's study situates the Court in the larger context of the legal and political system of the United States. Slightly dated but eminently readable is Charles Evans Hughes's *The Supreme Court of the United States* (New York: Columbia University Press, 1928). For a study of the Court and its procedures compared with courts in England and France, an indispensable source is Henry J. Abraham's *The Judicial Process* (7th ed., New York: Oxford University Press, 1998). On disagreements among the justices, an essential work is P. J. Cooper's *Battles on the Bench: Conflicts Inside the Supreme Court* (Lawrence: University Press of Kansas, 1995), as well as his and Howard Ball's *The United States Supreme Court from the Inside Out* (Englewood Cliffs, N.J.: Prentice-Hall, 1996). Also valuable is Donald E. Lively's *Foreshadows of the Law: Supreme Court Dissents and Constitutional Development* (Westport, Conn.: Praeger, 1992). More general works on the Court's decision-making processes include H. W. Perry's *Deciding to Decide* (Cambridge, Mass.: Harvard University Press, 1991) and Bernard Schwartz's *Decision: How the Supreme Court Decides Cases* (New York: Oxford University Press, 1996). Another excellent and accessible discussion

of the Court's procedures is Chief Justice William H. Rehnquist's *The Supreme Court: How It Was, How It Is* (New York: Morrow, 1987).

Philip A. Dynia

SEE ALSO *Bowers v. Hardwick*; Brandeis, Louis D.; Concurring opinions; Holmes, Oliver Wendell; Johnson, William; Marshall, John; *Nixon, United States v.*; Opinions, writing of; *Plessy v. Ferguson*; Seniority within the Court; Seriatim opinions; Stone, Harlan Fiske.

Diversity jurisdiction

DESCRIPTION: The authority of the federal courts to resolve disputes between citizens of different states or between a citizen and an alien when the total amount of damages in controversy exceeds seventy-five thousand dollars.

SIGNIFICANCE: Diversity jurisdiction, the requirements for which are clarified by the Supreme Court, accounts for a significant portion of the cases heard by the federal courts and was included in the Constitution to provide a forum in which litigants from different states could be assured of fairness.

Article III, section 2, of the U.S. Constitution grants authority to the federal courts to resolve disputes among citizens of different states. In the Judiciary Act of 1789, Congress provided that the federal courts had jurisdiction over cases between citizens of different states or between a citizen and an alien. Although the Constitution imposes no requirement as to a minimum amount of damages that must be involved in order to invoke diversity jurisdiction, Congress imposed a requirement that the amount in controversy, exclusive of interest and costs, must exceed a stated sum of damages. The requisite amount has increased over time and was set at seventy-five thousand dollars in the 1990's.

All cases brought under diversity jurisdiction can also be brought in a state court in which one of the litigants is situated. However, the framers of the Constitution created diversity jurisdiction out of a concern that state courts would be prejudiced against litigants from out of state. They believed that federal courts would serve as neutral forums in which citizens of one state would not be favored over those from another state. As Chief Justice

John Marshall explained in *Bank of the United States v. Deveaux* (1809), "However true the fact may be, that the tribunals of the states will administer justice as impartially as those of the nation, to parties of every description, it is not less true that the Constitution itself either entertains apprehensions on this subject, or views with such indulgence the possible fears and apprehensions of suitors."

The Supreme Court has clarified the two requirements for diversity jurisdiction. The Court has strictly interpreted the requirement that the case involve citizens from different states, holding in the case of *Strawbridge v. Curtiss* (1806) that there has to be "complete diversity" so that all the plaintiffs must be citizens of different states than all the defendants. In addition, the Court has held that the citizenship of an individual is determined by the state of his or her domicile at the time the case is filed, while a corporation is considered to be a citizen of its state of incorporation and the state where it has its principal place of business. In determining the required jurisdictional amount, the Court held in *St. Paul Mercury Indemnity Co. v. Red Cab Co.* (1938) that the sum claimed by the plaintiff controls whether the requirement is met, as long as it made in good faith.

FURTHER READING

James, Fleming, Jr., Geoffrey C. Hazard, Jr., and John Leubsdorf. *Civil Procedure.* 4th ed. Boston: Little, Brown, 1992.

Wright, Charles A. *Law of Federal Courts.* St. Paul, Minn.: West Publishing, 1994.

Kurt M. Saunders

SEE ALSO *Bank of the United States v. Deveaux;* Constitution, U.S.; Judiciary Act of 1789; Lower federal courts; *Strawbridge v. Curtiss.*

Dobbins v. Erie County

CITATION: 41 U.S. 435
DATE: March 4, 1842
ISSUE: State taxation
SIGNIFICANCE: In this important example of the nineteenth century view of federalism, the Supreme Court ruled that a state could not tax a person's federal income.

A U.S. ship captain on duty in Pennsylvania challenged the validity of that state's tax on his federal income. The state supreme court upheld the tax, but the Supreme Court unanimously reversed its decision, holding that such a tax would infringe on the taxing power of the national government.

Dobbins is historically significant as an example of the nineteenth century view of federalism. It followed Chief Justice John Marshall's landmark decision in *McCulloch v. Maryland* (1819) by interpreting the parallel immunities of both the federal and state governments broadly so that neither could tax the other. It remained valid until indirectly overturned in *Graves v. New York ex rel. O'Keefe* (1939) and is no longer a valid legal principle.

Richard L. Wilson

SEE ALSO *Collector v. Day; Graves v. New York ex rel. O'Keefe; Helvering v. Davis; McCulloch v. Maryland;* Separation of powers; State taxation; Tax immunities.

Dodge v. Woolsey

CITATION: 59 U.S. 331
DATE: February 6, 1856
ISSUES: Contracts; injunctions
SIGNIFICANCE: The Supreme Court's ruling that the state of Ohio's attempt to collect a tax from a bank chartered in its state constituted a breach of contract exemplifies the nineteenth century view of contracts and federalism.

Justice James M. Wayne wrote this 6-3 decision upholding an injunction against the collection of a tax by the state of Ohio on one of the banks chartered in the state. This bank was chartered under an Ohio statute pursuant to the state constitution that allowed it to pay 6 percent of its profits instead of paying taxes. That constitution and law were replaced in 1851 by a new law levying a higher tax than the old percentage of the profits, and John Woolsey, a bank shareholder, sued to enjoin collection of the tax on grounds that the original charter represented a contract that was being infringed by Ohio. The Court upheld this view of the contract and the injunction, although the Court later ruled that such a contractual provision had to be specific to a contract and not just a part of a general statute. However, *Dodge* was never overturned.

Richard L. Wilson

SEE ALSO Contracts clause; Injunctions and equitable remedies; Tax immunities.

Doe v. Bolton

CITATION: 410 U.S. 179
DATE: January 22, 1973
ISSUE: Abortion
SIGNIFICANCE: In a companion case to *Roe v. Wade* (1973), the Supreme Court ruled that Georgia's restrictions on a woman's right to terminate a pregnancy were unconstitutional.

Before the Supreme Court's 1973 decision in *Doe v. Bolton*, Georgia's abortion legislation stipulated that only medically necessary abortions were allowed and that abortions were available only to state residents. In addition, all abortions had to be performed in licensed hospitals and approved beforehand by a hospital committee, with two physicians concurring that the abortion was necessary. Based on the principles established in *Roe v. Wade* (1973), decided on the same day, the Court found that all these regulations infringed on a woman's fundamental right to terminate an unwanted pregnancy before the fetus attains viability. The *Doe* decision made it clear that the Court would apply the strict scrutiny test in deciding whether restraints on abortions were permissible.

Thomas T. Lewis

SEE ALSO Abortion; Due process, substantive; Judicial scrutiny; *Roe v. Wade*.

Dolan v. City of Tigard

CITATION: 512 U.S. 374
DATE: June 24, 1994
ISSUE: Takings
SIGNIFICANCE: The Supreme Court held that the government may not attach conditions to building permits that result in the taking of private property without just compensation, in violation of the Fifth and Fourteenth Amendments.

Florence Dolan applied for a building permit to expand her plumbing and electrical supply store in Tigard, Oregon. As part of a land-management program, the city refused to issue the permit unless she dedicated 10 percent of her land for two purposes: a public greenway for flood control and a pedestrian/bicycle pathway to relieve traffic congestion in the city. Dolan claimed that this requirement of dedicating land for a permit constituted a

taking of private property without compensation. The state's high court rejected her claim.

By a 5-4 vote, the Supreme Court remanded the case for reconsideration. Speaking for the majority, Chief Justice William H. Rehnquist concluded that in the circumstances, the city had the burden to show a "rough proportionality" between the building permit requirements and the individualized problems associated with the building project. Judging from the record, Rehnquist did not think the city had demonstrated a reasonable relationship between the project and the need for the greenway space and the pathway. If the city simply wanted some of Dolan's land for drainage and recreation purposes, it would be required to pay her just compensation. In a dissent, Justice John Paul Stevens criticized the majority for imposing a "novel burden of proof" on a city implementing a valid land-use plan.

Thomas T. Lewis

SEE ALSO *Nollan v. California Coastal Commission*; Property rights; Takings clause; Zoning.

Dombrowski v. Pfister

CITATION: 380 U.S. 499
DATE: April 26, 1965
ISSUES: Abstention doctrine; comity clause
SIGNIFICANCE: The Supreme Court held that a federal court may enjoin the enforcement of an excessively vague state statute when there is evidence of bad faith and harassment in the enforcement of the statute.

According to the doctrine of abstention, federal courts normally do not intervene in state court proceedings until after they are finalized. James Dombrowski, leader of a civil rights organization in Louisiana, alleged that state officials were using broad antisubversion statutes as an excuse to harass and intimidate members of his organization. Citing the abstention doctrine, a federal court refused Dombrowski's request for an injunction. By a 5-2 vote, however, the Supreme Court reversed the judgment. Justice William J. Brennan, Jr.'s opinion for the majority argued that the intervention was justified because the statutes were "overly broad and vague regulations of expressions" and because the harassment and bad faith of state officials produced a "chilling effect" on free speech. In dissent,

Justice John M. Harlan II argued that the Court's departure from the traditional abstention doctrine was contrary to principles of federalism and comity.

At first the *Dombrowski* decision led to a large number of lawsuits, but a narrow interpretation of the decision in *Younger v. Harris* (1971) greatly limited the scope of federal intervention.

Thomas T. Lewis

SEE ALSO Chase, Samuel; Federalism; Judicial review; *Younger v. Harris.*

Double jeopardy

DESCRIPTION: Guarantee, stated in the Fifth Amendment, that if a person has been acquitted or convicted of an offense, he or she cannot be prosecuted a second time for that same offense.

SIGNIFICANCE: For nearly two centuries the Supreme Court decided very few double jeopardy cases, but in the last three decades of the twentieth century, it decided many.

The second clause of the Fifth Amendment, part of the Bill of Rights, states "nor shall any person be subject for the same offense to be twice put in jeopardy of life or limb." For the first part of the United States' existence, federal criminal cases were not appealed to the Supreme Court, so it had no federal double jeopardy cases. In addition, in *Barron v. Baltimore* (1833), the Court said that the provisions of the Bill of Rights limited the power of only the federal government and were inapplicable to the states. Consequently, there were no state court double jeopardy cases for the Court to review. Not until *Benton v. Maryland* (1969) did the Court conclude that the double jeopardy clause was applicable to the states, relying on the selective incorporation doctrine of the due process clause of the Fourteenth Amendment. Since that time, so many, and sometimes contradictory, double jeopardy cases came before the Court that Chief Justice William H. Rehnquist referred to this area of the law as a Sargasso Sea—one in which even a skillful navigator could become entangled and lost.

The Basic Protection. Jeopardy—the immediate threat of conviction and punishment—attaches in a criminal case when a jury is sworn in or, if there is no jury, when a judge begins to hear evidence. Whether jeopardy has attached is important be-

cause events occurring before that time, such as dismissal of the charges, will not preclude a subsequent prosecution; a dismissal of the charges after jeopardy has attached would preclude their being brought again.

A defendant who has been acquitted cannot be reprosecuted for that offense. Even with a relatively weak case, a prosecutor who could try the case multiple times might be able to perfect the presentation of witnesses and evidence so that eventually a jury would agree to convict. The Court found that such a result would be fundamentally unfair and would violate double jeopardy in *Ashe v. Swenson* (1970). After an acquittal, no matter how strong the state's evidence may have been, the defendant may not be forced to undergo the stress and expense of another prosecution for that crime, regardless of whether the verdict in the second case is a conviction or an acquittal.

Similarly, the Court ruled that a person cannot be tried again after having previously been convicted of the same offense in *Brown v. Ohio* (1977). However, in *United States v. Ball* (1896), the Court found that a necessary exception to this rule does allow the reprosecution of an individual whose conviction was reversed on appeal. There are many reasons why a conviction might be reversed, such as the improper admission of prejudicial evidence or inaccurate instructions to the jury. In these situations, after the reversal of the first conviction, the case could be retried without using the inadmissible evidence and with proper instructions to the jury, and the retrial would not be double jeopardy.

Exceptions. The doctrine protects against only successive criminal prosecutions or punishments; it does not prohibit a criminal prosecution after a civil action or a civil action after a criminal action. For example, property used in the commission of certain crimes, such as houses, cars, and other vehicles used in the manufacture and distribution of illegal drugs, is subject to forfeiture to the government. Such forfeiture actions usually are deemed to be civil rather than criminal punishments. Therefore, in *United States v. Ursery* (1996), the Court ruled that a person's having to forfeit his or her house and car to the government because they were used in a drug transaction is not the imposition of double jeopardy, although the individual had previously been criminally convicted and sentenced for the same drug transaction.

Similarly, those who have served the entire sentence for conviction of a sexual offense, such as rape or child molestation, may subsequently be adjudicated as sexually violent predators and ordered confined and treated until it is safe for them to be released. Because the subsequent adjudication is deemed civil and not criminal, the Court, in *Kansas v. Hendricks* (1997), found there is no double jeopardy, even if such sexual offenders might end up being confined for the rest of their lives.

The dual sovereignty doctrine is another major exception to the protection against double jeopardy. The basic guarantee is that the same sovereign, or government, will not prosecute or punish an individual twice for the same offense. There is no double jeopardy violation, however, if different sovereigns prosecute an individual for the same offense. For these purposes, the federal government of the United States and the government of a given state, such as California, are deemed to be separate sovereigns.

Cities and counties derive their governmental authority from that of the state in which they are located, so that neither a city nor a county is considered a separate sovereign from the state. Consequently, prosecutions for the same offense in, for example, Chicago municipal court and Illinois state courts would violate double jeopardy. In *Heath v. Alabama* (1985), the Court ruled that because the states are separate sovereigns from one another, prosecutions for the same offense by two separate states do not violate double jeopardy. With traditional crimes, such as murder or rape, it would be unusual for two states to have sufficient contact with the crime to have jurisdiction to prosecute it, but many conspiracies, especially those involving illegal drugs, have sufficient contacts with several states to confer jurisdiction on more than one. Nonetheless, dual sovereignty prosecutions involving two or more states are relatively rare.

FURTHER READING

Lafave, Wayne, and Jerold Israel. *Criminal Procedure*. St. Paul: West Publishing, 1985.

McAninch, William. "Unfolding the Law of Double Jeopardy." *South Carolina Law Review* 44 (1993): 411.

Miller, Lenord. *Double Jeopardy and the Federal System*. Chicago: University of Chicago Press, 1968.

William Shepard McAninch

SEE ALSO Bill of Rights; Fifth Amendment; Fourteenth Amendment.

Douglas, William O.

IDENTIFICATION: Associate justice (April 17, 1939-November 12, 1975)

NOMINATED BY: Franklin D. Roosevelt

BORN: October 16, 1898, Maine, Minnesota

DIED: January 19, 1980, Bethesda, Maryland

SIGNIFICANCE: An associate justice for nearly thirty-seven years, Douglas served longer on the Supreme Court than anyone else. As an associate justice, he always followed the Bill of Rights closely.

Douglas was born in rural Minnesota but moved to Yakima, Washington, in 1904 with his newly widowed mother. Douglas, who contracted polio at

In 1999 an attorney for David Hale, a figure in the Whitewater investigations (shown here in 1994), argued before the Supreme Court that Hale's upcoming state trial constituted double jeopardy. (AP/Wide World Photos)

age three, improved his health by becoming an outdoorsman and throughout his life was a naturalist and conservationist. After graduation from Whitman College in 1920, Douglas attended Columbia University Law School and was graduated second in his class in 1925. He then worked for a Wall Street law firm and taught at Columbia, leaving New York in 1932 to assume Yale University's Sterling Chair of Commercial and Corporate Law.

Early Public Service. In 1934 Douglas, whose legal career focused on corporate reorganization and bankruptcy, joined the Securities and Exchange Commission (SEC). He was appointed SEC commissioner on January 21, 1936, and became chair of the SEC on September 21, 1937. The young lawyer continually impressed President Franklin D. Roosevelt, who considered him a possible candidate for the vice presidency in 1940 and again in 1944. On March 20, 1939, Roosevelt nominated Douglas to the Supreme Court, making him one of the youngest people ever nominated to such a position. Douglas was sworn in as an associate justice on April 17, 1939, at age forty-one.

President Harry S Truman approached Douglas to become his running mate in 1948, but Douglas demurred. In the early 1950's he had considerable support as a possible Democratic candidate for the presidency but had little interest in leaving the Court to enter politics. In any case, his divorce from his first wife, Mildred, in 1953 diminished his appeal as a major political contender.

Career as an Associate Justice. Douglas was among the Court's most controversial associate justices. He married four women and divorced three of them. In 1966, at age sixty-eight, he married his fourth wife, who was so much younger than he that many conservative Americans considered him immoral. Personal matters had an effect on the public's perception of this gifted and intelligent jurist. He was frequently threatened with impeachment, the earliest threat coming in 1951 when he aroused public ire by advocating that the United States recognize communist China. In 1970 conservative members of the House of Representatives, rankled by Douglas's liberal decisions in court cases but also appalled by his personal antics, sought his impeachment.

William O. Douglas. (Library of Congress)

A major factor in such efforts in the late 1960's and early 1970's was Douglas's dissent when the Court decided not to review several cases that challenged the legality of the Vietnam War. By that time, the nation was strongly divided by this conflict. The lines between liberals and conservatives were sharply drawn. Douglas, the ardent liberal, seemed to many in the opposition to be traitorous for suggesting that the Court consider the legality of the Vietnam engagement, which had already caused considerable social unrest in the United States.

Douglas was a strong advocate of enforcing and applying the Bill of Rights. He insisted that its guarantees be applied to people accused of crimes and tried in state courts. At this time, many courts in the South were particularly brazen in violating the rights of those who opposed segregation and who protested publicly for the rights of minorities, including the voting rights guaranteed them under the Constitution but often denied them by specious state and local ordinances that dictated how precinct lines were drawn and that applied unreasonable literacy tests to African Americans, thereby disfranchising them.

In 1961 *Mapp v. Ohio* became one of the most important cases in Douglas's career as a jurist. Prior to *Mapp*, Douglas had argued that the Bill of Rights applied to individual states under the due process clause of the Fourteenth Amendment. *Mapp*, however, involved the search of Dollree Mapp's home without a proper warrant. The police were seeking someone suspected in a bombing, but Mapp refused to admit them without a warrant. When they returned three hours later with a paper purported to be warrant, they refused to allow Mapp to read the paper. When she attempted to grab it, they manhandled her and subsequently searched her house.

The police did not find their suspect. They did, however, find a stash of pornography in Mapp's basement and arrested her for possessing that material. Douglas argued that Mapp's Fourth Amendment rights, protecting her against unwarranted search and seizure, had been violated. Four other justices were persuaded by Douglas's argument and ruled that the State of Ohio had violated the defendant's constitutional rights.

Douglas's Contribution. History has dealt kindly with the controversial rulings that originally brought the wrath of the community down on Douglas, who took courageous stands that were unpopular at the time. His flamboyant personal life also colored public images of him. After his death, most people who have viewed his career objectively have concluded that Douglas was a uniquely qualified jurist who fought strenuously to uphold the constitutional tenets of the fathers of the nation.

FURTHER READING

Ball, Howard, and Phillip J. Cooper. *Of Power and Right: Hugo Black, William O. Douglas, and America's Constitutional Revolution.* New York: Oxford University Press, 1992.

Countryman, Vern. *The Judicial Record of Justice William O. Douglas.* Cambridge, Mass.: Harvard University Press, 1974.

Durum, James C. *Justice William O. Douglas.* Boston: Twayne, 1981.

Simon, James F. *Independent Journey: The Life of William O. Douglas.* New York: Harper & Row, 1980.

Wasby, Stephen L., ed. *He Shall Not Pass This Way Again: The Legacy of William O. Douglas.* Pittsburgh: University of Pittsburgh Press, 1990.

R. Baird Shuman

SEE ALSO Bill of Rights; Due process, procedural; Due process, substantive; Fourth Amendment; *Mapp v. Ohio*; Roosevelt, Franklin D.; Vietnam War.

Due process, procedural

DESCRIPTION: Right not to be deprived by government of life, liberty, or property without notice and an opportunity to be heard according to fair procedures.

SIGNIFICANCE: The Supreme Court considers procedural due process to be one of the most fundamental constitutional rights.

The Supreme Court recognized that the constitutional right to procedural due process derives historically from the Magna Carta (1215), which prohibited the English monarch from depriving a certain class of subjects of their rights except by lawful judgment of their peers or by the law of the land. When the United States gained its independence, language modeled on the Magna Carta provision was included in some of the state constitutions. Soon after the ratification of the U.S. Constitution, the Fifth Amendment was adopted as part of the Bill of Rights. This amendment, applicable to the federal government, provided in part that "no person shall . . . be deprived of life, liberty, or property, without due process of law." In 1868 the Fourteenth Amendment formulated the same prohibition with regard to state—and, by implication, local—governments.

The due process clauses apply to criminal as well as civil procedures. However, because other constitutional protections are triggered in criminal matters by specific provisions of the Fourth, Fifth, Sixth, and Eighth Amendments, the Court has often invoked these more specific constitutional provisions in criminal procedure cases when it is unnecessary to address the more general requirements of the due process clauses.

Basic Principles. The Court ruled, in *Collins v. City of Harker Heights* (1992), that due process clauses provide a guarantee of fair procedure in connection with governmental deprivations of life, liberty, or property. In *Florida Prepaid Postsecondary*

Education Expense Board v. College Savings Bank (1999), it held that procedural due process does not prevent governmental deprivation of life, liberty, or property; it merely prevents such deprivation without due process of law. Furthermore, the governmental deprivation must be deliberate. According to its finding in *Daniels v. Williams* (1986), a civil action against a governmental entity cannot be predicated on a due process theory if the governmental conduct at issue was merely negligent.

The two major components of fair procedure are notice and an opportunity to be heard. A primary purpose of the notice requirement is to ensure that the opportunity for a hearing is meaningful, as the Court determined in *West Covina v. Perkins* (1999). In both judicial and quasi-judicial proceedings, the Court determined that due process requires a neutral and detached judge in the first instance in *Concrete Pipe and Products of California v. Construction Laborers Pension Trust* (1993). However, where an initial determination is made by a party acting in an enforcement capacity, it found that due process may be satisfied by providing for a neutral adjudicator to conduct a *de novo* review (complete rehearing) of all factual and legal issues in *Marshall v. Jerrico* (1980).

The Court often (but not always) evaluates procedural due process issues by considering the three factors brought out in *Mathews v. Eldridge* (1976): the private interest affected by the official action; the risk of erroneous deprivation of such interest through the procedures used and the probable value, if any, of other procedural safeguards; and the relevant governmental interest.

Criminal Procedure. The Court applied the due process clauses in the criminal law area in cases in which other constitutional provisions do not apply. For example, the Court held that the adjudication of a contested criminal case in a mayor's court violates due process where the mayor's executive responsibilities may create a desire to maintain a high flow of revenue from the mayor's court in *Ward v. Village of Monroeville* (1972). It also held that a child in delinquency proceedings must be provided various procedural due process protections in *In re Gault* (1967).

The Court also made two rulings regarding placement in mental institutions. In *Vitek v. Jones* (1980), it held that a convicted felon serving a sentence in prison may not be transferred to a mental institution without appropriate procedures to determine whether he or she is mentally ill, and in *Foucha v. Louisiana* (1992), it determined that a person found not guilty of a crime by reason of insanity who is accordingly confined in a mental hospital is entitled to constitutionally adequate procedures to establish the grounds for continued confinement when the original basis for the confinement no longer exists.

Other Applications. The Court applied the procedural component of the due process clause in many other contexts. For example, in *United States v. James Daniel Good Real Property* (1993), it held that, absent exigent circumstances, due process requires notice and a meaningful opportunity to be heard before the government can seize real property subject to civil forfeiture. In *Goldberg v. Kelly* (1970), the Court held that welfare recipients could not be deprived of their benefits without procedural due process protections. Similarly, in *Memphis Light, Gas and Water Division v. Craft* (1978), the Court established federal due process procedures for termination of public utility service to customers in states that have a just cause requirement for such termination.

In *Cleveland Board of Education v. Loudermill* (1985), the Court determined that tenured classified civil servants were entitled to at least some procedural due process before termination, such as notice of allegations and opportunity to respond, coupled with a full posttermination hearing. However, it found that defamatory statements by governmental officials, in the absence of other governmental action, do not trigger due process analysis in *Paul v. Davis* (1976).

FURTHER READING

American Bar Association. *Due Process Protection for Juveniles in Civil Commitment Proceedings.* Chicago: American Bar Association, 1991.

Decker, John F. *Revolution to the Right: Criminal Procedure Jurisprudence During the Burger-Rehnquist Court Era.* New York: Garland, 1993.

Galligan, Denis J. *Due Process and Fair Procedures: A Study of Administrative Procedures.* New York: Oxford University Press, 1996.

Roach, Kent. *Due Process and Victims' Rights: The New Law and Politics of Criminal Justice.* Toronto: Toronto University Press, 1999.

Alan E. Johnson

SEE ALSO Due process, substantive; Eighth Amendment; Fifth Amendment; Fourteenth Amendment; Fourth Amendment; Municipal corporations; Property rights; Self-incrimination, immunity against; Sixth Amendment.

Due process, substantive

DESCRIPTION: The doctrine that the liberty protected by the due process clauses of the Fifth and Fourteenth Amendments encompasses more than the procedural rights owed by the government when it seeks to punish someone for a crime.

SIGNIFICANCE: Substantive due process has become the chief means by which the Supreme Court defines and extends the constitutional rights enjoyed by people in the United States.

One of the intents of the framers of the Fourteenth Amendment was to protect the property and contract rights of newly freed slaves from state law. The amendment states that the state shall not take away any person's life, liberty, or property without "due process of law." The phrase "due process" usually meant proper legal procedure, especially in criminal law. However, in *Allgeyer v. Louisiana* (1897), the Supreme Court, most of whose members believed strongly in laissez-faire capitalism, decided that part of the "fundamental liberty" protected by the due process clause was a substantive right to make contracts. This new right was frequently used by the Court to strike down state economic regulations with which the justices disagreed. For example, in *Lochner v. New York* (1905), the Court declared unconstitutional a New York law restricting the number of hours per day that bakers could work because it interfered with the right of the bakers to contract with their employers for their services. Justice Oliver Wendell Holmes filed a powerful dissenting opinion in the case. The Court also found a few other fundamental rights applicable to the states. In *Gitlow v. New York* (1925), for example, it held that freedom of speech, a First Amendment right, limited state governments. However, Holmes's reasoning in the *Lochner* dissent eventually prevailed. In 1936 the Court upheld a Washington state minimum-wage law in *Morehead v. New York ex rel. Tipaldo*. Soon after *Morehead*, several older, more conservative justices retired from the court.

President Franklin D. Roosevelt appointed progressive justices, and a new era of judicial self-restraint began. To many observers, it appeared unlikely that substantive due process guarantees would surface again.

Substantive Due Process Reborn. The Court's interest in substantive liberty was rekindled in the 1960's. On November 1, 1961, the Planned Parenthood League of Connecticut opened a center in New Haven. On November 10, its executive director, Estelle Griswold, and its medical director, Dr. Harold Buxton, were arrested for violating the Connecticut birth control statute. This law, which had been on the state's books since 1879, prohibited the use of birth control devices and the provision of birth control information. Griswold and Buxton were the first people ever to have been charged under the statute. An earlier attempt to challenge the law had been defeated when the Court refused to take jurisdiction because no one had ever been prosecuted. Griswold and Buxton were convicted and appealed to the Court.

The Court's opinion in *Griswold v. Connecticut*, written by Associate Justice William O. Douglas for a 7-2 majority, struck down the Connecticut statute. Douglas reasoned that many constitutional provisions as well as many of the Court's cases had established a zone of privacy into which states are forbidden to intrude. The First Amendment, which protects speech and religion, also protects privacy in associations; the Third Amendment prevents the government from forcing the populace to house soldiers; and the Fourth Amendment limits "unreasonable" warrantless intrusions into the home. The Fifth Amendment includes some substantive liberties. Finally, the Ninth Amendment establishes that there may be constitutional rights that are not explicitly set forth in the Constitution. Taken together, Douglas argued, these provisions establish a constitutional marital privacy right that the Connecticut birth control statute infringed.

The two dissenters in the case, Associate Justices Hugo L. Black and Potter Stewart, argued that the decision would return the Court to the discredited era of substantive due process in which the justices had written their policy preferences into the Constitution. Black and Stewart pointed out that there was no explicit textual support in the Constitution for the new right of marital privacy. They were particularly perturbed by the majority's use of the

Ninth Amendment, which seemed completely open ended to them and would give the Court limitless authority to define rights beyond the text of the Constitution.

The same right to receive and use contraceptive devices was extended to unmarried persons in *Eisenstadt v. Baird* (1972). In this case a Massachusetts statute was declared unconstitutional by the Court on two grounds: It unconstitutionally discriminated against unmarried people, and it collided with "a fundamental human right" to control conception.

Abortion. The following year, conception and privacy rights were further extended by the Court in *Roe v. Wade* (1973). This famous case established that a pregnant woman has a constitutional right to an abortion on demand during the first trimester of pregnancy. Justice Harry A. Blackmun, writing for the seven-justice majority, argued that the Court's substantive due process cases had established a right of privacy that "is broad enough to encompass a woman's decision whether or not to terminate her pregnancy" and that outweighs the state's interest in protecting prenatal life, at least during the first trimester of pregnancy. Blackmun turned to historical medical and legal thinking about pregnancy and abortion to help define the extent of abortion rights. Some state regulation of abortions is permitted in the second trimester, and abortion may be prohibited altogether in the third.

The two dissenters, Justices William H. Rehnquist and Byron R. White, maintained that there is no "fundamental" right to an abortion on demand and referred to the historical tradition in England and the United States of prohibiting abortion. They argued that the Court should defer to the wishes of the majority, at least in the absence of a traditional fundamental right. *Roe v. Wade* is perhaps the boldest assertion of substantive due process rights by the Court. It has been immensely controversial and has resulted in a great deal of political action in opposition to the Court's decision and in occasional violence directed at abortion clinics, physicians, and patients. In the years since *Roe*, the Court has revisited the case often. Although the decree has been modified somewhat, the central holding—that a pregnant woman has a right to an abortion on demand in the first trimester—remains intact.

Limit on New Rights. At the end of the twentieth century, *Roe v. Wade* represented the high-water mark of the Court's protection of substantive liberties. The Court declined to extend the concept to protect homosexual sodomy in *Bowers v. Hardwick* (1986). A Georgia statute that prohibited anal or oral sex was challenged by Michael Hardwick, a gay man who had been threatened with prosecution under the law after he was found in bed with another man in the course of a police drug raid. In his opinion for the majority, Justice Byron R. White wrote that

Sodomy was a criminal offense at common law and was forbidden by the laws of the original 13 States when they ratified the Bill of Rights. In 1868 when the Fourteenth Amendment . . . was ratified, all but 5 of the 37 States in the Union had criminal sodomy laws. In fact, until 1961, all 50 States outlawed sodomy, and today, 24 States and the District of Columbia continue to provide criminal penalties for sodomy performed in private and between consenting adults. . . . Against this background, to claim that a right to engage in such conduct is "deeply rooted in this Nation's history and tradition" or "implicit in the concept of ordered liberty" is, at best, facetious.

White also pointed out that *Griswold, Eisenstadt,* and *Roe* had all spoken to the right to decide whether or not to bear children. This crucial element is absent in *Bowers*. Four justices—Harry A. Blackmun, William J. Brennan, Jr., Thurgood Marshall, and John Paul Stevens—argued that the case was really about a "fundamental right to be let alone," and that the Court's earlier privacy decisions established just that. Although *Bowers* is a 5-4 decision, the issue did not appear again before the Court. The Georgia supreme court struck down the statute in question on independent state constitutional grounds in 1999.

The Court resisted attempts to get it to establish substantive rights to die or to assisted suicide. In *Cruzan v. Director, Missouri Department of Health* (1990), the Court refused to order the removal of life-support equipment from Nancy Cruzan, a young woman in a "persistent vegetative state" as a result of injuries suffered in an automobile accident. The majority, perhaps unwilling to further politicize the Court's work in the wake of the controversy surrounding *Roe v. Wade*, made it clear that it preferred to allow state governments to resolve these newly arising life and death questions. Similarly, in 1997 the court refused to hear a claim that an Oregon assisted-suicide law is unconstitutional.

The "new" substantive due process has allowed the Supreme Court to define new individual constitutional rights. So far these have been limited to substantive rights already found in the First Amendment and additional reproductive privacy rights. The doctrine is very controversial because every time the Court limits state power, it is acting in an antimajoritarian way. It is not clear to the public why the right to an abortion is somehow "fundamental" while the "bedroom privacy" argued for in the Georgia sodomy case is not. Nothing appears to illuminate these decisions besides the wishes of the justices. The Constitution itself neither explicitly establishes these rights nor implies them with any clarity. The absence of textual support for these decisions puts perception of the Court's legitimacy at risk.

FURTHER READING

The property law and contract clause background of substantive due process is well discussed in *The Guardian of Every Other Right: A Constitutional History of Property Rights* by James Ely, Jr. (New York: Oxford University Press, 1992). *Private Property and the Limits of American Constitutionalism: The Madisonian Framework and Its Legacy* by Jennifer Nedelsky (Chicago: University of Chicago Press, 1990) provides less technical coverage of some of the same topics. There is a vast literature on the "true" meaning of the Fourteenth Amendment and whether it does or does not "incorporate" the Bill of Rights. The classic argument for the incorporationist position is *The Supreme Court in United States History* by Charles Warren (Boston: Little, Brown, 1937), while the opposition is best represented by Charles Fairman's *The Fourteenth Amendment and the Bill of Rights: The Incorporation Theory* (New York: Da Capo Press, 1970). A more recent work suggesting curtailing the judiciary's role is *The Fourteenth Amendment and the Bill of Rights* by Raoul Berger (Norman: University of Oklahoma Press, 1989). An argument supporting the Court's activities may be found in *Freedom and the Court: Civil Rights and Liberties in the United States* by Henry J. Abraham and Barbara A. Perry (6th ed., New York: Oxford University Press, 1994). Similarly the legitimacy of the privacy decisions and the natural law threads of thought that

produced them have engendered enormous comment. One balanced work is *The Supreme Court and the Second Bill of Rights: The Fourteenth Amendment and the Nationalization of Civil Liberties* by Richard C. Cortner (Madison: University of Wisconsin Press, 1981).

Robert Jacobs

SEE ALSO Abortion; Birth control and contraception; *Bowers v. Hardwick*; Contract, freedom of; *Cruzan v. Director, Missouri Department of Health*; Due process, procedural; *Eisenstadt v. Baird*; Fourteenth Amendment; *Griswold v. Connecticut*; Incorporation doctrine; Judicial activism; Judicial self-restraint; Privacy, right to; *Roe v. Wade*.

Duncan v. Kahanamoku

CITATION: 327 U.S. 304
DATE: February 25, 1946
ISSUE: Martial law
SIGNIFICANCE: The Supreme Court held that the establishment of military tribunals to try civilians in a U.S. territory was illegal because it was not authorized by an act of Congress.

In 1941, just after the attack on Pearl Harbor, the governor of Hawaii suspended the writ of *habeas corpus*, placed the territory under martial law, suspended all functions of the civilian government, and delegated executive and judicial powers to the military authorities. General Walter Short proclaimed himself military governor of Hawaii and established military courts that were not subject to review by the regular courts. Military authorities claimed that the Hawaiian Organic Act of 1900 authorized the temporary military regime. Duncan and another person imprisoned by the regime petitioned for a *habeas corpus* review.

By a 6-2 vote, the Supreme Court ordered the two prisoners released. Justice Hugo L. Black's majority opinion found that the Hawaiian Organic Act had not authorized a declaration of martial law except under conditions of actual invasion or rebellion. He pointed out that the 1900 statute had extended all the rights of the Constitution to the territory, and therefore, the civilians in Hawaii were entitled to all the constitutional guarantees of a fair trial. Although Black referred to the principles of *Ex parte Milligan* (1866), he carefully avoided any consideration of the constitutional limitations of Congress in the territories during time of war.

Thomas T. Lewis

SEE ALSO Military justice; *Milligan, Ex parte*; War powers; World War II.

Duncan v. Louisiana

CITATION: 391 U.S. 145
DATE: May 20, 1968
ISSUE: Trial by jury
SIGNIFICANCE: With this decision, the Supreme Court applied the Sixth Amendment's right to jury trial to the states through the Fourteenth Amendment under the incorporation doctrine.

Justice Byron R. White, writing for a 7-2 majority, held that a jury trial is mandatory in a state court if the same offense would be entitled to a jury trial in federal court. Through this ruling, he applied a portion of the Sixth Amendment through incorporation under the Fourteenth Amendment.

The defendant had been convicted of a misdemeanor without benefit of a jury because Louisiana's laws did not mandate jury trials for minor offenses. The Supreme Court held that a portion of the Bill of Rights must be considered part of due process if it is a part of the Anglo-American system of "ordered liberty," and juries were a part of that. This strengthened the theory of incorporation, which held that due process must include any feature without which one could not imagine civilized society existing. Justices John M. Harlan II and Potter Stewart dissented because they feared a further erosion of states' rights.

Richard L. Wilson

SEE ALSO *Batson v. Kentucky*; Due process, procedural; *Edmonson v. Leesville Concrete Co.*; Fourteenth Amendment; Incorporation doctrine; Jury, trial by; Sixth Amendment.

Duplex Printing Co. v. Deering

CITATION: 254 U.S. 443
DATE: January 3, 1921
ISSUE: Labor
SIGNIFICANCE: An antilabor Supreme Court majority severely curtailed labor union activity by limiting the protections granted to these organizations by Congress.

Justice Mahlon Pitney wrote this 6-3 opinion for the Supreme Court ruling that the 1914 Clayton Act did not protect labor unions from conviction for illegal restraints of trade, such as secondary boycotts. Through passage of the act, Congress had attempted to stop antiunion judges from issuing injunctions against labor unions for using secondary boycotts as a part of collective bargaining efforts. However, antiunion sentiment was strong on the Court at the time, and it used antitrust legislation against the unions.

Justices Louis D. Brandeis, Oliver Wendell Holmes, and John H. Clarke dissented in *Duplex Printing*, arguing that the Court was ignoring a legitimate congressional power to enact legislation that stipulated that labor unions were not monopolies in the usual sense of the word. *Duplex Printing* was effective for more than a decade until the Great Depression dramatically changed public and legal opinion. The leading dissenters later saw their views become the law of the land. When Congress adopted prounion legislation such as the 1932 Norris-La Guardia Act, the New Deal era Court upheld exempting labor unions from antitrust legislation.

Richard L. Wilson

SEE ALSO Antitrust law; Labor; New Deal; Separation of powers.

Duvall, Gabriel

IDENTIFICATION: Associate justice (November 23, 1811-January 14, 1835)
NOMINATED BY: James Madison
BORN: December 6, 1752, Prince Georges County, Maryland
DIED: March 6, 1844, Prince Georges County, Maryland
SIGNIFICANCE: During his twenty-three year tenure on the Supreme Court, Duvall sided with Chief Justice John Marshall on most well-known decisions. Duvall favored a strong central government and nationalist interpretation of the Constitution.

Duvall had a multifaceted career. He studied law and was admitted to the bar in 1778. He served as a soldier in the Maryland militia during the Revolutionary War. He was clerk of the Maryland House of Delegates in 1777 and was elected a member in

Gabriel Duvall. (Library of Congress)

1787. He served until 1794 when he was elected to the U.S. House of Representatives; he was reelected in 1796 when he resigned to become chief justice of the General Court of Maryland. Duvall was then appointed comptroller of the treasury by President Thomas Jefferson, serving under Secretary of the Treasury Albert Gallatin until 1811, when he was nominated by President James Madison to the Supreme Court.

Most notable for agreeing with Chief Justice John Marshall and the minority in *Ogden v. Saunders* (1827), when the majority ruled that states could discharge debts as long as they did not affect contracts predating state relief laws, Duvall also was noted for opposing Marshall in *Dartmouth College v. Woodward* (1819), which limited state legislative power. Duvall is also remembered for the unanimous opinion he wrote in *LeGrand v. Darnall* (1829), in which property left to a slave brought about the freeing of that slave. Duvall's health declined in later years. Upon hearing that President Andrew Jackson intended to appoint a fellow Marylander, Roger Brooke Taney, to the Court, Duvall resigned in January, 1835. He lived another nine years in retirement.

Gregory N. Seltzer

SEE ALSO *Dartmouth College v. Woodward*; Marshall, John; *Ogden v. Saunders*; Taney, Roger Brooke.

Dworkin, Ronald

IDENTIFICATION: Legal philosopher and constitutional scholar
BORN: December 11, 1931, Worcester, Massachusetts
SIGNIFICANCE: Dworkin defended liberal jurisprudence and proposed that Supreme Court justices and lower court judges use critical moral judgment in interpreting the Constitution.

A self-described liberal scholar, Dworkin argued for expansive judicial review to advance causes such as sexual freedom, legal abortion, and euthanasia. He proposed a moral reading of the Constitution according to which judges, subject to certain constraints, bring critical moral judgment to bear in determining the meaning of such terms as the free speech clause of the First Amendment and the due process and equal protection clauses of the Fourteenth Amendment.

According to Dworkin, rights to pornography, abortion, and assisted suicide, for example, follow from a basic moral obligation of government to treat persons with equal concern and respect. In addition, courts are the forum of principle in which rights that ought not to be left to the vicissitudes of power politics can be protected by independent judges.

Dworkin's critics argued that laws restricting pornography or forbidding abortion and assisted suicide deny no one equal concern and respect. Moreover, they rejected Dworkin's implicit denial that legislatures are proper forums of principle for resolving controversial moral issues. Finally, they insisted that constitutional provisions such as those concerning freedom of speech and due process of law, when understood in textual and historical context, have a high degree of determinate legal meaning and are not generalities.

Robert P. George

SEE ALSO Abortion; Bill of Rights; Due process, substantive; First Amendment; Fourteenth Amendment; Judicial activism; Judicial powers; Obscenity and pornography; Right to die.

E

E. C. Knight Co., United States v.

CITATION: 156 U.S. 1
DATE: January 21, 1895
ISSUE: Sherman Antitrust Act
SIGNIFICANCE: In its first decision under the Sherman Antitrust Act (1890), the Supreme Court found that the framers of the act had not intended for it to apply to the manufacturing process.

During the 1890's, the American Sugar Company was a large monopoly controlling 98 percent of the refining industry. Responding to a public outcry, President Grover Cleveland's administration filed suit against the monopoly under the Sherman Antitrust Act (1890). By an 8-1 vote, the Supreme Court ruled that the law was not applicable because it had not been designed to prevent a monopoly in manufacturing. In the opinion for the majority, Justice Melville W. Fuller wrote that the power to regulate manufacturing belonged exclusively to the states under their police powers and that the regulatory authority of the federal government was limited to interstate commerce. An article manufactured for sale in another state did not become an article of interstate commerce until it was actually transported as commerce. Fuller did not rule on the constitutionality of the Sherman Act because he assumed that the act had been framed according to the "well-settled principles" of dual federalism.

In a strong dissent, Justice John Marshall Harlan broadly defined commerce so that it included the buying and selling of goods. He argued that the U.S. Congress could constitutionally regulate some manufacturers and that it had intended to do so in the Sherman Antitrust Act. He insisted, moreover, that only the federal government had the capacity to deal with large business combinations. Although the Court would accept the stream of commerce theory in *Swift and Co. v. United States* (1905), it did not fully accept Harlan's view of congressional authority over sugar refineries until *Mandeville Island Farms v. American Crystal Sugar Co.* (1948).

Thomas T. Lewis

SEE ALSO Commerce, regulation of; Federalism; *Hammer v. Dagenhart*; Sherman Antitrust Act; *Swift and Co. v. United States.*

Edelman v. Jordan

CITATION: 415 U.S. 651
DATE: March 25, 1974
ISSUE: Eleventh Amendment

Chief Justice Melville W. Fuller, center front, presides over his Court. Clockwise from Fuller, the justices are Stephen J. Field, Horace Gray, Howell E. Jackson, Henry B. Brown, George Shiras, Jr., Edward D. White, David J. Brewer, and John Marshall Harlan. Fuller's ruling in United States v. E. C. Knight Co. *eviscerated the Sherman Antitrust Act.* (C. M. Bell/Collection of the Supreme Court of the United States)

SIGNIFICANCE: This Supreme Court decision, reached by a conservative majority, protected states from class-action suits by citizens alleging that these states were undermining federal legislation by granting them benefits too late.

John Jordan sued Illinois by suing various of its state and county officials, asserting they were paying out benefits later than federal law mandated and therefore violating the Fourteenth Amendment rights of the beneficiaries. A federal district court agreed and ordered retroactive payments to the class-action beneficiaries. Illinois appealed and lost in the court of appeals. However, the Supreme Court ruled in favor of Illinois. In the 5-4 majority decision written by Justice William H. Rehnquist, the Court ruled that Illinois did not waive its Eleventh Amendment rights by participating in the federal program and that the Eleventh Amendment prohibited—within limits—federal court lawsuits against a state without the state's consent brought by citizens of that state or of other states. The Court reasoned that although *Ex parte Young* (1908) allowed injunctions against states in matters affecting future policies, it did not permit suits for retroactive payments.

Justices William O. Douglas, William J. Brennan, Jr., and Thurgood Marshall wrote separate dissents, and Justice Harry A. Blackmun joined Marshall. These dissenting justices opposed the majority holdings on more than one front. Later decisions limited the impact of *Edelman* and allowed Congress to circumvent this state immunity issue.

Richard L. Wilson

SEE ALSO Federalism; General welfare clause; *Young, Ex parte.*

Edmonson v. Leesville Concrete Co.

CITATION: 111 S.Ct. 2077
DATE: June 3, 1991
ISSUE: Jury composition
SIGNIFICANCE: The Supreme Court extended its ruling that potential jurors could not be peremptorily excluded on the basis of race from criminal trials to include civil trials.

In *Batson v. Kentucky* (1986), the Supreme Court ruled that litigants in criminal trials could not use peremptory challenges to exclude federal court jurors on the basis of race because such exclusions violated the excluded person's Fifth Amendment rights. In this 6-3 decision, it extended its decision to civil as well as criminal trials. In his opinion for the Court, Anthony M. Kennedy argued that even if the litigants' private attorneys, not the state, make the exclusion, state action is involved because the attorneys are using the public court forum. Private parties must follow the same rules the state does when it uses the courts. Justice Sandra Day O'Connor was joined in a forceful dissent by Justices William H. Rehnquist and Antonin Scalia, who argued that the attorneys' challenges of jurors were essentially private choices. The dissenters rejected the idea that state action was inherent in all court proceedings.

Richard L. Wilson

SEE ALSO *Batson v. Kentucky*; Due process, procedural; Fifth Amendment; Incorporation doctrine; Jury composition and size; State action; *Strauder v. West Virginia*; *Williams v. Mississippi.*

Education

DESCRIPTION: Process of being trained by formal instruction and directed practice. Responsibility of the state, rather than the federal government, according to the Tenth Amendment to the U.S. Constitution.
SIGNIFICANCE: Although education is largely a state issue, the operation of educational systems must conform to constitutional mandates. When an education case involves a federal issue, particularly constitutional freedoms or rights, the Supreme Court may review the case.

Educational cases involve two major concepts: *parens patriae* and *in loco parentis*. The first of these, *parens patriae*, maintains that the state, as a parent to all persons within its boundaries, has the inherent authority to provide for the individual and general welfare of its citizens. Through the exercise of its police power, the state legislature can establish laws and regulations for the common good, including mandatory school attendance. The state also has the power to care for those who are legally incompetent to act on their own behalf, including minor children. Because the state's interest may conflict with parental interest, this scheme often is the subject of litigation surrounding compulsory education and curriculum. The second concept is that the school board and educational authorities have the power to act in the parents' stead, *in loco parentis*, with the caveat that the state's action must be supported by a rational or compelling state interest before a child's or a parents' rights can be infringed on or restricted.

In *Pierce v. Society of Sisters* (1925), the Supreme Court ruled that although the state has fairly extensive authority to protect children from parental abuse, it has only limited authority to interfere with parents' control of their children's education. However, in *Prince v. Massachusetts* (1944), the Court stated that the family is not beyond regulation in the public interest and that the state as *parens patriae* may restrict the parents' control by requiring school attendance or regulating or prohibiting child labor. In *Wisconsin v. Yoder* (1972), the Court said that the power of the parent may be subject to limitation if it appears that parental decisions will jeopardize the health or safety of the child or have the potential to create significant social burdens. A common link in these cases is a judicial concern for the child, with the parental interest and the state interest secondary.

Challenges to compulsory attendance laws often deal with the question of whether parental judgment should prevail over that of the state. *Parens patriae* also extends to compulsory medical care over the objection of parents. This does not mean, however, that parental authority is restricted in all cases; at times it is strengthened. In *Yoder*, the Court held that a state cannot compel Amish children to attend public high school, balancing the state's power to impose reasonable regulations against the fundamental rights and interests of individuals whose beliefs constitute their philosophical ideology. Moreover, where parents show that enforcement of compulsory education will endanger their religious beliefs, the state's *parens patriae* power must yield to the free exercise clause of the First Amendment.

Religion and Public Schools. The First Amendment freedom of religion is found in two clauses: the establishment clause and the free exercise clause. In 1791 Thomas Jefferson declared that there should be a "wall of separation," high and impenetrable, between church and state. The essential meaning of this phrase is that the education provided in public schools must be secular and without religious content or intent. An important element of the secular state contained in Jefferson's words was a system of public education that could convey all necessary temporal knowledge but not impede religious freedom. The power of the state could not be used to inculcate religious beliefs, nor could the authority of the state to tax be used to assist religious training.

In *Illinois ex rel. McCollum v. Board of Education* (1948), the Court held that the practice called "released time" violated the separation of church and state. Under this practice, schools set aside a period in which religious instruction was conducted in regular classrooms. Students not participating were required to go to other rooms where they received secular instruction. The practice was upheld, however, in *Zorach v. Clauson* (1952), when the religious training was held off school premises. In *Everson v. Board of Education of Ewing Township* (1947), the Court held that the establishment clause does not prohibit spending tax funds to pay bus fare for parochial school students, and in *Board of Education v. Allen* (1968), it held that the loan of textbooks to parochial school students did not violate the establishment clause.

The line between state neutrality to and support of religion is not easily drawn. In its analysis, the Court examines the purpose and primary effect of the legislation—if it is designed to advance or inhibit religion, then it exceeds the scope of the legislative power. In *Lemon v. Kurtzman* (1971), the Court clarified the criteria to be applied. The legislation must have a secular purpose and a primary secular effect that neither advances nor inhibits religion. In addition, the statute must not foster "excessive government entanglements" with religion.

In *Engel v. Vitale* (1962), the Court disallowed a nondenominational prayer recited daily in New York classrooms because the purpose of the recitation appeared to constitute government-sanctioned official prayers. Similarly, a daily reading of ten verses of the Bible and recitation of the Lord's Prayer without comment were also held unconstitutional in *Abington School District v. Schempp* (1963) and *Murray v. Curlett* (1963) respectively. A nonsectarian prayer at a high school graduation was also held unconstitutional in *Lee v. Weisman* (1992) because the Court believed that it exerted subtle coercive pressures where students had no other reasonable alternative.

In *Epperson v. Arkansas* (1968), the Court declared unconstitutional a statute that prohibited teaching from a book containing a chapter on Charles Darwin's theory of evolution because it conflicted with the religious interpretation of the Book of Genesis. The Court also found, in *Board of Education of Kiryas Joel Village School District v. Grumet* (1994) that a statute creating a special school district as a religious enclave also violated the establishment clause because it destroyed impartiality or neutrality toward religion. A noticeable shift in policy was apparent in *Agostini v. Felton* (1997), in which the Court admitted that some interaction between church and state is inevitable and tolerable as long as the entanglement is not "excessive." It did not, however, define the parameters of that standard.

Several cases involving the free exercise clause centered on mandatory participation in flag salute ceremonies. In *Minersville School District v. Gobitis* (1940), the Court upheld such a statute in the name of discipline, cohesion, and unity, largely because the outbreak of World War II in Europe had produced a high level of nationalism in the United States. In contrast, only three years later, in *West Virginia State Board of Education v. Barnette* (1943), the Court ruled that the state had no power to require such a ritual. Remaining passive created no danger and did not interfere with the rights of others to participate. Moreover, compelling the ritual, according to the Court, violated First Amendment freedoms. In *Wisconsin v. Yoder*, the Court held that a state statute compelling school attendance to age sixteen unduly burdened the free exercise of religion of the Amish people and was unconstitutional.

Race and Education. The most notable civil rights case was *Brown v. Board of Education* (1954), in which the Court mandated school desegregation on equal protection grounds. In *Plessy v. Ferguson* (1896), the Court had upheld segregation, stating that separate but equal public facilities did not violate anyone's rights. In *Brown*, however, the Court ruled that separate facilities deprive individuals of equal protection of the laws and generate feelings of inferiority, producing an overall detrimental effect. Ruling that separate facilities are inherently unequal, the Court ordered the integration of all schools, creating a unitary school system. Desegregation was to proceed "with all deliberate speed."

Throughout the 1960's, however, states struggled with implementing integration. The Court examined both de jure and de facto segregation. De jure (by law) segregation is mandated by law or by the deliberate act of school officials and was more typically found in the South. De facto segregation results from residential housing patterns and was more typically found in the North. The Court's ruling in *Keyes v. Denver School District No. 1* (1973) was regarded as a signal indicating its approval of districtwide desegregation in northern school districts. In *Swann v. Charlotte-Mecklenburg Board of Education* (1971) the Court also ruled that busing to overcome racial segregation is a judicially acceptable remedy for de facto segregation.

Rights of Teachers and Students. In the 1940's and 1950's loyalty oaths for educational personnel were not unusual, although their provisions differed widely. The Court has upheld loyalty oaths provided that they are not so vague that their meaning is uncertain and oath takers could be accused of perjury if they did not understand their implications. Public secondary schoolteachers do not have unlimited liberty or authority to determine course structure or content. In order to plead denial of academic freedom, teachers must first buttress their cases with some substantive claim under the First Amendment or a similar provision. In general, the courts have developed a flexible rule that balances the public's interests against the private interests of the employee. Due to their sensitive position in the classroom, however, teachers must be held accountable for certain activities, and their rights are not absolute and can be overcome if the public necessity is great enough.

The case of *Tinker v. Des Moines Independent Community School District* (1969) established some guidelines by which to reconcile the constitutional rights of' students and the power of school officials. The case involved three students who wore black arm bands to school in silent protest against the government's Vietnam War policy in violation of the school's prohibition against the wearing of arm bands. When the students were asked to remove the arm bands, they refused and were suspended. The Court observed that the wearing of arm bands was "pure speech" totally divorced from actual or potentially disruptive conduct. Desire to avoid discomfort or unpleasantness accompanying an unpopular viewpoint is not sufficient reason for prohibiting expression of opinion. The Court held, however, that schools may regulate the content of school-sponsored newspapers when the speech is part of the curriculum in *Hazelwood School District v. Kuhlmeier* (1988) or when the speech is lewd, indecent, or offensive to both students and teachers in *Bethel School District No. 403 v. Fraser* (1986).

In *Davis v. Monroe County* (1999), the Court held that schools found to be "deliberately indifferent" to a student's claims of sexual harassment can be liable for monetary damages in cases in which the behavior is so severe, pervasive, and offensive that it denies its victims equal access to education.

FURTHER READING

Although it is a textbook and contains case excerpts, *American Public School Law* by Kern Alexander and M. David Alexander (4th ed., Belmont, Calif.: Wadsworth, 1998) contains excellent explanatory material and is a rich resource for further research. E. Edmund Reutter, Jr.'s *The Supreme Court's Impact on Public Education* (Bloomington, Ind.: Phi Delta Kappa and National Organization on Legal Problems of Education, 1982) contains an analysis and summary of Court opinions, explaining judgments directly affecting education and the Court's policies and procedures. *A Digest of Supreme Court Decisions Affecting Education* (3d ed., Bloomington, Ind.: Phi Delta Kappa Educational Foundation, 1995), compiled by Perry A. Zirkel, Sharon Nalbone Richardson, and Steven S. Goldberg, presents numerous cases in simple summary fashion without comment. Evelyn B. Kelly's *Legal Basics: A Handbook for Educators* (Bloomington, Ind.: Phi Delta Kappa Educational Foundation, 1998) contains basic explanations of everyday matters likely to be encountered by educators. *Teachers and the Law* (5th ed., New York: Addison Wesley Longman, 1999) by Louis Fischer, David Schimmel, and Cynthia Kelly provides information about teachers' legal rights and responsibilities. Written in question-and-answer format with case references, Robert J. Shoop and Dennis R. Dunklee's *School Law for the Principal: A Handbook for Practitioners* (Boston: Allyn and Bacon, 1992) is another practical source of information containing hypothetical situations and suggested answers.

Marcia J. Weiss

SEE ALSO Desegregation; Equal protection clause; *Lemon v. Kurtzman; Pierce v. Society of Sisters;* Police powers; Religion, establishment of; Religion, freedom of; School integration and busing; School prayer; Speech and press, freedom of; Tenth Amendment; *West Virginia State Board of Education v. Barnette.*

Edwards v. Aguillard

CITATION: 482 U.S. 578
DATE: June 19, 1987
ISSUE: Establishment of religion
SIGNIFICANCE: The Supreme Court struck down a state law requiring balanced treatment of "evolution science" and "creation science," based on the establishment clause of the First Amendment.

In *Epperson v. Arkansas* (1968), the Supreme Court infuriated many religious groups when it overturned a state law that prohibited the teaching of Darwinian evolution in the public schools. A Louisiana statute, designed to get around the ruling, prohibited schools from teaching evolutionary theory unless the theories of creationism were also taught. Proponents of the statute argued that evolutionary theory is an integral part of the religion of secular humanism and asserted that creationism is a respectable scientific theory. Principal Don Aguillard, supported by the American Civil Liberties Union, challenged the constitutionality of the law.

By a 7-2 vote, the Court agreed with the challengers. Applying the three-part *Lemon* test (established in *Lemon v. Kurtzman,* 1971), Justice William J. Brennan, Jr., emphasized that the purpose of the statute was to restructure the science curriculum in conformity with a viewpoint associated with particular religious sects. Rejecting the academic freedom defense, Brennan noted that science teachers in Louisiana already enjoyed the freedom to teach a variety of theories about the origins of life. In dissent, Justice Antonin Scalia criticized the majority for looking at the intent rather than the effect of the statute, and he also argued against the portion of *Lemon* requiring a secular purpose for statutes.

Thomas T. Lewis

SEE ALSO *Epperson v. Arkansas; Lemon v. Kurtzman;* Religion, establishment of; Religion, freedom of.

Edwards v. California

CITATION: 314 U.S. 160
DATE: November 24, 1941
ISSUE: Right to travel
SIGNIFICANCE: The Supreme Court, in striking down a law barring indigents from entering California, strengthened the constitutional right to travel, especially for poor citizens.

The Supreme Court unanimously ruled that California's Great Depression era "Okie Law" was unconstitutional in its attempt to bar any person from bringing an indigent person into California. Justice James F. Byrnes, in his opinion for the Court, relied on Article I, section 8 of the Constitution (the commerce clause) and viewed the issue as the transportation of people as if they were property in interstate commerce. In his concurrence, Justice Robert H. Jackson agreed with the result but attacked the reasoning. He objected to equating people with property to give them constitutional rights as U.S. citizens. Jackson argued that the Fourteenth Amendment's privileges and immunities clause should be used to grant people the right to travel across state lines, which he saw as a basic feature of U.S. citizenship. Jackson's view would strengthen the privileges and immunities clause, which is not frequently cited by the Court.

Richard L. Wilson

SEE ALSO Commerce, regulation of; Privileges and immunities; Travel, right to.

Edwards v. South Carolina

CITATION: 372 U.S. 229
DATE: February 5, 1963
ISSUE: Freedom of assembly
SIGNIFICANCE: In this incorporation case, the Supreme Court held that local officials could not block an otherwise lawful demonstration because they disliked the demonstrators' political views.

About two hundred African American students marched peacefully in small groups from a church to the South Carolina state capitol, an obviously public forum, to protest the state's racially discriminatory laws. A few dozen police officers initially told them they could march peacefully but about an hour later ordered them to disperse under threat of arrest. A crowd had gathered to watch the demonstrators but did not seem threatening, and the police presence was ample. The demonstrators responded by singing patriotic and religious songs until some two hundred demonstrators were arrested and convicted of breach of the peace. Their conviction was upheld by the South Carolina supreme court.

The Supreme Court, by an 8-1 vote, reversed the convictions of the civil rights demonstrators. Justice Potter Stewart, in the majority opinion, applied the First Amendment right to freedom of assembly to the states, refusing to let the states bar demonstrations of unpopular views in traditional forums. In line with other time, place, and manner decisions, the Court used the Fourteenth Amendment's due process clause to incorporate the peaceable assembly portion of the First Amendment and to apply it to the states. Justice Tom C. Clark dissented, defending the state's action

Richard L. Wilson

SEE ALSO Assembly and association, freedom of; *Brandenburg v. Ohio; DeJonge v. Oregon;* Due process, procedural; Fourteenth Amendment; *Hague v. Congress of Industrial Organizations;* Incorporation doctrine; Symbolic speech; Time, place, and manner regulations.

Eichman, United States v.

CITATION: 496 U.S. 310
DATE: June 11, 1990
ISSUES: Symbolic speech; flag desecration
SIGNIFICANCE: The Supreme Court reaffirmed its 1989 decision that flag burning was a constitutionally protected form of free speech.

The Supreme Court, by a 5-4 majority, struck down the 1989 Flag Protection Act, which Congress passed to void the Court's ruling in *Texas v. Johnson* (1989), which overturned a Texas flag burning statute. Justice William J. Brennan, Jr., in the opinion for the Court, suggested that the justices would probably regard virtually any law directed at forms of flag desecration as unconstitutional because such laws would inevitably imply governmental disapproval of the message inherent in flag burning.

In *Johnson,* the Court declared a Texas statute unconstitutional because it explicitly stated that the desecration must be done to "offend" someone. This provision flew in the face of the cardinal tenet of allowable time, place, and manner regulations, namely, that they may not be used by officials who do not like the ideas expressed. Congress sought to circumvent the *Johnson* holding by carefully avoiding the expression of ideas question, but the Court found that the government's purpose was clearly the suppression of ideas and, therefore, that the strict scrutiny test needed to be applied to the congressional enactment. The Court found the 1989 federal law could not pass such a strict test. Justices William H. Rehnquist, Byron R. White, John Paul Stevens, and Sandra Day O'Connor dissented, arguing that there were so many ways that demonstrators could exercise their First Amendment rights that laws preventing flag desecration were not a real infringement on their rights.

Richard L. Wilson

SEE ALSO *Brandenburg v. Ohio*; Flag desecration; *Gitlow v. New York*; *O'Brien, United States v.*; *Schenck v.*

Prohibition, a popular women's cause in the late 1800's and early 1900's, became law when the Eighteenth Amendment went into effect in 1920. (Library of Congress)

United States; Symbolic speech; *Texas v. Johnson*; *Tinker v. Des Moines Independent Community School District*; *Whitney v. California*.

Eighteenth Amendment

DATE: 1919

DESCRIPTION: Amendment to the U.S. Constitution, also known as the Prohibition amendment, that prohibited the manufacture, sale, or transportation of intoxicating beverages.

SIGNIFICANCE: Constitutional prohibition of alcoholic beverages lasted from 1920 to 1933. Supreme Court decisions from 1917 to 1920 supported the prohibition cause and defended the ratification of the Eighteenth Amendment.

The Eighteenth Amendment to the Constitution was ratified on January 16, 1919, and went into effect on January 16, 1920. The Supreme Court's decisions in such cases as *Crane v. Campbell* (1917), *Hawke v. Smith* (1920), and the *National Prohibition Cases* (1920) strengthened the basis for and strongly endorsed the amendment.

In *Crane*, the Court supported national prohibition by ruling that possessing alcohol for personal use was not a constitutional right. In *Hawke*, the Court upheld the ratification of the Eighteenth Amendment by the Ohio General Assembly over the referendum by Ohio voters who rejected the amendment. According to the Court, when Congress requested that a constitutional amendment be ratified by state legislatures, it neither authorized nor permitted a referendum. In the *National Prohibition Cases*, the Court completed the process of making national prohibition part of the law of the United States. In these cases, the justices upheld the constitutionality of the Eighteenth Amendment and approved the method by which the state legislatures had ratified it.

On December 5, 1933, the Twenty-first Amendment to the Constitution was ratified. This amendment repealed the Eighteenth Amendment and ended constitutional prohibition of alcoholic beverages.

Louis Gesualdi

SEE ALSO *Carroll v. United States*; *Clark Distilling Co. v. Western Maryland Railway Co.*; *Lanza, United States v.*; *Olmstead v. United States*; Taft, William H.; Twenty-first Amendment.

Eighth Amendment

DATE: 1791

DESCRIPTION: Amendment to the U.S. Constitution that forbids requiring excessive bail, imposing excessive fines, and inflicting cruel and unusual punishments.

SIGNIFICANCE: The three clauses of the Eighth Amendment are the only provisions in the Constitution that place substantive limits on the severity of punishments in criminal cases. The Supreme Court's role has been to interpret these clauses.

The Eighth Amendment is derived almost verbatim from the English Bill of Rights (1689). Adopted in 1791 as part of the Bill of Rights, the amendment was intended to prohibit the abuse of federal government power, but the precise meaning of the amendment is unclear and requires interpretation by the Supreme Court.

The first two clauses of the Eighth Amendment (prohibiting excessive bail and fines) have not been applied to the states. Although the Court has never established an absolute right to bail, it has re-

---

TEXT OF THE EIGHTH AMENDMENT

Excessive bail shall not be required, nor excessive fines imposed, nor cruel and unusual punishments inflicted.

---

viewed whether bail has been set higher than necessary to ensure that a defendant appears for trial.

The Court has taken a flexible interpretation of the cruel and unusual punishment clause, stating in *Trop v. Dulles* (1958) that punishments should be evaluated in light of the "evolving standards of decency" of a maturing society. The clause was formally applied to the states in *Robinson v. California* (1962). Barbaric punishments are prohibited, but the Court has refused to hold that the death penalty itself is cruel and unusual punishment. Punishments disproportionate to the crime, the treatment of prisoners, and conditions of confinement, may also violate the Eighth Amendment.

John Fliter

SEE ALSO Bail; Bill of Rights; Capital punishment; Cruel and unusual punishment; Due process, procedural; *Furman v. Georgia*; *Robinson v. California*; *Trop v. Dulles*.

Eisenstadt v. Baird

CITATION: 405 U.S. 438

DATE: March 22, 1972

ISSUES: Reproductive rights; right of privacy; equal protection

SIGNIFICANCE: Based on an individual's rights to privacy and equality, the Supreme Court struck down a Massachusetts law that made it a felony to provide contraceptives to unmarried persons.

In the landmark case *Griswold v. Connecticut* (1965), the Supreme Court recognized a constitutional right to privacy, which included the right of married persons to obtain contraceptives. In *Eisenstadt*, the justices voted six to one to extend the same right to single people. Speaking for the majority, Justice William J. Brennan, Jr., emphasized that the equal protection clause of the Fourteenth Amendment prohibited discrimination against single people. The right of privacy, grounded in a substantive due process reading of the Fourteenth Amendment, included "the right of the individual, married or single, to be free from unwarranted governmental intrusion into matters so fundamentally affecting a person as the decision whether to bear or beget a child." Going beyond *Griswold*, the *Eisenstadt* decision explicitly recognized that the right to privacy was inherent in the individual rather than in the marital relationship, and it did not justify the right on the basis of history and tradition. The two decisions helped lay the theoretical foundation for *Roe v. Wade* (1973).

Thomas T. Lewis

SEE ALSO Birth control and contraception; Due process, substantive; Equal protection clause; Fundamental rights; Privacy, right to; *Roe v. Wade.*

Elastic clause

DESCRIPTION: Last clause of Article I, section 8, of the U.S. Constitution, authorizing Congress to make all laws necessary and proper for exercising its enumerated powers and any other power granted by the Constitution to the national government.

SIGNIFICANCE: After an 1819 Supreme Court decision, the elastic clause provided the basis for the doctrine of implied powers, stretching the powers of the national government beyond those specifically granted by the Constitution.

In 1791, when advising President George Washington on the constitutionality of establishing a national bank, Thomas Jefferson and others opposed to a strong national government maintained that Congress was limited to exercising those powers expressly granted by the Constitution, for example, the power to coin money. All other powers were reserved for the states. Jefferson argued that the necessary and proper clause imposed additional limits on the powers of Congress. The clause limited any use of powers not expressly granted by the Constitution except when such powers were absolutely necessary or indispensable to the exercise of an enumerated power. A national bank, for example, was unconstitutional both because the Constitution did not expressly delegate the power to create corporations to Congress and because a bank was not an indispensable means for achieving Congress's legitimate ends. A broader interpretation of

the clause, Jefferson argued, would effectively create a national government with unlimited power.

Alexander Hamilton and others opposed Jefferson's strict construction of the clause, maintaining that the Constitution established an independent national government that, although exercising limited powers, was fully sovereign within the scope of its powers. Hamilton argued that the elastic clause had to be broadly interpreted as granting whatever additional powers would assist Congress in carrying out its enumerated powers. The clause allowed Congress to do not just what was indispensable but also whatever was convenient or helpful to achieving its ends. The incorporation of a bank, for example, was constitutional because it was a useful means for Congress to carry out its delegated power to collect taxes.

When the controversy over the incorporation of the Second Bank of the United States reached the Supreme Court in *McCulloch v. Maryland* (1819), Chief Justice John Marshall transformed Hamilton's loose construction of the clause into constitutional law. In his opinion, he stated that if the ends were legitimate and within the scope of the Constitution, all means that were appropriate and not prohibited, as well as consistent with "the letter and spirit" of the Constitution, were constitutional. His decision meant that the Constitution did not limit the federal government's powers to those expressly delegated, but included powers implied by Congress's freedom to choose the means by which it would carry out its responsibilities.

FURTHER READING

Fisher, Louis. *The Politics of Shared Power: Congress and the Executive.* College Station: Texas A&M University Press, 1998.

Gunther, Gerald. *John Marshall's Defense of "McCulloch v. Maryland."* Stanford, Calif.: Stanford University Press, 1969.

Joseph V. Brogan

SEE ALSO Implied powers; *McCulloch v. Maryland*; Marshall, John; States' rights; Tenth Amendment.

Elections

DESCRIPTION: Events at which the citizens of a nation vote to select governmental and other public officials and to approve or disapprove of various local propositions and measures.

SIGNIFICANCE: Though the U.S. Constitution leaves the regulation of elections largely to Congress and the state legislatures, the Supreme Court has been a major influence in making the electoral system more accessible and in ensuring that each individual's vote is equal to that of every other voter.

The U.S. Constitution left elections and suffrage almost totally to the states' discretion. Article I, section 2, provides that the electors (voters) of each state shall have the qualifications requisite for electors of the most numerous branch of the state legislature. Although this clause provides a constitutional basis for the right to vote in federal elections, such a right did not actually exist until conferred by the states. Consequently, no uniform national electorate existed for several decades.

The states gradually removed most of the barriers to voting for white men. However, they were slow to extend suffrage to others, and the courts hesitated to infringe on the traditional prerogative of state legislatures to confer the privilege of voting. For example, when the suffragettes (those seeking the right to vote for women) filed a suit claiming the right to vote under the equal protection clause of the Fourteenth Amendment, the Supreme Court ruled in *Minor v. Happersett* (1875) that the right to vote was not a constitutionally protected right but a privilege conferred by an individual state.

Civil War Amendments. Regulation of elections and suffrage remained the exclusive domain of the states through the Civil War (1861-1865). Following the war, a major concern of Congress during Reconstruction was the enfranchisement of former slaves. Congressional efforts produced the Thirteenth (1865), Fourteenth (1868), and Fifteenth (1870) Amendments. The Fourteenth Amendment implied suffrage for African Americans by providing that states' representation in Congress could be reduced if they denied African Americans their voting rights. The Fifteenth Amendment prohibited the states or the federal government from excluding a person from voting on the basis of race, color, or previous condition of servitude.

These post-Civil War amendments designed to enfranchise African American voters led to a variety of efforts to block their participation and

brought in a new player—the Supreme Court. The Court's early involvement was a delicate balancing act. It tried to provide some federal protection of voting rights while still accommodating the traditional state control of suffrage and elections. In the 1870's the lower federal courts at first held that the right to vote, even in federal elections, derived from state constitutions and laws. In *United States v. Reese* (1876), the Court pointed out that the Fifteenth Amendment did not confer suffrage on anyone but rather prohibited the states or the federal government from denying the franchise to anyone on the basis of race, color, or previous condition of servitude.

By the 1880's the Court was beginning to uphold the federal government's power to protect the right to vote in state elections against racially based denials by either state officials or private parties and in federal elections against denial from any source and for whatever reasons. In *Ex parte Siebold* (1880), *Ex parte Clarke* (1880), and *United States v. Gale* (1883), the Court upheld convictions of state officials for interfering with national elections. In *Ex parte Yarbrough* (1884), the Court declared that voters in national elections got their right to vote from the U.S. Constitution, though the states could determine voter qualifications. This case also established federal power to protect the right to vote in national elections against private as well as state discrimination whether racially based or not.

Attempts at Circumvention. In response to growing federal pressure, the states and private parties devised various strategies for either legally denying or discouraging African Americans from voting. Among these were such devices as grandfather clauses, poll taxes, literacy tests, white primaries, and outright intimidation. In the 1890's the Court acceded to such state disenfranchisement schemes in decisions such as *Williams v. Mississippi* (1898), in which the Court allowed to stand a Mississippi law that authorized literacy tests and a poll tax.

In the first half of the twentieth century, Congress and the Court began to address discrimination against voters more aggressively, and one by one the various discriminatory practices began to fall. In *Guinn v. United States* (1915), the Court declared grandfather clauses (stipulations that only those whose ancestors voted could also vote) to be unconstitutional violations of voting rights. This decision put the Court on record as regarding any attempts to disenfranchise voters because of their race or color as violations of the Fifteenth Amendment.

However, when the Court ruled in *Newberry v. United States* (1921) that party primaries were not an integral part of the election process, this put primaries outside the reach of federal regulatory power. After this ruling, a number of states proceeded to adopt laws allowing political parties to determine who could vote in their nominating elections. In some states, laws stipulated that only white people could vote in primaries, effectively disenfranchising African Americans in the Democratic Party-dominated South. In 1927 the Court tried to end the practice by nullifying Texas's white primary law in *Nixon v. Herndon*. However, this decision failed to completely close the door, and political parties in several states were organized as private clubs, which excluded African Americans from participation in the nomination of candidates. In 1935 in *Grovey v. Townsend*, the Court ruled that as private groups, the political parties were not subject to provisions of the Fourteenth and Fifteenth Amendments.

Six years later in *United States v. Classic* (1941), the Court, realizing that the time, places, and manner clause of Article I was meaningless if primaries were not covered, reversed its *Newberry* position and declared primaries an integral part of the election process. Three years later in *Smith v. Allwright* (1944), the Court struck down the private club claim, holding that when the political parties were acting as agents of the state in the primary election process, they were subject to provisions of the Fourteenth and Fifteenth Amendments. In one final effort, the Democratic Party in Texas formed the unofficial Jaybird Party to nominate candidates and thereby exclude African Americans from the process. However, in *Terry v. Adams* (1953), the Court ruled that even though "unofficial," the Jaybird Party was performing an official election function and was engaging in unconstitutional discrimination.

With the white primary finally circumscribed by the Court, those seeking to deny African American voting rights turned to more subtle and indirect means of challenging the Court's commitment to eliminating voter discrimination. In *Gomillion v. Lightfoot* (1960), the Court struck down an Ala-

bama law that redrew the boundaries of the city of Tuskegee in such a way that virtually all of the city's African Americans were placed outside the city limits. The Court stated that this clearly violated their voting rights under the Fifteenth Amendment. In 1964 the Twenty-Fourth Amendment went into effect, outlawing poll taxes as a qualification for voting in federal elections, and in 1965 Congress passed the Voting Rights Act, designed to address any remaining pockets of discrimination against minority voters. In *Harper v. Virginia State Board of Elections* (1966), the Court banned poll taxes for all elections, saying they violated the equal protection clause. Also in 1966 the Court upheld the Voting

In 1875, the Supreme Court ruled that the Fourteenth Amendment did not give women the right to vote. Not until the ratification of the Nineteenth Amendment in 1920 would women be able to vote. The League of Women Voters was formed to make the most of this new power. (Library of Congress)

Rights Act's ban on literacy tests as a voting qualification (*South Carolina v. Katzenbach*) and New York's English literacy requirement in *Katzenbach v. Morgan.*

Diluting the Vote. With the passage of the Voting Rights Act, the focus shifted slightly from voter access to efforts to dilute the voting power of minority voters or limit their chances of electoral success through such methods as at-large elections, multimember districts and gerrymandering of election districts. In *White v. Regester* (1973), the Court ruled that multimember districts violated voters' constitutional rights when their effect was to dilute the voting strength of minority voters. However, in *Mobile v. Bolden* (1980), the Court refused to strike down a system of at-large elections in the absence of evidence of "intent to discriminate." Congress responded by amending the Voting Rights Act in 1982 to include a "discriminatory results test" instead of the Court's "discriminatory intent" standard. In *Rogers v. Lodge* (1982), the Court blended the two, saying an intent to discriminate could be inferred from the results of an election that produced no African American office holders or a disproportionately small number of them.

Although the Court has generally sought to make the election processes more open and democratic, as is shown in its decisions on the election of judges and voter residency requirements, it also seeks to leave as much control as possible to the states. In *Chisom v. Roemer* (1991), the Court held that provisions of the Voting Rights Act apply to the election of judges as well as of other elected officials. In *Dunn v. Blumstein* (1972), the Court invalidated Tennessee's one-year residency requirement for state and local elections, expressing a preference for a thirty-day requirement. In *Growe v. Emison* (1993), the Court ruled that when parallel redistricting plans are pending in state and federal courts, the federal courts must defer to the state courts. In *Burson v. Freeman* (1992), the Court allowed Tennessee's ban on campaigning within one hundred feet of voting places on election day, and in *Burdick v. Takuski* (1992), the Court found that Hawaii's ban on write-in votes did not impose unreasonable or discriminatory limits on the right to vote.

Apportionment. Other than on the issue of minority voting rights, the most far-reaching actions of the Court have been in the area of apportionment and the instituting of the one person, one vote concept. Although most states had provisions calling for election districts to be redrawn after each U.S. Census, many either ignored this task or failed to take it seriously. Consequently, many election districts became badly malapportioned, with widely disparate populations. In California, Los Angeles County had 6 million residents while the least populous rural district had only 14,000. In Florida, the population of state senate districts ranged from 900,000 to 9,500. When this issue was brought to the Court in *Colegrove v. Green* (1946), the majority held that redistricting was a "political issue" that the Court could not address. Malapportionment became more widespread, making voting strength from district to district more unequal.

In 1962 the Court agreed to revisit the issue and in *Baker v. Carr* (1962) ruled that malapportionment was a justiciable issue under the equal protection clause of the Fourteenth Amendment. Although *Baker* set the precedent for Court-ordered apportionment, it left many questions unanswered. Further elaboration came quickly. In *Gray v. Sanders* (1963), the Court held that a Georgia election plan that worked to the disadvantage of the more populous counties denied equal voting rights. In an 8-1 decision, the Court laid down the one person, one vote concept. In *Wesberry v. Sanders* (1964), the Court applied the same concept to districts for electing members of the House of Representatives. Writing for the majority, Justice Hugo L. Black said that as nearly as possible one person's vote in a congressional election should be worth as much as another's.

Four months later in *Reynolds v. Sims* (1964), the Court ruled that both houses of state legislatures must be based on population. In this decision Justice Earl Warren declared that *Wesberry* had established the principle that representative government meant equal representation for equal numbers of people. In *Avery v. Midland County* (1968), the Court extended the one person, one vote concept to city and county governments. In *Kirkpatrick v. Preisler* (1969) and *Wells v. Rockefeller* (1969), the Court noted that the one person, one vote principle required that states make a good-faith effort to achieve precise mathematical equality in their distribution of population among districts.

Although its path has taken various twists and turns, generally the Court's involvement in the electoral process has been directed toward making the process more open and accessible and making the rights of all voters and the relative strength of their votes as equal as possible. Through its decisions on elections and voting, the Court has been a major force for a more egalitarian democracy in the United States.

FURTHER READING

For a good general discussion of elections and their role in democratic government, see Benjamin Ginsberg and Martin Shafter's *Politics by Other Means: The Declining Importance of Elections in America* (New York: Basic Books, 1990) and *Do Elections Matter?*, edited by Benjamin Ginsberg and Alan Stone (3d ed., New York: Sharpe, 1996). An excellent discussion of the legal and constitutional issues of elections and voting is Richard Claude's *The Supreme Court and the Electoral Process* (Baltimore, Md.: Johns Hopkins University Press, 1970). An account of the Court's earlier role in expanding voting rights is Ward Elliott's *The Rise of Guardian Democracy: The Supreme Court's Role in Voting Rights Disputes, 1845-1969* (Cambridge, Mass.: Harvard Political Studies, 1974). Useful works on the issue of race and voting rights are Abigail M. Thernstrom's *Whose Votes Count? Affirmative Action and Minority Voting Rights* (New York: Twentieth Century Fund, 1987) and Michael Dawson's *Behind the Mule: Race and Class in American Politics* (Princeton, N.J.: Princeton University Press, 1994). Timothy G. O'Rourke's *The Impact of Reapportionment* (New Brunswick, N.J.: Transaction Books, 1980) provides a detailed analysis of the effect of the Court's reapportionment decisions on voting and elections.

Carl P. Chelf

SEE ALSO Civil Rights acts; Equal protection clause; Fifteenth Amendment; Financing political speech; Gerrymandering; Grandfather clause; Political parties; Poll taxes; Representation, fairness of; Twenty-fourth Amendment; Understanding tests; Vote, right to; Voting Rights Act of 1965; White primaries.

Eleventh Amendment

DATE: 1795

DESCRIPTION: Amendment to the U.S. Constitution restricting the power of federal courts to hear lawsuits lodged against states by citizens of other states or of foreign countries.

SIGNIFICANCE: This forty-three-word amendment was cited as the justification for many Supreme Court decisions that extend far beyond what it states overtly.

The Eleventh Amendment was the first amendment to the U.S. Constitution following the adoption of the ten original amendments known as the Bill of Rights in 1791. The Eleventh Amendment was adopted specifically to overrule a Supreme Court decision, *Chisholm v. Georgia* (1793). In this decision, the Court ruled that a default judgment in favor of the plaintiff, who served as executor for the estate of a South Carolina merchant, was valid because the defendant, the state of Georgia, had refused to appear in its own defense at the trial. Georgia claimed that, as an independent and sovereign state, it enjoyed immunity from such litigation.

Article III, section 2, of the U.S. Constitution grants jurisdiction to federal courts in the case of controversies between a state and citizens of another state. In a 4-1 decision, with only justice James Iredell dissenting, the Court set a precedent by ruling that the plaintiff in *Chisholm* had the right to sue the state of Georgia and that the state of Georgia was legally remiss in not responding to that suit. Opinions by Justices John Jay and James Wilson reiterated the nationalist view that sovereignty rests in the people of the United States for the purposes of union. In regard to these purposes, Georgia, in the eyes of these justices, did not meet the criterion of being a sovereign state.

Passage of the Amendment. Within a year of the *Chisholm* decision, Congress, on March 4, 1794, drafted the Eleventh Amendment and urged its passage. By February 4, 1795, the legislatures of the requisite three-quarters of the states had ratified this amendment, which officially made it a law and a part of the U.S. Constitution. By an odd circumstance, however, the amendment was not officially declared a part of the Constitution until January 8, 1798, when President John Quincy Adams declared it so in a presidential message.

The date on which the Eleventh Amendment officially became a part of the Constitution is often given as January 8, 1798, although it is now conceded that presidents play no official role in the

---

TEXT OF THE ELEVENTH AMENDMENT

The Judicial power of the United States shall not be construed to extend to any suit in law or equity, commenced or prosecuted against one of the United States by Citizens of another State, or by Citizens or Subjects of any Foreign State.

---

amendment process, so the Eleventh Amendment officially became a part of the Constitution after its ratification in 1795. The only states not voting for it were Pennsylvania and New Jersey.

Provisions of the Eleventh Amendment. Under the Eleventh Amendment, federal courts are prohibited from deciding lawsuits brought against states by two specific classes of people, citizens of other states and citizens or subjects of foreign states. As time passed, however, the Eleventh Amendment was interpreted more broadly than had perhaps been originally intended by its framers.

In *New Hampshire v. Louisiana* (1883), the Supreme Court ruled that one state could not sue another state if it did so in the interests of one or more of its citizens rather than in its own interest. Shortly thereafter, in *Hans v. Louisiana* (1890), the Court held that citizens of a state could not sue their own state in the federal courts. A further extension of the Eleventh Amendment occurred in *Ex parte New York* (1921), when the Court found that the amendment applied to admiralty jurisdiction so that sovereign states, as defined by the Court, could not be sued in federal courts for events that took place in the waters that adjoined those states.

In *Monaco v. Mississippi* (1934), the Court clearly found that foreign sovereigns could not sue sovereign states of the United States in federal courts. The decision in *Edelman v. Jordan* (1974) established, again under the jurisdiction of the Eleventh Amendment, that in situations where state officials are sued and compensation for past misdeeds would have to be paid from state treasuries, the complainants cannot pursue their actions in federal courts.

Exceptions. To ensure fairness, however, certain exceptions have been made to this amendment. Al-

though a law exists stating that parties may not bestow jurisdiction on courts, individual states may, in some situations, waive their protection under the Eleventh Amendment and consent to being sued. Congress, under the enforcement powers accorded it in the Fourteenth and Fifteenth Amendments, may approve private causes of action against states, invoking the commerce clause of the Constitution.

Perhaps no amendment to the Constitution has been interpreted as variously as the Eleventh. Some noted legal scholars have called for its restatement and simplification. Others have proposed that the amendment be interpreted literally from the forty-three words that constitute it. At present, however, citizens who have cause to take action against states must resort to political action or work within the framework of exceptions that has resulted from the complexities that varying interpretations of the Eleventh Amendment have evoked.

FURTHER READING

Baum, Lawrence. *The Supreme Court.* 4th ed. Washington, D.C.: Congressional Quarterly, 1991.

Orth, John V. *The Judicial Power of the United States: The Eleventh Amendment in American History.* New York: Oxford University Press, 1987.

Spaeth, Harold J. *Studies in U.S. Supreme Court Behavior.* New York: Garland, 1990.

Wagman, Robert J. *The Supreme Court: A Citizen's Guide.* New York: Pharos Books, 1993.

R. Baird Shuman

SEE ALSO Bill of Rights; *Chisholm v. Georgia*; *Edelman v. Jordan*; Reversals of Court decisions by amendment; Separation of powers.

Elfbrandt v. Russell

CITATION: 384 U.S. 11
DATE: April 18, 1966
ISSUE: Loyalty oaths
SIGNIFICANCE: The Supreme Court invalidated an Arizona statute and its accompanying statutory gloss, which together required employees to take an oath to support the federal and state constitutions, threatening prosecution for perjury and immediate discharge of an employee belonging to any organization committed to overthrowing the government.

Barbara Elfbrandt, a teacher and a Quaker, refused to take the oath and sued on the grounds that the legislature had not adequately explained the meaning of the statute and its accompanying gloss. Her lawyers referred to *Baggett v. Bullitt* (1964) and other cases in which the Supreme Court had struck down loyalty oaths that had restricted individual rights to free expression of ideas and political association.

Speaking for a 5-4 majority, Justice William O. Douglas argued that the legislative gloss interfered with the freedom of association guaranteed by the First and Fourteenth Amendments. He referred to several precedents in which the Court had held that a blanket prohibition of association with groups having both legal and illegal purposes interfered with the freedom of political expression and association.

Elfbrandt was typical of a half dozen cases in which the Court overturned loyalty oaths on grounds of vagueness or overbreadth. However, in *Cole v. Richardson* (1972), the Court upheld a requirement that state employees take an oath or affirmation similar to the one in Article VI of the U.S. Constitution.

Thomas T. Lewis

SEE ALSO Assembly and association, freedom of; Cold War; *Keyishian v. Board of Regents*.

Ellsworth, Oliver

IDENTIFICATION: Chief justice (March 8, 1796-December 15, 1800)

NOMINATED BY: George Washington

BORN: April 29, 1745, Windsor, Connecticut

DIED: November 26, 1807, Windsor, Connecticut

SIGNIFICANCE: Ellsworth helped author the Judiciary Act of 1789, which established the federal judicial system. As an associate justice, he favored the expansion of the powers of the federal courts, but illness and a diplomatic assignment prevented him from having much impact.

Intended by his father to have a career in the church, Ellsworth entered Yale in 1762 but left two years later to complete his college education at Princeton, where he earned a B.A. in 1766. Soon after returning home, he gave up the study of theology for law. Admitted to the bar in 1771, he set up practice in Windsor, Connecticut. Four years later,

Oliver Ellsworth. (William Wheeler/Collection of the Supreme Court of the United States)

he moved to Hartford, where he quickly rose to prominence and recognition as a leader of the Connecticut bar.

In 1777 Ellsworth was appointed state's attorney for Hartford County. He became a member of the Governor's Council within three years and a judge of the Connecticut superior court shortly thereafter. During the Revolutionary War, as a member of the Committee of the Pay Table, he supervised the state's war expenditures; in 1779, he was chosen to serve on the Council of Safety. Also in 1777, the Connecticut general assembly appointed him a delegate to the Continental Congress, where he served for six years. As a delegate, Ellsworth gained recognition for the Connecticut compromise, which established two legislative houses and, to create a balance between states with large and small populations, granted each state two senators. He also recommended that the words "United States" be used instead of the word "nation" to designate the government.

One of the first U.S. senators from Connecticut, he served in this capacity for seven years until appointed chief justice of the United States in 1796. In the Senate, Ellsworth had earned respect for drafting the Judiciary Act of 1789, which established the circuit and district court system, but his three-year term as chief justice was fairly undistinguished. His decisions were more remarkable for common sense than for legal learning. Although he was known as a good lawyer, Ellsworth was more an advocate than a jurist. Noteworthy, however, is his decision on *Hylton v. United States* (1796), the first time the Supreme Court ruled on the constitutionality of an act of Congress.

In 1799 Ellsworth, although still chief justice, traveled to France, where he and other U.S. commissioners negotiated with Napoleon Bonaparte to avoid a war between the two countries. The combined effects of arduous travel and difficult negotiations broke his health, and he resigned from the Supreme Court in 1800, while still in France. After retiring to Connecticut in 1801, he served in that state's upper house and was appointed chief justice of Connecticut's highest court in 1807, the year of his death.

FURTHER READING

Brown, William Garrott. *The Life of Oliver Ellsworth.* New York: Macmillan, 1905. Reprint. New York: DeCapo Press, 1970.

Friedman, Leon, and Fred L. Israel, eds. *The Justices of the Supreme Court: Their Lives and Major Opinions.* 5 vols. New York: Chelsea House, 1997.

Bes Stark Spangler

SEE ALSO Chief justice; Constitutional Convention; *Hylton v. United States*; Jay, John; Judiciary Act of 1789; Washington, George.

Elrod v. Burns

CITATION: 427 U.S. 347
DATE: June 28, 1976
ISSUE: Freedom of association
SIGNIFICANCE: The Supreme Court held that patronage dismissals of nonpolicy-making employees infringed on First Amendment rights to political beliefs and association.

In Cook County, Illinois, an elected Democratic sheriff attempted to remove several noncivil service employees who had been appointed by the previous sheriff, a Republican. By a 5-3 vote, the Court upheld a court of appeals judgment for injunction relief. Speaking for a plurality, Justice William J. Brennan, Jr., concluded that the First Amendment prohibited patronage dismissals except in policy-making positions. A few years later, the Court expanded the immunity of most noncivil service employees from penalties based on political affiliation in *Branti v. Finkel et al.* (1980) and *Rutan v. Republican Party of Illinois* (1990).

Thomas T. Lewis

SEE ALSO Assembly and association, freedom of; Political parties; *Robel, United States v.*; *Rutan v. Republican Party of Illinois*.

Employment discrimination

DESCRIPTION: Act of making decisions related to hiring and promoting workers based on nonjob-related characteristics such as race, color, religion, national origin, gender, age, and disability.
SIGNIFICANCE: The Fourteenth Amendment prohibits state-sponsored discrimination, and Congress, through its authority to regulate interstate commerce, passed several important statutes preventing employment discrimination. Through the Supreme Court's power to interpret these statutes, it influences employment discrimination law and policy.

Title VII of the Civil Rights Act of 1964 (including its amendments) is the most important employment discrimination statute in U.S. law. It forbids employment discrimination on the grounds of race, color, religion, sex, or national origin by private companies (with at least fifteen employees), labor unions, employment agencies, and federal, state, and local governments. The statute also created the Equal Employment Opportunity Commission (EEOC) to investigate charges of discrimination, attempt to work an agreement, and if necessary file suit in federal court on behalf of the plaintiff. Congress also passed the Age Discrimination in Employment Act of 1967 and the Americans with Disabilities Act of 1990, which extend similar protections against age and disability discrimination in the workplace. Although some Supreme Court litigation addressed employment discrimination in religion, national origin, disability, and age, the bulk of the Court's influence was in the areas of race and gender.

Race. Because racial discrimination has been so prominent in U.S. history, most of the Court's rulings involving Title VII concern race. In *Griggs v. Duke Power Co.* (1971), the Court had to decide whether African Americans could pursue a Title VII claim for employment practices that were not intended to discriminate but nevertheless put them at a disadvantage. The Duke Power Company used an examination as a standard for hiring and promotion. On this test, not directly related to job duties, blacks generally scored lower than whites. The Court ruled unanimously that even if there is no discriminatory intent, a practice that has a disparate impact on a protected class constitutes a Title VII violation. However, in *Wards Cove Packing Co. v. Atonio* (1989), the Court held that to establish disparate impact, plaintiffs needed to go beyond demonstrating that a particular practice caused a statistical disparity. Plaintiffs must also prove that the disparity did not result from a business necessity. The Civil Rights Act of 1991 reversed the Court's interpretation in *Wards Cove*, shifting the burden of proof to the employer to show that the employment practice is directly related to the position in question and is necessary for the normal operation of the business.

Furthermore, in *McDonnell Douglas Corp. v. Green* (1973), the Court addressed how to prove discriminatory intent (disparate treatment). McDonnell Douglas refused to rehire a black worker who had protested his layoff by criminally trespassing on McDonnell Douglas property. Although the Court sided with McDonnell Douglas, it did articulate a procedure for proving disparate treatment, which generally favors plaintiffs. First, the employee must show only that he/she is a member of a racial minority, applied and was qualified for the job, was rejected, and the position remained open. Then, the employer has a chance to provide a nondiscriminatory reason for its practice, but the plaintiff still has an opportunity to demonstrate that the employer's claim is a pretext for discrimination. In short, when a plaintiff alleges disparate treatment, the employer shoulders the burden of justifying the employment practice.

Not all racial employment discrimination litigation is based on Title VII. In *Johnson v. Railway Express Agency* (1975), the Court ruled that the Civil Rights Act of 1866 prohibited racial discrimination in private contracts, including discriminatory hir-

Albert Wynn (left) and Elijah Cummings, both Democratic representatives from Maryland, hold a news conference in Washington, D.C., in 1997 to protest alleged discrimination in the federal workforce, especially at the management level. (AP/Wide World Photos)

ing. In *Patterson v. McLean Credit Union* (1989), the Court refused to apply this statute to racial harassment in the workplace. However, the Civil Rights Act of 1991 amended the 1866 act to cover racial harassment.

Gender. Because gender discrimination is covered under Title VII, the landmark rulings for race apply to women as well, although there are several issues that are distinct for sex discrimination. First, Title VII allows for discrimination in cases in which it may be reasonably necessary for the operation of the business in question, thus establishing the bona fide occupational qualification exception. In upholding Alabama's exclusion of women from guard positions in maximum security prisons, the Court nevertheless articulated a stringent standard for allowing an occupational qualification exception in *Dothard v. Rawlinson* (1977). Any bona fide occupational qualification must be a "business necessity," which is usually difficult for an employer to establish. In *Automobile Workers v. Johnson Controls* (1991), the Court ruled that a battery manufac-

314 Employment Division, Department of Human Resources v. Smith

turer may not use the bona fide occupational qualification to exclude women of childbearing age from jobs that expose them to toxic materials that may damage a potential fetus.

Another gender discrimination issue concerns sexual harassment. In *Meritor Savings Bank v. Vinson* (1986), the Court ruled that sexual harassment did constitute sexual discrimination under Title VII. It decided further that a plaintiff could bring Title VII action even if she does not suffer any physical or psychological damage (*Harris v. Forklift Systems*, 1993) or is unable to establish employer negligence (*Burlington Industries v. Ellerth*, 1998).

FURTHER READING

Bloch, Farrell. *Antidiscrimination Law and Minority Employment.* Chicago: University of Chicago Press, 1994.

Epstein, Richard A. *Forbidden Grounds: The Case Against Employment Discrimination Laws.* Cambridge, Mass.: Harvard University Press, 1992.

Friedman, Joel William, and George M. Strickler. *Cases and Materials on the Law of Employment Discrimination.* Westbury, N.Y.: Foundation Press, 1997.

Player, Mack A., Elaine W. Shoben, and Risa L. Liebowitz. *Employment Discrimination Law Cases and Materials.* St. Paul, Minn.: West Publishing, 1995.

Steven C. Tauber

SEE ALSO Affirmative action; Age discrimination; *Albemarle Paper Co. v. Moody*; *Automobile Workers v. Johnson Controls*; Gender issues; *Griggs v. Duke Power Co.*; *Patterson v. McLean Credit Union*; Race and discrimination; *Wards Cove Packing Co. v. Atonio.*

Employment Division, Department of Human Resources v. Smith

CITATION: 494 U.S. 872
DATE: April 17, 1990
ISSUE: Freedom of religion
SIGNIFICANCE: Narrowly interpreting the free exercise clause of the First Amendment, the Supreme Court ruled that the states were not required to make a religious exception for the use of illegal drugs.

Alfred Smith and another Native American were fired from their jobs after their employer discovered that they occasionally smoked the hallucinogenic drug peyote as a part of tribal religious ceremonies. The use of peyote was illegal in Oregon, and the state's policy was to deny unemployment benefits to anyone discharged for work-related misconduct. The two men argued that the denial of benefits unconstitutionally infringed on their right to religious freedom. Their lawyers referred to *Sherbert v. Verner* (1963), which had required states to justify any indirect restraints on religion according to the "compelling state interest" standard.

In the *Smith* case, however, the Supreme Court voted six to three to uphold Oregon's policy. Justice Antonin Scalia argued that states had no obligation to make exceptions for laws that were reasonable, secular in intent, and generally applicable to all persons. Such matters were left up to legislative discretion, even if an unfortunate consequence was an "incidental burden" on unconventional religious practices. Although Justice Sandra Day O'Connor joined the majority in upholding Oregon's policy, she joined the three dissenters in wanting to continue *Sherbert*'s standards of strict scrutiny. Religious leaders and civil libertarians were outraged at the *Smith* decision. In the Religious Freedom Restoration Act of 1993, Congress required courts to return to the standards of *Sherbert*, but the Court overturned this requirement in *Boerne v. Flores* (1997).

Thomas T. Lewis

SEE ALSO *Boerne v. Flores*; Fundamental rights; Judicial scrutiny; Religion, freedom of; *Sherbert v. Verner.*

Engel v. Vitale

CITATION: 370 U.S. 421
DATE: June 25, 1962
ISSUE: Establishment of religion
SIGNIFICANCE: The Supreme Court, by invalidating a nondenominational prayer, first banned prayers in public schools as an unconstitutional establishment of religion.

Justice Hugo L. Black wrote the 7-1 opinion, in which Justice Byron R. White did not participate. The Supreme Court invalidated a twenty-two-word nondenominational school prayer composed by New York's educational authority as an unconstitutional establishment of religion. Having previously applied the prohibition against the establishment

After the Supreme Court banned school prayer, school teachers found other ways to start the day. Here, an elementary school teacher in Pittsburgh reads from a book called The School Day Begins. *(Library of Congress)*

of religion to the states under the Fourteenth Amendment in *Everson v. Board of Education of Ewing Township* (1947), the Court needed only to clarify what it meant by a "wall of separation between church and state." *Engel* raised the wall much higher.

Black provided a lengthy review of British and American history to justify his decision but did not cite any specific Court precedent. He opined that this decision would not block all public expression of religion but held that schools could not sponsor such expressions. Although the Court was supported by a number of groups that filed *amicus curiae* (friend of the court) briefs, when it sided with those who wanted a high wall, it provoked an intense reaction from many conservative religious groups. The storm of criticism did not deter the Court, which persisted in its position. Justice Potter Stewart was the lone dissenter, accusing the majority of misreading the First Amendment's religious clauses, which forbade only governmental establishment of an official church. To do otherwise was to open up unnecessary conflicts with the free exercise provision that Stewart thought was preeminent.

Richard L. Wilson

SEE ALSO *Abington School District v. Schempp; Everson v. Board of Education of Ewing Township;* Religion, establishment of; School prayer.

Environmental law

DESCRIPTION: Legislation dealing with and often designed to protect the natural and physical surroundings—the air, earth, and water—in which humans, other animals, and plants exist, or with the plants and animals themselves.

SIGNIFICANCE: The Supreme Court often interpreted the wording of environmental laws and regulations, determined the intended environmental policy goals, ensured that agencies enforce these laws, and resolved conflicting interests among the state and national governments on environmental issues.

Recognizing that technical expertise is necessary to implement environmental public policies, legislators have delegated considerable policy-making power to administrative agencies. Federal environmental legislation is often written in very general terms to provide considerable discretion to administrative agencies in the administration and enforcement of environmental law. The agencies' use of this discretion is subject to challenge in the judicial system. Industry groups and environmental organizations often challenge the processes and rationale by which agency decisions are made and the agencies' interpretation of the words and concepts in the legislation. Judicial interpretation of constitutional provisions and legislative acts permitted the federal government and federal regulatory agencies increased authority in regulation of environmental issues. Requests to the court system for judicial administrative oversight and for interpretation of legislation have allowed industry and environmental organizations to delay implementation of administrative decisions, to obtain specific policy goals within the context of environmental legislation, and to encourage legislative amendments and administrative alterations to environmental legislation.

Until the late 1960's, control of land use, pollution, and environmental nuisances was limited to state and local laws implemented under the police powers of the state. These powers were upheld by the Supreme Court in *Euclid v. Ambler Realty Co.* (1926) and *Georgia v. Tennessee Copper Co.* (1902). Federal government regulation of the environment was limited because the Constitution included no specific grant of authority to the federal government to act in this area. The Court upheld the federal government's power to regulate treatment of migratory wildfowl by treaty in *Missouri v. Holland* (1920) and to regulate pollution in navigable waters in *United States v. Republic Steel Corp.* (1960). Federal environmental legislation was largely limited to conserving and protecting nationally owned park lands, forests, and prairies; to constructing harbor facilities; to constructing irrigation, power generation, and flood control structures on navigable waters; to promoting agricultural soil and water conservation issues; and to

The experiences of civil lawyer Jan Schlichtmann, standing before the Norfolk Superior Court in Dedham, Massachusetts, in trying a Woburn environmental pollution case were made into a book, A Civil Action, *by John Grisham, and then a 1998 movie. Since the late 1960's, the Supreme Court and Congress have played an increasing role in environmental protection.* (AP/Wide World Photos)

studying air and water quality conditions. In *Hodel v. Indiana* (1981), the Court permitted the federal government to use its commerce power to establish environmental regulations, thereby increasing the range of federal government activity in environmental regulation.

Beginning with the enactment of the National Environmental Policy Act (NEPA) of 1969, the federal government began taking responsibility for the quality of the natural environment and for setting standards for environmental quality. As each subsequent act was passed by the legislature, appeals were made to the courts to modify the impact of each of those acts. As a consequence of judicial decisions, agency administration and enforcement of the laws and the public policy impact of the laws were modified. Many of the acts were subsequently amended by the legislature to clarify the legislature's intent and to remedy omissions in the original legislation.

The 1969 Act. The NEPA was intended to force nonenvironmental agencies to include environmental considerations in making agency decisions by requiring environmental impact statements (EIS) for government projects and by allowing citizens to sue in federal court when government agencies failed to fully assess environmental impact. Citizens used the judicial process to delay permitting for private and governmental projects affecting the environment. These delaying actions raised the costs of the proposed projects but also provided the time and the incentive for industry and government to review and modify their original proposals to lessen unfavorable effects on the environment.

Subsequent suits brought to the Court gradually eroded the effectiveness of environmental impact statements. For example, in *Kleppe v. Sierra Club* (1976), involving the strip-mining industry, the Court postponed the need for an EIS until late in the proposed project's planning and limited the EIS to impact on the local area rather than an entire geographic region. In *Vermont Yankee Nuclear Power Corp. v. Natural Resources Defense Council* (1978), the Court held that the technical expertise of the Nuclear Regulatory Commission to manage nuclear power policy could not be challenged by the technical expertise of environmental experts, thus severely limiting the use of EIS by environmental cause organizations to ensure that environmental issues were considered in agency policy decisions. The Court also instructed lower courts that only arbitrary and capricious agency actions or actions clearly beyond agency statutory authority are to be invalidated.

Andrus v. Sierra Club (1979) exempted budget processes from EIS review and *Strycher Bay v. Karlen* (1980), *Baltimore Gas and Electric v. Natural Resources Defense Council* (1983), and *Metropolitan Edison Co. v. People Against Nuclear Energy* (1983) had the combined effect of reducing the substantive content requirements for environmental impact statements and limiting their effectiveness as vehicles for ensuring that environmental considerations would be included in government agency and private industry decision making.

Water and Air Pollution Cases. The Federal Water Pollution Control Act of 1972 (also known as the Clean Water Act) gave the Environmental Protection Agency (EPA) authority to control private and state activities to reduce water pollution in an effort to make the waterways "swimmable and fishable" and free of manmade pollutants. The EPA set industry standards for the effluent permitted to flow into streams and pollution reduction standards for each pollution source discharging effluent into the streams. The EPA also set standards for use of the "best practicable" or "best available" technology for achieving required pollution reductions. In subsequent litigation, the Court required the EPA to provide numerous variances from EPA requirements and challenged the expertise of the EPA to classify pollutants or to set standards for their discharge into streams.

The Court also interpreted the wording in the 1972 act to erode previous federal common-law remedies available to downstream citizens affected by upstream pollution. In *Illinois v. Milwaukee* (1972) and *Middlesex County Sewerage Authority v. National Sea Clammers* (1981), the Court held that industries or agencies with EPA permits for effluent discharge could not be sued for the environmental damage their effluent caused downstream water users.

Other Court decisions effectively reduced the authority of the EPA to limit water pollution, prevented citizens from suing for damages, limited citizen standing to sue in order to require agencies to implement environmental protections, and provided public policy gains for polluting industries

and municipal governments at the expense of citizens living downstream.

The Clean Air Act Amendments of 1970 gave the EPA authority to set national ambient air quality standards similar to the clean water standards authorized under the Clean Water Act. The EPA chose to enforce those standards only in areas with high levels of air pollution. The Court ruled in *Sierra Club v. Ruckelshaus* (1972) and *Fri v. Sierra Club* (1973) that standards must also be set and enforced for areas with low pollution levels, thus requiring the EPA to either expand the scope of its activities or cease enforcing its standards in areas with substantial air pollution. Congress subsequently required the expansion of EPA activity in the 1977 amendments to the Clean Air Act.

The Court made other decisions concerning Clean Air Act enforcement that reduced the impact of the act and provided considerable relief to industry. In *Chevron, U.S.A. v. Natural Resources Defense Council* (1984) and *Alabama Power v. Castle* (1979), the Court allowed industries to offset increases in air pollution in one area of their plants with reductions in other areas and permitted some increase in air pollution by individual industries in geographic areas where overall pollution was on the decline. In the 1990 Amendments to the Clean Air Act and other legislation, Congress began to micromanage air pollution public policy in response to the actions of the courts.

Hazardous Waste. Congress passed the Resource Conservation and Recovery Act (RCRA) of 1976 and the Comprehensive Environmental Response, Compensation, and Liability Act (also known as the Superfund Act) of 1980 to control the transportation and disposal of hazardous wastes and to identify and clean up abandoned hazardous waste dumps. The Superfund requirement that the costs of dump cleanup should be recovered from those who owned the site or profited from its operation brought numerous lawsuits. In *United States v. Monsanto* (1988) and *United States v. Northeastern Pharmaceutical and Chemical Co.* (1986), the Court established strict liability and joint liability of all concerned. The decision to assign joint liability for any entity that profited from the waste dump brought a flood of civil suits as industries, banks, insurance companies, and others argued as to how much of the costs of cleaning up abandoned dumps each should bear. The Court's subsequent interpretation of strict and joint liability resulted in banks, lending institutions, and governments becoming liable for cleanup costs simply because of loans, defaults on loans, confiscation of property for nonpayment of property taxes, and other "innocent" acts. Congress amended the Superfund Act with the Superfund Amendments and Reauthorization Act of 1986 in an effort to relieve innocent parties of the liabilities assigned by the courts.

Other Judicial Limits. The Constitution's Fifth Amendment mandate that private property may not be taken for public use without just compensation (the takings clause) was applied by the Court in *Nollan v. California Coastal Commission* (1987) as a signal that government environmental regulations limiting an owner's land use must be substantially in the state interest. The Court invalidated state and local laws that interfered with federal regulations in *Burbank v. Lockheed Air Terminal* (1973) and that seek to regulate areas already regulated by the federal government in *Exxon Corp. v. Hunt* (1986) and *International Paper Co. v. Ouillette* (1987). In these and other cases, the Court held that federal law supplants and preempts state and local law on environmental issues on which the federal government chooses to act. In those cases in which federal laws contain nonpreemption provisions intended to allow states to enact complementary laws, the Court narrowly interpreted these nonpreemption provisions and restricted states from acting in areas in which comprehensive federal environmental laws and regulations already exist. The Court's use of the doctrine of federal preemption to invalidate state and local environmental laws when national legislation is enacted serves to erode the power of state and local governments within the federal system.

During most of the late twentieth century, the Court permitted Congress and federal agencies to increase the number of environmental issues addressed through law and regulation and generally upheld agency discretion in interpreting and applying rules and regulations.

FURTHER READING

James P. Lester's text *Environmental Politics and Policy: Theories and Evidence* (Durham, N.C.: Duke University Press, 1995) describes the role and the interrelationship of each branch of government in environmental law. Nancy K. Kubasek describes the administrative law and judicial adversary processes for resolving a variety of environmental disputes in a basic text aimed at an audience with little legal or scientific training in *Environmental Law* (Paramus, N.J.: Prentice Hall, 1996). Stephen R. Chapman's *Environmental Law and Policy* (Paramus, N.J.: Prentice Hall, 1998) describes the formulation, application, and interpretation of laws, rules, and regulations to resolve specific environmental problems. *Better Environmental Decisions: Strategies for Governments, Businesses, and Communities* (Washington, D.C.: Island Press, 1998), edited by Ken Sexton and others, reviews a variety of decision-making styles, discusses some legal issues related to each, and recommends improvements for more effective decisions. Other books describing environmental case law include Jeffrey Graba's *Environmental Law* (St. Paul, Minn.: West Publishing, 1994), Rosemary O'Leary's *Environmental Change: Federal Courts and the EPA* (Philadelphia: Temple University Press, 1995), Robert V. Percival's *Environmental Regulation: Law, Science, and Policy* (New York: Little, Brown, 1996), and Benjamin Davy's *Essential Injustice: When Legal Institutions Cannot Resolve Environmental and Land Use Disputes* (New York: Springer Verlag, 1997).

Gordon Neal Diem

SEE ALSO Commerce, regulation of; *Euclid v. Ambler Realty Co.*; Fifth Amendment; *Missouri v. Holland*; *Nollan v. California Coastal Commission*; Property rights; Public use doctrine; Takings clause; Zoning.

Epperson v. Arkansas

CITATION: 393 U.S. 97
DATE: November 12, 1968
ISSUE: Establishment of religion
SIGNIFICANCE: The Supreme Court found laws banning the teaching of evolution to be an unconstitutional establishment of religion.

The Supreme Court unanimously overturned an Arkansas supreme court ruling that upheld Arkansas "Monkey Law" statutes banning the teaching of evolution in public elementary schools, secondary schools, and universities. The Court held that Arkansas violated the freedom of religion mandate of the First Amendment as applied to the states by the

Fourteenth Amendment under the incorporation doctrine. Justice Abe Fortas wrote the majority opinion, with Justices John M. Harlan II and Hugo L. Black concurring. In 1982 Arkansas responded by passing a new law that required all public schools to "balance" any teaching of evolution with the teaching of creation by a "supreme power." This was declared unconstitutional in a federal district court in *McLean v. Arkansas Board of Education* (1982). This case was very similar to one covering a Louisiana policy later declared unconstitutional by the Court in a 7-2 decision in *Edwards v. Aguillard* (1987).

Richard L. Wilson

See also Academic freedom; *Edwards v. Aguillard*; *Engel v. Vitale*; Evolution and creationism; *Illinois ex rel. McCollum v. Board of Education*; *Lee v. Weisman*; Religion, establishment of; School prayer; *Wallace v. Jaffree*.

Equal protection clause

Date: 1868

Description: Provision of the Fourteenth Amendment to the U.S. Constitution that prohibits certain forms of discrimination.

Significance: Though the Supreme Court initially gave the equal protection clause a narrow construction, in the last half of the twentieth century, the clause was reinvigorated and used first to eliminate official racial segregation and then to prohibit a variety of other forms of discrimination.

Thomas Jefferson securely linked the ideal of equality to the U.S. political tradition when he argued in the Declaration of Independence that "all men are created equal." However, his tribute to equality did not immediately find a home in the U.S. Constitution. No clause within the Constitution guaranteed equal treatment by the law, and in fact, the accommodation of slavery within the original constitutional text amounted to an obvious breach of the principle of equality. Not until after the Civil War (1861-1865), when the Reconstruction Congress attempted to secure the political and civil rights of the newly freed slaves, would equality enter the constitutional vocabulary. The ratification of the Fourteenth Amendment in 1868 added to the Constitution the principle that Jefferson had

championed almost a century earlier. Section 1 of the amendment declared that no state "shall deny to any person within its jurisdiction the equal protection of the laws."

Early Interpretations. In two early cases, the Supreme Court used the equal protection clause of the Fourteenth Amendment to unsettle official patterns of racial discrimination. *Strauder v. West Virginia* (1880) invalidated a state law that denied African Americans the right to sit on juries and thus submitted them to trial by juries in which people of their race could not sit. This disqualification from an important civil right, declared the Court, offended the equal protection clause. Later that decade, in *Yick Wo v. Hopkins* (1886), the Court held that the Fourteenth Amendment's equal protection guarantee extended beyond discrimination embedded in the text of laws to racial discrimination practiced in the administration of otherwise evenhanded laws.

In other cases, though, the Supreme Court minimized the transformative potential of the equal protection clause in ways that would endure well into the twentieth century. First, in the *Slaughterhouse Cases* (1873), the Court suggested that the clause, though written in general terms capable of application to many forms of inequality, nevertheless would probably not be applied to matters other than discrimination against African Americans. Second, in the *Civil Rights Cases* (1883), the Court limited the application of the clause to inequalities involving state action rather than private acts of discrimination. By this limitation, the Court deprived Congress of power under the Fourteenth Amendment to address private forms of racial and other impermissible discriminations. Finally, in *Plessy v. Ferguson* (1896), the Court grafted onto the equal protection clause the separate but equal doctrine, which permitted states to maintain systems of racial segregation, even though the significance of these systems was to treat African Americans as second-class citizens and thus deprive them of equal treatment under the laws. The commutative effect of these interpretations of the equal protection clause by the Court was to diminish the clause's usefulness as a source of constitutional protection from invidious discrimination. Even in the 1930's, Justice Oliver Wendell Holmes observed that applications to invoke the equal protection clause were the "last resort of constitutional argument."

Emerging Standards of Review. Though an able commentator on the law of the times, Holmes could not see the future. Beginning in the 1940's, the Court, chastened perhaps by the alarming spectacle of Nazi racism toward Jews, reinvigorated the equal protection clause. It did so by establishing two broad categories of cases in which the clause would prove to be most protective against forms of official discrimination. The narrowing of the clause's potential reach in this fashion was necessary because laws routinely classify individuals differently for a variety of purposes and thus discriminate among individuals. State traffic laws allow seventeen-year-olds to obtain a driver's license but not eight-year-olds. State universities grant admission to those who have graduated from high school or obtained comparable credentials but refuse those who drop out early and never make up their educational deficits. In these and innumerable other respects, laws discriminate without offending typical notions of equality. The task of the Court, beginning in the 1940's, was to identify particular forms of discrimination that might be singled out as constitutionally troublesome in a sense not shared by the kind of routine discriminations that characterize ordinary law.

The Court first ventured that the equal protection clause would demand special scrutiny of discriminations that affected fundamental rights or interests. In *Skinner v. Oklahoma* (1942), the Court held that a law that provided for compulsory sterilization of certain habitual criminals but not others discriminated with respect to the fundamental right of procreation. In such cases, the Court determined, it would strictly scrutinize the asserted justifications for the discrimination. Finding such justification lacking in *Skinner,* the Court ruled that the sterilization law violated the Fourteenth Amendment's equal protection clause. In the years following *Skinner,* the Court determined that matters such as the right to vote, the right to privacy (concerning one's choice to use contraceptives), the right to travel, and the right to access to justice were sufficiently fundamental to subject acts of discrimination affecting these rights to more rigorous scrutiny.

As the Court was striving to identify particular rights or interests worthy of protection from discriminatory treatment, it also began to study whether particular grounds for discriminating among individuals might be subjected to corresponding rigorous review. For example, the equal protection clause clearly had its genesis in suspicion of laws that classified individuals on the basis of their race. In *Korematsu v. United States* (1944), the Court, in an opinion by Justice Hugo L. Black, codified this suspicion against racial classifications in principle, though the Court approved an act of racial discrimination that relocated people of Japanese ancestry to internment camps during World War II. At the level of principle, the Court was adamant: Racial classifications called for the most stringent review. In the application of this principle, though, the Court deferred to the military's judgment that the prevention of a West Coast invasion required the relocation of people of Japanese ancestry. This holding would be the last in which the Court upheld a law burdening a minority on account of race.

Desegregation. After the Court gave a constitutional harbor to racial segregation through its adoption of the separate but equal doctrine, segregation in public schools and a variety of other public and private contexts became deeply entrenched in the South. In *Brown v. Board of Education* (1954), however, the Court repudiated the separate but equal doctrine and held that segregated public schools were inherently unequal. The following year, in *Brown v. Board of Education II* (1955), the Court ruled that desegregation efforts were to proceed "with all deliberate speed." However, the only haste exhibited with respect to desegregation by southern school districts was directed at eluding the Court's desegregation order. By 1964, ten years after the decision in *Brown,* only 2 percent of the schools segregated at the time of the decision had experienced any significant desegregation. The Court, in the meantime, summarily ruled that segregation in golf courses, state parks, beaches, and public transportation violated the equal protection guarantee.

In the 1960's and 1970's the Court presided over cases involving efforts of segregated school districts to frustrate desegregation efforts and of federal district courts to further them. In *Green v. County School Board of New Kent County* (1968), the Court made it clear that desegregation required not simply that school districts cease their previous segregation practices but that they dismantle the segregated school systems produced by those practices. Eventually, the Court approved radical strategies to secure desegregation. Most controversially, in *Swann v. Charlotte-Mecklenburg Board of Education* (1971), the Court upheld a district court order requiring widespread busing of students to create racially balanced schools. Importantly, though, the Court held that such remedies required a showing that a school district had engaged in illegal segregation practices—de jure segregation, or segregation by law. The existence in schools of segregation that could be traced to social practices rather than officially sanctioned practices—de facto segregation—was not sufficient to justify a federal court to order remedies such as busing.

Suspect and Quasi-Suspect Classifications. In the years that followed the Court's decisions in *Korematsu* and *Brown*, the Court ventured to determine whether other ways of classifying individuals should be treated with a constitutional suspicion comparable to that now applied to racial discrimination. Classification schemes treated to this kind of suspicion are referred to as "suspect classifications," and are presumptively invalid except in those cases in which the government demonstrates that the classification is necessary to achieve some compelling government interest. In its inquiry into whether other forms of classifications were suspect, the Court was guided by one of constitutional law's most famous footnotes: footnote 4 from the opinion of Justice Harlan Fiske Stone in *United States v. Carolene Products Co.* (1938). In an otherwise unremarkable decision, Justice Stone suggested for the Court that heightened scrutiny might be justified for laws reflecting prejudice against "discrete and insular minorities." In practice, the Court has identified race, religion, and national or ethnic origin as suspect classifications. Additionally, laws discriminating among individuals on the basis of whether they are U.S. citizens are suspect, except in a narrow range of cases involving citizenship requirements for voting or for holding positions closely related to democratic self-government.

The Court wrestled at length over the question of whether laws that classified individuals on the basis of their gender should receive the strict scrutiny applied to suspect classifications. Discrimination on the basis of gender classifies individuals according to an immutable characteristic, and the Court has often expressed its suspicion of using immutable traits as grounds for distinguishing among individuals. Nevertheless, whether men or women

receive less favorable treatment under a particular gender classification, neither group can readily be identified as a discrete and insular minority. Accordingly, the Court eventually fashioned an intermediate level of scrutiny for gender classifications, more rigorous than the scrutiny applied to normal legislative classifications but not so rigorous as that applied to suspect classifications such as laws discriminating on the basis of race. Classification schemes subjected to this intermediate scrutiny are sometimes referred to as "quasi-suspect classifications." The Court included within this category both laws that discriminate on the basis of gender and those that discriminate on the basis of illegitimacy. The Court will uphold these kinds of laws only if they are supported by some important government purpose and the discrimination at issue is substantially related to achieving this important purpose.

Other Classifications. The Court turned away a variety of other claims that particular forms of classifying individuals should be treated as suspect or quasi-suspect. For example, except in cases involving access to certain aspects of justice, the Court declined to treat with any special suspicion laws that classify individuals on the basis of wealth. Furthermore, the Court refused to recognize classifications on the basis of age as inherently suspect, leaving the protection of individuals from age discrimination to the political process.

Nevertheless, the Court did not automatically sustain classification schemes when they were neither suspect nor quasi-suspect. For a classification that is neither suspect nor quasi-suspect, the Court applies what it refers to as rational basis scrutiny. In these circumstances, classifications are upheld as long as they are rationally related to a legitimate government interest. Although the application of this standard of review normally upholds a government classification scheme, occasionally it does not. For example, in *Cleburne v. Cleburne Living Center* (1985), the Court declined to classify mental infirmity as a suspect or quasi-suspect category. Nevertheless, it declared unconstitutional a zoning ordinance that required a special permit for the operation of a group home for the mentally retarded on a particular site, even though the ordinance allowed a wide variety of other land uses on the site. The Court concluded that the negative reactions of nearby residents and the unsubstantiated fears of elderly residents concerning the mental retardation home were not legitimate justifications for discriminatory treatment of the home. Similarly, in *Romer v. Evans* (1996), the Court invalidated a Colorado constitutional amendment that discriminated against homosexuals by providing that no state or municipal law could accord them any special protection from discrimination. Although the Court did not determine that sexual orientation was a suspect or quasi-suspect classification, a majority of the justices reasoned that the amendment reflected "bare animus" against gays and lesbians, and that this animus was not a legitimate basis for upholding the amendment from an equal protection challenge.

Affirmative Action. In his well-known dissent to the opinion of the Court in *Plessy v. Ferguson* (1896), Justice John Marshall Harlan rejected the separate but equal doctrine embraced by the majority. Instead, in his view the equal protection clause mandated that the law be color-blind. Understood literally, this color-blind reading of the equal protection clause would prevent laws designed to benefit racial minorities as well as those designed to burden and harass them. Beginning in the 1960's and 1970's, though, many American observers contended that the legacy of past and continuing racial discrimination in the United States could not be rectified with taking affirmative steps. These affirmative actions typically consisted of laws and policies that singled out racial minorities for beneficial or even preferential treatment as a way of remedying past discriminatory laws and policies.

Beginning with the Court's decision in *Korematsu*, it was clear that laws intentionally burdening racial minorities would be subjected to strict scrutiny. More than forty years would pass before the Court finally concluded that laws the singled out racial minorities for beneficial treatment would also receive the same rigorous scrutiny. The path to this ultimate conclusion was neither direct nor widely supported. In its first important consideration of affirmative action plans, a majority of the Court concluded in *Regents of the University of California v. Bakke* (1978) that the equal protection clause prevented a state university from using racial quotas in its admissions process but permitted the university to consider race as one factor in striving to create a diverse student body. Therefore, while the university could not set aside a particular number of seats for minority students, it could treat minority status as one among several favorable factors in the admissions process. A few years later, in *Fullilove v. Klutznick* (1980), the Court upheld a challenge against a federal set-aside program that gave certain preferences to minority businesses in the award of federal contracts. In neither *Bakke* nor *Fullilove* did the Court determine the standard of review to be applied in affirmative action cases.

The final years of the twentieth century witnessed a conservative majority on the Court becoming increasingly hostile to affirmative action programs. In closely divided decisions, the Court eventually determined, first in *Richmond v. J. A. Croson Co.* (1989) and then in *Adarand Constructors v. Peña* (1995), that equal protection principles required that *all* racial classifications, including those intended to benefit racial minorities, be subjected to strict scrutiny. Though at least some forms of affirmative action might be justified as necessary to serve compelling governmental interests such as remedying past racial discrimination, it nevertheless appeared that many affirmative action programs would no longer survive challenge under equal protection.

FURTHER READING
A general treatment of the equal protection clause can be found in Darien A. McWhirter's *Equal Protection: Exploring the Constitution* (Phoenix, Ariz.: Oryx Press, 1995). For historical coverage of the idea of equality in U.S. history, see J. R. Pole's *Pursuit of Equality in American History* (2d ed., Berkeley: University of California Press, 1993) and Charles Redenius's *The American Ideal of Equality: From Jefferson's Declaration to the Burger Court* (Port Washington, N.Y.: Kennikat Press, 1981). *The Fourteenth Amendment: From Political Principle to Judicial Doctrine* by William E. Nelson (Cambridge, Mass.: Harvard University Press, 1988) provides a useful analysis of the broader context of the equal protection clause in the Fourteenth Amendment. *The Civil Rights Era: Origins and Development of National Policy, 1960-1972*, by Hugh Davis Graham (New York: Oxford University Press, 1990), examines a crucial period in the enforcement of the equal protection guarantee through civil rights laws. Particular treatments relating to racial equality include *African Americans and the Living Constitution*, edited by John Hope Franklin and Genna Rae McNeil (Washington,

D.C.: Smithsonian Institution Press, 1995), and *Simple Justice: The History of "Brown v. Board of Education" and Black America's Struggle for Equality,* by Richard Kluger (New York: Alfred A. Knopf, 1976). Useful sources for further reading concerning gender discrimination issues are Cathy Young's *Ceasefire! Why Women and Men Must Join Forces to Achieve True Equality* (New York: Free Press, 1999), and Robert Max Jackson's *Destined for Equality: The Inevitable Rise of Women's Status* (Cambridge, Mass.: Harvard University Press, 1998). For treatments of the controversy regarding affirmative action, one may consult *Affirmative Discrimination: Ethnic Inequality and Public Policy* by Nathan Glazer (New York: Basic Books, 1975), *A Conflict of Rights: The Supreme Court and Affirmative Action* by Melvin I. Urofsky (New York: Scribner's Sons, 1991), and *The Color-Blind Constitution,* by Andrew Kull (Cambridge, Mass.: Harvard University Press, 1992).

Timothy L. Hall

SEE ALSO Affirmative action; Age discrimination; Civil Rights acts; Civil Rights movement; Desegregation; Fourteenth Amendment; Fundamental rights; Judicial scrutiny; Race and discrimination; Separate but equal doctrine; Suspect classifications.

Erie Railroad Co. v. Tompkins

CITATION: 304 U.S. 64
DATE: April 25, 1938
ISSUE: Diversity jurisdiction
SIGNIFICANCE: In ruling that under the Rules of Decision Act, federal courts were to proceed if multistate lawsuits occurred, the Supreme Court not only overturned one of its previous decisions but also declared it to have been unconstitutional.

The Supreme Court decided *Erie* by an 8-0 vote (Benjamin N. Cardozo did not participate), but the three separate concurrences by Justices Pierce Butler, James C. McReynolds, and Stanley F. Reed weakened the impact of this decision. The issue in this case is complicated and still partially unresolved. The Court has diversity jurisdiction if it is faced by lawsuits in which the parties are citizens of different states and often subject to different laws. Because it would be unfair to choose one state's law over another arbitrarily, the Judiciary Act of 1789 provided that "the laws of the several states . . . shall

be regarded as rules of decision in trials at common law" in federal courts. This provision, known as the Rules of Decision Act in contemporary law, indicates that federal courts should follow state "substantive" law in cases where diversity jurisdiction occurs but does not establish clearly the appropriate sources of state law.

Erie is one of a number of attempts to resolve the matter, which remains the subject of some confusion. An earlier attempt can be found in Justice Joseph Story's opinion in *Swift v. Tyson* (1842), in which he held that the federal courts should use the various statutes and real property laws but should rely on general doctrines or principles of commercial law for contracts and commercial transactions. This in effect created a federal common law, but this was problematic. After the middle of the nineteenth century, this common law expanded dramatically as did the power of the federal courts. When coupled with substantive due process and freedom of contract, the *Swift* decision was often used to nullify federal and state attempts to regulate corporations.

In this politically and economically charged atmosphere, Justice Louis D. Brandeis asserted in his opinion for the Court that there was no "federal general common law," thereby declaring the *Swift* ruling unconstitutional. However, this did not end the matter, as even Brandeis found it necessary to recognize the necessity of some types of specialized federal common law. Several attempts to establish guidelines have failed to fully resolve this matter.

Richard L. Wilson

SEE ALSO Common law, federal; Diversity jurisdiction; Federalism; *Swift v. Tyson.*

Ernst, Morris L.

IDENTIFICATION: Civil liberties attorney and writer
BORN: August 23, 1888, Uniontown, Alabama
DIED: May 21, 1976, New York, New York
SIGNIFICANCE: An attorney who fought against censorship and supported reproductive freedom, Ernst developed strategies and arguments that garnered civil liberties victories in the Supreme Court.

Ernst's parents moved to New York City when he was two, and he grew up there. He graduated from

Morris L. Ernst. (Archive Photos)

Williams College in 1909 and completed his law degree at New York Law School in 1912. Three years later, he began a law practice that concentrated on cases involving censorship law and questions of artistic freedom. He gained national fame when he argued the case to have James Joyce's novel *Ulysses* (1922) admitted to the United States. Ernst succeeded in having the case heard by a sympathetic judge who ruled that the publication of the book in the United States should be allowed because of its literary merits. Ernst's arguments provided the basis for later Supreme Court rulings in cases involving the rights of artists to be free of censorship. For the rest of his career, Ernst served as a general counsel for the American Civil Liberties Union and for the Planned Parenthood Federation. In both roles, he argued for freedom of thought and expression. Behind the scenes, he cooperated with the Federal Bureau of Investigation in identifying and exposing communists. A prolific author, Ernst wrote *The Great Reversals* (1973), a volume that explored cases in which the Court had changed its earlier rulings. He was a strong admirer and confidant of Justice Louis D. Brandeis.

Lewis L. Gould

SEE ALSO Abortion; American Civil Liberties Union (ACLU); Brandeis, Louis D.; Censorship.

Escobedo v. Illinois

CITATION: 378 U.S. 478
DATE: June 22, 1964
ISSUE: Defendants' rights
SIGNIFICANCE: The Supreme Court overturned a murder conviction because the accused was never warned of his right to remain silent. This decision helped transform police behavior toward those accused of committing crimes.

In this early defendants' rights case, Danny Escobedo was taken to the police station as a murder suspect but was denied repeated requests to speak to his lawyer. His lawyer was, in turn, denied repeated requests to speak to his client. Never warned of his right to remain silent, Escobedo made some incriminating statements and ultimately confessed. His confession was key evidence at the trial, which resulted in his conviction. On reaching the Supreme Court, his confession was thrown out as improperly taken and his conviction overturned.

Justice Arthur J. Goldberg wrote the decision for the Court, which ruled five to four that neither federal nor state courts could admit into evidence statements taken by police from a defendant who was not allowed to talk to a lawyer or warned to remain silent. Goldberg's decision was not clearly written, apparently reflecting divisions among the justices as to the proper rule to adopt. The confusion among police, lawyers, and judges led the Court to take up the issue again in *Miranda v. Arizona* (1966) when a clearer, broader ruling was provided. Both decisions were controversial; critics charged that the Court was turning criminals loose on technicalities. In both cases, Justices Tom C. Clark, Potter Stewart, Byron R. White, and John M. Harlan II dissented.

Richard L. Wilson

SEE ALSO Fourteenth Amendment; *Gideon v. Wainwright*; Incorporation doctrine; *Miranda v. Arizona.*

Espionage acts

DATE: 1917-1918
DESCRIPTION: Laws passed during World War I outlawing the unauthorized transmission of information that might injure the nation's defense and banning a wide range of expressions

of opinion critical of governmental policies or symbols during wartime.

SIGNIFICANCE: Espionage act prosecutions led to the first significant attempts by the Supreme Court to interpret the free speech provisions of the First Amendment, including the original espousal of the clear and present danger test.

On June 15, 1917, two months after the United States entered World War I, Congress passed the Espionage Act. In addition to outlawing a wide variety of acts that fit the commonsense definition of "espionage," including the gathering, transmission, or negligent handling of information that might harm U.S. defense efforts, the law forbade, during wartime, the willful making or conveying of false information with intent to interfere with the nation's armed forces or to promote the success of its enemies, as well as willful attempts to cause insubordination, disloyalty, mutiny, or refusal of duty within the military or the obstruction of military recruitment or enlistment. In practice, this law was used as the springboard for massive prosecutions of antiwar speeches and publications of all kinds across the United States, based on the theory that many such viewpoints were false and, in any case, aimed at undermining recruitment or other aspects of the war effort.

Despite the sweeping language and even more sweeping prosecutions associated with the 1917 law, a far more draconian amendment to the Espionage Act, sometimes known as the Sedition Act, was enacted in 1918 in response to complaints that the original law was not stringent enough to suppress antiwar sentiment. The 1918 amendments outlawed virtually all conceivable criticism of the war, including any expressions of support for "any country with which the United State is at war" or that opposed "the cause of the United States therein." Also banned was the oral or printed dissemination of all "disloyal, profane, scurrilous, or abusive language" about the "form of government" of the country, the Constitution, the flag, the military, and military uniforms, as well as any language intended to bring any of the above into "contempt, scorn, contumely, or disrepute."

Under these laws, more than two thousand people were indicted for written or verbal criticism of the war and more than one thousand were convicted, resulting in more than one hundred jail terms of ten years or more. No one was convicted under the espionage acts during World War I for spying activities. The 1918 amendments to the Espionage Act were repealed in 1920. Although the original 1917 law remains in effect, it was virtually never used after World War I to prosecute expressions of opinion (partly because the 1940 Smith Act included more updated sedition provisions); it has, however, been used in cases involving alleged theft of information, including in the prosecutions of Julius Rosenberg and Ethel Rosenberg during the Cold War and the Vietnam War-era prosecution of Daniel Ellsberg for dissemination of the Pentagon Papers.

Court Rulings. The Supreme Court handed down six rulings concerning the constitutionality of Espionage Act prosecutions in 1919-1920, during a severe "red scare." In every case, it upheld lower court convictions. Although the Court's rulings no doubt reflected the anticommunist cli-

In 1927 people gather in New York City to protest the upcoming executions of Nicola Sacco and Bartolomeo Vanzetti. The atmosphere of intense political repression that produced the Espionage Acts is also believed to have affected the outcome of the trial of the two anarchists. (AP/Wide World Photos)

mate, they had long-term significance because they were the first cases in which the Court sought to interpret the free speech clauses of the First Amendment and thus helped shape decades of subsequent debate and interpretation of this subject. In *Schenck v. United States* (1919), the Court upheld the conviction (under the original 1917 law) of a group accused of seeking to obstruct enlistment in the armed forces by mailing antidraft leaflets. Despite the lack of evidence that Schenck's mailings had any effect whatsoever, the Court, in a famous ruling penned by Justice Oliver Wendell Holmes, rejected Schenck's First Amendment claims. Holmes wrote that although the defendants would have been within their constitutional rights in saying what they did in ordinary times, the character of "every act depends upon the circumstances in which it is done." Just as "the most stringent protection of free speech would not protect a man in falsely shouting fire in a theater and causing a panic," the question was always whether the expression was used in such circumstances and was of such a nature as to create a "clear and present danger" that it would cause the "substantive evils" that Congress has the right to prevent.

In *Abrams v. United States* (1919), a second landmark case (based on the 1918 amendment), the Court upheld the conviction of a group of defendants who had thrown from a New York City rooftop leaflets critical of U.S. military intervention against the new Bolshevik government in Russia. This case became known especially because of a dissent by Holmes, who essentially maintained that no clear and present danger had been demonstrated and that Congress could not constitutionally forbid "all effort to change the mind of the country." In words that became famous both for their eloquence and because, after 1937, most Court rulings in First Amendment cases reflected their sentiment more than the those of the majorities in either *Abrams* or *Schenck*, Holmes declared that U.S. constitutional democracy was based on giving all thought an opportunity to compete in the free trade in ideas, and as long as that experiment remained part of the Constitution, Americans should be "eternally vigilant against attempts to check the expression of opinions that we loathe and believe to be fraught with death, unless they so imminently threaten interference with the lawful and pressing purposes of the

law that an immediate check is required to save the country."

In the only significant Espionage Act case involving First Amendment claims to be decided by the Court after 1920, a Court majority reflected Holmes's *Abrams* dissent. In *Hartzel v. United States* (1944), involving a man who had mailed articles attacking U.S. policies during World War II to Army officers and draft registrants (circumstances almost identical to *Schenck*), the Court reversed Hartzel's conviction on the grounds that there was no proof he had willfully sought to obstruct the activities of the armed forces.

FURTHER READING

Chafee, Zechariah. *Free Speech in the United States.* New York: Atheneum, 1969.

Goldstein, Robert Justin. *Political Repression in Modern America: 1870 to the Present.* Boston: G. K. Hall, 1978.

Polenberg, Richard. *Fighting Faiths: The Abrams Case, the Supreme Court, and Free Speech.* New York: Viking Penguin, 1987.

Robert Justin Goldstein

SEE ALSO *Abrams v. United States*; Clear and present danger test; First Amendment; First Amendment speech tests; *Schenck v. United States*; Sedition Act of 1798; Seditious libel; Smith Act; Speech and press, freedom of; War and civil liberties.

Euclid v. Ambler Realty Co.

CITATION: 272 U.S. 365
DATE: October 12, 1926
ISSUE: Zoning
SIGNIFICANCE: The Supreme Court, in a landmark decision, established the constitutionality of zoning ordinances by concluding they were a legitimate form of police power.

When comprehensive zoning ordinances began to be adopted in the first two decades of the twentieth century, many legal scholars and courts doubted their constitutionality on a number of grounds. Ambler Realty owned a large tract of land it was holding for industrial development, but it found the value of its property significantly reduced as the result of the city of Euclid's decision to adopt a zoning ordinance. Ambler sued on multiple grounds including the takings clause, due process, and equal protection. The lower court ruled that Ambler had suffered a taking without just compensation, but the Supreme Court reversed its decision, upholding Euclid's zoning law—and by analogy—most other zoning laws. Although criticism of many zoning laws continues, the Court does not appear ready to change its decision. Justice George Sutherland wrote for a 6-3 majority, facing dissents by Justices Willis Van Devanter, James C. McReynolds, and Pierce Butler.

Richard L. Wilson

See also Fourteenth Amendment; Takings clause; Zoning.

Evans v. Abney

CITATION: 396 U.S. 435
DATE: January 29, 1970
ISSUE: Restrictive covenants
SIGNIFICANCE: The Supreme Court imposed a racially neutral principle to decide a question of the legitimacy of race-based restrictions on park land donated to a municipality.

Justice Hugo L. Black wrote the 6-2 majority opinion upholding a decision of a Georgia court that a park built on land donated to the city of Macon explicitly for use as a whites-only park had to be closed and the property returned to the heirs of the person donating the land. Previous decisions made it clear that Macon was barred on equal protection grounds from operating the park on a racially restrictive basis. Because the benefactor had been explicit in his instructions, the Court decided the only proper course of action was to return the land to the heirs. Although African Americans were still denied access to the park, so were whites, thus preserving racial neutrality. Justices William O. Douglas and William J. Brennan, Jr., dissented, and Thurgood Marshall did not participate.

Richard L. Wilson

SEE ALSO Fourteenth Amendment; Restrictive covenants; *Shelley v. Kraemer*; Takings clause.

Everson v. Board of Education of Ewing Township

CITATION: 330 U.S. 1
DATE: February 10, 1947
ISSUE: Establishment of religion

SIGNIFICANCE: The Supreme Court upheld bus fare reimbursements for private school students in the first case to use the Fourteenth Amendment to apply the First Amendment's establishment of religion clause to the states.

Justice Hugo L. Black wrote the 5-4 opinion for the Supreme Court; Justices Robert H. Jackson, Felix Frankfurter, Wiley B. Rutledge, Jr., and Harold H. Burton dissented. On one level, all nine justices agreed that the establishment of religion clause applied to the states and that government should be neutral with respect to religion, neither aiding nor obstructing it. The disagreement was over whether the principle of neutrality toward religion was properly applied in this case.

New Jersey law authorized school boards to reimburse parents for the cost of bus transportation to attend school, whether public or parochial. Arch Everson was a local taxpayer in Ewing township who believed this violated the establishment clause. The four dissenting justices agreed with him, but the majority on the Court believed bus fare payment was remote from any religious purpose. They believed that the money for bus transportation would have been paid to all parents regardless of the kind of school their children attended. Depriving Roman Catholic parents of the payments forced them to pay taxes to support the transportation of other children while not receiving the benefit themselves. The larger point of this case was to establish that neither the state nor the federal government could support a religious institution, and on that point, all agreed.

Richard L. Wilson

SEE ALSO *Engel v. Vitale*; *Epperson v. Arkansas*; *Illinois ex rel. McCollum v. Board of Education*; Religion, establishment of.

Evolution and creationism

DESCRIPTION: Modern scientific theories of natural and human origins and religious beliefs about the world's creation.

SIGNIFICANCE: The battle between the teaching of evolution versus creationism entered the public schools and arrived before the Supreme Court, which found that the establishment clause forbids public schools from lending their authority to advance creationism.

Although the Supreme Court has ruled laws prohibiting the teaching of evolution to be unconstitutional, new laws and measures attempt to get around this ban. In 1999 this Shawnee Mission, Kansas, biology teacher expressed relief that his district opted out of state guidelines omitting the theory of evolution from state science standards. (AP/Wide World Photos)

The emergence of the theory of evolution as a scientific account of human origins has, since the nineteenth century, created conflicts with religious beliefs. Conservative Christians, in particular, have often viewed evolution as inconsistent with biblical teaching concerning creation. They viewed the gradual nature of the evolutionary process as contradicted by the biblical account of creation. They read the Bible as describing a relatively brief creation process—in some views, six literal days—and one not characterized by a progression from primitive to higher lifeforms.

Early Attempts to Ban the Teaching of Evolution. The debate between science and religion over natural origins inevitably arrived in the public schools. In areas controlled by conservative religious sensibilities, opponents of evolution were able, for a time, to prevent public school teachers from teaching the evolutionary account. As the twentieth century progressed, these prohibitions eventually took the form of law. The most celebrated attempt to enforce such a legal prohibition against teaching evolution was the Scopes trial in Tennessee in the 1920's. *State of Tennessee v. John Thomas Scopes* (1925), which eventually came to be

known as the "Monkey Trial," involved the criminal prosecution of a Tennessee schoolteacher for teaching evolution in violation of a state law prohibiting such teaching. For eight scorching days in July of 1925, the trial pitted William Jennings Bryan as a special prosecutor for the state of Tennessee against Clarence Darrow as attorney for the defendant. Bryan secured a conviction in the case, and the presiding judge imposed a $100 fine on Scopes. However, in the court of public opinion, Bryan faired more poorly. During the trial, he agreed to be cross-examined by Darrow and, at least in the minds of many observers, allowed Darrow to tar him and other evolution opponents as unsophisticated religious fundamentalists. On appeal, the Tennessee appellate court affirmed the constitutionality of the Tennessee anti-evolution statute but held that a jury rather than a judge should have assessed the fine in the case. The state of Tennessee, its law thus vindicated, declined to prosecute the case again, and so Scopes and others who wished to take their challenge to the Supreme Court were frustrated.

Several decades would pass before the Court finally considered the constitutionality of laws prohibiting instruction concerning evolution. When it did, in *Epperson v. Arkansas* (1968), the Court found a law prohibiting the teaching of evolution to be a violation of the First Amendment's establishment clause. During the 1960's, the Court had begun to examine the influence of religion in the public schools, declaring unconstitutional school-sponsored prayers in *Engel v. Vitale* (1962) and *Abington School District v. Schempp* (1963). With these precedents in mind, the Court concluded that attempts to ban the teaching of evolution in public schools amounted to an impermissible intrusion of religion on the public school curriculum.

Creation Science and the Public School Curriculum. The battle that began as an attempt to keep evolution out of public schools metamorphosed over the next two decades into a rear-guard attempt to return creationism to the schools. In the early 1980's, for example, the Louisiana legislature passed the Balanced Treatment for Creation-Science and Evolution-Science in Public School Instruction Act. This law essentially provided that public schools that chose to teach "evolution-science" also had to teach "creation-science" and was justified by the legislature as necessary to preserve academic freedom. The Supreme Court disagreed, however. By the time the matter arrived before the justices in the last half of the 1980's, the Court had interpreted the First Amendment's establishment clause as imposing a three-part requirement on state and federal laws. According to the three-part test adopted in *Lemon v. Kurtzman* (1971), laws had to have a secular purpose, a secular effect, and entail no excessive entanglement between government and religion.

The Louisiana law was challenged in *Edwards v. Aguillard* (1987), and a majority of the Court agreed that the law offended the establishment clause. According to the Court, the Louisiana statute stumbled over the first prong of the three-part *Lemon* test. In spite of the Louisiana legislature's assertion that the act was necessary to preserve academic freedom, a majority of the Court concluded that the act was, in fact, supported by an essentially religious purpose—that of restoring the religion-rooted view of natural origins represented by "creation-science" to the public school classroom. Finding that the law lacked any real secular purpose, therefore, the Court concluded that it violated the establishment clause.

FURTHER READING

Ecker, Ronald L. *Dictionary of Science and Creationism.* Buffalo, N.Y.: Prometheus Books, 1990.

Gilkey, Langdon. *Creationism on Trial: Evolution and God at Little Rock.* Charlottesville: University Press of Virginia, 1998.

Larson, Edward J. *Summer for the Gods: The Scopes Trial and America's Continuing Debate over Science and Religion.* New York: Basic Books, 1997.

_____. *Trial and Error: The American Legal Controversy over Creation and Evolution.* New York: Oxford University Press, 1985.

Webb, George Ernest. *The Evolution Controversy in America.* Lexington: University Press of Kentucky, 1994.

Timothy L. Hall

SEE ALSO *Abington School District v. Schempp*; Education; *Edwards v. Aguillard*; *Engel v. Vitale*; *Epperson v. Arkansas*; First Amendment; *Lemon v. Kurtzman*; Religion, establishment of; School prayer.

Ex post facto laws

DESCRIPTION: Statutes that render an act committed in the past illegal, although that act was legal when it took place.

SIGNIFICANCE: The Supreme Court examined the extent of the restriction against ex post facto laws, which are banned by the Constitution, prohibiting their use in criminal but not civil law.

Ex post facto laws, regarded as tools of oppression when the U.S. Constitution was written, were banned in Article I, section 9, of the Constitution, where they are excluded from the powers of Congress, and in Article I, section 10, where the exclusion is applied to state legislatures.

The Supreme Court specified the extent and meaning of this restriction on the powers of U.S. government. Its principal interpretation came in *Calder v. Bull* (1798), where plaintiffs challenged the right of a state legislature to legislate against their interests in a civil case. Justice Samuel Chase ruled, however, that the ex post facto exclusion applied only to criminal not to civil law.

Besides laws criminalizing actions that were committed before the law was passed, Chase's decision excluded laws that make crimes greater or subject to more severe punishments than when committed and laws that alter rules of evidence, making conviction easier.

Later Court cases extended the ex post facto restriction. In the *Test Oath Cases* (1867), the court voided laws requiring oaths regarding past loyalties that disqualify individuals from holding office or practicing certain professions. In *Beazell v. Ohio* (1925), changes in laws regarding evidence that "operate only in a limited and unsubstantial manner to [the defendant's] disadvantage, are not prohibited." In *Weaver v. Graham* (1981), the Court held that laws that reduce a prisoner's "good time" credits, thereby extending punishment, are prohibited, but those acting to defendants' benefit are allowed. The Court has also held that deportation of aliens and the denial of a passport are not banned as ex post facto because they are not criminal punishments.

Charles F. Bahmueller

SEE ALSO Bill of attainder; *Calder v. Bull*; Chase, Samuel.

Exclusionary rule

DESCRIPTION: Judicially created doctrine proscribing the admissibility at trial of evidence obtained illegally through violation of a defendant's constitutional rights.

SIGNIFICANCE: The Supreme Court ruling in 1914 excluded the use of physical evidence gathered through unreasonable search or seizure, and later rulings prohibited any evidence obtained in violation of the Fifth Amendment right against self-incrimination, the Sixth Amendment right to counsel, and Fifth and Fourteenth Amendment rights to due process of law.

The exclusionary rule, as applied to Fourth Amendment search and seizure provisions, originated with the Supreme Court's 1914 decision in *Weeks v. United States.* Although no emergency conditions existed, police officers had twice conducted nonconsensual, warrantless searches of Freemont Weeks's home, obtaining letters and documents that were later used as evidence against him over his objections at trial. Weeks was ultimately convicted, and the Supreme Court addressed his appeal. In a unanimous opinion, the Court noted that the Framers of the Constitution intended through the passage of the Bill of Rights to protect the American people from the general warrants that had been issued under the authority of the British government in colonial times. The Court declared that the courts, which are charged with the support of the Constitution, should not sanction the tendency of those who enforce the criminal laws of the country to obtain conviction by means of unlawful seizures. The Court concluded that if letters and private documents can be seized illegally and used in evidence against a citizen accused of an offense, the protection of the Fourth Amendment against unreasonable searches and seizures is of no value.

This newly minted rule was strengthened by *Silverthorne Lumber Co. v. United States* (1920), and *Agnello v. United States* (1925), which made clear that illegally acquired evidence could not be used by the government, regardless of the nature of the evidence. However, the mandatory exclusion of illegally obtained evidence pertained only to federal law enforcement and trials. Although the Court eventually agreed in *Wolf v. Colorado* (1949) that the due process clause of the Fourteenth Amendment prohibited illegal state governmental searches and seizures, it initially maintained that the states did not necessarily have to use the exclusionary rule as a method of enforcing that right. The states were allowed to come up with other safeguards to protect the constitutional rights of their citizens.

Silver Platter Doctrine. The incorporation of the prohibitions of the Fourth Amendment into the due process clause of the Fourteenth Amendment did not secure compliance by state law enforcement officers. In fact, because no real means of regulating unlawful state law enforcement behavior existed, state law enforcement agents cooperated with federal agents by providing them with illegally seized evidence, which was admissible in federal court because it was not obtained by federal agents. This practice became known as the "silver platter doctrine" because federal agents were being served up evidence much like food on a platter.

The silver platter doctrine was denounced by the Court in *Elkins v. United States* (1960), which disallowed the admission of evidence obtained by state officers during a search that, if conducted by federal officers, would have violated a defendant's Fourth Amendment rights. The Court decided that it hardly mattered to victims of illegal searches whether their rights had been abridged by federal agents or by state officers, and that if the fruits of an illegal search conducted by state officers could no longer be admitted in federal trials, no incentive would exist for federal and state agents to cooperate in such abhorrent schemes.

Partially because of state law enforcement officers' disregard for the Fourth Amendment's proscriptions, in *Mapp v. Ohio* (1961), the Court reconsidered its stance on extending the exclusionary rule to state action.

Mapp v. Ohio. In 1957 Cleveland, Ohio, police officers went to Dollree Mapp's home with the goal of finding and questioning a bombing suspect. When the officers requested entry, Mapp refused to let them in without a search warrant. The officers returned a few hours later and forcibly entered Mapp's house. A struggle ensued; officers handcuffed Mapp and carried her upstairs, then searched her entire house, including the basement. They found obscene materials during their search, and she was charged and convicted of possessing them. During her trial, no warrant was introduced into evidence. The Ohio supreme court upheld Mapp's conviction, although it acknowledged that the methods used to obtain the evidence offended a sense of justice.

In the *Mapp* majority opinion, the Court deplored the futility of protecting Fourth Amendment rights through remedies such as civil or criminal sanctions. It noted the failure of these remedies and the consequent constitutional abuses and suggested nothing could destroy a government more quickly than its failure to observe its own laws. The Court declared that if the Fourteenth Amendment did not bar improperly seized evidence, the Constitution would consist of nothing more than empty words. In addition, more than half of the states had already adopted the exclusionary rule through either statutory or case law. Therefore, the Court ruled that the exclusionary rule applied to the states as well as the federal government. This avoided the incongruity between state and federal use of illegally seized evidence. Through *Mapp*, the Court altered state criminal trial procedures and investigatory procedures by requiring local officials to follow constitutional standards of search and seizure or suffer exclusion of evidence at trial.

Rationale for the Rule. Some legal experts theorize that the exclusionary rule is a natural outgrowth of the Constitution. The government cannot provide individual rights without protecting them, and the exclusionary rule provides this function. Therefore, the rule is an implicit part of the substantive guarantees of the Fourth Amendment prohibition against unreasonable search and seizure, the Fifth Amendment right against self-incrimination, the Sixth Amendment right to counsel, and the Fifth and Fourteenth Amendment rights to due process. The exclusionary rule also involves the concept of maintaining judicial integrity. The introduction into evidence of illegally gathered materials must be proscribed to maintain judicial integrity and deter police misconduct.

The most common reason invoked for assertion of the exclusionary rule is that it effectively deters constitutional violations and that this deterrent effect is crucial to the vitality of the constitutional amendments. Beginning with *United States v. Calandra* (1974), the Court viewed the rule as primarily a judicial creation designed to deter police misconduct. Therefore, the Court felt free to balance the costs of excluding evidence against the benefits of the rule's effect as a deterrent and produced an ever-expanding list of judicially acknowledged exceptions to the exclusionary rule.

Exceptions to the Rule. After 1961, when the Court held that the states must apply the exclusionary rule to state investigatory and trial procedures, the rule came under increasing attack by those who argued that it exacts too great a price from society by allowing guilty people to either go free or to receive reduced sentences.

The Court, reflecting societal division over the exclusionary rule, fashioned a number of exceptions to it. For example, in *Calandra*, the Court refused to allow a grand jury witness the privilege of invoking the exclusionary rule in refusing to answer questions that were based on illegally seized evidence, as any deterrent effect that might be achieved through application of the rule was too uncertain. For the same reason, the Court also held that illegally seized evidence may be admitted at trial in civil cases (*United States v. Janis*, 1976) and when it would "inevitably" have been discovered through other legal means (*Nix v. Williams*, 1984) as well as used to impeach a witness's credibility (*United States v. Havens*, 1978) and against third persons (*United States v. Paynor*, 1980).

However, what most eroded the exclusionary rule was the good faith exception, first approved for criminal cases by the Court in *United States v. Leon* (1984). The good faith exception permitted the use of illegally acquired evidence if the officers who seized it did so in good faith. In *Leon*, the Court found no reason to apply the exclusionary rule to a situation in which an officer relied on a search warrant issued by a neutral magistrate that later was found not to be supported by probable cause. The Court reasoned that in such a case, the exclusion of evidence would have no deterrent effect on police officers and would exact too great a price from society. In *Illinois v. Krull* (1987), the Court ruled that the exclusionary rule did not bar the admissibility of evidence seized in good faith reliance on a statute, subsequently found to be unconstitutional, which authorized warrantless administrative searches.

In 1995 the Court again extended the good faith exception when it held in *Arizona v. Evans* that the exclusionary rule does not require suppression of evidence seized in violation of the Fourth Amendment because of inaccurate information based on a court employee's clerical errors. In *Evans*, a police officer made an arrest following a routine traffic stop when his patrol car computer erroneously indicated there was an outstanding misdemeanor warrant for Evans's arrest. When the issue of suppression reached the Court, it again applied the rationale of *Leon*. There was neither any evidence that court employees were inclined to ignore or subvert the Fourth Amendment nor any basis for believing that application of the rule would have an effect on the future behavior of court employees. Therefore, the Court decided that it would not serve the purposes of justice to apply the exclusionary rule in *Evans*.

FURTHER READING

Joel Samaha discusses the history of the exclusionary rule, rationales that justify it, and its social costs and deterrent effects in *Criminal Procedure* (4th ed., St. Paul, Minn.: West Publishing, 1999). For basic information regarding the exclusionary rule and its exceptions, see Louis Fisher's *Constitutional Rights: Civil Rights and Civil Liberties* (2d ed., New York: McGraw-Hill, 1995), Lee Epstein and Thomas G. Walker's *Constitutional Law for a Changing America: Rights, Liberties, and Justice* (3d ed., Washington, D.C.: Congressional Quarterly, 1998), Craig Ducat and Harold Chases's *Constitutional Interpretation: Rights of the Individual* (6th ed., St. Paul, Minn.: West Publishing, 1996), and Joan Biskupic's *The Supreme Court and Individual Rights* (3d ed., Washington, D.C.: Congressional Quarterly, 1997).

Rebecca Davis

SEE ALSO Due process, substantive; Fifth Amendment; Fourth Amendment; Fundamental rights; Incorporation doctrine; *Mapp v. Ohio*; Search warrant requirement; Self-incrimination, immunity against; Silver platter doctrine; Sixth Amendment; *Weeks v. United States*; *Wolf v. Colorado*.

Executive agreements

DESCRIPTION: International agreements made by presidents on their own constitutional authority or in cooperation with Congress.

SIGNIFICANCE: Executive agreements enhanced presidential leadership in foreign affairs and served as the form for key international commit-

ments from the Yalta Agreement to the North American Free Trade Agreement. On several occasions, the Supreme Court was asked to rule on the constitutionality of an executive agreement.

Executive agreements vary widely in formality and importance. Many address routine economic, military, and political subjects such as postal regulations and trade agreements, and others, such as the Yalta Agreement in 1945, the Vietnam War peace settlement in 1973, and the North American Free Trade Agreement (NAFTA) in 1993, had significant international political and economic consequences.

The U.S. Constitution's Article I, section 10, implicitly recognizes executive agreements by its prohibition on states making agreements and compacts with foreign powers, but it does not indicate how executive agreements are related to treaties made by the president with the advice and consent of two-thirds of the Senate. The Supreme Court provided some assistance in *Weinberger v. Rossi* (1982) when it observed that the word "treaty" in international law referred to a compact between sovereign states, but the Constitution distinguished Article II treaties from those governed by Article IV, section 2, the supremacy clause, which also included executive agreements. As the Court said in *United States v. Pink* (1942), this meant that a state law inconsistent with an executive agreement had to yield, because the agreement, like a treaty, was the supreme law of the land. Executive agreements and treaties also have to comply with personal constitutional guarantees. In *Reid v. Covert* (1957), the Court held that an executive agreement providing for trial by courts-martial for U.S. military personnel and their dependents violated the constitutional right to trial by jury. However, the Court never clearly indicated how treaties and agreements differ or defined the president's sole power to make agreements without the Senate and to collaborate with both chambers.

Sole Executive Agreement. Presidents have used their Article II power as commander in chief to make armistice and cease-fire agreements, enter into agreements to protect troops, control occupied areas, and arrange postwar territorial and political matters as at Yalta and Potsdam. Presidents have also construed their Article II diplomatic powers broadly to argue that their authority to settle claims lies within the penumbra of their power to recognize foreign governments. In 1933 President Franklin D. Roosevelt recognized the Soviet Union, established diplomatic relations, and negotiated a claims settlement agreement. In *United States v. Belmont* (1937) and *Pink*, the Court held that the Litvinov claims settlement agreement was a legally enforceable international compact that the president, as the sole organ of the federal government in foreign relations, had the authority to negotiate without consulting the Senate. In 1980 President Jimmy Carter negotiated the release of diplomatic personnel held hostage by Iran on the basis of an executive agreement that provided for the arbitration of claims, but in *Dames and Moore v. Regan* (1981), the Court was more cautious. *Pink* gave the president a measure of authority to enter into an agreement providing for claims settlement when it was necessary to resolve a major foreign policy dispute, but the Court emphasized that the crucial factor in upholding the agreement was a history of congressional acquiescence that had invited similar presidential actions.

Congressional-Executive Agreements. Presidential collaboration with Congress is based on Article I's requirement that revenue bills originate in the House of Representatives and its grant to Congress of the power to oversee foreign commerce and, under the necessary and proper clause, to make all laws reasonably related to foreign commerce and to the president's foreign relations powers. Congress at times took the initiative and provided presidents with prior authorization to make agreements on postal rates, trademark and copyright regulations, foreign assistance, and reciprocal trade agreements. Presidents also took the initiative and negotiated agreements with foreign governments and then sought authorization from Congress in the form of a statute or a joint resolution. The Congress-initiated agreement has a long historical pedigree, but the use of the president-initiated agreement dates back to World War II (1941-1945) and takes its current form from the Trade Act of 1974. This act stipulated congressional involvement in the negotiation process and a fast-track approval procedure (limited debate, and a thumbs up or down vote with no amendments) that President Bill Clinton used with NAFTA.

Executive agreements initiated by presidents have become a largely interchangeable alternative to treaties. They substitute the one-third plus one Senate veto for a simple majority of both chambers, provide the House of Representatives with an equal voice, and eliminate the danger that the House may refuse to approve the appropriation of funds necessary to implement a treaty. The Court has not addressed the constitutional status of these agreements. If it does, its reliance in *Dames and Moore* on Justice Robert H. Jackson's concurring opinion in *Youngstown Sheet and Tube Co. v. Sawyer* (1952) could allow it to frame a decision in terms of whether the president's action was taken with the support of, in opposition to, or in the absence of congressional authorization. However, the Court is unlikely to address the larger issue of a president's use of an agreement instead of treaty because it is a political question inappropriate for judicial inquiry.

Presidents' use of executive agreements will continue to be defined by their relationship with Congress and by their awareness that the Senate has objected to extensive use of these agreements. The Bricker Amendment (1954), though it would have conferred explicit constitutional recognition on executive agreements, sought to curtail and regulate them by providing that they would be effective as internal law only if they were supported by legislation. Congress has also been troubled by covert agreements and in the Case Act (1972), required their publication. As a consequence, presidents' use of executive agreements will be shaped by their respect for the Senate and its treaty power, their awareness that treaties have greater dignity, and their knowledge that the constitutional status of agreements is beyond doubt.

FURTHER READING

Akerman, Bruce, and David Golove. *Is NAFTA Constitutional?* Cambridge, Mass.: Harvard University Press, 1995.

Fisher, Louis. *Constitutional Conflicts Between Congress and the President.* 4th ed. Lawrence: University Press of Kansas, 1997.

Henkin, Louis. *Foreign Affairs and the Constitution.* New York: W. W. Norton, 1972.

William C. Green

SEE ALSO *Dames and Moore v. Regan*; Foreign affairs and foreign policy; Presidential powers; Treaties; *Youngstown Sheet and Tube Co. v. Sawyer.*

Executive immunity

DESCRIPTION: Limited right of a government executive official not to be sued in civil court for certain acts of official misconduct. It differs from executive privilege, which is a limited right to refuse to come before or furnish information, documents, or items to the legislature or judiciary.

SIGNIFICANCE: Although most state and federal executive officials have qualified immunity from civil suit, the Supreme Court ruled that some officials, acting within their official capacities, have absolute immunity from civil suit.

The U.S. Constitution expressly provides some immunity for federal legislative but not executive or judicial officials. Article I, section 6 protects speech and debate and related functions of members of Congress and certain aides. It also protects members from some arrests. The implications of Article I, sections 2 and 3, and Article II, section 4, all relating to impeachment, are equivocal concerning any executive or judicial immunities. Nevertheless, depending on the context, the Court found support for modern executive and judicial immunity in the common law of England in *Spalding v. Vilas* (1896), in constitutional notions of separation of powers and federalism, including the superiority of federal law, and in implications in particular laws. Within limits, immunity may be changed by law.

Types of Immunity. The majority of state and federal executive officials, in most civil suits arising from their discretionary functions, enjoy immunity, which takes a number of forms. Temporary immunity limits lawsuits while the official is in office. Permanent immunity limits lawsuits even after the official leaves office. Legislators have both types, and executive and judiciary officials have permanent immunity.

Immunity also can be absolute or qualified. Qualified, as currently defined by the Court in such executive immunity cases as *Harlow v. Fitzgerald* (1982) and *Wilson v. Layne* (1999), means immunity is not granted if the official knew or reasonably should have known at the time that his or her actions violated a clearly defined right under the law or Constitution. Absolute immunity is complete immunity from civil suit, provided the officer was acting within the perimeters of his or her office, irrespective of the officer's intention. In *Imbler v. Pachtman* (1976) and *Butz v. Economou* (1978), the Court granted absolute immunity from civil suit in a narrow, exceptional class of cases. Specifically, it granted absolute immunity from civil suit to presidents, as long as they acted anywhere within the "outer perimeter" of the scope of their official presidential functions, to judges and prosecutors, for suits based, respectively, on judging, or on initiating, pursuing, or presenting a case but not necessarily on other functions (such as conducting an investigation), and to executive branch officials engaged in functions analogous to those absolutely immunized for judges and prosecutors.

The Court's approach to executive immunity is also influential in state courts, even when those courts may have freedom to differ. The availability of immunity, and whether the immunity, if granted, is to be qualified or absolute, depends on the particular laws under which the suit is being filed, the activity being challenged, and the level of the executive being sued. The emphasis is on the importance of the function, rather than the loftiness of the person or office. The Court decides how sensitive and vital the particular executive function is, how much encouragement of it is needed as a matter of policy, and the relative importance of the ends served by the law under which the suit is being filed. Despite this flexibility, generalization is possible: Most state and federal executive officials, in most civil suits arising out of their discretionary functions, enjoy qualified immunity—although it may not apply on the particular facts.

As a general rule, the Court holds there is no distinction between state and federal executive officers. In *Wood v. Strickland* (1975), it ruled that school administrators had qualified immunity, and granted qualified immunity to the superintendent of a state hospital in *O'Connor v. Donaldson* (1975). Most of the Court's executive immunity decisions concern immunity from federal lawsuits, but a number, like presidential immunity, bind state courts as well.

Presidents. U.S. presidents have absolute permanent immunity covering their official functions, although unofficial functions are not covered by any immunity. Therefore they cannot be sued in civil court for official acts even after leaving the presidency. However, civil suits can be entered against presidents during their presidency or after for unofficial acts (including any acts done preceding their presidencies). *Nixon v. Fitzgerald* (1982) absolutely immunized Richard M. Nixon (former president at the time of the suit) against a civil lawsuit by a former government employee who alleged Nixon as president had illegally conspired to terminate the employee's job. In a companion case decided at the same time, *Harlow v. Fitzgerald*, the Supreme Court held that the Nixon aide who allegedly conspired with Nixon had only qualified immunity.

Although the act at issue was official, the *Nixon* decision advanced grounds that were broad enough to support presidential immunity for both official and unofficial acts. Immunity, it was argued, was necessary to avoid chilling the exercise of official discretion and distracting presidents from the duties of office. The latter part of this argument suggested that a sitting president could not be sued even for unofficial acts or those committed before assuming the presidency.

Clinton's Case. Subsequently, however, the Court, in *Clinton v. Jones* (1997), termed the distraction argument to be both gratuitous (because *Nixon* did not involve a sitting president) and somewhat preposterous. That left the argument that the lack of immunity chilled official conduct. However, this problem can arise only when the challenged act is an official one. Therefore, the Court ruled, Paula Jones could pursue a civil suit against sitting president Bill Clinton for alleged sexual harassment that predated his presidency. The president had asked for temporary immunity, lasting only until he left office, but the Court refused to grant any immunity at all. The Court, encouraging considerable deference to the president's schedule, stated that the trial judge had discretion to control timing, appearances, and other court matters to accommodate legitimate obligations of the president.

The Court did not believe that denying immunity would precipitate many potentially illegitimate or significantly distracting civil lawsuits, noting there had been only three apposite suits against presidents in the past, and they were either dismissed or settled. Normal judicial summary dismissal of obviously unfounded lawsuits would take care of problems. In any event, the personal attention of presidents would not necessarily be required, and their schedules could always be accommodated.

Justice Stephen G. Breyer, concurring, expressed several reservations. The Court's predictions might be wrong, and lawsuits might multiply and become unduly distracting. Breyer believed that, at the very least, accommodating the president's schedule should be constitutionally mandated. In addition, the president's word as to specific identified needs of his office should be taken by the trial judge without too much inquiry. Breyer also believed that the issue of immunity should probably be revisited down the road.

Jones does leave open the possibility of a different view of immunity should events later require it, and the Court noted that Congress can always enact a broader definition of immunity. Conceivably some claims should be deferred. The decision to defer is generally based on the degree of immediate need of the particular claimant, the degree of difficulty of preserving the specific proof, the kind of pending national presidential business and particular lawsuit distractions, the importance of the rights pressed by the claimant, the chances of ulti-

In 1997 the Supreme Court ruled that Paula Jones could pursue a civil suit against sitting President Bill Clinton for sexual harassment that allegedly took place in 1991 while Clinton was governor of Arkansas. (AP/Wide World Photos)

mate success, and the claimant's motivation. Some public tasks are important enough to derail normal legal procedures that would interfere. For example, under current law, claims against members of the armed forces must wait until their active duty is over. Evidentiary privileges recognize that normal legal procedures must be sacrificed to promote the public interest served by the husband-wife, doctor-patient, psychotherapist-patient, or lawyer-client relationship. For now, the Court does not wish to make these very difficult and perhaps inappropriate individualized judgments.

The Court has never determined whether a sitting president can be criminally prosecuted for official acts, unofficial acts, or acts done before taking the office. There may be some constitutional constraints on what punishment could be levied. It is generally assumed that a president may, at least in some of these circumstances, be criminally prosecuted after leaving office. These questions have been posed most recently by allegations that Clinton criminally lied both in a civil court deposition in the *Jones* case and before a criminal grand jury concerning the same matter, all while he was president.

Executive immunity is distinct from questions of the extent to which, if any, executive officials must respond to subpoenas and similar processes of the legislative and executive branches and of whether a court, having found acts of the executive to be illegal, can enforce its decision by, for example, enjoining the executive from doing the acts. The Court in *Jones* relied on the permissibility of some of these exertions of power over the executive to refute the president's separation of powers claim.

FURTHER READING

Cunningham, Thomas M. "*Nixon v. Fitzgerald*: A Justifiable Separation of Powers Argument for Absolute Presidential Civil Damages Immunity?" *Iowa Law Review* 68 (March, 1983): 557.

Jaffee, Louis L. "Suits Against Governments and Officers: Damage Actions." *Harvard Law Review* 77 (1963): 209-239.

Kirgis, Paul Frederic. "Section 1500 and the Jurisdictional Pitfalls of Federal Government Litigation." *American University Law Review* 47 (December, 1997): 301.

Schuck, Peter H. "Suing Our Servants: The Court, Congress, and the Liability of Public Officials for Damages." *Supreme Court Review* 1980 (1981): 281-368.

Woolhandler, Ann. "Patterns of Official Immunity and Accountability." *Case Western Reserve Law Review* 37 (1987): 396.

Paul F. Rothstein

SEE ALSO *Butz v. Economou; Clinton v. Jones*; Common law, federal; Congress, arrest and immunity of members of; Constitutional law; Executive privilege; Judicial immunity; Judicial review; *Nixon, United States v.*; Presidential powers; Restrictions on court power; Reversals of Court decisions by Congress; Separation of powers; Speech and debate clause.

Executive privilege

DESCRIPTION: Inherent power of the president to withhold information from Congress and the courts or to refuse to testify in a legislative or judicial proceeding.

SIGNIFICANCE: The Supreme Court recognized a constitutionally based limited privilege grounded in the doctrine of the separation of powers.

Presidential discretion to refuse to appear before a legislative or judicial proceeding is sometimes considered a separate category of executive discretion called executive privilege, or presidential privacy. According to William Safire, the phrase "executive privilege" was first used in the 1950's, but the concept dates back to the practice of the royal prerogative, privilege of clergy, and privileges of Parliament.

Origins and Early Uses. Executive privilege is also considered an implied power under Article II of the U.S. Constitution. George Washington claimed the authority to withhold information from Congress during a 1792 congressional investigation into the St. Clair Affair, in which General Arthur St. Clair, governor of the Northwest Territory, suffered a devastating defeat when ambushed by Indians in 1791. Although Washington gave the House of Representatives the documents it requested regarding the St. Clair expedition, the president argued that if he deemed it in the national interest, he could withhold the information.

Because of its opaque historical roots, disagreement exists regarding the meaning and scope of executive privilege, its application in U.S. government, and its constitutional basis. As a result of these disagreements, in the post-World War II period, federal courts frequently were asked to decide cases involving executive privilege. Constitutional scholars such as Raoul Berger represent one side of the debate that argues that executive privilege is a myth, not a constitutional reality. Proponents of a broad interpretation of executive privilege tend to be presidents and executive officials who argue for it in a particular political context rather than on principle. The debate over its application has been colored by the specific controversies that engendered its use. For example, President Dwight D. Eisenhower used executive privilege to prevent Defense Department officials from revealing information sought by the House of Representatives during the Army-Joe McCarthy hearings in 1953-1954.

Only a president can invoke executive privilege because in the Constitution, all executive power rests in that office. Executive privilege is justified by the president's need to receive frank advice from advisers, to protect national security, and to check and balance the subpoena power of Congress and the courts. In each of these cases, the justification for keeping information within the executive branch is national interest or the public good, often in combination with national security. Although executive privilege has no textual mooring in the Constitution, it emanates from the principle of the separation of powers.

A Limited Privilege. The Supreme Court set limits to executive privilege in the landmark precedent *United States v. Nixon* (1974), which led to the resignation of President Richard M. Nixon. In the 8-0 decision written by Chief Justice Warren E. Burger, the Court ruled that the president may not give privileged status to information that is instrumental to a criminal investigation. Nixon's use of executive privilege regarding the Watergate tapes was considered inconsistent with the idea that this privilege exists to serve the national interest, not to protect the president from criminal prosecution or impeachment.

Although post-World War II presidents have tended to argue for an absolute privilege, the federal courts have rejected the idea based largely on the legitimate needs of the other branches of government to acquire information from the execu-

Richard Nixon smiles and displays the victory sign as he says a final farewell to his supporters outside the White House on August 9, 1974, after resigning the presidency. Earlier that year, a Supreme Court ruling placed limits on executive privilege, forcing Nixon to produce evidence that made his impeachment seem likely. (AP/Wide World Photos)

tive. The Court has accepted a constitutionally based limited privilege. The closest the Court came to accepting an absolute privilege power was in *Spalding v. Vilas* (1896) and *Barr v. Matteo* (1959). The Court's position, however, was reshaped by the Watergate affair, and the effects of the *United States v. Nixon* decision were apparent in *Butz v. Economou* (1978). In the *Butz* decision, the majority, represented by Justice Byron R. White, denied absolute immunity based in part on its inconsistency with the rule of law.

In the 1990's, the federal courts ruled that President Bill Clinton's use of executive privilege was unfounded because, as with Nixon, it was invoked to avoid criminal prosecution and impeachment, not to serve the needs of the nation. During the investigation involving the president and Monica Lewinsky by independent council Kenneth Starr, the Clinton administration attempted to expand the meaning and application of executive privilege to new areas of the president's life. Two such areas were the attempt to extend executive privilege to the president and his attorneys and to the Secret Service agents who protect the president. U.S. District Judge Norma Holloway Johnson and a three-judge appeals court panel rejected Clinton's claims of executive privilege in the Lewinsky investigation. Johnson ruled that White House attorney Bruce Lindsey and White House aide Sidney Blumenthal must testify before a federal grand jury. President Clinton's attorneys appealed the decision to the Supreme Court, but the Court refused to hear the case.

In a related matter, the Clinton administration argued that Secret Service agents are covered by "protective-function privilege" because requiring them to testify about the president before a federal grand jury or to be deposed by the independent council's office is incompatible with their duty to protect the president. Acceptance of this claim would have significantly expanded the extent of executive privilege. However, the Court also refused to hear this case, letting stand the lower court's decision to deny the president's claim of a protective-function privilege.

FURTHER READING

Berger, Raoul. *Executive Privilege: A Constitutional Myth*. Cambridge, Mass.: Harvard University Press, 1974.

Rozell, Mark J. *Executive Privilege: The Dilemma of Secrecy and Democratic Accountability*. Baltimore, Md.: Johns Hopkins University Press, 1994.

Safire, William. *Safire's New Political Dictionary*. New York: Random House, 1993.

Michael P. Federici

SEE ALSO Burger, Warren E.; *Butz v. Economou*; Clinton, Bill; Executive immunity; Nixon, Richard M.; *Nixon, United States v.*; *Nixon v. Administrator of General Services*; White, Byron R.

Extrajudicial activities

DESCRIPTION: Actions undertaken by Supreme Court justices, usually at the command of the president or Congress, that are outside the scope of their judicial function of hearing and deciding cases.

SIGNIFICANCE: Congress and the president have ordered Supreme Court justices to perform a variety of duties unrelated to their work on the Court. Critics believe that such appointments adversely affect the efficiency of the Court, create a conflict of interest for the justices, and violate the constitutional principle of separation of powers.

From the earliest days of the Supreme Court, justices have served in a variety of official capacities beyond their strictly judicial duties. The practice was always controversial and became less common after Earl Warren's term as chief justice of the United States. The four principal criticisms of accepting such appointments from Congress or the president are that these appointments reduce the efficiency of the Court, may place justices in a conflict of interest, may weaken public respect for the judiciary, and violate the principle of separation of powers. Justices sometimes engage in questionable extrajudicial activities on their own volition, such as campaigning for the presidency or serving as a legal or political consultant. Business dealings may easily violate the code of judicial conduct that the justices swear to uphold. Judges must not only be honest, they must appear to be above reproach.

During the colonial period, Americans lived under the British parliamentary system. In this scheme of government, there is no separation of powers. The executive, the prime minister, is the leader of the legislature's lower house, the House of Commons, and the highest court, the House of Lords, is the upper house of Parliament. It was common for the justices, or Law Lords, to serve in legislative and executive capacities. This tradition survived the American Revolution and the establishment of constitutional government in the United States. During the Constitutional Convention of 1787, James Madison proposed a council of revision, in which the president and "a convenient number of the National Judiciary" would review statutes enacted by Congress and veto them if they were repugnant to the Constitution. The convention rejected the proposal and gave the veto to the president alone. In Canada and other countries based on the British parliamentary model, it is common for justices of the highest court to perform extrajudicial functions such as giving advisory opinions to the chief executive and serving on commissions of inquiry. The U.S. presidential system of government, based on the separation of powers, makes such assignments problematic for justices of the Supreme Court.

Early Rejection of Nonjudicial Duties. In two early cases, the Court asserted its independence of Congress and the president by refusing to engage in extrajudicial activities. In *Hayburn's Case* (1792), five of the six justices refused to perform duties imposed on the federal courts by an act of Congress. The law required U.S. circuit courts (consisting of district and Supreme Court justices riding circuit) to hear disability claims by Revolutionary War veterans and to make recommendations to the secretary of war. The secretary, however, could modify or reject the judges' recommendations. In their letters to President George Washington, the justices pointed out that the act imposed nonjudicial duties on the courts and was, therefore, unconstitutional.

In July, 1793, President Washington requested advice from the Court on whether the United States could remain neutral in the war between Great Britain and France under the 1778 treaty between the United States and France. In August, the justices of the Court replied in a letter to the president that they could not give advisory opinions. The constitution made the judiciary a separate and independent branch of government. Its opinions on matters of law must be final and unreviewable by the executive and legislative departments. In essence, the president was asking the court to perform the duties of the attorney general, the executive officer entrusted with proffering advice to the president on matters of law, advice that the president could always ignore.

Diplomatic Appointments. Although the Court twice refused extrajudicial assignments in the 1790's, individual justices were not so scrupulous. In 1794 while still holding the office of chief justice of the United States, John Jay accepted a presidential appointment as envoy to Great Britain. He negotiated Jay's Treaty, which resolved disputes between the two countries over unpaid debts. He did not resign his position as chief justice until 1795, when he was elected governor of New York. Oliver Ellsworth, also while serving as chief justice, accepted a diplomatic appointment from President Washington in 1799. He negotiated an end to the undeclared war with France.

Associate Justices Samuel Nelson and John A. Campbell accepted appointments as mediators in the conflict between the North and South in an unsuccessful attempt to avoid civil war. In 1871 President Ulysses S. Grant appointed Justice Nelson as a U.S. representative to the Alabama Claims Commission. The commission arbitrated U.S. claims against Great Britain arising from its support for the Confederacy during the Civil War. Five Supreme Court justices received appointments to the Electoral Commission that resolved the disputed presidential election of 1876, awarding the presidency to the Republican candidate, Rutherford B. Hayes.

Chief Justice Melville W. Fuller and Justice David J. Brewer served as arbitrators in a boundary dispute between Venezuela and British Guiana. Associate Justice John Marshall Harlan accepted an appointment as arbitrator in a conflict over fur seals. Justice William R. Day in the 1920's served on the American-German War Claims Commission. Chief Justice Charles Evans Hughes served as chairman of a tribunal authorized to settle a dispute over the border between Guatemala and Honduras. Justice Willis Van Devanter served as an arbitrator in a conflict between the United States and Great Britain over British seizure of a U.S. vessel. Justice Owen J. Roberts accepted an appointment to a commission to hear claims against the United States from Mexico.

Commissions of Inquiry. In addition to appointments to diplomatic posts, Court justices have received presidential commissions to conduct investigations of controversial or embarrassing public events. Justice Henry Baldwin, associate justice from 1830 to 1844, participated in an investigation of General Andrew Jackson's military campaign against the Seminole Indians. President Franklin D. Roosevelt appointed Justice Owen J. Roberts to a commission to investigate the Japanese surprise attack on Pearl Harbor. President Lyndon B. Johnson persuaded Chief Justice Earl Warren to chair the commission investigating the assassination of John F. Kennedy.

Justice Stephen J. Field served as a member of a California commission to revise the state's statutes. In 1911 Justice Charles Evans Hughes served as a commissioner empowered to set postal rates. President Harry S Truman tapped Justice Robert H. Jackson to serve as chief U.S. prosecutor in the

Nuremberg War Trials following the Allied victory in World War II.

The chief justice has several nonjudicial obligations. By statute, the chief justice serves as chairman of the National Gallery of Art's Board of Trustees and as chancellor of the Smithsonian Institute's Board of Regents. The chief justice also chairs the Judicial Conference of the United States, the body responsible for the administration of the federal courts. Most commentators rank Chief Justice Warren E. Burger rather low as a leader of the Court but give him high marks for his administrative work. He enjoyed his extrajudicial roles more than his strictly judicial duties of resolving constitutional disputes and helping the justices reach consensus on difficult issues of doctrine.

Private Activities. Not all extrajudicial activities are the result of congressional statutes or presidential appointments. The justices engage in many off-the-bench activities on their own initiatives. The ones that lead to controversy typically involve conflicts of interest or breaches of the expectation of impartiality. Several justices have served as advisers to members of Congress and the president. Justice Joseph Story was an adviser to President James Madison and to members of Congress. He even provided drafts of legislation he wanted Congress to adopt. One of the most notorious examples of such advice was a letter written by Justice John Catron to President James Buchanan, in which Catron informed the president of the Court's decision in *Dred Scott v. Sandford* (1857) before it was made public. President Lyndon B. Johnson relied on Justice Abe Fortas for counsel on a variety of issues. Several justices, including John McLean, Salmon P. Chase, and Charles Evans Hughes, have sought the presidency. Hughes resigned, however, before accepting the Republican presidential nomination in 1916.

The greatest scandal involving a justice's extrajudicial private acts led to the resignation of Justice Fortas in 1969. Fortas was not only an adviser to President Johnson but also the recipient of a high fee for giving a law school lecture and, most damning of all, of payments from a private foundation established by Louis Wolfson, a former client and businessperson indicted for federal crimes. Questions of propriety were also raised regarding Associate Justice Louis D. Brandeis's extrajudicial activities. Brandeis attempted to influence U.S.

domestic and foreign policy by financially supporting Felix Frankfurter, an adviser to President Franklin D. Roosevelt. Some of the issues of importance to Brandeis, a Progressive, were likely to come before the Court. The Brandeis-Frankfurter-Roosevelt connection was unknown at the time, however, so the justice was able to maintain the appearance of open-mindedness and impartiality.

Criticisms of Extrajudicial Activities. When justices leave the bench, even temporarily, they impair the efficiency of the Court. Justice Robert H. Jackson was away from the Court for more than a year. Several chief justices, including Edward D. White, William H. Taft, and Harlan Fiske Stone, have complained that taking justices away from their judicial tasks slows down the processing of cases.

The Court runs a risk when its justices agree to serve on extrajudicial commissions. The public may perceive their work as biased and politically motivated. This perception can lead to a loss of public respect for the Court. The 1876 Electoral Commission was criticized for voting along strict party lines. The task placed the justices in a conflict of interest, and they did not appear to be impartial. The Roberts Commission exonerated the Roosevelt administration of responsibility for the surprise attack on U.S. forces at Pearl Harbor and placed the blame on the military commanders in Hawaii. The Warren Commission concluded that assassin Lee Harvey Oswald acted alone. The commission's findings were attacked as soon as they were released, and criticism continued to grow as additional evidence and theories arose.

Extrajudicial activities became increasingly questionable. As the caseload of the Court increased, the demands of the office have reached the point where justices have little time for work outside their judicial duties. In the twentieth century, the Court grew bolder and struck down dozens of congressional statutes and presidential actions. Examples include *Youngstown Sheet and Tube Co. v. Sawyer* (1952), in which the Court ordered President Truman to return the steel mills he had nationalized in order to prevent a strike, and *United States v. Eichman* (1990), in which the Court invalidated the Flag Protection Act of 1989 as an infringement on freedom of expression. For the Court to be an effective check on the executive and legislative branches, it must maintain its distance from Congress and the president. The salaries and benefits of Supreme Court justices rose to the point where justices no longer need to be involved in questionable business dealings. The attention of the media also increased to a point where it is nearly impossible for justices to engage in the kind of clandestine lobbying in which Justices Story and Brandeis were involved.

FURTHER READING

Russell Wheeler provides a good overview of the early Court's efforts to claim its independence in "Extrajudicial Activities of the Early Supreme Court," *Supreme Court Review* (1973): 123-158. One of the justices who strongly opposed taking justices from the bench to serve on commissions and tribunals was Harlan Fiske Stone, who is the subject of Alpheus Thomas Mason's *Harlan Fiske Stone: Pillar of the Law* (New York: Viking Press, 1956). Bruce Allen Murphy revealed the full extent of Justice Brandeis's efforts to influence U.S. domestic and foreign policy in *The Brandeis-Frankfurter Connection* (Garden City, N.Y.: Anchor Books, 1983). He also documents the extrajudicial activities of Justice Fortas in *Fortas: The Rise and Ruin of a Supreme Court Justice* (New York: W. Morrow, 1988). A good account of Chief Justice Warren's reluctance to chair the Kennedy assassination commission can be found in Bernard Schwartz's *Super Chief: Earl Warren and His Supreme Court: A Judicial Biography* (New York: New York University Press, 1983). Eugene Gerhart's *America's Advocate: Robert H. Jackson* (Indianapolis, Ind.: Bobbs-Merrill, 1958) contains an account of Jackson's service as chief prosecutor at the Nuremberg War Trials.

Kenneth M. Holland

SEE ALSO Advisory opinions; British Law Lords; Chief justice; Fortas, Abe; *Hayburn's Case*; Judicial codes and rules; Supreme Court of Canada; Warren, Earl; Washington, George.

F

Fairfax's Devisee v. Hunter's Lessee

CITATION: 11 U.S. 203
DATE: March 15, 1813
ISSUE: Federal supremacy
SIGNIFICANCE: In this case and one in 1816, the U.S. Supreme Court engaged in a constitutional power struggle with the Virginia supreme court over seized Loyalist property and the state's treaty obligations.

Justice Joseph Story wrote the opinion for himself and only two other justices because three others, Chief Justice John Marshall and Justices Bushrod Washington and Thomas Todd, were not present. Justice William Johnson dissented. The most obvious issue was whether Virginia could pass a law upholding the seizure of property from Tory Loyalists during the Revolutionary War and whether Virginia had to fulfill its obligations under the controversial 1794 Jay Treaty. The Virginia supreme court of appeals upheld the state's seizure of property from British Loyalists and Virginia's position on its treaty obligations. Story ruled in favor of the Loyalist claim, but the authority of the Supreme Court was under attack partly because of the narrowness of the Court's majority. Virginia refused to accept the Court's authority and declared section 25 of the 1789 Judiciary Act to be unconstitutional. The case returned to the Court as *Martin v. Hunter's Lessee*.

Richard L. Wilson

SEE ALSO Federalism; Judiciary Act of 1789; *Martin v. Hunter's Lessee*; States' rights.

Family and children

DESCRIPTION: Men, women, their offspring, and other relatives. The Supreme Court has applied constitutional protection to family issues such as the right to marry, the right to privacy, the right of parents to raise and educate children, and in some cases the rights of children.
SIGNIFICANCE: Although the right to marry and the right to raise a child are not explicitly mentioned in the Constitution, the Court has ac-

corded these liberties constitutional protection through the equal protection and due process clauses.

Family law in the United States is created largely by the states rather than the federal government. Historically the Supreme Court was reticent to interfere in state family policy, but it overturned state and local law when constitutional rights were at issue. The Court also had an indirect effect on families by refusing to accept many cases that challenge state family law and policy. In this way, the Court has sanctioned a variety of family policies that can differ a great deal from state to state.

A threshold question in family law is the definition of a family. When government stepped in to create its own definition, the Court at times upheld the government and at other times declared this action in violation of the Constitution. A local government was prohibited from limiting the definition of family to include only a nuclear family for purposes of zoning in *Moore v. City of East Cleveland* (1977). A grandmother living with her son, his son, and another grandchild, faced eviction because hers was not considered a "single family" under the city ordinance.

The Court denied a free exercise claim from the Church of Jesus Christ of Latter-day Saints (Mormons) opposing a federal law banning polygamy in *Reynolds v. United States* (1879). The Court considered the practice to be "odious" and therefore a threat to public morality. This decision protected the public policy of monogamous marriages and allowed the government to define "family."

Applying the equal protection clause in *Levy v. Louisiana* (1968), the Court determined that illegitimate children cannot be given treatment that is substantially unequal to that of children who are born to parents who are married. Children who are born to parents who are not married have both equal protection and due process protection against arbitrary state laws.

Marriage and Privacy. The Court protected the right of people of different races to marry by declaring unconstitutional state laws that prohibited interracial marriage (miscegenation laws) in

Loving v. Virginia (1967). The right of prison inmates to marry was protected from arbitrary government restriction in *Turner v. Safley* (1987). A state law prohibiting a person who had not made child support payments from obtaining a marriage license was declared unconstitutional in *Zablocki v. Redhail* (1978). Although whether the corresponding right to divorce exists is not clear, the Court ruled that indigent people seeking to go to court to "adjust their fundamental human relationships" must not be prevented from doing so by nominal court fees.

In *Griswold v. Connecticut* (1965), the Court shielded marital privacy by protecting the right of married couples to use contraceptives. The Court expressed its disdain for governmental intrusion into the marriage relationship. Following the precedent of *Griswold,* the Court decided in 1973 that the word "liberty" in the due process clause of the Fourteenth Amendment, which encompasses an implied right of privacy, protects a woman's right to have an abortion in *Roe v. Wade.* This decision has both directly and indirectly had a major impact on the issues of family and children.

Parents and Children. In *Pierce v. Society of Sisters* (1925), the right of parents to educate their children in parochial school was protected when a state attempted to require that all children be educated in public schools. In *Wisconsin v. Yoder* (1972), the parental right to educate a child at home was protected when Amish parents refused to send their children to public high schools under the state's compulsory education law. In both cases, the free exercise clause of the First Amendment was applied through the due process clause of the Fourteenth Amendment to protect parental religious freedom.

The Court declared in *Stanley v. Illinois* (1972) that an unwed father who has an established relationship with his child must be given the due process protections of notice and a hearing before parental rights can be terminated. In the case of *Lehr v. Robertson* (1983), an unwed father challenged his child's adoption be- cause he had not been given notice and a hearing. This case was important in establishing constitutional protection for parental rights because the Court went further than the requirement for notice and hearing by asserting that the biological parent's right to establish a relationship with his (or her) child held constitutional status as a liberty interest under the due process clause of the Fourteenth Amendment. However, the unwed father in *Lehr* failed to meet state statutory guidelines to assert paternity, and his constitutional rights to challenge his child's adoption and to establish a relationship with his child were considered to be forfeited. *Lehr* served as a precedent in the 1994 case of *Baby Richard v. Kirchner* (1994), in which the biological father gained custody of his son even though the child had lived with an adoptive family for four years. The father in that case had not forfeited his constitutional liberty interest to establish a relationship with his son and had spent most of those four years attempting to gain legal custody of his son through the courts.

A man who fathered a daughter by a woman who was married to another man, however, was not granted constitutional protection in seeking custody or visitation rights. In *Michael H. v. Gerald D.*

The Supreme Court grants constitutional protection to parental rights; however, it and lower courts must struggle to define these rights in complex situations. In 1987 William Stern holds his daughter after her visit to Mary Beth Whitehead, the surrogate mother for Stern and his wife. The New Jersey supreme court gave the Sterns custody and granted visitation rights to Whitehead. (AP/Wide World Photos)

(1989), the Court determined that a state may refuse to recognize the rights of a biological father when, as in that case, an ongoing family unit is the subject of protection. The Court expressed that the family unit is an important component of American society and that it is the appropriate role of government to protect the family.

Fathers and mothers cannot be given substantially unequal treatment by state courts in custody and adoption decisions according to *Caban v. Mohammed* (1979). The unwed father in that case, protected by the equal protection clause of the Fourteenth Amendment, was allowed to block his children's adoption by their stepfather even though state statute had protected only the mother's right to block adoption.

In *Palmore v. Sadoti* (1984), the states were prohibited under the equal protection clause from making custody decisions solely on the basis of race. A white mother had lost custody of her daughter because she was living with, and later married, an African American man. The Court did not, however, prohibit race from being used as one of several factors in making custody and adoption decisions.

In *Lassiter v. Department of Social Services* (1981), the Court ruled that indigent parents do not have the constitutional right to counsel appointed by the state in proceedings in which parental rights may be terminated. One year later, the Court addressed the issue of what standard of proof should be required in termination proceedings in *Santosky v. Kramer* (1982). The Court declared that the lower standard of "preponderance of evidence" was not sufficient to protect parental rights but required states to satisfy the higher standard of "clear and convincing evidence" before parental rights may be terminated. Both cases were decided under the due process clause of the Fourteenth Amendment.

The Court was not particularly generous in protecting parents who abuse their children. One parent attempted to use the Fourth Amendment protection against unreasonable searches (a protection ordinarily within the province of criminal law) by government authorities involved in family welfare issues. The Court declined, in *Wyman v. James* (1971), to constitutionally protect a mother from an allegedly unreasonable visit by an Aid to Families with Dependent Children worker who discovered that the child had multiple injuries. In a simi-

lar decision in 1990 the Court refused to use the Fifth Amendment protection against self-incrimination on behalf of a mother who was required by court order to bring her abused child to court (*Baltimore City Department of Social Services v. Bouknight*).

In response to the high number of tribal children who were leaving the reservations under state court custody and adoption decisions, Congress passed the Indian Child Welfare Act of 1978, which took jurisdiction of such cases away from state courts. Under this act, the Supreme Court upheld the right of a Native American tribe to have jurisdiction, with some exceptions, over custody and adoption decisions that involved tribal children in *Mississippi Band of Choctaw Indians v. Holyfield* (1989). Ultimately the tribal court in that case made the decision to allow the child to remain with the adoptive non-Indian family, but in many other cases, Indian children were placed with extended family members, a reflection of tribal tradition, and remained on the reservation.

Rights of Children. In the 1940's the Court decided two cases affecting the interests of children. In *West Virginia State Board of Education v. Barnette* (1943), the Court protected the free exercise right of a student to refuse to salute and pledge allegiance to the flag for religious reasons. In *Prince v. Massachusetts* (1944), the Court upheld an ordinance that protected children from being put in danger near a public road. In that case, a woman was passing out religious literature with her nine-year-old niece when she was ordered to cease in the interests of the child. The ordinance, according to the Court, did not violate the free exercise of religion.

During the Vietnam War, the Court protected the rights of students to use symbolic speech in public schools. When a student was suspended for wearing a black armband to school in protest of the war, the Court protected her free speech rights in *Tinker v. Des Moines Independent Community School District* (1969) because her actions were not disruptive to the educational process.

Justice William O. Douglas raised an issue about the rights of children in his partial dissent in the *Yoder* case. Although he had agreed that the Amish had a right to educate their children at home, he disagreed that the decision should be based on the right of the parents to educate their children. He thought instead that the Court should be concerned about whether the children wanted to be educated at home or in public school. At times the Court protected the right of parents to raise their children, and at others it protected the rights of children. A problem arises, according to Justice Douglas, if these rights are in opposition.

FURTHER READING

Sources of information on the family and legal issues include E. Bartholet's *Family Bonds* (Boston: Houghton Mifflin, 1993) and Janet Dolgin's *Defining the Family* (New York: New York University Press, 1997). David Westfall's *Family Law* (St. Paul, Minn.: West Publishing, 1994) and *Cases, Comments and Questions on Family Law* (4th ed., St. Paul, Minn.: West Publishing, 1998) by Harry Krause et al. examine the basics of family law. Margaret Conway's *Women and Public Policy* (Washington, D.C.: Congressional Quarterly Press, 1995) looks at the relationship between women and public policy. Ziba Mir-Hosseini's *Marriage on Trial* (New York: St. Martin's, 1993) focuses on marriage-related legal issues.

Carol Tebben

SEE ALSO Abortion; Birth control and contraception; Due process, substantive; Education; Marriage; Native American law; Pregnancy, disability, and maternity leaves; Privacy, right to.

Fay v. Noia

CITATION: 372 U.S. 391
DATE: March 18, 1963
ISSUE: Procedural due process
SIGNIFICANCE: The Supreme Court upheld the right of those convicted of state offenses to use *habeas corpus* petitions in federal courts, notwithstanding minor time limitations in state law.

Justice William J. Brennan, Jr., wrote for the 6-3 majority, upholding the right of state prisoners to use *habeas corpus* petitions in federal courts even if they have failed to comply strictly with state statute-of-limitation provisions. Basically, the Supreme Court abandoned its earlier ruling that the exhaustion of state remedies had to include a petition to be heard by the Court (certiorari). Because so few certiorari petitions are granted and the process is so time-consuming, it is a burdensome requirement. In this case, defendant Noia had been convicted of

murder with the use of a coerced confession in a state court despite the Court's prior prohibition on the use of coerced confessions. The state admitted this and relied solely on Noia's failure to file a timely appeal from the state appellate court, a technicality that the Court did not find compelling under the circumstances, although it did satisfy the dissenting justices: Tom C. Clark, John M. Harlan II, and Potter Stewart.

Richard L. Wilson

SEE ALSO Certiorari, writ of; Federalism; *Habeas corpus*.

Federal Tort Claims Act

DATE: 1946
DESCRIPTION: Statute that enabled private citizens to sue the government in civil tort actions in federal court.
SIGNIFICANCE: The Federal Tort Claims Act allows people to sue when a federal employee harms a third party or private property by committing an intentional tort or by negligence. The Supreme Court later barred military personnel from suing the federal government for injuries suffered while performing their jobs.

The Federal Tort Claims Act was passed in 1946 to protect third parties injured by the actions of federal government employees. If a federal employee, acting within the scope of his or her employment, injures a third party, then the federal government can be held liable for the employee's actions.

Historically, the federal government was protected by the doctrine of sovereign immunity, which prevented a lawsuit's being filed against a government authority without the government's consent. The 1946 act limits the protection of the doctrine and allows third parties to seek compensation.

However, when the lawsuit arises out of injury to military personnel, acting within the scope of their service, the Supreme Court held that the government cannot be sued under the act. Vietnam veterans exposed to the herbicide Agent Orange filed a class action suit against the federal government and the herbicide's manufacturers. In one case, *In re "Agent Orange" Product Liability Litigation* (1980), the manufacturers reached a pretrial settlement with several of the veterans and their families. The suit against the federal government was dismissed by the lower court, and the Court refused to hear the appeals by the veterans. The Court continued to maintain that the act does not extend to suits filed by military personnel. In *Hercules v. United States* (1996), the Court stated that this exclusion is still viable.

Additionally, the Court refuses to impose liability when a private business contracting with the federal government attempts to hold the government responsible for negligent acts performed by the business. The injured third party can seek compensation from the business but not from the government.

However, when the federal government is liable, the Court has enforced the provisions of the act. In *Molzof v. United States* (1992), a veteran suffered irreversible brain damage because of negligence at a Veterans' Administration hospital. The lower court granted damages under the act but refused to award damages for future medical expenses and for loss of enjoyment of life. The lower court held that awarding such damages would be providing punitive damages, which the act expressly prohibits; the act prohibits awarding damages solely for the purpose of punishing the government for its actions. The Court reversed the decision, finding that although the award of such damages may have a punitive effect, it should be considered compensatory.

Patricia Jackson

SEE ALSO Contracts clause; Judicial immunity; Military and the Court.

Federalism

DESCRIPTION: Political union and the resulting constitutional structures that configure relationships among the states and institutions of national governance.

SIGNIFICANCE: Problems of federalism involve questions of constitutional structure. The Supreme Court has expressed its position on relationships among institutions of national and state governance and enforced federal constitutional limitations against the states.

Even before the U.S. Constitution went into effect, there were serious debates about what type of political system it would create—and what type of union

had already been formed. Part of the problem was multiple and shifting word usages. Those advocating the Constitution's ratification identified themselves as Federalists, described the new structures as partly federal, and claimed those structures were necessary to preserve the federal union. At the same time, members of the founding generation identified federalism with a confederation of sovereign states, as distinct from a consolidated or national government. Relying on these distinctions, James Madison in *The Federalist* (1788), No. 39, argued that the proposed Constitution was neither purely federal nor entirely national but instead included features of each.

Federalism in the American context has since become identified with this hybrid political system—especially the Constitution's configuration of national and state governing powers. Unlike the Articles of Confederation, the Constitution establishes a centralized government, which has institutions that directly represent the people and are capable, in turn, of acting directly on them. As a result of the Constitution's delegation of limited powers to these institutions, however, the states continue to hold independent governing powers. The states also play other important roles within the constitutional order, through, among other mechanisms, their equal representation in the Senate and their participation in constitutional amendment.

Not surprisingly, controversies involving problems of federalism survived the Constitution's ratification. Some such controversies—but certainly not all those of constitutional significance—have arisen in the context of litigation. Accordingly, the Supreme Court played an important role in the development of American federalism on several fronts. In the process, the Court articulated a range of competing conceptions of the constitutional design.

Questions of Federal Jurisdiction. One set of issues centered on problems of jurisdiction and matters of interpretive or decisional authority. Article III of the U.S. Constitution defines the jurisdiction of federal courts as including cases or controversies "between Citizens of a State and Citizens of another State." In *Chisholm v. Georgia* (1793), the Court held that this provision authorized federal courts to decide a suit against Georgia brought by two citizens of South Carolina. Two years later,

Congress and the states overturned this holding by passing the Eleventh Amendment, which restricts federal courts from hearing suits against states brought by citizens of other states or by citizens of foreign nations. In subsequent decisions, the Court held that this amendment also bars suits against a state by its own citizens without its consent. However, the significance of these exceptions has been diluted by the Fourteenth Amendment, along with distinctions between the states and state officials. As explained below, a fertile area of constitutional litigation involves federal courts' enforcing the U.S. Constitution and federal laws against the states and state actors.

Article III delegates to federal courts the authority to decide some cases based on the identity of the litigants, as with lawsuits between citizens of different states. Federal courts also have authority to decide controversies based on the subject matter, including cases "arising under th[e] Constitution, the Laws of the United States, and Treaties." Especially during the republic's first 100 years, substantial conflict surrounded the Court's assertions of appellate power to review decisions by state courts in cases raising such "federal questions." Most prominently, in *Martin v. Hunter's Lessee* (1816), a civil case, and *Cohens v. Virginia* (1821), a criminal case, the justices insisted that they had final authority to review decisions by state courts. In both contexts, state courts denied that the Supreme Court had authority to review or reverse their decisions.

Challenges of federal authority by state judges, legislatures, and others continued through the antebellum period and into the twentieth century. The Court responded to one such challenge in *Ableman v. Booth* (1859), in the context of efforts by the Wisconsin supreme court to authorize the release of prisoners from a local jail based on the state judges' position that the federal Fugitive Slave Act of 1850 was unconstitutional. In response, Chief Justice Roger Brooke Taney unflinchingly reasserted the Supreme Court's interpretive supremacy. He claimed that "no power is more clearly conferred by the Constitution and laws of the United States, than the power of this court to decide, ultimately and finally, all cases arising under such Constitution and laws." (Ironically, however, the Court's position on the constitutional status of slavery was soon overruled by the Civil War and Reconstruction amendments.)

Almost one hundred years later, Chief Justice Earl Warren echoed Taney's position on the pre-eminence of the Court's interpretive powers in *Cooper v. Aaron* (1958). In that case, the justices sought to overcome resistance to their previous ruling in *Brown v. Board of Education* (1954). Collapsing the constitutional text into its interpretation by the justices, Warren proclaimed that "the interpretation of the Fourteenth Amendment by this Court in the Brown Case is the supreme law of the land, and Article 6 of the Constitution makes it of binding effect on the States."

Early Views of Federal-State Relations. Woven through these cases raising questions of jurisdictional and decisional authority were controversies over the scope of Congress's powers (or federal powers more generally) and their relationships to state powers, along with efforts to enforce other limitations on the states. Among other things, the Supreme Court justices took positions on the constitutional status of slavery, the scope of the Constitution's delegation of commercial powers and their negative implications, implied powers, and taxing and spending powers. The Tenth Amendment was at the center of these debates because it both presupposes that federal powers are intrinsically limited and refers to reserved powers of "the states" and "the people." The Fourteenth Amendment was also centrally relevant, as it was the vehicle for the Court's applying much of the Bill of Rights to the states, along with additional guarantees of due process and equal protection.

During the republic's early years, the federal government's role was relatively limited compared to that of the states. Nevertheless, in cases such as *McCulloch v. Maryland* (1819) and *Gibbons v. Ogden* (1824), Chief Justice John Marshall offered a vigorous conception of federal powers and emphasized the supremacy of delegated over reserved powers. He presumed that federal powers were intrinsically limited and thus were consistent with the states' continuing to have substantial regulatory autonomy. However, he did not regard state powers as affirmative limitations on congressional powers or as capable of interfering with their exercise. Therefore, he claimed that state powers must give way to legitimate assertions of federal power.

Taney, Marshall's successor, developed the idea of state police powers and placed greater emphasis on the limited scope of federal powers. Beneath the surface if not always transparently, there was recurring concern during Taney's tenure with problems of slavery. In some contexts, he and his colleagues treated federal and state powers as potentially overlapping, as with powers of commercial regulation in general. At the same time, the justices treated some federal and state governing powers as mutually exclusive and reciprocally limiting. Taney relied on a version of the latter approach, characteristically dual federalist, in *Scott v. Sandford* (1857). Among other things, he argued that limitations on Congress's powers relating to slavery corresponded to—and protected—powers reserved exclusively to the states.

The predominant view during the antebellum period, as articulated by Chief Justice Marshall in *Barron v. Baltimore* (1833), was that federal judges lacked authority to enforce the Bill of Rights against the states. Other parts of the constitutional text, such as Article I, section 10, imposed limitations directly on the states. The Court interpreted some constitutional delegations of power to Congress as preempting state regulations within certain "spheres." However, the Court, along with Congress, allowed large measures of state autonomy. Accordingly, dual federalism largely prevailed in both theory and practice.

Constitutional Transformations. The Civil War and Reconstruction substantially altered these relationships between institutions of federal and state governance, along with their respective relationships to the people at large. During the war itself, governing power became increasingly centralized, supporting further consolidations of national power after the war. These tendencies were exacerbated, moreover, by problems of reconstruction. The Thirteenth, Fourteenth, and Fifteenth Amendments altered representational structures, imposed additional limitations on the states, and otherwise sought to reduce state autonomy and enhance national powers.

During these transformative periods, the Court's role was mixed. In *Ex parte Merryman* (1861), the Taney Court denied that President Abraham Lincoln had authority to suspend the writ of *habeas corpus*. However, the president refused to comply with this decision, and in the *Prize Cases* (1863), a majority of the justices upheld Lincoln's blockade of Southern ports. After the war, in *Ex parte Milligan* (1866), the Court reasserted itself,

with Salmon P. Chase as chief justice, by invalidating the military trial of a civilian when civil courts were open. In *Mississippi v. Johnson* (1867), *Georgia v. Stanton* (1868), *Ex parte McCardle* (1869), and *Texas v. White* (1869), however, the justices refrained in various contexts from taking a position on the validity of military reconstruction. In the last of these cases, Chase supported the cause of the Union by proclaiming that "the Constitution in all its provisions looks to an indestructible Union composed of indestructible states." Thus, he denied that states could legitimately secede from the Union, claimed that the war had altered relationships between the rebellious states and the Union, and affirmed congressional power to restore republican governments in the South.

The judges initially interpreted the Thirteenth, Fourteenth, and Fifteenth Amendments as supporting Congress's power to secure civil rights from abridgement by the states or individuals. However, soon the justices joined a broader retreat from Reconstruction, as signaled by the opinions in *Slaughterhouse Cases* (1873) and *Civil Rights Cases* (1883). Justices Samuel F. Miller and Joseph P. Bradley wrote the respective majority opinions. In the former case, the Court upheld a monopoly on the slaughtering of meat in New Orleans; in the latter, it invalidated the Civil Rights Act of 1875. From opposite directions, these two decisions perpetuated models of dual federalism.

Dual Federalism. In *Slaughterhouse Cases*, Miller claimed that the "one pervading purpose" of the Thirteenth, Fourteenth, and Fifteenth Amendments was "the freedom of the slave race, the security and firm establishment of that freedom, and the protection of the newly-made freeman and citizen." Though he suggested that other races might benefit from their guarantees, Miller denied that these amendments "radically changed the whole theory of the relations of the State and Federal governments to each other and of both these governments to the people." More specifically, he denied that the privileges or immunities clause of the Fourteenth Amendment "was intended to bring within the power of Congress the entire domain of civil rights heretofore belonging exclusively to the States." Nor did that clause "constitute this court a perpetual censor upon all legislation of the States, on the civil rights of their own citizens." He staked out corresponding positions on the Thirteenth

Amendment and the Fourteenth Amendment's due process and equal protection clauses.

In *Civil Rights Cases*, Bradley likewise argued that the Fourteenth Amendment did not "invest Congress with power to legislate upon subjects which are within the domain of State legislation." In his view, the amendment provided remedies for abridgements of rights by states, not individuals. Relying on the Tenth Amendment, a majority of the justices claimed that the law regulating individual actions exceeded Congress's delegated powers.

Although the Court would subsequently adhere to aspects of the majority opinions in these two cases, many of the dissenters' arguments would eventually prevail in one form or another. The dissents of Justices Stephen J. Field and Bradley in *Slaughterhouse* anticipated judicial enforcement of commercial rights as limitations on the states in reliance on the due process clause of the Fourteenth Amendment. Federal judges went even further by relying on that clause as the primary vehicle for enforcing much of the Bill of Rights against the states, making prescient Justice Noah H. Swayne's characterization of the amendment as "a new Magna Charta." Justice John Marshall Harlan's dissent in the *Civil Rights Cases* likewise anticipated national regulation of individual actions. Relying on the Fourteenth Amendment and Article I's delegation of commercial powers, Congress in the twentieth century would assert—and the justices would uphold—sweeping national civil rights legislation, economic regulations, and other expansions of national power.

In the meantime, the Court enlisted the Fourteenth Amendment, along with the Fifth and Tenth, to promote economic laissez-faire. *Lochner v. New York* (1905) and *Hammer v. Dagenhart* (1918) epitomize the restrictive decisions of this era. Both dealt with matters of federalism: the first through the justices' invalidation of a state law in reliance on the U.S. Constitution; the second because the majority relied on dual federalist premises to strike down an act of Congress. In *Lochner*, the Court held that a state maximum-hour workday law for bakers deprived them of liberty without due process of law in violation of the Fourteenth Amendment's due process clause; and in *Hammer*, they argued that a federal law regulating child labor exceeded Congress's powers, conflicted with the Fifth Amendment, and encroached on powers reserved exclu-

sively to the states. The combined result of such decisions was to treat a wide range of commercial transactions (but not all) as beyond the legitimate reach of governmental restriction, federal or state.

The Modern Era. Controversy over this issue erupted during the New Deal. In response to intense pressure from President Franklin D. Roosevelt, Congress, state legislatures, and various constituencies, the Court shifted its posture in the late 1930's and early 1940's. *West Coast Hotel Co. v. Parrish* (1937) and *United States v. Darby Lumber Co.* (1941) both signaled and epitomized this change, often described as "revolutionary." In *West Coast*, the Court employed deferential reasoning to uphold a state minimum-wage, maximum-hour law, and in *Darby*, it affirmed Congress's powers to regulate terms of employment. In the process, the Court rejected dual federalist premises: Instead of presuming that federal and state powers were mutually exclusive and reciprocally limiting, they treated such powers as substantially overlapping, in many ways complementary, but with federal powers supreme.

The Court did not, however, entirely withdraw from enforcing constitutional limitations on the states. On the contrary, *United States v. Carolene Products Co.* (1938) suggested that the Court would continue to enforce enumerated rights, seek to guard political processes, and ensure fidelity to requirements of equal protection. Such efforts and their extensions gained momentum through the Civil Rights and women's movements and social change more generally, culminating in Warren and post-Warren Court precedents such as *Brown v. Board of Education* (1954), *Mapp v. Ohio* (1961), *Miranda v. Arizona* (1966), *Griswold v. Connecticut* (1965), and *Roe v. Wade* (1973).

Chief Justice Earl Warren's successors, Warren E. Burger and William H. Rehnquist, led modest retreats from these overall trends toward the Court's upholding greater concentrations of central governing power along with increased supervision of state actions. For example, in *National League of Cities v. Usery* (1976), the Court invalidated provisions in the Fair Labor Standards Act (1938) as they applied to the states. However, a majority of the justices overruled this decision nine years later in *Garcia v. San Antonio Metropolitan Transit Authority* (1985). Once again invoking principles of federalism, the Court in *United States v. Lopez* (1995) invalidated a federal law limiting possession of guns near schools. For the first time since 1937, a majority of the justices held that Congress had exceeded its commercial powers. Then in *Seminole Tribe v. Florida* (1996) and *Printz v. United States* (1997), respectively, the justices revitalized the Eleventh Amendment and held that Congress could not command state and local officials to enforce a federal law. These cases, along with others involving issues of affirmative action, term limitations, criminal processes, and other matters, have been at the center of ongoing debates involving matters of federalism in the United States.

Cases from the founding period exemplify ways that constitutionalism in the United States rests on a premise that the states and the people may act through representational structures in some capacities while acting independently of them in others. Principles of federalism are at the heart of these interactions, forming and being reformed by ongoing commitment to constitutional governance. Rather than being settled by more than two hundred years of practice, these principles have remained radically contestable.

FURTHER READING

Charles Warren's "Legislative and Judicial Attacks on the Supreme Court of the United States: A History of the Twenty-fifth Section of the Judiciary Act," *American Law Review* 47 (1913-1914):1-34, 161-189, reviews the history of jurisdictional problems confronted by the Court. Edward S. Corwin's "The Passing of Dual Federalism," *Virginia Law Review* 36 (1950): 1-23 contains a concise account of the Court's shifting approach to federalism during the New Deal, and the special 1985 issue of the *Georgia Law Review* titled "Federalism: Allocating Responsibility Between the Federal and State Courts" explores subsequent constitutional developments. Federalism is placed in its historical and theoretical context in *A Nation of States: Essays on the American Federal System* (Chicago: Rand McNally, 1963), edited by Robert A. Goldwin; Raoul Berger's *Federalism: The Founders' Design* (Norman: University of Oklahoma Press, 1987); and *How Federal Is the Constitution?* (Washington, D.C.: American Enterprise Institute for Public Policy Research, 1987), edited by Robert A. Goldwin and William A. Schambra. Similar treatments of federalism can be found in Wayne D. Moore's *Constitutional Rights and Powers of the People* (Princeton, N.J.: Princeton

University Press, 1996) and Daniel J. Elazar's *Covenant and Constitutionalism: The Great Frontier and the Matrix of Federal Democracy* (New Brunswick, N.J.: Transaction, 1998). For a progressive approach to federalism, see the essays in "Constructing a New Federalism: Jurisdictional Competence and Competition," Symposium Issue, *Yale Law and Policy Review/Yale Journal on Regulation* (1996).

Wayne D. Moore

SEE ALSO *Ableman v. Booth*; *Civil Rights Cases*; Constitution, U.S.; Eleventh Amendment; Fourteenth Amendment; Implied powers; Judiciary Act of 1789; New Deal; Nullification; Reconstruction; *Slaughterhouse Cases*; State constitutions; States' rights; Tenth Amendment.

Federalist, The

DATE: 1788

DESCRIPTION: A collection of essays written by Alexander Hamilton, James Madison, and John Jay supporting the adoption of the U.S. Constitution.

SIGNIFICANCE: *The Federalist*, considered by many scholars to be the most important publication in political science in the United States, was a major milestone in the adoption of the Constitution. Essays Nos. 78 through 82 are devoted to the Supreme Court.

In 1787 the Framers of the Constitution of the United States were seeking support for its adoption. An important battleground was the large and influential state of New York, whose governor, George Clinton, strongly opposed adoption of the new Constitution. In hopes of swaying public opinion toward ratification, Alexander Hamilton, a lawyer who had been a delegate to the Constitutional Convention in Philadelphia earlier that year, began writing a series of essays that explained and defended the proposed Constitution. He enlisted the support of two equally respected and learned politicians, John Jay and James Madison. Writing under the joint pseudonym "Publius," the three published eighty-five essays in New York City newspapers between October, 1787, and August, 1788. Because supporters of the Constitution were known as Federalists, the collection of essays, published in 1788, was known as *The Federalist*. The collected essays were used in both Virginia and New York by supporters of the Constitution during the final debates on ratification. The identities of the authors were kept secret, but it later became generally accepted that Hamilton wrote fifty-one essays, including all those related to the Supreme Court. Six of the last eight essays dealt with the judicial system that would be established by the new Constitution, and Nos. 78 through 82 are devoted to the Supreme Court.

Judicial Review. That the Supreme Court was the subject of only five of the eighty-five essays is not surprising because Publius considered the judicial branch to be the weakest of the three proposed sectors of government. However, one of the major points of opposition to the concept of a supreme court with the power of judicial review was the fear that it would become the most powerful branch of the government, able to overturn acts of Congress unimpeded.

One of the most influential and well-known essays, No. 78, is Hamilton's defense of judicial review. Here, Hamilton argues that judicial review does not invalidate the supremacy of the will of the people as expressed through their legislators but is a necessity for the principle of separation of powers. He points out that "the executive not only dispenses the honors but holds the sword of the community. The legislature not only commands the purse but prescribes the rules by which the duties and rights of every citizen are to be regulated. The judiciary . . . can take no active resolution whatever. It may truly be said to have neither FORCE nor WILL but merely judgment; and must ultimately depend upon the aid of the executive arm even for the efficacy of its judgments." Hamilton also argues for permanent tenure for judges as long as they exhibit good behavior.

Nos. 79 to 82. No. 79 is relatively brief and primarily addresses the need for adequate pay for judges. No. 80 enumerates the types of cases to be reserved for the federal judiciary: "all cases in law and equity, arising under the Constitution and the laws of the United States"; cases involving treaties, ambassadors, and consuls; cases of admiralty and maritime jurisdiction; controversies to which the United States is a party; disputes between states or between citizens of different states; disputes between citizens of one state claiming land under grants of different states; and cases between states or citizens and foreign countries.

James Madison, along with Alexander Hamilton and John Jay, authored The Federalist, *an important document in the development of the Supreme Court.* (Library of Congress)

"No man [should] be a judge in his own cause, or in any cause in respect to which he has the least interest or bias," Hamilton asserts in No. 80. He continues this argument in No. 81, when he disputes the argument advanced by certain opponents of establishing a supreme court that the British Parliament reviews its own laws; as Hamilton points out, the House of Lords must reconstitute itself as a special court, rather than acting as a legislative body. No. 81 also reiterates Hamilton's assertion that the need for one supreme court cannot be disputed, referring back to No. 22, in which it was argued that having one supreme court in each state would be unworkable for cases involving the whole country. He also argues that while the Supreme Court will have appellate jurisdiction in cases of both law and fact, it still will be subject to any exceptions and regulations prescribed by Congress, and that the Court will have only two areas of original jurisdiction.

No. 82 discusses the relationship between the state courts and the Supreme Court. Here Hamilton refers back to No. 32, in which the relationship between state and federal governments in matters of taxation is discussed. In No. 82, it is also noted that the legislature will decide if the authority of the lower federal courts will be original or appellate or both.

FURTHER READING

Bailyn, Bernard, ed. *The Debate on the Constitution: Federalist and Antifederalist Speeches, Articles, and Letters During the Struggle over Ratification.* New York: The Library of America, 1993.

Cox, Archibald. *The Court and the Constitution.* Boston: Houghton Mifflin, 1987.

Hamilton, Alexander, James Madison, and John Jay. *The Federalist Papers.* New York: Penguin Books, 1961.

Smith, Page. *The Constitution: A Documentary and Narrative History.* New York: William Morrow, 1978.

Wills, Garry. *Explaining America: The Federalist.* Garden City, N.Y.: Doubleday, 1981.

Irene Struthers Rush

SEE ALSO Constitution, U.S.; Constitutional Convention; Hamilton, Alexander; Jay, John; Judicial review; Madison, James; Reversals of Court decisions by amendment; Reversals of Court decisions by Congress.

Feiner v. New York

CITATION: 340 U.S. 315
DATE: January 15, 1951
ISSUE: Freedom of speech
SIGNIFICANCE: In this street oratory case, the Supreme Court tolerated a level of government control of speech that is no longer acceptable.

Chief Justice Fred M. Vinson wrote the opinion for the 6-3 majority over strong dissents from Justices Hugo L. Black, William O. Douglas, and Sherman Minton. Irving Feiner, a college student, stood on a box making a speech to a racially and politically mixed audience of more than seventy people who had a strongly mixed reaction to the speech and seemed to become unruly. Feiner refused to stop even after requested to do so by a police officer and was arrested for violating a New York law making it a "breach of the peace" to use intentionally "abusive language." Despite Feiner's assertion of First Amendment protection, the Supreme Court upheld his conviction as necessary to stop a "clear and

present danger to public safety." Black's strong dissent argued that Feiner was being punished for unpopular political views. Similar speech was judged to be under First Amendment protection in *Brandenburg v. Ohio* (1969).

Richard L. Wilson

SEE ALSO Bad tendency test; *Brandenburg v. Ohio*; Clear and present danger test; *Gitlow v. New York*; *Schenck v. United States*; Speech and press, freedom of; *Whitney v. California.*

Feist Publications v. Rural Telephone Service Co.

CITATION: 499 U.S. 340
DATE: March 27, 1991
ISSUE: Copyright
SIGNIFICANCE: The Supreme Court rejected the notion that copyrights should be granted to those whose only claim to copyright is that they gathered information.

Rural Telephone Service Company published a directory containing information that Feist Publications used in preparing its own somewhat different but overlapping directory. Rural sued, alleging copyright infringement and arguing that the effort they made to collect even public domain data was entitled to copyright protection. The Supreme Court did not accept Rural's view, asserting the more traditional view that quality or creativity was entitled to copyright protection but not the simple compilation of material. Justice Sandra Day O'Connor wrote the unanimous opinion of the Supreme Court; Justice Harry A. Blackmun concurred. This case amplified the Court's position set forth in *Harper and Row Publishers v. Nation Enterprises* (1985).

Richard L. Wilson

SEE ALSO Copyright; O'Connor, Sandra Day; Property rights.

Ferguson v. Skrupa

CITATION: 372 U.S. 726
DATE: April 22, 1963
ISSUE: Regulation of business
SIGNIFICANCE: In upholding a state regulation, the Supreme Court declared that the concept of substantive due process had been repudiated.

This case involved a Kansas statute that prohibited anyone except lawyers from engaging in the business of debt adjustment. By a 9-0 vote, the Supreme Court upheld the constitutionality of the Kansas law. Writing the majority opinion, Justice Hugo L. Black took the opportunity to express his strong animosity to the earlier practice of overturning such regulations with the doctrine of substantive due process. Without inquiring whether there was any rational justification for the law, Black declared that it was entirely up to the state legislature to decide on the "wisdom and utility" of economic regulations. Justice John M. Harlan II, concurring in the result, wrote that the law had a rational relation to a constitutionally permissible objective. It was clear that Black and Harlan disagreed about substantive due process, but their differences would become much more pronounced in the landmark case of *Griswold v. Connecticut* (1965).

Thomas T. Lewis

SEE ALSO Contract, freedom of; Due process, substantive; *Griswold v. Connecticut*; *West Coast Hotel Co. v. Parrish*.

Fetal rights

DESCRIPTION: Constitutional rights accorded to a fetus, or a developing human being within a womb.

SIGNIFICANCE: The Supreme Court ruled in *Roe v. Wade* (1973) that a fetus is a "potential life" and is not recognized as a person in the legal sense with Fourteenth Amendment rights. The Court has, however, granted a number of protections to fetuses.

The legal notion that fetuses have rights results in part from the 1973 Supreme Court decision on abortion in *Roe v. Wade*. The majority in *Roe* held that "the unborn have never been recognized in the law as persons in the whole sense," and that "the word 'person,' as used in the Fourteenth Amendment, does not include the unborn."

The Texas statute at issue in *Roe* was typical of U.S. state laws at the time. It prohibited abortion except when necessary to save the life of the pregnant woman. A pregnant woman seeking an abortion brought suit against the statute under the pseudonym Jane Roe (she was later identified as Norma McCorvey). The Court declared the statute unconstitutional and legalized abortion nationwide for approximately the first six months of pregnancy—technically the point of fetal viability. The Court reasoned that women's freedom in the decision to terminate their own pregnancies was part of constitutionally protected privacy.

The Rationale. Justice Harry A. Blackmun specifically considered the state's interest or duty in preserving fetal life (the basic justification put forth by Texas for its law) and the question of protecting the pregnant woman's health. Blackmun first examined Texas's claim that the fetus was a person "from the moment of conception" and therefore protected by the mandate of the Fourteenth Amendment. Blackmun rejected this argument, ruling instead that the fetus is not a person for purposes of the Fourteenth Amendment. He noted that all three branches of government have consistently treated personhood for legal purposes as beginning at birth. Blackmun stated that the Court did not need to resolve the question of when life begins.

Regarding the state's interest in protecting maternal health, Blackmun wrote that after the point of fetal viability, the state could proscribe abortion except when it was necessary to preserve "the life or health of the mother." The Court created the trimester approach, dividing pregnancy into three periods of approximately three months each. In the first trimester, the state cannot regulate abortion. In the second, it can regulate only to protect the mother's health. In the third trimester, however, after the fetus becomes "viable," the state may proscribe abortions unless necessary to save the woman's life or health.

Later Opinions. The Court affirmed *Roe* in *Planned Parenthood of Central Missouri v. Danforth* (1976), *Akron v. Akron Center for Reproductive Health* (1983), *Thornburgh v. American College of Obstetricians and Gynecologists* (1986), *Webster v. Reproductive Health Services* (1989), and *Planned Parenthood of Southeastern Pennsylvania v. Casey* (1992). Each of these cases involved, at least in part, some sort of parental or spousal notification prior to the performance of an abortion. The plurality decision in *Casey* struck down as unconstitutional a state law providing that no abortion could be performed on a married woman without a signed statement that she had notified her husband of her plan to undergo the abortion. The Court gave the following explanation of why this notice requirement constituted an undue burden on the right to an abortion.

> If a husband's interest in the potential life of the child outweighs a wife's liberty . . . perhaps next in line would be a statute requiring pregnant married women to notify their husbands before engaging in conduct causing risks to the fetus. After all, if the husband's interest in the fetus' safety is a sufficient predicate for state regulation, the state could reasonably conclude that pregnant wives should notify their husbands before drinking alcohol or smoking.

The Court set aside the *Roe* trimester framework for legal abortions in *Webster* in 1989, although it retained the viability standard. After viability, when the fetus was judged to be capable of "meaningful life outside the mother's womb," state interference was judged to have both "logical and biological justifications." In *Webster,* the Court upheld a Missouri statute that contained numerous restrictions on abortion. In its preamble, the statute stated that life began at conception and that "unborn children have protectable rights in life, health and well-being." Another provision of the statute required physicians to ascertain the viability of a fetus in excess of twenty weeks of gestational age before performing an abortion. *Webster* did not overturn *Roe.* A majority of the Court held that the preamble had no operative legal effect and therefore did not conflict with *Roe.* Justice Sandra Day O'Connor argued that because of a four-week margin of error in determining gestational age, the fetus's age might actually be twenty-four weeks, which falls in the third trimester. Regulation of third-trimester abortions was allowable under *Roe;* therefore, the viability test was not inconsistent with the 1973 ruling.

Nevertheless, both sides of the abortion controversy saw *Webster* as a ruling that might be used politically. Abortion foes saw the ruling as a sign that the Court would allow state legislatures to pass more restrictive abortion statutes, and those favoring a woman's right to choose abortion saw the ruling as a possible threat to this right.

FURTHER READING

Mathieu, Deborah. *Preventing Prenatal Harm: Should the State Intervene?* 2d ed. Washington, D.C.: Georgetown University Press, 1996.

Morgan, Lynn, ed. *Fetal Subjects, Feminist Positions.* Philadelphia: University of Pennsylvania Press, 1999.

Samuels, Suzanne. *Fetal Rights, Women's Rights.* Madison: University of Wisconsin Press, 1995.

Susan L. Thomas

SEE ALSO Abortion; Family and children; Gender issues; *Planned Parenthood of Southeastern Pennsylvania v. Casey; Roe v. Wade; Webster v. Reproductive Health Services.*

The establishment of fetal rights led to the passage of fetal protection laws, such as the 1999 Arkansas law that led to the arrest on murder charges of this Little Rock man. Prosecutors allege that Erik Bullock hired three young men to kick his pregnant girlfriend in the stomach, an attack that resulted in the death of the fetus. (AP/Wide World Photos)

Field, Stephen J.

IDENTIFICATION: Associate justice (May 20, 1863-December 1, 1897)

NOMINATED BY: Abraham Lincoln

BORN: November 4, 1816, Haddam, Connecticut

DIED: April 9, 1899, Washington, D.C.

SIGNIFICANCE: For thirty-four years, Field used his position as a Supreme Court justice to effect a broad interpretation of the Constitution in restricting government regulation of property rights.

Born in Connecticut, Field was the son of a clergy-man. His brother, David Dudley Field, was a prominent Democratic politician and lawyer in New York. Stephen followed a less conventional path. After earning his law license, he moved to California in 1849 at the height of the gold rush. There he established his reputation as a judge on the state supreme court, creating legal order out of the chaos of the booming state.

His prominent position earned him the attention of President Abraham Lincoln when the U.S. Congress created a tenth seat on the Supreme Court. Lincoln recognized the political rewards of appointing a prowar Democrat from one of the fastest expanding states in the union. The president also knew he would receive the gratitude of the powerful David Dudley Field if his brother Stephen were appointed.

Upon his confirmation to the Court in 1863, Field performed as Lincoln had hoped, supporting the Civil War effort and the expansion of presidential power during the era. He was less friendly to executive prerogatives in the postwar period; in *Ex parte Garland* (1867) and *Cummings v. Missouri* (1867), he voted to strike down loyalty oaths for former confederates seeking political office.

Economic Rights. Field was also protective of individual economic rights. He broadly interpreted the newly ratified Fourteenth Amendment, arguing that the equal protection, due process, and privileges and immunities clauses protected property owners from state economic regulation. His support for property rights was seen in the first of the *Legal Tender Cases* (1870) as he voted to strike down the federal government's issuing of paper money to finance the Civil War. Field agreed that the inflation created by the printing of money represented the government taking property without compensation. In the second of the *Legal Tender Cases* (1871), Field dissented as the Court reversed course and upheld the Legal Tender Act.

Field's support of economic rights continued. In the *Slaughterhouse Cases* (1873), a narrow 5-4 majority ruled that the Fourteenth Amendment did not prevent the government from granting monopolies. Field dissented on the basis that the amendment's privileges and immunities clause protected the right of an individual to work at a trade without government interference.

Stephen J. Field. (Library of Congress)

The philosophy was reiterated by Field over the next quarter century. Dissenting from such cases as *Munn v. Illinois* (1877), which upheld the regulation of grain elevators, Field maintained the broad view that the Fourteenth Amendment could be used to protect the property rights of individuals and corporations.

Field continued to air his views before the Court, vigorously dissenting whenever the Court upheld state regulation of business. Eventually his dogged determination and changes in the Court's personnel produced a shift in doctrine. In *Santa Clara County v. Southern Pacific Railroad Co.* (1886), the Court ruled that corporations were recognized as persons under the Fourteenth Amendment. This advanced Field's argument that the amendment should protect corporate property rights. It also opened the door for the Court to use the due process clause of the Fourteenth Amendment to protect those rights.

The Terry Affair. Before Field could witness his final victory, he was embroiled in a personal controversy that made him the only justice to ever experience an assassination attempt. The Terry affair, as it became known, centered on a former California judge, David S. Terry. When Field made a ruling detrimental to Terry's wife, the California judge threatened the justice's life. In response, the federal government provided a marshal as Field's personal bodyguard when he traveled to California. That marshal, David Neagle, and Field were confronted by Terry. A struggle followed and Neagle shot Terry dead. Neagle was arrested, producing a legal case that made its way to the Supreme Court. With Field not participating, the justices ruled in *In re Neagle* (1890) that the marshal could not be prosecuted under state law because he was acting under the direction of federal law in protecting Field.

The Terry affair did not dampen Field's determination to use the Constitution to protect property rights. It was during the 1890's that Field's views took center stage, dominating the Court's decisions. Between 1895 and 1897 Field's colleagues followed his lead in striking down laws that restricted economic liberty.

Field's Success. In *United States v. E. C. Knight Co.* (1895), the Court narrowed the scope of antitrust laws, preventing the government from breaking up monopolies that involved the manufacturing of goods. This prevented antitrust prosecutions of corporate monopolies, a result favored by Field. In *Pollock v. Farmers' Loan and Trust Co.* (1895), the Court struck down the federal income tax as unconstitutional. Field wrote a separate opinion in the case, denouncing the income tax as a move toward communism and warning against legislation that might cause class warfare. Finally in one of the last decisions in which Field participated, *Allgeyer v. Louisiana* (1897), the Court recognized a freedom to contract. In *Allgeyer*, a unanimous Court agreed that the Fourteenth Amendment protected an individual's right to make contracts without government interference.

Field's victory in *Allgeyer* marked the end of his judicial career. Throughout the 1890's his mental abilities had declined, and he was unable to fully function on the Court. He retired on December 1, 1897, having served longer than any other justice up to that time. During his thirty-four years, he was able to move the Court toward a dynamic reading of the Fourteenth Amendment that protected economic rights. His career marked the success of a man whose strength of character and determination allowed him to reshape American law.

FURTHER READING
Ely, James. *The Chief Justiceship of Melville Fuller.* Columbia: University of South Carolina Press, 1995.
Friedman, Leon, and Fred L. Israel, eds. *The Justices of the United States Supreme Court: Their Lives and Major Opinions.* 5 vols. New York: Chelsea House, 1997.
Gillman, Howard. *The Constitution Besieged.* Durham, N.C.: Duke University Press, 1993.
Kens, Paul. *Justice Stephen Field.* Lawrence: University of Kansas Press, 1997.
Swisher, Carl Brent. *Stephen J. Field: Craftsman of the Law.* Hamden, Conn.: Archon Books, 1963.
Douglas Clouatre

SEE ALSO *Allgeyer v. Louisiana*; *E. C. Knight Co., United States v.*; Fourteenth Amendment; Lincoln, Abraham; *Neagle, In re*; *Pollock v. Farmers' Loan and Trust Co.*; Presidential powers; Property rights.

Fifteenth Amendment

DATE: 1870
DESCRIPTION: Amendment to the U.S. Constitution forbidding discrimination in voting rights on the basis of race, color, or previous condition of servitude. Section 2 gives enforcement power to Congress.
SIGNIFICANCE: The Supreme Court decided many cases involving discrimination in access to voting, especially after the passage of the Voting Rights Act of 1965. The law and the Court's interpretive decisions ended racially discriminatory voting restrictions in the United States.

The original U.S. Constitution tied the right of individuals to vote in federal elections to state election laws. A person who was eligible to vote in elections for the lower house of the state legislature was entitled to vote in federal elections. The result was that eligibility to vote was determined by state, not federal, law. If a national decision on voting rights was to be made, a constitutional amendment such as the Twenty-fourth, which ended poll taxes, was required.

In 1868, after the Northern victory in the Civil War, the Fourteenth Amendment established citizenship and civil rights for the newly freed slaves. On February 3, 1870, the Fifteenth Amendment was adopted to prevent state governments from denying freed slaves the right to vote. Its language however, is much broader, because it prohibits denial of the right to vote "on account of race, color, or previous condition of servitude." Section 2 of the amendment gives Congress the power to enforce its terms by remedial legislation.

Discriminatory Laws. Immediately after the ratification of the amendment, Congress passed the Enforcement Act of 1870, which made it a crime for public officers and private persons to obstruct the right to vote. Enforcement of this law was spotty and ineffective, and most of its provisions were repealed in 1894. Meanwhile, beginning in 1890, most of the states of the former Confederacy passed laws that were specifically designed to keep African Americans from voting. Literacy tests were a major disqualifier because at that time more than two-thirds of adult African Americans were illiterate. At the same time, white illiterates were allowed to vote under grandfather clauses, property qualifications, and "good character" exceptions, from which African Americans were excluded. Racially discriminatory enforcement of voting qualifications became the principal means by which African Americans were barred from the polls.

In the absence of a statute, the only remedy for these discriminatory practices was case-by-case litigation. The Supreme Court, in case after case, struck down the discriminatory state practices. Grandfather clauses were invalidated in *Guinn v. United States* (1915). The state-mandated all-white primary was outlawed in *Nixon v. Herndon* (1927); party-operated all-white primaries were forbidden by *Smith v. Allwright* (1944) and *Terry v. Adams* (1953). The Court held in *United States v. Thomas* (1959) that phony polling place challenges to African Americans seeking to vote—by the time the challenges had been resolved, the polls had closed—were improper under the Fifteenth Amendment. Racial gerrymandering was forbidden by *Gomillion v. Lightfoot* (1960). In that case, Alabama had redefined the shape of the city of Tuskegee so as to exclude all but four or five of its four hundred African American voters, thus denying this group the opportunity to influence city government. The Court also dealt with discriminatory administration of literacy tests in several cases, most important, *Schnell v. Davis* (1949), in which Justice William O. Douglas, writing for the Court, remarked that "the legislative setting and the great discretion it vested in the registrar made it clear that . . . the literacy requirement was merely a device to make racial discrimination easy."

TEXT OF THE FIFTEENTH AMENDMENT

Section 1. The right of citizens of the United States to vote shall not be denied or abridged by the United States or by any State on account of race, color, or previous condition of servitude.

Section 2. The Congress shall have power to enforce this article by appropriate legislation.

Voting Rights Act of 1965. The mass disenfranchisement of African Americans could not be reached efficiently or fully by means of individually brought cases. Although some of the discriminatory state practices were halted, every voting registration decision could be made on the basis of race if voting registrars wished to do so. Against this background, Congress passed the Voting Rights Act of 1965. Section 2 of the Fifteenth Amendment provided constitutional authority for this law, which was aimed at "ridding the country of racial discrimination in voting," according to the statute's preamble. The law forbade a number of discriminatory practices. Literacy tests were "suspended" for five years in areas where voting discrimination had been most flagrant. To deal with voting discrimination through outright intimidation and violence, the law provided for federal voting registrars and protection by federal marshals.

The first important cases arising under this law came to the Court in 1966. In *South Carolina v. Katzenbach* (1966), the Court held unanimously that the most important provisions of the Voting Rights Act were constitutional. Chief Justice Earl Warren wrote that "the record here showed that in most of the States covered, various tests and devices have been instituted with the purpose of disenfranchising Negroes, have been framed in such a way as to facilitate this aim, and have been administered in a discriminatory fashion for many years. Under these circumstances, the 15th Amendment has clearly been violated." Because Congress's power under the amendment is remedial, this finding of fact was necessary to invoke federal power. The broad construction of Congress's power to deal with discrimination in voting in *South Carolina v. Katzenbach* established an important precedent to which the Court consistently adhered.

Congress renewed the Voting Rights Act in 1970 and extended the literacy test ban to the entire country. The extension reached New York State's English-language literacy test, which had the practical effect of disenfranchising many Puerto Rican voters. The English-language literacy test had been in place long before any substantial Puerto Rican migration to New York City had taken place. The extension was upheld by the Court in *Oregon v. Mitchell* (1970). Although the justices disagreed on some aspects of the new law, they were unanimous in upholding the constitutionality of the literacy test ban, even though there was no showing that New York had attempted to discriminate against Puerto Ricans. However, in *Rome v. United States* (1980), the Court became enmeshed in the question of the extent to which Congress may control state and local government under the Fifteenth Amendment. The question arose as to whether the remedial power reached only deliberate attempts by states and municipalities to deny Fifteenth Amendment voting rights or whether it was the effect of state practices on African American—and by extension, other minority group—voting that authorized federal action. The Court has not fully settled this extraordinarily complex constitutional question. Congress renewed and further extended the requirements of the Voting Rights Act again in 1982, this time for a period of twenty-five years.

The effect of the Court's Fifteenth Amendment decisions coupled with the broader provisions of the Voting Rights Act has been immense. In 1961 only 1.2 million African Americans were registered to vote in the South—one-quarter of voting-age blacks. By 1964 nearly 2 million were registered. In 1975 between 3.5 and 4 million blacks were registered to vote in the South. By the end of the century, although electoral turnout among African Americans and other persons of color in the United States is still lower than that of whites, the gap has nearly been closed. Formal legal discriminatory barriers to voting no longer exist.

FURTHER READING

Jack Greenberg's *Race Relations and American Law* (New York: Columbia University Press, 1959) offers a good place to start for a comprehensive view of the constitutional rules before the passage of the Civil Rights Act of 1964 and the Voting Rights Act of 1965. John Braeman's *Before the Civil Rights Revolution: The Old Court and Individual Rights* (New York: Greenwood Press, 1988) discusses the developing jurisprudence of the Court in the area of civil rights. For insight into the inner workings of the Warren Court, Bernard Schwartz's *Inside the Warren Court* (Garden City, N.Y.: Doubleday, 1983), with Stephen Lesher, is based not only on the documentation but also on personal acquaintance. *Compromised Compliance: Implementation of the 1965 Voting Rights Act* (Westport, Conn.: Greenwood Press, 1982) by Howard Ball, Dale Krane, and Thomas P. Lauth contains one of the first important discussions of the remedial versus effects morass in which the Court finds itself.

Using cases, Daniel Hays Lowenstein's *Election Law* (Durham, N.C.: Carolina Academic Press, 1995) analyzes how the Supreme Court has treated questions regarding electoral structures and processes. J. Morgan Kousser's *The Shaping of Southern Politics: Suffrage Restriction and the Establishment of the One-Party South, 1880-1910* (New Haven, Conn.: Yale University Press, 1974) and *Colorblind Injustice: Minority Voting Rights and the Undoing of the Second Reconstruction* (Chapel Hill: University of North Carolina Press, 1998) analyze the right to vote in the South, covering the Reconstruction era in the first volume and the post-World War II years in the second. Michael Dawson's *Behind the Mule: Race and Class in American Politics* (Princeton, N.J.: Princeton University Press, 1994) examines voting rights in connection with race as does Abigail M. Thernstrom's *Whose Votes Count? Affirmative Action and Minority Voting Rights* (Cambridge, Mass.: Harvard University Press, 1987).

Robert Jacobs

SEE ALSO Fourteenth Amendment; *Gomillion v. Lightfoot*; Grandfather clause; *Oregon v. Mitchell*; Poll taxes; Smith v. Allwright; *South Carolina v. Katzenbach*; Thirteenth Amendment; Twenty-fourth Amendment; Vote, right to; Voting Rights Act of 1965; White primaries.

Fifth Amendment

DATE: 1791

DESCRIPTION: Amendment to the U.S. Constitution and part of the Bill of Rights that provides a right to avoid self-incrimination, a right to a grand jury indictment in capital or infamous crime cases, a right to be free from double jeopardy, and a right to just compensation for property taken by the government.

SIGNIFICANCE: The Supreme Court has used the Fifth Amendment to protect citizens against government coercion.

The Fifth Amendment includes more than just a right against self-incrimination, yet it is virtually synonymous with the right against self-incrimination. This right reflected the framers' judgment that in a society based on respect for the individual, the government shouldered the entire burden of proving guilt and the accused need make no unwilling contribution to his or her conviction.

The Fifth Amendment is restricted on its face to "criminal cases." However, the Supreme Court ruled that the Fifth Amendment applies to criminal and civil cases and extends to nonjudicial proceedings, such as legislative investigations and administrative hearings. The protection of the clause extends only to people, not organizations such as corporations or unions, and is applicable to witnesses as well as to the accused.

The self-incrimination clause is violated if evidence compelled by the government incriminates the person who provides it. Given these standards, self-incrimination violations occur most commonly during police interrogations and government hearings. Although the purpose of the clause is to eliminate the inherently coercive and inquisitional atmosphere of the interrogation room, a person may voluntarily answer any incriminating question or confess to any crime, subject to the requirements for waiver of constitutional rights, even if his or her statements are intended as exculpatory but lend themselves to prosecutorial use as incriminatory.

A Definition. The Court first addressed the meaning of the self-incrimination clause in *Twining v. New Jersey* (1908). The question was whether the right against self-incrimination was "a fundamental principle of liberty and justice which inheres in the very idea of free government" and therefore should be included within the concept of due process of law safeguarded from state abridgment. The Court decided against the right. It reaffirmed this position in *Palko v. Connecticut* (1937),

---

TEXT OF THE FIFTH AMENDMENT

No person shall be held to answer for a capital, or otherwise infamous crime, unless on a presentment or indictment of a Grand Jury, except in cases arising in the land or naval forces, or in the Militia, when in actual service in time of War or public danger; nor shall any person be subject for the same offence to be twice put in jeopardy of life or limb, nor shall be compelled in any criminal case to be a witness against himself, nor be deprived of life, liberty, or property, without due process of law; nor shall private property be taken for public use without just compensation.

---

in which the Court held that the right against compulsory self-incrimination was not a fundamental right; it might be lost, and justice might still be done if the accused "were subject to a duty to respond to orderly inquiry."

The Court abandoned this position in its 1966 decision in *Miranda v. Arizona*, a tour de force on self-incrimination. The opinion announced a cluster of constitutional rights for defendants held in police custody and cut off from the outside world. The atmosphere and environment of incommunicado interrogation was held to be inherently intimidating and hostile to the privilege against self-incrimination. To prevent compulsion by law enforcement officials, before interrogation, people in custody must be clearly informed that they have the right to remain silent and anything they say may be used in court against them and that they have the rights to consult an attorney, to have a lawyer present during interrogation, and to have a lawyer appointed if they are indigent.

When Chief Justice Warren E. Burger replaced Chief Justice Earl Warren in 1964 and Justice Harry A. Blackmun replaced Justice Abe Fortas in 1970, they joined Justices Byron R. White, John M. Harlan II, and Potter Stewart in support of a narrow application of *Miranda*. These five justices constituted the majority in *Harris v. New York* (1971), indicating the beginning of a contracting trend for *Miranda*. Chief Justice Burger held that the prosecution is not precluded from the use of statements that admittedly do not meet the *Miranda* test as an impeachment tool in attacking the credibility of an accused's trial testimony.

The erosion of *Miranda* continued in several rulings in the 1970's. In *Michigan v. Tucker* (1974), the Court held that failure to inform a suspect of his or her right to appointed counsel before interrogation was only a harmless error in the total circumstances of the case. Then one year later in *Oregon v. Haas* (1975), the Court reaffirmed *Harris* and allowed the use of a suspect's statements for impeachment purposes though they had been made before arrival of counsel that he had requested before making any statements. And the next year in *Michigan v. Mosley* (1976), the Court did not construe *Miranda* as invoking a "proscription of indefinite duration on any further questionings . . . on any subject." This ruling approved an interrogation process in which a suspect had initially used the shield of Miranda rights to remain silent but several hours later in a different room was administered the Miranda rights again and proceeded to respond to questions about a different crime.

By the mid-1980's it was clear that the Court under Chief Justice William H. Rehnquist would continue to construe *Miranda* very narrowly. In *New York v. Quarles* (1984), for example, the Court held that when a danger to public safety exists, police may ask questions to remove that danger before reading Miranda warnings. Answers given to the police may be used as evidence. In *Illinois v. Perkins* (1990), the Court ruled that Miranda warnings are not required when a suspect is unaware he or she is speaking to the police and gives a voluntary statement. The case concerned a jailed defendant who implicated himself in a murder when talking to an undercover agent placed in his cell. Justice Anthony M. Kennedy wrote in the opinion, "*Miranda* forbids coercion, not mere strategic deception." Finally, in *Arizona v. Fulminante* (1991), the Court admitted that the defendant's confession was coerced by the threat of physical attack. However, the Court held that if such testimony is erroneously admitted as evidence, a conviction need not be overturned if sufficient independent evidence supporting a guilty verdict is also introduced.

At the turn of the century, the Court's decision to maintain the precedent with continued narrow application of *Miranda* appeared well entrenched. The majority of the justices appeared to be comfortable with that approach, and changes appeared unlikely.

Double Jeopardy Clause. Also under the Fifth Amendment, a person shall not be subject "for the same offense to be twice put in jeopardy of life or limb." The underlying premise of the double jeopardy clause is to prohibit the government from making repeated attempts to convict an individual. Acquittal acts as an absolute bar on a second trial. The meaning of acquittal, however, often divides the Court.

The Court ruled that there is no double jeopardy in trying someone twice for the same offense if the jury is unable to reach a verdict—in *United States v. Ball* (1896), the jury is discharged—in *Logan v. United States* (1892), or an appeals court returns the case to the trial court because of defects in the original indictment—in *Thompson v. United States* (1894). The Court also unanimously ruled in three cases—*Jerome v. United States* (1943), *Herbert v. Louisiana* (1926), and *United States v. Lanza* (1922)—that a person may be prosecuted for the same act under federal law and state law. The theory is that the person is being prosecuted for two distinct offenses rather than the same offense.

The double jeopardy clause also prohibits prosecutors from trying defendants a second time for the express purpose of obtaining a more severe sentence. However, in 1969 the Court decided that there is no constitutional bar to imposing a more severe sentence on reconviction (after the first conviction is thrown out), provided the sentencing judge is not motivated by vindictiveness. In *North Carolina v. Pearce, Chaffin v. Stynchcombe* (1973), it ruled that the guarantee against double jeopardy requires that punishment already exacted must be fully credited to the new sentence.

The double jeopardy clause also bars multiple punishments for the same offense. In *United States v. Ursery* (1996) and *Kansas v. Hendricks* (1997), the Court narrowly construed this right. The latter case involved a challenge to a statute that permitted the state to keep certain sexual offenders in custody in a mental institution after they had served their full sentence. The Court ruled that the civil confinement was not a second criminal punishment but a separate civil procedure, thus not a violation of the double jeopardy clause.

Right to a Grand Jury. The Fifth Amendment also provides that "no person shall be held for a capital, or otherwise infamous crime, unless on a presentment or indictment of a grand jury, except in cases arising in the land or naval forces, or in the militia, when in actual service in time of war or public danger." The grand jury procedure is one of the few provision in the Bill of Rights that has not been incorporated into the due process clause of the Fourteenth Amendment and applied to the states. Instead the Court ruled that states may prosecute on a district attorney's "information," which consists of a prosecutor's accusation under oath in *Hurtado v. California* (1884) and *Lem Wood v. Oregon* (1913). The Court held in *Costello v. United States* (1956) that, unlike in a regular trial, grand juries may decide that "hearsay" evidence is sufficient grounds to indict. In 1992 the Court issued an opinion in *United States v. Williams* (1992) indicating that an otherwise valid indictment may not be dismissed on the ground that the government failed to disclose to the grand jury "substantial exculpatory evidence" in its possession. In 1974 the Court decided in *United States v. Calandra* that witnesses before a grand jury may invoke the Fifth Amendment privilege against self-incrimination. This privilege is overridden if the government grants immunity to the witness. Witnesses who then refuse to answer questions may be jailed for contempt of court. Witnesses may not refuse to answer because questions are based on illegally obtained evidence.

The Takings Clause. Finally, the Fifth Amendment provides that private property shall not "be taken for public use, without just compensation." This is referred to as the takings clause, or the just compensation clause. The Court incorporated the takings clause under the due process clause of the Fourteenth Amendment in *Chicago, Burlington, and Quincy Railroad Co. v. Chicago* (1897); therefore, states are also forbidden from taking private property for public use without just compensation. Not every deprivation of property requires compensation, however. For example, the Court held in *United States v. Caltex* (1952) that under conditions of war, private property may be demolished to prevent use by the enemy without compensation to the owner. When compensation is to be paid, a plethora of 5-4 decisions by the Court—including *United States v. Fuller* (1973) and *Almota Farmers Elevator and Wholesale Co. v. United States* (1973)—demonstrate fundamental disagreements among the

justices about the proper method of calculating what is "just."

Court decisions in the early and mid-1990's underscore the complexity and reach of the takings clause. Several cases broadened the powers of the states, and others expanded property rights. In *Yee v. Escondido* (1992), a unanimous Court held that a rent-control ordinance did not amount to a physical taking of the property of owners of a mobile home park. A more significant ruling, *Lucas v. South Carolina Coastal Council* (1992), narrowed the rights of states to rely on regulatory takings that completely deprive individuals of the economic use of their property. To be exempt from compensating a property owner, a state must claim more than a general public interest or an interest in preventing serious public harm.

The Court broadened property rights by holding that land use requirements may be "takings." The decision in *Dolan v. City of Tigard* (1994) dealt with the practice of local governments giving property owners a permit for building a development only on the condition that they donate parts of their land for parks, bike paths, and other public purposes. These conditions are valid only if the local government makes "some sort of individualized determination that the required dedication is related both in nature and extent to the impact of the proposed development." This 5-4 decision underscores the Court's inability to reach agreement on constitutional principles under the Fifth Amendment.

FURTHER READING

Two general works on the Fifth Amendment are Harvey Fireside's *The Fifth Amendment: The Right to Remain Silent* (Springfield, N.J.: Enslow, 1998) and Burnham Holmes's *The Fifth Amendment* (Englewood Cliffs, N.J.: Silver Burdett Press, 1991). David Bodenhamer's *Fair Trial: Rights of the Accused in American History* (New York: Oxford University Press, 1992) presents a useful account of double jeopardy and self-incrimination rights. Also recommended is Anthony Lewis's *Gideon's Trumpet* (New York: Vintage, 1964). A well-written and thorough account of the takings clause is found in Richard Epstein's *Takings: Private Property and the Power of Eminent Domain* (Cambridge, Mass.: Harvard University Press, 1985). A more scholarly account is James Ely's *The Guardian of Every Other Right: A Con-*

stitutional History of Property Rights (New York: Oxford University Press, 1992).

Susan L. Thomas

SEE ALSO Double jeopardy; Grand jury; *Miranda v. Arizona*; Self-incrimination, immunity against; Takings clause.

Finality of decision

DESCRIPTION: Under the law, the Supreme Court may review final decisions made by the highest court available to a petitioner in a state if a decision is sought in matters involving federal laws.

SIGNIFICANCE: When state remedies have been exhausted and a final decision rendered by the state's highest court, plaintiffs have the right to petition the Court to reach a judgment that will stand as the final decision in the case.

Title 28, section 1257, of the U.S. Code gives the Supreme Court jurisdiction to review final decisions or judgments made by the highest court of a state. Such reviews are permitted when the legitimacy of a federal law is questioned, when a state law is questioned as being inimical to a federal statute, or when a claim is filed under a federal law.

The Constitution does not specifically grant the Court authority to review decisions of state courts. This authority is generally assumed although it has never been precisely spelled out. It certainly is not usual, as Charles Alan Wright has written, "for the court of one sovereign to have appellate jurisdiction over the courts of other sovereigns, but federalism is—or was when the Constitution was adopted—an unusual system, and the supremacy clause is a sufficient basis on which to rest the appellate jurisdiction over state court decisions." It must be remembered that when the Constitution was being drafted, the form of government for which it was designed was experimental.

The Code's Mandates. In order to conform to the mandates of section 1257 of the U.S. Code, the decision of a state court must be final in two specific ways. First, such a decision must not be subject to review by any other state court; the court rendering the final verdict must be as far as the case can be appealed within that state's jurisdiction. Second, the Court, in *Catlin v. United States* (1945), declared a judgment or decree to be functionally final if it "ends the litigation on the merits and leaves noth-

ing for the court to do but execute the judgment."

An example of the first instance occurs in *Thompson v. City of Louisville* (1960). In this case, the Court considered a decision made by the police court of Louisville, Kentucky, under whose rules that case could be reviewed no further within the state. The only additional remedy available to the defendant was through the Supreme Court.

The question of finality is determined by how section 1257 is interpreted. The Court has permitted some latitude in this matter, sometimes deciding on practical grounds to consider some types of judgments sufficiently final to warrant further review by the Court.

Section 25 of the Judiciary Act. In the quarter century between 1790 and 1815, the Court reviewed and rendered decisions in seventeen cases that had been adjudicated by state courts. Section 25 of the Judiciary Act of 1789 authorized such reviews if a state court decision contradicted and nullified a federal statute or treaty or ruled against a claim that had been based on federal law. In other words, federal law was considered superior to all other laws in cases involving it.

It was not until 1816 that this concept was challenged. In that year, the court of appeals of Virginia refused to accept an opinion of the Supreme Court, declaring section 25 unconstitutional. In the Court hearing that followed, *Martin v. Hunter's Lessee* (1816), the Court denied Virginia's accusations in an opinion written by Joseph Story, who categorically declared section 25 to be within the bounds of the Constitution. A further challenge to the constitutionality of section 25 occurred in the case of *Cohens v. Virginia* (1821). John Marshall wrote the opinion in this case, upholding the constitutionality of section 25 and the authority of the Court to review and, if appropriate based on the evidence, to reverse the final decisions of a state's highest court in matters involving federal law.

A much later challenge to section 25 came in *Ableman v. Booth* (1859), a decision that sustained the highly controversial Fugitive Slave Act of 1850 shortly before the beginning of the Civil War. In this instance, Roger Brooke Taney reaffirmed the earlier opinions of justices Story and Marshall, holding that section 25 was, indeed, constitutional.

State Versus Federal Supremacy. The question of finality is fundamentally intertwined with the matter of judicial efficiency and of the federalist philosophy that undergirds the U.S. system of justice. The Court is placed in the position of having to balance two opposing forces. On one hand, it must demonstrate that it respects the sovereignty of state courts. On the other, it often is called on to reconsider the boundaries between the judicial sovereignty of the states and federal supremacy in the matters that come before it.

Perhaps the best succinct overview of the question of finality is that of William O. Douglas in the case of *North Dakota State Board of Pharmacy v. Snyder's Drug Stores* (1973). Douglas pointed out that the requirement of finality prevents the piecemeal review of decisions made by state courts. Further, it protects the Court from offering advisory opinions in cases that are not legitimate in terms of Article III of the Constitution. Finally, it limits intrusion of the federal government in the affairs of the individual states.

FURTHER READING

Spaeth, Harold J. *Studies in U.S. Supreme Court Behavior.* New York: Garland, 1990.

Stern, Robert L., Eugene Gressman, and Stephen M. Shapiro. *Supreme Court Practice: Jurisdiction, Procedures, Arguing and Briefing Techniques, Terms, Statutes.* 6th ed. Washington, D.C.: Bureau of National Affairs, 1986.

Wright, Charles Alan. *The Law of Federal Courts.* 5th ed. St. Paul, Minn.: West Publishing, 1994.

R. Baird Shuman

SEE ALSO *Cohens v. Virginia*; Douglas, William O.; Judiciary Act of 1789; Marshall, John; *Martin v. Hunter's Lessee*; States' rights; Story, Joseph.

Financing political speech

DESCRIPTION: Process by which money is raised and spent to promote candidates for public office and their platforms and to publicize views on public issues, legislation, ballot questions, and other political matters.

SIGNIFICANCE: Congress first passed regulations regarding campaign finance in 1867, and state legislatures also passed similar regulations. The Supreme Court has ruled on the constitutionality of many provisions of these regulations.

Beginning in 1867, Congress attempted to regulate various kinds of political finance. The earliest ef-forts limited solicitation of political funds from government employees or on government property. Later laws prohibited contributions from corporations or national banks to candidates for federal office. In 1911 Congress enacted spending limits and disclosure requirements for House and Senate campaigns. Many states passed similar laws during the late 1800's and early 1900's.

In 1925 Congress consolidated its regulations in the Corrupt Practices Act. One reason for the passage of this act was the 1921 Supreme Court decision in *Newberry v. United States*, which held that primary elections could not be regulated by Congress. The Court reversed that ruling in *Smith v. Allwright* (1944). In 1939 Congress passed the Hatch Act prohibiting participation in politics by employees of the U.S. government. The Court upheld this restriction in *United Public Workers v. Mitchell* (1947) and reaffirmed that holding in *United States Civil Service Commission v. Letter Carriers* (1973).

A Campaign Act. The Corrupt Practices Act was replaced in 1971 with the Federal Election Campaign Act. Its primary objectives were strengthening reporting requirements and limiting spending for media advertising. Although the act did accomplish some of what it was intended to do in the 1972 presidential campaign, that campaign also experienced the Watergate scandal and numerous abuses of campaign finance laws, which led to the passage of amendments to the act in 1974. The new provisions included limits on campaign expenditures, limits on campaign contributions, creation of an enforcement agency (the Federal Election Commission), public funding of presidential campaigns, and strengthened disclosure requirements.

The Federal Election Campaign Act amendments were immediately challenged in the courts. In *Buckley v. Valeo* (1976), the government defended the law on the grounds that it regulated conduct (the giving and spending of money) and was a reasonable regulation of such conduct. The Court held, however, that even though there was a nonspeech element (monetary transactions) involved, the law was basically a regulation of political communication, and therefore, the government had to demonstrate that the law was designed to achieve a compelling interest and that it was narrowly tailored to achieve that objective. The Court found that the compelling interest involved was the avoidance of corruption or the appearance of corruption. This interest supported the disclosure requirements; the contribution limits to candidates for individuals, political action committees (PACs), and political parties; and the public funding of presidential campaigns. Unconstitutional were limits on expenditures by campaigns not publicly funded, by candidates in support of their own campaigns (if not publicly funded), and by groups and individuals spending in support of candidates but independently of their campaigns. In 1978, in the case of *First National Bank of Boston v. Bellotti*, the Court expanded the right to spend money to promote one's political views to corporations seeking to influence state referendum campaigns on public issues.

Independent Expenditures. *Buckley* remains the cornerstone of Court doctrine on the financing of political speech. The Court has expanded its ruling that independent expenditures in support of candidates may not be limited. That right was extended to political action committees in *Federal Election Commission v. National Conservative Political Action Committee* (1985) and to political parties in *Colorado Republican Campaign Committee v. Federal Election Commission* (1996). The 1985 case allowed a political action committee unlimited independent expenditures in support of a presidential candidate who had accepted public funding. In the *Colorado* case, the Court held that money spend by the Colorado Republicans for attack ads against the expected Democratic candidate before the GOP had chosen its own candidate was an independent expenditure that could not be limited under the Federal Election Campaign Act.

In the only exception to its *Buckley* ruling that disclosure requirements are constitutional, the Court held in *Brown v. Socialist Workers '74 Campaign Committee* (1982) that an Ohio statute requiring disclosure of the names and addresses of campaign contributors to every political party could not be enforced against the Socialist Workers Party because of the threat of harassment of its supporters, an excessive burden on their right to freedom of association.

The Court reaffirmed its *Buckley* ruling on contribution limitations in *California Medical Association v. Federal Election Commission* (1981). In that case the Court upheld Federal Election Campaign Act limitations on contributions by individuals and

unincorporated associations to multicandidate political committees. Later the same year, however, the Court held unconstitutional a local ordinance that placed a $250 limit on individual contributions to committees supporting or opposing ballot questions. The act limits individual contributions to $1000 per candidate in any election. The low local limit placed too much of a burden on freedom of association, the Court said in *Citizens Against Rent Control v. Berkeley* (1981).

Corporations and PACs. Several Court decision have dealt with the relationship between corporations and political action committees. In *Federal Election Commission v. National Right to Work Committee* (1982), the Court upheld the electoral campaign act's provisions making it unlawful for a corporate PAC to solicit money from outside the corporation for contribution to federal election campaigns. In a later decision, *Federal Election Commission v. Massachusetts Citizens for Life* (1986), the Court ruled that a nonprofit corporation could not be required to finance expenditures in connection with elections by creating a separate fund for collection of voluntary contributions (that is, a political action committee). With respect to small nonprofits, the burden on First Amendment rights was too great, the Court held.

The Court revisited this issue in *Austin v. Michigan State Chamber of Commerce* (1990), which involved a Michigan campaign finance law modeled after the Federal Election Campaign Act. The Michigan chamber of commerce, a nonprofit corporation with more than eight thousand members, of whom more than 75 percent were for-profit corporations, wanted to fund political expenditures from its general treasury, as the Massachusetts Citizens for Life had been allowed to do. The Court found that although the Massachusetts group had been formed almost exclusively to promote political viewpoints and was not funded by for-profit corporations, the chamber of commerce was a general-purpose organization and was funded by for-profit corporations. Therefore although the Massachusetts group had been exempt from the requirement that it form a PAC to promote its political views, the chamber of commerce was not.

FURTHER READING

Bibby, John F. *Politics, Parties, and Elections in America.* 4th ed. Chicago: Nelson-Hall, 1999.

Sorauf, Frank J. *Inside Campaign Finance: Myths and Realities.* New Haven, Conn.: Yale University Press, 1992.

_____. *Money in American Elections.* Glenview, Ill.: Scott, Foresman and Co., 1988.

Tribe, Laurence H. *American Constitutional Law.* 3d ed. Mineola, N.Y.: Foundation Press, 1999.

Daryl R. Fair

See also *Buckley v. Valeo;* Elections; *First National Bank of Boston v. Bellotti;* Political parties; Political party system; *Smith v. Allwright;* United Public Workers v. Mitchell.

First Amendment

Date: 1791

Description: Amendment to the U.S. Constitution and part of the Bill of Rights that guarantees freedom of speech, freedom of the press, religious liberty, separation of church and state, and the rights to peaceably assemble and to petition the government for redress of grievances.

Significance: The wellspring of individual rights protected by the U.S. Constitution, the First Amendment presented the Supreme Court with endless challenges to decide the limits of governmental power and the scope of personal liberties.

Although the First Amendment, together with the other nine amendments known as the Bill of Rights, became part of the U.S. Constitution on December 15, 1791, the Supreme Court took little note of it until the beginning of the twentieth century. This was not for lack of federal laws impinging on free speech, from the Sedition Act of 1798 and the Comstock Act of 1873 to the Alien Immigration Act of 1930 and a wide variety of postal regulations. However, the Court never found that any of these laws violated the First Amendment. Indeed, in 1907 the Court upheld the conviction of an editor for contempt, rejecting a defense based on the First Amendment on the grounds that it only prohibited prior restraint.

It was inevitable that the Court and the First Amendment would travel together through U.S. constitutional law, frequently crossing paths, sometimes diverging, often forced by circumstances to retrace the same ground. Each clause of the First Amendment invites, indeed demands, judicial interpretation.

Freedom of Speech. Beginning at the end of World War I, the Court tackled the task of devising a series of tests to determine whether particular speech was constitutionally protected. The Court could not merely cite the general language of the First Amendment; it had to apply those opaque terms to the real world of real cases.

The first test was articulated by Justice Oliver Wendell Holmes in 1919 in a series of cases challenging the convictions of antiwar activists under the Espionage Act of 1917. The clear and present danger test looked at whether the speech posed a real and immediate risk of a substantive evil that Congress had a right to prevent. Holmes captured the test in a powerful, albeit often misquoted, metaphor that persists to this day: "The most stringent protection of free speech would not protect a man in falsely shouting fire in a theatre and causing a panic."

Later in 1919, Holmes and his ally, Justice Louis D. Brandeis, dissented in *Abrams v. United States,* arguing for greater constitutional protection for controversial or even subversive speech. The majority of the Court continued to use the clear and present danger test to uphold the punishment of such speech.

Six years later, the majority of the Court tightened the noose on free speech by focusing on whether the expression had a bad tendency. Over bitter dissent from Holmes and Brandeis, the Court upheld a conviction under the New York State Criminal Anarchy Act, stating that a "single revolutionary spark may kindle a fire," and therefore the state may "suppress the threatened danger in its incipiency."

Text of the First Amendment

Congress shall make no law respecting an establishment of religion, or prohibiting the free exercise thereof; or abridging the freedom of speech, or of the press, or the right of the people peaceably to assemble, and to petition the Government for a redress of grievances.

In 1951 the Court used a slightly reformulated test to uphold the convictions of eleven members of the Communist Party under the Smith Act (1940). Chief Justice Fred M. Vinson, writing for the Court, asked "whether the gravity of the 'evil' discounted by its improbability" would justify government limits on speech.

In 1964 Justice William J. Brennan, Jr., introduced a test that was far more protective of free speech. In the landmark case of *New York Times Co. v. Sullivan*, the Court held that false criticism of public officials was constitutionally protected unless it was made with knowledge that it was false or in reckless disregard of the truth. Instead of tilting the constitutional balance in favor of the government, the *Sullivan* test gave the advantage to the speaker.

The Holmes-Brandeis view in favor of more robust protection for free speech was finally vindicated in 1967 in *Brandenburg v. Ohio*, in which the Court declared that mere advocacy of the use of force or violation of the law could no longer be punished unless "such advocacy is directed to inciting or producing imminent lawless action and is likely to produce such action."

The Religion Clauses. As in the field of free speech, the perplexing issues surrounding freedom of religion have required the Court to fashion several constitutional tests to ensure the free exercise of religion, without establishing a state-sponsored religion. As the twentieth century ushered in an era of secularization, the dominance of religion in public life began to be seen as inconsistent with the First Amendment's promise of neutrality when it came to religious faith. Religion was seen as a part of the private sphere of life, leaving the public sphere, including most visibly public schools, free of religious symbols, let alone indoctrination.

In several decisions spanning more than twenty years, from *Everson v. Board of Education of Ewing Township* in 1947 to *Lemon v. Kurtzman* in 1971, the Court developed the test that any governmental action touching on religion would survive invalidation under the establishment clause only if it had a secular purpose that neither endorsed nor disapproved of religion, had an effect that neither advanced nor inhibited religion, and avoided creating a relationship between religion and government that entangled either in the internal affairs of the other. The *Lemon* test has been criticized by all

ends of the political and constitutional spectrum, but it has provided lower courts and legislators with some level of guidance in dealing with such thorny issues as prayer in schools and financial aid to religious institutions.

Meanwhile, the Court had to interpret the free exercise clause of the First Amendment in numerous cases in which believers claimed a right to ignore laws that required them to perform an act that violated their religious beliefs or that prohibited them from performing an act that was required by their religious beliefs.

Beginning in 1879 in *Reynolds v. United States* and for almost a hundred years, the Court dealt with most free exercise cases by upholding laws that punished *actions* but struck down laws that punished *beliefs*. However, the easy dichotomy began to break down when, in *Sherbert v. Verner* (1963), the Court ordered a state to pay unemployment benefits to a Seventh-Day Adventist even though she would not make herself available for work on Saturday (her Sabbath). In 1972, in *Wisconsin v. Yoder*, the Court held that the Amish were not required to send their children to public school past the eighth grade in violation of their religious beliefs.

By the 1980's, the pendulum had begun to swing against religious liberty as the Court issued a succession of decisions ruling against a Native American who sought to prevent the government from assigning his daughter a social security number, an Orthodox Jew who sought to wear a yarmulke in violation of Air Force uniform regulations, a Native American tribe that sought to prevent construction of a federal highway that would interfere with their worshiping, and two Native Americans who sought unemployment compensation after they were fired from their jobs for smoking peyote as part of tribal religious rituals.

The Court has found the religion clauses of the First Amendment fraught with interpretative dangers. Inevitably, the Court is criticized either for going too far in promoting religion or for exhibiting hostility toward religion. That alone may be evidence that the Court is doing its job as conceived by the Founders.

The Right to Peaceably Assemble. Although freedom of speech and freedom to worship protect highly personal rights, the First Amendment's guarantee of the right "of the people peaceably to assemble," protects the right of association. These are the rights of the people as a community to join together to achieve certain political, social, economic, artistic, educational, or other goals.

For the Court, interpreting the right to assemble has been even more difficult than construing other aspects of the First Amendment, because by its very nature, assembly involves both speech *and* conduct. At first blush, the First Amendment has nothing to do with conduct. However, when the Court is confronted with cases involving public demonstrations, protests, parades, and picketing, it is apparent that these activities are intended to send a message—and communicating messages is clearly protected by the First Amendment.

However, blocking traffic, littering the streets, or physically obstructing others from going about their business is not protected by the First Amendment. Consequently, when it comes to freedom of assembly, the Court has used a balancing test, seeking first to determine whether the law regulating assembly is in fact a ruse to suppress a particular viewpoint, and if not, whether the law serves a compelling state interest unrelated to the suppression of free speech.

For example, in 1940 in *Thornhill v. Alabama*, the Court struck down a state law that prohibited all picketing. Although the First Amendment does not afford an absolute right to picket, the Court overturned the statute because instead of regulating specific aspects of labor demonstrations, it prohibited "every practicable method whereby the facts of a labor dispute may be publicized."

Closely aligned with freedom of assembly is freedom of association or the right of the people to form and join organizations in order to educate themselves and influence public policy on important issues of the day. Even during the hysteria of the Cold War in the 1950's, the Court held in *Yates v. United States* (1957) that when membership in the Communist Party involved nothing more than the advocacy or teaching of the abstract doctrine of the forcible overthrow of the government (as contrasted with the advocacy or teaching of direct action to achieve that end) convictions under the Smith Act were unconstitutional.

In 1958, in *National Association for the Advancement of Colored People v. Alabama*, the Court found that the forced disclosure of an organization's membership list violated the members' rights to pursue their lawful interests and to freely associate

with like-minded persons. Although freedom of association is not expressly set forth anywhere in the Constitution, the Court nevertheless found freedom of association to be an integral part of the First Amendment.

The Right to Petition the Government. The least controversial (and least litigated) right in the First Amendment is the right "to petition the government for redress of grievances." Aside from a doomed attempt in 1836 by the House of Representatives to impose a gag rule against the receipt of petitions from abolitionists who opposed slavery, Congress has not had the temerity to even attempt to restrict this quintessential right to write to your Congressperson, thereby sparing the Court the task of striking down such legislation.

FURTHER READING

Steven H. Shiffrin and Jesse H. Choper's *The First Amendment: Cases, Comments, Questions* (St. Paul, Minn.: West Publishing, 1996) provides a basic introduction to the First Amendment. *The First Amendment: The Legacy of George Mason* (London: Associated University Presses, 1985), edited by T. Daniel Shumate, focuses on the origin and meaning of the amendment. Louis E. Ingelhart's *Press and Speech Freedoms in the World, from Antiquity Until 1998: A Chronology* (Westport, Conn.: Greenwood Press, 1998) covers the concept of freedom of speech and press from ancient times until the modern period, and Margaret A. Blanchard's *Revolutionary Sparks: Freedom of Expression in Modern America* (New York: Oxford University Press, 1992) covers the concept from the beginning to the end of the twentieth century. The First Amendment and the freedoms of association and assembly are examined in *Freedom of Association* (Princeton, N.J.: Princeton University Press, 1998), edited by Amy Gutmann, and Paul L. Murphy's *Rights of Assembly, Petition, Arms, and Just Compensation* (New York: Garland, 1990). The First Amendment and religion are examined in *Toward Benevolent Neutrality: Church, State, and the Supreme Court*, edited by Ronald B. Flowers and Robert T. Miller (Waco, Tex.: Baylor University Press, 1998), *The Believer and the Powers That Are: Cases, History, and Other Data Bearing on the Relation of Religion and Government*, by John Thomas Noonan, Jr. (New York: Macmillan, 1987), and *Religious Liberty in the Supreme Court: The Cases That Define the Debate over Church and State*, edited by Terry Eastland (Grand Rapids, Mich.: Wm. B. Eerdmans, 1995).

Stephen F. Rohde

SEE ALSO Assembly and association, freedom of; Bad tendency test; Brandeis, Louis D.; Brennan, William J., Jr.; Censorship; Clear and present danger test; Dissents; First Amendment absolutism; First Amendment balancing; First Amendment speech tests; Holmes, Oliver Wendell; Religion, establishment of; Religion, freedom of.

First Amendment absolutism

DESCRIPTION: Position that protections given by the First Amendment to the U.S. Constitution are absolute, not subject to qualification or abridgement in any way.

SIGNIFICANCE: Very few First Amendment absolutists sat on the Supreme Court, and the Court never made a First Amendment decision based on the absolutist approach.

Among the Supreme Court justices who could be called First Amendment absolutists is Justice Hugo L. Black. He argued that when the First Amendment said "Congress shall make no law" it meant that Congress should make absolutely no laws abridging First Amendment rights. Almost all other justices have taken that with a grain of salt, opining that "no law" meant something other than absolutely no laws.

Justice William O. Douglas joined Black in most of his absolutist decisions, and he wrote that the government should take an enabling position regarding First Amendment issues, especially freedom of the press, creating opportunities for citizens to publish opinions. However, the Court majority never took an absolutist approach to First Amendment issues.

The First Amendment can be separated into three divisions: the religion clauses (establishment and freedom), the speech and press clauses, and the clauses guaranteeing peaceable assembly and the right to petition. Most of the Court's First Amendment decisions relate to speech and press, and a substantial number of cases relate to religion. Only a handful are about assembly and petition rights.

Speech and Press. The Court clearly stated that no absolute freedom of speech or the press exists.

It found in *Cohen v. California* (1971) that there is no absolute freedom to speak wherever or whenever one chooses and in *Dennis v. United States* (1951) that the "societal value of speech must on occasion be subordinated to other values and considerations." It should be noted that *Dennis*, a case involving the trial of people charged with preaching the violent overthrow of the government by the Communist Party, is not unanimously considered good law today. Neither is *Schenck v. United States* (1919), a case involving people convicted of distributing leaflets urging draftees not to bear arms; this violated the Espionage Act of 1917. Their conviction was unanimously upheld by the Court. In his opinion, Justice Oliver Wendell Holmes wrote that freedom of speech does not give one the right to shout a false "fire" warning in a crowded theater. Holmes's words served as the foundation of the clear and present danger test. The Court used the clear and present danger test as well as a balancing test (which examines the gravity of the danger to see if it justifies suppressing freedom of speech) in numerous decisions to determine when First Amendment freedom of speech and press rights could be abridged.

Hugo L. Black, pictured here, is the only justice who is said to have been a First Amendment absolutist. He was joined, however, in many decisions by William O. Douglas. (AP/Wide World Photos)

When Justice Joseph Story, a friend and colleague of Chief Justice John Marshall, wrote his commentaries on the law, he argued that the government has a right to protect its survival, and the Court upheld that line of reasoning in *American Communications Association v. Douds* (1950). The free speech and free press clauses must be balanced against compelling public interests, the Court ruled, and it appears that every effort to challenge that ruling has been denied certiorari. The Court ruled that regulation of speech and the press must not be content-based, must bear a reasonable relationship to a significant government interest, and must allow for other channels of communication.

Religion. The Court comes closest to the absolutist position when it rules on religion cases. The religion clauses are absolute "as far as they go," the Court ruled, but they do not require complete separation of church and state. What they do require is that the government avoid regulating religious beliefs, establishing a state religion, and showing any preferences among religions or between religion and irreligion. When religious belief is translated into action, the state can intervene to regulate or prevent the action. Any legislation, the Court ruled in *Larkin v. Grendel's Den* (1982), must meet three rules: First, it must meet a secular legislative purpose; second, it must neither advance nor inhibit religion; and third, it must not entangle the government with religion.

Assembly and Association. Neither the right to assemble nor that to associate was judged to be absolute. For example, in *Cox v. New Hampshire* (1941), the Court upheld a license requirement for public parades and processions. In various cases, it endeavored to establish where and how people could assemble. The Court also examined association issues, trying to determine whether membership in certain clubs or organizations could be denied to members of various groups and whether those institutions were public or private.

FURTHER READING

Alderman, Ellen, and Caroline Kennedy. *In Our Defense: The Bill of Rights in Action.* New York: Morrow, 1991.

Black, Hugo LaFayette. *One Man's Stand for Freedom: Mr. Justice Black and the Bill of Rights.* New York: Alfred A. Knopf, 1971.

Dennis, Everett, Donald M. Gillmore, and David L. Grey, eds. *Justice Hugo Black and the First Amendment: "'No law' means no law."* Ames: Iowa State University Press, 1978.

Duran, James C. *Justice William O. Douglas.* Boston: Twayne, 1981.

Fellman, David. *The Constitutional Rights of Association.* Chicago: University of Chicago Press, 1963.

Hocking, William Ernest. *Freedom of the Press: A Framework of Principle.* New York: Da Capo Press, 1972.

Levy, Beth, and Denise M. Bonilla. *The Power of the Press.* Bronx, N.Y.: H. W. Wilson, 1999.

Miller, William Lee. *The First Liberty: Religion and the American Republic.* New York: Alfred A. Knopf, 1986.

St. John, Jeffrey. *Forge of Union, Anvil of Liberty: A Correspondent's Report on the First Federal Elections, the First Federal Congress, and the Bill of Rights.* Ottawa, Ill.: Jameson Books, 1992.

Smolla, Rodney A. *Free Speech in an Open Society.* New York: Alfred A. Knopf, 1992.

Dwight Jensen

SEE ALSO Assembly and association, freedom of; Black, Hugo L.; Douglas, William O.; First Amendment; First Amendment balancing; Petition, right of; Religion, establishment of; Religion, freedom of; Speech and press, freedom of.

First Amendment balancing

DESCRIPTION: Weighing of different interests involved in cases raising First Amendment claims, typically the free speech rights of an individual versus the potential harm posed to society as a whole.

SIGNIFICANCE: Although all Supreme Court First Amendment rulings involve the balancing of different claims and interests, the Court explicitly or implicitly invoked the balancing test most consistently during the 1947-1957 period. It almost invariably placed a higher value on social than individual claims in free speech cases, thus often upholding convictions.

The Supreme Court's First Amendment jurisprudence gradually evolved after World War I. Earlier, the Court had invoked various tests for resolving First Amendment conflicts, including the well-known clear and present danger test first invoked

Allen Ginsberg reads his poetry in a New York park in 1966 after a state supreme court decision that allowed him to present his uncensored works in public parks. In deciding cases such as this, the Supreme Court and lower courts must weigh the interests of the general public against the individual's freedom of speech rights. (AP/ Wide World Photos)

in *Schenck v. United States* (1919). During the 1947-1957 period, the Court, usually implicitly but sometimes explicitly, appears to have been guided by a balancing test, through which the Court sought to weigh competing interests and claims against each other.

Ten Years of Balancing. All legal cases, by definition, involve competing considerations, and therefore any jurisprudence involves balancing, as indeed does virtually all private decision making. However, the concept of First Amendment balancing is particularly apparent in the Court's First Amendment jurisprudence during the 1947-1957 period because of the manner and outcome of its rulings. When the Court seems to have invoked balancing during this period, it invariably gave more weight to perceived societal interests over First Amendment claims of individuals and organizations. Therefore, in the view of its critics, the Court claimed to be impartially balancing compet-

ing interests while in fact placing a thumb on the social side of the scales. After 1957, the Court largely abandoned the balancing test in First Amendment cases, instead generally relying on other tests such as the preferred freedoms doctrine, which tended to yield results favoring individual rights.

American Communications Association v. Douds (1950) is one of the relatively few cases in which the Court explicitly elaborated balancing considerations. At issue was a provision of the 1947 Taft-Hartley (Labor-Management Relations) Act that required all union officials to sign noncommunist affidavits in order to maintain their offices and for their unions to qualify for various benefits under existing federal labor laws. Chief Justice Fred M. Vinson's majority opinion upholding the validity of the contested provision declared that the clear and present danger standard of *Schenck* was not intended to create an absolutist test. He stated that when a statute's effect on a person's ability to exercise First Amendment rights was relatively small but the public interest to be protected was significant, a rigid test that necessitated the demonstration of imminent danger to the nation's security was an "absurdity." Instead, Vinson said, the Court's duty was to determine which interest needed greater protection under the particular circumstances of the case. He weighed the likely effects of the statute on the free exercise of First Amendment rights against the "congressional determination that political strikes are evils of conduct which cause substantial harm to interstate commerce" and that communists "pose continuing threats to the public interest when in positions of union leadership."

In *Dennis v. United States* (1951), the Court upheld the conviction of top U.S. Communist Party leaders for conspiracy to advocate and organize the overthrow of the government. In his concurring opinion, Justice Felix Frankfurter, a leading advocate of balancing, stated, "The demands of free speech in a democratic society as well as the interest in national security are better served by candid and informed weighing of the competing interests, within the confines of the judicial process, than by announcing dogmas too inflexible for the non-Euclidean problem to be solved."

Criticisms. Frankfurter's reference to inflexible "dogmas" was a response to critics of balancing, who claimed that it was consistently invoked in a manner that overlooked or watered down compelling free speech claims. Among the critics of balancing was Justice Hugo L. Black, who was associated with the absolutist view that held that absolutely no law should be passed that abridged First Amendment rights. In *Barenblatt v. United States* (1959), Black declared that the Court's application of balancing amounted to amending the First Amendment to read, "Congress shall pass no law abridging freedom of speech, press, assembly, and petition unless Congress and the Supreme Court reach the joint conclusion that on balance the interest of the government in stifling these freedoms is greater than the interest of the people in having them exercised."

Similarly, in *Smith v. California* (1959), Black argued that because the First Amendment said Congress could pass "no law abridging" free speech rights, this meant that the Constitution placed these rights above any competing claims, and therefore no federal agency, including the Court, had the power or authority to subordinate speech and press to what they think are more important interests.

FURTHER READING

Abernathy, M. Glenn, and Barbara Perry. *Civil Liberties Under the Constitution.* Columbia: University of South Carolina Press, 1993.

Barker, Lucius, and Twiley W. Barker, Jr. *Civil Liberties and the Constitution.* Englewood Cliffs, N.J.: Prentice-Hall, 1994.

Emerson, Thomas. *The System of Freedom of Expression.* New York: Vintage Books, 1970.

Robert Justin Goldstein

SEE ALSO *American Communications Association v. Douds*; Bad tendency test; Clear and present danger test; *Dennis v. United States*; First Amendment absolutism; First Amendment speech tests; Preferred freedoms doctrine; Speech and press, freedom of.

First Amendment speech tests

DESCRIPTION: Rules set forth in several twentieth century Supreme Court decisions by which the Court judged later claims of protected speech.

SIGNIFICANCE: To First Amendment absolutists and civil libertarians, the speech tests employed by the Supreme Court severely weakened individuals' constitutional rights to free speech. To others, the tests balanced the rights of government and society with those of individuals.

Beginning in the early twentieth century, the Supreme Court adopted tests by which to decide claims of First Amendment protection. The first and most frequently applied test is that of clear and present danger and its subsequent modifications. Developed by Justices Oliver Wendell Holmes and Louis D. Brandeis, this test weighs an individual's First Amendment rights against the government's right to protect itself and its citizens.

The clear and present danger test was set forth by Justice Holmes in *Schenck v. United States* (1919). Charles Schenck and his codefendants were convicted under the 1917 Espionage Act for disrupting military recruiting by distributing antiwar leaflets. Schenck appealed, citing First Amendment protection, but the Court unanimously upheld the conviction. In the opinion for the Court, Holmes wrote, "The question in every case is whether the words used are used in such circumstances and are of such a nature as to create a clear and present danger that they will bring about the substantive evils that Congress has a right to prevent. It is a question of proximity and degree." The clear and present danger at the time was World War I, and the substantive evil was the hindering of national defense.

Changing Applications. However, just as free speech is not absolute, according to the Court, speech tests also are not absolute. Chief Justice Fred M. Vinson, in the majority opinion in *Dennis v. United States* (1951), wrote, "Neither Justice Holmes nor Justice Brandeis ever envisioned that a shorthand phrase should be crystallized into a rigid rule to be applied inflexibly without regard to the circumstances of each case. . . . Nothing is more certain in modern society than the principle that there are no absolutes, that a name, a phrase, a standard has meaning only when associated with the considerations which gave birth to the nomenclature." Therefore, the Court continuously modified and reinterpreted the clear and present danger test.

For example, in *Gitlow v. New York* (1925), the test was further qualified. Despite a lack of clear and present danger, the Court upheld Benjamin

Gitlow's conviction for publishing the *Left-wing Manifesto,* which urged a violent government overthrow. The majority opinion of Justice Edward T. Sanford put forth that speech is not protected "if its natural tendency and probable effect was to bring about the substantive evil which the legislative body might prevent." The Court applied this new bad tendency test again in *Whitney v. California* (1927) to uphold the conviction of Charlotte Anita Whitney, a communist. She was guilty under California's criminal syndicalism law because the organization in which she participated promoted violent political action. In upholding the conviction, the Court cited a state's right to protect itself from organizations advocating criminal acts.

In addition to changing the definitions for tests, the Court also inconsistently applied them. For example, in *Terminiello v. Chicago* (1949), Father Arthur Terminiello's conviction was narrowly overturned, despite a riot by protestors during his inflammatory speech. In writing the majority opinion, Justice William O. Douglas modified the clear and present danger test by adding that it must be "of a serious substantive evil that rises far above public inconvenience, annoyance, or unrest." This particular Court was of the opinion that speech is necessarily provocative and that the ensuing disturbance was mild enough to be quelled by police.

In *Dennis,* the Court again modified the definition of clear and present danger. In upholding the convictions of communists under the Smith Act (1940), Chief Justice Fred M. Vinson restated Chief Judge Learned Hand's lower court ruling: "In each case [courts] must ask whether the gravity of the 'evil,' discounted by its improbability, justifies such invasion of free speech as is necessary to avoid the danger." The Court thus created the grave and probable danger test, which removed the burden of the state to prove the existence of an immediate danger to itself. Consequently, civil liberties were severely weakened.

Dissenting Views. First Amendment speech tests are not without criticism, as Justice Hugo L. Black's dissenting opinion in *Dennis* illustrates: "I cannot agree that the First Amendment permits us to sustain laws suppressing freedom of speech and press on the basis of Congress' or our own notions of mere 'reasonableness.' Such a doctrine waters down the First Amendment so that it amounts to little more than an admonition to Congress." Black's dissent is important because the Court seemed to favor the side of government in the First Amendment cases brought to it.

By *Brandenburg v. Ohio* (1969), however, the Court redefined clear and present danger, and in so doing, began to favor civil liberties. Ku Klux Klan leader Clarence Brandenburg was convicted under Ohio's criminal syndicalism law, which was modeled on the California statute under which Whitney was convicted decades earlier. The Court overturned the conviction and established the incitement test. In its unsigned majority opinion, the Court distinguished between speech and action. It stated that speech advocating force or lawlessness is protected; however, speech "directed to inciting or producing imminent lawless action" or "likely to incite or produce such action" is unprotected. The Court referred to this ruling in subsequent cases.

FURTHER READING

Killian, Johnny H., ed. *The Constitution of the United States of America: Analysis and Interpretation.* Washington, D.C.: Government Printing Office, 1987.

Rabban, David M. *Free Speech in Its Forgotten Years.* New York: Cambridge University Press, 1997.

Beau David Case

SEE ALSO *Brandenburg v. Ohio;* Clear and present danger test; *Dennis v. United States;* First Amendment; First Amendment absolutism; First Amendment balancing; *Gitlow v. New York; Schenck v. United States; Terminiello v. Chicago; Whitney v. California.*

First English Evangelical Lutheran Church of Glendale v. County of Los Angeles

CITATION: 482 U.S. 304
DATE: June 9, 1987
ISSUES: Zoning; takings clause
SIGNIFICANCE: In this case involving buildings in a flood plain, the Supreme Court first ruled that a zoning ordinance could result in a taking, thus requiring just compensation under the Fifth Amendment.

A flood destroyed buildings that belonged to the First English Evangelical Lutheran Church in Southern California. The church found it could not rebuild because the buildings had been constructed on a flood plain, and a county ordinance banned building in such areas. The church challenged the ordinance, and California courts found the church could recover only if the ordinance was ruled an unlawful taking and the county refused to withdraw the ordinance. The Supreme Court found that the rescinding of an invalid ordinance was not an adequate remedy and the county must pay for excessive interference during the time the ordinance was in effect. The Court did not determine exactly when the taking actually occurred and how the damages might be calculated but did say that small delays that are a normal part of the process are not a taking. Justice John Paul Stevens expressed his concern, in his dissent, that this ruling would have a chilling effect on land-use planning because local governments might worry about potential liability. The case was returned to the lower courts, which found that the ordinance was not a taking.

Richard L. Wilson

SEE ALSO Property rights; Stevens, John Paul; Takings clause; Zoning.

First Monday in October

DESCRIPTION: Opening day of the Supreme Court session.

SIGNIFICANCE: Although the agenda for the First Monday in October has changed over the years, this day still holds symbolic meaning for the Court.

In 1916 Congress moved the opening session of the Supreme Court from the second Monday in October to the first Monday in October (beginning in 1917) to allow the Court more time to handle its increasing agenda. Some rituals of first Monday include tributes offered to deceased and retired associates and court officers and judicial oaths taken by new justices.

From 1917 to 1975, opening day and week were spent in conference. The justices examined cases

Visitors line up outside the Supreme Court building on Monday, October 7, 1996, the day that the Court began its 1996-1997 session. (AP/Wide World Photos)

that were still open from the previous term and discussed new cases that appeared on the Court's docket during summer recess. During this week agreement on which cases to accept for oral argument was reached, and the announcement of these cases was made on the second Monday of October.

At the start of the October, 1975, session, this custom was changed. Thereafter the justices gathered for their conference during the last week in September. Oral arguments started when the justices formally met on the first Monday in October.

Andrea E. Miller

SEE ALSO Conference of the justices; Oral argument; Workload.

First National Bank of Boston v. Bellotti

CITATION: 435 U.S. 765
DATE: April 26, 1978
ISSUE: Campaign finance
SIGNIFICANCE: This decision extended the impact of *Buckley v. Valeo* to referendum campaigns.

The Supreme Court, by a 5-4 vote, struck down a clause in Massachusetts law restricting the amount of money corporations could contribute to support or oppose referenda. Justice Lewis F. Powell, Jr., wrote the 5-4 majority opinion, which extended the *Buckley v. Valeo* (1976) distinction between contributions to campaigns to influence opinion and those to candidates. Although corporations could contribute freely to referenda, unlike individuals, they could be prohibited from spending money directly on a candidate or outside a candidate's campaign to benefit his or her efforts. Justices Byron R. White and William H. Rehnquist separately dissented strongly, asserting that states should be able to limit corporate campaign expenditures.

Richard L. Wilson

SEE ALSO *Buckley v. Valeo*; Elections; Financing political speech.

Fiscal and monetary powers

DESCRIPTION: Taxation, government expenditures, and management of the public debt; creation and regulation of the money supply and banking system.

SIGNIFICANCE: The Supreme Court's monetary decisions have generally supported broad federal authority, particularly in crisis periods. Its fiscal decisions affected development of federal income tax and intergovernmental relations.

The U.S. Constitution bestowed extensive monetary powers on the new central government and restricted possible monetary actions by state governments. In 1792 Congress chartered the Bank of the United States, which operated branches in major cities. The bank's constitutionality was much in dispute, and it closed in 1812 when its charter expired. Monetary disorder attending the War of 1812 led to the chartering of a second Bank of the United States in 1816, intended to aid in managing the government's finances and also in forcing state banks to restrict their issue of bank notes. Maryland levied a punitive tax against the bank, which was challenged in the landmark Supreme Court case of *McCulloch v. Maryland* (1819). In his opinion for the Court, Chief Justice John Marshall stated that the creation of the bank was an acceptable exercise of implied powers, principally because of the bank's usefulness in managing the government's financial transactions, and therefore, the tax was invalid.

A severe business depression in 1819 led several states to experiment with methods of increasing the money supply. Missouri created paper near-money in the form of loan certificates that paid interest but were designed to circulate as currency. This practice was struck down by the Court as an unconstitutional issue of bills of credit in *Craig v. Missouri* (1830). Kentucky achieved the same result by creating the Bank of the Commonwealth of Kentucky, which could lend newly printed bank notes to residents. The Court refused to bar this action, holding that the bank was a separate entity from the state in *Briscoe v. Bank of the Commonwealth of Kentucky* (1837). State authority to create banks remained a major loophole in federal monetary authority for nearly another century.

Civil War. The financial predicament of the federal government during the Civil War (1861-1865) led to several major monetary developments. The government began in 1862 to issue legal tender paper currency ("greenbacks") with no fixed parity to gold. The greenbacks depreciated relative to gold, and debtors claimed the right to use greenbacks to repay debts that had initially called for repayment in gold. In *Hepburn v. Griswold* (1870), the Court held that the legal tender provision could not apply to debts incurred before the greenbacks were created. However, this decision was reversed in *Knox v. Lee* (1871) and *Parker v. Davis* (1871), after President Ulysses S. Grant appointed two more justices. Therefore, greenbacks could be used to pay off any (private) debts, even those dating from before greenbacks were issued. In *Juilliard v. Greenman* (1884), the Court upheld the right of the government to maintain inconvertible legal tender paper money even in peacetime.

The National Banking Act of 1863 authorized the federal government to charter national banks, which were permitted to issue national banknotes, secured by deposit of government bonds. To induce banks to take national charters, Congress in 1865 levied a punitive tax on state-bank note issues. The tax was upheld as a legitimate act of federal monetary authority in *Veazie Bank v. Fenno* (1869). The tax did not wipe out state-chartered banks but obliged them to stick to deposit business rather than issuing bank notes.

Echoes of the greenback cases arose during the Great Depression. In 1933 Congress abolished the gold standard, required holders of gold coins to turn them in, and invalidated contracts calling for payment of debts in gold. The Court upheld the government's action in *Norman v. Baltimore and*

Ohio Railroad Co. (1935), stating that people "cannot remove their transactions from the reach of dominant constitutional power by making contracts about them."

Fiscal Matters. The Constitution provided that "direct taxes shall be apportioned among the several states . . . according to their respective numbers." An early federal tax on the ownership of carriages was held in *Hylton v. United States* (1796) not to be a direct tax and therefore exempt from the proportionality requirement.

The Civil War fiscal crisis led to the first federal income tax, enacted in 1862. It was removed in 1872 but revived in 1894. The Court repeatedly upheld the tax's constitutionality, especially in *Springer v. United States* (1881). However, surprisingly in *Pollock v. Farmers' Loan and Trust Co.* (1895), the Court held that the 1894 tax was a direct tax and therefore invalid. Political support for an income tax was sufficient in 1913 to bring adoption of the Sixteenth Amendment, which specifically allowed the tax. Income taxes on individuals and corporations have been a major fiscal factor ever since.

After *McCulloch v. Maryland*, numerous cases arose concerning the authority of one level of government to tax instrumentalities and operations of another. Many decisions of this "much litigated and often confused field" are reviewed in *United States v. New Mexico* (1982) and *South Carolina v. Baker* (1988). In the latter case, the Court concluded that "the States can never tax the United States directly but can tax any private parties with whom it does business, . . . as long as the tax does not discriminate." After *Weston v. Charleston* (1829), states were prohibited from taxing interest incomes from federal government bonds, and federal statutes have exempted interest on state and local government bonds from the federal income tax.

Similarly the Court often upheld the use of federal tax and spending policies to influence state policy. In *South Dakota v. Dole* (1987), it upheld federal law withholding federal highway funds from states that did not prohibit purchase or public possession of alcohol by persons under twenty-one years of age. The Court frequently ruled on cases where taxation or government expenditures involved issues of discrimination or issues of church-state relations. In *Bob Jones University v. United States* (1983), it upheld withholding tax exemption from institutions practicing racial discrimination.

An important issue relating to federal expenditure policy was the Court's position denying the authority of the president to refuse to spend funds authorized by Congress in the 1975 cases *Train v. City of New York* and *Train v. Campaign Clean Water.*

FURTHER READING

Cohen, William, and Jonathan D. Varat. *Constitutional Law: Cases and Materials.* Westbury, N.Y.: Foundation Press, 1997.

Dunne, Gerald T. *Monetary Decisions of the Supreme Court.* New Brunswick N.J.: Rutgers University Press, 1960.

Ratner, Sidney. *American Taxation.* New York: W. W. Norton, 1942.

Paul B. Trescott

SEE ALSO *Briscoe v. Bank of the Commonwealth of Kentucky*; Civil War; *Craig v. Missouri*; *Hylton v. United States*; Income tax; *Legal Tender Cases*; *McCulloch v. Maryland*; *Pollock v. Farmers' Loan and Trust Co.*; Presidential powers; Sixteenth Amendment; State taxation; Tax immunities; Taxing and spending clause.

Flag desecration

DESCRIPTION: Act of physically "harming" the U.S. flag, usually through such means as burning or tearing; at times the term was also applied to verbal criticism of the flag or what it represents.

SIGNIFICANCE: The Supreme Court upheld the right, under the First Amendment, of people to both verbally and physically assault the flag and, in so doing, helped define and extend the meaning of constitutionally protected symbolic speech.

The U.S. flag, a symbol of the nation, is displayed widely in front of government buildings, private homes, and commercial enterprises and used extensively as a design springboard for clothing, advertising, and a wide variety of other products. However, it attracted little interest and received little public display for more than eighty years after its original adoption as a symbol of the nation by the Continental Congress on June 14, 1777. Only the outbreak of the Civil War (1861-1865) transformed the flag into an object of public adoration—although only, of course, in the North.

The newly found Northern love for the flag continued after the Civil War, but the flag's growing popularity was not accompanied by any sense that it should be regarded as a sacred object or relic. During the nation's rapid postwar industrialization, as the modern advertising industry developed, the flag became increasingly popular as a decorative accompaniment in the commercialization of a wide range of products. Gradually, after 1890, Union veterans and members of patriotic-hereditary groups such as the Sons of the American Revolution began to protest alleged commercial debasement of the flag, which they declared would ultimately cause the significance of both the flag and patriotism to degrade among the general public. After about 1900 the supposed threat to the flag shifted from commercialization to that allegedly posed by its use as a means of expressing political protest by political radicals, trade union members, and immigrants (who were often indiscriminately lumped together).

Between 1897 and 1932 veterans and hereditary-patriotic groups lobbied for stringent laws to "protect" the flag from all forms of alleged "desecration" (the harming of sacred religious objects) and succeeded in obtaining passage of flag desecration laws in all forty-eight states, with thirty-one states

acting between 1897 and 1905 alone. The laws generally outlawed attaching anything to or placing any marks on the flag, using the flag in any manner for advertising purposes, and physically or verbally "harming" flags in any way, including, typically, publicly mutilating, trampling, defacing, defiling, defying, or casting contempt on the flag. The term "flag" was generally defined to mean any object of any form, size, or material that resembled the U.S. flag.

Early Court Rulings. The earliest state flag desecration laws were quickly and, at first, successfully challenged in local and state courts as illegally restricting property rights by adversely affecting commercial interests. However, in *Halter v. Nebraska* (1907), the Supreme Court upheld Nebraska's law in sweeping terms that made clear the futility of any further legal challenges for the foreseeable future. In a case involving sales of Stars and Stripes beer, which had pictures of flags on the bottle labels, the Court declared that the state was entitled to restrict property rights for the valid and worthy purpose of fostering nationalism. In a ruling that did not address free speech rights, the Court declared that "love both of the common country and of the State will diminish in proportion as respect for the flag is weakened," that advertising usage of the flag tended to "degrade and cheapen it in the estimation of the people," and that the state was entitled to "exert its power to strengthen the bonds of the Union and therefore, to that end, may encourage patriotism and love of country among its people."

The Court did not consider another flag desecration case until 1969, and during the interim period, the constitutionality of flag desecration laws was essentially considered beyond review by the lower courts. The Court revisited the issue during the Vietnam War, when flags were widely burned or used in other unorthodox ways to express political dissent (resulting in hundreds of flag desecration prosecutions).

A group of Vietnam War protesters in Portland, Oregon, in 1970 burned an American flag before marching through the city's downtown. A year earlier, the Supreme Court struck down several flag desecration statutes. (AP/Wide World Photos)

In *Street v. New York* (1969), the Court relied heavily on its rulings in *Stromberg v. California* (1931) and *West Virginia State Board of Education v. Barnette* (1943) to strike down flag desecration provisions that outlawed *verbal* disrespect for the flag as violating the First Amendment. The Court, by a 5-4 vote, overturned Street's flag desecration conviction on the grounds that because he had been charged under a provision of New York's law outlawing casting contempt on the flag by words or acts and evidence concerning his statements had been introduced at trial, he might have been convicted for his words alone. Any such conviction, in the absence of any evident threat to the peace or incitement to violence, was held to violate the First Amendment because "it is firmly settled that under our Constitution the public expression of ideas may not be prohibited merely because the ideas are themselves offensive to some of their hearers," even opinions about the flag "which are defiant or contemptuous." The Court completely avoided addressing the constitutionality of laws that banned *physical* flag desecration on the grounds that there was no need to decide the case "on a broader basis than the record before us imperatively requires." Aside from *Street*, the Court in 1974 overturned convictions in two other Vietnam-era flag desecration cases, *Goguen v. Smith* and *Spence v. Washington*, which were both decided on narrow grounds that again avoided directly addressing the validity of state interests in protecting the physical integrity of the flag in light of First Amendment questions.

A Texas Flag Burning. In *Texas v. Johnson* (1989), which arose from a 1984 Dallas flag-burning incident, the Court directly faced the question of physical desecration of the flag, ruling by a 5-4 vote that Texas's venerated objects law had been unconstitutionally applied to Johnson. Texas advanced two interests as overriding Johnson's First Amendment rights, but the Court dismissed them. First, it found that the state's interest in maintaining order was not implicated because no disturbance of the peace occurred or threatened to occur because of Johnson's act. Second, regarding a need to preserve the flag as a national symbol, the Court held that because Johnson's guilt depended on the communicative nature of his conduct, the Texas statute violated the main principle behind the First Amendment, that the government cannot ban the

expression of an idea because society finds that idea offensive or disagreeable. Citing its holding in *Street* that a state cannot criminally punish a person for speech critical of the flag, the Court declared flatly that Texas's attempt to distinguish between written or spoken words and nonverbal conduct "is of no moment where the nonverbal conduct is expressive, as is here, and where the regulation of that conduct is related to expression, as it is here."

Furthermore, the Court declared that the government cannot ban expression of ideas that it does not like because the expression takes a particular form; therefore, the state cannot criminally punish a person for burning a flag in political protest on the grounds that other means of expressing the same idea were available. The Court concluded that the principles of freedom reflected in the flag would be reaffirmed by its decision: "We do not consecrate the flag by punishing its desecration, for in doing so we dilute the freedom that this cherished emblem represents."

Johnson touched off an intense and massive uproar across the United States. Virtually every member of Congress endorsed resolutions condemning the ruling. To circumvent the ruling, most Democrats maintained that an ordinary law would suffice, but President George Bush and most Republicans maintained that a constitutional amendment would be required. The Democratic congressional leadership noted that *Johnson* struck down a Texas statute that forbade flag desecration likely to cause "serious offense" to observers, rather than, as the Court noted at one point, "protecting the physical integrity of the flag in all circumstances" and argued that the court might uphold such a "content neutral" law.

The 1989 Flag Protection Act. Whether due to a perceived cooling of public sentiment, to increasing signs of growing opposition to a constitutional amendment, or to increased acceptance of the argument that trying a statute first was preferable to a constitutional change, by October, 1989, the drive for a constitutional amendment, seemingly unstoppable in late June after President Bush endorsed it, was sputtering. On October 19, the constitutional amendment failed to reach the two-thirds majority it required in the Senate. However, both houses of Congress passed the proposed statutory alternative, the Flag Protection Act of 1989.

The Flag Protection Act provided penalties of up to one year in jail and a one thousand dollar fine for anyone who "knowingly mutilates, physically defiles, burns, maintains on the floor or ground, or tramples upon any flag of the United States" with "flag" defined as "any flag of the United States, or any part thereof, made of any substance, of any size, in a form that is commonly displayed." Although the stated purpose of the act was to end flag burnings, its immediate impact was to spur perhaps the largest single wave of such incidents in U.S. history, as flags were burned in about a dozen cities shortly after the law took effect in late October.

Acting under an extraordinary expedited review procedure mandated by the act, the Court struck down the Flag Protection Act by a 5-4 vote in *United States v. Eichman* on June 11, 1990. The *Eichman* ruling essentially underlined *Johnson*, finding that the government's interest in protecting the flag's position as a symbol of the United States and certain ideals did not justify the infringement on First Amendment rights. Although conceding that the new law, unlike the Texas statute in *Johnson*, did not explicitly place content-based limits on the scope of prohibited conduct, the Court held that the Flag Protection Act still suffered from the same fundamental flaw as the Texas law, namely that it could not be justified without reference to the content of the regulated speech. The Court added, "Punishing desecration of the flag dilutes the very freedom that makes this emblem so revered, and worthy of revering."

The *Eichman* decision sparked an immediate renewal of calls by President Bush and others for a constitutional amendment. However, the proposed amendment was defeated in both houses of Congress in 1990. After Republicans gained control of both houses of Congress in 1994, the amendment was passed by the required two-thirds majority in the House in 1995, 1997, and 1999. However, in the Senate, it failed to gain a two-thirds vote (by three votes) in 1995, was never taken up during the 105th Congress (1997-1998), and appeared unlikely to be voted on in the 106th Congress.

FURTHER READING

Curtis, Michael, ed. *The Flag Burning Cases.* Vol. 2 in *The Constitution and the Flag.* New York: Garland, 1993.

Goldstein, Robert Justin. *Burning the Flag: The Great 1989-1990 American Flag Desecration Controversy.* Kent, Ohio: Kent State University Press, 1996.

_____, ed. *Desecrating the American Flag: Key Documents of the Controversy from the Civil War to 1995.* Syracuse, N.Y.: Syracuse University Press, 1996.

_____. *Saving "Old Glory": The History of the American Flag Desecration Controversy.* Boulder, Colo.: Westview Press, 1995.

Miller, J. Anthony. *"Texas v. Johnson": The Flag Burning Case.* Springfield, N.J.: Enslow, 1997.

Robert Justin Goldstein

SEE ALSO *Eichman, United States v.*; Speech and press, freedom of; Symbolic speech; *Texas v. Johnson.*

Flast v. Cohen

CITATION: 392 U.S. 83
DATE: June 10, 1968
ISSUES: Establishment of religion; standing
SIGNIFICANCE: For the first time since the 1920's, the Supreme Court ruled that a taxpayer could sue the government for the misuse of government money but carefully limited the right of suit.

By an 8-1 vote, the Supreme Court ruled that a group of taxpayers could sue to stop federal funds from being spent on teaching secular subjects in parochial schools. After *Frothingham v. Mellon* (1923), federal taxpayers lacked standing and were unable to sue on the constitutionality of federal expenditures. However, in *Flast v. Cohen*, the Court allowed such suits if taxpayers could demonstrate that a logical link existed between their status and the type of enactment attacked and show that the challenged enactment exceeded specific constitutional limitations. Chief Justice Earl Warren wrote the majority opinion and was supported by concurrences from Justices William O. Douglas, Abe Fortas, and Potter Stewart. Justice John M. Harlan II dissented, fearing a large increase in inappropriate taxpayer challenges to the government. Subsequently, more conservative justices were named to the Court and the Harlan view increased in importance. In particular, the Court indicated that it would not expand the *Flast* ruling in *United States v. Richardson* (1974).

Richard L. Wilson

SEE ALSO *Engel v. Vitale*; *Illinois ex rel. McCollum v. Board of Education*; *Lee v. Weisman*; Religion, establishment of; *Richardson, United States v.*; Standing; Taxing and spending clause.

Fletcher v. Peck

CITATION: 6 Cranch (10 U.S.) 87
DATE: March 16, 1810
ISSUES: Contracts clause; property rights
SIGNIFICANCE: The Supreme Court's broad construction of the contracts clause enhanced protection from legislative interference for vested rights in private property. For the first time, moreover, the Court declared that a state law was unconstitutional and therefore invalid.

In 1795 the Georgia legislature granted thirty-five million acres of prime cotton land along the Yazoo River to speculative companies. The price was 1.5 cents per acre. Informed observers believed that members of the legislature had been influenced by bribes and personal interests. The following year, a newly elected legislature rescinded the Yazoo grant and invalidated all property rights deriving from it. Meanwhile, however, third parties in several states had already purchased much of the land. One such person, Robert Fletcher, sued John Peck in federal court, with the goal of having the title restored.

In one of its most unpopular decisions, the Supreme Court found that the rescinding statute had violated the contract clause. Speaking for the Court, Chief Justice John Marshall broadly defined a contract as "a compact between two or more parties," which included a grant made by a state legislature. Possible corruption in the motives of the legislators was a political question and not germane to the contract's validity. Marshall wrote that the offending statute was prohibited "either by the general principles which are common to our free institutions, or by the particular provisions of the Constitution." Justice William Johnson's concurrence relied solely on the vested law and higher law concept, without reference to the constitutional text.

Thomas T. Lewis

SEE ALSO Contracts clause; *Dartmouth College v. Woodward*; Ex post facto laws; Natural law; Property rights.

Florida v. Bostick

CITATION: 501 U.S. 429
DATE: June 18, 1991
ISSUE: Search and seizure
SIGNIFICANCE: The Supreme Court held that the Fourth Amendment allows the controversial police practice of randomly approaching individuals in public places and asking them for permission to search their belongings, as long as the request is not coercive in nature.

It is an elementary principle of law that persons may waive their constitutional rights. In *Schneckloth v. Bustamonte* (1973), the Court held that, when a suspect is not in custody, the evidence obtained in a consensual search may be used in a criminal trial even when the suspect did not know that he could refuse to agree to the search. Encouraged by this ruling, some police officers routinely boarded buses or trains and asked individual passengers for permission to search their luggage. Using this technique, two officers found cocaine in a bag belonging to Terrance Bostick. The police claimed that they advised Bostick of his right to refuse the search, but he denied that he gave his permission. After the trial court denied Bostick's motion to suppress the evidence, the Florida supreme court held that Bostick had been unconstitutionally seized because a "reasonable person" would not have felt free to leave the bus to avoid police questioning.

By a 6-3 vote, the Supreme Court reversed the judgment. Justice Sandra Day O'Connor's majority opinion quoted earlier decisions holding that the police did not need reasonable suspicion in order to ask questions of a person in a public place and that such questioning did not constitute a seizure. Because there were many circumstances preventing Bostick from leaving the bus, O'Connor concluded that the legal issue was not whether a reasonable person would have felt free to leave but rather whether a reasonable person would have felt free to refuse to submit to the search. The "reasonable person test," moreover, presupposes "an innocent person." Thus, the Court remanded the case to the state courts for a reexamination of "all the circumstances" of the search in order to decide whether Bostick had given his consent voluntarily.

Expanding upon *Bostick* in *Ohio v. Robinette* (1996), the Court ruled that the police are not required to inform motorists who are stopped for other reasons that they are "free to go" before their consent will be recognized as voluntary.

Thomas T. Lewis

SEE ALSO Automobile searches; Fourth Amendment; Search warrant requirement; *Terry v. Ohio.*

Foreign affairs and foreign policy

DESCRIPTION: Domain of public policy making whereby the national government orders its relations with other countries.

SIGNIFICANCE: Although foreign affairs and policy are mainly the concern of the president and, to a lesser degree, Congress, the Supreme Court arbitrates in disputes between the political branches. Its original jurisdiction includes cases involving foreign ambassadors, ministers, and consuls, and its appellate jurisdiction embraces disputes involving foreign governments, citizens, and subjects as well as admiralty and maritime law.

The Supreme Court typically defers to the political branches of the government in the area of foreign policy making. The president is constitutionally the lead actor in dealing with foreign governments. Article II of the U.S. Constitution invests the president with the power to make treaties, to conduct foreign relations, and, as commander in chief, to make war. Congress is not without authority in these areas, but its powers are more limited. The Senate advises and consents to the ratification of treaties, while the president negotiates and ratifies them and determines which agreements will be submitted for formal Senate consideration. Only Congress may declare war, but it does so only after a presidential request, and it is the president who, as commander in chief, conducts the war. The president nominates ambassadors subject to congressional approval. In each case the president acts and Congress reacts in matters involving foreign affairs.

The one area in which Congress has primary power is in the authorization of budgets for the conduct of foreign policy, but rarely does it use this power to contradict a president's foreign policy. Although the Constitution nowhere says definitively that the president is the primary constitutional authority in foreign affairs, and indeed both the president and Congress are invested with certain powers relative to the making and conduct of foreign policy, the deck is stacked in the president's favor. Still, the interpretation and relationship of the checks and balances that exist in this area have proved an invitation throughout U.S. history to struggle and contest between the executive and legislative branches, and the Supreme Court has ruled in several important cases in ways that have supported the assertion of presidential authority.

The Supreme Court's Role. Presidential authority in foreign policy increased in the twentieth century, as the United States rose to a position of prominence in international affairs. The Court, although not a direct player in the foreign policy arena, provided, in a series of rulings, an interpretation of the Constitution that supported the growth of presidential authority in this arena. In *Missouri v. Holland* (1920), the Court upheld the supremacy of treaties as the law of the land, giving the president and Congress the power to override state legislation where foreign policy interests and international obligations were involved. In the *United States v. Curtiss-Wright Export Corp.* (1936), which was advanced on appeal by an individual who had violated an arms embargo established by the president with the authorization of Congress concerning the Chaco War in South America, the Court upheld the legislative authorization and the presidential action as valid. Justice George Sutherland, writing for the majority, argued that the president had authority for his action not only from Congress but also from the "very delicate, plenary and exclusive power of the president as the sole organ of the federal government in the field of international relations." This case established a tone that the president, not Congress, conducts foreign relations, and that his or her powers are extensive.

Political Questions. The Court proved extremely reluctant to interfere with political disputes between Congress and the president over the conduct of foreign policy. In *Goldwater v. Carter* (1979), when Senator Barry Goldwater challenged President Jimmy Carter's authority to terminate a treaty with Taiwan without the advice and consent of the Senate, the Court dismissed the case on the grounds that this was a nonjusticiable political question. Legal challenges by members of Congress to the authority of the president to conduct military actions overseas without congressional authorization were also rebuffed by the Court as nonjusticiable political questions. Here, too, the Court was reluctant to interfere. Court abstention from interference in cases where legislative and executive claims were at odds concerning foreign policy often worked to the advantage of the chief executive rather than the legislature.

However, although a president's powers are considered to be broad in the foreign policy area, they are limited. The Court ruled in *Youngstown Sheet and Tube Co. v. Sawyer* (1952) that President Harry S Truman could not, under his powers as commander in chief during time of war, seize steel mills because he feared an impending strike by workers, especially in view of congressional opposition to such action. In this case, the Court displayed a reluctance to acknowledge as constitutional actions that, although related to foreign affairs, had no clear constitutional basis, had chiefly a domestic impact, and defied congressional wishes.

FURTHER READING

Bland, Randall W. *The Black Robe and the Bald Eagle: The Supreme Court and Foreign Policy, 1789-1960.* Bethesda, Md.: Austin & Winfield, 1998.

Corwin, Edward S. *The President: Office and Powers.* New York: New York University Press, 1984.

Goldwin, Robert A., and Robert A. Licht, eds. *Foreign Policy and the Constitution.* Washington, D.C.: American Enterprise Press, 1990.

Henkin, Louis. *Foreign Affairs and the Constitution.* Mineola, N.Y.: Foundation Press, 1996.

Westerfield, Donald L. *War Powers: The President, the Congress, and the Question of War.* Westport, Conn.: Praeger, 1996.

Robert F. Gorman

SEE ALSO *Curtiss-Wright Export Corp., United States v.*; Executive agreements; *Goldwater v. Carter*; National security; Presidential powers; Treaties; War powers; War Powers Act of 1973; Wartime seizure power; *Youngstown Sheet and Tube Co. v. Sawyer.*

Fortas, Abe

IDENTIFICATION: Associate justice (October 4, 1965-May 14, 1969)
NOMINATED BY: Lyndon B. Johnson
BORN: June 19, 1910, Memphis, Tennessee
DIED: April 5, 1982, Washington, D.C.

Abe Fortas. (Library of Congress)

SIGNIFICANCE: Associate justice and nominee for chief justice who resigned from the Supreme Court in disgrace.

A gifted student, Fortas received a scholarship to study at Yale Law School. After graduating in 1933, Fortas taught at Yale and worked for various New Deal government agencies. He worked full-time for the U.S. government from 1941 to 1946, when he went into private practice. Fortas earned recognition as a brilliant legal mind and as an advocate of liberal causes. He successfully argued the case of *Gideon v. Wainwright* (1963) before the Supreme Court, guaranteeing the indigent a right to counsel in state criminal cases.

Fortas was a close friend of Lyndon B. Johnson, and when Johnson became president in 1963, he relied heavily on Fortas for counsel. Johnson wanted Fortas to serve on the Supreme Court, both as an advocate for his Great Society programs and as a source of information concerning the attitudes and opinions that prevailed among the justices. Fortas also had the support of Justice William O. Douglas, whom he had known since his days as a Yale law student. In order to create a vacancy on the Court, Johnson offered Justice Arthur J. Goldberg the United Nations ambassadorship. Goldberg accepted and Johnson nominated Fortas. During his confirmation hearings, Fortas downplayed his close relationship with the president, and he received little opposition from the Senate, which quickly confirmed his nomination.

As an associate justice, Fortas served as an advocate for liberal issues. He provided the fifth and crucial vote in the ruling in the 1966 case of *Miranda v. Arizona*, which required that suspects be informed of their constitutional rights when arrested. Fortas wrote the majority opinion in the 1967 case *In re Gault*, which concerned the rights of juveniles accused of a crime. In his opinion, Fortas argued that accused juveniles possessed most of the rights of adults. He also wrote the majority opinion in the 1969 case *Tinker v. Des Moines Independent Community School District*, in which wearing an armband as a sign of protest was protected as a First Amendment right.

The Nomination. During his years on the Court, Fortas remained in close contact with President Johnson, offering him advice on both foreign policy and domestic issues. In 1968 when Chief Justice Earl Warren resigned, Johnson sought to provide a defense against possible future conservative attacks on his liberal programs by nominating Fortas for the vacant position. In order to gain support for the Fortas nomination from southerners who were less than enthusiastic at the notion of a liberal Jewish chief justice, Johnson planned to nominate Texas judge William H. Thornberry to take Fortas's position as associate justice.

The Fortas nomination proved to be a disaster for the Democratic Party. Because Johnson was a lame duck, Republicans had everything to gain by slowing the nomination process in the hope that a Republican would be elected to the White House in the upcoming election. Southerners were not mollified by the Thornberry nomination, and several southern senators voiced their antagonism toward Fortas. Senate hearings revealed the depth of opposition to the nomination. Senators expressed their concern that Fortas's close relationship with the president had constituted a violation of the separation of powers. In addition, Fortas was criticized for his liberal positions.

The September, 1968, revelation that Fortas had received $15,000 from wealthy private individuals for teaching a seminar at American University made little difference, as opposition to Fortas had become so intense that he had no chance of being confirmed. Although the Senate Judiciary Committee approved his nomination, Senate Republicans began a filibuster. Fortas asked Johnson to withdraw his nomination, and Johnson complied with his request on October 1.

Fortas's trials were not yet over. On May 5, 1969, *Life* magazine reported that while serving as associate justice, Fortas had accepted $20,000 from the Wolfson Family Foundation for assisting with foundation efforts. Fortas had returned the money after Louis Wolfson was indicted on stock fraud charges. Nonetheless, Fortas's relationship with Wolfson showed a lack of judgment and pointed to possible ethical violations. Fortas quickly issued an unconvincing statement regarding his dealings with Wolfson. He did not reveal that he and Wolfson had originally signed a contract ensuring him $20,000 a year for life, and $20,000 a year to his wife should she survive him.

Fortas's enemies, including members of President Richard M. Nixon's administration who hoped to create a vacancy on the Court, went into action. Members of Congress began discussing impeachment. Despite the enormous pressure and media attention, Fortas struggled to retain his position on the Court. However, Fortas's fate was sealed when the Justice Department learned of the lifetime contract with Wolfson. On May 14, 1969, Fortas resigned. He continued to practice law after his resignation. In 1982 the final year of his life, he argued a case before the Court.

Although widely recognized as an outstanding lawyer, Fortas showed considerable lack of judgment during his tenure on the Court. His relationship with Johnson went beyond offering advice—at times Fortas shared confidential information regarding the operations of the Court. Always concerned with money, he engaged in financial dealings that raised doubts about his ability to serve as an impartial jurist.

FURTHER READING

Kalman, Laura. *Abe Fortas: A Biography*. New Haven, Conn.: Yale University Press, 1990.

Murphy, Bruce Allen. *Fortas: The Rise and Ruin of a Supreme Court Justice*. New York: William Morrow, 1988.

Shogan, Robert. *A Question of Judgment: The Fortas Case and the Struggle for the Supreme Court*. Indianapolis, Ind.: Bobbs-Merrill, 1972.

Thomas Clarkin

SEE ALSO *Gault, In re*; *Gideon v. Wainwright*; Goldberg, Arthur J.; *Miranda v. Arizona*; Nominations to the Court; Thornberry, William H.; *Tinker v. Des Moines Independent Community School District*.

Fourteenth Amendment

DATE: 1868

DESCRIPTION: Amendment to the U.S. Constitution that provides legal protections for individuals against actions by state governments.

SIGNIFICANCE: The Supreme Court used the due process and equal protection clauses of this amendment in order to expand both the number and breadth of rights protecting individuals. More than any other amendment, the Fourteenth provided the basis for the range of rights that Americans came to take for granted during the twentieth century.

The Fourteenth Amendment was ratified after the Civil War (1861-1865) to provide protection for individuals, including the African Americans newly freed from slavery, against actions taken by state governments. Before ratification of the amendment, the rights provisions within the Constitution were aimed at preventing the federal government from violating individuals' legal protections. There were serious concerns that the former Confederate states might undertake actions that would threaten the liberty of individuals, especially African Americans, who resided within those states.

The amendment guarantees three primary rights: due process of law, equal protection of the law, and privileges or immunities of citizens. Section 5 of the amendment also grants Congress the power to enact legislation to enforce the rights specified in the amendment. Because the words describing Fourteenth Amendment rights are so vague, the Supreme Court had to use its interpretive powers to give meaning to the rights contained within it.

The Court's first major interpretation of the Fourteenth Amendment was in the *Slaughterhouse Cases* (1873), in which butchers in New Orleans complained that they had been denied due process, equal protection, and privileges or immunities of citizenship when the State of Louisiana gave one company an exclusive monopoly to slaughter livestock. The Court found that there was no Fourteenth Amendment violation. The justices declared that the equal protection clause was intended to protect newly freed African Americans, not occupational groups such as butchers. They said that the due process clause did not apply and that the privileges or immunities clause was similarly inapplicable. Although the Court's initial interpretation of the Fourteenth Amendment did not identify any specific protections provided for citizens, subsequent cases began to identify how the Fourteenth Amendment protected rights.

The Due Process Clause. During the twentieth century, the Court began to use the Fourteenth Amendment's due process clause as the mechanism for applying the protections of the Bill of Rights against the states. Through a process that scholars call "incorporation," the Court gradually decided that many provisions of the Bill of Rights, which protect individuals against actions by the federal government, should be incorporated in the due process clause in order to provide protection for individuals against actions by state and local governments. Some justices argued that the Court should declare that all of the rights from the Bill of Rights are contained in the Fourteenth Amendment due process clause. However, most justices preferred to examine each right individually to determine whether that particular right should be applied to state governments.

Beginning with the Court's decision in *Gitlow v. New York* (1925), which determined that the First Amendment's protection for freedom of speech applied to the states through the Fourteenth Amendment's due process clause, the justices examined specific rights from the Bill of Rights in a series of cases extending through the 1960's. By the time the Court declared in *Duncan v. Louisiana* (1968) that the Sixth Amendment's right to trial by jury was incorporated into the due process clause, the Court had applied nearly the entire Bill of Rights to the states through the incorporation process. Along the way, the Court incorporated the Fifth Amendment privilege against self-incrimination, the Sixth Amendment right to counsel, the Eighth Amendment prohibition on cruel and unusual punishments, and other important rights. Only a few rights remained unincorporated and still applicable against the federal government only. These rights include the Second Amendment

TEXT OF THE FOURTEENTH AMENDMENT

Section 1. All persons born or naturalized in the United States and subject to the jurisdiction thereof, are citizens of the United States and of the State wherein they reside. No State shall make or enforce any law which shall abridge the privileges or immunities of citizens of the United States; nor shall any State deprive any person of life, liberty, or property, without due process of law; nor deny to any person within its jurisdiction the equal protection of the laws.

Section 2. Representatives shall be apportioned among the several States according to their respective numbers, counting the whole number of persons in each State, excluding Indians not taxed. But when the right to vote at any election for the choice of electors for President and Vice President of the United States, Representatives in Congress, the Executive and Judicial officers of a State, or the members of the Legislature thereof, is denied to any of the male inhabitants of such State, being twenty-one years of age, and citizens of the United States, or in any way abridged, except for participation in rebellion, or other crime, the basis of representation therein shall be reduced in the proportion which the number of such male citizens shall bear to the whole number of male citizens twenty-one years of age in such State.

Section 3. No person shall be a Senator or Representative in Congress, or elector of President and Vice President, or hold any office, civil or military, under the United States, or under any State, who, having previously taken an oath, as a member of Congress, or as an officer of the United States, or as a member of any State legislature, or as an executive or judicial officer of any State, to support the Constitution of the United States, shall have engaged in insurrection or rebellion against the same, or given aid or comfort to the enemies thereof. But Congress may by a vote of two-thirds of each House, remove such disability.

Section 4. The validity of the public debt of the United States, authorized by law, including debts incurred for payment of pensions and bounties for services in suppressing insurrection or rebellion, shall not be questioned. But neither the United States nor any State shall assume or pay any debt or obligation incurred in aid of insurrection or rebellion against the United States, or any claim for the loss or emancipation of any slave; but all such debts, obligations and claims shall be held illegal and void.

Section 5. The Congress shall have power to enforce, by appropriate legislation, the provisions of this article.

---

right to bear arms, the Fifth Amendment right to a grand jury, and the Seventh Amendment right to a jury in civil cases. In effect, the Fourteenth Amendment's due process clause served as the vehicle for expanding the scope of constitutional rights so that citizens would enjoy the same protections against all levels of government.

In the late nineteenth century and early twentieth century, the Court used the due process clause as a general source of protection for economic liberty. It relied on the Fourteenth Amendment to strike down a variety of state laws seeking to regulate businesses and enhance social welfare. For example, in *Lochner v. New York* (1905), the Court struck down a state law regulating bakers' working hours on the grounds that the law violated the due process-based right for workers to freely contract to provide their labor as they wished for their employers. Historians view the Court's decisions as primarily advancing the interests of businesses rather than those of the individual workers whose rights were supposedly violated by the economic regulation and social welfare laws. These decisions viewed the right to due process as a substantive right rather than as merely a guarantee that the government would follow certain processes before affecting individuals' lives and property. The Court's use of substantive due process theories to protect economic rights disappeared in the late 1930's as the Court's composition changed and other political actors, especially President Franklin D. Roosevelt, grew more vocal in their criticism of Court decisions blocking economic legislation intended to alleviate the effects of the Great Depression.

The due process clause has also been interpreted to provide other protections for individuals. For example, in *Brown v. Mississippi* (1936), police officers' actions in torturing suspects to obtain confessions were found to violate the suspects' right to due process of law. In other words, the torture deprived the suspects of the proper processes due to them in the criminal justice system. In addition to decisions to ensure procedural fairness in criminal justice, due process has also been referred to by the Court as the source of other personal rights not explicitly specified in the Constitution, such as a right for competent adults to decline unwanted medical care, as in *Cruzan v. Director, Missouri Department of Health* (1990).

The Equal Protection Clause. Initially, the Court did not interpret the equal protection clause as a strong vehicle for eliminating discrimination. In *Plessy v. Ferguson* (1896), for example, the Court found no violation of equal protection when Louisiana mandated that African Americans ride in separate railroad cars. Because the Court found no equal protection problem with racial segregation, various states imposed segregation on many facets of their societies. During the mid-twentieth century, the Court began to shift its interpretation of the equal protection clause. Eventually this provision of the Fourteenth Amendment was used in *Brown v. Board of Education* (1954) to declare that racial segregation in public schools violated the Constitution. In subsequent decisions, the Court interpreted the clause to bar other forms of racial discrimination by the government.

In interpreting and applying the equal protection clause, the Court developed a special analytical approach that requires the government to show compelling reasons for any policy or program that involves racial discrimination. The only time that state governments have been able to successfully justify treating people differently with regard to their race has been in cases concerning affirmative action programs that seek to remedy the country's long history of discrimination by giving extra consideration to school and job applicants who are members of racial groups that have been victimized by discrimination. In *Regents of the University of California v. Bakke* (1978), for example, although the Court ruled against racial quotas and ordered that Bakke, a white applicant, be admitted, it held that a university could give members of racial minorities groups extra consideration in the admissions process for medical school without violating the equal protection clause.

The Court rejected efforts to apply the equal protection clause to private discrimination, even when state support arguably existed for that discrimination. For example, in *Moose Lodge v. Irvis* (1972), the Court refused to accept the argument that the state's granting of a liquor license to a club that denied membership to African Americans meant that state action was a component of the discrimination and therefore prohibited by the equal protection clause.

During the 1970's, the Court expanded the applicability of the equal protection clause by interpreting it to prohibit many kinds of discrimination by gender in government policies and programs. In its interpretation of the Fourteenth Amendment, the Court did not provide the same level of protection against gender discrimination that it provided against racial discrimination. Therefore, in *Rostker v. Goldberg* (1981), the Court held that the Selective Service program, which registers young men and not women for a potential military draft, is permissible despite its different treatment of men and women. The Court rejected equal protection claims based on other alleged forms of discrimination, such as a claim that the equal protection clause bars discrimination by government based on people's wealth in *San Antonio Independent School District v. Rodriguez* (1973). The Court has interpreted the equal protection clause to provide protection against discrimination based on race, gender, national origin, and a few other categories only. In most instances not involving one of these categories, the government may treat people differently as long as there is a rational basis for distinguishing people as part of a legitimate governmental program.

Because the Fourteenth Amendment was the first constitutional provision explicitly aimed at giving individuals protection against state actions, the due process and equal protection clauses of the

Fourteenth Amendment have been relied on by the Court for broadly expanding the scope and reach of constitutional rights. The Court paid little attention to the privileges or immunities clause until its decision in *Saenz v. Roe* (1999), which used the clause to protect citizens' right to travel, including a right for people moving to new states to be treated equally with established residents in receiving benefits from social welfare programs. The rediscovery of the privileges and immunities clause opens further possibilities for the Fourteenth Amendment's use as a vehicle for the expansion of constitutional rights.

FURTHER READING

The history of the Fourteenth Amendment and its role in expanding the scope of rights is examined in Michael Kent Curtis's *No State Shall Abridge: The Fourteenth Amendment and the Bill of Rights* (Durham, N.C.: Duke University Press, 1986). The incorporation process is analyzed in Henry J. Abraham's *Freedom and the Court* (5th ed., New York: Oxford University Press, 1988). Raoul Berger's *Government by Judiciary: The Transformation of the Fourteenth Amendment* (Cambridge, Mass.: Harvard University Press, 1977) provides a critique of the Court's expansion of constitutional rights. The Court's use of the due process clause to protect economic liberties is analyzed in Howard Gillman's *The Constitution Besieged: The Rise and Demise of "Lochner" Era Police Powers Jurisprudence* (Durham, N.C.: Duke University Press, 1993). Richard Kluger's *Simple Justice* (New York: Random House, 1975) provides a detailed account of the Court's use of the equal protection clause to attack racial discrimination. A comprehensive presentation of the Court's interpretation of the Fourteenth Amendment is contained in William B. Lockhart, Yale Kamisar, Jesse H. Choper, and Steven H. Shiffrin's *The American Constitution* (6th ed., St. Paul, Minn.: West Publishing, 1986). The justices' voting records on Fourteenth Amendment issues are analyzed in Thomas R. Hensley, Christopher E. Smith, and Joyce A. Baugh's *The Changing Supreme Court: Constitutional Rights and Liberties* (St. Paul, Minn.: West Publishing, 1997).

Christopher E. Smith

SEE ALSO Affirmative action; *Brown v. Mississippi*; Citizenship; Desegregation; Due process, procedural; Due process, substantive; Equal protection clause; Incorporation doctrine; Privileges and immunities; Race and discrimination; *Rostker v. Goldberg; San Antonio Independent School District v. Rodriguez; Slaughterhouse Cases.*

Fourth Amendment

DATE: 1791

DESCRIPTION: Amendment to the U.S. Constitution and part of the Bill of Rights that protects people against unreasonable searches and seizures.

SIGNIFICANCE: In the early 1900's the Supreme Court began expanding the applications of the Fourth Amendment, balancing the rights of the accused against the safety of other people.

The Framers of the Bill of Rights were concerned with the old English practice of issuing general warrants and writs of assistance. These two legal tools authorized searches with few stipulations on searching agents, allowing searches day or night on bare suspicion. Authorized by the monarch, they were valid for the duration of his or her lifetime. They were not required to name a specific person or place but could be stated in more general terms. No oath before a magistrate was necessary to secure a warrant, and probable cause was not required. Everything was left to the discretion of the holder of the warrant. The result was harassment. The colonists were victims of these general warrants and writs of assistance and purposely set out to outlaw them.

James Madison revised his initial draft of the Fourth Amendment, changing the word "secured" to "secure" and adding the clause "against unreasonable searches and seizures." Although Madison's goal was to eliminate general warrants and writs of assistance, scholars believe these alterations made the meaning of the amendment ambiguous. The Fourth Amendment outlaws only unreasonable searches and seizures, logically allowing those deemed reasonable. The Framers envisioned that searches conducted with a warrant, which required specifics such as who is to be searched, what is to be seized, and when, were constitutionally permissible. The warrant clause stipulated what was expected of police when conducting searches. However, left unanswered were the questions of whether there are times when it is reasonable to search without a warrant, what constitutes probable cause, and whether the amendment restricts only police or other governmental agents with searching authority.

The Court in *Wolf v. Colorado* (1949) made clear that search warrants had to be supported by probable cause and issued by a neutral and impartial magistrate. However, often searches are conducted without a search warrant.

Exceptions to the Warrant Requirement. The Court created a number of exceptions to the search warrant requirement. Using the reasonableness clause of the amendment rather than the warrant provision, the Court rejected the idea of a bright-line rule in favor of a more fact-bound, case-by-case approach. The police do not need a warrant for searches incident to arrest; stop-and-frisk situations; when illegal or stolen items are in plain view during a legal search; administrative, consensual, and border searches; and searches involving exigent circumstances such as automobile searches.

When an individual is arrested on probable cause, a police officer is permitted to conduct a warrantless search of the person. This exception to the warrant requirement, search incident to arrest, rests on the understanding that the arresting officer must have the power to disarm the accused and preserve any evidence. Protecting the officer's safety and retaining probative evidence is reasonable. The officer may search not only the person but the areas of immediate control. In *Chimel v. California* (1969), the Court reasoned that the scope of a search incident to arrest included wherever the arrestee might reach to grab a weapon or piece of evidence.

If in the course of a valid search, an officer comes on stolen or illegal items in plain view, they may be seized and used as evidence. This inadvertent windfall is permissible and reasonable under the Fourth Amendment as long as the officer happens on the evidence in the course of conducting a legal search. Related is the plain feel exception. In *Minnesota v. Dickerson* (1993), the Court held that if an officer feels what seems to be contraband or evidence of a crime when patting down the outside of a suspect's clothing, the items can be seized.

In *Terry v. Ohio* (1968), the Court allowed for searches on the street that did not meet the standard of probable cause. In this case, it upheld the brief detention of a suspect for weapons on the grounds of reasonable suspicion rather than probable cause. Only a limited frisk was permitted with the lowered standard of cause. If the pat-down yielded a basis for an arrest, however, a full search incident to arrest could follow.

The Court has applied the Fourth Amendment to the increasing problems arising in a mobile society. Planes, buses, trains, and boats all raise exigency concerns because of the highly mobile nature of the place to be searched and the futility of the police in executing search warrants on moving objects. The most common exigent circumstance is created by the automobile. As early as 1925 in *Carroll v. United States*, the Court made clear that the automobile would not be afforded the same level of privacy rights protection as an individual's home or person. Stopping an automobile and searching it on the street without a warrant was reasonable. However, the particulars of the car have generated a volume of litigation aimed at answering questions such as whether the police can lawfully open the glove box, the trunk, or containers in the automobile or search the driver, passengers, and their personal items. Given the lower expectation of privacy in automobiles, the Court in *Michigan Department of State Police v. Sitz* (1990) allowed roadblocks to briefly stop all drivers to catch those driving under the influence of drugs and alcohol.

Employees of other governmental agencies, such as housing, fire, health, welfare, and safety inspectors, also have searching capabilities. These agents have a lesser standard than probable cause and often invoke an element of surprise, such as unannounced inspections of restaurants. Related to these types of searches are those to ensure safety

---

TEXT OF THE FOURTH AMENDMENT

The right of the people to be secure in their persons, houses, papers, and effects, against unreasonable searches and seizures, shall not be violated, and no Warrants shall issue, but upon probable cause, supported by Oath or affirmation, and particularly describing the place to be searched, and the persons or things to be seized.

in the workplace or school by drug-testing employees and students. In *National Treasury Employees Union v. Von Raab* (1989), the Court upheld suspicionless mandatory urinalysis testing for promotion on the grounds of safety (the employees would have access to firearms and secure information). By 1995 in *Vernonia School District v. Acton*, the Court upheld the right to drug-test all student athletes without requiring suspicion of individuals.

The courts have long recognized that individuals and items entering the United States may be searched at the international border without warrant or probable cause. The Court has placed some limits on these searches, such as the level of intrusion. Strip searches, for example, must be justified by real suspicion. In an attempt to stop the influx of illegal drugs, law enforcement developed the drug courier profile, a composite of variables that indicates the likelihood an individual is trafficking drugs. In *United States v. Sokolow* (1989), the Court upheld the use of the profile as a basis for detaining and searching individuals both at the border and within the continental United States.

In *Schneckloth v. Bustamonte* (1973), the Court acknowledged the use of consent searches, noting that individuals may waive their Fourth Amendment rights and allow a search without a warrant or probable cause. The key to the validity of such searches is that they must be voluntary; an individual must knowingly and freely consent to be searched. The waiver must be uncoerced, given without trickery or fear or promise of reward. Consent can be withdrawn at any time, and a refusal to give consent cannot then be used to establish probable cause.

The Fourth Amendment also applies to wiretapping and other forms of police surveillance. The Court in *Katz v. United States* (1967) reasoned that a person's expectation of privacy includes the seizure of intangible items such as words.

Exclusionary Rule. The Fourth Amendment describes the right to be secure against unreasonable searches and seizures without mentioning a remedy. The common-law remedy for search and seizure violations was a suit of trespass. This was used until *Weeks v. United States* (1914) when the Court adopted the exclusionary rule, which excludes illegally seized evidence from trials. The twofold purpose of the rule is to preserve the integrity of the judiciary and deter police misconduct. *Weeks* mandated the application of the exclusionary rule to searching agents of the federal government. In 1949 in *Wolf*, the Court incorporated the Fourth Amendment, thereby requiring states not to abridge the search and seizure rights of their citizens, yet allowing them to choose the remedy. This choice was eliminated in *Mapp v. Ohio* (1961) when the Court incorporated the remedy of exclusion from trials for all Fourth Amendment violations, by either state or federal officials.

Mapp's scope was limited by the Court. In *Linkletter v. Walker* (1965), the Court refused to apply the exclusionary rule retroactively. The exclusion remedy was limited in scope so that it did not include grand jury proceedings in *United States v. Calandra* (1974). The Court ruled in *United States v. Havens* (1980) that illegally seized evidence could be used to impeach the credibility of the defendant at trial and in *Nix v. Williams* (1984) that it could also be admitted into evidence if the police would have inevitably discovered the evidence by lawful means. In 1984 in *United States v. Leon* and *Massachusetts v. Sheppard*, the Court allowed the use of illegally obtained evidence if the police error was made in objective good faith. The Court was unwilling to exclude reliable probative evidence when the error made by the police was unintentional and made in the course of attempting to follow the law.

FURTHER READING

One of the better historical treatments of the Fourth Amendment is Nelson B. Lasson's *The History and Development of the Fourth Amendment to the United States Constitution* (Baltimore, Md.: Johns Hopkins University Press, 1937). Several classic and often cited works about the Fourth Amendment are Jacob W. Landynski's *Search and Seizure and the Supreme Court* (Baltimore, Md.: Johns Hopkins University Press, 1966), Wayne LaFave's *Search and Seizure: A Treatise on the Fourth Amendment* (Mineola, N.Y.: Foundation Press, 1978), Erwin N. Griswold's *Search and Seizure: A Dilemma of the Supreme Court* (Lincoln: University of Nebraska Press, 1975), and Telford Taylor's *Two Studies in Constitutional Interpretation* (Columbus: Ohio State University Press, 1969). A general treatment of Fourth Amendment rights can be found in David M. O'Brien's *Constitutional Law and Politics: Civil Rights and Liberties*. 3d ed. 2 vols. New York: W. W. Norton, 1997. Some law review articles debating the policy implications of the Fourth Amendment and its remedy are Anthony Amsterdam's "The Supreme Court and the Rights of Suspects in Criminal Cases," *New York University Law Review* 45 (1970): 785, Yale Kamisar's "Is the Exclusionary Rule an 'Illogical' or 'Unnatural' Interpretation of the Fourth Amendment?" *Judicature* 62 (1978): 67, and Malcolm Wiley's "Constitutional Alternatives to the Exclusionary Rule," *South Texas Law Journal* 23 (1982): 531. Warren E. Burger expressed his views on the Fourth Amendment in "Who Will Watch the Watchman?" *American University Law Review* 14 (1964): 1.

Priscilla H. Machado

SEE ALSO Automobile searches; Bill of Rights; *Carroll v. United States*; *Chimel v. California*; Exclusionary rule; *Leon, United States v.*; *Mapp v. Ohio*; Search warrant requirement; Stop and frisk rule; *Weeks v. United States*; *Wolf v. Colorado*.

Frank v. Mangum

CITATION: 237 U.S. 309
DATE: April 19, 1915
ISSUES: Trial by jury; *habeas corpus*
SIGNIFICANCE: The Supreme Court refused federal relief for a defendant convicted of murder in state court under conditions of mob intimidation.

When Leo Frank, a Jewish capitalist, was tried in Georgia for the murder of a young woman, a large anti-Semitic mob intimidated the jury as it reached a guilty verdict. Almost all observers agreed that the trial did not conform to the due process requirements of the Fourteenth Amendment. Based on traditional notions of federalism, nevertheless, the federal district court rejected Frank's petition for a writ of *habeas corpus*. Speaking for the 7-2 majority, Justice Mahlon Pitney upheld and defended the lower court's hesitancy to intervene in a state criminal proceeding. Several years later, the Court in *Moore v. Dempsey* (1923) agreed to grant *habeas corpus* relief for defendants convicted in a similar mob-dominated trial. Justice Oliver Wendell Holmes dissented in *Frank* and wrote the majority opinion in *Moore*.

Thomas T. Lewis

SEE ALSO Due process, procedural; Federalism; *Habeas corpus*; *Moore v. Dempsey*; Review, process of.

Frankfurter, Felix

IDENTIFICATION: Associate justice (January 30, 1939-August 28, 1962)
NOMINATED BY: Franklin D. Roosevelt
BORN: November 15, 1882, Vienna, Austria
DIED: February 22, 1965, Washington, D.C.
SIGNIFICANCE: During his twenty-three years as an associate justice, Frankfurter, a dedicated liberal in his personal life, was a major advocate of judicial self-restraint. As a justice, he attempted to decide cases procedurally rather than to reconstruct the judicial system.

Frankfurter was twelve when he arrived in the United States from his native Austria. He learned English quickly and in 1902 was graduated third in his class from the City College of New York. Four years later, he received a law degree with highest honors from Harvard University. He soon left the private practice of law to take a position as assistant to Henry L. Stimson, U. S. attorney for New York's southern district. In 1914 he became a faculty member at Harvard University Law School.

During World War I (1917-1918), Frankfurter became a legal adviser on industrial matters to Secretary of War Newton D. Baker. In 1917 he served as secretary and later as counsel to President Woodrow Wilson's Mediation Commission. The following year, he chaired the War Labor Policies Board. These government appointments gave Frankfurter the opportunity to deal with a broad variety of circumstances involving labor unrest. They also brought him to the attention of a broad range of government officials, some of whom were distressed by his liberal stands in relation to matters involving labor but many of whom admired his ability to deal objectively with controversial situations.

Frankfurter was Woodrow Wilson's legal adviser at the Paris Peace Conference in 1919, after which he resumed his teaching career at Harvard. During the next decade, he was instrumental in founding the American Civil Liberties Union and helped to launch the *New Republic*, a magazine of political opinion. He was highly visible as a liberal activist, writing an impassioned article for the March, 1927, issue of *The Atlantic Monthly* in which he called for a new trial in the famous Sacco-Vanzetti case, whose defendants were both sentenced to death for a

Felix Frankfurter. (AP/Wide World Photos)

murder committed during a payroll robbery even though their trial was tainted in several ways.

When Franklin D. Roosevelt became president in 1933, Frankfurter became a frequent legal adviser to him. The president's respect for Frankfurter grew through the years, and Roosevelt became increasingly dependent upon him for legal guidance as he proceeded with implementing the New Deal.

Appointment to the Court. On January 5, 1939, Roosevelt nominated Frankfurter to serve as an associate justice of the Supreme Court. The nomination was unanimously confirmed in the Senate and, on January 17, 1939, Frankfurter was sworn in. The United States was in the midst of the New Deal, and Washington officials rejoiced at the appointment of a liberal activist who had proved his mettle as a champion of civil liberties. The *Nation* magazine proclaimed that Frankfurter's whole life had been a preparation for service on the Court.

Even the conservative press applauded the appointment, acknowledging Frankfurter's even-handedness in judicial matters. Frankfurter's qualifications as a jurist could hardly be questioned. Few feared that his decisions would reflect narrow prejudices or unbalanced partisanship.

Frankfurter as a Justice. Frankfurter, the quintessential liberal when appointed to the Court, in time came to be known as one of the Court's

staunch conservatives. This transformation occurred because the Court, during the Roosevelt administration, came to be dominated by liberals who viewed it as their duty to promote liberal goals through their decisions. Some of these liberals felt hostility toward Frankfurter and considered him a turncoat.

Frankfurter believed fervently in Justice Oliver Wendell Holmes's dedication to judicial self-restraint, which grew out of the Court's tendency, when it was dominated by conservatives at the beginning of the twentieth century, to vote against cases brought before it that promoted progressive social legislation. During Frankfurter's term, the Court had a majority of liberal justices, and he feared that it was becoming more concerned with making law than with interpreting the Constitution as it related to the cases brought before it. Because he realized the necessity of the separation of powers that characterizes democratic societies, Frankfurter frequently voted with the conservative minority rather than with the liberal majority, often casting the deciding vote in 5-4 decisions.

Frankfurter's greatest contribution as a justice was to maintain to the best of his ability the separation of powers that assures government by the people rather than government by the government. Ironically, it was Frankfurter's deep-seated liberalism that forced him into taking conservative stands. He recognized that a Court dominated either by liberals or conservatives bent on changing society rather than on interpreting the law as it is set forth in the Constitution overstepped its authority, taking on duties specifically assigned by the Constitution to the legislative branch of government. The Constitution is, after all, the U.S. government's contract with its citizens.

Frankfurter's transformation into a judicial conservative did not represent a contradiction in his thinking. Rather, it was totally consistent with his most closely held beliefs. He never at any point in his life failed to support the concept of government by the people.

FURTHER READING

Baker, Leonard. *Brandeis and Frankfurter: A Dual Biography.* New York: Harper & Row, 1984.

Burt, Robert A. *Two Jewish Justices: Outcasts in the Promised Land.* Berkeley: University of California Press, 1988.

Mendelsohn, Wallace. *Justices Black and Frankfurter: Conflict in the Court.* Chicago: University of Chicago Press, 1961.

Parrish, Michael. *Felix Frankfurter and His Times: The Reform Years.* New York: Free Press, 1982.

Simon, James F. *The Antagonists: Hugo Black, Felix Frankfurter and Civil Liberties in Modern America.* New York: Simon & Schuster, 1989.

Urofsky, Melvin I. *Felix Frankfurter: Judicial Restraint and Individual Liberties.* Boston: Twayne, 1991.

R. Baird Shuman

SEE ALSO Constitution, U.S.; Judicial self-restraint; New Deal; Roosevelt, Franklin D.; Separation of powers.

French Constitutional Council

DESCRIPTION: French government council, not part of the judicial branch, that examines proposed laws to ensure that they are constitutional, oversees certain elections, and certifies extraordinary actions in times of national emergency.

SIGNIFICANCE: Although the French Constitutional Council rules on matters of constitutionality, unlike the U.S. Supreme Court, it hears appeals referred by members of the government rather than by average citizens.

The Constitutional Council of France, while similar to the U.S. Supreme Court, is not its equivalent. Although both are charged with reviewing the constitutionality of government actions, they differ in many ways. The Constitutional Council is an innovation of the French constitution adopted in 1958, which established France's Fifth Republic. Unlike the Supreme Court of the United States, the Constitutional Council does not hear appeals from criminals or from the average citizens of France. Before it was amended, the 1958 constitution gave only the president of France, the prime minister, the president of the Senate (the upper legislative house), and the president of the National Assembly (the lower legislative house) the right to appeal decrees, laws, or treaties to the Constitutional Council. However, under a 1982 amendment, the right to appeal was extended to members of the National Assembly and the Senate, although sixty members of one house must sign the appeal to initiate the process. Certain institutional acts must always be referred to the council before they can be applied, including rules of procedure for the legislature.

When an item is referred to the Constitutional Council, a reasoned decision as to its constitutionality has to be made within one month. However, for urgent items, the government can request that a decision be made within eight days. Only the decision of the majority is published; dissenting opinions are not made public. The decisions of the council cannot be appealed.

When deciding whether the issue before the Constitutional Council is constitutional, the council interprets the constitution broadly, unlike the U.S. Supreme Court, which must base its opinions more closely on what is contained within the articles of the U.S. Constitution. The council recognizes the preamble of the French constitution as an integral part of the document. The preamble to the constitution includes references to the 1946 French constitution (which established the Fourth Republic) and to the 1789 Declaration of Human and Civic Rights. Therefore, these two historic texts, as well as all parts of the 1958 constitution, are binding legal documents.

Political Orientation. The U.S. Supreme Court is part of the judicial branch of government and is charged with judicial responsibilities in addition to interpreting the Constitution. The Constitutional Council of France is separate from the judicial branch of government and deals only with matters relating to the French constitution. The U.S. Supreme Court is viewed as an entity whose members are outside day-to-day politics. Its decisions are usually seen as reflections of the U.S. Constitution, laws enacted by the national government, and the legal institutions established to govern the country. Generally, respected jurists and legal scholars are appointed to the U.S. Supreme Court. Contrary to this tradition, the Constitutional Council of France was viewed as political from its inception. The majority of its members were politicians who had previously served in the upper levels of the government. Therefore, the decisions of the Constitutional Council are seen by most French citizens as political in nature, reflecting the need to check the actions of either the executive or legislative branches of government.

COMPARISON OF THE HIGHEST U.S. AND FRENCH COURTS

	United States	*France*
Name of court	Supreme Court	Constitutional Council
Power of judicial review?	yes	yes
Number of judges	9	9
How selected	presidential appointment with Senate confirmation	president appoints 3; speaker of upper house appoints 3; speak of lower house appoints 3
Length of terms	life	9 years
Legal tradition	common law	Roman or code law
Written constitution	yes	yes
Criminal system	adversarial	procuratorial inquisitional
Bill of rights	yes	yes
Degree of protection of the accused	moderate	low
Habeas corpus	yes, for 48 hours	no
Type of review	concrete; cases and controversies only may be brought by citizens; no abstract jurisdiction; no advisory opinions	No concrete cases by citizens; only abstract jurisdiction in form of advisory opinions asked by executive or legislature within 15 days of passage

The nine members of the Constitutional Council are appointed for nine-year terms. Every three years, one new member is appointed by the president of France, another by the president of the Senate, and a third by the president of the National Assembly. However, in addition to these nine regular members, all former presidents of France may sit on the Constitutional Council, participate in its deliberations, and vote on the issue being decided. There are no age or professional requirements for the members. However, an individual cannot serve on the Constitutional Council and at the same time be an elected official or hold certain other governmental offices. The members of the council may not be reappointed. It takes a quorum of seven members for the council to conduct business.

Electoral and Emergency Functions. In addition to its interpretive duties, the Constitutional Council has a role to play in the electoral process. The Constitutional Council oversees the election of the president of France, which takes place every seven years. This includes drawing up the lists of candidates, regulating the campaign, and certifying the results. If a dispute arises as to who won a seat in the National Assembly or the Senate, the Constitutional Council will decide the winner. From time to time, an issue is brought before the voters in the form of a referendum. When this occurs, the Constitutional Council administers the election.

The president of France has very strong powers in times of emergency. However, to legally use these powers, the president must first declare a state of emergency. Then the Constitutional Council confirms that the emergency exists and that the steps proposed by the president are appropriate for ending the emergency. One type of emergency act is the removal of elected officials from office. One step in the process of impeaching the president of France is to obtain agreement with the charges from a majority of the members of the Constitutional Council. If a member of the legislative branch is being removed from office, the specific charge must be recorded by the council. The council also decides if a conflict of interest exists when a member of the legislature also holds some other governmental position.

FURTHER READING

Banks, Arthur S., and Thomas C. Muller. *Political Handbook of the World: 1998.* Binghamton, England: CSA Publication, 1998.

De Gaulle, Charles. *Memoirs of Hope: Renewal and Endeavor.* New York: Simon & Schuster, 1971.

Pierce, Roy. *French Politics and Political Institutions.* New York: Harper & Row, 1968.

Williams, Philip M., and Martin Harrison. *Politics and Society in de Gaulle's Republic.* Garden City, N.Y.: Doubleday, 1972.

Donald A. Watt

SEE ALSO British Law Lords; Constitutional interpretation; Court of Justice of the European Communities; German Federal Constitutional Court; International perspectives on the Court; Judicial review; Rule of reason; Separation of powers; Supreme Court of Canada.

Freund, Ernst

IDENTIFICATION: Professor and scholar of administrative and constitutional law

BORN: January 30, 1864, New York, New York

DIED: October 20, 1932, Chicago, Illinois

SIGNIFICANCE: A legal scholar, Freund influenced the Supreme Court through his treatise on police powers and his theoretical defense of free speech.

Freund was born in New York while his German parents were visiting the United States but grew up and was educated in their homeland. He moved to the United States shortly after completing legal studies at Heidelberg. After briefly practicing law in New York City, he began teaching, first at Colum-

bia College and later at the University of Chicago. He received a Ph.D. from Columbia in 1897.

Freund brought special awareness of administrative law to writing and teaching. A precise analyst, he was for almost twenty-five years a member of the National Conference of Commissioners on Uniform State Laws. His practical experience made him a pioneering and enduring figure in U.S. law.

As a scholar, Freund concentrated on the issue of governmental regulation. One of his early works, *The Police Power: Public Policy and Constitutional Rights* (1904), dealing with the boundaries between community needs and individual rights, was noted and cited by the Supreme Court. Freund was both analytic and systematic in his treatment, with a unique style and point of view. He welcomed extensive judicial control over legislative action in a fashion unusual for legal writers of his time.

His most important work, *Standards of American Legislation* (1915), which emerged from a series of lectures, touches on a number of issues more lightly than some of his other works. Drawing on a lifetime of research, teaching, and bill drafting, Freund attempted to formulate both positive and negative tenets for legislation at its inception. In the work, he pointed out that freedom of assembly and free speech could without great assumption of authority be held to imply a right to association and political participation.

Samuel Krislov

SEE ALSO British background to U.S. judiciary; Police powers; Speech and press, freedom of.

Frontiero v. Richardson

CITATION: 411 U.S. 677

DATE: May 14, 1973

ISSUE: Sex discrimination

SIGNIFICANCE: The Supreme Court reaffirmed that discrimination based on sex is contrary to the equal protection clause of the Fourteenth Amendment, but only a plurality of the justices recognized all gender classifications as inherently suspect.

A federal law automatically allowed a male member of the armed service to claim his spouse as a dependent, but a female member did not receive this benefit unless she could show that her spouse depended on her for more than half of his support.

Sharron Frontiero, a married Air Force lieutenant, asserted that the policy was unconstitutional. By an 8-1 vote, the Supreme Court upheld her claim.

Justice William J. Brennan, Jr., speaking for a four-member plurality, wanted to declare that all gender classifications were suspect, which would require that they be judged by the same stringent standards accorded to classifications based on race. He noted that sex was an immutable characteristic, that it had long been the basis of invidious discrimination, and that congressional endorsement of the Equal Rights Amendment demonstrated public acknowledgment of the problem. Justice Lewis F. Powell, Jr., speaking for three justices, argued that a decision on the level of scrutiny was not necessary to decide the case. In addition, because the ratification of the Equal Rights Amendment (which never took place) might settle the scrutiny issue, the Court should not preempt a political decision, which the Constitution reserved to the states.

In *Craig v. Boren* (1976), the Court returned to the issue of whether to apply the rational basis or strict scrutiny test when examining allegations of sex discrimination, and the majority agreed on a compromise: heightened, or intermediate, scrutiny.

Thomas T. Lewis

SEE ALSO *Craig v. Boren*; Equal protection clause; Gender issues; Judicial scrutiny; *Reed v. Reed*; *Rostker v. Goldberg*.

Frothingham v. Mellon

CITATION: 262 U.S. 447
DATE: June 4, 1923
ISSUE: Taxing and spending clause
SIGNIFICANCE: The Supreme Court held that payment of taxes does not establish the standing to sue necessary to challenge the constitutionality of congressional spending statutes.

Harriet Frothingham filed suit as a federal taxpayer to prevent the secretary of the treasury from spending money under the Maternity Act of 1921, which provided grants to the states for programs designed to reduce maternal and infant mortality. She alleged that the statute violated the Tenth Amendment and that it also deprived taxpayers of property without due process of law.

By a 9-0 vote, the Supreme Court ruled that the suit was not a legitimate judicial controversy because Frothingham lacked standing to sue. Justice George Sutherland reasoned that the plaintiff in the case would have to show an immediate and direct personal injury from the enforcement of the statute and not merely a remote and uncertain interest shared with all taxpayers. Sutherland wrote that a taxpayer of a municipality would have the necessary standing to sue, but he did not mention possible taxpayer challenges to spending by the states. The Court substantially modified the rule against federal taxpayer standing in *Flast v. Cohen* (1968).

Thomas T. Lewis

SEE ALSO *Everson v. Board of Education of Ewing Township*; Federalism; *Flast v. Cohen*; *Richardson, United States v.*; Separation of powers; Standing.

Fugitive slaves

DESCRIPTION: Slaves who had escaped from their masters. Under the institution of slavery that existed in the United States until 1865, many African Americans were classified as property with no political or legal rights.

SIGNIFICANCE: The Supreme Court repeatedly upheld fugitive slave laws that denied that slaves had any rights and permitted their capture and return to a slave state without a jury trial.

In 1619 the first African slaves were brought to Virginia. By the late 1700's, there were more than a million blacks in the United States. The battle between the proslavery and antislavery factions reflected an economic and moral divide. The proslavery faction threatened not to ratify the U.S. Constitution at the 1787 Constitutional Convention if the institution of chattel slavery was not allowed. The antislavery faction in the North posited that slavery was a moral outrage and contrary to the law of nature and, therefore, that international and national slave trade activities should be terminated.

George Washington, James Madison, and some of the other Founders owned a large number of slaves and were reluctant to ban slavery because they derived profit from their slaves' free labor and feared the potential damage to the fledgling American economy, especially in the South. The divisive debate at the Constitutional Convention created two strategic outcomes. First, the North forbade slavery in its territories and passed the 1787 Northwest Ordinance, which outlawed slavery in Illinois, Indiana, Michigan, Ohio, and Wisconsin. Second, the South was permitted in its territories to equate black slaves to property, enforce the subservience of blacks to whites by all means necessary, and ensure the legal subjugation and dehumanization of blacks required to maximize both economic productivity and wealth creation.

The institution of slavery in the United States was explicitly protected by four provisions in the Constitution. Article I, section 2, clause 3, known as the Three-Fifths Compromise, stated that a slave was counted as three-fifths of a free person for the purposes of taxation and the apportionment of seats in the House of Representatives. Article I, section 9, clause 1, called the slave trade clause, prevented Congress from stopping the slave trade for twenty years and taxed each slave brought into the nation. Article IV, section 2, clause 3, called the fugitive slave clause, demanded that escaped slaves be returned to their owners. Article V prevented constitutional amendments on the international slave trade until after 1808. Moreover, ten other provisions in the Constitution supported the institution of slavery. This legal superstructure laid the foundation for Supreme Court rulings that would follow, especially with regard to fugitive slaves.

The First Law. Congress passed the Fugitive Slave Act in 1793. The act ordered free states in the North to turn over fugitive slaves to slave catchers and to expedite their eventual return with a federal certificate of removal to their masters in the South. When the act was implemented in the North, problems arose concerning the legal status of free African Americans. Northern states passed laws against kidnapping and personal-liberty statutes to protect free African Americans from Southern slave catchers. However, the steady rise in slave insurrections and runaway slaves amplified Southern whites' fears concerning property losses and personal safety and caused them to increase their support for fugitive slave measures.

In *Groves v. Slaughter* (1841), in a 5-2 vote, the Court ruled that the commerce clause in the Con-

This 1851 poster cautions free blacks living in Boston against dealing with the authorities lest they be mistaken for a fugitive slave and returned to slavery. (Library of Congress)

stitution did not interfere with the institution of slavery in the South. This major ruling advanced states' rights over federal rights in the slavery domain. In *Prigg v. Pennsylvania* (1842), Justice Joseph Story, speaking for the 8-1 majority, upheld the constitutionality of the 1793 Fugitive Slave Act and struck down state personal-liberty laws interfering with the return of slaves. Chief Justice Roger Brooke Taney, a proslavery Southerner, argued that states had the right to enforce the act and certainly were not prohibited from doing so. In *Jones v. Van Zandt* (1847), the antislavery faction along with free blacks contested the constitutionality of the 1793 act. In this case, an Underground Railway conductor, John Van Zandt, was accused of hiding and assisting fugitive slaves. Attorney and future chief justice Salmon P. Chase defended Van Zandt, arguing that the act was unconstitutional and that Congress had no enforcement power with regard to slavery. However, the Court found that the 1793 act was consistent with Congress's enforcement power under the slave trade clause and that the 1787 Northwest Ordinance had not been negatively affected.

The Second Law. In 1850 Congress passed a revised, strengthened fugitive slave act, supporting the capture and return procedure and providing penalties for anyone who interfered. Federal commissioners were appointed to enforce the law. The Fugitive Slave Act of 1850 stated that these federal commissioners could return slaves to their owners' plantations based on proof of ownership by claimants, without a jury trial or hearing the alleged slave's testimony. In this second act, Congress considerably strengthened the property rights of Southern slave owners. In *Strader v. Graham* (1851), Chief Justice Taney argued that states had the legitimate right to determine the legal status of all blacks within their territory. In *Moore v. Illinois* (1852), Judge Robert C. Grier wrote that a state using its inherent police powers had the right to both arrest and detain fugitive slaves as it would paupers, idlers, and vagabonds. Furthermore, a state could exercise such powers legally under the fugitive slave clause of the Constitution.

In *Scott v. Sandford* (1857), the Court, in a 7-2 vote, ruled that African Americans were not citizens of the United States because they were both slaves and black. The decision denied African Americans access to the federal court system in civil cases, prevented them from exercising the rights of citizenship, and eroded the limited rights of blacks in free states. Moreover, in his opinion for the Court, Chief Justice Taney argued that the Missouri Compromise of 1820 was unconstitutional because Congress went far beyond its powers in legislating where chattel slavery could exist in the new territories. Taney asserted that blacks "had no rights that the white man was bound to respect." In *Abelman v. Booth* (1859), the Court unanimously ruled that all provisions of the 1850 Fugitive Slave Law were constitutional. In *Kentucky v. Dennison* (1861), the Taney Court held that the interstate extradition for trial and punishment from Ohio to Kentucky of a free black who had assisted a black slave could not be allowed nor could Congress force a state official to perform any duty to that effect. This ruling upheld states' rights over federal rights in the fugitive slave domain.

Enforcement of the Fugitive Slave Act of 1850 met with opposition in the North, and riots and rescues took place in several Northern cities. Northerners, many of whom were opposed to slavery, disliked being forced to participate in the return of slaves, and Southerners were angry because the North was not obeying the law. The outbreak of the Civil War in 1861 and the succession of the Southern states ended the return of slaves to the South. In 1865 the passage of the Thirteenth Amendment outlawed slavery in the United States.

FURTHER READING

For a fugitive slave's perspective, read William Wells Brown's "Narrative of William W. Brown, A Fugitive Slave," in *From Fugitive Slave to Free Man* (New York: Mentor, 1993), edited by William L. Andrews. Also read Austin Steward's "Twenty Years a Slave and Forty Years a Freeman," in *In Four Slave Narratives* (Reading, Mass.: Addison-Wesley, 1969), by Robin A. Winks, Larry Gara, Jane H. Pease, William H. Pease, and Tilden G. Edelstein. *Plantation Society and Race Relations* (Westport, Conn.: Praeger, 1999), edited by Thomas J. Durant, Jr., and J. David Knottnerus, presents a wide-ranging discussion of Southern plantation slave society and the everyday conditions that led to an estimated fifty thousand slave escapes per year. For a review of the beginning and end of the slavery system in the United States, see Louis Filler's *The Rise and Fall of Slavery in America* (New York: Van Nostrand, 1980). Merton L. Dillon's *The Abolitionists: The Growth of a Dissenting Minority* (De Kalb: Northern Illinois University Press, 1974) provides a good review of the abolitionist movement. For an excellent political and historical chronology of the African and African American experience, read *The Atlas of African-American History and Politics: From the Slave Trade to Modern Times* (New York: McGraw-Hill, 1998), edited by Arwin D. Smallwood and Jeffrey M. Elliot.

Michael J. Siler

SEE ALSO *Ableman v. Booth*; Fugitives from justice; *Groves v. Slaughter*; *Kentucky v. Dennison*; *Prigg v. Pennsylvania*; Property rights; Race and discrimination; *Scott v. Sandford*; Slavery; States' rights; Taney, Roger Brooke.